Organizations

ORGANIZATIONS

Rational, Natural, and Open Systems

W. Richard Scott

Stanford University

Prentice Hall, Upper Saddle River, New Jersey 07458

Library of Congress Cataloging-in-Publication Data

Scott, W. Richard.
    Organizations : rational, natural, and open systems / W. Richard
Scott. — 4th ed.
      p. cm.
    Includes bibliographical references (p.   ) and indexes.
    ISBN 0-13-266354-6
    1. Organizational sociology.   I. Title.
HM131.S385 1998
302.3'5—dc21   97-9352
                                                                     CIP

Editorial director: Charlyce Jones Owen
Editor-in-chief: Nancy Roberts
Sociology editor: Stephen T. Jordan
Associate editor: Sharon Chambliss
Project manager: Merrill Peterson
Prepress and manufacturing buyer: Mary Ann Gloriande
Marketing manager: Christopher DeJohn

Credits appear on page xvi.

This book was set in 10/11 Baskerville by DM Cradle Associates
and was printed and bound by Courier Companies, Inc.
The cover was printed by Phoenix Color Corp.

ISBN   0-13-266354-6

PRENTICE-HALL INTERNATIONAL (UK) LIMITED, *London*
PRENTICE-HALL OF AUSTRALIA PTY. LIMITED, *Sydney*
PRENTICE-HALL CANADA INC., *Toronto*
PRENTICE-HALL HISPANOAMERICANA, S.A., *Mexico*
PRENTICE HALL OF INDIA PRIVATE LIMITED, *New Delhi*
PRENTICE-HALL OF JAPAN, INC., *Tokyo*
SIMON & SCHUSTER ASIA PTE. LTD., *Singapore*
EDITORA PRENTICE-HALL DO BRASIL, LTDA., *Rio de Janeiro*

Again for
Jennifer, Elliot, and Sydney

Contents

11. Goals, Power, and Control, *285*

PART IV.   ORGANIZATIONS AND SOCIETY _____ 319

12. Organizational Pathologies, *321*

13. Organizational Effectiveness, *343*

Preface

This fourth edition allows me to continue my attempt to comprehend and make meaningful developments—recent as well as earlier—in the study of organizations. This effort commenced almost forty years ago when, in 1962, I coauthored an early text-treatise on organizations with the distinguished organizational scholar, Peter M. Blau. The field of organizational sociology was just beginning to see the light of day at that time, and I believe that our joint effort helped to give the fledgling field some intellectual coherence and perhaps even provided some guidelines for its development.

It was considerably later, in 1981, that I returned again to the task of codification and synthesis, resulting in the first edition of this book. The title and the general format have not changed over the intervening years up to and including this new, fourth edition. While it is possible that this persistence only signifies intellectual laziness or atrophy, I prefer to believe that it is because the fundamental categories—rational, natural, and open systems—still serve as containers within which we can fruitfully sort our ideas about and approaches to studying organizations. I believe my original typology still functions to tame and order a field of study that, at first exposure, appears to be chaotic and, indeed, is crowded with competing theories and paradigms.

While the broad typology of theories has not changed throughout this period of nearly two decades, the content certainly has. A reader of the first edition would recognize the basic framework and would be reminded again of the contributions of early pioneers, but could not help but be impressed by how much has changed: the number of new perspectives being employed, the reversal of trends in the development of organization size and form, the range of new and different topics being addressed. In particular, new theories have been developed to encompass processes and structures operating at more and more macro levels, as organizational analysts increasingly turn their attention to the ways in which organizations act as members of populations of organizations and as component units in larger fields and networks of organizations.

More generally, in comparing the fourth with the first and subsequent editions, I call attention to two general trends. First, organizations and organizational theory have become—fitfully and reluctantly—ever more open over time. As I note in the text, earlier organizations endeavored to seal themselves off from their environments in a variety of ways: Although open systems, they acted to artificially restrict the impact of environmental factors on their structure and activities. Little by little, over time, the boundaries separating organizations from environments have been breached and bridged. The "new" organization is more closely attuned and interdependent with its suppliers and buyers; it is less likely to have a large body of permanent, full-time employees, and much of its structure is shaped and the logics controlling its operation are provided by experts and specialists imported from the outside who have less stake in the welfare of their specific employer. Older models emphasized the organization's drive for autonomy; newer models recognize the reality of interdependence and stress the importance of developing appropriate alliances and alignments (see Ancona et al., 1996). Theory, which has long given lip service to open systems, is still trying to catch up with the fundamental changes that are transforming organizations in our time and to grasp the full implications of openness.

Second, the distinction between rational and natural systems, which the typology emphasizes and which still exists as a major watershed distinguishing among contrasting assumptions and approaches to organizations, shows signs of softening, if not disappearing. More analysts recognize that rationality is situationally located and that its rules or logics vary over time and place. There is increased awareness that much rationality may reside in sets of established rules or in existing routines for carrying out certain types of tasks. More analysts acknowledge that what appears to be rational behavior from one point of view or given a short time perspective does not appear so from another or longer-term vantage point. Developments in the areas of organizational learning and in evolutionary economics have helped us to appreciate the intelligence embedded in rules and routines. And the resurgence of institutional theory, which I review at some length in this edition, appears to provide the basis for an improved dialog between these ancient protagonists.

While there is much that is new, this edition adheres to several tenets that guided earlier editions and that, in my view, distinguish it from most other general books on organizations. Among these are the following:

- I give roughly equal time to describing changes in the "real world" of organizations and to examining changes in theories of organizations—our ideas about what they are and what we think they should be. While events shape our ideas, it is no less true that our ideas shape events.
- I give roughly equal time to presenting and evaluating organizational theory and to describing and commenting on empirical research. Scientific inquiry is characterized, as Whitehead (1925) reminds us, by the confrontation of "general principles" with "irreducible and stubborn facts."

- I give substantial time, particularly in Chapters 2 through 5, to discussing the contributions of early theorists and students of organizations. While attending to the new ideas, I believe it is important to remember and to understand our origins.

- Because I was trained as a sociologist, I give primary attention to sociological approaches to organizations, but I am keenly aware of the extent to which the study of organizations is an interdisciplinary enterprise, and I attempt to recognize and take into account salient contributions from the other social sciences as well as from management theory.

- While I am not happy about the micro-macro divide that tends to unduly segregate work that focuses primarily on individuals within organizations from work that focuses primarily on organizations as complex social systems and as actors in still wider systems, this volume gives primary attention to work at the more macro levels of analysis.

- I try to write about organizations not only from a manager's point of view, but also from the view of various participants and audiences (stakeholders), including the general public. While most current books are addressed to the interests of managers, I see organizations as a broad and socially significant topic of interest to any thoughtful person. Most of us, not just managers, spend a great deal of time working within organizations, and all of us are significantly affected by their actions. Organizations are too important a topic to be left to the managers.

Prefaces provide a welcome opportunity to acknowledge the assistance of others who have helped along the way—with intellectual insights, constructive criticism, or, most important, the gift of friendship. Forty years in professional harness is a long time, and it is not possible to acknowledge all of those who have made a difference in my work, but there are some who must be named and publicly thanked.

At the University of Kansas, where I completed my undergraduate and master's degrees in sociology, I remember fondly Marston M. McCluggage and Charles K. Warriner, who enlisted me in the company of sociologists and responded supportively to my early efforts.

At the University of Chicago, the site of my doctoral training, three mentors stand out: Everett C. Hughes, who shared with me his insights on what has come to be termed the Chicago school of institutional analysis; Otis Dudley Duncan, who along with Beverly Duncan gave me research experience, methodological training, and friendship; and Peter M. Blau, who allowed me to collaborate with him in joint research on organizations and to coauthor an early text on this newly developing field of study.

I have spent my entire professional career on the faculty at Stanford University, so the list of friends and colleagues there is necessarily long. Harold J. Leavitt and Eugene Webb provided early support and stimulation. During the first part of my career at Stanford, I was involved in a productive collaboration with Sanford M. Dornbusch examining authority systems, and he remains one of my closest friends. Somewhat later, I conducted research on organizational factors influencing the quality of care in hospitals, and I was aided greatly by Byron Wm. Brown, Jr., and William H. Forrest, Jr., of the Stanford Medical School. More recently, and over a period of many years, I have worked closely with John W. Meyer on studies of institutional structures and processes, and I have benefitted greatly from his creativity and insights. While we have never collaborated in a research project, James G. March and I have engaged in a collective, long-term effort to build interdisciplinary and interschool connections and training forums for graduate students at Stanford as well as scholarly linkages between Stanford and other universities. Jim has been and remains a major source of intellectual stimulation and friendship.

Stanford University hosts an embarrassment of riches—or what Jim March describes as a "density of competence"—in the faculty it has assembled in the area of organization studies matched by few if any other universities. Other valued colleagues at this institution (a few have since moved elsewhere) who have made my time here both stimulating and, for the most part, pleasant include: Stephen R. Barley, William P. Barnett, James N. Baron, Terrence E. Deal, Kathleen M. Eisenhardt, Roberto Fernandez, Mark Granovetter, Michael T. Hannan, James Jucker, Roderick Kramer, William G. Ouchi, Joanne Martin, Milbrey McLaughlin, Jeffrey Pfeffer, Joel Podolny, Francisco Ramirez, Philippe C. Schmitter, Ann Swidler, and Robert I. Sutton.

An equally valued source of intellectual stimulation and social support has been a remarkable set of doctoral students with whom I have worked and from whom I have learned. These include Jeffrey A. Alexander, Victoria Alexander, Elaine Backman, Karen Bradley, Bruce C. Busching, Carol A. Caronna, Glenn Carroll, Randi C. Cohen, Karen S. Cook, Andrew Creighton, Gerald F. Davis, Jacques Delacroix, Frank Dobbin, Lauren Edelman, Mary L. Fennell, Ann Barry Flood, P. Devereaux Jennings, Ronald L. Jepperson, James D. Laing, Barbara Levitt, Peter Mendel, Stephen J. Mezias, Weifan Min, Anne S. Miner, Brian Mittman, Susanne C. Monahan, Andrew E. Newman, Willie Ocasio, Seth S. Pollack, Amy Elizabeth Roussell, Brian Rowan, Martin Ruef, Claudia Bird Schoonhoven, Jitendra V. Singh, David Strang, Mark Suchman, John Sutton, Azumi Takata, Sharon Takeda, Patricia Thornton, Marc Ventresca, Gayle Watkins, and Lynne G. Zucker. Many of these former students are now full professors, and all are productive members of the profession.

Not all of the talent is at Stanford. Over the years, I have profited enormously from the association of a collection of esteemed friends and scholars, including Andrew Abbott, Howard E. Aldrich, Joel A. C. Baum, Janice M. Beyer, Nicole Woolsey Biggart, Robert E. Cole, Thomas A. D'Aunno, Paul DiMaggio, Neil Fligstein, J. Richard Hackman, Peter A. Hall, Robert I. Kahn, John R. Kimberly, David Knoke, Edward O. Laumann, Peter Marsden, Marshall W. Meyer, Christine Oliver, Donald Palmer, Charles Perrow, Walter W. Powell, Philip Selznick, Neil J. Smelser, Barry Staw, Arthur L. Stinchcombe, Rosemary C. R. Taylor, James D. Thompson, Andrew Van de Ven, Karl E. Weick, D. Eleanor Westney, Oliver E. Willamson, Sidney G. Winter, and Mayer N. Zald.

In recent years, my list of colleagial connections and obligations has become increasingly international. These valued associates include Nils Brunsson, Søren Christensen, Tom Christensen, Lex Donaldson, Lars Engwall, David Hickson, Christian Knudsen, Cornelius Lammers, Helge Larsen, Keri Lilja, Renata Mayntz, Johan Olsen, Risto Tainio, and Chu-Tao John Wu.

My life companion, Joy, continues to tolerate my scholarly activities and to gently remind me that there is more to life than work and things of interest in the world apart from organizations.

Finally, the book is again dedicated to our three children, Jennifer, Elliot, and Sydney, who are now quite grown up, married, almost financially independent, and have given us the gift of grandchildren. Most important, while they have remained our children, they, along with their spouses, have also become our best friends.

W. Richard Scott

Acknowledgments

The author wishes to thank the copyright owners for permission to reprint in the text the following figures, tables and quotations:

Table 6–1. Adapted from Scott, *Institutions and Organizations*, p. 35, copyright © 1995 by Sage Publications. Reprinted by permission of Sage Publications, Inc.

Fig. 7–1. Reprinted with permission of The Free Press, a division of Simon & Schuster from *Markets and Hierarchies: Analysis and Antitrust Implications* by Oliver E. Williamson. Copyright © 1975, 1983 by The Free Press.

Fig. 7–3. From Michael T. Hannan and John Freeman, The ecology of organizational founding: American labor unions, 1836–1985. *American Journal of Sociology*, 92 (1987), Figure 3, p. 927. Reprinted by permission of the University of Chicago.

Fig. 8–1. Adapted from Gerard F. Davis, Robert L. Kahn, and Mayer N. Zald, "Contracts, Treaties, and Joint ventures." In R.L. Kahn and M.N. Zald (eds.), *Organization and Nation States: New Perspectives on Conflict and Cooperation*, Figure 2.1 (p. 34) and Figure 2.2 (p. 35). Copyright 1990 Jossey-Bass, Inc., Publisher.

Table 10–1. Reprinted by permission of JAI Press from W.W. Powell, "Neither markets nor hierarchy," in B. Staw and L. Cummings, *Research in Organization Behavior*, Vol. 12, 1990.

Figure 10-1. Reprinted from Alfred D. Chandler, Jr., *Strategy and Structure*, p. 10, by permission of MIT Press, Cambridge, Massachusetts. Copyright © 1962 by Massachusetts Institute of Technology.

AN INTRODUCTION TO ORGANIZATIONS

Organizations play a leading role in our modern world. Their presence affects—some would insist that the proper term is *infects*—virtually every sector of contemporary social life. Peter Drucker thus observes, "Young people today will have to learn organizations the way their forefathers learned farming." Chapter 1 endeavors to amplify and justify this advice by examining both the practical and theoretical benefits to be gained from a better understanding of organizations.

Part One pursues the two major themes of commonality and diversity. Organizations share certain features, which serve to differentiate them from other social forms. Students of this field believe that we can understand much about a specific organization from knowing about other organizations. Understanding how a factory functions can illuminate the workings of a hospital; and knowledge of a governmental bureau can help us understand the workings of a union.

Diversity appears in many guises. While organizations may possess common, generic characteristics, they exhibit staggering variety—in size, in structure, and in operating processes. Just as organizations vary, so do those who study them. Students of organizations bring to their task varying interests, tools, and intellectual preconceptions. Of particular importance are differences in the level of analysis employed and in the theoretical perspectives utilized.

Three influential perspectives are introduced in Chapter 1 as competing definitions of organizations. Part Two is devoted to an intensive examination of these perspectives, which have shaped and continue to govern our understanding of organizations.

CHAPTER 1

The Subject Is Organizations

> The recurrent problem in sociology is to conceive of corporate organization, and to study it, in ways that do not anthropomorphize it and do not reduce it to the behavior of individuals or of human aggregates.
>
> *Guy E. Swanson (1976)*

THE IMPORTANCE OF ORGANIZATIONS

There is no need to belabor the assertion that ours is an organizational society—that organizations are a prominent, if not the dominant, characteristic of modern societies. Organizations were present in older civilizations—Chinese, Greek, Indian—but only in modern industrialized societies do we find large numbers of organizations engaged in performing many highly diverse tasks. To the ancient organizational assignments of soldiering, public administration, and tax collection have been added such varied tasks as discovery (research organizations), child and adult socialization (schools and universities), resocialization (mental hospitals and prisons), production and distribution of goods (industrial firms, wholesale and retail establishments), provision of services (organizations dispensing assistance ranging from laundry and shoe repair to medical care and investment counseling), protection of personal and financial security (police departments, insurance firms, banking and trust companies), preservation of culture (museums, art galleries, universities, libraries), communication (radio and television studios, telephone companies, the post office), and recreation (bowling alleys, pool halls, the National Park Service, professional football teams). Even such a partial listing testifies to the truth of Parsons's statement that "the development of organizations is the principal mechanism by which, in a highly dif-

3

ferentiated society, it is possible to 'get things done,' to achieve goals beyond the reach of the individual" (1960: 41).

Even though organizations are now ubiquitous, their development has been sufficiently gradual and uncontroversial that they have emerged during the past few centuries almost unnoticed. The spread of public bureaucracies into every sector and the displacement of the family business by the corporation "constitutes a revolution" in social structure, but one little remarked until recently.

> Never much agitated, never even much resisted, a revolution for which no flags were raised, it transformed our lives during those very decades in which, unmindful of what was happening, Americans and Europeans debated instead such issues as socialism, populism, free silver, clericalism, chartism, and colonialism. It now stands as a monument to discrepancy between what men think they are designing and the world they are in fact building. (Lindblom, 1977: 95)

Organizations in the form that we know them emerged during the nineteenth century in Europe and America, during the period of economic expansion occasioned by the industrial revolution. Not only did organizations rapidly increase in number and range of applications, they also underwent a transformation of structure as formerly "communal" forms based on the bonds of kinship and personal ties gave way to "associative" forms based on contractual arrangements among individuals having no ties other than a willingness to pursue shared interests or ends (see Starr, 1982: 148).

The increasing prevalence of organizations in every arena of social life is one indicator of their importance. Another, rather different index of their significance is the increasing frequency with which organizations are singled out as the source of many of the ills besetting contemporary society. Thus, writing in 1956, C. Wright Mills pointed with alarm to the emergence of a "power elite" whose members occupied the top positions in three overlapping organizational hierarchies: the state bureaucracy, the military, and the larger corporations. At about the same time, Ralf Dahrendorf (1959 trans.) in Germany was engaged in revising and updating Marxist doctrine by insisting that the basis of the class structure was no longer the ownership of the means of production but the occupancy of positions that allowed the wielding of organizational authority. Such views, which remain controversial, focus on the effects of organizations on societal stratification systems, taking account of the changing bases of power and prestige occasioned by the growth in number and size of organizations. More recently, concerned critics point with alarm to the increasing power of the multinational corporations as they search for cheap labor, dispoil the environment, and disrupt the continuity of stable communities (see Korten, 1995).

A related criticism concerns the seemingly inexorable growth in the power of public-sector organizations. The two great German sociologists, Max Weber (1968 trans.) and Robert Michels (1949 trans.), were among the first to insist that a central political issue confronting all modern societies is the enormous influence exercised by the (nonelected) public officials—the bureaucracy—over the ostensible political leaders.

Other criticisms point to the negative consequences of the growth of organizations in virtually *every* area of social existence. Borrowing from and enlarging on a theme pervading the thought of Weber, these critics decry the rationalization of modern life—in Weber's phrase, the "disenchantment of the world" (1946 trans.: 51). The essence of this view is graphically captured by Norman Mailer: "Civilization extracts its thousand fees from the best nights of man, but none so cruel as the replacement of the good fairy by the expert, the demon by the rational crisis, and the witch by the neurotic female" (1968:83). Organizations are viewed as the primary vehicle by which, systematically, the areas of our lives are rationalized—planned, articulated, scientized, made more efficient and orderly, and managed by "experts." (See, for example, Mannheim, 1950 trans.; Ellul, 1964 trans.; Goodman, 1968; and Galbraith, 1967.) A prosaic but powerful example is provided by the world-wide success of fast-food chains—the "Macdonaldization of Society" (Ritzer, 1993)—which have rationalized food preparation and depersonalized employee-customer relations.

A new generation of feminist critics reminds us that women as well as men are trapped within organizational cages. Glennon (1979) decries the growth of bureaucracy, but on the feminist grounds that it feeds the "dualism of private-expressive and public-instrumental selves and worlds" and engenders a ruthless rationality that extends instrumental and administrative orientations into everyday—including private—life. Ferguson is even more direct in her criticism:

> The organizational forms and discourse of bureaucratic capitalism institutionalize modes of domination that recreate the very patterns of oppression that feminism arose to combat. (1984: 203)

Bureaucratic structures are argued to give priority to masculine virtues and values. The principles by which organizations are structured—inequality, hierarchy, impersonality—devalue alternative modes of organizing that are alleged to be more characteristic of women's values: equalitarian and personalized associations. And the criteria associated with achievement—aggressive competition and independence—are very different from the nurturant and relational virtues often associated with feminine styles (see Gilligan, 1982; Calas and Smircich, 1996). Feminist critics assert that formal organizations are gender biased not only in their application of criteria for appointment and promotion but, more fundamentally, in their choice of criteria—in their conception of what is entailed in creating a rational system for supporting collaborative action. Contemporary organizations are said to be modeled on military systems and sports teams.

These critics thus add their voices to others who have called attention to the ways in which organizational structures damage the personalities and psyches of their participants. Alienation, overconformity, and the stunting of normal personality development are among the consequences attributed, not to such special cases as prisons and concentration camps, but to everyday, garden-variety organizations (see Argyris, 1957; Maslow, 1954; Whyte, 1956).

We attempt to evaluate such criticisms of organizations at appropriate points throughout this volume. Here we simply note that these wide-ranging accusations and concerns regarding the pervasive negative consequences of organizations provide further testimony to their importance in the modern world.

In addition to their being mechanisms for accomplishing a great variety of objectives and, perhaps as a necessary consequence, the source of many of our current difficulties, organizations have yet another important effect on our collective lives. This effect is more subtle and less widely recognized, but it may be the most profound in its implications. It is, perhaps, best introduced by an analogy: "The medium is the message." This twentieth-century aphorism was coined by Marshall McLuhan to focus attention on the characteristics of the mass media themselves—print, radio, movies, television—in contrast with the content transmitted by these media. McLuhan defines media very broadly as "any extension of ourselves"; elaborating his thesis, he notes, "The message of any medium is the change in scale or pace or pattern that it introduces into human affairs" (1964: 23, 24).

McLuhan's thesis appears to be more clearly applicable to our subject—organizations—than to any specific media of communication. First, like media, organizations represent extensions of ourselves. Organizations can achieve goals that are quite beyond the reach of any individual—from building skyscrapers and dams to putting a person on the moon. But to focus on what organizations do may conceal from us the more basic and far-reaching effects that occur because organizations are the mechanisms—the media—by which those goals are pursued. A few examples may suggest some of these unanticipated and, often, unrecognized organizational effects:

- In his crucial decision on how to react to the installation of Russian missiles in Cuba, President Kennedy had to select from among a naval blockade, a "surgical" air strike, and a massive land invasion, not because these were the only conceivable responses, but because these were the principal organizational routines that had been worked out by the Pentagon (see Allison, 1971).
- Although we seek "health" when we visit the clinic or the hospital, what we get is "medical care." Clients are encouraged to view these outputs as synonymous although there may be no relation between them. In some cases, the relation can even be negative; more care can result in poorer health (see Illich, 1976).
- Organizations may exert only weak effects on the activities of their participants, but still exert influence on external audiences because they embody and exemplify purposeful and responsible action. They depict rationality, enabling providers to offer a rational account of how resources were used and policies pursued (see Meyer and Rowan, 1977).

To suggest that our organizational tools shape the products and services they produce in unanticipated ways and, in some cases, substitute "accounts" for outcomes indicates the quite substantial impact that organizations have on individual activity. However, even this expanded view does not reveal the full significance of these forms.

We will fail to perceive the importance of organizations for our lives if we view them only as contexts—as arrangements influencing the activities of individual actors. Organizations must also be viewed as actors in their own right, as *collective* actors. They can take actions, utilize resources, enter into contracts, and own property. Coleman (1974) describes how these rights and capacities have gradually developed since the Middle Ages to the point where now it is accurate to speak of two kinds of persons—*natural* persons (such as you and me) and *collective* or juristic persons (such as the Red Cross and General Motors). The social structure of the modern society can no longer be described accurately as consisting only of relations among natural persons; our understanding must be stretched to include as well those relations between natural and collective persons, and between two or more collective persons.[1] In short, we must come to "the recognition that the society has changed over the past few centuries in the very structural elements of which it is composed" (Coleman, 1974: 13).

To this point, we have assembled a variety of evidence and arguments to support the case that organizations merit attention. All of these claims relate to their social significance: their ubiquity, their impact on power and status, their effects on personality and performance. A different kind of rationale for justifying the study of organizations points to their sociological significance: the contribution their study can make to our understanding of the social world.

George Homans points to the value for social science of studying organizations when he asserts:

> The fact is that the organization of the large formal enterprises, governmental or private, in modern society is modeled on, is a rationalization of, tendencies that exist in all human groups. (Homans, 1950: 186–87)

To say that organizations exhibit "tendencies that exist in all human groups" is to suggest that organizations provide the setting for a wide variety of basic social processes, such as socialization, communication, ranking, the formation of norms, the exercise of power, and goal setting and attainment. If these generic social processes operate in organizations, then we can add as much to our knowledge of the principles that govern their behavior by studying organizations as by studying any other specific type of social system. But Homans asserts something more.

---

[1]These developments were associated with and facilitated by changes in legal codes, as described in Chapter 7. Lawyers' practice also reflects the distinction in an interesting way, as described by Heinz and Laumann. They point out that much of the variation in current legal practice is accounted for by:

> one fundamental distinction—the distinction between lawyers who represent large organizations (corporations, labor unions, or government) and those who represent individuals. The two kinds of law practice are the two hemispheres of the profession. Most lawyers reside exclusively in one hemisphere or the other and seldom, if ever, cross over the equator. (Heinz and Laumann, 1982: 379)

It is also instructive to learn that lawyers who represent collective actors rather than natural persons are the more powerful, prosperous, and prestigious segment.

To say that we can perceive in organizations "a rationalization of tendencies that exist in all human groups" is to suggest that organizations are characterized by somewhat distinctive structural arrangements that affect the operation of the processes occurring within them. For example, social-control processes occur within all social groups, but there are some forms or mechanisms of control—for instance, a hierarchical authority structure—that are best studied in organizations, since it is within these systems that they appear in their most highly developed form.[2] The processes of interest can occur at various levels of analysis, as will be discussed in the following section. Also, decidedly, one of the important tasks is to spell out clearly what is meant by distinctive structural arrangements. We begin this task in the present chapter but will find it sufficiently challenging that we will need to keep it before us throughout this volume.

At this point, however, we assert our belief that the study of organizations can contribute to basic sociological knowledge by increasing our understanding of how generic social processes operate within distinctive social structures.

ORGANIZATIONS AS AN AREA OF STUDY

Emergence of the Area

The study of organizations is both a specialized field of inquiry within the discipline of sociology and an increasingly recognized focus of multidisciplinary research and training. It is impossible to determine with precision the moment of its appearance, but it is safe to conclude that until the late 1940s, organizations did not exist as a distinct field of sociological inquiry. Precursors may be identified, but each lacked some critical feature. Thus, there was some empirical research on organizations by, for example, criminologists who studied prisons (for example, Clemmer, 1940), political analysts who examined party structures (for example, Gosnell, 1937), and industrial sociologists who studied factories and labor unions (for example, Whyte, 1946). But these investigators rarely attempted to generalize beyond the specific organizational form they were studying. The subject was prisons or parties or factories or unions—not organizations. Similarly, in the neighboring disciplines, political scientists were examining the functioning of legislative bodies or public agencies, and economists were developing their theory of the firm, but they were not attempting to generalize beyond these specific forms.

Industrial psychologists did pursue such general problems as low morale, fatigue, and turnover within several types of organizational settings, but they did not attempt to determine systematically how the varying charac-

---

[2]This general argument has been elaborated elsewhere (Scott, 1970). The basic premise is that a set of generic social processes—such as socialization, integration, status, power, adaptation—may be identified in all social structures. However, each of these processes operates differently depending on the structural context in which it is acting so that, for example, the process of integration is effected in a small group differently than in an organization, and both differ from the same process occurring within a community, and so on.

teristics of different organizational contexts influenced these worker reactions. And although, from early in this century, administrative and management theorists such as Taylor (1911), Fayol (1949 trans.), and Gulick and Urwick (1937) did concentrate on the development of general principles concerning administrative arrangements, their approach was more often prescriptive than empirical. That is, they were interested in determining what the proper form "should be" in the interests of maximizing efficiency and effectiveness rather than in examining and explaining organizational arrangements as they existed. They also focused primary attention on managerial activities and functions rather than on the wider subjects of organizations and organizing (see Guillen, 1994).

Within sociology, the emergence of the field of organizations may be roughly dated from the translation into English of Weber's (1946 trans., 1947 trans.) and, to a lesser extent, Michels's (1949 trans.) analyses of bureaucracy. Shortly after these classic statements became accessible to American sociologists, Robert K. Merton and his students at Columbia University attempted to outline the boundaries of this new field of inquiry by compiling theoretical and empirical materials dealing with various aspects of organizations (Merton et al., 1952). Equally important, a series of pathbreaking and influential case studies of diverse types of organizations was launched under Merton's influence, including an examination of the Tennessee Valley Authority (Selznick, 1949), a gypsum mine and factory (Gouldner, 1954), a state employment agency and a federal law-enforcement agency (Blau, 1955), and a union (Lipset, Trow, and Coleman, 1956). For the first time, sociologists were engaged in the development and empirical testing of generalizations dealing with the structure and functioning of organizations viewed as organizations.

At about the same time, an important interdisciplinary development was under way at the Carnegie Institute of Technology (now Carnegie-Mellon University). Herbert Simon became head of the Department of Industrial Management in 1949, assembled an eclectic group of political scientists, economists, engineers, and psychologists, and encouraged them to focus their energies on building a behaviorally oriented science of administration. Following Simon's lead, emphasis was placed on decision making and choice within organizations (Simon, 1976). The unrealistic assumption of a single, towering entrepreneur, rational and all-knowing, that dominated economic models of the firm was replaced first by the view of intendedly rational but cognitively limited actors (March and Simon, 1958), and subsequently by models emphasizing the multiple and competing objectives of participants in organizations (Cyert and March, 1963). Economic models of administrative behavior were modified and enriched by the insights of psychologists and political scientists.

These central and other related efforts gave rise to the identification of a new area of study—organizations; an area defined at a level of *theoretical abstraction* sufficiently general to call attention to similarities in form and function across different arenas of activity; and a subject matter that exhibited sufficient diversity and complexity to encourage and reward *empirical investigation*. The key elements for creating a new arena of scientific study were in place. As Alfred North Whitehead (1925: 3–4), the astute philosopher of science, observes:

All the world over and at all times there have been practical men, absorbed in "irreducible and stubborn facts": all the world over and at all times there have been men of a philosophical temperament who have been absorbed in the weaving of general principles. It is this union of passionate interest in the detailed facts with equal devotion to abstract generalization which form the novelty of our present society.

Accompanying the creation of the new subject area was a search for appropriate intellectual ancestors to provide respectability and legitimacy—Machiavelli, Saint-Simon, Marx, and Weber were obvious candidates. And more recent forebears, such as Taylor, Barnard, and Mayo, were rediscovered and reprinted. Even a couple of token women contributors were identified, in the persons of Lillian M. Gilbreth—who collaborated with her husband in finding ways to improve work efficiency in factories but also applied the techniques to organizing her housework and whose feats are celebrated in the book and movie *Cheaper by the Dozen* (see Gilbreth and Gilbreth, 1917)—and Mary Parker Follett (1942), an early student of management and change working in the human relations tradition. After about a decade of empirical research and theory development, three textbook-treatises—by March and Simon (1958), Etzioni (1961), and Blau and Scott (1962)—provided needed integration and heightened interest in the field. Also, a new journal, *Administrative Science Quarterly*, beginning publication in 1956 under the editorship of James D. Thompson, emphasized the interdisciplinary character of the field.[3]

Common and Divergent Interests

What features do all organizations exhibit in common? What are the general organizational issues analysts began to perceive among the great diversity of tasks and structural arrangements? Most analysts have conceived of organizations as *social structures created by individuals to support the collaborative pursuit of specified goals.* Given this conception, all organizations confront a number of common problems. All must define (and redefine) their objectives; all must induce participants to contribute services; all must control and coordinate these contributions; resources must be garnered from the environment and products or services dispensed; participants must be selected, trained, and replaced; and some sort of working accommodation with the neighbors must be achieved.

In addition to these common operational requirements, some analysts have also emphasized that all organizations are beset by a common curse. Not all resources can be devoted directly to goal attainment; some—in some cases a high proportion—must be expended to maintain the organization itself. Although organizations are viewed as means to accomplish ends, the

---

[3]Other brief histories of the development of organizations as an identifiable field of inquiry are provided by March (1965: ix–xvi) and Pfeffer (1982: 23–33). An entertaining, if jaundiced, view of the evolution of organization theory can be found in Perrow (1973). Summaries of the contributions of major organizational theorists together with brief biographical information have been assembled by Pugh and Hickson (1996).

means themselves absorb much energy, and in the extreme (but perhaps not rare) case, become ends in themselves.

There is a convergence of interest around these common features, but we must not overlook the many bases of divergence. These include differences among the organizations themselves as objects of study, differences in the interests and backgrounds of those who study organizations, and differences in the level of analysis at which inquiry is pitched.

Diverse organizations. Organizations come in a bewildering variety of sizes and shapes. The largest of them are immense. Although the exact numbers depend on how the boundaries are defined, there is little doubt that the largest organizational units found in modern society are the military services. The U.S. Department of the Navy includes over 4 million people if we count active officer and enlisted ranks, reservists, civil service employees, and contractor employees; the Army and the Air Force generate similar numbers (Cote and Sapolsky, 1990). Within the civilian world, the largest industrial corporation, General Motors, employed over 370,000 employees in its North American plants, although it eliminated 75,000 workers in its "downsizing" operations during the early 1990s. AT&T, before divestiture, counted more than 3 million stockholders. Most workers in this country are employees of someone else; only about 8 percent of the workforce is self-employed. And more workers are employed by fewer and larger companies: by 1975, 3 percent of the employing organizations accounted for 55 percent of the employed, and about one quarter of the total workforce was employed by firms with more than 1,000 employees.

Size, however, should not be equated with success. Perhaps for a time in the industrial age size as measured by employees or productive capacity was instrumental to success (survival, profitability), but such an association is ill suited to the postindustrial era. Recent years have seen efforts to restructure and downsize many of the corporate giants. Indeed, it is somewhat ironic that the largest corporate enterprise in the United States in the mid-1990s is Manpower Temporary Services, with over 800,000 workers. More generally, Carroll (1994) reports that the average size of business organizations in the United States has declined from about 50 employees per company in 1960 to about 31 employees in 1989. The most productive and innovative businesses are often small or intermediate in size.

In an age when giant organizations seem to dominate the landscape, it is important to emphasize that small organizations are actually in the majority: 51 percent of all employing organizations in the United States in 1975 employed three or fewer individuals (U.S. Department of Labor, 1979). And the predominant ownership form remains the sole proprietorship, with more than 12 million establishments, compared with about 2.8 million corporations and about 1.5 million partnerships. Of course, the corporation far outstrips the other forms in assets, employees, and earnings (U.S. Bureau of the Census, 1984). These employment organizations also vary greatly in the types of goods and services provided: from coal mining to computers, from fortune-telling to futures forecasting.

Large numbers of people are employed in the public sector. In 1990, in the United States, over 18 million individuals—about 15 percent of the number working in the private sector—were employed in federal, state, and local governments. The number of units or agencies involved is difficult to determine because of the nested character of governmental forms. *The United States Government Manual* (U.S. Office of the Federal Register, 1992) provides organizational charts and brief descriptions of the principal agencies. It currently numbers almost 1,000 pages! Federal employees make up only about 17 percent of all governmental officials, the vast majority of whom are employed at the state (4.5 million) and local levels (10.7 million), where there exists great variation in organizational arrangements.

The shift in type of employment settings has been dramatic. In 1960 roughly half as many jobs were to be found in manufacturing as in services (including public sector employment). By 1992, the ratio had shifted to one out of five, in favor of the services sector. Indeed, more Americans are now employed in government service than in all of manufacturing. The gender composition of the workforce has also changed greatly in a relatively short period. In the 1940s women made up only about 20 percent of the workforce. By 1994, over 46 percent—nearly half—of all workers were women. And women are not only employees of organizations. By the beginning of the 1990s, women owned about 30 percent of U.S. firms, accounting for about 14 percent of all sales.

Employing organizations do not exhaust the list of organizational forms. Verba and Nie (1972) estimate that about two-thirds of adult Americans belong to one or more voluntary associations, not counting churches. The number and variety of such forms is large, and includes labor unions, political parties, professional societies, business and trade associations, fraternities and sororities, civic service associations, reform and activist groups, and neighborhood organizations. Two "slices" into this world suggest how diverse it is. A vertical slice, extracting only one occupational group, doctors of medicine, reveals over 380 specialty associations listed in the *Directory of Medical Specialists*. A horizontal slice, an attempt to compile a detailed list of all voluntary associations in Birmingham, England, reported 4,264 such organizations (Newton, 1975).

In addition to size and sector, organizations vary greatly in structural characteristics. The relatively flat authority and control structure found in many voluntary associations stands in sharp contrast with the multilayer hierarchy of a military unit or a civil service bureaucracy. And both seem relatively clean and simple in comparison with the project team or matrix structures (discussed in Chapter 9) found in research and development units of high-tech companies. Much attention has recently been directed to "network" or alliance forms: cooperative connections among formally independent organizations that enable them to enjoy simultaneously the benefits associated with being small, such as rapid response, and with being large, such as economies of scale. (These forms are discussed in Chapter 10.)

Some organizations are capital intensive, placing most of their resources in machinery and automated equipment. Others invest heavily in the "human capital" of their workforce, selecting highly qualified personnel, underwriting their further, specialized training, and then struggling to keep them from carrying off their expertise to some other company. Some organizations directly employ most of the personnel that carry on the activities of the enterprise; others contract out much of their work, even the functions of general management.

Organizations also vary greatly because they relate to and draw on different surrounding environments. Public agencies differ from private firms even when they carry on the same kinds of work because they function in different contexts. It matters considerably whether you operate to satisfy the demands of many decentralized customers or one centralized budget or oversight bureau. Much of what we know about organizations is drawn from organizations operating in the last decades of the twentieth century in capitalist, democratic societies—and in one such society in particular, the United States. Only recently have there been extensive efforts to examine the structure and operation of organizations in different times, using historical documents, and in different kinds of societies.

Large-scale organizations devoted to the pursuit of specialized goals developed in this country during the middle of the nineteenth century. Many of the characteristics we associate with modern organizations—the specialized equipment, the sizable administrative hierarchy, the collection of specialists—first appeared in association with the development of the railroads. Handling the problems of scale and scope, of distance and tight scheduling precipitated the development of the "managerial revolution" (see Chandler, 1977). Organizations developing at this time were different in structure from those developing later: the unified structures soon gave way to diversified and conglomerate forms, which in turn are now being replaced by more flexible, network arrangements. More generally, as Stinchcombe (1965) first observed, organizational forms exhibit different structures that reflect the times in which they were created. Thus, at any given time, much of the diversity exhibited by a collection of organizations is due to the varying conditions present at the time of their birth.

The remarkable recent economic performance of the East Asian "tigers"—especially Japanese, South Korean, and Indonesian firms—has stimulated great interest in these organizations, and investigations of their operation have confirmed the importance of context. For example, one cannot understand the Japanese corporation without attention to the distinctive belief systems governing employment, the connections between a company and its family of firms (the Zaibatsu), and the relations between private firms and the state (Hamilton and Biggart, 1988). Less dramatic but significant differences are associated with organizations operating on the European continent as well as in other areas of the world (see Hofstede, 1984; Chandler, 1990; Whitley, 1992b). Among all the other sources of variation, we must not overlook temporal, regional, and cultural factors.

Diverse interests. Another basis for divergence in work on organizations resides not in the differences among organizations as objects of study but in the interests, training, and employment settings of those who study organizations. As already noted, researchers from different disciplines vary to some extent in the kinds of organizations they choose to study. Political scientists continue to focus on political parties and state administrative structures, economists on business firms, sociologists on voluntary associations and on agencies engaged in social welfare and social control functions, and anthropologists on comparative administration in primitive, colonial, and developing societies. Disciplinary differences remain even when a single type of organization is selected for study: specialists tend to look not only at different objects but also at different aspects of the same object. Thus, the political scientist will be likely to emphasize power processes and decision making within the organization; the economist will examine the acquisition and allocation of scarce resources within the organization and will attend to such issues as productivity and efficiency; the sociologist has quite varied interests, but if there is a focus it will likely be on status orderings, on the effect of norms and sentiments on behavior, and on organizational legitimacy; the psychologist will be interested in variations in perception, cognition, and motivation among participants; and the anthropologist will call attention to the effects of diverse cultural values on the functioning of the system and its members. The study of organizations embraces all these interests, and students of organizations work to develop conceptual frameworks within which all these topics and their interrelations may be examined. And, increasingly, organizational analysts attempt to specify what is distinctive about power, or status, or motivation, or cultural processes because they occur within the context of organizations.

Cutting across these disciplinary divisions is another, more general basis of divergence among those who study organizations: the adoption of a *basic* versus an *applied* research orientation. Some studies (basic) are aimed primarily at accurately describing existing features and relations of organizations in order simply to better understand their nature and operation. Others (applied) seek knowledge in order to solve specific problems or to bring about desired changes in these systems. Of course, there is not a hard-and-fast line between these interests. Basic research, particularly in the long run, can lead to practical applications, and applied research often contributes importantly to general knowledge. Both rest on interests and values—neither is value-free; and the same investigators often conduct both basic and applied studies.

Still, there are important differences in these orientations. Basic research is driven more by theory—in its choice both of problems and of variables. Particular concepts—authority, legitimacy, institutionalization—are of interest because of their place in theoretical arguments, not because of their practical significance. Basic research is more likely to focus on the independent variables—on understanding the effects of certain concepts of interest—than on the dependent variables. Conversely, applied research is driven by an interest in solving some identified problem—low morale or productivity, high turnover—and is willing to incorporate any kinds of variables, whether economic, psychological, or cultural, that may shed light on it. Thus, applied studies are much more likely to be interdisciplinary: practical problems do not respect disciplinary boundaries.

Although there are many exceptions, applied research is more likely to be conducted by researchers located in nonacademic settings: in governmental bureaus, research units of corporations, consulting firms, or policy-research organizations. The results of these studies are less likely to be published in scholarly journals; often they result in no publications at all, only a report to the client group and/or chief executive officer. Basic research is conducted largely within the academic departments of colleges and universities. This work is either unfunded—and hence subsidized by the academic institution (which may, for example, permit low teaching loads and reward faculty for their research productivity)—or funded largely through research grants from government sources or private foundations.[4] These organizations support research primarily because of "public interest" arguments: it is better to know than not to know, and all benefit from the discovery of new knowledge.

An intermediate group of scholars "swings" both ways. These academics are faculty members in professional schools: business, educational administration, public administration, public health, engineering management, social-work administration, and so forth. These faculty are more likely to engage in consulting work for private companies or public organizations than those located in academic departments, and they are generally more likely to carry out applied studies, in part because of pressures from their students—past (alumni) and present—who are interested in usable practical information and in skills that will affect the "bottom line," such as profits. At the same time, these individuals are confronted by demands from their school and university to contribute to basic knowledge—that is, to publish in scholarly journals. As faculty members of a university, they are subject to the academic culture and its requirements, although the strength of these pressures varies from campus to campus and school to school.

Both the basic and the applied science orientations have made and may be expected to continue to make important contributions to our knowledge of organizations—what they are and how they work. In the long run, each orientation depends on and complements the other, and a healthy scientific enterprise requires that both types of research receive attention and support.

Diverse levels of analysis. Although organizations furnish a common locus of research for many social scientists, they vary greatly in the types of questions they seek to address. Even apart from the variety of conceptual schemes and orientations that guide inquiry and the differences in methodological tools, investigators differ in the level of analysis at which they choose to work (see Blau, 1957). For present purposes, the level of analysis is determined by the nature of the dependent variable—that is, by whether the phenomenon to be explained is (1) the behavior or interpersonal relations involving individual participants within organizations, (2) the structural features or processes that characterize organizations; or (3) the characteristics or actions of the organization viewed as a collective entity operating in a larger system of relations. We will briefly discuss each of these levels.

Some investigators are interested in explaining individual behavior within an organization. At this *social psychological* level, organizational characteristics are viewed as context or environment, and the investigator attempts to explore their impact on the attitudes or behavior of individuals.

---

[4]Increasingly, however, scholars within academic departments are also affiliating with other organizational units—laboratories, centers, institutes—both within the university and outside. These organizations serve as a research base for studies that are often applied in character.

Such a perspective is exemplified by the work of Katz and Kahn (1978) and of Porter, Lawler, and Hackman (1975).

At the second level, the major concern is to explain the structural features and social processes that characterize organizations and their subdivisions. The investigator working at this *structural* level may focus on the various subunits that make up the organization (for example, work groups, departments, authority ranks) or may examine various analytical components (for example, specialization, communication networks, hierarchy) that characterize the structural features or operational routines of organizations. Researchers working at this level include Udy (1959b) and Blau and Schoenherr (1971).

At the third level of analysis, the focus is on the organization as a collective actor functioning in a larger system of relations. At this *ecological* level, the analyst may choose either to examine the relation between a specific organization or class of organizations and the environment (for example, Selznick, 1949; Pugh et al., 1969) or to examine the relations that develop among a number of organizations viewed as an interdependent system (for example, Pfeffer and Salancik, 1978; Miles, 1982). Admittedly, distinguishing among these three levels of analysis is somewhat arbitrary and ambiguous.[5] Many levels of analytical complexity can be identified as one moves from organizational-individual to societal-organizational relations.[6] Nevertheless, if only to remind us of the complexity of the subject matter and the variety of aims and interests with which analysts approach it, the three distinctions are helpful in providing a rough gauge for distinguishing among broad categories of studies.

Early research on organizations was conducted almost exclusively at the social-psychological level. The structural level of analysis became prominent in the early 1960s and continues to be heavily utilized by sociologists. The ecological level was the last to develop, emerging in the late 1960s, but it is this level that is associated with much of the intellectual excitement and energy that have characterized the field during the past three decades.

Yet another base of divergence among those who study organizations is the *theoretical perspective* employed by the analyst. However, this is, in our view, such a fundamental difference that it provides the basic themes around which we have organized this volume. Whether the analyst employs a rational, natural, or open system perspective, or some combination, is viewed as central to interpreting the work. Chapters 2, 3, and 4 are devoted to reviewing these perspectives while the subsequent chapters explicate the ways in which they have been developed and combined.

Because so much of our attention in succeeding chapters will be devoted to emphasizing divergent perspectives, it is prudent in the next section to return to the theme of the basic characteristics shared by all organizations.

---

[5]The most commonly employed distinction is that between "micro" and "macro" organizational studies. The former is equivalent to the social psychological level; the latter encompasses both the structural and the ecological levels.

[6]In Chapter 6 we introduce and define several additional levels of analysis, all of which are distinctions made within the ecological level.

THE ELEMENTS OF ORGANIZATIONS

Organizations are diverse and complex, and so it may be helpful to begin with a simplifying model focusing on their central features. The proposed model shown in Figure 1–1 is adapted from Leavitt (1965).[7] Let us briefly consider each element.

Social Structure

Social structure refers to the patterned or regularized aspects of the relationships existing among participants in an organization. The social structure of any human grouping can be analytically separated into two components. As Kingsley Davis suggests:

> Always in human society there is what may be called a double reality—on the one hand a normative system embodying what *ought* to be, and on the other a factual order embodying what *is*. . . . These two orders cannot be completely identical, nor can they be completely disparate. (1949: 52)

We shall refer to Davis's first component as the *normative structure*, including values, norms, and role expectations. Briefly, *values* are the criteria employed in selecting the goals of behavior; *norms* are the generalized rules governing behavior that specify, in particular, appropriate means for pursuing goals; and *roles* are expectations for or evaluative standards employed in assessing the behavior of occupants of specific social positions. A social position is simply a location in a system of social relationships. (For a basic formulation of positions and roles, see Gross, Mason, and McEachern, 1958.) In any social grouping, values, norms, and roles are not randomly arranged, but are organized so as to constitute a relatively coherent and consistent set of

[7]Leavitt identifies the four "internal" elements but does not include the environment as a separate factor. As will be obvious from our discussion, we regard the environment as an indispensable ingredient in the analysis of organizations.

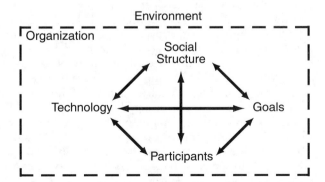

FIGURE 1–1 Leavitt's Diamond: A Model of an Organization.
Source: Adapted from Leavitt (1965), Figure 1, p. 1145.

beliefs and prescriptions governing the behavior of participants. It is for this reason that we speak of a normative *structure*.

The second component, which Davis refers to as "a factual order," we will call the *behavioral structure*. This component focuses on actual behavior rather than on prescriptions for behavior. Homans's (1950: 33–40) well-known classification of social behavior into activities, interactions, and sentiments suggests the types of elements that constitute the behavioral structure. Because our concern is with the analysis of behavioral *structure*, rather than simply behavior, we focus on those activities, interactions, and sentiments that exhibit some degree of regularity—the recurrent behavior of a given individual or similarities in the behavior of a class of individuals. Such actions, exhibiting some consistency and constancy in their general characteristics, are themselves arranged into larger patterns or networks of behavior. For example, we may observe in a group over a period of time which individuals attempt to influence others and with what degree of success, and in this way obtain a description of the power structure within that group. Or by observing the patterning of sentiments among group members—who is attracted to or rejected by whom—we can describe the sociometric structure of the group. Both the power structure and the sociometric structure are specific instances of behavioral structures.

As the passage from Davis reminds us, the normative structure and the behavioral structure of a social group are neither independent nor identical, but are to varying degrees interrelated. The normative structure imposes an important set of constraints on the behavioral structure, shaping and channeling behavior and helping to account for much of the regularity and patterning that exists. On the other hand, much behavior departs from the normative structure and is an important source of changes in that structure. Behavior shapes norms just as norms shape behavior. Groups vary in the extent to which their normative and behavioral structures are aligned. In some situations precept corresponds closely to practice: this appears to be the case in many utopian communities or communes—at least in their early stages of development (see Kanter, 1972). In many prisons, on the other hand, there is a large gap between what the rules specify and how the guards and inmates actually behave. Nevertheless, in every existing social structure, the normative and behavioral structures are always in a state of dynamic tension—each existing and changing somewhat independently of the other while at the same time exerting continuing influence on the other.

All social groups—or *collectivities*, to use the more general sociological concept—are characterized by a normative structure applicable to the participants and by a behavioral structure linking participants in a common network or pattern of activities, interactions, and sentiments. These two interrelated structures constitute the *social structure* of a collectivity.

Organizational participants are likely to emphasize the amount of confusion, the indeterminacy, and the unpredictability of the actions of their coworkers, in part because such matters draw their attention and require their energies. However, to focus on the social structure of organizations is to emphasize the impressive amount of order exhibited by the behavior of participants in organizations. Every day hundreds or thousands of persons in organizations perform millions of individual acts, yet the outcome is not bedlam, not total confusion or chaos, but a reasonable approximation of order. This remarkable achievement merits our attention.

Emphasizing the importance of the social structure of organizations does not commit us to the view that relations among participants are all sweetness and light: social structure does not connote social harmony. Conflict is always present and has helped to shape the social structure. An emphasis on social structure should enable us to see that much of whatever conflict is present in the organization is patterned, in the sense that it is built into the structure of relations between individuals and groups and is not due to innately aggressive individual participants. Not only stability and order, but tension and stress, deviance and change, can often be attributed to structural factors (see Merton, 1957: 131–60).

The social structure of an organization varies in the extent to which it is formalized. A *formal* social structure is one in which the social positions and the relationships among them have been explicitly specified and are defined independently of the personal characteristics and relations of the participants occupying these positions. By contrast, in an *informal* social structure, it is impossible to distinguish between the characteristics of the positions and the prescribed relations and the characteristics and personal relations of the participants. In an informal structure, when specific participants leave or enter the system, their roles and relationships develop and change as a function of their personal characteristics and the interpersonal relations they develop.[8]

Participants—Social Actors

Organizational participants are those individuals who, in return for a variety of inducements, make contributions to the organization (Barnard, 1938; Simon, 1976). All individuals participate in more than one organization (recall that, by definition, organizations are specialized in their purposes), and the extent and intensiveness of their involvement may vary greatly; the decision as to who is to be regarded as a participant is thus often a difficult one and may legitimately vary with the issue at hand. For example, a single individual may simultaneously be an employee of an industrial firm, a member of a union, a church member, a member of a fraternal lodge or sorority, a "member" of a political party, a citizen of the state, a client of a group medical practice, a stockholder in one or more companies, and a customer in numerous retail and service organizations. For some purposes, analysts might wish to treat customers as organizational participants; for other purposes, they might be excluded. Analysts disagree, as we shall see, on the extent to which organizations do and should incorporate facets of partici-

[8]Of course, at any given point in the history of a particular structure, new jobs are being created around the particular skills and interests of specific individuals. Miner (1987) has labeled these positions idiosyncratic jobs and notes two subtypes: "evolved jobs," created around current organizational members, and "opportunistic hires," created around people outside the organization. The number of such positions appears to vary considerably by type of organization, as does the extent to which such informal positions become codified and formalized. Informal job redefinition followed by codification appears to be a significant form of mobility in some organizations.

pants. How much of the personality and private life of individual participants is relevant to the functioning of the organization also varies from one type of organization and role to another: consider the situation of a novice in a religious order versus that of an occasional customer in a supermarket.

The demographic characteristics of participants—for example, their age, gender, ethnic distributions—have important consequences for many aspects of organizational structure and functioning; we will explore these implications in Chapter 7. And the structural features of organizations—the opportunities they create and the sorting rules they use for selection, retention, and promotion—have equally fateful consequences for participants, as we discuss in Chapter 8.

However, it is essential to emphasize that participants are, first and foremost, the social actors. It is their energy, their conformity, their disobedience that constitutes and shapes the structure of the organization. Without their participation, there is no social structure, no organization. Early sociological theories privileged social structure. More recent theorists remind us that social structures do not exist unless—and only exist to the extent that—social actors carry out the requisite activities. They also insist that social actors are the instruments of both continuity—the reproduction of structure—and change—the production of novelty and innovation (see Bourdieu, 1977 trans.).

Giddens usefully explicates this conception of the "duality" of social structure: it is, at one and the same time, both medium and outcome. Structure influences ongoing actions and it is constituted by—made up of—such actions:

> Every process of action is a production of something new, a fresh act; but at the same time all action exists in continuity with the past, which supplies the means of its initiation. Structure thus is not to be conceptualized as a barrier to action, but as essentially involved in its production, even in the most radical processes of social change. (Giddens, 1979: 70)

This conception helps to correct for an all-too-common sociological bias: an emphasis on the power and weight of existing social arrangements coupled with a discounting of the importance of individual imagination and initiative. On the other hand, it also guards against the more common individualistic bias, particularly pervasive in the American culture, which attributes all events to individual interest and will.

Goals

The concept of organizational goals is among the most important—and most controversial—to be confronted in the study of organizations. Some analysts insist that goals are indispensable to the understanding of organizations; others question whether goals perform any function other than to justify past actions. Behaviorists are fond of pointing out that only individuals have goals; collectivities, such as organizations, do not. We will not attempt to tackle these prickly issues here but promise not to duck them indefinitely.

For most analysts, goals constitute a central point of reference in the study of organizations. *Goals* are tentatively defined as conceptions of desired ends—ends that participants attempt to achieve through their performance of task activities.

Since goals figure prominently in some definitions of organizations, we will consider them further in the following section, and we will discuss the major issues and problems bearing on their analysis in Chapter 11.

Technology

To focus on the technology of an organization is to view the organization as a place where some type of work is done, as a location where energy is applied to the transformation of materials, as a mechanism for transforming inputs into outputs. The connotations of the term technology are narrow and hard, but we will insist that every organization does work and possesses a technology for doing that work. Some organizations process material inputs and fabricate new equipment and hardware. Others "process" people, their products consisting of more knowledgeable individuals, in the case of effective school systems, or healthier individuals, in the case of effective medical clinics. Still others process primarily symbolic materials, such as information or music. The *technology* of an organization is often embedded in part in machines and mechanical equipment but also comprises the technical knowledge and skills of participants.

All organizations possess technologies, but organizations vary in the extent to which these techniques are understood, or routinized, or efficacious. Some of the most interesting theoretical and empirical work in recent years has focused on the relation between the characteristics of technology and the structural features of organizations. This work is described and evaluated in Chapter 9.

Environment

Every organization exists in a specific physical, technological, cultural, and social environment to which it must adapt. No organization is self-sufficient; all depend for survival on the types of relations they establish with the larger systems of which they are a part. Early analysts of organizations, as we will see, tended to overlook or underestimate the importance of organization-environmental linkages, but recent work places great emphasis on these connections. And, indeed, the number and variety of these connections are impressive. Let us briefly reconsider each of the four organizational components in this light.

Consider organizational participants. Very few organizations assume full responsibility for the socialization and training of their participants. Employees come to the organization with heavy cultural and social baggage obtained from interactions in other social contexts. With very few exceptions—such as inmates in "total institutions," for example, concentration camps or cloisters (Goffman, 1961)—participants are involved in more than one organization at any given time. These outside interests and commitments inevitably constrain the behavior of participants in any given organization and, in some instances, strongly influence it. To regard participants as completely contained by the organization is to misperceive one of the fundamental characteristics of modern organizations: that they are systems built on the partial involvement of their members.

What about technologies? Few organizations create their own technologies; rather, they import them from the environment in the form of mechanical equipment, packaged programs and sets of instructions, and trained workers. Any specific organization must also adapt to the larger occupational structure—for example, union rules or professional norms—in the selection and deployment of workers within the organization. Moreover, the environment is the source of the inputs to be processed by the organization, just as it is the "sink" to which all outputs are delivered—as products to be sold, clients restored to function, or waste materials to be eliminated.

How do goals relate to environments? Parsons (1960) has called attention to the importance of this connection. He points out that what is termed a goal or objective by a specific organization is, from the point of view of the larger society, its specialized function. An organization may thus expect societal support for its activities to reflect the relative value society places on those functions: if health represents a strong positive value for a society, for example, then those organizations that supply health care may expect to receive a disproportional share of resources to support their work.

Finally, the social structure of the organization will reflect important features borrowed from or impressed on it by the environment. Structural forms, no less than technologies, are rarely invented and are usually borrowed from the environment. Part Three of this volume explores the thesis that environmental complexity tends to be incorporated within and reflected by the structural features of organizations. These incorporations may give rise to formal components such as rules or offices or departments, or they may form the basis for informal cliques or for work patterns not sanctioned by the formal structure. Both formal and informal structures can have their roots in the environment.

While insisting on the pervasive and critical importance of environmental influences on organizational forms and operations, we must not assume that the causal processes work in only one direction. Organizations not only are influenced by but also affect their environments. Although modern theorists differ in their views of the relative importance of these causal connections, as we will discuss in later chapters, they generally agree that the relations between organizations and environments are vital, complex, and interdependent. Each of the four organizational elements shapes and is sigificantly shaped by the wider environment. To complete the diagram of Leavitt's diamond depicted in Figure 1–1, we should add double-headed arrows linking the environment to each of the "internal" elements. As reframed, Leavitt's diamond might better be renamed the thistle.

Each of these organizational elements—social structure, participants, goals, technology, environment—represents an important component of all organizations. Indeed, each element has been regarded as of surpassing importance by one or another analyst of organizations. However, the chief value of Leavitt's model is as a graphic reminder that no one element is so dominant as to be safely considered in isolation from the others. Organizations are, first and foremost, systems of elements, each of which affects and is affected by the others. Goals are not the key to understanding the nature and functioning of organizations, any more than are the participants, the technology, or the social structure. And no organization can be understood in isolation from the larger environment. We will miss the essence of organization if we insist on focusing on any single feature to the exclusion of all others.

THE BENEFITS OF ORGANIZATIONS

The foregoing discussion represents an opening attempt to identify some of the key elements or ingredients of organizations: to specify their building blocks. However, such an approach does not go far toward explaining what they are good for. What are their distinctive capacities and benefits? We briefly address this question here but will return to it again throughout the volume.

Hannan and Carroll (1995) identify a number of features that help to explain why organizations are much in demand as vehicles for conducting the myriad of activities associated with modern social life. First, more so than many other types of social structures, organizations are *durable:* they are designed in such a way as to persist over time, routinely and continuously supporting efforts to carry on a set of specified activities. More so than other types of social structures, they are expected to operate as long-distance runners. Attaining stability over time and in spite of shifting participants is one of the major functions of formalization, as we will emphasize in Chapter 2. Durability is not to be mistaken for rigidity. Many of the newer forms of organizations are designed to combine great flexibility with the maintenance of an organizational core that persists across changing combinations of personnel and structure and even goals.

A second benefit associated with organizations is their *reliability* (Hannan and Carroll, 1995: 20). Organizations are good at doing the same things in the same way, over and over, and for many types of activities there are many advantages associated with this characteristic. In later chapters we will describe the numerous means of control utilized in organizations, including formalization, authority structures, elaborate rules and routines, strong cultures, and the use of specialized machinery. All of these factors and more are designed in part to increase the reliability of the work activities being performed. Reliability of performance is not, of course, an unmixed blessing. To the extent that conditions change and new activities are called for, the very factors associated with effective performance may prevent organizations from changing their rules and procedures quickly enough to develop new ways of behaving. Still, for many types of activities and many situations, there are great advantages associated with the ability to reliably produce goods and services.

Third, organizations exhibit the trait of being *accountable* (Hannan and Carroll, 1995: 21; see also, Meyer and Rowan, 1977). Behavior takes place within a framework of rules that provide both guidelines and justifications for decisions and activities. They establish a framework of rationality that allows participants to give an accounting of their past behaviors. This framework is connected to and supported by legal codes that define the powers and limits of the vast majority of organizations. Records are kept and a "paper trail" created so that, if necessary, the bases for past actions can be reviewed. The hierarchy of authority is expected, at least in part, to ensure that rules are being followed and work performed in accordance with agreed-on standards and procedures. Of course, not all organizations measure up to these standards: there is much evidence of both incompetence and corruption. More important, as we will learn, the type of rationality involved—formal rationality—is itself a limited and flawed basis for ensuring reasonable, let alone moral, conduct. Nevertheless, in an imperfect world, there is much to be said for systems in which individuals attempt to operate within an explicit framework of rules nested in wider legal systems to which they are accountable.

DEFINING THE CONCEPT OF ORGANIZATION

Consistent with the objectives of this volume, not one but three definitions of organizations are offered. These definitions pave the way for our description and evaluation in Part Two of three major perspectives employed in the analysis of organizations. Thus, we leave to later chapters the considerable task of spelling out the implications of these differing definitions. Special attention is accorded to the first definition because it continues to be the dominant perspective in the field, not only in guiding the work of the majority of organizational scholars but in being embraced at least implicitly by most real-world managers and other participants. Moreover, this definition served to establish organizations as a distinctive field of study. The first definition underpins the *rational system* perspective on organization. Two other definitions—one associated with the *natural system* perspective and the other with the *open system* perspective—will be briefly described here and examined more fully in later chapters.

A Rational System Definition

Because a primary function of a definition is to help us distinguish one phenomenon from another, most definitions of organizations emphasize the distinctive features of organizations—those that distinguish them from related social forms. Many analysts have attempted to formulate such definitions, and their views appear to be similar, as illustrated by the following four influential definitions.

According to Barnard:

> formal organization is that kind of coöperation among men that is conscious, deliberate, purposeful. (1938: 4)

According to March and Simon:

> Organizations are assemblages of interacting human beings and they are the largest assemblages in our society that have anything resembling a central coordinative system. . . . The high specificity of structure and coordination within

organizations—as contrasted with the diffuse and variable relations among organizations and among unorganized individuals—marks off the individual organization as a sociological unit comparable in significance to the individual organism in biology. (1958: 4)

According to Blau and Scott:

Since the distinctive characteristic of . . . organizations is that they have been formally established for the explicit purpose of achieving certain goals, the term "formal organizations" is used to designate them.[9] (1962: 5)

And, according to Etzioni:

Organizations are social units (or human groupings) deliberately constructed and reconstructed to seek specific goals. (1964: 3)

All of these early definitions point to the existence of two structural features that distinguish organizations from other types of collectivities.

- Organizations are collectivities oriented to the pursuit of relatively specific goals. They are "purposeful" in the sense that the activities and interactions of participants are coordinated to achieve specified goals. Goals are *specific* to the extent that they are explicit, are clearly defined, and provide unambiguous criteria for selecting among alternative activities.
- Organizations are collectivities that exhibit a relatively high degree of formalization. The cooperation among participants is "conscious" and "deliberate"; the structure of relations is made explicit and can be "deliberately constructed and reconstructed." As previously defined, a structure is *formalized* to the extent that the rules governing behavior are precisely and explicitly formulated and to the extent that roles and role relations are prescribed independently of the personal attributes and relations of individuals occupying positions in the structure.

It is the combination of relatively high goal specificity and relatively high formalization that distinguishes organizations from other types of collectivities. Note that both goal specificity and formalization are viewed as variables: organizations may be characterized by higher or lower levels of each. Nevertheless, as a structural type, organizations are expected to exhibit higher levels of formalization and goal specificity than other types of collectivities, such as primary groups, families, communities, and social movements. In general—there certainly are exceptions—families and kinship structures

---

[9]This definition, which I developed with Blau a good many years ago, now strikes me as somewhat misleading. Emphasis is placed on the conditions present at the founding of the organization: on whether the unit was "formally established for the explicit purpose of achieving certain goals." The wording suggests that factors associated with the founding of the unit—in particular, the intent of the founders—are of critical importance. Such historical considerations seem much less important to me now than the current state of the system—that is, the extent of goal specificity and of formalization.

tend to rank relatively high on formalization but low on goal specificity (Litwak and Meyer, 1966); social movements tend to exhibit low levels of formalization combined with higher levels of goal specificity,[10] although the specificity of goals varies greatly from movement to movement and from time to time (Gusfield, 1968); and communities are characterized by low levels of both goal specificity and formalization (Hillery, 1968: 145–52).

We arrrive, then, at the first definition, compatible with the rational system perspective: *Organizations are collectivities oriented to the pursuit of relatively specific goals and exhibiting relatively highly formalized social structures.* Note that this definition focuses not only on the distinctive characteristics of organizations but also on their normative structure.

A Natural System Definition

Gouldner (1959) reminds us that the distinguishing features of a phenomenon are not its only characteristics and, indeed, may not be the most important ones. Although organizations often espouse specific goals, the behavior of participants is frequently not guided by them, nor can they be safely used to predict organizational actions. Similarly, formal role definitions and written rules may have been developed, but they sometimes exhibit little or no influence on the behavior of members. Thus, if the behavioral structure is attended to, rather than the normative structure—if we focus on what participants actually do rather than on what they are supposed to do—the first definition of organizations can be quite misleading.

Focusing attention on the behavioral structure produces a view of organizations quite different from that proffered by the rational system theorists. The goals pursued become more complex, diffuse, differentiated, and subject to change; participants are viewed as motivated by their own interests and as seeking to impose these on the organization. It is recognized that the organization itself is a major asset, a valuable resource. Rather than being only a means, an instrumentality to pursuing other ends, its maintenance and strengthening become ends in themselves. Informal and interpersonal structures are seen to be of greater importance than formal structures, which often serve only as a decorative canopy concealing the "real" agenda and structure, and power is recognized as stemming from many sources other than occupancy of a formal position.

Hence, a second definition of organizations, useful for viewing them as natural systems, is proposed: *Organizations are collectivities whose participants are pursuing multiple interests, both disparate and common, but recognize the value of perpetuating the organization as an important resource. The informal structure of relations that develops among participants provides a more informative and accurate guide to understanding organizational behavior than the formal.*

---

[10]In recent years, analysts of movements have placed more emphasis on their organizational features—for example, the extent to which they are guided by a full-time, paid staff and have regularized mechanisms for obtaining resources and recruits and for setting goals (see Zald and McCarthy, 1987). It would appear that this shift in emphasis reflects both changes in the perspectives employed by social analysts, who are increasingly sensitive to organizational features, and changes in the nature of social movements, which are more likely to adopt organizational models.

The natural system view emphasizes that organizations are social collectivities—just one among many forms that socially structured behavior assumes. Thus, it should not be surprising that, just as there are two contrasting versions of the bases of social order in the sociological literature at large, there are replicas of these two views in the natural system view of organizations.

The first, *social consensus* version, emphasizes a view of collectivities as composed of individuals sharing primarily common objectives. The assumption underlying this conception is that social order (of any type) is a reflection of underlying consensus among the participants; that organizational stability and continuity reflect the existence of cooperative behaviors and shared norms and values. This widely held and influential version of the basis of social order is generated in the writings of Durkheim (1961 trans.) and Parsons (1951), among others, and reflected in the organizational theories of Barnard (1938), Mayo (1945), and others whose work is described in Chapter 3.

The contrasting, *social conflict,* version views social order as resulting from the suppression of some interests by others. Order results not from consensus, but from coercion, the dominance of weaker by more powerful groups. And analytic attention needs to be devoted not to the appearance of consensus, but to the reality of underlying conflicts, which provide a basis for understanding instability and change. The sociological progenitors of this view include Marx (1954 trans.) and Coser (1956), among others. Applications to organizations are provided by such theorists as Gouldner (1954) and Bendix (1956).

In Chapter 3 we review the development of the basic assumptions of the natural system perspective and examine the two subtypes associated with this perspective: the consensus and the conflict models.

An Open System Definition

The previous definitions tend to view the organization as a closed system, separate from its environment and encompassing a set of stable and easily identified participants. However, organizations are not closed systems, sealed off from their environments, but are open to and dependent on flows of personnel, resources, and information from outside. From an open system perspective, environments shape, support, and infiltrate organizations. Connections with "external" elements can be more critical than those with "internal" components; indeed, for many functions the distinction between organization and environment may be shifting, ambiguous, and arbitrary.

All three perspectives agree that if an organization is to survive, it must induce a variety of participants to contribute their time and energy to it. However, open system theorists emphasize that individuals have multiple loyalties and identities. They join and leave or engage in ongoing exchanges with the organization depending on the bargains they can strike—the relative advantage to be had from maintaining or ending the relation. Viewed from this perspective, participants cannot be assumed to hold common goals or even to routinely seek the survival of the organization. Thus, much of the work of organizing entails hard bargaining and "horse training"—as well as creating affective ties and common interpretive systems—as participants attempt to form and reform transitory coalitions.

An open system perspective is less concerned with distinguishing formal from informal structures; instead, organizations are viewed as a system of interdependent activities. Some of these activities are tightly connected; others are loosely coupled. All must be continuously motivated—produced and reproduced—if the organization is to exist. The arrival of this perspective has triggered the elaboration and elevation of levels of analysis. No longer is the single organization the privileged unit of analysis. Rather, analysts recognize that many organizational phenomena are better understood and explained by seeing individual organizations as representatives of a given type of structure or by viewing organizations as components in larger systems of relations. The open system perspective is associated with the development of studies aimed at understanding organizational sets, populations, and fields—topics we pursue in Chapters 6, 7, and 8.

We arrive, then, at a third definition, useful for viewing organizations as open systems: *Organizations are systems of interdependent activities linking shifting coalitions of participants; the systems are embedded in—dependent on continuing exchanges with and constituted by—the environments in which they operate.*

It is no doubt unsettling to be confronted so early with three such diverse views of organizations. But better to know the worst at the outset! The definitions are quite different in that they not only encompass somewhat divergent types of collectivities but also emphasize different facets of a given organization. But this is precisely why they are useful. It is essential to remember that definitions are neither true nor false but are only more or less helpful in calling attention to certain aspects of the phenomenon under study. With the assistance of these definitions, and the more general perspectives with which they are associated, we can expect to see and learn more about organizations than would be possible were we to employ a single point of view. As we proceed, we will call attention to the stimulating vistas and profound depths charted by each of the conceptions. Each has its own charms as well as its own blemishes; and each carries its own truths as well as its own biases.

SUMMARY

Organizations are important objects of study and concern for many reasons. They are vital mechanisms for pursuing collective goals in modern societies. They are not neutral tools because they affect what they produce; they function as collective actors that independently possess certain rights and powers. Both as instruments and as actors, organizations are alleged to be the source of some of contemporary society's most serious problems. Organizations encompass generic social processes but carry them out by means of distinctive structural arrangements.

Although an interest in organizational forms and processes may be traced far back in history, a distinctive field of sociological inquiry focusing on the creation and empirical testing of generalized knowledge concerning organizations did not develop until after 1950. This development was linked with and greatly stimulated by the translation into English of Max Weber's historical and comparative studies of administrative organizations, conducted during the first two decades of this century. The field of organizational studies is becoming increasingly interdisciplinary.

Organizations are studied for many purposes and from many points of view. Among the most important bases of divergence are the tremendous variation in types of organizations; the diverse disciplinary background of the investigators; whether the research is addressed to more immediate and applied problems or seeks more long-term basic understanding; and the level of analysis selected. Three levels of analysis are identified: the social psychological, which emphasizes the interaction of individuals and groups within organizations and examines the impact of organizational characteristics on these processes; the structural, which attempts to examine and account for variations in the patterned, structural features of organizations; and the ecological, which views the organization as a collective actor or a component in some more comprehensive system of relationships.

Three contrasting definitions of organizations are presented. Each is associated with one of three perspectives on organizations to be elaborated in Part Two: the rational system, the natural system, and the open system perspectives. The first definition views organizations as highly formalized collectivities oriented to the pursuit of specific goals. The second definition views organizations as social systems forged by consensus or conflict but seeking to survive. And the third definition views organizations as coalitions of participants with varying interests highly influenced by their environments. The three definitions are viewed as opening up analytically useful, if partial, views of organizations.

THREE PERSPECTIVES ON ORGANIZATIONS

In this century, three more or less distinct perspectives have been employed in the study of organizational structure.[1] The term *perspective* is used advisedly since we will be dealing in each case not with a single, unified model of organizational structure but rather with a number of varying approaches or three schools of thought, the notion of perspective serving as a conceptual umbrella under which we may gather the related views. To add further to the complexity, the three perspectives partially conflict, partially overlap, and complement one another.

An understanding of these perspectives is valuable for several reasons. It is very difficult to comprehend or to fruitfully utilize the large literature on organizations without knowledge of the differing perspectives underlying this work. Why do some investigators assume that organizational goals are central and obvious whereas others presume that goals are dispensable and cannot be taken at face value? Why does one analyst assert that organizations have great difficulty in changing their structures while another assumes that change is easy and continuous? These are the kinds of issues that cannot be understood without knowledge of the underlying perspectives that frame the work. Also, we should expect to receive help not only in making sense out of past studies but also in examining the current efforts of organizational analysts. For although these perspectives emerged at different times, later perspectives have not succeeded in supplanting earlier ones: the three perspectives continue to coexist and to claim their share of advocates.

---

[1] Others have also classified organizational theories into broader categories. Among the more interesting schemas are those proposed by Burrell and Morgan (1979), Pfeffer (1982), Astley and Van de Ven (1983), and Guillen (1994).

The perspectives need to be understood in two senses. On the one hand, they are historical products—systems of ideas and practice that developed and held sway in specific times and circumstances. To completely divorce them from their context would be a mistake, since much of their meaning is historically situated. But at the same time, the perspectives selected are not just of historical interest. Each has shown great resilience and has been invented and reinvented over time so that each has persisted as an identifiable, analytic model. In our discussion, we try to do justice to both moments: the historical specific versions and the underlying enduring analytical features. In their pure form, the perspectives share many of the features of paradigms as described by Kuhn in his influential essay on scientific revolutions. Kuhn describes paradigms as "models from which spring particular coherent traditions of scientific research" (1962: 10).

The three perspectives to be considered are the rational, the natural, and the open system perspectives. They are considered in the order of their emergence. For each, we first discuss the basic model that forms its core. Then we consider three or four representative theorists or schools within that tradition. Each discussion concludes with an evaluation of the contributions and limitations of the perspective. Chapter 2 reviews the rational system perspective, following its development from Taylor to Simon. In Chapter 3, we describe the natural system perspective, following developments from early in this century, beginning with Michels, up to the work of Parsons. And Chapter 4 reviews the open system perspective, from its origins in the general systems theory as advanced by Bertalanffy through its application to organizations by analysts ranging from Boulding to Weick. Most of the work reviewed in these introductory chapters extends only through the 1960s.

Beyond this point, matters become more complex and, we think, more interesting. There have been a number of attempts to combine the perspectives into more complex models. In Chapter 5 we review three of these integrative efforts by other theorists and propose a fourth of our own. Combining the perspectives provides a framework that enables us to locate conceptually a number of the more important, recent theoretical developments, including transaction costs, resource dependence, population ecology, Marxist approaches, and institutionalization theory, in a broader analytic framework.

2

Organizations
as Rational Systems

A well-designed machine is an instance of total organization, that is, a series of interrelated means contrived to achieve a single end. The machine consists always of particular parts that have no meaning and no function separate from the organized entity to which they contribute. A machine consists of a coherent bringing together of all parts toward the highest possible efficiency of the functioning whole, or interrelationships marshalled wholly toward a given result. In the ideal machine, there can be no extraneous part, no extraneous movement; all is set, part for part, motion for motion, toward the functioning of the whole. The machine is, then, a perfect instance of total rationalization of a field of action and of total organization. This is perhaps even more quickly evident in that larger machine, the assembly line.

John William Ward (1964)

From the rational system perspective, organizations are instruments designed to attain specified goals. How blunt or fine an instrument they are depends on many factors that are summarized by the concept of rationality of structure. The term *rationality* in this context is used in the narrow sense of technical or functional rationality (Mannheim, 1950 trans.: 53) and refers to the extent to which a series of actions is organized in such a way as to lead to predetermined goals with maximum efficiency. Thus, rationality refers not to the selection of goals but to their implementation. Indeed, it is perfectly possible to pursue irrational or foolish goals by rational means. Captain Ahab in Melville's classic, *Moby Dick*, chases the white whale across the seven seas musing; "All my means are sane, my motive and my object mad." Nazi Germany provides a more terrible, nonfiction example. Adolf Hitler's insane objective of eradicating Europe's Jewish population was efficiently pursued by hosts of functionaries who, like Adolph Eichmann, took the goal as given and worked faithfully to rationally bring it about (Arendt, 1963). It is essential to keep in mind the restricted definition of rationality used within the rational system perspective.

THE DEFINING CHARACTERISTICS

From the standpoint of the rational system perspective, the behavior of organizations is viewed as actions performed by purposeful and coordinated agents. The language employed connotes this image of rational calculation: such terms as *information, efficiency, optimization, implementation,* and *design* occur frequently. But another somewhat different set of terms also occurs within this perspective; it indicates the cognitive limitations of the individual decision maker and the effects of the organizational context in which rational choices are made. These terms—*constraints, authority, rules, directives, jurisdiction, performance programs, coordination*—imply that the rationality of behavior within organizations takes place within (some analysts would argue, because of) clearly specified limits.

It is no accident that the key features of organizations emphasized by rational system theorists are the very characteristics identified as distinguishing organizations from other types of collectivities. Rational system theorists stress goal specificity and formalization because each of these elements makes an important contribution to the rationality of organizational action.

Goal Specificity

Goals are conceptions of desired ends. These conceptions vary in the precision and specificity of their criteria of desirability. Specific goals provide unambiguous criteria for selecting among alternative activities. As viewed by economists or by decision theorists, goals are translated into a set of preference or utility functions that represent the value of alternative sets of consequences. Without clear preference orderings among alternatives, rational assessment and choice are not possible.

Specific goals not only supply criteria for choosing among alternative activities; they guide decisions about how the organization structure itself is to be designed. They specify what tasks are to be performed, what kinds of personnel are to be hired, how resources are to be allocated among participants. The more general or diffuse the goals, the more difficult it is to design a structure to pursue them.

It is important to note that some organizations espouse quite vague and general goals, but in their actual daily operation are guided by relatively specific goals that do provide criteria for choosing among alternative activities and for designing the organization structure itself. Consider the case of schools. Although both educators and lay people will argue endlessly about the true function of education and about the virtues of liberal arts versus more practical types of programs, within a given school there will be considerable agreement on such matters as what disciplines should be represented among the faculty, what courses will count toward graduation (or, at least, who has the right to make these decisions), and how many units are required for a student to graduate. With agreement on such matters as these, administrators can safely allow the faculty occasionally to debate the ultimate aims of education. Similarly, although physicians cannot agree on abstract definitions of health or illness, they do successfully organize their work in clinics and hospitals around such proximate outcomes as relieving pain and prolonging life.

Vague goals do not provide a solid basis for formal organizations. Either the goals become more specific and limited over time, as often happens, or the structures developed are likely to be unstable and amorphous. Collective movements such as radical political sects or protest groups may temporarily succeed in mobilizing resources and participants around vague concepts such as human liberation or environmental protection. Indeed, their generality may broaden their appeal and enlist the support of diverse groups. But such generalized movements are usually sustained and their energy focused by the definition of more specific and limited objectives that can provide the basis for stable organizations. Organizations such as the Sierra Club and Greenpeace gain legitimacy from the broader environmental movement, but carve out limited goals around which to mobilize attention and resources.

The most precise description of the manner in which specific goals support rational behavior in organizations is that developed by Herbert Simon, whose classic, *Administrative Behavior*, first appeared in 1945. His ideas on this subject are summarized later in this chapter as an example of one of the major contributions to the rational system perspective.

Formalization

All rational system theorists assume the existence and presume the importance of a formalized structure, but few make explicit the contributions that formalization makes to rationality of behavior in organizations. Let us attempt to do so.

Recall that a structure is formalized to the extent that the rules governing behavior are precisely and explicitly formulated and to the extent that roles and role relations are prescribed independently of the personal attributes and relations of individuals occupying positions in the structure. Formalization may be viewed as an attempt to make behavior more predictable by standardizing and regulating it. This, in turn, permits "stable expectations to be formed by each member of the group as to the behavior of the other members under specified conditions. Such stable expectations are an essential precondition to a rational consideration of the consequences of action in a social group" (Simon, 1976: 100).

Formalization may also be viewed as an attempt to make more explicit and visible the structure of relationships among a set of roles and the principles that govern behavior in the system. It enables participants or observers to diagram the social structures and the work flows, allowing them to depict these relationships and processes with the possibility of consciously manipulating them—designing and redesigning the division of responsibilities, the flow of information or materials, or the ways in which participants report to one another. As Gouldner notes:

> Fundamentally, the rational model implies a "mechanical" model, in that it views the organization as a structure of manipulable parts, each of which is separately modifiable with a view to enhancing the efficiency of the whole. Individual organizational elements are seen as subject to successful and planned modification, enactable by deliberate decision. (1959: 405)

Thus, in a fundamental sense, the organizational structure is viewed as a means, as an instrument, that can be modified as necessary to improve performance. Organizational designers and managers draw and redraw the organizational chart; coaches attempt to improve performance by diagraming plays and giving chalk talks; and consultants are employed to recommend better arrangements for achieving business goals. In recent years, highly technical managerial systems, such as management by objectives (MBO), planning, programming, and budgeting systems (PPBS), program evaluation review techniques (PERT)—all designed to provide greater visibility and, hence, greater accountability for the critical work flows—have been developed and widely adopted to facilitate rational decision making within complex organizational systems (see Haberstroh, 1965; Odione, 1965; Drucker, 1976; Wildavsky, 1979: 26–40).

Formalization can contribute to rationality in other, less obvious ways. In addition to making behavior more available for conscious design, the structuring of expectations prior to interaction carries with it another distinct advantage. Laboratory research by Bales (1953) documents the strains and tensions generated when a status structure begins to emerge among individuals who entered the situation as presumed status-equals. These status battles and their associated interpersonal tensions are reduced by the prestructuring of differentiated role expectations in which an individual is assigned a role prior to his or her participation. Thus, in an experimental study, Carter and his colleagues (1953) found that group leaders who had been appointed to their position by the experimenter spent less time attempting to assert their power and defend their position and encountered less resistance to their leadership efforts than leaders who emerged on their own (see also Verba, 1961: 161–72).

Formalization also serves to objectify the structure—to make the definitions of roles and relationships appear to be both objective and external to the participating actors. These qualities contribute substantially to the efficacy of the systems in controlling behavior. A series of experiments conducted by Zucker (1977) demonstrates this effect. Subjects placed in an ambiguous situation were much more likely to accept influence from another when that person was defined as holding a specified organizational position (not, by the way, a position of authority but simply a named office) than when the person was described simply as "another person."

The social cement that binds and regulates activities and interactions in informal groups is the *sociometric structure*—the patterning of affective ties among participants. The creation of a formal structure constitutes an important functional alternative to the sociometric structure. With formalization, the smooth functioning of the organization is to some degree made independent of the feelings—negative or positive—that particular members have for one another. As Merton (1957: 195) notes, "formality facilitates the interaction of the occupants of offices despite their (possibly hostile) private attitudes toward one another." Indeed, many organizations even discourage the development of positive sentiments among their members for fear that such emotional ties will undermine discipline and judgment and interfere with attempts to deploy participants rationally.

Formalization makes allowances for the finitude and inconstancy of human actors. The process of succession—the movement of individuals into and out of offices—can be routinized and regularized so that one appropriately trained person can replace another with minimal disturbance to the functioning of the organization. In this sense, organizations can—although few actually do—achieve a kind of immortality. The Roman Catholic church provides a notable example.

Formalized structures are thus rendered independent of the participation of any particular individual; a related consequence is that it becomes less essential to recruit unusually gifted individuals for the key positions. The power and influence of leaders can be determined in part by the definition of their offices and not made to depend on their personal qualities—their charisma. In his discussion of political structures, MacIver notes, "The man who commands may be no wiser, no abler, may be, in some sense no better than the average of his fellows; sometimes, by any intrinsic standard, he is inferior to them. Here is the magic of government" (1947: 13). More generally, here is the magic of formalization. To explain more clearly the alchemy of this process, Wolin draws an analogy between the formalization of structure and scientific method:

> Method, like organization, is the salvation of puny men, the compensatory device for individual foibles, the gadget which allows mediocrity to transcend its limitations. . . . Organization, by simplifying and routinizing procedures, eliminates the need for surpassing talent. It is predicated on "average human beings." (1960: 383)

In the highly formalized organization, the innovating entrepreneur is supplanted by a corps of administrators and technical specialists. Leadership, even innovation, is routinized and regularized by being incorporated into the formal structure (see Schumpeter, 1947; Galbraith, 1967).

Note that in describing the contributions of formalization to rational functioning of the organization, emphasis has been placed simply on formalization per se—on the existence of role specifications—without attention to content, to the particular rules prescribing preferred behaviors. Most rational system theorists, examples of which are described in the following section, assume the importance of formalization and devote their energies to developing precise guidelines to govern participants' activities. They attempt to describe or to prescribe principles that will conduce to rational organizational behavior.

SELECTED SCHOOLS

The preceding discussion represents an effort to distill the central elements characterizing the rational system perspective. As noted, this perspective does not reflect a unitary theory but encompasses a set of generically related but distinctive approaches. Four such approaches will be briefly described: Taylor's scientific management; administrative theory as developed by Fayol and others; Weber's theory of bureaucracy; and Simon's discussion of administrative behavior.

Taylor's Scientific Management

The scientific management approach received its primary impetus from the work of Frederick W. Taylor (1911) in the late nineteenth and early twentieth centuries but was carried forward by the contributions of others, such as Frank and Lillian Gilbreth, Henry Gantt, and Charles Bedeaux. Taylor may be viewed as the culmination of a series of developments occurring in the United States between 1880 and 1920. As Shenhav (1995) points out, with the maturation of the industrial revolution, engineers, particularly mechanical engineers, began to organize to promote rationalization of practice through standardization of, first, "fittings, screws, nuts, [and] bolts" and, subsequently, "the human element in production" (Calvert, 1967: 178; Noble, 1977: 83). The extension of standardization principles to workers was associated with an increase in industrial unrest during the period 1900–1920 (Shenhav, 1995), whether as cause or effect is less clear. Unlike similar developments in Europe, the drive toward "systematization" in the United States appeared to be largely a professional project rather than one championed by the state (see Guillen, 1994).

Taylor and his followers insisted that it was possible to scientifically analyze tasks performed by individual workers in order to discover those procedures that would produce the maximum output with the minimum input of energies and resources. Efforts were concentrated on analyzing individual tasks, but attempts to rationalize labor at the level of the individual worker inevitably led to changes in the entire structure of work arrangements. Ward describes the sequence of changes that resulted from Taylor's efforts to improve the efficiency of performing such menial tasks as shoveling coal and iron ore in a steel mill:

> First, a variety of kinds of shovels had to be designed to handle different kinds of materials. That also meant building shovel rooms in the various parts of the yard, so that a gang would have the proper tools at hand. To eliminate the waste motion of wandering about so large a yard, it meant, as Taylor said, "organizing and planning work at least a day in advance," so that when men checked in, they would be at that day's work. This meant, Taylor reported, building a labor office for a planning staff—a bureaucracy, as we would say. Large maps of the yard were then necessary to show at a glance the location of different kinds of work and the location of men. Furthermore, the installation of a telephone network was essential for more effective interior communication. Once the yard was mapped so that one could see at a glance the relationships in time and sequence between different jobs, it led, naturally enough, to the reorganization of the yard itself, so that materials could be delivered or dumped in a more logical sequence.
>
> One can see readily enough what happened. Taylor's attempt to make the crudest physical act of labor efficient led inexorably to a further organization of every aspect of the production process. (Ward, 1964: 64–65)

It was not only, or even primarily, the lot of workers that was to be altered by the introduction of scientific management: the role of management was also to be transformed. Taylor aspired to replace the arbitrary and capricious activities of managers with analytical, scientific procedures:

> Under scientific management arbitrary power, arbitrary dictation, ceases; and every single subject, large and small, becomes the question for scientific investigation, for reduction to law. . . .
>
> The man at the head of the business under scientific management is governed by rules and laws which have been developed through hundreds of experiments just as much as the workman is, and the standards which have been developed are equitable. (Taylor, 1947: 211, 189)

The activities of both managers and workers were to be rationalized; both were equally subject to the regimen of science.

Taylor believed that the adoption of scientific management principles by industrial concerns would usher in a new era of industrial peace. The interests of labor and management would be rendered compatible. Workers would be scientifically selected to perform those tasks for which they were best suited. Scientifically determined procedures would allow them to work at peak efficiency, in return for which they would receive top wages. "Once work was scientifically plotted, Taylor felt, there could be no disputes about how hard one should work or the pay one should receive for labor. 'As reasonably might we insist on bargaining about the time and place of the rising and setting sun,' he once said" (Bell, 1960: 228). Managers would cooperate with workers in devising appropriate work arrangements and pay scales and would enjoy the fruits of maximum profits.

Many of the elements that Taylor pioneered were employed to provide the basis for the mass production technologies—known after their most famous exemplar, Henry Ford, as "Fordism"—that represented the highwater mark of the industrial revolution. To Taylor's meticulous time-motion study and perfection of each worker movement, Ford added the specialized machines and conveyor belts that greatly enhanced the productivity of workers turning out standardized products for mass markets. Zuboff (1988: 47) summarizes the key elements of Fordism:

> This formula has dominated the design of mass-production techniques throughout the twentiety century. Effort is simplified (though its pace is frequently intensified) while skill demands are reduced by new methods of task organization and new forms of machinery.

Taylor was also a leader in formulating the elements of what Cole (1994) has referred to as the "traditional quality paradigm." This approach stressed the "importance of identifying work tasks and then making that method the standard," together with an emphasis on inspection, involving elaborate designs to ensure that the inspectors' activities were themselves subject to careful review. In contast to the contemporary emphasis on total quality management, which we discuss in Chapter 13, the traditional approached devised by Taylor and others viewed quality as a specialized staff function and embraced "an inspection-oriented rather than a prevention-oriented approach" (Cole 1994: 69).

The underlying spirit of Taylor's approach—an amalgam of the Protestant ethic, social Darwinism, and a faith in technical expertise—found widespread acceptance among many American managers and support from the Progressive movement early in the twentieth century. However, many managers increasingly were disquieted by Taylor's vision of their own new role: "After all, Taylor had questioned their good judgment and superior ability which had been the subject of public celebration for many years. Hence, many employers regarded his methods as an unwarranted interference with managerial prerogatives" (Bendix, 1956: 280). Workers for their part resisted time-study procedures and attempts to standardize every aspect of their performance and rejected incentive systems requiring them to perform continuously at a peak level of efficiency. Given the increasing resistance of both managers and workers, scientific management has persisted more in the guise of a set of technical procedures than as an overarching managerial ideology.[1]

Fayol's Administrative Theory

A second approach, developing concurrently with scientific management, emphasized management functions and attempted to generate broad administrative principles that would serve as guidelines for the rationalization of organizational activities. Whereas Taylor and his disciples proposed to rationalize the organization from the "bottom up"—changes in the performance of individual tasks affecting the larger structure of work relations—the administrative management theorists worked to rationalize the organization from the "top down." Henri Fayol, a French industrialist writing in the early part of this century, was probably the earliest exponent of this approach, but his ideas did not become widely available in this country until 1949, when his major work was translated. Influential participants in this movement in the United States included two General Motors executives, Mooney and Reiley (1939), whose treatise on management principles gained a wide following, and Gulick and Urwick, who in 1937 collaborated to edit the volume *Papers on the Science of Administration*.

The various contributors to this perspective did not reach agreement as to the number of principles required or the precise formulation of many specific principles, but there was considerable consensus on the importance of two types of activities: coordination and specialization (Massie, 1965). The major principles developed to guide *coordination* activities include the scalar principle, which emphasizes the hierarchical organizational form in which all participants are linked into a single pyramidal structure of control relations; the unity-of-command principle, specifying that no organizational par-

---

[1]Perhaps the most useful overview of Taylor's conception is contained in his testimony before the Special House Committee to Investigate the Taylor and Other Systems of Shop Management in 1912. This testimony is reprinted in Taylor (1947). Summaries of and commentaries on his contribution will be found in Bell (1960: 222–37), Bendix (1956: 274–81), and Guillen (1994: 30–58). A severe critique of Taylor's work from a Marxist perspective is provided by Braverman (1974: 85–138).

ticipants should receive orders from more than one superior; the span-of-control principle, which emphasizes that no superior should have more subordinates than can be effectively overseen (theorists were unable to agree on the precise number of subordinates who could be supervised); and the exception principle, which recommends that all routine matters be handled by subordinates, leaving superiors free to deal with exceptional situations to which existing rules are inapplicable.

Specialization issues include decisions both about how various activities are to be distributed among organizational positions and about how such positions can most effectively be grouped into work units or departments. Among the principles espoused to guide these types of decisions is the departmentalization principle, which maintains that activities should be grouped so as to combine homogeneous or related activities within the same organizational unit. Homogeneity might be based on similarity of purpose (activities contributing to the same subgoal—for example, marketing), process (activities requiring similar operations—for example, typing), clientele (activities performed on the same set of recipients—for example, a medical team organized around the care of a specific group of patients), or place (for example, services provided to individuals in a given geographical territory). Also proposed is the line-staff principle, by which all activities directly concerned with achieving organizational goals are designated as line functions, to be distinguished from staff activities, which consist primarily of advice, service, or support. Staff units are to be segregated from the scalar organization of power and made responsible and subordinate to appropriate line units.

Note the heavy emphasis on formalization implicit in these principles. Careful specification of work activities and concern for their grouping and coordination is the hallmark of the formalized structure. Mooney makes explicit this call for formalization by distinguishing between jobs (positions) and the person on the job:

> In every organization there is a collective job to be done, consisting always of the sum of many individual jobs, and the task of administration, operating through management, is the co-ordination of all the human effort necessary to this end. Such co-ordination, however, always presupposes the jobs to be coordinated. The job as such is therefore antecedent to the man on the job, and the sound co-ordination of these jobs, considered simply as jobs, must be the first and necessary condition in the effective co-ordination of the human factor. (1937: 92)

The more astute administrative theorists recognized that their managerial principles furnished at best only broad guidelines for decision making. Thus, Fayol reminds practitioners:

> The soundness and good working order of the body corporate depends on a certain number of conditions termed indiscriminately principles, laws, rules. For preference I shall adopt the term principles whilst dissociating it from any suggestion of rigidity, for there is nothing rigid or absolute in management affairs, it is all a question of proportion. Seldom do we have to apply the same

principle twice in identical conditions; allowance must be made for different changing circumstances. (1949 trans.: 19)

And Gulick cautions:

> Students of administration have long sought a single principle of effective departmentalization just as alchemists sought the philosopher's stone. But they have sought in vain. There is apparently no one most effective system of departmentalism. (Gulick and Urwick, 1937: 31)

In spite of such disclaimers, the managerial principles enunciated by the administrative theorists soon drew considerable criticism. Much of this criticism came from natural system proponents and will be discussed in Chapter 3, but a good deal of the fire came from other rational system theorists on the ground that the so-called principles were mere truisms or commonsense pronouncements (see Massie, 1965: 406). No doubt the most devastating critique was provided by Herbert Simon, whose classic, *Administrative Behavior*, commenced with "an indictment of much current writing about administrative matters" (1976: 36).[2] He examines one principle after another, observing that many occur in pairs that are, on close inspection, contradictory; others lack specificity or reveal "a deceptive simplicity— a simplicity that conceals fundamental ambiguities" (1976: 21).

Without gainsaying any of these criticisms, we can admire what the administrative theorists attempted to do. They were pioneers in identifying the fundamental features of formal organizational structure, audaciously clinging to the view that all organizations contain certain common structural characteristics. With the improved vision of hindsight, it is now apparent that their search was confounded in part by their failure to develop conditional generalizations—statements that specify the limits of their applicability to particular situations or types of organizations.[3]

Weber's Theory of Bureaucracy

Our consideration of Weber's work must begin with an important disclaimer. Although Weber's writings had a profound influence on the development of organization theory in the United States from the time they were first translated into English, because his arguments were available in disconnected fragments, they were taken out of context and incorrectly interpreted. As Collins (1975: 286) has observed:

> there is nothing better known in the field of organizations, perhaps in all of sociology, than Weber's model of bureaucracy. It also happens that there is no

---

[2]Simon's basic work, *Administrative Behavior*, first appeared in 1945. However, all our references are to the third edition of this work, published in 1976, which contains an extensive new introduction.

[3]This is the major insight that underlies the contingency theory of organizations, described in Chapter 4.

more complete misunderstanding of a major sociological theory than the way Weber's organizational theory was treated in American sociology.

There are two major ways in which early interpretations of Weber's work were flawed. First, his famous depiction of the central features of rational-legal "bureaucratic" structures was decontextualized, taken out of historical context and treated as a kind of caricature of modern administration forms. Second, most of his arguments were interpreted as belonging within the framework of a conventional technical rationality, whereas his theoretical framework was more complex, paving the way to an alternative conception of rationality. We begin our review by attempting to place Weber's work back in its proper historical frame.

Max Weber, the influential German sociologist/political economist was a contemporary of Taylor and Fayol but worked along quite different lines. Weber's analysis of administrative structures was only a limited aspect of his much larger interest in accounting for the unique features of Western civilization (see Bendix, 1960). In his view, what was distinctive was the growth of rationality in the West, and his active mind roamed across legal, religious, political, and economic systems, as well as administrative structures, as he searched for materials to test and extend his notions by comparing and contrasting differing cultures and historical periods. Weber's analysis of administrative systems can be fully appreciated only if it is seen in this larger context, since his listing of the structural characteristics of bureaucracy was generated in an attempt to differentiate this more rational system from earlier forms.

In his justly famous typology, Weber distinguishes three types of authority:

- *Traditional authority*—resting on an established belief in the sanctity of immemorial traditions and the legitimacy of those exercising authority under them
- *Rational-legal authority*—resting on a belief in the "legality" of patterns of normative rules and the right of those elevated to authority under such rules to issue commands
- *Charismatic authority*—resting on devotion to the specific and exceptional sanctity, heroism, or exemplary character of an individual person, and of the normative patterns or order revealed or ordained by him or her (1968 trans.: vol. 1: 212–301).

Clearly, the basis for the typology is differences in the beliefs by which legitimacy is attributed to an authority relation. (See the discussion of power and authority in Chapter 11.) Associated with each authority type is a distinctive administrative structure. Traditional authority gives rise to the particularistic and diffuse structures exemplified by patrimonialism and its various manifestations, including gerontocracy, patriarchalism, and feudalism (see Dibble, 1965).[4] The simplest way to visualize a patrimonial system is

---

[4]Such traditional structures are not simply of historical interest. Many contemporary societies contain various traditional and "neotraditional" elements in their political and economic organizations. For example, Walder (1986) provides an interesting account of such arrangements in today's China.

as a household writ large: an estate or production organization governed by a ruler-owner who in managing the enterprise relies for assistance on a variety of dependents, ranging from slaves to serfs to sons and daughters. Rational-legal authority provides the basis for the more impersonal specific and formal structures of which the most highly developed form is the bureaucracy. And charismatic authority is associated with the "strictly personal" relations linking an impressive leader with his or her devoted coterie of followers or disciples.

In Weber's view, only traditional and rational-legal authority relations are sufficiently stable to provide the basis for the formation of permanent administrative structures. And, during recent centuries, particularly in Western societies, traditional structures are viewed as gradually giving way to rational-legal structures, most notably in "the modern state" and in "the most advanced institutions of capitalism," due to their "purely technical superiority over any other form of organization" (Weber, 1946 trans.: 196, 214). Charismatic forms arise in periods of instability and crisis when extraordinary measures are called for and seemingly offered by individuals perceived as possessing uncommon gifts of spirit and mind. Lenin, Hitler, Gandhi, Mao, and Martin Luther King are only a few recent examples of such charismatic leaders, illustrating their diversity and their power to inspire the fanatical devotion of others around their personal vision of "reform." However, for such movements to persist, they must move in the direction of one or the other stable form, by establishing "new" traditional structures or new bureaucratic structures.[5] Charisma becomes routinized: the circle of adherents expands to include more but less committed participants; systematic sources of support replace voluntary and heartfelt, but irregular, contributions; personal ties between leader and followers are replaced by more orderly but impersonal arrangements; and rules of succession are developed in recognition of the truth that no one lives forever—not even a superhuman leader.

Weber's typology of authority is of interest not only because it underlies his conception of basic changes occurring in administrative systems over time. The distinction between traditional and rational-legal forms also serves as the basis for his influential conception of the characteristics of bureaucratic structures. Before describing Weber's conception, however, it is necessary to briefly comment on the concept of bureaucracy because this term is used in so many ways. For many, bureaucracy is employed as an epithet, signifying rule-encumbered inefficiency or mindless overconformity (see, for example, Mises, 1944; Parkinson, 1957). While acknowledging that this description fits all too many organizations, we shall define bureaucracy in a more neutral manner, following the lead of Bendix. He observes:

> Seen historically, bureaucratization may be interpreted as the increasing subdivision of the functions which the owner-managers of the early enterprises had performed personally in the course of their daily routine. (1956: 211–12)

Such functions include supervision, personnel selection, accounting and financial management, record keeping, job design, and planning. This defi-

---

[5]The art of "inventing" traditions is described by Hobsbawm and Ranger (1983).

nition excludes the head of the organization—whether president, dictator, or owner—as well as those who carry out the direct work of the organization: the production personnel. A useful way of thinking about a bureaucracy is that it consists of those positions or activities whose function is to service and maintain the organization itself. In short, we define *bureaucracy* as the existence of a specialized administrative staff. Like formalization and goal specificity, bureaucracy should be viewed as a variable; organizations vary in terms of how much of their personnel resources are devoted to administrative as compared with production activities.

Weber's definition of bureaucracy differs from our own. In his conception, bureaucracy is a particular type of administrative structure, developed in association with the rational-legal mode of authority. In many discussions of Weber's work, his model of bureaucracy is depicted as a simple list of administrative characteristics present in bureaucratic forms, characteristics such as:

- a fixed division of labor among participants
- a hierarchy of offices
- a set of general rules that govern performance
- a separation of personal from official property and rights
- selection of personnel on the basis of technical qualifications
- employment viewed as a career by participants

However, his contribution can be better appreciated if these bureaucratic elements are described in relation to the traditional features they supplanted. Thus, according to Weber, bureaucratic systems are distinguished from traditional administrative forms by the following features:

1. Jurisdictional areas are clearly specified: the regular activities required of personnel are distributed in a fixed way as official duties (in contrast with the patrimonial arrangement, in which the division of labor is not firm or regular but depends on assignments made by the leader, which can be changed at any time).
2. The organization of offices follows the principle of hierarchy: each lower office is controlled and supervised by a higher one. However, the scope of authority of superiors over subordinates is circumscribed, and lower offices enjoy a right of appeal (in contrast with the patrimonial form, where authority relations are more diffuse, being based on personal loyalty, and are not ordered into clear hierarchies).
3. An intentionally established system of abstract rules governs official decisions and actions. These rules are relatively stable and exhaustive, and can be learned. Decisions are recorded in permanent files. (In patrimonial systems, general rules of administration either do not exist or are vaguely stated, ill defined, and subject to change at the whim of the leader. No attempt is made to keep permanent records of transactions).
4. The "means of production or administration"—for example, tools and equipment or rights and privileges—belong to the office, not the office-holder, and may not be appropriated. Personal property is clearly separated from official property, and working space from living quarters.

(Such distinctions are not maintained in patrimonial administrative systems since there is no separation of the ruler's personal household business from the larger public or corporate business under his direction.)

5. Officials are personally free, selected on the basis of technical qualifications, appointed to office (not elected), and compensated by salary. (In more traditional administrative systems, officials are often selected from among those who are personally dependent on the leader—for example, slaves, serfs, relatives. Selection is governed by particularistic criteria, and compensation often takes the form of benefices—rights granted to individuals that, for example, allow them access to the stores of the ruler or give them grants of land from which they can appropriate the fees or taxes. Benefices, like fiefs in feudalistic systems, may become hereditary and sometimes are bought and sold.)

6. Employment by the organization constitutes a career for officials. An official is a full-time employee and looks forward to a lifelong career in the agency. After a trial period he or she gains tenure of position and is protected against arbitrary dismissal. (In patrimonial systems, officials serve at the pleasure of the leader and so lack clear expectations about the future and security of tenure.) (1968 trans.: vol. 3: 956–1005)

When we thus juxtapose Weber's list of bureaucratic characteristics and the related aspects of patrimonial systems, a clearer view emerges of Weber's central message. He viewed each bureaucratic element as the solution to a problem or defect contained within the earlier administrative systems.[6] Further, each element operates not in isolation but as part of a system of elements that, in combination, are expected to provide more effective and efficient administration. To capture both the notions of distinctive elements and their interrelation, Weber employed what is termed an *ideal-type* construct. This approach attempts to isolate those elements regarded as most characteristic of the phenomenon to be explored. The term *ideal-type* is somewhat misleading, since it does not refer to a normatively preferred type but rather to the construction of a simplified model that focuses attention on the most salient or distinctive features.

Even though Weber's model of administrative systems emphasized that they were composed of many, interrelated factors, in his own analysis he focused primarily on organizations as systems of power or domination in which the leader exercises control over and through a hierarchy of officials who both receive and give orders. It is administration based on discipline; and discipline is "nothing but the consistently rationalized, methodically prepared and exact execution of the received order" (Weber, 1968 trans.: vol. 3: 1149).

In contrasting the rational-legal with the other two (nonrational) types, Weber stressed two seemingly contradictory points. First, the rational-legal

---

[6]For a revealing description of the gradual replacement of a patrimonial by a bureaucratic structure, see Rosenberg's (1958) account of the emergence of the Prussian state during the eighteenth century. This "German" case was, of course, well known to Weber, whose father was a municipal official in Berlin and subsequently a member of both the regional and imperial parliament.

form provides the basis for a more stable and predictable administrative structure for both superiors and subordinates. The behavior of subordinates is rendered more reliable by the specificity of their role obligations, the clarity of hierarchical connections, and their continuing dependence on the hierarchy in the short run for income and in the longer term for career progression. And superiors are prevented from behaving arbitrarily or capriciously in their demands made on subordinates.

On the other hand, the rational-legal structure permits subordinates to exercise "relatively greater independence and discretion" than is possible in the other types of administrative systems (Smith and Ross, 1978). Because obedience is owed not to a person—whether a traditional chief or a charismatic leader—but to a set of impersonal principles, subordinates in bureaucratic systems have a stronger basis for independent action, guided by their interpretation of the principles. They also have a clear basis for questioning the directives of superiors, whose actions are presumably constrained by the same impersonal framework of rules. By supporting increased independence and discretion among lower administrative officials constrained by general administrative policies and specified procedures, bureaucratic systems are capable of handling more complex administrative tasks than traditional systems. (This argument is amplified in Chapter 10.)

Weber's analysis of bureaucratic structure, while influential, has also been controversial. We briefly review two important criticisms. Since type of authority relation goes a long way toward determining the nature of administrative structures in Weber's conception, criticisms of his views of the type of authority prevailing in bureaucratic systems take on special significance. Both Parsons and Gouldner have suggested that Weber tended to conflate two analytically distinguishable bases of authority. On the one hand, in his discussion of the administrative hierarchy of bureaucracies, Weber asserts that authority rests on "incumbency in a legally defined office." On the other hand, in his discussion of criteria for recruitment and advancement, Weber argues that authority is based on "technical competence" (Parsons, 1947: 58–60). Indeed, at one point Weber states, "Bureaucratic administration means fundamentally the exercise of control on the basis of knowledge" (1947 trans.: 339). Gouldner underlines the contradiction:

> Weber, then, thought of bureaucracy as a Janus-faced organization, looking two ways at once. On the one side, it was administration based on discipline. In the first emphasis, obedience is invoked as a means to an end; an individual obeys because the rule or order is felt to be the best known method of realizing some goal.
>
> In his second conception, Weber held that bureaucracy was a mode of administration in which obedience was an end in itself. The individual obeys the order, setting aside judgments either of its rationality or morality, primarily because of the position occupied by the person commanding. The content of the order is not examinable. (1954: 22–23)

One might defend Weber by insisting that there is a high positive correlation between a person's position in the hierarchy and his or her degree of technical competence. Such may have been the case in Weber's day, when on-the-job experience was a major source of technical competence, but seems far off the mark in today's world of minute specialization supported by prolonged and esoteric training in institutions separated from the work setting. Thompson convincingly portrays the ever-widening gap between ability and authority in modern organizations, asserting that:

> Authority is centralized, but ability is inherently decentralized because it comes from practice and training rather than from definition. Whereas the boss retains his full rights to make all decisions, he has less and less ability to do so because of the advance of science and technology. (1961: 47)

Staff-line arrangements, in which the positional authority of the line administrator is distinguished from the technical expertise of the staff specialist, appear to be not so much a solution to the difficulty (see studies by Dalton [1950; 1959] of staff-line conflict) as a structural recognition of the distinctiveness of the two sources of authority sloughed over in Weber's analysis.

A second criticism of Weber's formulation is that his ideal-type construct of bureaucracy is "an admixture of a conceptual scheme and a set of hypotheses" (Blau and Scott, 1962: 33), the difficulty being that Weber does not clearly distinguish definitions from propositions in his model. Weber's conception not only calls attention to what he regards as the key elements of bureaucracy—a set of characteristics—but also contains numerous propositions linking the various elements. For example, it is implied that organizations having a well-developed hierarchy of authority also attempt to standardize the performance of tasks by applying rules and formalized procedures, and that these same organizations also employ technical criteria in recruiting and promoting personnel, and so on. Weber's conception contains numerous propositions about the interrelations of structural characteristics in organizations, some explicit but many implicit. For a long time sociologists following in Weber's footsteps took as given the interrelations posited in his schema.

Udy (1959a; 1959b) was among the first to suggest that Weber's model could be regarded as identifying a set of structural variables whose interrelations should not be taken as a matter of definition but as a subject for empirical exploration. His lead was quickly followed by numerous others, including Hall (1963; 1968), Pugh and colleagues (1968; 1976), and Blau and associates (1966; 1971), all of whom documented the great variety exhibited by structural systems (see Chapter 10).

As noted at the beginning of our discussion, a number of recent commentators have suggested that early generations of organizational analysts, especially Americans, misread Weber's work and distorted his views (see Collins 1975; McNeil, 1978; Thompson, 1980). In particular, contemporary Weberian scholars point out that Weber identified a number of types of rationality that his early readers tended to conflate or confuse (see Albrow, 1970; Kalberg, 1980). Early influential interpreters such as Blau (1956) and Thompson (1967) assumed that Weber equated bureaucratic rationality with efficiency. A closer reading, however, makes it clear that Weber distinguished between technical rationality—emphasizing instrumental means-ends efficiency—and formal rationality, and that he defined bureaucracy as rational primarily in the latter sense. *Formal rationality* refers to the orientation of action to formal rules and laws (Kalberg, 1980: 1158).

> At the heart of Weber's idea of formal rationality was the idea of correct calculation, in either numerical terms, as with the accountant, or in logical terms, as with the lawyer. . . . Each of the propositions involved in his pure type of bureaucracy referred to a procedure where either legal norms or monetary calculation were involved, and where impersonality and expert knowledge were necessary. Any such procedure was for Weber intrinsically rational, irrespective of its relation to organizational objectives. In short, he was not offering a theory of efficiency, but a statement of the formal procedures which were prevalent in modern administration. (Albrow, 1970: 65)

Employing this conception of formal rationality, Weber recognized the potential for conflict between the abstract formalism of legal certainty on the one hand and objective accomplishments on the other. He understood the difference between, for example, the perfection of legal procedures and the attainment of justice. He realized the possibility that formalization can degenerate into formalism. Most important, he recognized in his work alternative meanings of rationality and, in so doing, anticipated truths that contemporary institutional theorists have rediscovered and amplified (see Meyer, 1990). We pursue these insights in Chapter 6.

Early readers of Weber also failed to recognize his strong ambivalence about the developments he charted: his recognition that bureaucratic forms were capable of growing with an inexorable logic of their own, concentrating great power in the hands of their masters, reducing individual participants to the status of "cog in an ever-moving mechanism," and having the potential to imprison humanity in an "iron cage" (Weber, 1946 trans.: 228; 1958 trans.: 181). These concerns are discussed in Chapter 12.

Finally, early conveyers of Weber's work decontextualized it, extracting Weber's ideal-type characterization of bureaucratic structure from its historical context. But, as we will see, Weber was ahead of his time in recognizing the importance of the wider social context on the form and functioning of organizations.

In sum, Weber was clearly a rational system theorist even though early interpreters may have misconstrued the type of rationality Weber had in mind. While there remains controversy over some aspects of Weber's conceptions and arguments, there is virtually universal agreement that he was and remains the premiere analyst of organizations, an intellectual giant whose conceptions continue to shape and enrich our understandings of how and why organizations arose, and how their operation affects the wider social structure.

Simon's Theory of Administrative Behavior

Herbert Simon, both in his early work on administration and in his later collaborative work with March, has clarified the processes by which goal specificity and formalization contribute to rational behavior in organizations (Simon, 1976; March and Simon, 1958). We have already observed that

Simon was critical of the platitudes developed by Fayol and others searching for management principles. He also criticized the assumptions made by Taylor and other early theorists about the actors in organizations. For the "economic man" motivated by self-interest and completely informed about all available alternatives, Simon proposed to substitute a more human "administrative man," who seeks to pursue his or her self-interests but does not always know what they are, is aware of only a few of all the possible alternatives, and is willing to settle for an adequate solution in contrast with an optimal one.

Following the lead of Barnard (1938), Simon distinguishes between (1) an individual's decisions to join and to continue to participate in an organization and (2) the decisions an individual is asked to make as a participant in the organization. Only the latter set of decisions is of interest in the present context.[7] A scientifically relevant description of an organization, according to Simon, details what decisions individuals make as organizational participants and the influences to which they are subject in making these decisions. In general, in Simon's view, organizations both simplify decisions and support participants in the decisions they need to make.

A primary way in which organizations simplify participants' decisions is to restrict the ends toward which activity is directed. Simon points out that goals affect behavior only as they enter into decisions about how to behave. Goals supply the value premises that underlie decisions. *Value premises* are assumptions about what ends are preferred or desirable. They are combined in decisions with *factual premises*—assumptions about the observable world and the way in which it operates. The more precise and specific the value premises, the greater their impact on the resulting decisions, since specific goals clearly distinguish acceptable from unacceptable (or more from less acceptable) alternatives. Typically, participants higher in the hierarchy make decisions with a larger value component, whereas lower participants are more apt to make decisions having a larger factual component. Those closer to the top make decisions about what the organization is going to do; those in lower positions are more likely to be allowed to make choices as to how the organization can best carry out its tasks. Simon (1976: 45–56) insists that quite different criteria of correctness underlie these two classes of decisions: choice of ends can be validated only by fiat or consensus; choice of means can be validated empirically.

Ultimate goals served by organizations are frequently somewhat vague and imprecise. Some organizations exist to develop and transmit knowledge, others to maintain public order, and others to care for and cure patients. Such general goals in themselves provide few cues for guiding the behavior of participants. However, as March and Simon argue, they can serve as the starting point for the construction of *means-ends chains* that involve:

(1) starting with the general goal to be achieved, (2) discovering a set of means, very generally specified, for accomplishing this goal, (3) taking each of these

---

[7]Factors affecting the first type of decision—decisions to participate—are discussed in Chapter 7 of this volume. See also March and Simon (1958: 52–111).

means, in turn, as a new subgoal and discovering a set of more detailed means for achieving it, etc. (1958: 191)

In this manner, there is established a hierarchy of goals in which each level is:

considered as an end relative to the levels below it and as a means relative to the levels above it. Through the hierarchical structure of ends, behavior attains integration and consistency, for each member of a set of behavior alternatives is then weighted in terms of a comprehensive scale of values—the "ultimate" ends. (Simon, 1976: 63)

For example, in a manufacturing organization, an assignment to an individual worker to construct a specific component of a piece of equipment such as an engine provides that worker with an end toward which to direct his or her activities. This end, viewed from the level of his or her supervisor, is only a means toward the creation of the engine. The supervisor's end is to ensure that all parts are available when needed and are correctly assembled to produce the engine. However, this objective, when viewed from the next higher level, is only a means to the end of completing the final product, such as a lawn mower, containing the engine. The completion of all parts and assembly operations required to produce the lawn mower, while an end for the manufacturing division, is only a means at a higher level to the ultimate end of selling the lawn mower for profit to retail outlets. Viewed from the bottom up, the rationality of individual decisions and activities can be evaluated only as they relate to higher-order decisions; each subgoal can be assessed only in terms of its consistency or congruency with more general goals. Viewed from the top down, the factoring of general purposes into specific subgoals that can then be assigned to organizational subunits (individuals or departments) enhances the possibility of rational behavior by specifying value premises and hence simplifying the required decisions at every level. From this perspective, then, an organization's hierarchy can be viewed as a congealed set of means-ends chains promoting consistency of decisions and activities throughout the organization. Or, as Collins (1975: 316) suggests, March and Simon describe organizational structure "as a nested set of plans for action."

The ultimate goals—making a profit, achieving growth, prolonging life—are those that, by definition, are not viewed as means to ends but as ends in themselves. They may be determined by consensus or by decree. In either case, any challenge to these ultimate objectives is likely to be met with strong resistance. Physicians, for example, are reluctant to consider the merits of euthanasia, and capitalists react with righteous indignation to any questions concerning their rights to profits. Apart from any considerations of self-interest, such emotional reactions are partly caused by the half-conscious realization that any challenge to the ultimate objectives calls into question the premises around which the entire enterprise is structured.

Organizations also support participants in the decisions they must make. A formalized structure supports rational decision making not only by parceling out responsibilities among participants but also by providing them with the necessary means to handle them: resources, information, equipment. Specialized roles and rules, information channels, training programs, standard operating procedures—all may be viewed as mechanisms both for restricting the range of decisions each participant makes and for assisting the participant in making appropriate decisions within that range. As Perrow (1986: 128–131) notes, Simon's model of organizational influence stresses unobtrusive control of participants: training and channeling of information and attention play a larger role in producing dependable behavior than do commands or sanctions.

Underlying Simon's model of organizational decision making is a conception of the cognitive limits of individual decision makers.[8] Simon stresses that:

> It is impossible for the behavior of a single, isolated individual to reach any high degree of rationality. The number of alternatives he must explore is too great, the information he would need to evaluate them so vast that even an approximation to objective rationality is hard to conceive. Individual choice takes place in an environment of "givens"—premises that are accepted by the subject as bases for his choice; and behavior is adaptive only within the limits set by these "givens." (1976: 79)

By providing integrated subgoals, stable expectations, required information, necessary facilities, routine performance programs, and in general a set of constraints within which required decisions can be made, organizations supply these "givens" to individual participants. This is the sense in which March and Simon (1958: 169–71) intend the concept *bounded rationality*—a concept that both summarizes and integrates the two key elements of the rational system perspective: goal specificity and formalization.[9]

Also, in his later collaboration with March, Simon gave substantial emphasis to the importance of rules and routines in supporting rational behavior within organizations. As DiMaggio and Powell (1991: 19) stress, "March and Simon (1958) taught us that organizational behavior, particularly decision making, involves rule following more than the calculation of consequences." Thus, Simon, like Weber, was among those who began to identify formal rationality as distinct from technical rationality.

The model developed by Simon also can be used to explain how the very structures developed to promote rationality can, under some conditions,

---

[8]Simon and the Carnegie School led the way in introducing students of organizations to the "new" cognitive psychology with its emphasis on heuristics and organizational routines as a means of responding to complexity and uncertainty. Rationality does not always entail thoughtful choice but the following of rules. Later studies by cognitive psychologists have pursued in detail some of the specific types of biases underlying judgment and decision making by individuals (see Kahneman, Slovic, and Tversky, 1982; Nisbett and Ross, 1980). Organizational routines are designed to overcome such limitations.

[9]A good overview of Simon's contributions to the analysis of decision making in organizations is provided by Taylor (1965). An interesting critique of Simon's work is provided by Krupp (1961), and useful applications and extensions of Simon's framework are carried out by Allison (1971), Steinbruner (1974), and Ocasio (1997).

have the opposite effect. These and other sources of organizational pathologies will be discussed in Chapter 12.

SUMMARY AND TENTATIVE CONCLUSIONS

Any conclusions reached at this point must be tentative; it is difficult to appraise the strengths and limitations of any one perspective in isolation from the others. Nevertheless, a few general observations on the rational system approach can be made at this time.

From the rational system perspective, structural arrangements within organizations are conceived as tools deliberately designed for the efficient realization of ends or, from Weber's perspective, for the disciplined performance of participants. As Gouldner notes, "the focus is, therefore, on the legally prescribed structures—i.e., the formally 'blue-printed' patterns—since these are more largely subject to deliberate inspection and rational manipulation" (1959: 404–5). All theorists utilizing this perspective focus on the normative structure of organizations: on the specificity of goals and the formalization of rules and roles. There are, however, important differences among the various schools in their approach to the normative structure.

Taylor was highly pragmatic in his approach, placing his faith in a method by which, beginning with individual jobs, superior work procedures could be developed and appropriate arrangements devised for articulating the various tasks to be performed. Work planning was distinguished from work performance, the former becoming the responsibility of management. Taylor was concerned primarily with devising methods for the planning of work and working arrangements. The administrative theory group led by Fayol was less pragmatic and more prescriptive in its approach. They believed that general principles of management could be devised to guide managers as they designed their organizations, and so they busied themselves constructing lists of "do's and dont's" as guides to managerial decision making. Weber was less concerned with discovering ways—whether pragmatic or prescriptive—for improving organizations than with attempting to develop a parsimonious descriptive portrait of the characteristics of the newly emerging bureaucratic structures. Like Weber, Simon was also descriptive in his approach, examining the effect of structural features on individual decision makers within the organization. Simon's conception, in particular, enables us to understand better how thousands and even hundreds of thousands of individual decisions and actions can be integrated in the service of complex goals. Such rational, purposeful collective behavior requires the support of an organizational framework.

The four theorists also differ in the level of analysis at which they work. Taylor and Simon operate primarily at the social psychological level, focusing on individual participants as they perform tasks or make decisions; they treat structural features as contexts affecting these behaviors. By contrast Fayol and Weber work at the structural level, attempting to conceptualize and analyze the characteristics of organizational forms.

Thompson provides a simple summary of the general argument underlying the rational system perspective: "structure is a fundamental vehicle by which organizations achieve bounded rationality" (1967: 54). The specification of positions, role definitions, procedural rules and regulations, value and factual inputs that guide decision making—all function to canalize behavior in the service of predetermined goals. Individuals can behave rationally because their alternatives are limited and their choices circumscribed.

In a larger sense, however, rationality resides in the structure itself, not in the individual participants—in rules that assure participants will behave in ways calculated to achieve desired objectives, in control arrangements that evaluate performance and detect deviance, in reward systems that motivate participants to carry out prescribed tasks, and in the set of criteria by which participants are selected, replaced, and promoted. Because of its emphasis on the characteristics of structure rather than the characteristics of participants, Bennis has dubbed the rational system perspective one of "organizations without people" (1959: 263).[10]

Let us not forget, however, that the conception of rationality employed by this perspective is limited. At the top of the organization, the value premises that govern the entire structure of decision making fall outside the system: as long as they are specific enough to provide clear criteria for choice, these premises can support a "rational" structure no matter how monstrous or perverted their content. And at the bottom of the organization, "rational" behavior often consists in turning off one's mind and one's critical intellectual judgment and blindly conforming to the performance program specified by the job description.

We have noted the great emphasis the rational system theorist places on control—the determination of the behavior of one subset of participants by the other. Decision making tends to be centralized, and most participants are excluded from discretion or from exercising control over their own behavior. Most rational system theorists justify these arrangements as being in the service of rationality: control is the means of channeling and coordinating behavior so as to achieve specified goals. Few perceive the possibility that interpersonal control may be an end in itself—that one function of elaborate hierarchies and extensive divisions of labor is to allow some participants to control and, perhaps, to exploit others. The critical or Marxist perspective calls attention to these possibilities. We examine this critique in Chapter 7.

With the important exception of Weber, the early rational system theorists did not take much notice of the effect of the larger social, cultural, and technological context on organization structure or performance. Attention was concentrated on the internal features of organizations.

By concentrating on the normative structure, these rational system analysts virtually overlooked the behavioral structure of organizations. We learn much from them about plans and programs and premises, about roles and

---

[10]Consistent with this conclusion, Boguslaw has pointed out that whereas the classical utopians strove to achieve their end of the perfect social system by "populating their social systems with perfect human beings," the "new utopians"—systems engineers and control-systems experts—have become impatient with human imperfections, so that "the theoretical and practical solutions they seek call increasingly for decreases in the number and in the scope of responsibility of human beings within the operating structures of their new machines systems. . . . the new utopians are concerned with nonpeople and with people-substitutes" (1965: 2).

rules and regulations, but very little about the actual behavior of organizational participants. Structure is celebrated; action is ignored.

The natural system perspective, the second perspective to be considered, developed in response to these perceived inadequacies and limitations of the rational system perspective.

CHAPTER 3

Organizations as Natural Systems

To administer a social organization according to purely technical criteria of rationality is irrational, because it ignores the nonrational aspects of social conduct.

Peter M. Blau (1956)

Although the natural system perspective developed in large measure from critical reactions to the inadequacies of the rational system model, it should not be seen as merely providing a critique of another perspective. Rather, it defines a novel and interesting view of organizations that deserves to be considered and evaluated in its own right. As in our discussion of the rational system approach, we begin by identifying the more general or basic ideas common to natural system advocates and then briefly examine selected schools within this perspective.

IMPORTANT VERSUS DISTINCTIVE CHARACTERISTICS

Whereas the rational system theorists conceive of organizations as collectivities deliberately constructed to seek specific goals, natural system advocates emphasize that organizations are, first and foremost, collectivities. The rational system perspective stresses those features of organizations that distinguish them from other types of social groups, while the natural system theorists remind us that these distinguishing characteristics are not their only characteristics (Gouldner, 1959: 406). Indeed, they are not the most important characteristics.

We have already seen that much is made by rational system theorists of goal specificity and formalization as characteristics differentiating organizations from other types of collectivities. Natural system theorists generally acknowledge the existence of these attributes but argue that other characteristics—characteristics shared with all social groups—are of greater significance. Take first the matter of organizational goals and goal specificity.

Goal Complexity

Organizational goals and their relation to the behavior of participants are much more problematic for the natural than for the rational system theorist. This is largely because natural system analysts pay more attention to behavior and hence worry more about the complex interconnections between the normative and the behavioral structures of organizations. Two general themes characterize their views of organizational goals. First, there is frequently a disparity between the stated and the "real" goals pursued by organizations—between the professed or official goals that are announced and the actual or operative goals that can be observed to govern the activities of participants. Second, natural system analysts emphasize that even when the stated goals are actually being pursued, they are never the only goals governing participants' behavior. They point out that all organizations must pursue *support* (or "maintenance") goals in addition to their output goals (Gross, 1968; Perrow, 1970: 135). No organization can devote its full resources to producing products or services; each must expend energies maintaining itself.

These distinctions, though useful, do not go quite far enough. They do not capture the most profound difference between these two perspectives on organizational goals. The major thrust of the natural system view is that organizations are more than instruments for attaining defined goals; they are, fundamentally, social groups attempting to adapt and survive in their particular circumstances. Thus, formal organizations, like all other social groups, are governed by one overriding goal: survival. Gouldner emphasizes this implication of the natural system perspective:

> The organization, according to this model, strives to survive and to maintain its equilibrium, and this striving may persist even after its explicitly held goals have been successfully attained. This strain toward survival may even on occasion lead to the neglect or distortion of the organization's goals. (1959: 405)

Under many conditions, organizations have been observed to modify their goals so as to achieve a more favorable adjustment. If their survival is at stake, organizations will abandon the pursuit of their avowed objectives in order to save themselves. It is because of such tendencies that organizations are not to be viewed primarily as means for achieving specified ends, but as ends in themselves.

Two types of explanations have been proposed to account for the survival instincts of organizations. The first, and more elaborate, argues that the organizations are social systems characterized by a number of needs that must be satisfied if they are to survive. This view is linked to a broader theoretical framework known as functional analysis, which we briefly describe later in this chapter. Other theorists reject such assumptions as being anthropomorphic at worst and unnecessary at best. They suggest instead that one does not have to posit a survival need for the collectivity itself. It is sufficient to assume that some participants have a vested interest in the survival of the organization. Because it is a source of power, or resources, or prestige, or pleasure, they wish to see it preserved and include among their own goals that the organization itself be protected and, if possible, strengthened. This view is developed by the conflict theorists.

One of the earliest and most influential analyses of how some participants seek to preserve an organization even at the sacrifice of the goals for which it was originally established is that provided by Robert Michels (1949 trans.), a contemporary of Weber's writing in pre–World War I Germany. His analysis of the changes that occurred in the largest socialist party in Europe, Germany's Social Democratic party, is rightly regarded as a classic. This work is most famous for its formulation of "the iron law of oligarchy," which equates the processes by which complex administrative work is carried out in an organization with the processes by which power shifts from the rank-and-file members to a small group of leaders. "Who says organization says oligarchy" (see Chapter 12). But of greater interest for present purposes are Michels's views on the consequences of these oligarchical tendencies for the professed goals of the organization. The leaders of the party continue to give lip service to its revolutionary objectives, but over time become increasingly conservative, reluctant to risk the gains they have achieved or to endanger the party, which is their source of power. Michels gloomily concludes:

> Thus, from a means, organization becomes an end. To the institutions and qualities which at the outset were destined simply to ensure the good working of the party machine (subordination, the harmonious cooperation of individual members, hierarchical relationships, discretion, propriety of conduct), a greater importance comes ultimately to be attached than to the productivity of the machine. Henceforward the sole preoccupation is to avoid anything which may clog the machinery. (1949 trans.: 390)

Another way of viewing differences in the uses of goals by rational and natural system analysts is suggested by Brunsson (1985). He argues that the rational system decision-making model is in fact rational only if attention is focused on the decision as outcome. If instead we attend to actions (goal implementation) as outcome, then a more "irrational" decision process produces better results. Irrational decision processes speedily remove alternative possibilities and overestimate probabilities of success attached to the chosen alternative in order to structure participants' expectations, eliminate conflicts, and mold commitment to the selected course of action. Rational system theorists emphasize the normative structure and so focus on decisions—designs or proposals for action—as if they were the principal outcomes. Natural system theorists stress the behavioral structure and are more interested in examining what is done rather than what is decided or planned. Commitment and motivation loom as more salient variables than search and choice if action rather than decision is the focus.

Informal Structure

If the ends that organizations are designed to serve are not pure and simple and specific in the view of the natural system analysts, then neither are the structures that exist to attain them. The natural system theorists do not deny the existence of highly formalized structures within organizations, but they do question their importance, in particular their impact on the behavior of participants. Formal structures purposefully designed to regulate behavior in the service of specific goals are seen to be greatly affected—supplemented, eroded, transformed—by the emergence of *informal* structures. As first discussed in Chapter 1, we equate formal structures with those norms and behavior patterns that exist regardless of the characteristics of the individual actors. Informal structures are those based on the personal characteristics and relations of the specific participants. Thus, for example, formal authority refers to those control rights that are available to and exercised by all incumbents of a given position, such as supervisor or teacher; informal authority would indicate those rights that become available to a particular supervisor or teacher because of his or her special qualities or interpersonal ties. Obviously, one of the clearest ways to distinguish empirically between the formal and the informal elements in a given situation is to observe what happens to beliefs and behaviors when there is a change in personnel.

Natural system analysts emphasize that there is more to organizational structure than the prescribed rules, the job descriptions, and the associated regularities in the behavior of participants. Individual participants are never merely "hired hands" but bring along their heads and hearts: they enter the organization with individually shaped ideas, expectations, and agendas, and they bring with them differing values, interests, and abilities.

Expressed through interaction, these factors come together to create a reasonably stable informal structure. One of the most important insights of the natural system perspective is that the social structure of an organization does not consist of the formal structure plus the idiosyncratic beliefs and behaviors of individual participants but rather of a formal structure and an informal structure: informal life is itself structured and orderly. Participants within formal organizations generate informal norms and behavior patterns: status and power systems, communication networks, sociometric structures, and working arrangements.

In the early studies exploring informal structures, it was presumed that these "irrational" relations characterized only the lower strata of the organization: managers and executives were immune to such developments. But empirical studies by Dalton (1959) and others dispelled such notions. Also, early studies emphasized the dysfunctional consequences of the informal structures as private and irrational concerns that impeded the implementation of the rational formal design. Thus, Roethlisberger and Dickson equated the formal structure with the "logic of cost and efficiency" while the informal structure expressed the "logic of sentiments" (1939: 562–64). Later analysts emphasized the positive functions performed by informal structures—in increasing the ease of communication, facilitating trust, and correcting for the inadequacies of the formal systems (see Gross, 1953).

Greater appreciation for the functions of informal systems was coupled with increasing skepticism that formalization was conducive to rationality. Natural system analysts emphasize that formalization places heavy and often intolerable burdens on those responsible for the design and management of an organization. No planners are so foresighted or omniscient as to be able to anticipate all the possible contingencies that might confront each position in the organization. Attempts to program in advance the behavior of participants are often misguided, if not foolhardy. Such programming can easily become maladaptive and lead to behaviors both ineffective and inefficient, giving rise to the "trained incapacity" that Veblen (1904) called attention to long ago and for which some organizations have become notorious (see also Merton, 1957: 197–200). Further, formal arrangements that curtail individual problem solving and the use of discretion undermine participants' initiative and self-confidence, causing them to become alienated and apathetic. Such restrictive arrangements not only damage participants' self-esteem and mental health but prevent them from effectively contributing their talents and energies to the larger enterprise (Argyris, 1957; McGregor, 1960). In sum, natural system analysts insist that highly centralized and formalized structures are doomed to be ineffective and irrational in that they waste the organization's most precious resource: the intelligence and initiative of its participants.

Functional Analysis

Functional analysis served as an important underpinning for the work of some of the most influential natural system analysts. The origins of this widely used model are to be found in the work of a group of British social anthropologists, most notably Malinowski and Radcliffe-Brown. Merton's essay (1957: 19–84) is the most influential statement of this approach in sociology, while Stinchcombe (1968: 80–129) provides a valuable guide to the logical structure and causal imagery of functional arguments. The paradigm is complex, and there are many variants; nevertheless, its central features can be quickly summarized. As Stinchcombe (1968: 80) notes, a functional explanation is "one in which the *consequences* of some behavior or social arrangement are essential elements of the *causes* of that behavior."

The existence of some practice or behavior is explained in terms of its consequences—the functions it performs—rather than by reference to its origins. A number of natural system theorists implicitly or explicitly assumed an organic imagery, in which the organization was treated as a social system with certain needs or requirements that must be met if it was to survive. Just as the human body requires a continuing flow of oxygen, a need met by the lungs and circulation of blood, social systems were presumed to require the development of mechanisms to meet their needs to gather and circulate relevant information to decision makers. All functional explanations assume that the ends or consequences attained are "homeostatic" variables: the system remains in equilibrium so long as certain conditions are maintained.

Most analysts employ functional arguments in a rather casual manner rather than as a rigorous explanation. To be a valid functional explanation, it is not sufficient to simply show that a given practice is associated with the desired consequence. In addition, the analyst must identify the causal feed-back loop by which the forces maintaining the structure are themselves acti-vated by forces threatening the equilibrium (Stinchcombe 1968: 88). As Elster (1983) notes, most functionalists are content to argue "as if" rather than to "demonstrate that" such forces are at work. Even though few socio-logical theories of organizational stability and survival achieve this level of logical sophistication, many of our most important insights into the nature of organization structure and process have their origins in functional rea-soning.

SELECTED SCHOOLS

As with the rational system perspective, the natural system perspective is an umbrella under which a number of rather diverse approaches can be gath-ered. While they share certain generic features, they differ in important par-ticulars. We will discuss briefly four influential variants of the *social consensus* subtype—Mayo's human relations school, Barnard's conception of coopera-tive systems, Selznick's institutional approach, and Parsons's AGIL model—and then briefly describe and illustrate the *social conflict* model.

Mayo and the Human Relations School

We will not recount in detail the famous series of studies and experiments conducted at the Hawthorne plant of the Western Electric Company outside Chicago during the late 1920s and early 1930s. This research is meticulous-ly described by Roethlisberger and Dickson (1939) and given its most influ-ential interpretation by Elton Mayo (1945). Mayo, along with Roethlisberger, was a member of the Harvard Business School faculty. He was trained as an industrial psychologist, and his early work grew out of the scientific management tradition established by Taylor. Like Taylor, Mayo studied individual factors such as fatigue in an attempt to determine the optimum length and spacing of rest periods for maximizing productivity. The early work in the Hawthorne plant followed the scientific management approach: the researchers set about to determine the optimal level of illu-mination for the assembly of telephone relay equipment. Mayo summarizes the surprising results:

> The conditions of scientific experiment had apparently been fulfilled—experi-mental room, control room; changes introduced one at a time; all other con-ditions held steady. And the results were perplexing. . . . Lighting improved in the experimental room, production went up; but it rose also in the control room. The opposite of this: lighting diminished from 10- to 3-foot-candles in the experimental room and the production again went up; simultaneously in the control room, with illumination constant, production also rose. (1945: 69)

The researchers were in confusion. Other conditions were run with similar inexplicable results. In desperation, they asked the workers themselves what was going on and learned that the workers were so pleased to be singled out for special attention that they had worked very hard to please the researchers and the company. The "Hawthorne effect" was discovered. Although this effect has been variously interpreted, a summary translation of its lessons might be stated: Change is interesting; Attention is gratifying!

Additional studies carried out by the Harvard group—the second relay-assembly group, the mica-splitting test room, the bank-wiring observation room—all served to call into question the simple motivational assumptions on which the prevailing rational models rested. Individual workers do not behave as "rational" economic actors but as complex beings with multiple motives and values; they are driven as much by feelings and sentiments as by facts and interests; and they do not behave as individual, isolated actors but as members of social groups exhibiting commitments and loyalties stronger than their individualistic self-interests. Thus, in the bank-wiring observation room, workers were observed to set and conform to daily work quotas—group norms restricting production—at the expense of their own higher earnings. And informal status hierarchies and leadership patterns developed that challenged the formal systems designed by managers (see Roethlisberger and Dickson, 1939: 379–447; Homans, 1950: 48–155). At the social psychological level, the Hawthorne studies pointed to a more complex model of worker motivation based on a social psychological rather than an economic conception of the individual;[1] at the structural level, the studies discovered and demonstrated the importance of informal organization.

In drawing general conclusions from this work, Mayo adopted a reactionary intellectual stance: he emphasized the evils of industrialism and nostalgically longed for the stability and socially cohesive ways of the preindustrial past (see Guillen, 1994; Trahair, 1992). Later researchers discarded this metaphysical pathos but pursued his insights regarding the complexity of human motivation and the importance of informal structure.

The Hawthorne trunk gave rise to a rich assortment of research and reform offshoots, each of which has produced many individual branches. The major research issues pursued include studies of the work groups in the organizational environment, leadership behavior, and the impact of worker background and personality attributes on organizational behavior. Reform attempts include the use of personnel counselors, leadership training, job redefinition, and participation in decision making. Each of these interests merits a brief description; all of them are still flourishing.

The discovery of informal group processes in organizational settings both stimulated and received impetus from the study of small-group behavior carried on by social psychologists and sociologists. Among the former, Likert (1961) and Katz (Katz, Maccoby, and Morse, 1950), together with their colleagues at the Institute for Social Research, University of Michigan, were particularly influential; among the latter, Homans (1950) and Whyte (1951; 1959) were effective in analyzing group processes in organizational settings. A few analysts, such as Sayles (1958), attempted to understand how organi-

---

[1]After inspecting the results of the bank-wiring observation room study at the Hawthorne plant, Mayo concluded: "It is unfortunate for economic theory that it applies chiefly to persons of less, rather than greater, normality of social relationships. Must we conclude that economics is a study of human behavior in non-normal situations, or alternatively, a study of non-normal human behavior in ordinary situations?" (1945: 43)

zational factors affected the number, types, and tactics of groups that emerged; but most focused not on the determinants but on the consequences of group membership—for example, the impact of group cohesiveness on individual conformity to production norms (Roy, 1952; Seashore, 1954).

From the human relations perspective, leadership is conceived primarily as a mechanism for influencing the behavior of individual participants. Early studies sought a set of leadership traits or characteristics that would stimulate individual performance in the service of organizational goals. Thus, studies by White and Lippitt (1953) reported that participants in experimental task groups performed more effectively under "democratic" than under "laissez-faire" or "authoritarian" leaders. Later research stressed the relational aspects of leadership. For example, a series of studies conducted at the Ohio State Leadership Studies Center (Stogdill and Coons, 1957) isolated two basic dimensions of leadership behavior: *consideration*, the extent to which trust, friendship, and respect mark the relation between the supervisor and his or her workers, and *initiating structure*, the degree to which the supervisor is a good organizer who can "get the work out." These dimensions were observed to vary independently, and in general, the more effective leaders—that is, the leaders whose subordinates performed better and had higher morale—were those who scored high on both dimensions.

Later efforts emphasized that leadership characteristics vary with the nature of the situation (Fiedler, 1964; 1971) and the specific needs or motivations of the individual subordinates (Cartwright, 1965). Studies by Pelz (1952) suggested that a supervisor's relation to his or her own superior—specifically, the extent of his or her influence upward—is a powerful determinant of the supervisor's influence over his or her own subordinates. Likert (1961) built on this finding to create his model of the supervisor's critical function as a "linking pin" relating lower to higher levels of the hierarchy. Most of these leadership studies ignored the effects of incumbency in a formal office on an individual's influence, either by overlooking this aspect of the situation or by deliberately holding it constant—for example, by studying differences in leadership behavior among all first-line supervisors in a given office or factory situation (see Katz and Kahn, 1952).[2]

From the very beginning, human relations analysts emphasized the great variability of individual characteristics and behaviors and insisted on the relevance of these differences in understanding organizational behavior. Early research demonstrated that such officially irrelevant differences as race (Collins, 1946), class (Warner and Low, 1947), and cultural background (Dalton, 1950) had strong effects on allocation to work roles and organizational behavior. These studies are important forerunners of the more recent interest in the relation between stratification and organizations, which we discuss in Chapter 8.

---

[2]Blau (1964: 210) has pointed out that "although managerial authority in organizations contains important leadership elements, its distinctive characteristic, which differentiates it from informal leadership, is that it is rooted in the formal powers and sanctions the organization bestows upon managers." It is in keeping with the natural system perspective to ignore this distinctive component of leadership in formal organizations. (We examine it in Chapter 11.)

Many of the lessons learned by the human relations researchers were codified by Douglas McGregor in his influential book, *The Human Side of Enterprise* (1960). McGregor emphasized that the most significant differences between classical (rational system) management theory, which he labeled "Theory X," and the human relations approach, termed "Theory Y," was the nature of the assumptions made about human actors. Principal assumptions underlying Theory X were:

- individuals dislike work and will seek to avoid it (p. 33)
- therefore, "most people must be coerced, controlled, directed, threatened with punishment to get them to put forth adequate effort toward the achievement of individual objectives" (p. 34)
- "the average human being prefers to be directed, wishes to avoid responsibility, has relatively little ambition, wants security above all" (p. 34)

By contrast, human relations theory was constructed on the assumption that:

- most individuals do not "inherently dislike work . . . the expenditure of physical and mental effort in work is as natural as play or rest" (p. 47)
- "external control and threat of punishment are not the only means for bringing about effort toward organizational objectives" (p. 47)
- the most significant rewards are those associated with "the satisfaction of ego and self-actualization needs" (p. 47–48)

One constructs very different kinds of organizational structures based on such contradictory assumptions concerning human nature.

The human relations school has also given rise to much effort directed at changing organizations—modifying and improving them as social environments. The original Hawthorne researchers were themselves interested in pursuing practical applications of their findings. Stressing the positive relation in their studies between worker satisfaction and productivity, they sought techniques to improve the adjustment and morale of individual workers. One approach involved the introduction of a set of personnel counselors, distinct from the line hierarchy, whose task it was to listen sympathetically to workers' complaints (Roethlisberger and Dickson, 1939: 189–376, 590–604). The interviewing techniques devised for this program contributed to the development of nondirective counseling techniques now in wide use.

Another change strategy devised by the human relations school stressed the importance of supervisory skills in promoting worker morale. Supervisors required special training if they were to become more sensitive to the psychological and social needs of their subordinates. Mayo (1945), influenced in part by Barnard, stressed the important role to be performed by supervisors and managers whose social function it was to elicit cooperation among workers—cooperation that could not be assumed to be automatic (see Bendix and Fisher, 1949). Thus, the human relations approach helped to spawn many diverse efforts in leadership training, from simple attitude-change efforts to more intensive Bethel-type sensitivity or T-group training (see, for example, Blake and Mouton, 1964; National Training Laboratories, 1953).

Yet another reform approach focused on the need to redefine and enlarge the role definitions specified for workers. Contrary to the assumptions of the rational system model, the human relations group stressed the dangers of excessive formalization with its emphasis on extreme functional specialization. Job enlargement or, at least, job rotation, was advocated as a method of reducing the alienation and increasing the commitment and satisfaction of workers performing routine work (see Herzberg, 1966).

Still other reformers stressed the importance of worker participation in decision making within the organization, particularly decisions directly affecting them. Although the notion of linking participation to motivation and commitment was given encouragement by the Hawthorne studies, more direct support has come from the experimental and theoretical work of Lewin (1948) and his colleagues (for example, Coch and French, 1948). From the outset, attempts to encourage participation by workers in organizational decisions has received more attention and support in Europe than in the United States (see Jaques, 1951; Blumberg, 1968).

Virtually all of these applications of the human relations movement have come under severe criticism on both ideological and empirical grounds. Paradoxically, the human relations movement, ostensibly developed to humanize the cold and calculating rationality of the factory and shop, rapidly came under attack on the grounds that it represented simply a more subtle and refined form of exploitation. Critics charged that workers' legitimate economic interests were being inappropriately deemphasized; that actual conflicts of interest were denied and "therapeutically" managed; and that the roles attributed to managers represented a new brand of elitism. The entire movement was branded as "cow sociology": just as contented cows were alleged to produce more milk, satisfied workers were expected to produce more output (see Bell, 1960: 238–44; Bendix, 1956: 308–40; Landsberger, 1958; Braverman, 1974: 139–51).

It is important to recognize that in spite of the label "human" relations, humanizing the workplace was viewed primarily as a means to increasing productivity, not an end in itself. It was not until well into the 1960s that employee well-being came to be recognized as a valid objective of organization design, and even then and up to the present time, this emphasis has been stronger in European than in United States organizations and organization theories (see Kahn, 1990).

The ideological criticisms were the first to erupt, but reservations raised by researchers on the basis of empirical evidence may in the long run prove to be more devastating. Several decades of research have demonstrated no clear relation between worker satisfaction and productivity (see Brayfield and Crockett, 1955; Schwab and Cummings, 1970); no clear relation between supervisory behavior or leadership style and worker productivity (see Hollander and Julian, 1969); no clear relation between job enlargement and worker satisfaction or productivity (see Hulin and Blood, 1968); and no clear relation between participation in decision making and satisfaction or productivity (see Vroom, 1969: 227–39). Where positive relations among these variables have been observed, the direction may be opposite to that predict-

ed: productivity producing satisfaction (Porter and Lawler, 1968) or productivity influencing supervisory style (Lowin and Craig, 1968), rather than vice
versa. Even the original Hawthorne results have been reanalyzed and questioned (Carey, 1967; Franke and Kaul, 1978; Jones, 1990; 1992).

Our brief survey of the human relations school cannot do justice to the
variety of theoretical implications, empirical studies, and practical reform
efforts it has generated. Guillen (1994) argues that there is evidence to show
that the human relations programs and techniques had a substantial impact
both in reducing conflict and in increasing productivy in United States
industrial firms between 1930 and 1960, in part because they were adopted
and promoted by the rapidly developing personnel profession. In terms of
intellectual impact, it is only a small exaggeration to suggest that the academic field of industrial sociology first saw the light of day at the Hawthorne
plant, with Mayo serving as midwife. Moreover, sociological work on organizations well into the 1960s was shaped primarily by the human relations
model—whether it was attempting to fill in the model's missing pieces or
attacking its shortcomings and biases. And all of the thousands of studies
concerned with motivation, morale, and leadership either have been directly stimulated by or are indirectly beholden to a tiny group of workers who
kept increasing their output even though the lights were growing dimmer.[3]

Barnard's Cooperative System

At the same time that Mayo and his associates were conducting their studies
and extrapolating from them to underline the importance of interpersonal
processes and informal structures, Chester I. Bernard was expanding his own
views of the nature of organizations. Barnard was not a researcher but an
executive, president of New Jersey Bell Telephone company. Although
Barnard's major book, *The Functions of the Executive* (1938),[4] was a very personal work reflecting his rather distinctive views and concerns, he was in regular contact with the human relations group at Harvard, including Mayo and
Roethlisberger. Barnard's influence on the field has been great, in part
because his treatise was one of the first systematic attempts to outline a theory of organization available to U.S. readers, since Weber's work had not yet
been translated. Barnard's ideas contributed to human relations approaches
and provided a foundation for both Selznick's institutionalist views and
Simon's theory of decision making.

Barnard stressed that organizations are essentially cooperative systems,
integrating the contributions of their individual participants. As already
reported in our review of organizational definitions in Chapter 1, Barnard
defined a formal organization as "that kind of coöperation among men that
is conscious, deliberate, purposeful" (p. 4).[5] Two separable ideas are embed-

---

[3]For a more extensive summary of the human relations work, see Waring (1991). Perrow
(1986: 79–114) provides a review and highly critical assessment.

[4]Unless otherwise indicated, all references in this section are to this work.

[5]Like many natural system theorists, Barnard defined organizations so as to emphasize
their rational system features—their distinguishing features—but then concentrated on other,
more generic aspects in his analysis.

ded in this definition. First, organizations rely on the willingness of participants to make contributions. Participants must be induced to make contributions—a variety of incentives can be used to motivate them to do so, including material rewards, opportunities for distinction, prestige, personal power, and associated attractions—and make them in sufficient quantities, or the organization cannot survive.[6] Second, whatever the specific motives that procure contributions to the enterprise, these efforts must be directed toward a common purpose. "The inculcation of belief in the real existence of a common purpose is an essential executive function" (p. 87).

Thus, Barnard attempts to combine and reconcile two somewhat contradictory ideas: goals are imposed from the top down while their attainment depends on willing compliance from the bottom up. This view of accepted direction is developed most fully in Barnard's conception of authority. He argues that it is a "fiction that authority comes down from above" (p. 170), noting the many situations in which leaders claim authority but fail to win compliance. This is because authority depends ultimately on its validation from the response of those subject to it: "the decision as to whether an order has authority or not lies with the persons to whom it is addressed, and does not reside in 'persons of authority' or those who issue these orders" (p. 163). Still, some types of orders have a greater "potentiality of assent of those to whom they are sent" (p. 173). These are orders that are products of a well-designed and integrated communications system that links all contributions in a purposeful cooperative framework.

> At first thought it may seem that the element of communication in organization is only in part related to authority; but more thorough consideration leads to the understanding that communication, authority, specialization, and purpose are all aspects comprehended in coördination. All communication relates to the formulation of purpose and the transmission of coördinating prescriptions for action and so rests upon the ability to communicate with those willing to coöperate. (p. 184)

This conception of an organization as a purposefully coordinated system of communications linking all participants in such a manner that the purposes of superordinates are accepted as the basis for the actions of subordinates became the foundation for Simon's theory of decision making, as described in Chapter 2.

Barnard's views thus contain many ideas that are consistent with a rational system conception of organizations. What sets them apart is his insistence on the nonmaterial, informal, interpersonal, and, indeed, moral basis of cooperation. Material rewards are viewed as "weak incentives" that must be buttressed by other types of pyschological and social motivations if cooperative effort is to be sustained. As for informal organization, Barnard argued that "formal organizations arise out of and are necessary to informal organization; but when formal organizations come into operation, they create and require informal organizations" (p. 120). Informal structures facili-

---

[6]Simon later adopted and elaborated upon Barnard's "contributions-inducements" theory of organizational equilibrium. We review these developments in Chapter 7.

tate communication, maintain cohesiveness, and undergird "the willingness to serve and the stability of objective authority" (p. 122). Interpersonal ties at their best create a "condition of communion": "the opportunity for commandership, for mutual support" forming the "basis of informal organization that is essential to the operation of every formal organization" (p. 148).

But the most critical ingredient of successful organization is the formation of a collective purpose that becomes morally binding on participants. Developing and imparting this mission is the distinctive function of the executive.

> The distinguishing mark of the executive responsibility is that it requires not merely conformance to a complex code of morals but also the creation of moral codes for others. The most generally recognized aspect of this function is called securing, creating, inspiring of "morale" in an organization. This is the process of inculcating points of view, fundamental attitudes, loyalties, to the organization or coöperative system, and to the system of objective authority, that will result in subordinating individual interest and the minor dictates of personal codes to the good of the coöperative whole. (p. 279)

On the one hand such views sound quaint and hopelessly old fashioned; they have been subjected to scathing attack by critics such as Perrow (1986: 62–68), who scoff at Barnard's moral imperialism and point out the duplicity inherent in "willing" cooperation that is managed from above. On the other hand, many of these themes have again become highly fashionable as students of organizations rediscover the importance of organizational cultures shaped by zealous managers supplying strongly held values to their members. Barnard is the godfather of contemporary business gurus, such as Peters and Waterman (1982), who advocate the cultivation of "strong cultures." We discuss these neo-Barnardian developments in Chapters 9 and 11.[7]

More so than his contemporaries, Barnard did give some attention to the environment. His conception of organizations as systems of consciously coordinated *activities* rather than persons allows him to recognize that individuals "stand outside all organizations and have multiple relations with them" (p. 100). And, more generally, he recognizes that many organizations are "incomplete, subordinate, and dependent" (p. 98). However, unlike the open system theorists, he did not systematically pursue these insights (see Scott, 1990a).

Consistent with the natural system framework, however, Barnard recognized the existence of organizational forces even more powerful than purpose:

> Finally it should be noted that, once established, organizations change their unifying purposes. They tend to perpetuate themselves; and in the effort to survive may change the reasons for existence. (p. 89)

The necessity of survival can override the morality of purpose.

---

[7]A collection of essays edited by Williamson (1990) celebrates the fiftieth anniversary of the publication of *The Functions of the Executive* as a number of organizational scholars appraise Barnard's intellectual legacy and continuing influence. For a general review of his managerial career and an appraisal of his impact on organization theory, see W. G. Scott (1992).

Selznick's Institutional Approach

Philip Selznick, a student of bureaucracy under Merton at Columbia, but an intellectual descendant of Michels and Barnard, developed his own unique natural system model—which has recently been refurbished and elaborated to constitute an influential approach to the analysis of organizations known as institutional theory (see Chapter 5). We restrict attention now, however, to Selznick's seminal early contributions and to the related work of his immediate intellectual followers. Unlike Barnard, Selznick did not present his approach in one single, unified statement, but scattered his ideas through several books and articles. We attempt to provide a short but coherent sketch of his framework.

For Selznick, "the most important thing about organizations is that, though they are tools, each nevertheless has a life of its own" (1949: 10). He agrees with the rational system analyst that the distinguishing characteristic of formal organizations is that they are rationally ordered instruments designed to attain goals. However, these formal structures can "never succeed in conquering the nonrational dimensions of organizational behavior" (1948: 25). The sources of these nonrational features are (1) individuals, who participate in the organization as "wholes" and do not act merely in terms of their formal roles within the system; and (2) organizational structures, which include the formal aspects but also the complex informal systems that link participants with one another and with others external to the official boundaries. Organizational rationality is constrained by "the recalcitrance of the tools of action": persons bring certain characteristics to the organization and develop other commitments as members that restrict their capacity for rational action; organizational procedures become valued as ends in themselves; the organization strikes bargains with its environment that compromise present objectives and limit future possibilities (1949: 253–59).

Although Selznick's earlier work emphasized the constrains imposed by individual and environmental commitments, his later work increasingly recognized that these same processes could be a source of strength. In some cases, participants come to share a common set of commitments and a unity of purpose that create a formidable weapon (Selznick, 1952). The underlying theme stresses the importance of *institutionalization*: the processes by which an organization "takes on a special character" and "achieves a distinctive competence or, perhaps, a trained or built-in incapacity" (Selznick, 1996). Thus, institutionalization refers to a morally neutral process: "the emergence of orderly, stable, socially integrating patterns out of unstable, loosely organized, or narrowly technical activities" (Broom and Selznick, 1955: 238). Selznick argued that the most significant aspect of institutionalization is the process by which structures or activities became "infused with value beyond the technical requirements at hand" (Selznick, 1957: 17).

Selznick views organizational structure as an adaptive organism shaped in reaction to the characteristics and commitments of participants as well as to influences from the external environment. He explicitly embraces a functional form of analysis, explaining:

> This means that a given empirical system is deemed to have basic needs, essentially related to self-maintenance; the system develops repetitive means of self-defense; and day-to-day activity is interpreted in terms of the function served by that activity for the maintenance and defense of the system. (1948: 29)

Insisting that the overriding need of all systems "is the maintenance of the integrity and continuity of the system itself," Selznick attempts to spell out certain more specific "derived imperatives," including the security of the organization as a whole in relation to its environment, the stability of lines of authority and communication, the stability of informal relations within the organization, and a homogeneity of outlook toward the meaning and role of the organization.

Institutional commitments develop over time as the organization confronts external constraints and pressures from its environment as well as changes in the composition of its personnel, their interests, and their informal relations. No organization is completely immune from these external and internal pressures, although the extent of institutionalization varies from one organization to another.

To examine these processes Selznick proposes that, rather than following the lead of experimental psychologists who study routine psychological processes, we should imitate the clinical psychologists who examine the dynamic adaptation of the organism over time. Instead of focusing on the day-to-day decisions made in organizations, we should concentrate on those critical decisions that, once made, result in a change in the structure itself. The pattern of these critical decisions, viewed over time, results in the development of a distinctive character structure for each organization, just as an individual's critical decisions and typical mode of coping with problems give rise to the development of a distinctive personality (Selznick, 1957).

Following Barnard, Selznick believes that leadership can play a critical role in this evolutionary process. Leaders must define the mission of the enterprise: it is their responsibility to choose and to protect its distinctive values and "to create a social structure which embodies them" (1957: 60). Among the critical decisions confronting any enterprise are the selection of a social base—what clientele, what market to serve; the building of an institutional core—the selection of central personnel; and the determination of the nature and timing of formalization of structure and procedures.

Selznick thus invites us to observe the process by which an organization develops its distinctive structures, capacities, and liabilities; he proposes, in sum, that we carry out a natural history of organizations.

If we examine some of the empirical work stimulated by Selznick's institutional model, we will obtain a clearer picture of both the strengths and weaknesses of the proposed approach. Selznick's most famous study is of the Tennessee Valley Authority (TVA), a decentralized government agency created during the depression to improve the economic status of the entire Tennessee Valley, a chronically depressed, flood-ravaged region. Massive federal funds—at least by the standards of the 1930s—were provided to support a broad-gauged attack on the problems of the area. Flood control, hydroelectric power, and soil conservation were to be provided in an integrated manner. Top agency officials were located at the site, not in far-off

Washington, so that officials would not be inclined to impose solutions from above but would work with the local inhabitants and community agencies in developing acceptable projects (see Lilienthal, 1944).

As we would expect, Selznick (1949) focuses on the "internal relevance"—the consequences for the agency—of these strategies. He points out that the democratic ideology not only served to recruit and motivate talented participants but also enabled the New Deal agency to gain access to a suspicious and conservative area. Agency officials employed co-optation as a strategy to gain legitimacy and political support. *Co-optation* is a mechanism by which external elements are incorporated into the decision-making structures of an organization: in the case of the TVA, local leaders were recruited to participate in the agency's decision-making and advisory bodies. This tactic ensured that the agency would enjoy local political support for its programs, but such support always comes at a price: local leaders exchanged support for a measure of influence on the agency's programs and goals. As a consequence, some public interest goals were subverted to serve private interests. For example, improved land values surrounding water projects that were supposed to benefit the public often fell into private hands, and reforested land intended as watershed was taken over by lumber interests.[8]

Selznick's analysis set the pattern for a number of similar studies that examined the ways in which the original goals of an organization can be displaced or undermined. Thus, Clark's (1956) study of an adult education program in Los Angeles argues that its professed goals of providing cultural and intellectual programs could not be realized because of its marginal organizational and institutional status. Because the program lacked full legitimacy, only those parts of it that could attract large numbers of students were retained, with other academically valuable but less popular offerings losing out to the "enrollment economy." And Zald and Denton (1963) describe the transformation of the YMCA from a religious organization performing rehabilitative and welfare services for the urban poor into a social and recreational center for suburban and middle-class young people.

These and related studies exhibit several common features. The analyst focuses on the administrative history of the organization: the structural features and programs of the organization are viewed as changing over time in response to changing conditions. The methodology employed tends to be that of the case study, and heavy reliance is placed on the analysis of organizational documents and interviews with informants knowledgeable about the organization's history. Given this approach, most of the organizations selected for study have been relatively recently founded. Selznick (1957: 142) insists that he is interested not in recounting the history of any given organization for its own sake but in seeking "to discover the characteristic ways in which types of institutions respond to types of circumstances." However, this interest in generalization is somewhat at odds with the intensive case-study approach. Cohen points out: "As the desire to explain more and more aspects of a single study, situation, or phenomenon increases, the possibility

---

[8]A reanalysis of the data concerning the early development of the TVA by Colignon (1996) utilizes a conflict model to provide a somewhat divergent interpretation of the agency's formative years.

of using this explanation outside the situation for which it was created approaches the vanishing point" (1972: 402).

Thus, in these earlier uses of the institutional approach, a rather consistent pattern emerges. Fundamentally, analysts sought to explain changes in the goals of the organization—not the professed goals, but the ends actually pursued, the operative goals. The general mode of explanation is similar to that offered by Michels: to increase their own security, organizational participants modify controversial goals in the face of hostile environments. As Perrow notes, the literature spawned by the approach—to which Perrow himself has contributed (see Perrow, 1961)—takes on an "exposé" character: "The major message is that the organization has sold out its goals in order to survive or grow" (1986: 163). This early work stimulated by Selznick's conception appears to go out of its way to inspect the seamy side of organizational life, although in doing so it perhaps served as a useful antidote to the paean to organizational rationality being sung during this era by overexuberant rational system theorists.

However, with time, this negative emphasis has been tempered by more constructive concerns about the ways in which precarious values can be protected. Selznick himself, as we have noted, began to emphasize that leaders could and should act to defend and, if necessary, reinterpret and renew the mission of their organization (1957). And Clark (1970; 1972) turned his attention to how such "distinctive" and successful colleges as Antioch, Reed, and Swarthmore managed to survive and to preserve their special character. This broadened research agenda has gained a number of adherents. Not only is Selznick's work recognized as providing the underpinnings for the institutionalist perspective, which has garnered much attention in the most recent decades, but his concern for the role of leaders in making critical decisions and in defining institutional values has contributed to the current interest in strategic decision making and the creation of organizational cultures. We consider these developments in later chapters, especially Chapters 9 and 11.

Parsons's AGIL Schema

More so than other analysts working within the natural system tradition, Talcott Parsons developed a very explicit model detailing the needs that must be met if a system is to survive. Parsons's approach is the product of a lifetime devoted to perfecting a general analytic model suitable for the analysis for all types of collectivities—from small, primary groups to entire societies (see Parsons, 1951; Parsons, Bales, and Shils, 1953; Parsons, 1966). He first applied the model to formal organizations in two papers published in the late 1950s and collected in his book on societies (1960).

Parsons's model is identified by the acronym AGIL, which represents the four basic functions that all social systems must perform if they are to persist:

Adaptation: the problem of acquiring sufficient resources.

Goal attainment: the problem of setting and implementing goals.

Integration: the problem of maintaining solidarity or coordination among the subunits of the system.

Latency: the problem of creating, preserving, and transmitting the system's distinctive culture and values.

In addition to being applicable to all types of social systems, the schema may be applied at more than one level in analyzing a given type of system. Thus, Parsons applies his model to organizations at the ecological, the structural, and the social psychological levels. Linkages across these levels are also stressed. First, at the ecological level, Parsons relates organizations to the functioning of the larger society. Applying AGIL at the societal level, Parsons suggests that subordinate social units such as organizations can be classified according to their social function (see Table 3–1). For example, economic organizations such as firms are said to serve the adaptive needs of the larger society. As Parsons (1960: 19) points out:

> What from the point of view of the organization is its specified goal is, from the point of view of the larger system of which it is a differentiated part or subsystem, a specialized or differentiated function.

Because of this functional linkage, the place or role of the subsystem is legitimated, and it may expect to receive societal approval and resources in accordance with the value placed in the society on the particular functions it performs.

Shifting to the structural level of analysis, Parsons notes that each formal organization may also be analyzed as a social system in its own right, and each must develop its own differentiated subsystems to satisfy the four basic needs. Thus, each organization must develop structures that enable it to adapt to its environment and must mobilize resources needed for its continued operation. Arrangements are also needed to enable the organization to set and implement its goals. To solve its integrative problems, an organization must find ways to command the loyalties of its members, enlist their effort, and coordinate the operations of its various sectors. And mechanisms must be developed to cope with latency problems, to promote consensus on

TABLE 3–1   Parsons's Typology Based on Societal Functions

Societal Function	Organizational Type	Examples
Adaptation	Organizations oriented to economic production	Business firms
Goal attainment	Organizations oriented to political goals	Government agencies Other organizations that allocate power, such as banks
Integration	Integrative organizations	Courts and the legal profession Political parties Social-control agencies
Latency	Pattern-maintenance organizations	Cultural organizations, such as museums Educational organizations Religious organizations

the values that define and legitimate the organization's output and system goals.

While Parsons does not insist that a specific structural unit will develop to manage each of these functional needs, he does argue that structural differentiation will tend to occur along these divisions. Functional imperatives generate the fault lines along which a social structure becomes differentiated. The explanation for this linkage between functional requirements and structural arrangements is simply that the various functional needs are somewhat in conflict, so that efforts directed at solving one functional problem interfere with efforts directed toward the others.[9] Specifically, energies devoted to adapting the organization to its environment partially conflict with efforts toward goal attainment—a problem emphasized by Selznick and his colleagues—and efforts directed toward integration—a tension emphasized by Bales (1953)—and so on.

A structural "solution" to these tensions is to create roles and subsystems focused on each problem area. For example, Bales and his colleagues argue that in informal groups the inherent tensions involved in goal attainment (for example, winning the game) versus integration (for example, providing satisfaction for all participants) is partially resolved by the emergence of a "task" leader, who specializes in directing and controlling goal attainment activities, and a "socio-emotional" leader, who specializes in motivating members and reducing tensions (Bales, 1953; Slater, 1955). And in formal organizations, specialized departments and roles—supervisors, maintenance workers, personnel counselors, inspectors—emerge to carry out the multiple, and somewhat conflicting, functions.

This solution only simplifies the definitions of individual roles and subsystems and does not, of course, eliminate the incompatibilities: these are merely pushed to a higher level of the system for resolution. For example, at the level of the informal group, Bales (1953) argues that the differentiated leader roles provide a stable basis for group functioning only if the two leaders form a coalition of mutual support. At the organizational level, Lawrence and Lorsch (1967) have argued that organizations characterized by a higher level of structural differentiation are in greater need of integrative and conflict-resolution mechanisms (see Chapter 5).

In moving toward a more micro or social psychological level, Parsons again employs the AGIL schema, arguing that each subsystem within the organization itself comprises finer subdivisions that can be distinguished in terms of the functional requirements. However, because these applications become excessively complex and esoteric, we will not pursue them here.

---

[9]Parsons's reasoning at this point is illuminated by knowledge of the intellectual origins of the AGIL schema. His conception of these system problems grew out of his work on the "pattern variables"—basic value dichotomies representing the dimensions along which structures are arranged. The pairs of opposing values—universalism-particularism, affectivity–affective neutrality, ascription-achievement, and specificity-diffuseness—were cross-classified, producing the four system needs. Thus, values identified as most appropriate for solving the problem of adaptation are universalism, affective neutrality, specificity, and achievement; at the opposite extreme, values appropriate for improving integration are particularism, affectivity, diffuseness, and ascription (see Parsons, 1951; Parsons, Bales, and Shils, 1953).

Like many natural system models, Parsons's framework emphasizes a set of functional needs that all social systems must satisfy in order to survive. As noted, this approach emphasizes the similarities between organizations and other types of social systems. But unlike other natural system models, Parsons's formulation also provides a clear basis for distinguishing between organizations and other social systems. Parsons states, "As a formal analytical point of reference, primacy of orientation to the attainment of a specific goal is used as the defining characteristic of an organization which distinguishes it from other types of social systems" (1960: 17). Within the Parsonian framework, this definition implies more than the widely shared view that organizations tend to pursue specific goals. Parsons calls attention to the relative importance placed on the goal-attainment subsystem in organizations. That is, organizations are social systems placing greater priority on those processes by which goals are set and resources are mobilized for goal attainment than is the case in other social systems.

Finally, we review one other useful set of distinctions proposed by Parsons. In addition to his analysis of the functional differentiation that occurs along a horizontal axis at any given level of analysis, Parsons also distinguishes three major levels of organizational structure. At the bottom layer is the *technical* system, where the actual "product" of the organization is processed. This level is exemplified by the activities of workers on assembly lines, scientists in the laboratory, and teachers in the classroom. Above the technical level is the *managerial* system, whose primary functions are to mediate between the organization and the task environment, including those who consume the organization's products and supply its raw materials, and to administer the organization's internal affairs. At the top of the organization is the *institutional* system, whose function is to relate the organization to the larger society: "the source of the 'meaning,' legitimation, or higher-level support which makes the implementation of the organization's goals possible" (Parsons, 1960: 63–64). Parsons makes the interesting point that there exists a "qualitative break" in the line-authority relation at the two points where the three systems are linked (p. 65). (This distinction among levels anticipates some of the concerns of open system theorists, described in Chapters 4 and 5. The significance of the break between levels is discussed in Chapter 10.)

Parsons's theoretical model has been employed by some, but not many, researchers to guide their empirical studies of organizations. Georgopoulos (1972) adapted it in his analysis of hospitals, and Lyden (1975) makes use of it in his study of public organizations. Of course, Parsons's generalized social system paradigm has had considerable impact on the work of sociologists (see Alexander, 1982), and many of his specific concepts and ideas have influenced work in the area of organizations.

We restrict ourselves to a few general comments in assessing Parsons's contributions. On the positive side, his work attempts to develop and perfect a limited set of abstract concepts to be used in examining the structure and functioning of diverse social groupings. Using the same generic concepts helps us to see similarities in social structure and process across systems that appear to be quite different. Also, more than those of other natural system theorists, Parsons's framework is quite comprehensive, encompassing the formal and rational aspects of organizations as well as the informal. Further,

Parsons is more explicit than others in identifying the system needs that must be served for survival. Finally, in important respects, Parsons, like Selznick, proposes an instutional analysis of organizations. His concern for the relation between an organization's goals and the wider societal norms and values is a clear example of one mode of instutional analysis (see Chapter 6).

The problems with the Parsonian approach are numerous, but perhaps its most important limitation is that his formulation tends to be more of a conceptual framework than a substantive theory. We are provided with numerous concepts that help us to see interesting distinctions, but given relatively few testable propositions. The functional paradigm underlying the approach does provide some implicit hypotheses—such as, unless the system needs are met the organization will not survive—but such predictions are difficult to test.[10]

Early Exemplars of the Social Conflict Model

As previewed in Chapter 1, the natural system perspective exhibits two subtypes: the social consensus and the social conflict variants. Both have their adherents although the consensus version has always had more support among United States scholars while the social conflict version enjoys greater receptivity in Europe. Both are grounded in general sociological theory with applications made to organizations, the conflict version developing later than the consensus model.

Conflict theory traces its origins most directly to the writings of Marx (1954 trans.; 1963 trans.), although a number of conflict scholars claim Weber as an early progenitor because of his recognition that organizations were systems of power or domination. This school emphasizes the extent to which participants' interests diverge and values conflict. Change is seen to be as natural and common as is stability, and much of the stability of social order results from the dominance of one group or coalition of interests over others. A fully developed Marxist theory of organizations did not emerge until the 1970s following the appearance of open system models (we review this later work in Chapter 7), but conflict models appeared much earlier. We briefly comment on four influential examples of this work.

As already noted, Dalton (1950; 1959) was among the first to extend the concept of informal organization beyond the study of workers to include managers. His work is based on extended participant observation—"the aim is to get as close as possible to the world of managers" (1959: 1) and, as a consequence, we learn much more about the behavioral than the normative structure, the unofficial world of power struggles rather than the official realm of rules and organizational charts. He studied four organizations over a ten-year period—three factories and a department store. He concludes: "If our cases are typical, then conflict is typical." Conflict is not depicted as abnormal or pathological. "Conflict fluctuates around some balance of the constructive and disruptive" (p. 263). Rather than adopting "bureaucratic

---

[10]Alexander (1982) provides an overview of Parsons's overall contributions to social theory, while Landsberger (1961) offers an excellent description and critique of Parsons's model as it applies to organizations.

theory," which assumes that members of the organization are relatively inert and ready to follow the intent of rules, he recognizes the "active seeking nature of man, his ancient and obvious tendency to twist the world to his interests" (p. 165). Dalton depicts in elaborate detail the multiple bases of conflict arising within organizations: between departments, between higher and lower ranks of line officials, between staff and line officers, between cliques, and between personalities.

As a member of Columbia University's pioneering cohort of organizational scholars, Gouldner (1954) attempted to uncover some of the tensions in Weber's theory of bureaucracy. Picking up on Weber's (1947 trans.: 329) statement that "any given legal norm may be established by agreement or by imposition," Gouldner insisted that these two processes would lead to quite different consequences. In his study of the gypsum factory, Gouldner identified several classes of rules varying in terms of the degree of consensus or conflict and examined the implications of these differences for the managers and workers involved. He also raised other questions about Weber's schema:

> First, to whom did the rules have to be useful, if bureaucratic authority was to be effective? Secondly, in terms of whose goals were the rules a rational device? Whose end did they have to realize to operate effectively? . . . Had he [Weber] focused on the factory bureaucracy with its more evident tensions between supervisor and supervised, as this study shall, he would have been immediately aware that a given rule could be rational or expedient for achieving the ends of one stratus, say managment, but might be neither rational nor expedient for the workers. (Gouldner 1954: 20–21)

To assume that organizations are rational instruments for the pursuit of goals ignores the question of whose goals are being served. It assumes that there is consensus rather than conflict over goals. More generally, to adopt an approach that posits the existence of "organizational goals" masks the reality that the goals served by organizations are selected by individuals and may favor the interests of some parties over those of others.

One of the most important early comparative studies in organizations, conducted by Bendix (1956), examined the contrasting nature—across time and space—of managerial ideologies. Building on the insights of both Marx and Weber, Bendix contrasted social class—"the universal tendency of men who are similarly situated socially and economically to develop common ideas and to engage in collective action"—with bureacuracy—"the universal tendency of men who are employed in hierarchical organizations to obey directives and to identify their own interests and ideas with the organization" (p. xx). How is this possible? Bendix argues:

> Employers, entepreneurs, and managers typically act in such a way as to combine these tendencies. To safeguard and advance their interests they will join with others like them in the collective actions of a social class. But within each of their separate economic enterprises they will use their authority to have the workers identify their ideas and interests with the enterprise rather than with each other. Ideologies of managment are attempts by leaders of enterprises to justify the privilege of voluntary action and association for themselves, while

imposing upon all subordinates the duty of obedience and the obligation to serve their employers to the best of their ability. (1956: xxi)

Different ideologies are developed to fit varying circumstances. Bendix contrasts the ideologies developed by managerial elites during the time of industrialization in England and in imperial Russia, contrasting these with the twentieth-century ideologies utilized in the United States and in the Soviet Union. Among the ideologies examined in the United States are scientific management and human relations (Bendix, 1956: 274–340).

The most explicit early application of Marxist theory to organizations was provided by the German theorist Dahrendorf (1959), who, as noted in Chapter 1, attempts to revise Marx's arguments by insisting that the basis of power in modern society is no longer ownership of the means of production—increasingly in the hands of widely dispersed stockholders—but occupancy of managerial and executive positions within organizations. In explicit contrast to Taylor, Parsons, and others emphasizing "social integration," Dahrendorf elaborates a theory of organizations built on an assumption of the existence of socially structured conflicts of interest.

Scholars proposing a social conflict model of organizations were a distinct minority, particularly among students of organizations in the United States, and they remain so to this day. Nevertheless, the concerns they addressed are real: conflict and change are a part of organizational life no less than consensus and stability. Interest in these issues developed rapidly in the 1970s, and has been reactivated recently by feminist theorists. We consider these developments elsewhere, particularly in Chapter 11.

SUMMARY AND TENTATIVE CONCLUSIONS

Whereas the rational system model focuses on features of organizations that distinguish them from other social groupings, the natural system model emphasizes commonalities among organizations and other systems. The natural system theorists do not deny that organizations have distinctive features, but they argue that these are overshadowed by the more generic systems and processes. Thus, the specific output goals of organizations are often undermined or distorted by energies devoted to the pursuit of system goals, chief among which is the concern to survive. And the formal aspects of organizational structure that receive so much attention from the rational system analysts are treated as faded backdrops for the "real" informal structures. More generally, whereas the rational system model stresses the normative structure of organizations, the natural system model places more emphasis on the behavioral structure. And where the rational system perspective stresses the importance of structure over the characteristics of participants, the natural system perspective reverses these priorities—so much so that Bennis labels this orientation as one of "people without organizations" (1959: 266).

Most of the early theorists who shaped the natural system perspective embrace a functional model of analysis, although they vary considerably in how explicitly and how fully they pursue its development. The human relations analysts tend to be less overt and less complete in their use of this model than is Barnard or Selznick or Parsons. All schools within the consensus branch of the natural system framework presume the existence of certain needs that must be met if the system is to survive, and all direct attention to discovering the mechanisms by which these needs are satisfied. This is less so with the conflict models, although some versions emphasize the "functions" of social conflict for attaining and preserving social order.

Varying views of the environment appear to be associated with the natural system theorists. Most of the human relations analysts simply overlook it as a factor. Like the early rational system theorists, they concentrate on the internal organizational arrangements and their effects on participants, treating the organization as a closed system. This neglect is especially striking in the case of the Hawthorne studies, which were conducted during the 1930s, in the depths of the Great Depression. In the bank-wiring observation room study, for example, the workers' efforts to restrict production were viewed as irrational conformity to group norms. Given the larger economic situation, however, these activities may have been a highly rational response to the threat of being laid off (see Landsberger, 1958: 58; Blau and Scott, 1962: 92–93). Indeed, during the period of the research there were many layoffs at the Hawthorne plant; in fact, the bank-wiring room study had to be discontinued because so many workers were let go! (Roethlisberger and Dickson, 1939: 395).

Barnard takes somewhat more account of the environment than does the human relations group (see Scott, 1990a). He shows awareness that organizations must attract participants by providing them with inducements, indeed must compete with other organizations that are attempting to attract their services and loyalties. Moreover, he recognizes that a given individual participates in many cooperative groups simultaneously, so that his involvement in any single organization is both partial and intermittent. It is undoubtedly such insights that cause Barnard to put such emphasis on obtaining contributions and inspiring commitment. However, Barnard does not attempt to explicitly conceptualize the environment or to examine the extent to which organizations vary in their environment locations.

Selznick and his students, by contrast, do explicitly consider the environment in their analyses of organizations. However, their view is a highly selective one: the environment is perceived primarily as an enemy, as a source of pressures and problems. In most of the pioneering studies in this tradition, the organization is viewed as capitulating to a tyrannical and hostile environment as the price of its survival.

In the work of Parsons we begin to have a more balanced view of the environment. Great stress is placed on the importance of the organization-environment relation, the organization being viewed as a subsystem within a more comprehensive social unit, and the environment seen more as a stabilizing element sustaining and legitimating the organization in its special mission than as a source of resistance. In these ways, Parsons anticipates the view of the open system theorists.

Two quite different perspectives on organizations have now been described. How could two such different viewpoints have arisen? Several explanations have been proposed. Since each sheds additional light on the subject, they will be briefly reviewed.

Lawrence and Lorsch (1967: 163–84) propose that some of the differences in perspective were produced by variations in the experience and background of the analysts themselves. They point out that among the rational system or "classical" theorists, as they label them, Fayol, Mooney, and Urwick were all practical men with managerial experience. Taylor's training was as an industrial engineer. By contrast, among the natural system theorists, Mayo, Roethlisberger, Selznick, McGregor, Parsons, Bendix, Dalton, Gouldner, and Dahrendorf were all from academic backgrounds with experience largely in the university. (Exceptions to this division were, on the one side, Weber, who was a university professor—although, in terms of lifestyle and experience he is more accurately described as a recluse scholar—and Gulick, who was also an academic. On the other side, of course, was Barnard, a company executive.) Lawrence and Lorsch argue that divergent backgrounds shaped the reactions of these analysts to organizations. Coming from the relatively unstructured context of a university, the natural system analysts would be prone to react negatively to the formalism of an industrial plant, and might even be inclined to attribute their own needs for autonomy to workers in this situation.

A second explanation offered is that the two types of analysts concentrated on different types of organizations. The rational system analysts were more likely to investigate industrial firms and state bureaucracies, while the natural system analysts tended to focus on service and professional organizations—schools, hospitals, and the YMCA. Since the degree of formalization and of goal specificity clearly varies greatly across the spectrum of organizations, it is quite possible that the rational system analysts concentrated on the relatively highly structured end of the continuum and the natural system analysts on the less structured end.

A related explanation for the differences between the two perspectives is also proposed by Lawrence and Lorsch, who argue that the two types of analysts are looking at different types of organizations, and that the organizations differ because they are operating in different types of environments. They conclude:

> In simplified terms, the classical [rational system] theory tends to hold in more stable environments, while the human relations [natural system] theory is more appropriate to dynamic situations. (Lawrence and Lorsch, 1967: 183)

This important thesis is simply introduced at this point; it is elaborated in Chapter 5 and elsewhere throughout the remainder of this volume.

Although differences in the analysts' backgrounds or in the particular organization on which they chose to focus may account for some of the variance in these two perspectives, it is our view that these points of view represent more fundamental divisions than are suggested by these explanations. Underlying the perspectives are quite basic differences in moral and philosophical views and assumptions.

The natural and the rational system theorists tend to hold differing conceptions of the actual and the proper relation of individual participants to organizations. Rational system theorists argue that only selected behaviors of participants are relevant as far as the organization is concerned and that only these "task-related" behaviors are at issue. Natural system theorists tend to expand the definition of organizationally relevant behavior to include more and more aspects of the individual's activities and attitudes. They have done so on two grounds: that such behaviors do in fact have an impact on the task behavior of participants, and thus are *empirically* relevant to an understanding of organizational behavior, and that organizations as social contexts affect the participant's well-being, a relation that has *normative* significance to anyone concerned with bettering the human condition. Many of these theorists point to the dysfunctions arising from the partial inclusion of participants and argue, partly on moral grounds, that organizations should take more responsibility for the "whole person." These arguments are not without merit, but all of the morality is not on one side. It is important to recognize that formal organizations developed in part out of efforts to place limits on the demands superiors could make on their subordinates. The development of formal role definitions—definitions of the limits of a participant's obligations—was an important step in increasing the freedom of individuals. Whether the organization's purview should incorporate more or fewer facets of the lives of its participants is a basic philosophical difference separating the two perspectives.

Further, the two approaches are characterized by quite divergent views of the fundamental nature of social systems. These differences are reflected in the contrasting imagery or metaphors employed by the two schools. For the mechanistic model of structure of the rational system perspective, the natural system substitutes an organic model. Rational systems are designed, but natural systems evolve; the former develop by conscious design, the latter by natural growth; rational systems are characterized by calculation, natural, by spontaneity. Lest we regard these images of social structure as being of recent vintage, Wolin (1960: 352–434) reminds us that they have a long history in political and social thought. The view of organizations as economic, technological, efficient instruments is associated with the work of such social theorists as Hobbes, Lenin, and Saint-Simon—the precursors of Taylor, Weber, Fayol, and Simon. The view of organizations as communitarian, natural, arational, organic systems may be traced back to the social theories of Rousseau, Proudhon, Marx, Burke, and Durkheim, the intellectual ancestors of Mayo, Barnard, Selznick, Parsons, Gouldner, and Bendix. With such lengthy and distinguished pedigrees, it is unlikely that either of these two lines of thought will soon end, or that their differences will be quickly resolved.

CHAPTER 4

Organizations as Open Systems

That a system is open means, not simply that it engages in interchanges with the environment, but that this interchange is an essential factor underlying the system's viability.

Walter Buckley (1967)

The open system perspective emerged as a part of the intellectual ferment following World War II, although its roots are much older. This general theoretical movement created new areas of study, such as cybernetics and information theory; stimulated new applications, such as systems engineering and operations research; transformed existing disciplines, including the study of organizations; and proposed closer linkages among scientific disciplines. The latter interest has been fostered especially by general system theory. Its founder, biologist Ludwig von Bertalanffy, was concerned about the growing compartmentalization of science:

> The physicist, the biologist, the psychologist and the social scientist are, so to speak, encapsulated in a private universe, and it is difficult to get word from one cocoon to another. (Bertalanffy, 1956: 1)

Bertalanffy and his associates argued that certain general ideas could have relevance across a broad spectrum of disciplines. In particular, they endeavored to show that many of the most important entities studied by scientists— nuclear particles, atoms, molecules, cells, organs, organisms, ecological communities, groups, organizations, societies, solar systems—are all subsumable under the general rubric of system.[1]

[1]In his monumental book, *Living Systems*, Miller (1978) identifies seven basic levels: cell, organ, organism, group, organization, society, and supranational system.

All systems are characterized by an assemblage or combination of parts whose relations make them interdependent. While these features underlie the similarities exhibited by all systems, they also suggest the bases for the differences among them. The parts of which all systems are composed vary from being quite simple in structure to very complex, from being highly stable in their state to highly variable, and from being relatively impervious to system forces to being highly reactive to the workings of the system to which they belong. As we move from mechanical through organic to social systems, the parts of which systems are composed become more complex and variable. Similarly, the nature of the relations among the parts varies from one type of system to another. In this connection, Norbert Wiener, the founder of cybernetics, notes "Organization we must consider as something in which there is an interdependence between the several organized parts but in which this interdependence has degrees" (1956: 322). In mechanistic systems, the interdependence among the parts is such that their behavior is highly constrained and limited. The structure is relatively rigid and the system of relations determinant. In organic systems, the connections among the interdependent parts are somewhat less constrained, allowing for more flexibility of response. In social systems, such as groups and organizations, the connections among the interacting parts become relatively loose: less constraint is placed on the behavior of one element by the condition of the others. Social organizations, in contrast with physical or mechanical structures, are loosely coupled systems (see Ashby, 1968; Buckley, 1967: 82–83).

Also, as we progress from simple to complex systems, the nature and relative importance of the various flows among the system elements and between the system and its environment change. The major types of system flows are those of materials, energy, and information. And, as Buckley notes:

> Whereas the relations among components of mechanical systems are a function primarily of spatial and temporal considerations and the transmission of energy from one component to another, the interrelations characterizing higher levels come to depend more and more on the transmission of information. (1967: 47)

The notion of types or levels of systems that vary both in the complexity of their parts and in the nature of the relations among the parts has been usefully elaborated by Boulding, who has proposed a classification of systems by their level of complexity. Briefly, Boulding identifies the following system types:

1. *Frameworks:* systems comprising static structures, such as the arrangements of atoms in a crystal or the anatomy of an animal.
2. *Clockworks:* simple dynamic systems with predetermined motions, such as the clock and the solar system.
3. *Cybernetic systems:* systems capable of self-regulation in terms of some externally prescribed target or criterion, such as a thermostat.
4. *Open systems:* systems capable of self-maintenance based on a throughput of resources from their environment, such as a living cell.
5. *Blueprinted-growth systems:* systems that reproduce not by duplication but by the production of seeds or eggs containing preprogrammed instruc-

tions for development, such as the acorn-oak system or the egg-chicken system.

6. *Internal-image systems:* systems capable of a detailed awareness of the environment in which information is received and organized into an image or knowledge structure of the environment as a whole, a level at which animals function.

7. *Symbol-processing systems:* systems that possess self-consciousness and are capable of using language. Humans function at this level.

8. *Social systems:* multicephalous systems comprising actors functioning at level 7 who share a common social order and culture. Social organizations operate at this level.

9. *Transcendental systems:* systems composed of the "absolutes and the inescapable unknowables." (Boulding, 1956: 200–207)

Boulding's typology is illuminating in several respects. It quickly persuades us of the great range and variety of systems present in the world. Levels 1 to 3 encompass the physical systems; levels 4 to 6, the biological systems; and levels 7 and 8, the human and social systems. From levels 1 to 8, systems become progressively more complex, more loosely coupled, more dependent on information flows, more capable of self-maintenance and renewal, more able to grow and change, and more open to the environment. Boulding adds level 9 so that his classification will not be closed but open to new possibilities not yet envisioned.

Although the nine levels can be distinctly identified and associated with specific existing systems, they are not meant to be mutually exclusive. Indeed, each higher-level system incorporates the features of those below it. For example, it is possible to analyze a social organization as a framework, a clockwork, a cybernetic system, and so on up to level 8, the level that captures the most complex, the higher-level, processes occurring in organizations. Boulding argues that because each level incorporates those below it, "much valuable information and insights can be obtained by applying low-level systems to high-level subject matter." At the same time, Boulding reminds us that "most of the theoretical schemes of the social sciences are still at level 2, just rising now to 3, although the subject matter clearly involves level 8" (1956: 208). This is an important criticism of current theoretical models of organizations, one we need to keep before us as we review recent attempts to develop open system models.

The most systematic and influential introduction of open system concepts and models into organization theory was provided by Katz and Kahn (1966).

SPECIAL EMPHASES AND INSIGHTS

Broadly speaking, the contributions of the general systems perspective to organization theory up to this time have been to raise the level of our theoretical models up to level 3, where organizations are viewed as cybernetic systems, and to level 4, where they are viewed as open systems. Although Boulding's typology suggests we still have a long way to go before our models capture the complexity of organizational behavior, the insights obtained by moving to levels 3 and 4 are of great value. Along with our consideration of organizations as cybernetic and as open systems, we also take note of two other concepts emphasized by this perspective: organizations as loosely coupled systems and organizations as hierarchical systems.

Organizations as Cybernetic Systems

Systems functioning at Boulding's level 3 are capable of self-regulation. This important feat is attained through the development of specialized parts or subsystems related by certain processes or flows. Consider the mechanical example of the thermostat related to a source of heat. As Figure 4–1 illustrates, the system contains differentiated parts: a component for converting inputs into outputs—in this case, a heater that converts fuel and oxygen into heat; and a component for comparing the actual and desired temperatures—the thermostat. The parts are interrelated: the heater produces changes in temperatures detected by the thermostat; the thermostat controls a switch on the heater, turning it on or off based on information provided by comparing the actual and desired temperatures.

The key mechanism that effects the control process, that renders the system capable of self-regulation, however, is the program. Beniger provides an illuminating discussion of programs, which he defines as "any pre-arranged information that guides subsequent behavior" (1986: 39). He continues:

> Programs control by determining decisions. . . . the process of control involves comparison of new information (inputs) to stored patterns and instructions (programming) to decide among a predetermined set of contingent behaviors (possible outputs). (p. 48)

The identification of programs that exercise control through information processing and decision making circumvents the problem of teleology: the attempt to explain present activities by reference to their future conse-

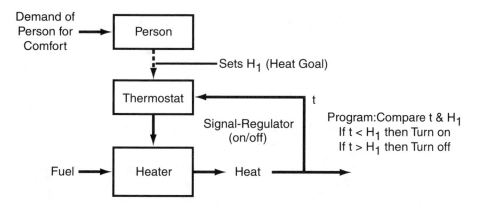

FIGURE 4–1 Illustration of a Cybernetic System: The Thermostat and the Heater. *Source:* Adapted from Swinth (1974), Figure 2–1, p. 18.

quences.[2] Programs "must exist prior to the phenomena they explain"; "their effects precede rather than follow their causes" (Beniger, 1986: 40).

Figure 4–1 also depicts a person who sets the standards that govern the cybernetic system functions. The person is capable of altering the system by reprogramming it, that is, by changing the desired temperature level. However, the person is not a component in the basic cybernetic system, which is, in its simplest manifestation, a closed system consisting, in the current example, of simply the thermostat, heater, and their interconnections. If the standard-setting and programming functions are included as a part of the system, then the model is transformed into a powerful, general model of control, depicted in Figure 4–2: a type of control that is widely employed in organizational settings.

To view an organization as a cybernetic system is to emphasize the importance of the operations, control, and policy centers, and the flows among them (Swinth, 1974). The policy center sets the goals for the system. This activity occurs in response to demands or preferences from the environment (flow 1 in Figure 4–2); some of the environmental demands take the form of orders (flow 2) from, for example, customers or from a higher-level organizational system. Note that the setting of goals is based on information received from the environment so that favorable exchanges between the environment and organization can occur. The policy center transmits goals or performance standards (flow 3) to the control center. This unit applies its program(s) to the operations level (flow 4), where raw materials

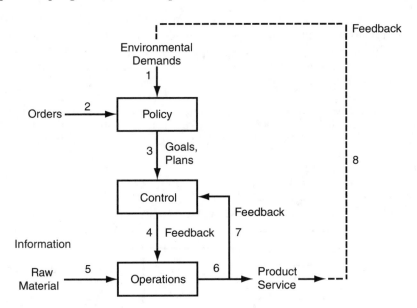

FIGURE 4–2 Abstract Model of Cybernetic System. *Source:* Adapted from Swinth (1974), Figure 2–4 p. 23.

[2]Functional arguments, described in Chapter 3, suffer from the difficulties of teleological explanation.

are transformed into products and services (flows 5 and 6). It is also the task of the control center to monitor the outputs, comparing their quality and/or quantity with the standards set by the policy center (flow 7). Discrepancies are the occasion for corrective actions as prescribed by the program. The figure also displays a second feedback loop (flow 8) to illustrate the possibility that reactions to the system's outputs by those outside the system, for example, customers, may lead the organization to revise its goals. Ashby (1952) points out that in such double feedback systems, the primary loop handles disturbances in "degree," applying existing decision rules, while the secondary loop handles disturbances in "kind," determining whether it is necessary to redefine the rules controlling the operating levels. Argyris (1982) labels such adaptive behaviors that result not simply in different activities but in different rules for choosing activities *double-loop learning.* Monitoring environmental feedback on the system's past performance—for example, a company reviewing records on sales by product lines—is an important mechanism of adaptation for any open system.[3]

Buckley stresses that cybernetic systems result in behavior that is "goal-*directed,* and not merely goal-*oriented,* since it is the deviations from the goal-state itself that direct the behavior of the system, rather than some predetermined internal mechanism that aims blindly" (1967: 53). Further, a feedback mechanism detects departures from the established goals no matter what their cause, an important control characteristic when systems become so complex that all the potential sources of disturbance cannot be identified in advance (see Beer, 1964: 29–30).

The cybernetic model places great emphasis on the operational level of the organization—the level at which the production processes of the system are carried out. The analysis of these technical flows—inputs, throughputs, and outputs—is regarded as vital to an understanding of the system; indeed, the control and policy centers are examined chiefly in terms of their impact on these technical flows.

This analytic framework can be applied to the organization as a whole or to any of its subsystems. It can be used, for example, to analyze the operation of a company's personnel subsystem, which must meet the demands of other subsystems for trained employees and must control the recruitment and training of new workers and monitor their turnover (see Carzo and Yanouzas (1967: 345–47). Or it can be used to examine the working of an entire organization, for example, a company producing, distributing, and exercising quality control over its products and attempting to monitor past sales and customer preferences so as to keep abreast of a changing marketplace.

Organizations as Loosely Coupled Systems

The cybernetic model gives the impression of a taut system—an arrangement of parts such that each is highly responsive to changes in the others. Such system elements are certainly found within organizations, but we should guard

---

[3]We must also note, however, that many organizations do not routinely collect this type of information (see Chapter 13).

against overgeneralization. One of the main contributions of the open system perspective is the recognition that many systems—especially social systems—contain elements that are only weakly connected to other elements and that are capable of fairly autonomous actions (see Ashby, 1968; Glassman, 1973).

This insight can be applied to many different components or elements of organizations and their participants. Thus, we have seen that from the standpoint of the natural system analysts, the normative structure of an organization is only loosely coupled with its behavioral structure. Rules do not always govern actions: a rule may change without affecting behavior, and vice versa. A similar observation has been made at the social psychological level. Analysts have noted that an individual's goals or intentions may be only weakly linked to his or her actions (see March and Olsen, 1976; and Chapter 11). The concept of loose coupling can also be applied to the relationship among structural units such as work groups or departments. Inspection of official organizational charts may lend the impression that these units are all highly interrelated and closely coordinated, whereas observation of their actual behavior may reveal that they are weakly and occasionally connected.

A particularly important application of the loose coupling image is that proposed by Cyert and March (1963) and adopted by Pfeffer and Salancik (1978). As noted in Chapter 1 in the open system definition of the concept of organization, these theorists propose to view the key participants in organizations not as a unitary hierarchy or as an organic entity, but as a loosely linked coalition of shifting interest groups. According to Pfeffer and Salancik:

> The organization is a coalition of groups and interests, each attempting to obtain something from the collectivity by interacting with others, and each with its own preferences and objectives. (1978: 36)

Rather than being rigidly oriented to the pursuit of consistent, common objectives, these coalitions change:

> their purpose and domains to accommodate new interests, sloughing off parts of themselves to avoid some interests, and when necessary become involved in activities far afield from their stated purposes. (1978: 24)

Contrary to first impressions and to rational system assumptions, open system theorists insist that loose coupling in structural arrangements can be highly adaptive for the system as a whole (see Weick, 1976; Orton and Weick, 1990; see also Chapter 10). It appears that loose coupling need not signify either low moral or low managerial standards.

On the other hand, the loose coupling of organizational elements no doubt contributes to what has been termed the "productivity paradox," the situation in which a great many organizations have made enormous investments in information processing technologies without appreciable effects on the overall rate of productivity growth in this country (see Harris, 1994). Enhancements in the productivity of individual workers do not quickly or easily translate into gains in productivity assessed at the departmental or firm level, let alone that of the industry.

The Characteristics of Open Systems

Organizations may be analyzed as cybernetic systems, but they also function at higher levels of complexity (recall Boulding's typology). They operate as open systems. *Open systems* are capable of self-maintenance on the basis of a throughput of resources from the environment. As Buckley (1967: 50) observes, this throughput is essential to the system's viability. Note that the heating unit that was one of the components in our example of a cybernetic system is not an open system as we have defined it. Although the heater receives inputs such as fuel from its environment, it is not capable of using the fuel to replace or repair its own elements: it cannot transform its inputs in such a way as to enhance its own survival or self-maintenance.

Some analysts have mistakenly characterized an open system as having the capacity for self-maintenance despite the presence of throughput from the environment; their assumption is that because organizations are open, they must defend themselves against the environment. This view is misleading, since interaction with the environment is essential for open system functioning. As Pondy and Mitroff (1979: 7) argue, rather than suggesting that organizational systems be protected "against environmental complexity," one should realize that "it is precisely the throughput of nonuniformity that preserves the differential structure of an open system."

This is not to say that open systems do not have boundaries. They do, of course, and must expend energy in boundary maintenance. But it is of equal importance that energies be devoted to activities that span boundaries. Because of the openness of organizations, determining their boundaries is always difficult and sometimes appears to be a quite arbitrary decision. Does a university include within its boundary its students? Its alumni? Faculty during the summer? The spouses of students in university housing? Pfeffer and Salancik (1978: 30) propose to resolve this type of problem by reminding us that individual persons are not enclosed within the boundaries of organizations, only certain of their activities and behaviors. Although this interpretation helps, we all know that many actions have relevance for more than one system simultaneously. For example, a sale from the standpoint of one system is a purchase when viewed from another, and what is an act of conformity for one system can be an act of deviance for another. Moreover, as will be emphasized, all systems are made up of subsystems and are themselves subsumed in larger systems—an arrangement that creates linkages across systems and confounds the attempt to erect clear boundaries around them. Finally, our determination of whether a system is open is itself a matter of how the boundaries of the system are defined. As Hall and Fagen note:

> whether a given system is open or closed depends on how much of the universe is included in the system and how much in the environment. By adjoining to the system the part of the environment with which an exchange takes place, the system becomes closed. (1956: 23)

General systems theorists elaborate the distinction between closed and open systems by employing the concept of *entropy*: energy that cannot be turned into work. According to the second law of thermodynamics, all systems spontaneously move toward a state of increasing entropy—a random arrangement of their elements, a dissolution of their differentiated structures, a state of maximum disorder. Open systems, because they are capable of importing energy from their environment, can experience negative entropy, or negentropy. By acquiring inputs of greater complexity than their outputs, open systems restore their own energy and repair breakdowns in their own organization. Bertalanffy concludes, "Hence, such systems can maintain themselves at a high level, and even evolve toward an increase of order and complexity"[4] (1962: 7).

To emphasize these twin properties of open systems, Buckley (1967: 58–62) distinguishes between two basic sets of system processes: morphostasis and morphogenesis. The term *morphostasis* refers to those processes that tend to preserve or maintain a system's given form, structure, or state. Morphostatic processes in biological systems would include circulation and respiration; in social systems, socialization and control activities. *Morphogenesis* refers to those processes that elaborate or change the system—for example, growth, learning, and differentiation. In adapting to the external environment, open systems typically become more differentiated in form, more elaborate in structure. Thus, in biological systems, organs whose sensitivities to external stimuli are coarse and broad are succeeded by more specialized receptors capable of responding to a wider range and finer gradations of stimuli. Biological organisms move toward greater complexity through the process of evolution: individual organisms are little affected, but over time, as mutations occur and are selected for their survival value, species are gradually transformed. Social organizations, more variable and loosely coupled than biological systems, can and do fundamentally change their structural characteristics over time. The General Motors of today bears little if any structural resemblance to the company of the same name of fifty years ago. Indeed, social organizations exhibit such an amazing capacity to change their basic structural features that researchers who study organizations over time have difficulty deter-

---

[4]Information theorists posit a close relation between the concepts of organization and entropy: they are viewed, in effect, as opposite states. If entropy is a state of randomness, or zero organization, it is also the state that provides maximum variety, maximum information, to someone observing a set of elements. As organization develops, constraints and limitations grow, restricting the number of states that may be present among the elements. Miller elaborates this point:

> A well-organized system is predictable—you know what it is going to do before it happens. When a well-organized system does something, you learn little that you didn't already know—you acquire little information. A perfectly organized system is completely predictable and its behavior provides no information at all. The more disorganized and unpredictable a system is, the more information you get by watching it. (1953: 3)

Based on such reasoning, information theorists Shannon and Weaver (1963) have proposed a measure of information, H, which assesses the amount of entropy present in a set of elements—their variation, their relative frequency of occurrence, and their interdependence. The higher the H level, the more information and the less organization is present (see also Buckley, 1967: 82–89).

mining when the units they are studying are the "same" organizations with reorganized structures and when they represent the emergence of new organizations.

To repeat, the source of system maintenance, diversity, and variety is the environment. From an open system point of view, there is a close connection between the condition of the environment and the characteristics of the systems within it: a complex system cannot maintain its complexity in a simple environment. Open systems are subject to what is termed the *law of limited variety*: "A system will exhibit no more variety than the variety to which it has been exposed in its environment" (Pondy and Mitroff, 1979: 7). Although the processes by which such "laws" operate are not clearly understood, Part Three of this volume is devoted to explicating and illustrating the interdependence of organizations and environments.

Organizations as Hierarchical Systems

General systems theorists also stress that hierarchy is a fundamental feature of complex systems—not so much hierarchy in the sense of status or power differences, but hierarchy in the guise of clustering and levels. Systems are composed of multiple subsystems, and systems are themselves contained within suprasystems. This is such a common feature of virtually all complex systems that it is easily overlooked. Books like this one are made up of letters, words, sentences, paragraphs, sections, and chapters. The United States political system is constituted of precincts, special districts, counties, states, and regions, all contained within the nation-state. And organizations are made up of roles contained within work groups, within departments, within divisions; many organizations are themselves subsystems of larger systems: corporate structures, or associations, or some branch of the government. (See Figure 10–1 for a diagram illustrating the major clusters to be found in a modern corporate organization.)

Combining the notion of hierarchy with that of loose coupling, we note a common feature of complex systems: the connections and interdependencies within a system component are likely to be tighter and greater than those between system components. In a well-written book, for example, the ideas expressed in a single paragraph should be more closely interrelated than those expressed in different paragraphs. Similarly, interactions within a given academic department within a university are likely to be more frequent and more intense than those occurring between departments. Indeed, as will be discussed in Chapter 9, this generalization provides the basis for an important principle of organizational design.

When subsystems take the form of "stable subassemblies"—units capable of retaining their form without constant attention from superior units—then hierarchical forms have an important survival advantage over other systems (Simon, 1962). Many seemingly complex organizational systems are made up of, and depend for their stability on, units that are highly similar and capable of relatively autonomous functioning—for example, similarly organized work teams or departments; franchise units; and chain stores. From this perspective, the apparent complexity of many systems becomes simpler: everything is *not* connected to everything else; there are loose connections and missing connections; and many components of systems are identical or nearly so (see Aldrich, 1979: 75–80).

To this point, we have emphasized that all systems are composed of subsystems. Of equal significance is the observation that all systems are also subsumed by other, more encompassing systems. This suggests that to understand the operation of a system, it may be as important to look outside the system and its context as to look inside the system at its component units. Schwab (1960) has termed this perspective "rationalism," the opposite of reductionism. Rationalism occurs when explanation comes by looking outside an entity to the environment or a higher system in which it is embedded (see also McKelvey, 1982: 5). In these many ways, the open system perspective points to the significance of the wider environment.

SELECTED SCHOOLS

As with the previous perspectives, we turn now to several schools that exemplify the open system approach. We briefly describe the systems design approach; contingency theory, which can be regarded as a school growing out of the systems design approach; and Weick's social psychological model of organizing. Although open system approaches to organizations were the last of the three perspectives to emerge, they have spread very rapidly and have had an enormous effect on organization theory. We discuss in this section only a few early developments; in Chapter 5 and later chapters we consider other approaches embodying open system assumptions and insights.

Systems Design

A large and growing number of organization theorists look to general systems theory as a source of ideas to improve the design of organizations—determining proper work flows, control systems, and planning mechanisms, and their interrelations—for carrying out their designated functions (see Carzo and Yanouzas, 1967; Khandwalla, 1977; Swinth, 1974; Mintzberg, 1979). Unlike some of the schools devoted to the study of organizations, the orientation of this group is pragmatic and applied: they seek to change and improve organizations as viewed from a managerial perspective, not simply to describe and understand them.

Many of the analysts attempting to apply systems ideas to organizations are aware both of the great complexity of organizations as one type of system and of the danger of misapplying or overextending analogies based on the operation of other, less complex systems. Beer (1964) proposes a classification of systems ranging from those that are both simple and deterministic, such as the behavior of a block and tackle system, to those that are complex and probabilistic, such as the operation of an assembly line in a factory, to those that are "exceedingly complex" and probabilistic, such as an entire organization (for example, a company). Complex probabilistic systems, whose behavior can be generally described and predicted with statistical procedures, are the province of operations research; exceedingly complex probabilistic systems have given rise to the fields of cybernetics and systems design

(Beer, 1964: 18). Because of their great complexity, the latter systems currently defy conventional mathematical modeling approaches. Instead, the most widely employed technique of analysis is to simulate the operation of the system. "Here, all the variables and relationships of interest are linked as understood into a model and then the manager-analyst-researcher manipulates certain ones and observes how others change as the simulation of the system plays itself out" (Swinth, 1974: 11). Note that this approach emphasizes the importance of treating the system as a system.

A recent branch of systems theory, termed "complexity" or "chaos" theory, pursued with most vigor by scientists at the Santa Fe Institute in New Mexico, examines the behavior of nonlinear dynamic systems. This theory was developed to account for the behavior of the flow of fluids or the behavior of metal balls suspended over two or more magnets in which "a single set of deterministic relationships can produce patterned yet unpredictable outcomes" (Levy, 1994: 168). Scholars have begun to explore the applicability of such models to the study of probabilistic, nonlinear systems such as the economy or the behavior of a firm. Nonlinear dynamics systems can reach three types of equilibrium: systems governed by negative feedback loops such that after a time, the system returns to its initial state; systems driven by positive feedback loops that amplify the initial disturbances so that small changes over time lead to explosive outcomes; and complex systems in which the interaction of positive and negative feedback loops gives rise to unpredictable but patterned outcomes (see Thietart and Forgues, 1995). Organizations, as systems that combine elements that suppress variation (for example, control systems) and elements that create and amplify variation (for example, diversity of personnel, attempts to innovate) would appear to be likely candidates for the useful application of complexity models.

No complex system can be understood by an analysis that attempts to decompose the system into its individual parts in order to examine each part and relationship in turn. This approach, according to Ashby, one of the founders of the general systems movement:

> gives us only a vast number of separate parts or items of information, the results of whose interactions no one can predict. If we take such a system to pieces, we find that we cannot reassemble it! (1956: 36)

Simulation techniques are popular with systems analysts because they are consistent with this image of a unit whose behavior can be understood only as the resultant of complex and probabilistic interactions among its parts. They also support the systems view that to understand organizations one must focus on the operational level of the organization. Thus, a systems design analyst would be more interested in obtaining diagrams depicting the flows of information, energy, and materials throughout the organization than in inspecting the formal table of organization. In examining a football team, for example, such an analyst would rather inspect the play books—the programs—governing the activities of the various players during the course of a game than the formal authority arrangements among the players, coaches, managers, and owners of the club.

It is consistent with the holistic emphasis of the systems analyst that the approach can accommodate parts of systems, the detailed structure of which is unknown or regarded as irrelevant. These basic units are the so-called "black boxes," elements of the system under study (Haberstroh, 1965: 1174). For the purposes of systems analysis, all the information that is required is a description of the inputs to and the outputs from each of the basic elements (or the relation between the inputs and the outputs). It is not necessary to know the internal working of these system components to understand or simulate the workings of the larger system.

An important characteristic of exceedingly complex, probabilistic systems is that the whole is more than the sum of its parts in the pragmatic sense that given the properties of the parts and the laws of their interaction, it is not a trivial matter to infer the behavior of the larger system. As a consequence, it is virtually impossible to predict and protect against all the ways in which such systems can fail—for example, move rapidly toward an explosive state. When the systems are characterized by high levels of interactive complexity and tight coupling—for example, nuclear power plants—then, Perrow argues, accidents should be regarded as normal. The odd term "normal accident" is meant to signal that, given the system characteristics, "multiple and unexpected interactions of failures are inevitable" (1984: 5). From an in-depth analysis of the near disaster at the Three Mile Island nuclear plant in Pennsylvania, Perrow notes the more obvious and ever-present problems of design and equipment failures and operator error but emphasizes the role played by "negative synergy."

> "Synergy" is a buzz word in business management circles, indicating that the whole is more than the sum of its parts, or in their congenial familiarity, two plus two equals five. But minus two plus minus two can equal minus five thousand in tightly-coupled, complex, high risk military and industrial systems . . . where complex, unanticipated, unperceived and incomprehensible interactions of off-standard components (equipment, design, and operator actions) threaten disaster. (Perrow, 1982: 18)

Gall (1978: 97) indentifies concisely the dilemma posed by these systems: "When a fail-safe system fails, it fails by failing to fail safe."

A lively debate has developed between analysts adopting the normal accidents view and others who insist that it is possible to develop "high reliability" organizations. Both camps agree the hallmark of these systems is the combination of interactive complexity and tight coupling, but those insisting that high reliability can be achieved point to the construction of redundant systems, reliance on extensive training and simulation of crisis situations, and the creation of a "culture of safety" (see LaPorte, 1982; Roberts, 1990; Weick, 1987). Those insisting that accidents cannot be completely avoided point to our inability to anticipate all the ways in which complex systems can fail and to the ways in which excessive concern for perfection can cause lower-level personnel to cover up inevitable lapses and shortcomings, so that safety is undermined by procedures designed to ensure its attainment (see Sagan, 1993; Vaughn, 1996). We revisit these issues in Chapter 13.

Among the various flows connecting system elements, the flow of information is the most critical. The gathering, transmission, storage, and retrieval of information are among the most fateful activities of organizations, and design theorists devote much attention to them (see Sage, 1981). We described in Chapter 2 Simon's views on the cognitive limits of decision makers. From the perspective of systems design, Simon is pointing out the limitations of individuals as information processors.[5] Viewing individuals in this manner, Haberstroh asserts that they exhibit "low channel capacity, lack of reliability, and poor computational ability." On the other hand, individuals possess some desirable features: "The strong points of a human element are its large memory capacity, its large repertory of responses, its flexibility in relating these responses to information inputs, and its ability to react creatively when the unexpected is encountered" (Haberstroh, 1965: 1176). The challenge facing the systems designers is how to create structures that will overcome the limitations and exploit the strengths of each system component, including the individual participants.

Of course, not all environments place the same demands on organizations and their participants for information processing. Recognition of this important point has given rise to a special perspective known as contingency theory, which we briefly summarize next.[6]

Contingency Theory

Jay Galbraith (1973: 2) states succinctly two assumptions underlying contingency theory:

- There is no one best way to organize.
- Any way of organizing is not equally effective.

The first assumption challenges the conventional wisdom of those administrative theorists who have sought to develop general principles applicable to organizations in all times and places. Such a quest not only overlooks the vast diversity of existing organizational forms but also fails to recognize the great variety of tasks undertaken by organizations. The second assumption challenges the view, held by early economists developing the theory of the firm, that organizational structure is irrelevant to organizational performance. Only relatively recently have economists begun to embrace Williamson's conclusion that: "Organization form matters" (1985: 274).

A third assumption can be formulated to represent the position of the contingency theorist:

---

[5]Simon has made important contributions to both the rational system and the open system perspective. As we discuss in Chapter 5, we do not consider these perspectives to be inconsistent.

[6]Recent economic theorists, especially Arrow (1974) and Williamson (1975; 1985) also place great emphasis on the cognitive inadequacies of individuals confronted by complex situations. They view these conditions, however, not simply as posing special problems for organizational designers but as a general explanation for the existence of organizations. These arguments are considered in Chapter 7.

- The best way to organize depends on the nature of the environment to which the organization relates.

As a branch of systems design, contingency theory emphasizes that design decisions depend—are contingent—on environmental conditions.

Contingency theory is guided by the general orienting hypothesis that organizations whose internal features best match the demands of their environments will achieve the best adaptation. To the extent that the markets within which the organization is operating are competitive, adaptation should entail effective performance. The challenge facing those who embrace this orientation is to be clear about what is meant by "the organization's internal features," "the demands of their environments," "best adaptation," and, most difficult of all, "best match." Details of attempted answers to these questions are best postponed to Part Three, but two general approaches can be briefly described to illustrate the directions pursued within this theoretical tradition.

Lawrence and Lorsch (1967), who coined the label contingency theory, argue that different environments place differing requirements on organizations: specifically, environments characterized by uncertainty and rapid rates of change in market conditions or technologies present different demands—both constraints and opportunities—on organizations than do placid and stable environments (see also, Burns and Stalker, 1961). They conducted empirical studies of organizations in the plastics, food processing, and standardized container industries to assess the relation between these environments—ranging from high to low uncertainty—and the internal features of each type of organization. They also point out that different subunits within a given type of organization may confront different external demands. Thus, within plastics manufacturing companies, the research and development units face a more uncertain and more rapidly changing environment than do the production departments. To cope with these various environments, organizations create specialized subunits with differing structural features. For example, some subunits may exhibit higher levels of formalization than others; some may be more centralized in decision making; some may be oriented to longer planning horizons. The more varied the types of environments confronted by an organization, the more differentiated its structure needs to be. Moreover, the more differentiated the organizational structure, the more difficult it will be to coordinate the activities of the various subunits and the more bases for conflict will exist among participants. Hence, more resources and effort must be devoted to coordinating the various activities and to resolving conflicts among members if the organization is to perform effectively.

In sum, Lawrence and Lorsch propose that the match or coalignment of an organization with its environment occurs on at least two levels: (1) the structural features of each organizational subunit should be suited to the specific environment to which it relates; and (2) the differentiation and mode of integration characterizing the larger organization should be suited to the overall environment within which the organization must operate (see Chapter 10).

Galbraith's (1973; 1977) version of contingency theory is similar to the systems design school in its stress on information processing. As in Lawrence and Lorsch's view, the environment is characterized in terms of the amount of complexity and uncertainty it poses for the organization. Galbraith connects the extent of environmental challenge with organizational information systems by asserting that environmental uncertainty enters the organization by affecting the work or tasks it performs; and "the greater the task uncertainty, the greater the amount of information that must be processed among decision makers during task execution in order to achieve a given level of performance" (1977: 36). Various structural arrangements, including rules, hierarchy, and decentralization, are viewed as mechanisms determining the information-processing capacity of the system. The design challenge is to select a structural arrangement appropriate for the information-processing requirements of the tasks to be performed. We consider Galbraith's specific arguments in more detail in Chapter 9.

Over time, contingency theory has become greatly elaborated, partly as analysts discover more and more factors on which the design of organizations is, or should be, contingent. In a recent review article, Lawrence (1993) provides a partial list of factors that one or another theorist has considered important: size or scale, technology, geography, uncertainty, individual predispositions of participants, resource dependence, national or cultural differences, scope, and organizational life cycle. Such an elaboration of the conditions on which structural design is dependent indicates both the broadening interests of scholars as well as the looseness of many versions or applications of contingency theory. In spite or, perhaps, because of this expansion of concerns, contingency theory remains "the dominant approach to organization design" (Lawrence 1993: 9) as well as the most widely utilized contemporary theoretical approach to the study of organizations (see Donaldson, 1985).

Weick's Model of Organizing

While the design and contingency theorists developed their version of the open system approach at the structural level of analysis, Karl Weick has attempted to pursue some of the implications of this approach at the social psychological level (1969; rev. 1979). We cannot do justice to his subtle and imaginative ideas in this overview but will note some of his lines of argument and attempt to capture the flavor of his work.

Weick cites with approval Bateson's (1972: 334) motto "stamp out nouns." He argues:

> The word, organization, is a noun and it is also a myth. If one looks for an organization one will not find it. What will be found is that there are events, linked together, that transpire within concrete walls and these sequences, their pathways, their timing, are the forms we erroneously make into substances when we talk about an organization. (Weick, 1974: 358)

Rather than talking about organizations, the focus of our attention should be "organizing." This is a very explicit example of the manner in which the systems perspective attempts to shift attention from structure to process.

Weick defines organizing as "the resolving of equivocality in an enacted environment by means of interlocked behaviors embedded in conditionally related process" (1969: 91). Let us attempt to unpack this dense definition. Weick argues that organizing is directed toward information processing generally and, in particular, toward removing its equivocality. He explains that:

> The basic raw materials on which organizations operate are informational inputs that are ambiguous, uncertain, equivocal. Whether the information is embedded in tangible raw materials, recalcitrant customers, assigned tasks, or union demands, there are many possibilities, or sets of outcomes that might occur. Organizing serves to narrow the range of possibilities, to reduce the number of "might occurs." The activities of organizing are directed toward the establishment of a workable level of certainty. (1969: 40)

In short, Weick asserts that "human beings organize primarily to help them reduce the information uncertainty they face in their lives" (Kreps, 1986: 111).

Organizational activities become structured as sets of "interlocked behaviors—repetitive, reciprocal, contingent behaviors that develop and are maintained between two or more actors" (Weick, 1969: 91). The activities are carried on in three stages: enactment, selection, and retention.[7] "Enactment" involves the active process by which individuals, in interaction, construct a picture of their world, their environment, their situation. Weick argues that:

> Since human beings actively create the world around them through perception, organization members do not merely react to an objectively accepted physical environment but enact their environment through information and the creation of meaning. (Kreps, 1986: 116)

The concept of enactment emphasizes the role of perceptual processes but also recognizes that organizational members not only selectively perceive but also directly influence the state of their environments through their own actions.[8]

"The activities of organizing are directed toward the establishment of a workable level of certainty" (Weick, 1969: 40). Participants selectively attend to their environments and then, in interaction, make collective sense of what is happening (Weick, 1995). "Making sense" entails not only developing a common interpretation or set of common meanings, but also developing one or more agreed-upon responses that are "selected" from among the many possibilities. Among responses that are selected, some are more useful and robust than others and it is these that are "retained" in the form of rules or routines. In this manner, communal sense making gives rise to a reperto-

---

[7]It is instructive to note that these three stages are Weick's translation of the three phases of evolution—variation, selection, and retention—as formulated by Campbell (1969; see also Chapter 5). Weick substitutes the term *enactment* for Campbell's label of "variation" for the first stage to emphasize the active role played by individuals—including organizational participants—in defining the environments they confront.

[8]Enactment and other processes by which organizations "create" their environments are discussed in Chapter 7.

ry of repeated routines and patterns of interaction—which constitute the process of organizing.

Although the objective of the entire process is to reduce equivocality, some uncertainty does and must remain if the organization is to be able to survive into a new and different future. In other words, "organizations continue to exist only if they maintain a balance between flexibility and stability" (Weick, 1979: 215). The information received and selected by the organization must be both credited (retained) and discredited or questioned if the organization is to safely face a future that may resemble, but must inevitably differ from, its past.

Weick's major concern is to spell out the implications of the open system perspective when applied to the level of individual participants and the relationships among them. The semiautonomy of the individual actors is stressed: the looseness and conditionality of the relationships linking them is emphasized. Attention and interpretation processes are highlighted. And whereas conventional wisdom asserts that goals precede activities, that intention precedes action, Weick (1969: 37) insists that behavior often occurs first and then is interpreted—given meaning. In these and related ways, Weick has attempted to "open up" our conception of organizational structure and behavior.

Many other theories have expanded the range of insights and implications based on the open system perspective, but we reserve discussion of them to later chapters.

SUMMARY AND TENTATIVE CONCLUSIONS

The open system perspective developed later than the rational and natural system views, but it has gained adherents rapidly and has profoundly altered our conception of organizations and their central features and processes. The open system view of organizational structure stresses the complexity and variability of the individual parts—both individual participants and subgroups—as well as the looseness of connections among them. Parts are viewed as capable of semiautonomous action; many parts are viewed as, at best, loosely coupled to other parts. Further, in human organizations, as Boulding emphasizes, the system is multicephalous: many heads are present to receive information, make decisions, direct action. Individuals and subgroups form and leave coalitions. Coordination and control become problematic. Also, system boundaries are seen as amorphous; the assignment of actors or actions to either the organization or the environment often seems arbitrary and varies depending on what aspect of system functioning is under consideration.

Open system imagery does not simply loosen the more conventional views of the structural features of organizations: it shifts attention from structure to process. Whether viewed at the more abstract level through concepts such as enacting, selecting, and retaining processes, or at the more concrete level with concepts such as input, throughput, and output production flows and feedback-control loops, the emphasis is on organizing as against organization. Maintaining these flows and preserving these processes are viewed as problematic. As Weick insists, "processes are repetitive only if this repetitiveness is continuously accomplished" (1969: 36). Both morphostatic and morphogenetic processes are of interest: many processes are reproductive, but others are not recurrent cycles but actions that change the existing structures.

A process view is taken not only of the internal operations of the organization but of the organization itself as a system persisting over time. The organization as an arrangement of roles and relationships is not the same today as it was yesterday or will be tomorrow: to survive is to adapt, and to adapt is to change. As Leavitt and his colleagues conclude:

> The complex organization is more like a modern weapons system than like old-fashioned fixed fortifications, more like a mobile than a static sculpture, more like a computer than an adding machine. In short, the organization is a dynamic system. (Leavitt, Dill, and Eyring, 1973: 4)

The interdependence of the organization and its environment receives primary attention in the open system perspective. Rather than overlooking the environment, as tends to be true of most early rational and natural system theories, or viewing it as alien and hostile, as is true of some early theories, the open system perspective stresses the reciprocal ties that bind and relate the organization with those elements that surround and penetrate it. The environment is perceived to be the ultimate source of materials, energy, and information, all of which are vital to the continuation of the system. Indeed, the environment is seen to be the source of order itself.

With the arrival of open system arguments in the 1960s, it quickly became clear that to the extent that previous perspectives were grounded on closed system views of organizations, they would need to be radically revised. To remain credible, all subsequent theories have had to take into account the openness of organizations to their environments. So did these developments signal the end of rational and natural system models? Have these earlier perspectives been consigned to the dustbins of history? Hardly. As we will describe in the next chapter, they continue to flourish as viable perspectives, by moving into the halls of open systems.

Combining
the Perspectives

Political revolutions aim to change political institutions in ways that those institutions themselves prohibit. Their success therefore necessitates the partial relinquishment of one set of institutions in favor of another. Like the choice between competing political institutions, that between competing paradigms proves to be a choice between incompatible modes of community life. Because it has that character, the choice is not and cannot be determined merely by the evaluative procedures characteristic of normal science, for these depend in part upon a particular paradigm, and that paradigm is at issue. When paradigms enter, as they must, into a debate about paradigm choice, their role is necessarily circular. Each group uses its own paradigm to argue in that paradigm's defense.

Thomas S. Kuhn (1962)

The three preceding chapters have described and illustrated three perspectives on organizations as they emerged and have developed from the early part of this century into the 1960s. We have attempted to present these perspectives succinctly but fairly, discussing examples of the work of influential theorists that have contributed to them, and to assess their strengths and limitations. We have sought to avoid treating these viewpoints as caricatures or as approaches having only historical interest. In our opinion, each is valuable: each focuses on a set of significant and enduring features of organizations.

In this chapter, we begin by reviewing three important efforts to combine and reconcile these three perspectives. Then we propose an alternative framework. The latter approach is used both to briefly review theories previously discussed and to introduce new conceptions developed during the past three decades. Since there has been a flurry of theoretical activity during the period from 1960 up to the present, the catalog of possible candidates is embarrassingly long: too many new ideas have been proposed to be usefully reviewed or comprehended in a single chapter. Rather than attempting at this point to be comprehensive, we select a subset of the most influential and representative recent theories so that we can illustrate the utility of the framework. Additional theories will be introduced and folded into the schema in subsequent chapters.

As noted in the introduction to Part Two, the three perspectives operate as paradigms, as Kuhn (1962) defines this concept. Functioning as conceptual frameworks and as sets of assumptions guiding empirical investigations, paradigms are not themselves subject to verification. A paradigm is not so much disproved as it is dislodged or supplanted by a different paradigm providing a new map of the territory—indeed, not only a new map but new directions for mapmaking. As Kuhn observes:

> In learning a paradigm the scientist acquires theory, methods, and standards together, usually in an inextricable mixture. Therefore, when paradigms change, there are usually significant shifts in the criteria determining the legitimacy both of problems and of proposed solutions. (1962: 108)

Thus in some respects the differences between competing paradigms cannot be completely resolved by scientific evidence or argumentation.

Nevertheless, noting the selectivity of the perspectives, a number of theorists have attempted to develop more encompassing formulations, combining selected portions of the earlier traditions. We will briefly review three of these synthetic frameworks: models proposed by Etzioni, by Lawrence and Lorsch, and by Thompson.

THREE ATTEMPTS AT INTEGRATION

Etzioni's Structuralist Model

Etzioni (1964) has proposed a "structuralist" approach as a synthesis of the classical (rational) schools and the human relations (natural) schools (see also, Gross and Etzioni, 1985: 65–88). In contrast with our view, Etzioni does not regard Weber as a prime contributor to the classical approach but rather, together with Marx, as a theorist who attempted to synthesize the insights of the rational and natural system arguments. Marx and Weber both believed that regardless of the best efforts of managers and workers, their economic and social interests are inevitably in conflict. Marx (1972 trans.) viewed factory workers as alienated from their work since they owned neither the means of production nor the product of their labor. Weber (1946 trans.: 221–24) generalized this assertion, noting that soldiers in modern armies did not own their weapons, nor did research scientists own their equipment and supplies. In this sense, all employees, unless they are also owners, can be viewed as alienated from their labor (see Chapter 12). Both Marx and Weber viewed control as central to the concept of organizations.

Etzioni shares this conception and argues that both the rational and the natural system theorists have important, and different, things to say about control systems within organizations. The rational system theorists contribute to the analysis of control by focusing attention on the differential distribution of power among organizational positions. The natural system theorists make their contribution by insisting that naked power only alienates, that power must be acceptable to the subordinates in the power relation if control attempts are to be effective, as Barnard (1938) insisted. Weber, according to Etzioni, combines both of these points of view in his examination of the distribution of power, on the one hand, and of the bases on which it is seen to be legitimate by participants in the system, on the other (Etzioni, 1964: 50–51; 1961; Weber, 1968 trans.: vol 1: 212–301).[1]

In addition to combining the rational and natural system perspectives in the analysis of the central issue of power, Etzioni proposes that the structuralist model gives equal attention to formal and informal structures, and in particular to the relations between them; to the scope of informal groups and the relations between such groups both inside and outside the organization; to both social and material rewards and their interrelation; and to the interaction of the organization and its environment (Etzioni 1964: 41–49). In approaching all of these matters, however, the structuralist point of view recognizes fully:

> the organizational dilemma: the inevitable strains—which can be reduced but not eliminated—between organizational needs and personal needs; between rationality and non-rationality; between discipline and autonomy; between formal and informal relations; between management and workers, or more generically, between ranks and divisions. (1964: 41)

In sum, the structuralist model suggests that the rational and the natural system perspectives are complementary. Each view represents a partial truth. If the perspectives seem at times to conflict, this is because the organizational elements to which they point sometimes conflict. The recognition of such conflicts is an important part of the "whole" truth about organizations, their structural features, and their functioning.

Lawrence and Lorsch's Contingency Model

We have already reported Lawrence and Lorsch's various proposals for reconciling the rational and natural system perspectives (Chapter 3) and described their contingency model of organizations (Chapter 4). We briefly review these ideas at this point to emphasize that they may be viewed as providing a general framework within which all three perspectives can be reconciled.

In essence, Lawrence and Lorsch (1967) argue that if an open system perspective is taken—so that any given organization is viewed not in isolation but in relation to its specific environment—then the rational and the

---

[1]The relations among power, authority, legitimacy, and control are more fully discussed in Chapter 11.

natural system perspectives may be seen to identify different organizational types that vary because they have adapted to different types of environments. The rational and natural system perspectives are at variance because each focuses on a different end of a single continuum representing the range of organizational forms. At one extreme, some organizations are highly formalized, are centralized, and pursue clearly specified goals; at the other extreme, some organizations are less formalized, rely greatly on the personal qualities and initiative of participants, and cannot be as clear and determinant as to their goals. The two extreme types depicted by the rational and the natural system models are not viewed as differing aspects of the same organizations—as, for example, Etzioni's structuralist model suggests—but rather as different kinds of organizations. And, as emphasized by the open system perspective, the nature of the form is determined by the type of environment to which the organization must relate. Specifically, the more homogeneous and stable the environment, the more appropriate will be the formalized and hierarchical form. And the more diverse and changing the task environment, the more appropriate will be the less formalized and more organic form.

Thus we arrive at the contingency argument: there is no one best organizational form but several, and their suitability is determined by the extent of the match between the form of the organization and the demands of the environment. The argument is framed at the ecological level of analysis; it rests on the assumption that different systems are more or less well adapted to differing environments. Environmental conditions determine which systems survive and thrive: those best adapted are most likely to prosper. By this argument, Lawrence and Lorsch attempt to account both for the different forms of organizations and for the different theoretical perspectives that have developed to characterize them. Note that their views can also explain why the rational system perspective preceded in time the natural system perspective if it is assumed, as most open system analysts would contend, that the environments of organizations were more stable in the past and have become progressively more volatile.

The open system perspective is viewed by Lawrence and Lorsch as the more comprehensive framework within which the rational and natural system perspectives may be housed, since each of the latter constitutes only a partial view depicting particular organizational adaptations to differing environmental conditions.

Thompson's Levels Model

Simultaneously with the emergence of Lawrence and Lorsch's contingency model, James D. Thompson (1967) developed a somewhat different basis for reconciling the three perspectives. In his influential work *Organizations in Action*, Thompson argues that analysts should be mentally flexible enough to admit the possibility that all three perspectives are essentially correct and applicable to all portions of an organization. However, they do not all apply with equal force to all organizational locations. Thompson borrows the distinctions among organizational levels proposed by Parsons (1960: 60–65). As we described in Chapter 3, Parsons differentiated three levels:

- the *technical* level: that part of the organization carrying on the production functions that transform inputs into outputs;
- the *managerial* level: that part of the organization responsible for designing and controlling the production system, for procuring inputs and disposing of outputs, and for securing and allocating personnel to units and functions;
- the *institutional* level: that part of the organization that relates the organization to its wider environment, determines its domain, establishes its boundaries, and secures its legitimacy.

Thompson proposes that each of the three perspectives is suitable to a different level of the organization: the rational system perspective to the technical level, the natural to the managerial, and the open to the institutional level.

Thompson's thesis in a nutshell is that organizations strive to be rational although they are natural and open systems. It is in the interest of administrators—those who design and manage organizations—that the work of the organization be carried out as effectively and efficiently as possible. Since technical rationality presumes a closed system, Thompson (1967: 10–13) argues that organizations will attempt to seal off their technical level, protecting it from external uncertainties to the extent possible.[2] Thus, it is at the level of the core technology—the assembly line in the automobile factory, the patient care wards and treatment rooms in the hospital—that we would expect the rational system perspective to apply with the most force. At the opposite extreme, the institutional level, if it is to perform its functions, must be open to the environment. It is at this level, where the environment must be enacted and adapted to, that the open system perspective is most relevant. In the middle is the managerial level, which must mediate between the relatively open institutional and the closed technical levels. To do so effectively requires the flexibility that is associated with the less formalized and more political activities depicted by the natural system theorists. It is also the managers—whose power and status are most intimately linked to the fate of the organization—who have the greatest stake in and seek to secure the survival of the organization as a system.

There is much to be said for, and learned from, each of these efforts to reconcile the three perspectives. All contain valuable insights. Etzioni is surely correct in insisting that all organizations embody conflicting tendencies and interests: between formal and informal structures, rational and nonrational aspects of behavior, controlling and controlled participants. Lawrence and Lorsch are correct that some types of organizations exhibit higher levels of formalization and goal specificity than do others and that these differences are related to the environments in which they operate. And Thompson is correct that some parts or levels of organization are more protected from, while others are more open to, environmental influences; similarly, some parts are more strongly governed by rational system

---

[2]Specific techniques, termed *buffering* mechanisms, used to seal off the technical core, are described in Chapter 8.

concerns while others are more subject to natural system influences. All of these combinations and applications of the three general perspectives have illuminated additional facets of organizations, and in this way, the utility of the perspectives has been reinforced for a new generation of students of organizations.

A LAYERED MODEL

There is yet another sense in which the three perspectives may be seen as persisting up to the present time, albeit in new combinations. Our introduction to the perspectives in earlier chapters suggested that they fell into a neat time line with the rational perspective preceding the natural system view, and the open system perspective developing most recently. We will suggest now a slightly more complex view—namely, that there have been not three but four phases, created by cross-classifying or layering the three perspectives (see Table 5–1).

At the risk of considerable oversimplification, we suggest that theoretical models of organizations underwent a major shift about 1960, at the time open system perspectives supplanted closed system models. Analyses focusing primarily on the internal characteristics of organizations gave way at approximately that date to approaches emphasizing the importance for the organization of events and processes external to it. After 1960, the environments of organizations, conceived in terms of economic, political, cultural, social, technological, and interorganizational elements, figure prominently in all attempts to explain organizational structure and behavior.

On both sides of this watershed representing the transition from closed to open system models, a second trend can be identified: a shift from rational to natural system models of analysis. It appears that this shift has occurred twice! It occurred for the closed system models in the late 1930s and early 1940s, as we have already described in Chapters 2 and 3—the rational system formulations of Weber and Taylor giving way to the natural system approaches of Mayo and Barnard—and it appears to have occurred again during the late 1970s as the neorational approaches of Lawrence and Lorsch and Williamson were challenged by the neonatural perspectives of Hannan, Pfeffer, Meyer and others in ways to be discussed in this and later chapters.

We argue, in short, that the early rational and natural system models shared in common the fact of being layered under closed system assumptions. The open system models that developed in the 1960s did not supplant either the rational or the natural system arguments, but rather the (often implicit) closed system assumptions underlying both. When the open system models appeared, they were quickly combined with, first, rational systems and, later, natural systems perspectives.

Table 5–1 presents representative theories for each of the four periods: closed-rational; closed-natural; open-rational; and open-natural. The theories tend to fall into an orderly sequence with closed-rational models dominating during the period 1900–1930; closed-natural models during the period 1930–1960; open-rational models during the period 1960–1975; and

TABLE 5–1 Dominant Theoretical Models and Representative Theorists: A Layered Model

	Closed System Models		Open System Models	
Levels of Analysis	*1900–1930 Rational Models*	*1930–1960 Natural Models*	*1960–1970 Rational Models*	*1970–present Natural Models*
Social Psychological	Scientific Management Taylor (1911) Decision Making Simon (1945)	Human Relations Whyte (1959)	Bounded Rationality March & Simon (1958)	Organizing Weick (1969)
Structural	Bureaucratic Theory Weber (1968 trans) Administrative Theory Fayol (1919)	Cooperative Systems Barnard (1938) Human Relations Mayo (1945) Conflict models Gouldner (1954)	Contingency Theory Lawrence & Lorsch (1967) Comparative Structure Woodward (1965) Pugh et al. (1969) Blau (1970)	Socio-technical Systems Miller & Rice (1967)
Ecological			Transaction Cost Williamson (1975)	Population Ecology Hannan & Freeman (1977) Resource Dependence Pfeffer & Salancik (1978) Institutional Theory Selznick (1949) Meyer & Rowan (1977) DiMaggio & Powell (1983)

open-natural models dominant from the period 1975 up to the present.[3] The theories are also categorized by level of analysis, although this classification is only a rough guideline to the level at which the dependent variables are defined.[4] While closed system models were conducted at the social psychological or the structural levels, with the advent of open system models, ecological analyses became an important new source of theorizing about the determinants of organizational behavior and structure. A great deal of the recent theoretical work in organizations has occurred at the ecological level. (Indeed, as will be discussed in Chapter 6, several differing layers of analysis have emerged within this level.)

Before commenting in more detail on the four primary categories of layered models, we note the relation of these four types to the organization of the present volume. To this point, our discussions of the rational and the natural system models have emphasized their closed system versions. Although we have stressed the differences between a closed and an open system perspective, we have deliberately refrained from serious attention to the new generations of open-rational and open-natural system models, types that have emerged since the development of the open system perspective. These most recent contributions receive primary attention in succeeding chapters. Hence, our discussion of the closed-rational and closed-natural types serves as a brief review of the work of major theorists prior to 1960, as described in Part Two of this volume. And our discussion of the rational and natural open variants will serve to preview the work of major theorists since 1960, to be discussed in greater detail in Part Three.

Closed-Rational System Models

The representative theories and theorists listed in Table 5–1 for the closed-rational system models should by this time look very familiar: Taylor, Weber, and Fayol are old friends. Simon represents a transitional case: his early work (Simon, 1976, first published in 1945) fits into the closed-rational model, but his later work (for example, March and Simon, 1958) is more closely related to open-rational models. As emphasized in Chapter 2, all of these theories portray organizations as tools designed to achieve preset ends, and all of them ignore or minimize the perturbations and opportunities posed by connections to a wider environment. Thompson stresses the closed system assumptions of these theorists. Speaking of Taylor's contributions, he says:

[3] Although it is possible to thus identify a dominant theoretical orientation for each period, this is not to say that all of the important work associated with that orientation was produced during that period or that important work associated with the alternative orientations was not taking place at the same time. Note, for example, that Selznick (1949), in developing his institutional theory, was considerably ahead of his time. The time periods identify the dominant tendencies.

[4] For example, Williamson's work is classified as being at the ecological level because his primary objective is to explain how the boundaries of the organization are shaped by variations in transaction costs. However, the theory is sufficiently abstract so that it is useful at other levels, for example, the structural, to determine which specific services or products will be produced within the firm or purchased from outside.

> Scientific management achieves conceptual closure of the organization by assuming that goals are known, tasks are repetitive, output of the production process somehow disappears, and resources in uniform qualities are available. (1967: 5)

And of the work of Fayol, Gulick, and Urwick:

> Administrative management achieves closure by assuming that ultimately a master plan is known, against which specialization, departmentalization, and control are determined. (1967: 5)

And of Weber's model of bureaucracy:

> Bureaucratic theory also employs the closed system of logic. Weber saw three holes through which empirical reality might penetrate the logic, but in outlining his "pure type" he quickly plugged these holes. Policymakers, somewhere above the bureaucracy, could alter the goals, but the implications of this are set aside. Human components—the expert officeholders—might be more complicated than the model describes, but bureaucratic theory handles this by divorcing the individual's private life from his life as an officeholder through the use of rules, salary, and career. Finally, bureaucratic theory takes note of outsiders—clientele—but nullifies their effects by depersonalizing and categorizing clients. (1967: 5–6)

Thus, in all of these models, the variety and uncertainty associated with an organization's openness to its environment is stifled, curtailed, or denied.[5]

Closed-Natural System Models

Our prime candidates for natural system theorists working predominantly with a closed system conception are the human relations theorists. As described in Chapter 3, this conception originated with the empirical research of Roethlisberger and Dickson (1939) and the theoretical work of Mayo (1945) but expanded throughout the 1940s and 1950s to encompass a great deal of the sociological research on organizations and to incorporate both consensus and conflict models. Although this work caused our view of organizational structure to become more complex and flexible, as diffuse and conflicting goals were recognized and participants were endowed with multiple interests and motives, most of the work within this tradition restricted attention to the inside of the organization. We learn a great deal about the emergence of informal structures—interpersonal systems of power, status, communication, and friendship—and their impact on formal systems, but whether the concern was with formal or informal systems or the relations between them, the focus was primarily on the organization's internal arrangements.

---

[5]Again, we must point out that more recent readings of Weber's work on bureaucracy emphasize that he has been inappropriately regarded as a closed system theorist. Even though incorrect, this interpretation of his work greatly influenced organization theory up through the 1960s, as is illustrated by Thompson's view of Weber's work.

Barnard's (1938) model of organizations as cooperative systems also concentrated attention on internal structures and processes, as did most of the conflict models developed during this period, such as that of Gouldner (1954). However, neither Selznick (1949) nor Parsons (1960) can be characterized as a closed system theorist. As noted in Chapter 3, Selznick's view of the environment was often a rather jaundiced one, whereas Parsons's is more balanced, but both of these versions of natural system models represent more open system conceptions and, hence, are important precursors to later open-natural models.

Open-Rational System Models

Beginning in the late 1950s and continuing to the present, a new generation of theories have again focused on the organization as a rational system, but with a difference: now the organization is also viewed as an open system. An important figure in this transformation was Simon, whose major early contributions have already been described. His more recent work with March illustrates the joining of rational and open system concerns at the social psychological level of analysis.

The contingency theorists, whose work we discussed to illustrate open system approaches, also combine rational with open system concerns. We briefly review this work before describing two other types of theories combining these perspectives. Indeed, all of the discussions will be brief since the intent here is merely to introduce important contemporary theories that will be considered at length in Parts Three and Four.

Bounded rationality revisited. Important changes are apparent in Simon's view of administrative behavior as a result of his collaboration with March (March and Simon, 1958, especially chaps. 6 and 7). While there is still a concern with the cognitive limits of individual decision makers and with how structures can help to support improved decisions, there is more recognition of the variable nature of the challenges posed by tasks and environments. The organization is viewed as more open to its environment. March and Simon identify "performance programs" that guide the decisions of individuals, but whereas some of these programs can be routinized, others must be problem-solving responses, requiring the decision maker to exercise more discretion in the face of greater uncertainty (p. 139). Moreover, it is recognized that some organizations face such volatile environments that they must institutionalize innovation, devising meta programs for changing existing performance programs, often rapidly (p. 186).

March and Simon suggest a number of additional ways in which decision making is simplified within organizations. Organizations encourage participants to *satisfice*—to settle for acceptable as opposed to optimal solutions, to attend to problems sequentially rather than simultaneously, and to utilize existing repertoires of performance programs whenever possible rather than developing novel responses for each situation. There is a stronger sense in this later work that organizations face environments of varying complexity, that they must adjust their internal decision-making apparatus to take these variations into account, and that some environments pose levels of complexity that organizations cannot manage unless they impose simplifying restrictions on the information processed.

Contingency theory reviewed. We have described in Chapter 4 the central ideas of contingency theory as introduced by Lawrence and Lorsch (1967). Their realization that organizations—indeed, units within organizations—confront varying environments that pose differing challenges for them is a clear recognition of the open system character of organizations. Their further assumption that organizations will, or should in the interest of effectiveness, adapt their structures to these environmental requirements incorporates the rational system argument.

The combination of open and rational system assumptions also figures strongly in Thompson's (1967) approach. Thompson was among the first organization theorists to recognize the importance of the environment for the structure and performance of organizations, and, as noted, he argues that different locations or levels within structures are differentially open to environmental influences. More so than most theorists, Thompson is quite explicit about the rationalist assumptions that undergird his approach. He prefaces virtually all of his empirical predictions with the phrase "Under norms of rationality, organizations seek to . . ."

Thus, the problem that Thompson and the contingency theorists set for themselves may be stated: Given that an organization is open to the uncertainties of its environment, how can it function as a rational system? As hinted at in our review of Thompson's levels model, his principal answer to this question is that it can do so by creating some closed system compartments in critical parts of its structure. How this is done, by what sealing mechanisms and buffering strategies, will be described in detail in Chapter 8. For now, we simply underscore the juxtaposition of rational and open system perspectives that underlie this form of analysis.

Comparative structural analysis. Parallel to but somewhat distinct from the efforts of systems design and contingency theorists is the work conducted during the same period by analysts attempting to account for variations in organization structures. Whereas the efforts of the former group tend to be more qualitative and prescriptive, the work of the latter is more quantitative and descriptive. Among the leading figures in comparative structural analysis are Udy (1959b), Woodward (1965), Pugh and associates (1969), and Blau (1970) and his colleagues. These were the first analysts to collect systematic data on large samples of organizations rather than on individual participants or organizational subunits. In this work, formal structure is viewed as the dependent variable, its characteristics to be measured and explained. A large variety of explanatory (independent) variables have been examined—with most attention concentrated on size, technology, and uncertainty—but most studies have focused on characteristics of the environment in which the organization is located. In short, organizations are viewed as open systems.

At the same time, organizations are presumed to design their structures rationally. An assumption underlying most of these studies is that organizations are striving to develop effective and efficient structures. Environmental demand and organizational response are mediated by designers or managers who are concerned with cutting costs, developing adequate arrangements to cope with environmental complexity, and creating coordinative mechanisms to manage the requirements of information processing. These are the assumptions of a rational system model, and they dominate much of the empirical and theoretical work on organizations during the 1960s. The findings of these theorists are reviewed in Chapter 10.

Transaction cost analysis. An important new perspective combining open and rational systems assumptions was introduced in the mid-1970s by Oliver Williamson (1975; 1981). Based on the work of earlier institutional economists (such as Commons, 1924; Coase, 1937), Williamson proposed that analysts focus on the costs of entering into transactions—exchanges of goods or services between persons or across boundaries of any sort.

> With a well-working interface, as with a well-working machine, these transfers occur smoothly. In mechanical systems we look for frictions: do the gears mesh, are the parts lubricated, is there needless slippage or other loss of energy? The economic counterpart of friction is transaction cost: do the parties to the exchange operate harmoniously, or are there frequent misunderstandings and conflicts that lead to delays, breakdowns, and other malfunctions? (Williamson, 1981: 552)

To focus on transactions rather than on commodities or services is to shift attention away from technical production concerns to governance structures. For individuals to be willing to enter into exchanges, they must feel certain that their interests are safeguarded. Simple economic transactions that take place "on the spot" as one good or service is exchanged for another of equal value pose no problems and can be safely conducted in the free marketplace. However, as exchanges become more complex and uncertain— because the environment is not stable or predictable and because others cannot always be trusted to abide by the terms of the agreement—various kinds of external controls and supports must be devised to aid the exchanges—that is, to reduce the transaction costs. Organizational structures are viewed as one important arrangement for establishing and safeguarding transactions.

Williamson and his colleagues argue not only that organizations develop in order to reduce transaction costs, but also that organizational forms may be expected to vary with the types of exchanges to be governed. We reserve for Chapter 7 a fuller description of this approach to explaining organizations and their structural variety. Here we merely identify yet another approach that assumes that organizations are both open— responding to the differential demands of their environments—and rational—doing so in such a manner as to economize on the costs of engaging in transactions.

Williamson's work represents one variant of the "new institutionalism" in organizations research, a version that embraces rational system assumptions. As we discuss in the next section, other institutional approaches are more compatible with the natural system framework.

Open-Natural System Models

Toward the end of the 1970s, we again witness a transition from the dominance of rational system models to that of natural system models. These new models place great emphasis on the importance of the environment in determining the structure, behavior, and life chances of organizations: they are clearly open system models. However, the assumption that organizations behave as rational systems is strongly challenged in this work. In this section, we provide a quick sketch of the more important of these new open-natural models. We begin with a review of Weick's model and then introduce other work at the structural and ecological levels that continues to be important up to the present time.

Organizing revisited. Just as it was necessary, armed with our layered schema, to reclassify contingency theories as not only open but also rational, so it is necessary to re-view Weick's model as combining open with natural system assumptions. As noted in Chapter 4, Weick gives great attention to the cognitive processes entailed in creating and sustaining organizations, but his view of these processes, unlike those of Simon, for example, is that they operate in an evolutionary fashion: they involve trial and error, chance, superstitious learning, and retrospective sense-making. Also, Weick rejects the notion that evolution necessarily entails improvements in the surviving forms. He points out that successful interlocking of behaviors (that is, organized patterns of action) "can occur without any necessary increase in the productivity or viability of the system" (1979: 179) and insists that we must "free ourselves from the notion that selection is for environmental advantage" (p. 127). In these and many other respects, Weick's model is that of a natural, not a rational, open system.

We shift now to the structural level of analysis, briefly describing an influential approach developed in England which embraces the open-natural system perspective.

Sociotechnical systems. At the end of World War II, the Tavistock Clinic, a voluntary outpatient center for psychotherapy in England, reconstituted itself as the Tavistock Institute of Human Relations. Influenced by the human relations research in the United States, the Tavistock team of researchers conducted a series of studies in differing work organizations on ways to improve productivity and morale. From the beginning, the preferred approach was one of "action" research, the investigators working with management and labor to introduce change into a work setting and then attempting to learn from its results (Jaques, 1951). In addition to this somewhat distinctive research style, the group developed a particular problem focus. They proposed that the distinguishing feature of organizations is that they are both social and technical systems: "Their core interface consists of the relation between a nonhuman system and a human system" (Trist, 1981: 25).

Rather than insisting that individual and social units must conform to technical requirements, the sociotechnical system approach emphasizes that the needs of both should be served. Rather than obtaining the best "match" between technical and social components, the goal should be one of the "joint optimization" of the needs of both, since the two systems follow different "laws" and their relationship represents a "coupling of dissimilars" (Emery, 1959). The "grain of the fifties" was the celebration of top-down, manager-controlled, technical bureaucracies, but the Tavistock group attempted to go against this grain by designing systems that emphasized discretionary behavior, internalized regulation, and work-group autonomy (Trist, 1981).

Although their early empirical efforts were concentrated at the individual and work-group level, the Tavistock researchers discovered that changes made at these levels did not long survive unless there were compatible changes in larger structures. Further, they became increasingly aware that the organizations themselves were open to the wider environment. As Trist recalls:

> In our action research projects at that time, we and our organizational clients were baffled by the extent to which the wider social environment was moving in on their more immediate concerns, upsetting plans, preventing the achievement of operational goals, and causing additional stress and severe internal conflict. (1981: 50)

In addition to developing a widely influential typology of organizational environments and speculating on their effects on organizational forms (see Emery and Trist, 1965), to be described in the next chapter, the research group attempted to discover ways in which the larger enterprise is shaped by its needs to survive in a specific social and economic environment (Miller and Rice, 1967). The most resilient building blocks available to organizations as they respond to these demands are the sets of semiautonomous groups, capable of self-regulation as cybernetic systems, and the larger networks of groups organized into "primary work systems," which are functionally interdependent. Interest in the creation of these units is a common thread running throughout many specific studies describing the history of change attempts in particular industrial settings, and it is this emphasis that locates the perspective at the structural level of analysis. Throughout their work, the Tavistock group has remained strongly committed to creating organizational forms that serve the values of human community as well as the interests of technical efficiency.[6]

Finally, we introduce three quite different and influential approaches to analyzing organizations that have developed at the ecological level of analysis.

Population ecology. The population ecology or natural selection model originated in biology with the work of Darwin. Although the application of these ideas to social systems has a long and checkered history

---

[6]This general approach to the "design" of natural systems has been more influential and more often emulated in Europe than in the United States. Related research has been carried on, for example, by Thorsrud in Norway and Sweden (Emery and Thorsrud, 1969; 1976). In the United States, some socio-technical themes are to be found in research on the quality of working life (see O'Toole, 1972), and socio-technical action research strategies have been adopted by organizational development (OD) researchers and practitioners.

(see Hofstadter, 1945), more recent and promising efforts have been stimulated by the work of Hawley (1950) and Campbell (1969). Applications of these general ideas to organizations by Hannan and Freeman (1977) and by Aldrich (1979) have led to a rapidly growing body of research and theory.

This model differs from other approaches to organizations in that it applies primarily to populations of organizations rather than to individual units.[7] It is designed to explain organizational diversity: to answer the question, why are there so many—or so few—organizations? Although diversity occurs because individual organizations change their characteristics through *adaptation* over time, ecologists have devoted attention primarily to *selection* processes: "change in the composition of a set of organizations from differential replacement of one form by another" (Hannan and Carroll, 1995: 23). Organizations are formed and they die at varying rates. For example, an ecologist might examine factors associated with the decline of teachers' colleges and the growth in the numbers of community colleges over recent decades in the United States.

It is central to the natural selection thesis that environments differentially select organizations for survival on the basis of fit between organizational forms and environmental characteristics. Three processes are emphasized in evolutionary analysis: the creation of variety, the selection of some forms over others, and the retention of those forms (Campbell, 1969). In the first stage, variety is created by some process, planned or unplanned. In the second, some forms of organization are differentially selected for survival. And in stage three, the selected forms are preserved in some fashion, by reproduction or duplication. Positively selected variations survive and reproduce similar others, which then form the starting point for a new round of selection as mutants appear (Aldrich and Pfeffer, 1976). In the founding work primary emphasis was placed on selection as the prime process by which change occurs in organizations, but more recent work has incorporated adaptation by existing forms (see Singh, Tucker, and House, 1986).

This approach has created much interest among students of organizations: it employs a well-known and highly regarded intellectual framework and has been able to adapt for use quite sophisticated concepts and measures from the work of population biologists. Also, by emphasizing the population level of analysis, it has focused on a new set of issues largely ignored by earlier theorists. In particular, it is asserted that most change that occurs in the realm of organizations is the result, not of adaptation or change on the part of existing organizations, but of the replacement of one type of organization with another.

This conception is firmly grounded in an open system model: the importance of the environment can hardly be more strongly underlined than in the population ecology framework. The conception is also clearly a natural system approach. The bottom line is survival. And although based on an evolutionary framework, in its contemporary usage, "evolution is no

---

[7]The underlying evolutionary arguments can be applied to virtually any level, from components of organizations such as rules and routines, individual organizations, organizational communities or populations of organizations (see Aldrich, 1979; Carroll, 1984; Miner, 1990). We discuss some of these other applications in Chapter 8.

longer equated with progress, but simply with change over time" (Carroll, 1984: 72). The ability to perpetuate one's form is the hallmark of successful adaptation.[8]

Resource dependence. Whereas the population ecology approach stresses selection—attributing observed patterns in the distribution of organizational forms to the action of environmental selection, both in terms of what kinds of organizations are created and which survive—the resource dependence model emphasizes adaptation. It is assumed that existing organizations can act to improve their chances of survival.

The resource dependence approach focuses primary attention on one organization, examining the environment from its vantage point. The approach has been developed by a number of investigators and has received a variety of labels. Zald and his colleagues refer to their version as a political economy model (Zald, 1970; Wamsley and Zald, 1973). Thompson (1967), much of whose work employs this model, describes the approach as an exchange or a power-dependence model. The most comprehensive development to date of the resource dependence approach is found in the work of Pfeffer and Salancik (1978).

This perspective is strongly rooted in an open system framework: it is argued that one cannot understand the structure or behavior of an organization without understanding the context within which it operates. No organization is self-sufficient; all must engage in exchanges with the environment as a condition of their survival. The need to acquire resources creates dependencies between organizations and external units. How important and how scarce these resources are determine the nature and the extent of organizational dependency. Dependency is the obverse of power (Emerson, 1962). Economic dependencies give rise to political problems and may succumb to political solutions.

Much more so than in the population ecology approach, organizations are viewed as active, not passive, in determining their own fate. Organizational participants, particularly managers, scan the relevant environment, searching for opportunities and threats, attempting to strike favorable bargains and to avoid costly entanglements. All organizations are dependent on suppliers and consumers, but which specific exchange partners are selected and what are the terms of exchange are partly determined by the organization itself. Astute managers acquire the necessary resources but do so without creating crippling dependencies. Thus, the resource dependence model views organizations as:

> capable of changing, as well as responding to, the environment. Administrators manage their environments as well as their organizations, and the former activity may be as important, or even more important, than the latter. (Aldrich and Pfeffer, 1976: 83)

---

[8]Useful summaries and general statements of the population ecology approach to organizations are provided by Baum (1996), Hannan and Freeman (1989), and Singh (1990).

One of the major contributions of the resource dependence perspective is to discern and describe the strategies—ranging from buffering to diversification and merger—employed by organizations to change and adapt to the environment. We review these strategies in Chapter 8.

Institutional theory. Institutional theory, like resource dependence and population ecology, has developed quite rapidly during the 1970s and up to the present. In part because institutional analysis enjoys a long history— important institutional work was carried on at the turn of the nineteenth century—and in part because it has stimulated efforts across most of the social sciences—in particular, economics, political science, and sociology—a broad spectrum of arguments is encompassed by this perspective. The arguments converge around an interest in understanding the basis of social meaning and social stability. They diverge in the elements that are emphasized as providing these conditions. As we will discuss in more detail in Chapter 6, economists tend to emphasize the importance of legal and rule-based systems that are externally enforced by third parties, for example, the nation-state. Early sociologists, from Cooley (1902) to Selznick, emphasized the importance of normative controls: values and norms that are both internalized by actors and enforced by others in social situations. The most recent, "neo-institutional" approaches emphasize the importance of cognitive or cultural controls. As formulated by Berger and Luckmann (1967) and Geertz (1973) a set of beliefs, developed in social interaction, provides models and guidelines for governing and guiding behavior in varied social situations.

These general cultural arguments were first applied to organizations by Meyer and Rowan (1977) and amplified by DiMaggio and Powell (1983). These theorists argue that a set of rationalizing agents—in particular, the nation-state and the many types of scientists and professionals—provide an increasingly elaborate base of beliefs and rules that furnish the foundation for organizations: forms that embrace these models. One after another area of social life is in the process of being rationalized, with the construction of means-ends recipes around which behavior can be regularized, formalized, organized.

Institutional theory emphasizes that organizations are open systems— strongly influenced by their environments—but that it is not only rational or efficiency-based forces that are at work. Socially constructed belief systems and normative rules exercise enormous control over organizations—both how they are structured and how they carry out their work. While early applications of institutional theory to organizations tended to pit rational explanations of organizational structure against nonrational or legitimacy-based explanations (e.g., Meyer and Rowan, 1977; DiMaggio and Powell, 1983), later researchers suggest that organizations need to attend to the demands of both institutional and rational or technical environments (e.g, Meyer and Scott, 1983). And, more recently, a number of institutionalists have argued that institutional rules provide the context and the frame within which effectiveness criteria are constructed (see Fligstein, 1990; Whitley, 1992a; Scott, 1995).[9]

---

[9]Synthetic overviews of sociological institutional theory are provided by DiMaggio and Powell (1991) and by Scott (1995). Reviews of economic institutional theory are provided by Hodgson (1988) and by Langlois (1986).

PARADIGM WARS?

In layering the perspectives into four combinations of open-closed systems and rational-natural systems, we have created a "property space" that seeks to contain not only earlier but also contemporary approaches to understanding organizations. The review just concluded gives much evidence of an active— perhaps hyperactive—arena of study. Organizations are a central focus of current social science inquiry and have aroused the interest and claimed the attention of a widening array of social theorists—from rational choice economists to institutional sociologists.

As emphasized in our typology (Table 5–1), the theories vary in level of analysis. They also vary in terms of what aspects of organizations are privileged. For example, resource dependence emphasizes the power relations that grow out of asymetric economic exchanges; institutional theorists emphasize the role of ideas and belief systems in supporting and structuring organizations. Some of these theories may be complementary; others are based on contradictory assumptions or pose incompatible arguments. We attempt to sort out some of these matters in Part Three.

One of the characteristics of much of the work just introduced is that, in developing arguments and making claims, the analysts employ language that is sufficiently general to imply that the ideas are applicable to all types of organizations and to all or most conditions. We will be well-advised to question this assumption. In an insightful commentary on some of these recent theories, the Italian economist Grandori argues that each is more appropriate for some types of organizations or contexts than for others—that each has an "appropriate domain of application" (Grandori, 1987: xxii). Grandori emphasizes differences among theories in terms of how organizational goals are treated. We discuss her interpretations in the following chapters, especially Chapter 11. More generally, we attempt to consider throughout our evaluation of these and other approaches still to be introduced the conditions under which the various theories apply.

The development of so many competing theoretical perspectives necessarily poses difficult problems for all of us—from beginning student to seasoned scholar—working in this field. Aldrich (1992) has labeled the recent era of organization theory as one characterized by "paradigm wars." Pfeffer (1993) has argued that the multiplication of so many competing paradigms has numerous pernicious consequences, including increasing dissensus among scholars who cannot reach agreement on what articles should be published or what research should be funded and undermining intellectual and financial support for the field from universities and the state. Donaldson (1995) mounts an even stronger attack against the proliferation of paradigms, which, he asserts, reflect a pathological status contest among intellectuals who receive more attention and fame for creating new theories than from testing and improving existing models. Donaldson also asserts that many of the newer perspectives, such as that of population ecology and institutional theory, reflect an antimanagerial bias among American organization theorists. This is not the place to attempt to refute these criticisms of recent developments in the field. Suffice it to say that while the existence of multiple paradigms may reduce consensus and support, it does not thereby necessarily reduce the power of the ideas and the value of possessing multiple lens through which to observe our world. And while enhanced status does accompany the creation of new theories—as it should—that does not imply that the theory-creating process is only a status contest or that the products of this competition are not without intellectual merit. Moreover, as new theories have moved to higher levels of analysis, they necessarily defocalize the role of individual managers within organizations.

SUMMARY

The rational, natural, and open system perspectives for analyzing organizations provide contrasting paradigms. Because of the differing assumptions underlying these paradigms, one may replace another but cannot disprove it.

Nevertheless, several analysts have attempted to reconcile the three perspectives by combining them into more complex models of organizations. Etzioni suggests that the rational and natural system models are complementary, focusing on conflicting tendencies present in all organizations. Lawrence and Lorsch propose that all organizations are open systems, and that rational and natural forms emerge as varying adaptive structures in response to different environmental conditions. And Thompson suggests that the three perspectives are differentially applicable to various levels of an organization's structure, the open system being most suited to analyzing the institutional level, the natural system applying best to the managerial level, and the rational system, to the technical level.

An alternative basis for combining the perspectives is to suggest that they have appeared in varying combinations over time and that they are applicable to differing levels of analysis. This layered framework suggests that the earliest models, dominant between 1900 and 1930, were closed-rational system models. Some of these were developed at the social psychological level—for example, Taylor's scientific management approach—while others were advanced at the structural level—for instance, Weber's model of bureaucracy and Fayol's administrative theory. From the 1930s through the 1950s, a new set of perspectives developed that combined closed with natural system assumptions. Again, some of these approaches were developed primarily at the social psychological level—such as the human relations models of Roy and Katz—and others at the structural level—for example, Barnard's theory of cooperative systems and Mayo's version of human relations.

Beginning in the early 1960s, open system models largely replaced closed system assumptions, and analyses at the ecological level began to appear. At the same time, rational and natural system models persisted, providing competing theoretical explanations for organizational structure and behavior. During the 1960s, open-rational system models were dominant, represented by the work of March and Simon at the social psychological level and by contingency theory and comparative analyses at the structural level. Transaction cost analysis was added to these approaches in the 1970s. The open-rational system models were joined and challenged by the open-natural system models that became dominant in the 1970s and continue into the 1990s. These rapidly proliferating approaches range from the work of Weick at the social psychological level, through the sociotechnical model developed at the structural level, to the population ecology, resource dependence, and institutional theories at the ecological level.

Our classification emphasizes the historical evolution of organization theory. The types of theories guiding work today differ from those in use ten or forty years ago. A question to be pondered is why this is the case. Does it represent changes in the nature of organizations, changes in the interest of theorists, or both?

Many new and competing theories concerning organizations now occupy the landscape. We have reviewed some of the most influential of these, will add more in subsequent chapters, and consider their contributions to understanding some of the important processes and problems posed by organizations.

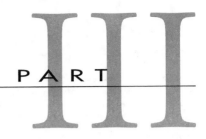

ENVIRONMENTS, STRATEGIES, AND STRUCTURES

Three general perspectives on the nature of organizations have been described, along with several attempts to combine or integrate them. If these perspectives are as useful as we have claimed, they will enable us not simply to comprehend past efforts to dissect organizations but to better fathom current work and perhaps even to discern future analytic directions.

Part Three combines topics that are often separated in contemporary treatments of organizations. It deals both with the ways in which organizations relate to their environments and with the determinants of organizational structure. With the help of the open system perspective, we see these topics as inseparable: how an organization relates to its environment—indeed, what its environment is—is influenced by the organization's structure and strategy, and, conversely, the characteristics of the structure are strongly affected by the organization's environment. External forces shape internal arrangements, and vice versa.

We learn from the open system perspective that organizations are not fortresses, impervious to the buffeting or the blessing of their environments. On the other hand, we learn from the rational and natural system perspectives that organizations are not wind tunnels, completely open and responsive to every perturbation of their context. Organizations construct and reconstruct boundaries across which they relate to the outside world. Between the organization and those outside there is not one barrier but many, and for most kinds of organizations these barriers become higher and more impenetrable as we come closer to the organization's technical core.

Part Three begins with an examination of organizational environments. Having been persuaded that the open system perspective is critically important, we distinguish among various levels at which environments may be analyzed and differentiate their technical from their institutional elements. The multiple ways in which organizations interact with their environments are stressed in Chapter 6.

Chapter 7 addresses the fundamental but difficult questions of why organizations exist and how they are created. These questions are pursued from both a historical and a comparative perspective. Rational system explanations stressing efficiency are contrasted with natural system accounts emphasizing power and conformity to external rules and symbols.

Organizations must both distinguish their systems from and connect themselves to their environment. Boundary-defining mechanisms as well as the strategies used by organizations to buffer their technical core and to build bridges to other organizations—both competitors and exchange partners—are examined in Chapter 8. Connections to both technical and instutional facets of the environment are considered.

Chapters 9 and 10 describe sources of structural complexity, Chapter 9 focusing on complexity within the technical core and Chapter 10 examining influences on the form of the peripheral sectors: the wider, encompassing structures. Characteristics of the type of work being performed—the technology—and of the technical and instutional environment pose opportunities and challenges to which organizations respond. These responses have significant consequences for the structure of the organization. The extent to which organizations change by adaptation—the modification of an existing organization—or by selection—the elimination of one form of organization and the generation of new forms—is currently under debate.

Environmental factors are also argued, in Chapter 11, to be critical in determining the size and composition of the dominant coalition—that set of an organization's participants who have sufficient power to set the goals to be pursued by the organization.

Environments shape organizations, but organizations also shape environments. Organizations in part choose which environments to enter and to exit, and they seek, individually and in coalition with others, to influence the contexts within which they function. Organizations relate strategically to environments.

In all of these ways, we challenge the sharp dichotomy between inside and outside, between organization and environment. The structures and processes of organizations and environments penetrate one another in interesting and unexpected ways that are revealed when we combine the open system perspective with the rational and natural system viewpoints.

Conceptions of Environments

For a given system, the environment is the set of all objects a change in whose attributes affect the system and also those objects whose attributes are changed by the behavior of the system.

The statement above invites the natural question of when an object belongs to a system and when it belongs to the environment, for if an object reacts with a system in the way described above should it not be considered a part of the system? The answer is by no means definite. In a sense, a system together with its environment makes up the universe of all things of interest in a given context. Subdivision of this universe into two sets, system and environment, can be done in many ways which are in fact quite arbitrary. Ultimately it depends on the intentions of the one who is studying the particular universe as to which of the possible configurations of objects is to be taken as the system.

A. D. Hall and R. E. Fagen (1956)

Since the emergence and increasing prominence of open system models, investigators are no longer able to comfortably ignore the effects of environments on organizations. To examine these causal connections, it is necessary to develop some working conceptions of environments themselves: it is not very helpful to regard the environment as simply "everything else." We need ideas as to how to circumscribe them and how to identify and assess their relevant features. This chapter describes the major conceptions that currently guide investigations in this area.

Over the past three decades, the arena of organizational studies has expanded both "up" and "out": up to include higher and wider levels of analysis and out to encompass more kinds of factors or forces shaping organizations. The first section of this chapter describes the new levels that have been identified; the second, the new facets of environments now being examined.

THE ANALYSIS OF ENVIRONMENTS

Levels of Environments

A basic source of variation among conceptions of environments stems from the level of analysis selected. In Chapter 1 we identified the social psychological, structural, and ecological levels, and we have made ample use of these distinctions in our examination of various theories of organizations. Since our current concern is with conceptions of organizational environments—the ecological level—all of the analyses to be developed in this chapter are within this level.[1] We distinguish four sublevels within the ecological level.

Organization sets.   The first level of analysis is that of the organization set (see Blau and Scott, 1962: 195–99; Evan, 1966). Blau, Evan, and I all acknowledge that the concept of organization set was developed by analogy from Merton's (1957: 368–80)concept of role-set. Merton noted that a single position such as "mother" is associated with not one but a cluster of different roles depending on the identity of the counterpositions. Thus, a mother has a number of specific role obligations toward her children, other obligations toward the father, still other obligations toward the children's teachers, and so on. Similarly, a given organization participates in a variety of relations depending on the identity of its specific partners. For example, a small grocery store will relate in one manner with its suppliers, another with its customers, yet another with its neighbors, and so on. The fundamental idea is a simple one, but its implications are quite rich. One is led to ask questions about the relative size of the organization set, the extent to which one group of role partners is aware of the demands made by another, the extent to which expectations held by partners coincide, and so on.

One of the more useful concepts to emerge at the analytical level of the organization set is that of organizational domain (Levine and White, 1961; Thompson, 1967). An organization's *domain* consists of the range of products or services it provides and the types of clients or consumers served. Producing goods and providing services necessarily relate each organization to a number of other organizations—suppliers, customers, competitors— that affect its behavior and outcomes. Some diversified corporations operate

---

[1]This does not mean the other levels of analysis are not relevant to examining the relation between organizations and environments. Thus, when boundary roles are considered (see Chapter 8), the level of analysis often employed is the social psychological, and when organizational strategies and structural modifications are examined as modes of organizational adaptation to environments (see Chapters 9 and 10), the level of analysis is the structural. The concern at this point, however, is to determine variations in the way in which environments of organizations are circumscribed. In this sense, the four approaches we consider here are at the ecological level.

in multiple domains. In such cases, an important consideration is the degree of overlap or extent of synergies between them.

A crucial, defining characteristic of the concept of organization set is that it views the environment from the standpoint of a specific (focal) organization. Relations or connections between other (counter) members of the set are of no concern unless they affect the activities or interests of the focal organization. Analysts employing the resource dependence approach, as described in Chapter 5, typically work at the level of the organization set, as do many of those utilizing transaction cost approaches. It is from this level that the interests, the resources, the dependencies of a given organization are best examined and its survival tactics probed. It is also at this level that most discussions of strategic decision making occur (Porter, 1980). And decisions about whether to perform activities within the organization or contract them out to other players involves an examination of the number of suppliers and the specificity of assets in the form of skills or equipment. Up to the present time, the great majority of studies of organization-environment connections have been conducted at the organization-set level of analysis.

While the organization-set level of analysis has proved extremely useful in directing attention to the impact of information and resource flows and relations on a select organization, it does so at the expense of detracting attention from the nature of the larger system of relations in which the focal organization is but one participant among many. Other approaches attempt to correct this shortcoming.

Organizational populations. A second level identified by analysts is that of the population of organizations. This concept is used to identify aggregates of organizations that are alike in some respect—for example, institutions of higher education or newspapers. This is the level at which most natural selection theories have been applied, such as the population ecology model, introduced in Chapter 5. Also, studies conducted of industry structure by economists employ a related level of analysis.[2]

Those concerned with studying populations have had to wrestle with the question of what it means to be "alike in some respect." How are populations identified? When one studies "colleges," for example, what organizations are included—private as well as public schools? Universities? Community or junior colleges? Technical institutes? Organizational ecologists borrow or adapt biological language and ideas in working on this problem. Hannan and Freeman (1977: 935) in their early formulation noted that biological species are defined in terms of genetic structure, and proposed that the appropriate analogue for organizations is to define them in terms of their "blueprint for organizational action, for transforming inputs into outputs." McKelvey (1982) adopts a similar stance, suggesting that all organizations in the same population contain "elements of dominant competence," or "comps," drawn from the same "compool," or collection of elements. By dominant competence McKelvey means essentially the technical core of the organization—that is, the activities that transform "inputs into those outputs

---

[2]Ecologists define populations as organizations exhibiting the same structural form, whereas economists define industries as including all organizations serving the same demand or function, which could include quite diverse types of providers of substitutable products.

critical to a population's survival" (p. 174). Both of these definitions of the boundaries of populations are conceptually clear, but neither is easy to apply. Blueprints and comps are hard to measure.

More recently, Hannan and Carroll have concluded that the basic key to identifying a population is the possession of a common organizational form:

> Form serves as the organizational ecologist's analogue to the biological ecologist's species. Form summarizes the core properties that make a set of organizations ecologically similar. . . . *Organizational populations* are specific time-and-space instances of organizational forms. (Hannan and Carroll, 1995: 29)

Returning to the educational example then, to the extent that community colleges and universities exhibit different structural forms—and they indeed do in many respects—then they would be considered to be different populations operating within the general sector (or industry) of higher education.

More generally, there are several approaches to the problem of defining organizational populations. First, one can use "native" commonsense categories—for example, hospitals, universities, newspapers; or researchers can employ more abstract, theory-based classification schemas, such as those proposed by Parsons (see Chapter 3). Alternatively, more empirically derived classifications can be developed based on statistical techniques that detect the existence of similar combinations of characteristics (see, for example, McPherson, 1983). Another solution involves the recognition that the boundaries that define organizational forms are dynamic, changing over time. Some organizational populations are more sharply demarcated than are others. Hannan and Freeman suggest that the boundary-defining process itself is among the more important subjects confronting not only ecological but all organizational theorists. We return to this topic in Chapter 7.

Up to now, most of the empirical studies of organizational populations have relied on commonsense definitions of the population and have employed geographical criteria for bounding it. For example, Freeman and Brittain (1977) studied mergers among national labor unions in the United States; Carroll and Delacroix (1982) studied mortality rates of Irish and Argentine newspapers; and Singh, Tucker, and House (1986) examined the formation and dissolution of social service organizations in Toronto. However, Hannan and colleagues (Hannan et al., 1995) have recently undertaken an investigation of the evolution of the automobile manufacturing industry as it has developed in five different European countries in a multinational context. (For general reviews of population studies, see Carroll, 1984; Singh and Lumsden, 1990; and Baum, 1996.)

In a population ecology approach, primary attention is given to the analysis of competition among similar organizations, to varying strategies of competition, and to the selection effects of changes in environments. Although this level of analysis clearly identifies an important set of questions and has attracted great interest, it directs attention away from connections among organizations, in particular those organizations whose relations are more symbiotic and cooperative than commensalistic and competitive. To examine these connections, we need other models that perhaps change not so much the level as the focus of analysis.

Interorganizational community. This level of analysis is employed when the investigator focuses on the relations among a collection of similar and diverse organizations within a delimited geographical area. Also labeled the ecological community model (Hawley, 1950; Astley, 1985), the interorganizational field model (Warren, 1967), and the collective-action model (Astley and Van de Ven, 1983), this approach emphasizes not the individual organizational units or even their characteristics as an aggregate, but rather the network of relations among them.

Of course, the extent of such networks among organizations varies from time to time and place to place. In a highly theoretical fashion, the influential paper by Emery and Trist (1965) attempts to classify environments by the way in which resources are distributed and the extent to which organizations sharing the same territory are obliged to take into account the behavior of others. They distinguish among four types of environments:

> *Placid, randomized environments,* in which resources required by organizations in the territory are unchanging and randomly distributed over the area;
>
> *Placid, clustered environments,* in which resources are unchanging but clustered, so that location becomes an important factor in survival;
>
> *Disturbed, reactive environments,* in which the availability of resources is partially determined by the actions of the organizations themselves, so that a given organization's survival is dependent on the use of strategies that take into account the behavior of competitors;
>
> *Turbulent environments,* in which all organizational actors are interconnected, so that the organizational relation or network itself becomes a force that each organization must attempt to take into account.

A related but more concrete typology based on the extent to which an "inclusive decision making structure" has come into existence has been proposed by Warren (1967). Four types of organizational contexts are identified:

> *Social-choice context:* no formal or informal inclusive structure exists within which the participating organizations make their decisions. All decisions are made at the level of the individual units. An example is the relations among diverse organizations that happen to reside in the same community.
>
> *Coalitional context:* each organizational unit has its own decision-making apparatus and set of goals but collaborates informally and on an ad hoc basis when some of its goals are similar to those of other member units. An example is a group of independent child-care agencies collaborating to obtain a federal grant.
>
> *Federative context:* Organizational units have individual goals but also participate in a structure in order to set more inclusive goals, which must be ratified by member units. An example is social agencies partic-

ipating in a community council of agencies that has only limited delegated powers.

Unitary context: Decision making on policies and programs takes place at the top of a hierarchy of organizations, where final authority rests. An example is a corporate hospital system that owns, operates, and coordinates the work of a set of hospital units, satellite outpatient clinics, and urgent care units.

The central message of both typologies—Emery and Trist's and Warren's—is that organizational communities vary greatly in the extent and nature of the relational and normative structures that develop among organizations. And in both typologies attention has shifted from the individual organization or organizational form to emphasize the nature of the relations that exist among the component organizations.

Interorganizational communities also vary in longevity. Aldrich and Whetten (1981: 387) have identified as an *action-set* a group of organizations "that have formed a temporary alliance for a limited purpose." Action-sets contrast with more permanent and stable organizational communities, although all communities evolve over time.

As Astley (1985) emphasizes, shifting attention to the community level allows us to examine relations among similar and different kinds of organizations so that we variously observe instances of cooperation or mutualism and of competition or conflict. It also allows us to observe not only the waxing and waning of a particular type of organization but also the disappearance of some types and the emergence of new forms. A substantial and continuing stream of research has examined the nature of the linkages that develop among similar or diverse organizations located within the same community or metropolitan area (see Litwak and Hylton, 1962; Warren, 1963; Turk, 1977; Lincoln, 1979; Galaskiewicz, 1979).

From an ecological perspective, the networks developing among organizations sharing the same territory are adaptive mechanisms. As Astley and Van de Ven point out:

> Rather than view organizations as pitched in a competitive battle for survival through a direct confrontation with the natural, or exogenous, environment, [community theorists] emphasize collective survival, which is achieved by collaboration between organizations through the construction of a regulated and controlled social environment that mediates the effects of the natural environment. (1983: 250–51)

The interorganizational community represents a significant shift in focus from that of the individual organization or the organization set. Organizations are treated as components of larger, overarching systems. However, two restrictions characterize this approach, one by definition and the other by usage. First, attention is restricted by definition to connections among organizations sharing the same territorial area. For many kinds of biological and social units, such a limitation would pose no problem, but for organizations, it is a serious and potentially biasing restriction. Modern transportation and communication systems are such that geographical boundaries are for many purposes meaningless. A large number of types of organizations are influenced by distant as well as proximate connections, and for many organizations, the former are more fateful. Numerous organizations are linked to national and even international corporate systems, and many buy from and distribute to national and international markets. Second, by convention, most of the studies at this level give primary attention to "horizontal" relations among organizations—that is, to connections among competing or cooperating organizations lacking formal rights over one another. Neglected are the "vertical" connections that relate organizations in hierarchical systems—regulatory systems linking public and private organizations, formal authority connecting headquarters and branch offices, informal power channels relating dominant and subordinate organizations.

The fourth and final level of analysis to be considered was developed by theorists seeking to emphasize extralocal and vertical connections among organizations.

Organization fields. As defined by DiMaggio and Powell (1983: 143), an *organization field* refers to:

> those organizations that, in the aggregate, constitute a recognized area of institutional life: key suppliers, resource and produce consumers, regulatory agencies, and other organizations that produce similar services and products.

Closely related concepts include Hirsch's (1985) concept of "industry system" and Scott and Meyer's (1991a) concept of "societal sector."

The organization field isolates for analysis a system of organizations operating in the same realm as defined both by relational linkages and by shared cultural rules and meaning systems. Local as well as distant connections are included as are both horizontal and vertical ties and linkages between similar and dissimilar organizations. The field concept also calls attention to organizations that are not linked by direct connections but, because they are operating under similar conditions, exhibit similar structural characteristics and types of relationships—a condition referred to as "structural equivalence" or "isomorphism" (see DiMaggio, 1986).

There is a useful tension in the fact that fields are bounded by both relational and cultural criteria. "The notion of field connotes the existence of a community of organizations that partakes of a common meaning system and whose participants interact more frequently and fatefully with one another than with actors outside of the field" (Scott, 1994: 207–8). In stable and more highly institutionalized fields, there is high consensus on the definitions as to who the critical players are, what activities and interactions are appropriate, and which organizations are included, marginal to, or outside field boundaries. For example, the field of higher education in the United States has enjoyed substantial stability throughout most of the latter half of this century. By contrast, during the same period a field such as mental health has exhibited little consensus regarding legitimate providers, diagnoses, or therapies. It is estimated that only about one-fifth of "mental health services" are provided by organizations considered by the professional community to be legitimate players (see Regier, Goldberg, and Taube, 1978). The relational patterns and cultural rules in this arena do not reinforce each other so as to create and sustain a coherent realm of activity (see Scott, 1985b).

A number of empirical studies of organization fields have been conducted. Hirsch (1975), for example, has compared the relations between artists and recording studios with those between authors and publishers; Laumann and Knoke (1987) carried out an ambitious investigation comparing how public and private organizations interacted over time in setting national policy in the United States during the 1970s in two arenas, health and energy. DiMaggio (1991) has examined factors affecting the development of art museums in the United States in the early decades of the twentieth century. And Suchman (1995) has studied the emergence of semiconductor firms in Silicon Valley with special attention to the role played by law firms and venture capitalists.

Studies at the organization field level have been primarily guided by the theoretical interests of resource dependence, institutional, and Marxist perspectives. In later chapters, we review some of the findings from these studies.

More so than the other approaches considered, the organization field can be viewed as encompassing the other levels: the individual organization, the organization set, and several populations of interdependent organizations. In this sense, it provides a basis for integrating previous approaches and supports efforts to examine not only the effects of wider structures and processes on populations, sets, and organizations but also the ways in which individual organizations and their participants can influence their environments[3] (see Scott, 1993).

Finally, organizational fields provide an important intermediate unit connecting the study of individual organizational structure and performance with broader social structures and processes. As DiMaggio (1986: 337) observes: "the organizational field has emerged as a critical unit bridging the organization and societal levels in the study of social and community change." For example, federal and state regulations directed at individual organizations (for example, pollution controls) seldom directly impact single organizations but are typically mediated by field-level structures and processes (for example, trade associations).

Obviously, each of the levels identified can be viewed as a useful way of depicting the environment of organizations.[4] The characteristics of and relations among the counterorganizations constitute an important environment for the focal organization. Similarly, the distribution of organizational forms in a population may be viewed as a salient aspect of the environment for any particular organization in that population, and the characteristics of organi-

---

[3]Note that this is yet another instance of the "structure-agency" problem discussed in Chapter 1. At the field level, the structure refers to the existence of patterned relations among organizations, while the agents of interest here are individual organizations. The actions of individual organizations both reproduce existing structural relations and alter them.

[4]While the levels we have discussed are those most employed by organizational analysts, they are not the only ones possible or in use. For example, Hopkins and Wallerstein (1986: 159) have identified *commodity chains*—"a network of labor and production processes whose end result is a finished commodity"—as a useful level of analysis. In today's complex world, such chains may stretch across many countries and continents (see Gereffi and Korzeniewicz, 1994).

zation fields—their degree of centralization or formalization—are of obvious significance for their component organizations. On the other hand, each of these levels—organization sets, populations, interorganizational communities, and fields—are systems that may themselves be the primary object of study. Recall from Chapter 1 that levels of analysis are defined in terms of the dependent variables on which they focus. Much of the research conducted during the past decade has centered on these new units of analysis, examining how sets or populations or fields of organizations come into existence, vary over time, grow, and decline. The identification of these and related levels allows us to examine not simply the environments of organizations but the organization of environments.

Characteristics of Environments: Institutional and Technical Aspects

Establishing the level at which organizations and systems of organizations are to be defined is an important step in determining how environments are to be conceived: the environment of a population of hospitals is assuredly different from the environment of a single hospital and its set of related organizations. But once the level of analysis is established, many choices remain. We distinguish broadly between institutional and technical features of environments. The *institutional* elements encompass the more symbolic, cultural factors affecting organizations; the *technical*, the more materialist, resource-based features. Technical factors remind us that organizations are production systems—systems for transforming inputs into outputs—and as such they require material, resource, and energy inputs and markets, that is, buyers who will provide capital resources in exchange for what they produce. Up to the mid-1970s, researchers concentrated primarily on these technical features and their effects on organization structure. The contingency, resource dependence, transaction cost, and population ecology theories all privilege the technical environment and its effects.

Organization theorists long overlooked the importance of the institutional environment. Only gradually, over a period of time, did analysts come to recognize that organizations were not just technical systems; they were also human systems (human relations), political systems (conflict, Marxist, and feminist theory), social systems (cooperative systems; socio-technical systems), and cultural systems (organizational culture; institutional theory).

As the institutional perspective has developed, it becomes more and more apparent that the distinction between technical and institutional facets is, at best, analytic, and at worst, misleading because institutional factors shape many aspects of the technical. Nevertheless, we begin by briefly describing important aspects of technical environments of organizations.

Technical environments. Perhaps the most commonly held conception of the environment of organizations is still that of the *task environment* as proposed by Dill (1958: 410). This concept is broadly defined as all aspects of the environment "potentially relevant to goal setting and goal attainment," but is typically narrowed in use to refer to the nature and sources of inputs, markets for outputs, and competitors. The conception emphasizes that most organizations are created to achieve goals and to perform some type of work. More important, no organization is self-sufficient; all must enter into exchanges with the environment. Managers are viewed as ensuring adequate suppliers of resources and suitable markets, designing efficient work arrangements, and coordinating and controlling technical activities. Organization structure is viewed as being closely linked to external technical requirements and to internal work systems.

Broadly speaking, two types of language were developed to describe what organizations exchange with their environments: some formulations emphasize environments as *stocks of resources* while others view them as *sources of information* (Aldrich and Mindlin, 1978). Those stressing the former are apt to focus on the degree to which the organization becomes dependent on others for vital resources. Investigators emphasizing the informational aspects of environments focus primarily on the degree of uncertainty confronting the organization. Both uncertainty and dependency are viewed as problematic situations confronting organizations and much attention has been devoted to examining the types of strategies and mechanisms organizations use to cope with them. We discuss these in Chapters 8 and 9. Here we note general conditions giving rise to these states.

Early theorists such as Dill (1958), Lawrence and Lorsch (1967), and Thompson (1967) emphasized factors contributing to the complexity or the uncertainty of environmental conditions. They identified numerous dimensions, including the degree of stability-variability, threat-security, homogeneity-heterogeneity, interconnectedness-isolation, and coordination-noncoordination, which characterized environmental elements with which the organization had to deal. In general, the higher the level of variability, threat, heterogeneity, interconnection, and noncoordination involved, the greater the level of complexity or uncertainty confronted.

Later theorists, such as Pfeffer and Salancik (1978) emphasized those aspects of the resource environment that increased the dependency of organizations on one or another source. They focused attention on dimensions such as munificence-scarcity and concentration-dispersion, as well as on coordination-noncoordination among environmental elements. In general, the higher the level of scarcity, concentration, and coordination, the greater the dependence of the organization was expected to be.

Attempts to empirically assess these environmental dimensions have not met with marked success and have raised numerous issues. First, there is the question of whether objective or subjective (perceptual) measures are more appropriate. (We discuss this issue later in this chapter.) Second, assessing environmental features is made more difficult by the differentiated nature of organizations: different components or subunits of an organization may confront quite different environmental conditions, as Lawrence and Lorsch (1967) first noted. Finally, DiMaggio (1986) has argued that the identification of disembodied dimensions of resource environments is not very helpful because (1) it treats all organizations as though they were in identical or similar positions in the environment, whereas organizations in the "same" environment may face quite different circumstances depending on their specific locations; and (2) it does not specify which particular other actors are causing the uncertainty or creating the dependency. An organizational field approach, which attempts to identify important relevant actors and their relations in a particular domain, seems better suited to assist investigators in gauging the amount and source of uncertainty or dependency confronting an organization. Network analytic techniques can be helpful in mapping and analyzing these relations (see Marsden 1990; Nohria and Eccles, 1992).

Institutional environments. Institutional concerns have a long and illustrious history in the social sciences, but did not become a central focus in the study of organizations until the 1970s. (For a review, see Scott, 1995.) Early work by political scientists, such as Burgess (1902), by economists, such as Commons (1924), and by sociologists, such as Cooley (1902) and Weber (1968 trans.), recognized the extent to which organizations were shaped by political and legal frameworks, the rules governing market behavior and general belief systems (recall Weber's typology of authority). Close examination of this work, however, reveals that while there is substantial overlap in themes and interests, theorists have singled out somewhat different aspects of institutions as the focus of attention. It is possible to throw a broad tent over these approaches by employing the following omnibus definition:

> Institutions consist of cognitive, normative, and regulative structures and activities that provide stability and meaning to social behavior. (Scott, 1995: 33)

In any fully developed institutional system, all three of these forces or elements are present and interact to promote and sustain orderly behavior.

Nevertheless, over the years and up the present, theorists vary in the extent to which they focus on one or another of these elements. Generally speaking, economists stress regulatory factors; political scientists and early sociologists, normative factors; and recent sociologists, anthropologists, and cognitive psychologists stress cognitive-cultural factors. Not only the focus, but the arguments and assumptions made by each collection of theorists tend to vary systematically and substantially, as suggested by Table 6–1. In addition, they differ in terms of the locus of institutional processes: some emphasize those occurring within or at the level of a specific organization; others emphasize the effects of wider environmental forces.

Analysts emphasizing the *regulative* features of institutions view institutions as systems of rules or as governance systems. For example, the economic historian, Douglass North, argues that:

> [Institutions] are perfectly analogous to the rules of the game in a competitive team sport. That is, they consist of formal written rules as well as typically unwritten codes of conduct that underlie and supplement formal rules. . . . The rules and informal codes are sometimes violated and punishments are enacted. Therefore, an essential part of the functioning of institutions is the costliness of ascertaining violations and the severity of punishment. (North, 1990: 4)

North observes that the major source of regulatory rules and enforcement mechanisms in modern society is the nation-state, although a variety of formal and informal regulatory structures exist at the sector and community

TABLE 6–1 Three Conceptions of Institutions

	Regulative	*Normative*	*Cognitive*
Basis of Compliance	expedience	social obligation	taken for granted
Mechanisms	coercive	normative	mimetic
Logic	instrumentality	appropriateness	orthodoxy
Indicators	rules, laws, sanctions	certification, accreditation	prevalence, isomorphism
Basis of Legitimacy	legally sanctioned	morally governed	culturally supported, recognizable

Source: Adapted from Scott (1995), Table 3.1, p. 35.

level—for example, trade associations and widely shared understandings regarding the limits of acceptable competitive practices.

In the regulatory view of institutions, it is assumed that the major mechanism by which compliance is effected is coercion. Individuals and groups comply to rules and codes out of expediency: to garner rewards or to avoid sanctions. Behavior is viewed as legitimate to the extent that it conforms to existing rules and laws.

For economic historians, such as North, institutions operate at the level of the environment: whether in the relatively uncodified and informal assumptions and understandings underlying many markets or the more direct intervention of governmental regulatory structures, institutions set the rules by which individual organizations must play. But for a newer generation of institutional economists, including Williamson and others, these wider institutions are viewed as "background conditions," whereas in the foreground are the institutional forms that serve as "governance structures" that manage economic transactions, including markets, organizational hierarchies, and various types of hybrid or network structures (see Williamson, 1994). As described in Chapter 5, transaction cost analysis defines its primary task as explaining why it is that these quite different ("discrete") institutional forms arise to govern economic activity (Williamson, 1991).

Early sociologists from Cooley and Weber to Selznick and Parsons viewed institutions primarily as *normative* structures providing a moral framework for the conduct of social life. Unlike externally enforced rules and laws, norms are internalized by participants; behavior is guided by a sense of what is appropriate, by one's social obligations to others, by a commitment to common values. While most sociologists have emphasized the more widely shared norms and values that give rise to stable social arrangements such as families and communities, sociologists like Selznick, as we have seen, emphasize the beliefs and commitments operating at the level of particular organizations that give them a distinctive character structure. This latter interest is also reflected in the work of contemporary students of corporate culture (see, for example, Schein, 1992; Trice and Beyer, 1993).

The most recent version of institutions—the view associated with "the new institutionalism in organizational analysis" (Powell and DiMaggio, 1991)—emphasizes the role of *cognitive-cultural* processes in social life. We employ the hyphenated concept to emphasize that we are not referring to individual mental constructs but to common symbolic systems and shared meanings that undergird much of the stability and order in social life. Based on philosophical underpinnings established by German idealists and by phenomenologists such as Dilthey and Husserl, and strongly shaped by the work of Schutz (1962 trans.), the most influential contribution to this sociological conception of institutions is that of Berger and Luckmann (1967). They argue that social life is only possible because and to the extent that individuals in interaction create common frameworks and understandings that support collective action. The process by which actions are repeated and given similar meaning by self and others is defined as institutionalization: it is the process by which social reality is constructed. The distinguished anthropologist Clifford Geertz has developed a very similar conception in his reformulation of culture as "the symbolic dimensions of social action" (1973: 300). He amplifies:

> The concept of culture I espouse . . . is essentially a semiotic one. Believing, with Max Weber, that man is an animal suspended in webs of significance he himself has spun, I take culture to be those webs. . . . (p. 5)

It is not necessary to insist that all reality is socially constructed. There exists what Searle (1995) defines as "brute" facts: the world of physical objects and forces. But there also exist a wide variety of "social facts" that are facts only by virtue of human agreement: language systems, legal institutions, monetary systems, national boundaries, to name only a few. Such facts, while dependent on human agreement, exist independently of your or my attitudes or preferences toward them.

These ideas concerning the construction of social reality were first introduced into organizational analysis at the micro or social psychological level by researchers working in the symbolic interactionist and ethnomethodological traditions. Their studies attend to the ways in which participants interact to develop shared understandings of their situation—collectively constructing their social reality. Analysts like Bittner (1967), Cicourel (1968), Zimmerman (1970), and Van Maanan (1973) have examined the ways in which participants interact to construct shared conceptions of their work situations.

Among the most influential applications of institutional ideas to the analysis of organizations is that of Meyer and Rowan (1977), who shift to the macro level, emphasizing the importance of cultural rules operating in wider institutional environments. They argue that modern societies contain many complexes of institutionalized rules and patterns—products of professional groups, the state, public opinion. These socially constructed realities provide frameworks for the creation and elaboration of formal organizations. According to Meyer and Rowan, in modern societies these institutions are likely to take the form of *rationalized myths*. They are *myths* because they are widely held beliefs whose effects "inhere, not in the fact that individuals believe them, but in the fact that they 'know' everyone else does, and thus that 'for all practical purposes' the myths are true" (Meyer, 1977: 75). They are *rationalized* because they take the form of rules specifying procedures necessary to accomplish a given end. Law provides a good example. How can property legitimately change hands? How can an organization become a corporation? Legal systems—as complexes of rationalized myths—provide solutions to such problems. Meyer and Rowan argue that these institutional belief systems powerfully shape organizational forms:

> Many of the positions, policies, programs, and procedures of modern organizations are enforced by public opinion, by the views of important constituents, by knowledge legitimated through the educational system, by social prestige, by the laws, and by the definitions of negligence and prudence used by the courts. Such elements of formal structure are manifestations of powerful institutional rules which function as highly rationalized myths that are binding on particular organizations. (1977: 343)

Organizations receive support and legitimacy to the extent that they conform to contemporary norms—as determined by professional and scientific authorities—concerning the "appropriate" way to organize. These beliefs are so powerful that organizations that conform to them receive public support and confidence even in situations where no specific technical advantages are obtained.

The impact of institutional rules and constructs can be pursued at varying levels. In its broadest version, institutional theorists argue that for too long organizations have been thought to be somehow insulated from culture. The received wisdom, as set forth by the dominant rational system theorists, has it that organizations—in particular, organizations competing in the marketplace—are technical instruments rationally designed to accord with universal economic laws. It is, these theorists assert, the other parts of society—families, classes, political parties, churches, schools—that carry the cultural baggage. Organizations (except perhaps for their "soft underbelly" of workers who sometimes abide by collective norms or behave out of sentiment rather than self-interest) are viewed as embodying rational rather than cultural principles.

It is primarily due to the work of Peter Berger and colleagues (Berger and Luckmann, 1967; Berger, Berger, and Kellner, 1973) that institutionalists have slowly begun to advance the argument that the modern conception of rationality is itself a social and cultural construction—a collective, socially realized and enforced agreement emphasizing the value of identifying specific ends and developing explicit, formalized means for pursuing them. We social scientists have been slow to recognize, as Dobbin (1994a: 118) points out, "that rationalized organizational practices are essentially cultural, and are very much at the core of modern culture precisely because modern culture is organized around instrumental rationality." Lecturing to contemporary generations of students about norms of rationality is like lecturing to fish about water! From this highly general vantage point, organizations embody the primary values that distinguish modern cultural beliefs from earlier, more romantic or traditional forms. Organizations are the archetypes of modern societal forms. They are, as Zucker (1983: 13) argues, "the focal defining institution in modern society." In order to demonstrate that we are serious about achieving some goal or protecting some value, we must create an organization to symbolize our commitment.

Most institutional work does not go on at this rarified level, but rather at the sector or organizational field level where the effects of particular rules and belief systems governing, for example, medical care systems are contrasted with those operating at a different time or in a different field. A number of these studies are reviewed in subsequent chapters.

Institutional foundations of technical environments. As noted, the distinction between technical and institutional environments can mislead analysts to the extent that they mistakenly assume that technical considerations are independent of institutional arrangements. We emphasize that all organizations operate in institutional environments (but also that there are many kinds of institutional environments). And many aspects of technical environments and systems rest on institutional underpinnings. All technologies are shaped by social intentions and concerns, a point we amplify in Chapter 9. Even more generally, all exchange processes take place in markets that are themselves socially constructed. Rather than being "natural" processes or following universal economic principles, markets are embedded in a complex of institutional rules and practices: rules regarding private property, norms governing fair exchange, definitions concerning the rights and capacities of economic actors such as partnerships and corporations, beliefs regarding the appropriate role of the state in governing economic transactions, and so on (see Fligstein, 1990; Fligstein and Mara-Drita, 1996; Whitley, 1992c).

Accounting systems are one of the most important conventions connecting institutionally defined belief systems with technical activities. For modern organizations to exist and operate, there must be institutionalized arrangements by which diverse activities are codified and valorized. Accounting rules focus primarily on the definition and monetarization of work processes, technologies, and means-ends relationships (see Hopwood and Miller, 1994). Accounting rules evolve over time, shaped by the practices of individual firms, the activities of accounting professionals, and regulatory structures established by the state (see Mezias, 1990). Accounting conventions necessarily privilege some types of activities and information over others. Johnson and Kaplan (1987), for example, argue that current accounting practices in the United States have deflected the attention of managers from critical organizational operations to give undue emphasis to measures of short-term financial performance.

DiMaggio (1988) has asserted that institutional theorists tend to "defocalize" interests in explaining human behavior. By emphasizing norms and taken-for-granted assumptions guiding behavior, he suggests that institutional arguments give insufficient attention to the reality of purposive, interest-driven behavior.[5] By contrast, we prefer to emphasize not that institutional forces repress or replace interests but that they shape them. Institutional frameworks define the ends and shape the means by which interests are

---

[5]Early formulations by Meyer and Rowan (1977) and DiMaggio and Powell (1983) implied that institutional patterns operated in opposition or as alternatives to rational forces. More recent views, which we embrace, view rationality as defined within an institutional framework.

determined and pursued. They define whether actors can legitimately pursue profits or are governed by other incentives (for example, reelection, esteem, salvation). They furnish the "vocabularies of motives" as well as the modes of practice. Moreover, institutional theorists emphasize that the rules themselves are important types of resources and that those who shape them possess a valuable form of power (see Burns and Flam, 1986).

Technical and institutional controls. Recognizing that technical environments are framed and shaped by institutional forces, it is nonetheless useful to distinguish between the types of control associated with these two contexts. Technical environments allow the use of controls based on the characteristics of the outputs produced by organizational production systems. Products or services are produced that can be assessed in terms of their relative cost or quality, giving rise to *outcome controls*. These are the controls that we tend to associate with technical rationality. By contrast, institutional environments emphasize the extent to which the organization is conforming to the norms of formal rationality, the extent to which the appropriate processes are being carried out and suitable structures are in place. The use of these *procedural* and *structural controls* is intended to garner legitimacy and to guarantee accountablity. In these environments it is more difficult to assess outcomes independently of knowledge of the processes that produced them.

The distinctions between these types of controls are more useful if they are treated as dimensions along which environments vary, not as exclusive alternatives. The two dimensions tend to be negatively correlated, but only weakly so, so that various combinations and mixed cases exist. Hence, some types of environments place greater emphasis on technical outcome controls, and less on institutional process controls, whereas other organizations face more stringent process controls and weaker outcome controls. Still other organizations confront both strong outcome and process controls; and some organizations exist in environments in which they are subject to only weak controls of each type. Table 6–2 illustrates the typology that results when the varying strength of the two modes of control are cross-classified.

As suggested in Table 6–2, organizations such as utilities and banks are subject to strong institutional as well as strong technical pressures. On the one hand, there are requirements that utilities produce energy, water, and other basic commodities effectively and reliably; on the other hand, there are equally strong demands that they conform to regulations governing safety,

TABLE 6–2 Technical and Institutional Controls, with Illustrative Organizations

| | | Institutional Controls | |
		Stronger	Weaker
Technical Controls	Stronger	utilities banks general hospitals	general manufacturing pharmaceuticals
	Weaker	mental health clinics schools; legal agencies churches	restaurants health clubs child care

distribution, pricing, pollution control, employment practices, and so on. In general, organizations in this cell carry out tasks that combine complex technical requirements with a strong "public good" component. Because they confront strong demands of both types, these organizations tend to exhibit more complex administrative structures than those confronting only one set of controls. Most manufacturing and other commercial organizations operate in environments characterized by strong technical and weaker institutional pressures. They confront various health, safety and employment standards, but their major concern is to compete effectively in the marketplace.

Other types of organizations, such as mental health clinics, legal agencies, and schools are subject to stronger institutional but weaker technical pressures. They tend to be rewarded not for the quality of their outputs but primarily for their conformity to professional standards or legal requirements. Note, however, that current efforts are under way to utilize test scores to put greater pressures on schools to meet minimal outcome criteria.

Finally, some types of organizations operate in environments characterized by neither strong technical nor strong institutional controls. Health clubs and child-care centers provide examples of such forms. The institutional infrastructure needed to support these organizations is still under development. In general, organizations operating in these types of environments tend to be less stable and durable than organizations in the other sectors. As discussed in Chapter 7, organizations tend to form around either reliable technologies or highly institutionalized formal rules. The absence of both these conditions does not provide fertile ground for growing strong organizations.

One final comment: This typology of environmental dimensions ignores the possible play of power and politics. Some organizations in each type of environment achieve resources more by the exercise of power than by conformity to institutional demands or by superior performance.

Both technical and institutional environments shape organizational forms and influence organizational behavior. To this point, we have reviewed some of the more important distinctions, concepts, and dimensions identified by analysts attempting to capture salient features of organizational environments. In later chapters, we review specific predictions and empirical studies attempting to explain how these features of the environment influence organizational structure and performance.

THE INTERDEPENDENCE OF ORGANIZATIONS AND ENVIRONMENTS

Enactment, Attention, and Outcomes

In research on organizational environments, a healthy controversy has developed about the relative merits of employing subjective or perceptual versus objective measures of environmental characteristics. (For a review, see Boyd, Dess, and Rasheed, 1993.) This is not simply a measurement issue, but raises important theoretical questions concerning how organizations relate to their environments. A number of analysts (Dill, 1958; Lawrence and Lorsch, 1967; Duncan, 1972) argue that it makes sense to measure the environment in terms of the perceptions of participants, since only factors that they perceive can enter into their decision-making behavior. Weick's formulation is even stronger. He argues, as discussed in Chapter 4, that participants do not merely perceive and react but actively construct or "enact" their environments. Weick (1979: 164) insists that "the concept of an enacted environment is not synonymous with the concept of a perceived environment." Rather, the label "enactment" is meant "to emphasize that managers construct, rearrange, single out, and demolish many 'objective' features of their surroundings." The process of enacting is one in which "the subject partly interacts with and constitutes the object" (p. 165). The organization does more than observe and interpret: it modifies the environment. Whereas a resource dependence approach would emphasize the ability of an organization to purposively intervene in its environments, Weick stresses less conscious effects: "the unforeseen effects and the undesired, nonpursued consequences arising from action taken by the firm," including "self-fulfilling prophecies" and "the magnifying effects of small variations" (Grandori, 1987: 86).

March and colleagues build on this work by introducing the concept of attention structure, a specific and important way in which our rationality is bounded:

> Time and capabilities for attention are limited. Not everything can be attended to at once. Too many signals are received. Too many things are relevant to a decision. Because of these limitations, theories of decision making are often better described as theories of attention or search than as theories of choice. They are concerned with the way in which scarce attention is allocated. (March 1994: 10)

Among the factors identified as structuring the attention of decision makers are deadlines, initiatives of others, well-defined options, and evidence of failure. In addition to these more "rational" bases, attention is also greatly structured and constrained by the office or identity of the person choosing—do I define myself as a professional sociologist or as an employee of Stanford University—as well as by the rules thought to be applicable to the situation (see March and Olsen, 1989; Ocasio, 1997).

Much of the empirical research on the structuring of attention involves case studies of particular decisions (see for example, March and Olsen, 1976), but Sproull (1981) points out that studies of time allocation by managers are also quite germane. For example, in a very influential study, Mintzberg (1971; 1973) observed and systematically recorded the activities and interactions of the chief executive officer in five diverse organizations for one week each in order to answer the question "What do managers do?" Among the relevant findings, which have been replicated in similar studies, were that managers engage in multiple activities characterized by brevity, such that the manager "is forced to treat issues in an abrupt and superficial way" (1971: B100). Managers were also observed to rely primarily on verbal rather than written communications, which provided them with more timely information. Meetings, scheduled and unscheduled, consumed most of their time. Such findings reinforce the importance of attention structures in understanding how organizational participants enact their environments.

Pfeffer and Salancik emphasize the importance of organizational arrangements for structuring attention and extend them by stressing the significance of the development of specialized units and routines for collecting and processing information.

> The information system is conceptualized as the reports, statistics, facts, or information that are regularly collected and their pattern of transmission through the organization. The fact that certain information is regularly collected focuses the organization's attention on it. The collection of certain information occupies the time and attention of the organization, which necessarily restricts the time and attention devoted elsewhere. (1978: 74)

Some information is important simply because it is collected and, hence, available as an input to decision making. In this manner, information systems help to determine attention structures and enactment processes.

Stinchcombe (1990: 6) argues that organizational structures "grow" in directions determined by the "sources of news, news about uncertainties that most affect their outcomes." Since different organizations confront different kinds of uncertainties, Stinchcombe asserts that this is one of the major factors determining the structure of organizations. While this "postulate of rationality" may explain important differences we observe in organizational forms, we must take care not to overestimate the rationality of the information systems devised by organizations. Recall in this connection Boulding's (1956) typology of system levels described in Chapter 4. Organizations and their participants are capable of responding to their environments at levels 7 and 8 by creating complex consensual images of environmental processes as a basis for doing so. At the other end of the spectrum, organizations also devise and employ simple, tightly coupled mechanisms to track specific environmental variables.

Ashby (1952) stresses the adaptive behavior of which simple systems are capable as they monitor particular variables linked to one or a few response rules: witness the "intelligence" of the thermostat. Simon (1962) suggests two terms to distinguish between these lower- and higher-level responses. He proposes that a cybernetic response works on the principle of the *recipe*: feedback variables trigger the performance of a specified sequence of activities. Steinbruner amplifies:

> The simplest cybernetic mechanisms do not confront the issue of variety at all, for they make no calculations of the environment. The mechanisms merely track a few feedback variables and beyond that are perfectly blind to the environment. (1974: 57)

Organizational systems relying on recipes can perform effectively as long as the signals they track are reliable indicators of the true state of the variables of concern. However, such is often not the case, because of random error, changed circumstances, or deception. Under any of these circumstances, "smart" systems suddenly act quite stupidly.

By contrast, higher-level responses entail the construction of what Simon terms a *blueprint*—an image of the environment that attempts to capture and reflect its salient complexity. Thus, some information systems create vastly simplified pictures of environments whereas others attempt to more fully capture and codify its complexity. But whether the system is relying on recipes or blueprints, these theorists conclude that the environment of an organization is as much if not more a function of the organization, the cognitive work of its participants and their structure of attention, and its information system as it is of the external situation.

It is not necessary to embrace fully these phenomenological arguments to accept a related, but different point. Even if we prefer objective measures of an organization's environment, we must still take into account the characteristics and goals of the organization in order to evaluate what aspects of the external world are likely to be salient. If a church replaces a factory on the corner lot of a small town, the environments of the two types of organizations will not be very similar; each defines and functions in a different domain. The demands a specific organization makes on its environment, as well as the demands made by the environment on the organization, will vary with each type of organization.[6] Hence, one cannot describe "objectively" the environment of an organization without knowledge of the organization and the domain in which it functions.

Still, we do not want to conclude that all is perception and enactment. The environment of a given organization does vary in its stability, its complexity, its threat—and such matters can be assessed apart from ascertaining what participants believe to be the case. For example, one can examine the density of competing organizations, or count the number of hostile takeovers in an industry, or examine fluctations in profit margins over time. Participants may or may not attend to these matters, but this does not mean that what they don't know can't hurt (or help) them! Pfeffer and Salancik (1978: 62–63) correctly observe that although environments must be perceived in order to influence actions taken by organizational participants, they can influence organizational *outcomes* whether or not they have been perceived. Outcomes are results. Organizations produce *outputs*—goods and services—over whose characteristics they typically exercise considerable control, but outcomes represent the joint product of organizational performance and environmental response. The surgeon may perform flawlessly, but the patient may die; the automobile may be well built but fail to sell. In this sense, environments directly influence outcomes (see Chapter 13).

Thus, one's measurement strategy should depend on what is being predicted: measures based on the perceptions and reports of participants are necessary if we hope to predict their choices, but they are not sufficient if we wish to predict the outcomes of these choices, since outcomes are a product of multiple forces, many of which are outside the control of the organization.

---

[6]These demands also vary within organizational type. Churches vary in the types of parishioners to whom they appeal as well as the larger systems with which they affiliate. Such differences within specified types are the concern of "strategy" (see Chapter 11).

For example, perceptions of the market held by recording-studio executives can better predict what types of artists are given contracts than how well their records sell.

In Figure 6-1 we collect some of the distinctions we have described and depict their relations to one another. The result is a cycle of interdependence of organizations and environments. Beginning, arbitrarily, with the organizational structure, we argue that its decision makers determine a domain of operation, selecting what goods and services are to be produced for what types of consumers. Domain selection will strongly affect what types of information will be required. An information system is designed that, in turn, gives rise to an attention structure that will help to determine what participants in varying locations attend to and what importance is assigned to their concerns. The attention structure contributes to the creation of the enacted environment—the constructed (and reconstructed) picture that participants have of the environment to which they relate.

But these organizational processes do not take place in a vacuum. Starting at the opposite point in the cycle, the objective environment directly influences the enacted environment. Environmental factors can also be expected to command attention, and will shape the information system of the organization. The objective environment will also affect the domain definition. An organization may claim to be a day-care center or an automobile-repair shop, but others—clients, distributors, regulators—must acknowledge and endorse these claims for them to have "reality."

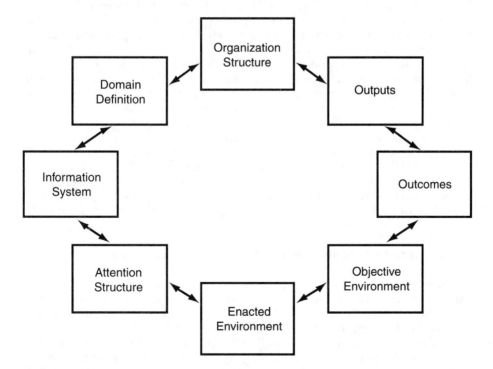

FIGURE 6–1 Organization-Environment Relations: A Cycle of Interdependence

Finally, as we have described, the environment can perform an "end run," influencing the structure of the organization indirectly by affecting its outcomes. Outcomes are joint products of organizational performance and environmental response.

Influence

To this point we have suggested that organizations and environments are interdependent in terms of information systems and cognitive processes, and in terms of environmental effects on organizational outcomes. They are also interdependent in more direct ways: organizations attempt to directly influence environments, and vice versa.

There is little doubt that environments profoundly shape organizations—their structures, their performances, their outcomes. How this occurs is subject to dispute. For example, contingency and resource dependence theorists argue that organizations consciously take steps to adapt to their environment, changing their structural features as required to better match its requirements. By contrast, population ecologists emphasize the structural inertia of organizations; they suggest that most organizations have great difficulty in changing their structures so that, if the environment changes, they fail and new organizational forms come into existence. Ecologists emphasize selection rather than adaptation processes (see Chapter 8).

Organizations are also recognized to influence their environments. Such effects are obvious in the case of large and powerful organizations, such as monopolies, but they can be observed in many other situations as well. Organizations attempt to influence demand for their products through advertising; they reduce some of the uncertainty they confront by entering into contracts with suppliers or wholesalers. They even change the boundaries separating them from the environment by entering into mergers or acquiring important competitors or exchange partners. They also attempt to influence their institutional environments: by lobbying for favorable legislation or against regulations; or by seeking the endorsement of a licensing or accrediting agency (see Chapter 8).

Perhaps most profoundly, organizations can and do select their environments. They can alter their product or service mix; they can exit one business and enter another, or diversify their operations by adding entirely new types of activities while retaining older types.

In sum, environments influence organizations but organizations also influence environments.

Absorption and Interpenetration

We have previously noted the open system assertion that the boundary separating the organization from its environment is somewhat arbitrarily drawn and varies with the flows or activities being examined. For example, if we wish to examine the authority system regulating faculty members at a university, we will want to include professional colleagues from other universities who serve as significant evaluators, helping to determine promotion and tenure decisions for the host school (see Hind, Dornbusch, and Scott, 1974; Clark,

1983). Thus, elements that for some purposes are usefully analyzed as parts of a system's environment are for other purposes included within the system itself.

Also, even arbitrary boundaries change over time. What today is a functioning system operating within the framework of a given organization may tomorrow be regarded as a service to be purchased. Universities, for example, may decide to "contract out" services such as building maintaintence or student health. On the other hand, if the service is viewed as critical, organizations are likely to attempt to acquire or absorb it, as discussed in Chapter 8. With increasing frequency, organizations acquire—and disaffiliate from—other systems. In this sense, organizational executives, like researchers, take a pragmatic view of the boundary separating their organization and its environment.

Even without "official" redefinitions, organizations constantly incorporate environmental elements into their own structures. In a fully developed open system conception, all of the "materials" used to create organizations—resources and equipment, but also personnel and procedures—are obtained from the environment. If we add to this the institutionalist ingredients—beliefs, meanings, conceptual categories, models for organizing—then it is no longer possible to think of the environment as something "out there"; its elements are part of the organization, not absorbed by it so that they become separated from the environment but interpenetrating it, infusing it with value, and connecting it with larger systems. Like most other ideas, however, these insights are better treated as variables: organizations are open systems, but some are more open than others.

The nested nature of organizational environments as well as the penetration of organizations by their environments raises serious problems for investigators who are trying to decide where to draw boundaries for analytical purposes (see Chapter 8). In studying educational systems, for example, is the proper unit of analysis the individual classroom, the individual school, the school district, or the state educational system? Clearly, there is no way to answer this question without knowing what processes or relations within the system are to be examined. There is always the danger that we will select the wrong unit of analysis for a given topic. We may elect to study the influence of teachers on curriculum and select a sample of classrooms, only to discover that the major curriculum choices are made at the district or state office. Such *specification* errors become more likely when the boundaries of systems are indefinite. The boundaries of many organizations are diffuse with respect to many processes and are variable with respect to space and time (see Freeman, 1978).

THE EVOLUTION OF ENVIRONMENTS

Is it possible to characterize the general direction of change taking place in the environments of organizations? Several theorists have offered their views on this important topic. Probably the most prevalent view is that first enunciated by Emery and Trist: "The environmental contexts in which organizations exist are themselves changing, at an increasing rate, and toward increasing complexity" (1965: 21). Except for noting that these conditions are occurring "under the impact of technological change" (p. 30), Emery and Trist are content to describe these developments rather than to explain them. Terreberry (1968) concurs with Emery and Trist's thesis, pointing out that organizations are open systems evolving from less to more complex states and since the environments of organizations predominately consist of other organizations, it follows that the environments of organizations are also becoming more complex.

There is no doubt that many organizations operate in very complex and uncertain environments. Perhaps the premier example is the multinational corporation, which must simultaneously operate in a number of global markets and in numerous host countries while, at the same time, confronting requirements to exhibit consistency among the various units of the enterprise (see Rosenzweig and Singh, 1991; Ghoshal and Westney, 1993).

However, we are not convinced by arguments that all environments of organizations are moving toward greater turbulence—increased uncertainty and interdependency. Although Terreberry is correct that open systems evolve from more to less complex states, increased complexity need not be synonymous with increased uncertainty. Indeed, as Galbraith (1967) and others have noted, differentiation permits specialization of function, and specialization, in turn, permits the application of scientific or engineering knowledge to the problem at hand. Thus, differentiation contributes to rationalization and routinization of a field of action and, in this manner, to increased certainty. Similarly, the spread of organizations into more arenas of activity often results in increased standardization and predictability. Why trust the uncertainty of small-town cuisine when you can count on the consistency of a Big Mac?

> On the modern McDonald's grills, winking lights tell countermen when to flip over the hamburger. . . . A small group of equipment makers furnished McDonald's with a stream of such continually updated gadgets designed to automate the serving and cooking of food to the ultimate degree: premeasured scoops, ketchup and mustard dispensers, computer-run fryers, infrared warning lights, instruments for testing the solidity of raw potatoes and the fluffiness of shakes. Nothing—as Hamburger Central proudly boasts—was left to chance. (Boas and Chain, 1977: 40–41)

Also, there is much evidence in the economics literature about the advantages that obtain to participants once industry standards are in place that allow firms to produce interchangeable components and benefit from network externalities (see Powell, 1991).

Increased certainty is produced not only by such technical "lock-in" processes, but also by the shared understandings, norms and rules created by institutional processes. Meyer (1978: 361, 363) argues that "in post-industrial societies, rationalized states expand their dominance over more and more aspects of social life, increasing centralization and homogeneity in these domains." He insists that through the creation of rationalized myths, institutional actors such as states and professional groups produce "vast new forms of certainty, which organizations may obtain by the mere process of conformity to environmental specifications." (See also, Meyer, 1994.)

Since Meyer stresses increased certainty in institutionalized environments, we will strike the opposing note. Although new laws, administrative agencies, and professional occupations are continually created, giving rise to new rationalized myths that provide a basis for organized action where none existed before, we should not overemphasize the amount of certainty that results. Laws are often ambiguous and variously interpreted, as Edelman (1992) reminds us. State and federal bureaus represent an increasingly vast and diverse collection of interests and programs that are often contradictory or competing, and professional occupations challenge one another's visions of truth (see Abbott, 1988).

While some arenas of organizational action are probably moving toward increasing certainty—whether because of the routinization of technical operations or the widespread acceptance of institutional rules—we also see evidence of increased uncertainty in many areas of social life. Given these contradictory processes—of standardization and rationalization on the one hand, and uncertainty and conflicting logics on the other—it seems inappropriate to make any assumption about the general direction of change in the environments within which organizations function. Empirical investigations, not a priori assumptions, should settle disputes over the rate and direction of environmental change.

SUMMARY

Determining how the environments of organizations can be usefully characterized and circumscribed is an issue that confronts analysts embracing the open system perspective. Conceptions of environments vary by level of analysis as well as by substantive focus. Analysis levels include the organizational set, organizational population, interorganizational community, and organizational field. Each focuses on a somewhat different aspect of organization-environment relations, and each is associated with different theoretical perspectives.

Analysts examining environments also differ in substantive interests. A great deal of research has been devoted to the technical aspects of environments—the ways in which stocks of resources and sources of information are distributed and arranged. More recently, investigators have pursued institutional features of environments, studying how regulative, normative, and cultural-cognitive systems shape organizational structures and activities. And, we have argued, institutional features shape and frame technical components of organizations.

Organizations are viewed as interdependent with environments in a number of senses. Participants' perceptions of their environments together with the attention structures of organizations result in enacted environments that are products of both environmental features and organizational information systems. Environments directly affect organizational outcomes, which in turn affect subsequent perceptions and decisions. Environments influence organizations, but organizations also modify and select their environments.

And environments supply the materials and ingredients of which organizations are composed.

Most observers argue that the environments of organizations are becoming more complex and uncertain over time. The increasing differentiation and interconnectedness of organizations cause increased uncertainty and interdependency for them. But other processes—routinization, standardization, the creation of rationalized myths—create new islands of certainty. We conclude that the extent and the direction of change in the environments of organizations is a matter to be settled not by assumption but by empirical investigation.

Creating Organizations

Questions about the diversity of organizations in society might seem to have only academic interest. In fact, these issues bear directly on important social issues. Perhaps the most important is the capacity of a society to respond to uncertain future changes. Organizational diversity within any realm of activity, such as medical care, microelectronics production, or scientific research, constitutes a repository of alternative solutions to the problem of producing sets of collective outcomes. These solutions are embedded in organizational structures and strategies. . . .

    A stock of alternative forms has value for a society whenever the future is uncertain. A society that relies on a few organizational forms may thrive for a time; but once the environment changes, such a society faces serious problems until existing organizations are reshaped or new organizational forms are created.

Michael T. Hannan and John Freeman (1989)

In this chapter we attempt to explain how and why organizations come into existence. It is helpful to separate this broad question into three categories of more specific questions. The first deals with the emergence of organizations as a distinctive type of collectivity. This category subsumes such questions as these: Have organizations always existed? If not, when did they first emerge? What are the social conditions under which organizations develop? What alternatives to organizations exist for carrying out complex tasks? It will quickly become apparent that "authorities differ" in the answers they give to these and related questions. In particular, we contrast the views of rational system theorists with those of natural system theorists.

    The second set of questions assumes the existence of organizations as one general type of social arrangement and asks how new and different types of organizations emerge. Whether defined more broadly as new industries or more specifically as new populations of organizations, this question has received increased attention from organization researchers in recent years. Questions asked about new forms of organizations include the following: What are the social conditions that give rise to new types of organizations? Why are many organizations of the same general type founded during specific periods? Do the growth patterns of new types of organizations exhibit a common pattern?

A third cluster of questions concerns the founding of a specific organization. What do we know about the entrepreneurs that are willing to assume the risks of creating a new organization? What means do organizations use to induce participants to contribute resources to them? What effects are associated with the use of particular types of incentives or with the recruitment of particular types of participants? How do the resource needs of organizations vary by type of organization and by time and place? Although such questions cannot be definitively answered, they serve to focus the discussion and point to areas of needed work.

THE EMERGENCE OF ORGANIZATIONS

It is only in modern, industrialized societies that organizations dominate the landscape. Their emergence, proliferation, and consolidation as a ubiquitous and significant building block of society is one of the great social transformations that distinguishes the modern from the premodern world. In a quite literal sense, the history of the development of modern society is also a history of the development of special-purpose organizations: organizations both were created by and helped to produce these changes. We shall not attempt to recount here this vast and complex history but will only note some of the changes scholars have identified as among the most fateful for the development of organizations.

The Changing Relations of Individual and Corporate Actors

When we speak of the emergence of organizations, we are not implying that previous societal arrangements exhibited disorganization. Indeed, in important ways some of the preexisting social systems exhibited higher degrees of order! The correct contrast, then, is between different types of ordered social arrangements. The principal ways in which modern social structures differ from earlier, traditional forms are (1) in the relation of individual actors to corporate actors, and (2) in the relation of corporate actors to one another.

Coleman's (1974; 1990: 531–52) analysis of these differences is most illuminating. Examining the corporate bodies of the Middle Ages, he observes that the basic units—the manor, the guild, the village—wholly contained their members and possessed full authority over them. What rights and interests individuals possessed, they acquired from their membership in these units. (Note that these bodies are the patrimonial systems dissected by Weber, as described in Chapter 2.) Moreover, the corporate actors were themselves organized in a strict hierarchy, the subordinate units being responsible to and contained within superordinate systems in a concentric pattern (see Simmel, 1955 trans.).

Gradually and fitfully, over several centuries, these relations were altered. Individuals were able to acquire rights and were recognized to have interests, and corporate actors were allowed to acquire rights and to pursue interests that were not simply aggregates of the interests of their members. Coleman summarizes these developments:

> Two things happened. First, men themselves began to break out of their fixed estates, began to have rights to appear before the king's court, rights to make contracts on their own; became, in effect, persons before the law with a certain set of rights (elevated by seventeenth-century philosophers to the status of "natural rights") to engage in a variety of activities at their own pleasure. But second, and as a direct consequence of this fragmentation of the feudal structure, a different kind of intermediate organization arose in society: a corporate actor which had, under charter from the king, a variety of rights to free and expansive action. This new corporate actor became the instrument through which men could jointly exercise their new-found rights. (Coleman, 1974: 28)

Under these altered conditions, corporate actors no longer contained their individual members but only the specific resources invested in them by persons acting as owners or investors; and they no longer fully controlled their members but only the specific behaviors contracted for by persons who agreed to function as their participants or agents. Individuals were only partially involved in these new organizations. Also, these organizations were no longer arranged in a concentric, hierarchical pattern, but were allowed to function somewhat independently of one another, competing for the loyalties and resources of individuals.

Coleman emphasizes the impact of individualism on the development of special-purpose organizations. Simmel (1955 trans.) in his brilliant essay "The Web of Group-Affiliations" stresses the reverse effect. When social arrangements consist of layers of concentrically related systems, the social spaces created tend to produce homogeneous individuals: batches of individuals are likely to share the same social location and perceive themselves as holding the same social identity. However, as social arrangements shift to contain overlapping and intersecting systems, a vastly increased variety of social spaces is created, and no two individuals are as likely to share the same social location or to hold the same social identity. As Simmel explains:

> The groups with which the individual is affiliated constitute a system of coordinates, as it were, such that each new group with which he becomes affiliated circumscribes him more exactly and more unambiguously. To belong to any one of these groups leaves the individual considerable leeway. But the larger the number of groups to which an individual belongs, the more improbable is it that other persons will exhibit the same combination of group-affiliations, that these particular groups will "intersect" once again in a second individual.
>
> . . . As individuals, we form the personality out of particular elements of life, each of which has arisen from, or is interwoven with, society. This personality is subjectivity par excellence in the sense that it combines the elements of culture in an individual manner. . . . As the person becomes affiliated with a social group, he surrenders himself to it. A synthesis of such subjective affiliations

creates a group in an objective sense. But the person also regains his individuality, because his pattern of participation is unique; hence the fact of multiple group-participation creates in turn a new subjective element. (1955 trans.: 140–41)

Combining the insights of Coleman and Simmel, we conclude that there was an intimate, reciprocal, supportive relation between the emergence of individualism and the development of special-purpose organizations. Given this historical association, it is somewhat ironic that numerous commentators in our own time perceive organizations as the enemy of individualism. (We explore this paradox in Chapter 12.)

Societal Conditions Favoring the Development of Organizations

Thus far we have described some quite basic changes in societal arrangements without attempting to determine what brought these changes about. Drawing on the insights of Weber, Durkheim (1949 trans.), and other social theorists, Stinchcombe (1965) suggests that the capacity of a population to develop and support special-purpose organizations is determined by such general factors as widespread literacy and specialized advanced schooling, urbanization, a money economy, and political revolution. To these primarily economic and political factors, theorists such as Eisenstadt (1958) and Parsons (1966) add institutional and normative variables such as increased role and institutional differentiation, allocation of roles by universalistic and achievement rather than particularistic and ascriptive criteria, and increased dissensus among societal groups concerning the priority of goals, together with competition among them for resources. Eisenstadt concludes, "The most important characteristics of the environment conducive to the development of bureaucracies are first, the availability of various 'free-floating' resources, and second, the development of several centres of power which compete over such resources" (1958: 111). To these characteristics, Parsons (1960: 20–21) adds that societal environments support the emergence of organizations by legitimating their specialized functions and independent existence.

These arguments are all at a very general level: most of them describe conditions that are conducive to rationalization of the social structure in general and do not point specifically to conditions favoring the creation of organizations. Stinchcombe (1965: 146–50) recognizes this problem and has attempted to construct more specific arguments that relate these general conditions to the creation of organizations through intermediate variables. He suggests that such general societal factors influence the development of organizations (1) by motivating individuals to form and join such social units, and (2) by improving the chances that these units, once formed, will survive. Thus, individuals are motivated to join organizations by increased literacy, which facilitates the learning of new roles and the keeping of rules and records; by urbanization, which increases social differentiation and encourages the formation of mechanisms for regularizing relations among strangers; by a money economy, which liberates resources, depersonalizes economic relations, and simplifies the calculation of benefits and future conditions; and by political revolutions, which dislodge vested interests and loosen resources for new uses. These same social conditions also improve the likelihood of survival of newly formed organizations. Stinchcombe asserts that organizations suffer the *liability of newness*: new organizations and in particular new forms of organization are likely to fail. New organizations require the creation and learning of new roles, reliance on strangers, and the generation of new markets and customer ties.

Although somewhat more specific, these arguments can still be sharpened. However, in doing so, we encounter once again the contrasting assumptions and arguments associated with the rational and the natural system views of the nature of organizations.

Rational System Explanations of the Origin of Organizations

Dividing labor. Certainly the most widely accepted and one of the most compelling arguments concerning the origins of organizations ties their emergence to the division of labor. The classic statement of this argument was provided by Adam Smith in 1776 in his celebrated account of the manufacture of pins. Smith observed that whereas an untrained worker without the proper machinery could "scarce, perhaps, with his utmost industry, make one pin in a day," vastly different results obtain when the work is properly divided into a number of branches.

> One man draws out the wire, another straights it, a third cuts it, a fourth points it, a fifth grinds it at the top for receiving the head; to make the head requires two or three distinct operations; to put it on is a peculiar business, to whiten the pins is another; it is even a trade by itself to put them into the paper; and the important business of making a pin is, in this manner, divided into about eighteen distinct operations. (Smith, 1957 ed.: 2)

So arranged, ten persons "could make among them upwards of forty-eight thousand pins a day."

This miracle of productivity is accomplished primarily by the application of technology to the work process. As Galbraith explains, "technology means the systematic application of scientific or other organized knowledge to practical tasks." This is possible only when the tasks are divided into their components in such a manner that they become "coterminous with some established area of scientific or engineering knowledge" (1967: 24). In addition to this prime benefit, specialization within the workforce allows the organization to take advantage of particular skills possessed by a member and also fosters the development of such skills through repetition and learning. And to the extent that the various skills required are of differential complexity, variable pay scales may be introduced, so that further economies are realized through task subdivision (Braverman, 1974: 79).

A related process, "agglomeration"—the gathering of workers together in a common location—was encouraged by the use of common energy sources, first water power, later steam engines (see Rosenberg and Birdzell, 1986). This, in turn, resulted in a more efficient and effective use of energy, centralized locations for shipping and receiving of raw materials and products, and economies of scale. Moreover, concentration of workers increased the observability of labor and allowed increased supervision and control, including the imposition of specified work hours and schedules (see E. P. Thompson, 1967).

These types of changes—the division of labor, advances in technology, agglomeration of the workforce in factories—are all associated with the general process of industrialization. In an influential volume, Kerr and his colleagues (1964) attempt to identify a set of developments that are generic to the process of industrialization as well as to examine specific variants of the process that occur under differing societal and cultural conditions. Among the universal consequences, they include the creation of organizations. "The technology and specialization of the industrial society," they assert, "are necessarily and distinctively associated with large-scale organizations" (p. 21). Rosenberg and Birdzell (1986: 145) also emphasize the import of "the change in the organization of production from the artisan's shop to the factory" as one of the most critical factors in advancing industrialization.

However, it is not only production organizations that are associated with work division and specialization. As we already know, Weber advanced similar arguments for systems of political administration. His ideal-type conception of bureaucracy places great emphasis on technical expertise and a fixed division of labor among officials. And he was quite explicit that this form replaced earlier, more traditional social structures because of its greater efficiency.

> Experience tends universally to show that the purely bureaucratic type of administrative organization . . . is, from a purely technical point of view, capable of attaining the highest degree of efficiency and is in this sense formally the most rational known means of exercising authority over human beings. It is superior to any other form in precision, in stability, in the stringency of its discipline, and in its reliability. (Weber, 1947 trans.: 337)

Giddens correctly notes the extent to which Weber's conception draws on technical and mechanical imagery:

> Weber's talk of "precision," "stability" and "reliability" points to the direct connection between bureaucracy and mechanisation that he sometimes makes quite explicit. Bureaucracy, he says, is a "human machine": the formal rationality of technique applies with equal relevance to human social organisation as to the control of the material world. (1983: 202)

On the other hand, work division entails overhead costs. Someone must design the work segments and someone must control and coordinate the divided work. A horizontal division of labor is usually accompanied by a vertical hierarchy providing oversight over those engaged in tasks of production. Also, the technologies associated with high levels of specialization are likely to be special-purpose machinery of a sort that is dedicated to the production of particular products. Such machines increase the rigidity of production so that long-term productivity requires the continuing expansion of markets for uniform goods (see Piore and Sable, 1984: 26–28).

According to these well-known arguments, the division of labor supports the application of technology or rationalized procedures to work, increases the scale of work organizations and of markets, and gives rise to a managerial hierarchy. These developments occur because they are associated with increasing productivity and with heightened efficiency of operations. Rational system analysts assume that they are fundamental to the appearance and growth of organizations. As the administrative theorist Luther Gulick concludes, "work division is the foundation of organization; indeed, the reason for organization" (Gulick and Urwick, 1937: 3).

Reducing transaction costs. As noted in Chapter 5, a more recent rational (and open) system perspective provides an alternative explanation for the emergence of organizations. This approach, first proposed by Coase (1937) but revived and extended by Williamson (1975; 1985; 1994), shifts attention from technology and production costs to transactions costs—the costs associated with reaching and policing agreements about the exchange of goods and services between persons or across boundaries. The typical neoclassical economic model conceived of firms as systems for managing production functions, with the primary decisions focused on the optimal mix of production factors—resources, labor, capital. In this model, variations in organizational structure are largely irrelevant. By contrast, the transactions costs perspective assumes that the major obstacle to creating wealth is getting individuals to cooperate—to agree to and abide by the terms of exchange. These costs range from those of obtaining information (about quality, alternatives, and so on), negotiating agreements, policing agreements, to settling disputes. Hence, this approach emphasizes the importance of the structures that govern these exchanges. Two broad types of governance structures are contrasted: the market and the organization (hierarchy).

In a market system, exchanges occur between buyers and sellers based on negotiated contractual agreements. These transactions are governed by the price system, which, in aggregate, provides a set of signals concerning what goods and services in what quantity are desired and hence profitable to produce. It is presumed that all parties are governed by self-interest. Several advantages are associated with a market arrangement as a basis for organizing transactions. Adam Smith (1957 ed.) was among the first to note that relatively little knowledge is required by the participants in such transactions. Assuming that individuals know their own preferences, price signals provide a comparatively simple basis on which to make decisions. And, as symbolized by Smith's famous simile of the "invisible hand," market and pricing mechanisms provide an overall basis for coordinating individual actions. Hence, it is not necessary to expend resources specifically to achieve coordination; no administrative overhead is required for planning, collective decision making, or control.[1]

Simple market transactions work well as a framework for *spot contracts*—contracts in which all obligations are fulfilled on the spot, such as

---

[1]But, as noted in Chapter 6, markets require institutional supports; in the simpler cases, shared norms and conventions will suffice; in the more complex, more formal governance mechanisms are required, often backed by state power.

the exchange of money for a commodity in hand. They fare less well when the transactions involve future values. When goods or services are not to be delivered on the spot, but at some future time, it is often possible to draw up a *contingent claims contract*. Such a document specifies the obligations of each party to the exchange, contingent upon possible future developments. For example, a farmer may agree to sell his grain to a warehouse if the price does not drop below a specified amount per ton. But as the future becomes more complex or uncertain, it becomes increasingly difficult and costly to draw up contracts that take into account all possible contingencies. In such circumstances, organizations are likely to be viewed as attractive alternatives to market-mediated transactions.

Arrow asserts that "organizations are a means of achieving the benefits of collective action in situations in which the price system fails" (1974: 33). The price system, viewed as a mechanism for the efficient allocation of personnel and resources to production tasks, fails when confronted with very complex relations among these factors or with uncertainty concerning future conditions. As such complexity and uncertainty increases, more information must be processed in order for contracts to be negotiated and transactions conducted. Both Arrow and Williamson conclude that organizations are superior to markets in managing complex and uncertain economic transactions because—and to the extent that—they reduce the cost of such transactions.

Williamson (1975) elaborates the argument by developing an elegant and simple model of the conditions under which markets tend to give way to organizations.[2] The basic elements of the model appear in Figure 7–1. Williamson uses the concept of bounded rationality simply to refer to the limitations of individuals as information processors. The cognitive limitations of individuals were noted by Simon (1976) and have already been described in Chapter 2. Williamson adds the idea that it is only under certain environmental conditions that an individual's cognitive capacities are insufficient. It is the coupling of cognitive limitations with high levels of uncertainty and complexity that encourage individuals to move the affected transactions out of markets and into organizations.

How do organizations help us when the factors of bounded rationality are coupled with uncertainty and complexity? We have already described, in Chapter 2, the ways in which organizational structures shore up individual cognitive activities. Simon's framework is the relevant one: the organization supports the subdivision of problems, simplifies choices, channels information, and restricts alternatives. Goal specificity and formalization overcome the cognitive limitations of individual actors. As Simon asserts:

> It is now clear that the elaborate organizations that human beings have constructed in the modern world to carry out the work of production and government can only be understood as machinery for coping with the limits of man's

---

[2]Williamson's terminology differs from our own and can cause confusion on first reading. He employs the term *organization* to refer to any social arrangement within which transactions are conducted. Thus, markets as well as organizations in our sense are regarded as organizations. This is why Williamson's discussion of the limitations of markets is presented in terms of an "organizational failures framework." Williamson's terms for organizations in our sense are, variously, *internal organizations, hierarchies,* and *firms.*

Human Factors	Environmental Factors	Organizational Solutions
Bounded rationality	Complexity	Support for decision making
	Uncertainty	Incomplete contracts
Opportunism	Few alternative partners	Auditing and control systems
		Incentives for contributing and cooperating

FIGURE 7–1 Organizational Solutions to Market Failures. *Source:* Adapted from Williamson (1975), Figure 3, p. 40.

abilities to comprehend and compute in the face of complexity and uncertainty. (1979: 501)

Simplifying and supporting decision making is particularly useful when confronting complexity. Uncertainty, by contrast, encourages the use of what economists term "incomplete contracts." These are agreements that replace the detailed and specific contracts that would be required to support transactions in the marketplace with a diffuse, open-ended contract: in short, the *employment contract.* The great institutional economist John Commons first called attention to the special nature of this contract, noting that what the worker sells "when he sells his labor is his willingness to use his faculties according to a purpose that has been pointed out to him. He sells his promise to obey commands" (1924: 284). Under conditions of uncertainty, the advantages of this open-ended contract are obvious: obedience is promised to a general range of commands,[3] the specific command being determined by the variable and unpredictable requirements of the changing situation.

Williamson uses the second pair of concepts in Figure 7–1—opportunism and few partners—to develop a different argument regarding the relative advantages of markets and organizations. Opportunism is revealed in individual actors who are capable of "self-interest seeking with guile" and of making "self-disbelieved threats and promises" (Williamson, 1975: 26). In short, some people lie, cheat, and steal! Those of us who are honest will try to avoid entering into transactions with these disreputable types, but we may have no choice if we are faced with a small-numbers condition—that is, few alternative exchange partners. Williamson cogently notes that many situations not characterized in the beginning by a small number of alternative partners may become so as transactions progress, because of first-mover advantages, natural monopolies, and the dependencies that develop over time when one party relies on another to provide specialized services.

---

[3]The range of commands that will be obeyed automatically in any organizational situation is, of course, restricted. Ordinarily a supervisor does not have the right to tell an employee to perform personal services or to carry out activities beyond those specified in the job description. These boundaries are also influenced by generalized social beliefs. For example, some contemporary secretaries have decided that making coffee is outside their appropriate job definition. Barnard refers to the arena within which employees will unquestioningly comply with directives as the *zone of indifference* (1938: 168–69); Simon refers to the same concept as the *zone of acceptance* (1976: 12).

The creation of organizations helps to solve the problem of opportunism among exchange partners. By bringing economic exchanges under a hierarchical structure, organizations can construct better auditing and surveillance systems. Also, incentive systems within an organization can be arranged so that individual participants are discouraged from behaving opportunistically. Further, arrangements by which individual performance can be more closely monitored are especially helpful when the work involves nonseparabilities—products of highly interdependent teams such that it is difficult to determine who has made what contributions. When outputs involve nonseparabilities, it is useful to be able to inspect inputs (see Alchian and Demsetz, 1972).

The transaction cost framework provides a general explanation for the origins of organizations as mechanisms for supporting decisions under conditions of uncertainty and suppressing opportunism under conditions of restricted exchange. It is also used to explain how specific organizations determine their boundaries and design their governance systems, but these matters are reserved for later chapters. The transaction cost approach, like other economic explanations, focuses primarily on efficiency. Governance structures, including markets, organizations, and various "hybrid" structures, are compared and assessed "in terms of their capacities to economize on transaction costs" (Williamson, 1981: 549; see also, Williamson, 1991). Such arguments reside within the rational system perspective.

Williamson's arguments have received much attention, both supportive and critical (see Francis, Turk, and Willman, 1983; Milgrom and Roberts, 1992). Since we elaborate these arguments in subsequent chapters, we note at this point only two general criticisms. One concerns the logical status of the type of explanation developed by Williamson and other institutional economists of the development of institutional structures. Oberschall and Leifer characterize their arguments as "the reverse of the functionalist mode":

> The functionalist starts at the societal or aggregate level and ends up analyzing individual behavior as it conforms to institutions. . . . The economist starts with individual wants and ends up analyzing institutions that produce social welfare and satisfy individual wants. (1986: 236)

To show that an institution functions to reduce transactions costs for individual actors does not explain how that institution came into being. A second issue is raised by Granovetter (1985), who asserts that conceptual frameworks such as Williamson's underestimate the extent to which economic behavior is embedded in a matrix of social relations. Opportunism, for example, should not be viewed as a constant, but as varying across different social situations. Overlooking the matrix of social relations surrounding all activities—including economic—causes the economist to overstate both the extent to which explicit contracts are required to govern economic behavior in the market and the effectiveness of hierarchical controls and incentive systems within the organization. We return to this issue in later chapters.

Efficient information processing.   Yet another explanation for the emergence of the organization is its superior capacity to manage flows of information. A hierarchical structure incorporates several features—including status distinctions and power differences among positions—but among its most significant components is a centralized communication system. What, if any, are the advantages of carrying on work within a hierarchical structure—specifically, a centralized communication structure—compared with a more informal and equalitarian arrangement? Experiments on communication structures conducted during the 1950s and 1960s examined the effects of centralized versus decentralized communication networks on the task performance of groups.[4] In a technique developed by Bavelas (1951), a small number of individuals are placed in cubicles and allowed to communicate only by means of written messages passed through slots in the cubicle walls. The slots connecting each cubicle can be opened or closed by the experimenter, so that differing communication patterns can be imposed on the interacting subjects. The most frequently studied communication networks are diagramed in Figure 7–2. The circle and all-channel networks are relatively decentralized communication structures; the chain and, particularly,

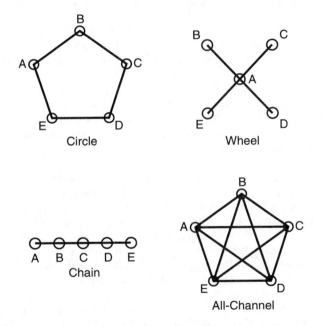

Circle

Wheel

Chain

All-Channel

FIGURE 7–2 Examples of Communication Networks (five-person groups)

[4]Some analysts are reluctant to generalize from findings based on "artificial" experiments to behavior in real-world organizations. However, we believe that, interpreted with caution, results from experimental studies can aid our understanding of natural phenomena. The great advantage of experimental settings is that they permit investigators to isolate certain variables from others whose presence may influence the effects being observed (see Zelditch, 1969). We just noted that hierarchies in organizations contain a number of elements only one of which defines the formal structuring of communication flows. Experiments allow us to examine the effects of these structured flows independently of those produced by formal status and power differences.

the wheel are more highly centralized. A typical task presented to groups placed in these networks is to provide each individual with a card containing several symbols, only one of which is present on the cards of all subjects, and ask all participants to identify the common symbol. Most researchers using this type of task report that groups working in more centralized structures are more efficient in their performance, as measured by the speed of attaining a solution or the number of messages transmitted to arrive at a solution, than groups in more decentralized structures (see Leavitt, 1951; Guetzkow and Simon, 1955).

Vroom accounts for these findings as follows:

> The centralized structures more rapidly organize to solve the problems. Participants in peripheral positions send information to the center of the network, where a decision is made and sent out to the periphery. Furthermore, this pattern of organization tends to be highly stable once developed. In less centralized structures the organization problem is more difficult and observed interaction patterns are less stable, as well as less efficient. (Vroom, 1969: 242)

Vroom stresses the functions of formalization, as discussed in Chapter 2. Arrow embraces the same conclusion, but his arguments concerning the superiority of centralized networks are based on efficiency of information processing:

> Since transmission of information is costly, in the sense of using resources, especially the time of individuals, it is cheaper and more efficient to transmit all the pieces of information once to a central place than to disseminate each of them to everyone. (Arrow, 1974: 68)

Noting that the gathering of information is also essential to arriving at a decision, Arrow applies the same arguments to this process, concluding, "Thus, authority, the centralization of decision-making, serves to economize on the transmission and handling of information" (Arrow, 1974: 69).

Williamson (1975:41–54) agrees that hierarchies are superior to peer groups or other types of decentralized communication networks in the economies of information flows effected. In addition, he asserts that the use of hierarchies reduces the likelihood of opportunistic behavior by improving surveillance of individual performance.

It would be incorrect, however, to conclude that hierarchies are superior to more decentralized or equalitarian arrangements under all conditions. Other studies employing the Bavelas networks have introduced more complex tasks—for example, mathematical problems—or provided subjects with more ambiguous information to process—for example, asking them to identify similar colors when the samples provided include unusual colors for which there are no common names (Shaw, 1954; Christie, Luce, and Macy, 1952). Such studies show that as tasks become more complex or ambiguous, decentralized nets are usually superior to centralized structures (Shaw, 1964). Note that these are the same conclusions reached by Burns and Stalker (1961) in their association of organic structures with innovation and mechanical structures with routine tasks.

Reviewing these communication-network studies, Blau and I (Blau and Scott, 1962: 116–28) concluded that formal hierarchies aid the performance of tasks requiring the efficient coordination of information and routine decision making, but they interfere with tasks presenting very complex or ambiguous problems. Specifically, we argued that hierarchies impede work on the latter by stifling free interactions that can result in error correction, by undermining the social support necessary to encourage all participants to propose solutions, and by reducing incentives for participants to search for solutions.

More generally, there appears to be a curvilinear relation between information-processing requirements and the utility of hierarchy. When little information is to be processed, there are no particular advantages to hierarchy and some clear disadvantages (for example, higher administrative overhead). As information-processing needs increase up to a certain point, hierarchies can be of benefit, reducing transmission costs and ensuring coordination. But as information-processing needs continue to increase, hierarchies become overloaded and the intellectual resources of peripheral participants underutilized. Such increased demands do not require a return to informal systems, but they do encourage the creation of more decentralized structures. (Specific types of decentralization strategies are described in Chapter 9.)

The same type of argument can be made with respect to the relation between surveillance requirements and hierarchies. The creation of hierarchies can result in improved surveillance and control of participants up to a point, but if extraordinary demands are required for secrecy or loyalty, formal hierarchical surveillance may have to be supplemented or replaced by clan systems relying on more diffuse, internalized controls (see Ouchi, 1980). For example, organizations confronting hostile environments, such as the FBI or the Mafia, are likely to rely heavily on procedures that induce a strong personal commitment (see Wilson, 1978) or on the creation of diffuse interpersonal ties (see Ianni, 1972) to effect tight controls (see Chapter 11).

New information technologies, which make possible all-channel connections such as electronic mail and the World Wide Web pose interesting problems for conventional, hierarchical organizations. While the use of e-mail has been demonstrated to influence the flow and direction of communication in organizations, studies also show that norms, both formal and informal, arise to prevent it from disrupting existing status and authority systems (see Sproull and Kiesler, 1991). Like all technologies, information technology is too often treated simply as a fixed input that determines human use rather than as a cluster of constraints and possibilities that requires interpretation and learning, and whose effects will vary across actors and situations (see Shulman, 1996; see also, Chapter 9).

We turn now, briefly, to consider one additional explanation for the existence of organizations from a rational system perspective.

Monitoring agents. In an approach closely related to transaction cost analysis, a number of microeconomists have developed "agency theory" explanations for the existence of hierarchical arrangements for carrying out cooperative tasks (see Jensen and Meckling, 1976).[5] When two or more people contribute to a common activity, how can each be certain that the other is doing his fair share? The language employed by agency theory pertains to the situation—one that is basic to the structure of all organizations—in which one party, termed the "principal," seeks to achieve some outcome but requires the assistance of another, the "agent," to carry out the necessary activities. Stockholder-manager and supervisor-worker are examples of principal-agent relations. It is assumed that both parties are motivated by self-interest, and that these interests may diverge.

> The challenge in the agency relationship arises whenever—which is almost always—the principal cannot perfectly and costlessly monitor the agent's action and information. The problems of inducement and enforcement then come to the fore. (Pratt and Zeckhauser, 1985)

That is, agents almost always know more about their tasks than do their principals—the problem of *information asymmetry*. Because their interests may not coincide, principals seek to gather information (for example, by inspection or evaluation), and they seek to design an incentive system such that agents will be rewarded to the extent that they pursue the principal's interests. The establishment of information and control systems is itself costly, so the design problem that agency theorists pose is how to structure effective control and incentive systems in such a manner as to minimize their costs. Different types of work situations that entail varying modes of risk sharing require different types of contracts.[6] But, in general, from an agency theory perspective, organizations emerge to support and sustain systems of complex cooperation.

To summarize the rational system perspectives on creating organizations, from Smith and Coase to Arrow, Demsetz, and Williamson, there is general agreement that organizations are called into existence by the increasing need to coordinate and control complex administrative and technical tasks and transactions. Enlarged political states, expanding markets, and improved technologies both require and are made possible by the development of organizations that can manage complex exchanges and coordinate diverse, interrelated activities.

[5] Williamson (1985: 26) describes agency theory as one of the two major branches of the "new institutional economics," the other dealing with transaction costs. Both emphasize efficiency-maximizing explanations of social arrangements, but agency theory focuses on *ex anti* (before the fact) "incentive alignments."

[6] If the behavior of agents can be readily monitored, then incentives are likely to be based on conformity to performance programs. For example, research by Eisenhardt (1988) reports that for salespersons in retail stores, the more routine (programmed) the job and the smaller the span of control, the more likely that workers were compensated by salary rather than by commission. If behavior is difficult to observe or to evaluate, then commissions—which align the interests of agents and principals—are more likely to be used.

Natural System Explanations of the Origins of Organizations

Institutional explanations. As described in Chapters 5 and 6, institutional theorists emphasize the extent to which the world is a product of our ideas and conceptions—the socially created and validated meanings that define social reality. Associated with the rise of the modern world is not only a set of production technologies and administrative structures for coordinating complex activities but also the growth of certain beliefs and cognitions about the nature of the world and the way in which things work. Technology and bureaucracy are more than hardware and filing cabinets filled with papers: they are new states of consciousness. The concomitants of technological production at the level of consciousness include the belief that the work process has a machinelike functionality, that all actions within the process are reproducible, that productive activity entails participation in a large organization and in a sequence of production, that the work being performed is measurable, and so on. Similarly, bureaucracy connotes distinctive spheres of competence, the importance of proper procedures, orderliness, predictability, and an attitude of "moralized anonymity" (Berger, Berger, and Kellner, 1973: 23–62).

While technical explanations for the existence of organizations stress their contributions to efficiency and reliability in the production of goods and services, institutional explanations stress that they provide accountability (see Hannan and Carroll, 1995; see also, Chapter 1). Conforming to authorized structures and to certified procedures—regardless of their outcomes—provides a rationale and justification to organizational participants. Formal rationality often stands in for functional rationality.

Rationalized beliefs are widely held by people in modern society and are continually being created and reinforced by a wide range of corporate actors and forces: universities, professional groups, public opinion, the mass media, the regulative and legislative arms of the state. Thus, these beliefs do not exist merely as general values that support organizations, but take on very specific and powerful forms in a variety of guises—as professional expertise, as procedural rules, and as legal requirements.

Someplace between the general concept of a formal organization and a particular type of organization, such as a labor union or a hospital, there exists a set of important intermediate models or forms; for example, corporations, partnerships, nonprofit institutions. A concrete example of the manner in which these models support the development of organizations is provided by historical changes in the corporation in American society. We earlier summarized Coleman's general survey of the emergence of the corporate form in Western Europe. These early corporate forms were typically reserved for broadly public purposes (for example, building a canal) and required specific action by a legitimating authority (for example, a royal decree or the passage of a special statute) (see Seavoy, 1982). However, early in the nineteenth century, and particularly in the United States, the legal environment began to change such that (1) a wide range of business enterprises could qualify for the form; and (2) the procedures were themselves regularized and simplified by the passage of general incorporation statutes. Research by Creighton (1990) shows how, over time, the legal form of incorporation, with its distinctive advantages of limited liability for shareholders, became increasingly standardized across state jurisdictions within the United States. These changes, occurring after 1850, supported, in turn, the rapid growth of corporate business enterprise in this country during the second half of the nineteenth century.

Both Zucker and DiMaggio and Powell suggest that there is a time ordering in the forces leading to the creation of organizations. Whereas the early impetus for creating organizations was their technical benefits, their more recent growth largely reflects an institutional process. Zucker (1983: 13) argues that:

> The rush to create organizations cannot be explained either by the need to counterbalance the power of existing organizations or by any distinct advantage inherent in organizational form (such as increased production efficiency). Rather, the rapid rise and continued spread of the organizational form is best interpreted as an instance of institutionalization: early in the process of diffusion, the organizational form is adopted because it has unequivocal effects on productivity, while later it becomes seen as legitimate to organize formally, regardless of any net benefit. (see also, Tolbert and Zucker, 1983)

In a similar vein, DiMaggio and Powell (1983: 147) assert that "the causes of bureaucratization and rationalization have changed," in that "structural change in organizations seems less and less driven by competition or by the need for efficiency" and is more likely to reflect institutional processes.

Although we agree that both technical and institutional processes give rise to organizations, it does not seem obvious that technical forces were dominant in earlier periods and have now given way to institutional forces. New technologies are constantly being created, and institutional forms that were once strong—such as religion—are no longer as robust. Moreover, professions such as medicine that earlier could make few supportable claims to a scientific base are in a far stronger position to do so today. Both institutional and technical forces appear to be vigorous, to varying degrees, across contemporary organizational domains.

Conflict or Marxist explanations.   In Chapter 3, we described early examples of a conflict theory approach to organizations. This work took a giant step forward during the 1970s because of the resurgence of Marxist theory, a perspective embraced earliest and most strongly by European social scientists. Of the two giants of European social thought, the influence of one of them, Max Weber, on organizational theory was apparent from the beginning—indeed, in many ways it was the beginning! The effect of the second, Karl Marx, though widely felt in many areas of inquiry, did not seriously begin to make waves in work on organizations until much later.[7] Organization theorists such as Albrow (1970), Burawoy (1982), Clegg and Dunkerley (1977), and, especially, Collins (1975) combined Weberian and

---

[7]For a lucid review of earlier theorists who link Marx's insights to this more recent organizational work, see Burrell and Morgan (1979: 279–392).

Marxian themes and connected the latter with the other work on social conflict to advance a general conflict theory of organizations.

Consistent with the origins of the natural system perspective, the Marxist approach began essentially as a critique of the dominant rationalist views, and of the mainstream natural system models as well, particularly those developed by Barnard and the human relations school. Marxists argue that organizational structures are not rational systems for performing work in the most efficient manner; rather, they are power systems designed to maximize control and profits. Work is divided and subdivided not to improve efficiency but to "deskill" workers, to displace discretion from workers to managers, and to create artificial divisions among the workforce (Braverman, 1974). While recognizing that all social structures involve role differentiation, most Marxists argue that the minute division of labor that developed in the early days of industrialization was aimed more at maximizing managerial control than at achieving productive efficiency. In their famous tract, Marx and Engels (1955 trans.: 65) described how in the factories of capitalist systems, the worker "becomes an appendage of the machine, and it is only the most simple, most monotonous and most easily acquired knack, that is required of him." Marx argued that the type of work division developed in these organizations destroyed the craft skills of workers:

> Hence, in the place of the hierarchy of specialized workmen that characterizes manufacture, there steps, in the automatic factory, a tendency to equalise and reduce to one and the same level every kind of work that has to be done by the minders of the machines. (Marx, 1954 trans.: 420)

Braverman and Marglin have amplified Marx's position. The dissection of work separates workers from their products; deskills workers, turning artisans into operatives; increases the potential pool of workers, thereby weakening the job security of each; and segments workers, fragmenting their common experience and undermining their class consciousness (Braverman, 1974).

Not only does the division of labor reduce the power of workers, it increases and legitimates the power of managers. Returning to Adam Smith's pin factory, Marglin insists that:

> Without specialization, the capitalist had no essential role to play in the production process. . . . Separating the tasks assigned to each workman was the sole means by which the capitalist could, in the days preceding costly machinery, ensure that he would remain essential to the production process as integrator of these separate operations into a product for which a wide market existed. (1974: 38)

Indeed, dividing work provides many managerial and technical roles: not only that of integrator but those of designer of the work process, hirer, trainer, inspector, troubleshooter, procurer of supplies, securer of markets, and so forth. In short, work division leads to the bureaucratization of organizations (Edwards, 1979).

Hierarchy develops not as a rational means of coordination but as an instrument of control and a means of accumulating capital through the appropriation of surplus value (Edwards, 1979; Marglin, 1974). Human relations and cooperative systems reforms are misguided because they do not challenge the fundamental exploitative nature of organizations; indeed, they help to shore it up by assuming a congruence of goals and by providing managers with new psychological tools for controlling workers and with new arguments justifying this control (Bendix, 1956; Braverman, 1974). From the Marxist perspective, rationality is an ideology—the use of ideas to legitimate existing arrangements and to deflect criticism of those with excessive power by depersonalizing the system of relations (see Zey-Ferrell and Aiken, 1981).

In addition to arguing that discretion was removed from workers and transferred to managers (and their growing technical staff), Marx insisted that the surplus value created by productive labor was stripped from workers and grasped by manager-capitalists. Although Marx and many other social analysts have condemned this practice, Marglin (1974: 34) acknowledges that this form of "enforced savings" created the surplus capital that led to the subsequent technological revolution. He argues that "the social function of hierarchical work organization is not technical efficiency, but accumulation."

On the one hand, Marx argued that the concentration of workers in factories would increase their class consciousness and the will and ability to collectively organize to protect their interests, while, on the other hand as noted, the specialization of workers undermined solidarity. But a division of interests is not restricted to workers. Both Stark and Burawoy suggest that Marx and Braverman have overstated the cohesion and unity of managers under capitalism and understated those of workers. Stark emphasizes the resourcefulness of workers who have found ways to counteract and undermine the effectiveness of the new control systems. Some changes introduced to improve managerial control have actually increased the power of workers:

> Assembly line production, for example, decreases the degree of direct cooperation among workers, but the objective interdependence of workers also increases their ability to disrupt production either through individual acts of sabotage, collective activity, or the more passive form of simply not showing up for work. (Stark, 1980: 93)

And, as we noted in our discussion of scientific management in Chapter 2, these attempts to rationalize the work process were resisted not only by workers but also by managers, who did not want to see their powers usurped by engineers. As Burawoy (1985: 46) points out, control over the labor process emerges as a result "not only of struggle between capital and labour, but also of struggle among the different agents of capital. . . . one cannot assume the existence of a cohesive managerial and capitalist class that automatically recognizes its true interests."

We also need to take into account the effects of the specific social circumstances within which interests develop and struggles take place. This more contextualized approach is stressed by Granovetter and Tilly:

> Differences in bargaining power among the actors . . . depend on the resources each actor brings to the bargaining and on the interpersonal networks in which the actors are embedded. Workers' success in strikes depends, for example, not

only on their ability to hold out without wages, but also on their capacity to keep out strikebreakers and to enlist the support of third parties, including government officials. (1988:181)

Wider political contexts, such as the posture and policies of the state, are highly relevant, as Burawoy (1985) and Sabel (1982) emphasize. It is also argued that more general social values, like the great importance placed in the United States on individualism, has undermined the power of unions in this country compared with those advocating more social democratic values.

Power contests are not restricted to factories. In his illuminating history of the rise of the Prussian bureaucracy, Rosenberg (1958) argues that many of the Prussian bureaucratic reforms were imposed by the newly emerging administrative elite on the Crown, restricting his or her arbitrary powers of appointment and promotion, rather than the reverse (see also Chapters 10 and 11).

In short, while it is important to recognize the power aspects of changes in the division of labor or in the structuring of work processes, it is an oversimplification to view all of the power advantages as being on any one side, or even to presume that there are only two sides. The work setting is indeed a "contested terrain," as Edwards (1979) has argued, with various parties vying for control and for a greater share of the value created there; the outcomes to date do not support the conclusion that any single party has been either omniscient or all-powerful.

We have tried to indicate some of the complexities and nuances involved in debates about power contests in organizations. But the main point remains that for conflict and Marxist theorists, organizations are more about power than they are about anything else. They are structures for attaining and sustaining power and for exercising control over others.

We have reviewed a variety of rational and natural open system explanations for the emergence of organizations as distinctive forms of social structure. Accounting for the origins of organizations is, however, not the same as explaining how specific types of organizational forms are created and maintained. We turn now to this topic.

CREATING NEW INDUSTRIES AND POPULATIONS OF ORGANIZATIONS

Although economists have long examined the conditions under which new industries develop and mature over time, they have not linked these processes to the fate of organizations that carry out and are caught up in them. During the past decade, organizational scholars have begun to examine the role played by organizations in these vital processes. To examine the emergence of new types of organizations or industries, the analysis needs to take place at either the interorganizational community or the organizational field level of analysis (see Chapter 6).

Whereas changes in social arrangements normally follow an incremental model of slow, gradual evolution, theorists argue that new industries are most likely to arise in periods of rapid and discontinuous change—referred to as a "punctuated equilibrium" model (see Gould and Eldredge, 1977; Astley, 1985). The great institutional economist Joseph Schumpeter (1934 trans.) characterizes these periods as unleashing "the gales of creative destruction." Schumpeter argued that the creation of new technologies was largely responsible for the development of new industries. Later researchers have refined this insight to distinguish between two types of technical innovations: those that enhance the competence of existing participants and those that "destroy" their competence in the sense that old ways of doing the work are not augmented but displaced by the new techniques. Destructive innovations are those most likely to be associated with the creation of new types of organizations and new industries (Tushman and Anderson, 1986). Indeed, because of organizational inertia and "sunk costs," existing forms confront major obstacles in adapting since they must "unlearn" before they can adapt. Thus, large and powerful electronics companies were not able to change quickly enough to capture the new computer technologies.

The creation of new industries, however, is not a simple matter of mastering new technologies. It requires for its success the development of an entire new community of organizations and supporting arrangements—financial, political, social. Van de Ven and Garud (1989) describe the multiple changes that were required to support the development of a new technology for improving hearing, including new ideas from inventors and risks taken by entrepreneurs, the development of a critical mass of people who believed in the new technology, and the creation of new institutional forms and mechanisms, including new panels of reviewers in the U.S. Food and Drug Administration and the creation of industry standards. In their theoretical discussion, Aldrich and Fiol (1994) give particular attention to these institutional supports, including the development of consensus on cultural-cognitive models of appropriate organizational structures, normative systems expressing consensus among technical and professional constituencies, and regulatory approval from state authorities.

Returning to the creation of new organizational forms—the basis of new populations of organizations—we confront again the question of how best to characterize differences among organizations. Ecologists have given most attention to this problem, seeking for the organizational equivalent of the human gene. Clearly, what we wish to focus on is *information about how to organize*—"constitutive information" (see Suchman, forthcoming). As we have noted, some theorists emphasize structural blueprints (Hannan and Freeman, 1989), others "comps" (McKelvey, 1982), and still others "routines" and rules. The latter view is emphasized by the evolutionary economists Nelson and Winter (1982: 99), who argue that "the routinization of activity in an organization constitutes the most important form of storage of the organization's specific operational knowledge."

How novel ways of organizations and routines arise and are transmitted from one organization to another is a subject of much current interest and research. While many students of entrepreneurship stress the role of genius and leadership, more macro and evolutionary versions stress the role of randomness, chance variations, trial and error, good timing, and luck. Evolutionary and learning theorists emphasize that most new ideas are wrong or flawed and lead to failure; it is more often than not the case that other firms exploit and benefit from the innovative work of first-movers (see March, 1991; Miner and Haunschild, 1995). Once created, models diffuse in a variety of ways: the movement of personnel, various intermediaries such as lawyers or accountants, organizational consultants—perhaps even the writings of organizational scholars.

New organizational forms must always draw on an existing stock of resources, knowledge, and supporting structures and so are always constrained by the conditions present in the environment at the time of their founding (Westney, 1987; Romanelli, 1991). Stinchcombe (1965) calls attention to the remarkable pattern exhibited by the founding of organizations of a given type:

> An examination of the history of almost any type of organization shows that there are great spurts of foundation of organizations of the type, followed by periods of relatively slower growth, perhaps to be followed by new spurts, generally of a fundamentally different kind of organization in the same field. (1965: 154)

Stinchcombe cites numerous U.S. examples: the founding of savings banks and the first factory industry, textiles, in the 1830s; the development of railroads and steel companies in the 1850s and 1870s; the founding of universities and labor unions from the 1870s to the 1900s; the development of department stores in the 1850s and mail-order houses in the 1870s; the growth of the oil, rubber, and automobile industries in the 1920s; the emergence of the airline manufacturing and transportation companies during and after World War II; and the development of data-processing and electronic equipment since the 1960s (1965: 154–55). Of course, as previously noted, new technologies often provide the occasion for such spurts, but existing social conditions shape the forms devised.

Because they confront similar circumstances, organizational cohorts arising during a given period tend to exhibit similar structural features. What is more remarkable is that, once established, an organization of a given type tends to retain the basic characteristics present at its founding. Organizational forms are *imprinted*: they are likely to retain the features acquired at their origin. For this reason, there tends to be a strong correlation between the structural form exhibited by an organization and the date of its founding.

Both rational and natural system explanations can help to account for this association between organizational characteristics and time of founding. The characteristics may provide a competitive advantage over alternative arrangements (a rational system argument) or they may be preserved by a set of "traditionalizing forces," including vested interests (a natural system explanation). Whatever the case, it is instructive to realize that the form organizations acquire at their founding is likely to affect the structure they retain over their life. The mix of initial resources out of which an organizational structure is created has lasting effects on the attributes of that structure.

Population ecologists have called attention to the general form that characterizes the growth of organizational populations as they move from birth to maturity or, eventually, death. Hannan and Freeman employ the concept of *density dependence* to account for the routinely observed trajectory of populations of organizations, which characteristically exhibit a period of growth the rate of which gradually increases up to some point (the carrying capacity of the environment) at which a leveling off occurs and is followed by a gradual decline (see Carroll, 1984; Hannan and Freeman, 1989). This pattern is illustrated in Figure 7–3 using data on U.S. labor unions. In the very early stages of the development of a population, founding rates tend to be low. There is no easy way to obtain relevant experience, and organizations suffer what Stinchcombe (1965: 148) has termed the "liability of newness." Not only are experienced participants lacking, the organizational form itself is being developed. It lacks both reliability and legitimacy. Thus, founding rates will be low and failure rates high. Hannan and Freeman argue that the growth in the number of organizations can itself be employed as an indicator of increasing institutionalization: the "simple prevalence of a form tends to give it legitimacy" (p. 132). In our terms, it becomes more cognitively and culturally recognizable and understandable.

As the form becomes more widely accepted, the rate of its growth increases up the point where competition among the organizations for relevant resources becomes sufficiently intense to end the period of growth and usher in a period of decline, as consolidation occurs and weaker forms are eliminated. Organizational density is a two-edged sword, having positive effects on foundings in the early phases of the development of a population and negative effects in the later phases.

The creation of new populations of organizations is supported and enhanced by the broader belief in and support for organizations per se that

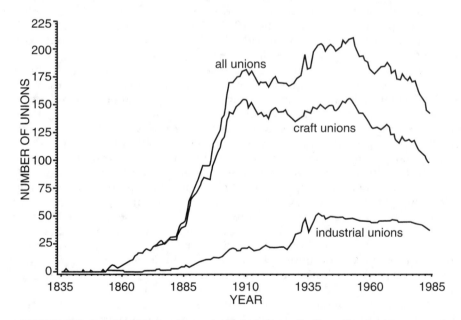

FIGURE 7–3 Density of Union Forms in United States by Year. *Source:* Hannan and Freeman, 1987, Figure 3, p. 927.

are widespread in all contemporary societies. Institutional theorists emphasize the extent to which rationalized elements in the modern social environments encourage the development of organizations:

> The growth of rationalized institutional structures in society makes formal organizations more common and more elaborate. Such institutions are myths which make formal organizations both easier to create and more necessary. After all, the building blocks for organizations come to be littered around the societal landscape; it takes only a little entrepreneurial energy to assemble them into a structure. (Meyer and Rowan, 1977: 345)

Population growth is also influenced by specific normative supports and regulatory systems. We note in Figure 7–3, which depicts the growth of labor unions in the United States, the spurt in growth that occurred in 1935 with the passage of the Wagner Act granting various legal protections to unions and to the organizing processes.

Recent research on population processes has given increased attention to numerous coevolutionary phenomena, including the ways in which two populations in the same community or field may act to compete for resources or, under other conditions, provide mutual support (see Barnett and Carroll, 1987); and the ways in which populations coevolve with the development of technologies or wider institutional environments (see Baum and Singh, 1994).

THE MOBILIZATION OF RESOURCES

Oberschall provides a useful definition of mobilization—"the process of forming crowds, groups, associations, and organizations for the pursuit of collective goals" (1973: 102). Organizations do not spontaneously emerge but require the gathering and harnessing of resources—materials, energy, information, and personnel. The availability of such resources varies from place to place and from time to time. In traditional societies, material resources are locked into landholdings and individuals into caste and kinship systems; in modern societies, to repeat the observation of Eisenstadt (1958), resources are more "free-floating" and easier to mobilize in the service of specialized goals. We have already reviewed, in the first section of this chapter, the general societal factors that facilitate the creation of these conditions.

Many factors affect the mobilization process, as we will see. As just described, the conditions present at the time of the founding of the organization have significant and enduring effects on an organization; what types of incentives are employed to induce contributions will affect the structure of the organization as will the characteristics of the members recruited; and the competitive environment confronting an organization will help to shape its distinctive strategies and structures.

Balance of Contributions and Inducements

Of all the many resources required by organizations, the most vital are the contributions of its human participants. Not only are these contributions themselves of infinite variety, they are also the ultimate means by which all other resources are acquired. More than other early theorists, Barnard (1938) stressed the importance of an organization's ability to motivate participants to continue to make contributions—of time, resources, effort—to it rather than to some competing system. Barnard's concerns were pursued by Simon (1976), the result being the Barnard-Simon theory of *organizational equilibrium*.[8] This equilibrium refers to the organization's ability to attract sufficient contributions to ensure its survival. The basic postulates of the theory are as follows:

1. An organization is a system of interrelated social behaviors of a number of persons whom we shall call participants in the organization.
2. Each participant and each group of participants receives from the organization inducements in return for which he makes contributions to the organization.
3. Each participant will continue his participation in an organization only so long as the inducements offered him are as great as or greater (measured in terms of his values and in terms of the alternatives open to him) than the contributions he is asked to make.
4. The contributions provided by the various groups of participants are the source from which the organization manufactures the inducements offered to participants.
5. Hence, an organization is "solvent"—and will continue in existence— only so long as the contributions are sufficient to provide inducements in large enough measure to draw forth these contributions. (Simon, Smithberg, and Thompson, 1950: 381–82)

Although it points to an essential truth about the survival of organizations, the theory "verges on the tautological," as Simon himself observes (March and Simon, 1958: 84). It is difficult to measure the balance of inducements and contributions independently of the individual's decision to stay with or leave the organization. Also, as noted by Krupp, since the concept of organizational inducement includes techniques for changing an individual's values or needs, it is difficult to distinguish between inducements that "win participation because they create satisfactions at a given level of willingness and inducements that shift the level of willingness" (1961: 107). Further, it is difficult to determine what utilities or values are attached by individual participants to the contributions they are asked to make and the inducements they are offered. Indeed, one of the major contributions of the human relations school in attempting to counteract the myth of the economic actor is its demonstration of the diversity of factors to which individuals attach importance—working conditions, tools, skills, personal relations, office furnishings, and raw materials, for example—whether they are processing fish or preparing desserts in a restaurant (see Whyte, 1948; Whyte et al., 1955).

---

[8]Recall from Chapter 2 that Barnard and Simon distinguish between the decisions a participant makes to join and continue to participate in an organization and those that he or she makes as a participant in the organization. The current discussion deals with the first category of decisions.

And related work emphasizes that level of satisfaction is not assessed on an absolute scale but depends on choice of reference or comparison group. That is, how one worker assesses his or her own benefits depends on those received by others regarded as comparable (see Adams, 1965; Homans, 1961; Patchen, 1961; Martin, 1981).

One of the most useful approaches to understanding how organizations attract and reward participants for their contributions is based on a simple typology developed by Clark and Wilson (1961: 134–36; see also Wilson, 1973). Clark and Wilson differentiate among three types of incentives:

- *material incentives*: tangible rewards; rewards with a monetary value—for example, wages, interest, fringe benefits, patronage;
- *solidary incentives*: intangible rewards derived from the act of association—for example, sociability, status, identification;
- *purposive incentives*: intangible rewards related to the goals of the organization—for example, satisfaction obtained from working on the election of a candidate whose position on issues is similar to one's own, or the rewards perceived by a pacifist who contributes money and time to antiwar groups.

Like Etzioni (1961), whose similar typology was developed at the same time, Clark and Wilson suggest that although all organizations use all three types of incentives, it is usually possible to identify a predominant type for each. And associated with each type are important structural and operational differences.

Organizations that rely primarily on material incentives are labeled *utilitarian organizations*; examples are business firms, labor unions, and political machines. Clark and Wilson predict that such organizations will explicitly seek material rewards for their members and develop fairly precise cost-accounting machinery. Executives will devote their energies first and foremost to obtaining the material resources needed to provide incentives; central conflicts within the organization will center on their equitable distribution. The substantive goals pursued by the organization will be of only secondary importance. Such organizations can be flexible about their goal-related activities: these "activities may change without disrupting member participation as long as material incentives continue to be available" (Clark and Wilson, 1961: 140).

Solidary organizations include most service-oriented voluntary associations and social clubs. Members make contributions in return for sociability and status. Executive efforts must therefore be devoted to obtaining organizational prestige, publicity, or good fellowship. The goals of such organizations need to be noncontroversial and socially desirable. Solidary organizations are tactically less flexible than utilitarian organizations: the means utilized must be acceptable to desirable participants, and projects must often be carried on publicly to stimulate the flow of approvals and publicity.

In many ways, *purposive organizations* represent the most interesting case. These organizations "rely almost exclusively on their stated purposes as incentives to attract and hold contributors" (Clark and Wilson, 1961: 146).

This would appear to be the ideal organizational arrangement: members join because they wish to help achieve the goals espoused by the organization, and the organization, in achieving its goals, supplies inducements to its members to secure their continuing contributions. Wilson's (1962; 1973; 1989) analyses, however, suggest that this "ideal" is very difficult to realize. Executives in these organizations—like their counterparts in other organizations—must secure a continuing flow of inducements to sustain the interests of members, but many of the types of goals sought by purposive organizations are difficult to achieve. Political parties do not always succeed in winning elections; religious organizations do not always succeed in transforming the world or converting the heathen; and social movements may not succeed in achieving their specific goals—which range from achieving equality for minority racial groups to protecting the environment.

Sometimes the goals of such organizations may be only vaguely stated—so that the organization can appeal to a large number of potential adherents—but when the time comes for action and goals are more specifically defined, many participants may feel betrayed or at least sense that their interests are not being served. In order to provide strong inducements to participants, the goals of purposive organizations are often relatively controversial, attracting "true believers." Developing strategies and tactics that will interest and motivate the more militant members yet not alienate the more moderate members requires delicate manuevering on the part of leaders, who must sometimes distance themselves from overzealous, sometimes illegal, actions of members while at the same time defending the cause. Leaders of Earth First! must condemn the spiking of trees while reminding the public of the benefits of protecting old-growth forests (see Elsbach and Sutton, 1992). Thus, the activities that provide the strongest inducements to the most committed members can undermine more general support for the movement.

Olson (1965) suggests yet another reason why purposive organizations are difficult to sustain. Under the classical economic assumption that individuals attempt to behave rationally and to pursue their self-interest, Olson points out that no individual should be expected to join an organization in order to achieve common or public interests. Rational persons will realize that their own act of joining, except under very special conditions, will not appreciably affect the chances of the organization to succeed in its mission. These individuals will also observe that because the goals served represent a collective good—one that cannot be differentially distributed but is available to all—they will share in the benefits of the organization's success whether or not they have contributed to its attainment.[9]

Thus, both the analysis by Clark and Wilson and that by Olson conclude that purposive organizations—those attempting to equate organizational goals with individual motives—are difficult to manage and to maintain. Purposive organizations typically supplement their primary incentives with material inducements—to retain a core staff and provide secondary incentives to members—and solidary incentives to help sustain the rank and file through the dry spells.

---

[9]Of course, this "free rider" problem is one of the important conditions that gives rise to public organizations—organizations that individuals are required to support, for example, through their taxes.

Harnessing Affect

Feminist theorists argue that most current views about why organizations are created and why individuals join them are overly rationalist. They argue that arguments which set aside emotion and affect reflect a masculine bias on the part of those who attempt to create and manage organizations as well as those who analyze them. For evidence, these analysts point to a broad new range of organizational forms—as well as some aspects of conventional organizations—that make use of participants' interest in finding outlets for the development of "consciousness, self-actualization, and the expression of subjective feelings, desires and experiences" as well as new individual and "collective identities" (Taylor, 1995: 226).

Organizations that provide such opportunities have been labeled *collectivist* organizations (Rothschild-Whitt, 1979; Rothschild and Whitt, 1986). They include many forms of client-oriented service organizations popular in the 1960s and early 1970s, such as neighborhood health centers, alternative schools, and legal collectives—as well as some earlier forms, such as food and producer cooperatives. More recently, many feminist organizations are of this type, including rape crisis centers and shelters for battered women (Ferree and Martin, 1995). More so than conventional organizations, these forms attempt to combine both purposive and solidarity incentives, giving attention to participants' needs for affiliation, emotional support, and meaningful work.

Many of these types of organizations eschew formalization as a structural characteristic.[10] Rothschild-Whitt's (1979) survey of the structural features of collectivist organizations suggests that many go to great lengths to eliminate or reduce formalization. They deny the authority of office, seek to minimize the promulgation of rules and procedures, attempt to eliminate status gradations among participants, and do away with role differentiation and specialization of function. Great stress is laid on equality in decision making, and differences in interests and preferences among individual members are deemed of great importance. (See also, Calas and Smircich, 1996.) Natural system assumptions prevail over rational system views: the personal qualities of members do matter!

The new feminist organizations often lack much in the way of physical capital—financial and real property assets—but attempt to make up for it by unleashing the substantial human capital of their participants—intelligence, creativity, and energy—as well as by creating social capital—the development of strong bonds among members that facilitate trust and support collective action. Even with these important types of resources, however, such organizations confront strong pressures toward structural isomorphism from their

---

[10]Although these forms would appear to be thereby excluded from the category "organizations" as defined by rational system theorists (see Chapter 1), these types of social structure are nevertheless illuminated by this definition. Collectivist forms do not simply exhibit relatively low levels of formalization; they are characterized by active hostility to this mode of organizing. They are self-consciously and energetically antiformal in practice and, more important, in their ideologies and normative systems. Indeed, much of the interest and energy they generate among their participants can be directly attributed to the ideological battle they wage against the more conventional formalized and hierarchical models. They are organized in opposition to the prevailing model of organizations—a model so widely shared that its *negation* can serve as a potent basis of organizing.

environments. Many, over time, move in the direction of increasing hierarchy and greater formalization—forms Acker (1990) refers to as a "gendered logic of organization."

Membership Demographics

We have seen that there are a variety of ways in which organizations induce participants to contribute their time and resources to them, and that the mix of inducements employed has important consequences for the organization. The mix of participants also has important consequences. Considering only those participants who are identified as members of the organization, who is recruited and how long they stay has a wide range of implications for the structure and performance of the organization. The demography of the organization—the aggregated characteristics of its members, including their age, sex, education, ethnicity, and length of service—is increasingly recognized as a major determinant of organizational structure and performance (see McNeil and Thompson, 1971; Pfeffer, 1983).

The demographic composition of organizations is determined by such factors as the growth rate of the organization and of the industry in which it is located, the rapidity with which the organization's technology is changing (the more rapid, the more likely the organization will be hiring new and better-educated workers), the personnel practices that are followed (for example, some types of organizations promote only from within their own ranks), and the extent of unionization (which is likely to promote longer tenure for workers) (Pfeffer, 1983).

The effects of demographic composition are wide-ranging and have yet to be fully explored. Their variety can be indicated by a few illustrations. Kanter (1977a) has examined the consequences of widely varying proportions of group members having one or another attribute—for example, the ratio of men to women, whites to blacks, or younger to older participants—on the attitudes and performance of the group. Focusing on a collection of women who occupied less than 10 percent of the exempt (salaried) jobs in a corporation, Kanter observed that the few women reaching the upper levels of management were treated as "tokens": because they were different they were highly visible, the ways in which they varied from the majority took on exaggerated importance, and performance pressures were heightened by their "life in the limelight." Kanter explains how tokenism can shape the behavior and expectations of those involved:

> Tokens of Type O who are successful in their professional roles face pressures and inducements to dissociate themselves from other O's, and thus they may fail to promote, or even actively block, the entry of more O's. At the same time, tokens who are less than successful and appear less than fully competent confirm the organization's decision not to recruit more O's, unless they are extraordinarily competent and not like most O's. And since just a few O's can make the X-majority people feel uncomfortable, X's will certainly not go out of their way to include more O's. (1977a: 241–42)

In this manner, tokenism can become a self-perpetuating system.

Another example of the importance of membership composition is provided by Reed's (1978) analysis of the effects of cohort composition on the operation of the American Foreign Service bureaucracy. A cohort is simply a population of individuals who have experienced the same events at the same periods of their life. Thus an organizational cohort would be composed of those individuals who are recruited at the same time and whose careers develop in a parallel manner. Cohorts can significantly influence individual careers. Obviously, an individual's chances for promotion are going to be greatly affected by the size of one's own and preceding cohorts, especially in a system like that of the Foreign Service, where all promotions are made from within and few persons voluntarily transfer into some other system. But Reed also suggests that cohort composition can have organization-level effects. He argues that the slowness with which the Foreign Service adapted to its rapidly changing environment during the period surrounding World War II was significantly influenced by the characteristics of the cohort in charge—a collection of officers recruited many years earlier and under very different political and social conditions. A closed-career service bureaucracy is not well suited to changed demands that require innovative responses.

A final example of the import of demography is suggested by the work of Ouchi (1980; 1981) on varying systems of organizational control. Ouchi argues that the Japanese-style model of the employment relation, which is based on the presumption of a lifetime commitment of organization to employee and vice versa, provides the basis for the creation of much more diffuse and informal control systems, which he terms "clan systems," that rely greatly on the socialization of employees and their internalization of company norms and values than can be developed when there is a more rapid turnover of personnel. (See the related discussion of internal labor markets in Chapter 8 and clans in Chapter 9.) More generally, Pfeffer (1983) argues that the fewer the average years of service of the employees of an organization, the larger and more elaborate the bureaucratic control apparatus.

Thus, it is not only the initial resource mix and the assortment of incentives that shape the structure and performance of organizations. The creation of an organization is not a one-time event but a continuing process, and particularly fateful for the later stages of this process are the numbers and types of participants recruited earlier.

Acquisition of Resources

How difficult it is to garner the necessary resources to support an organization depends greatly on the nature of the organization and its goals. Much work has been devoted to describing protest or social-movement organizations that pursue controversial or change-oriented programs. Such organizations face a decidedly uphill struggle in their search for resources—including adherents and constituents—and, more often than not, fail to survive (see Oberschall, 1973; Gamson, 1975).

Earlier theory and research on collective behavior—studies of crowds, mobs, riots, rebellions—stressed the importance of a common sense of grievance and discontent in motivating individuals to take collective action in behalf of their interests. Later views emphasized that collective action is more

a function of resource availability and mobilization, including organizational skills and connections, than of shared discontent (Zald and McCarthy,
1987; Tilly, 1978). Jenkins summarizes this approach:

> The main thrust of "resource mobilization" theory has been to argue that dis-
> content is at best secondary in accounting for the emergence of insurgency,
> that organizational resources and the changing power position of the aggriev-
> ed, not sudden increases in their grievances, are the major factors leading to
> the outbreak of disorders. (1979: 224)

Thus, research by Snyder and Tilly (1972) demonstrates that industrial
strikes in France were not associated with fluctuations in the discontent of
workers but were affected by the size and strength of union organization.

   This view of social mobilization has recently been challenged by a body
of work termed "new social movement theory," which focuses attention on
the organizing processes at work in the 1960s social movements—civil rights,
feminst, peace, environmental, and gay and lesbian (Klandermans and
Tarrow, 1988). As noted in our discussion above of affect as a source of organizational energy, these theorists "question the rationalist assumptions
underlying resource mobilization theory" (Taylor, 1995: 226), emphasizing
instead the importance of emotion and the creation of new individual and
collective identities.

   A particularly interesting situation confronting entrepreneurs who
must acquire and assemble resources is represented by ethnic communities,
or "enclaves." Studies suggest that while ethnic minorities often confront
economic and social barriers that restrict their enterprise, the very forces
that constrain their activities (for example, discrimination; ethnocentrism)
may create special opportunities and resources. Thus, discrimination may
create markets that only members of the ethnic group can service; and group
solidarity, including religious and kinship ties—can provide conditions of
high trust (social capital) that facilitate the raising of financial capital and
the pooling of resources (see Light and Bonacich, 1988; Aldrich and
Waldinger, 1990). Studies of entrepreneurship and resource mobilization
indicate that, while organizations require resources, organization is itself a
resource. New social movement theory adds that human and social capital
are also major assets.

   Population ecologists have reminded us of the difficult time faced by
many types of organizations in acquiring sufficient resources to survive.
While the birthrate of new organizations in a developed society such as the
United States is high, so is the failure rate. Although data on organizational
births and deaths are difficult to acquire and are limited largely to the business sectors, Aldrich (1979: 36) cites data from a discontinued census on the
numbers of new businesses, businesses transferred to a new owner, and businesses discontinued for nine selected years between 1940 and 1962. During
these years, roughly 3.4 million new businesses were started, 3.1 million were
transferred, and 2.5 million ceased to exist. As would be expected, the likelihood of failure is considerably higher among newer and smaller organizations. Records collected by Dun and Bradstreet reveal that over half (54
percent) of the businesses that failed in the United States during 1980 were

five years old or less (see Bedeian, 1984: 333). The "liability of newness" is often lethal. But it is not only the newer and smaller firms that fail or cease to exist as independent entities. If longer periods are used, then there is a surprising amount of turnover in the populations of all types of organizations (see Carroll, 1984).

If we shift the level of analysis from the population of organizations to that of the individual organization, it is useful to think of each organization as undergoing an evolutionary process from birth to maturity to old age and death. Although the organizational life cycle is not as distinct and regular as the life cycle of plants or animals or humans, it is nevertheless instructive to identify general phases of development and decline (see Kimberly, Miles, et al., 1980). Theorists have developed a variety of schemata for distinguishing stages of development (see Bedeian, 1984, for a review).

As an example of one such model, after examining a number of case studies of corporate development, Greiner (1972) identified five general evolutionary stages. He proposed that each stage ends in a predictable crisis calling for some type of appropriate adjustment by management if the organization is to survive and proceed to the next stage. For example, the first crisis typically encountered is that of leadership: the founding members of the organization—often technical experts or entrepreneurial types—give way to managers who are more skilled at consolidation and routine administration. The next crisis occurs because controls become too centralized; the solution is more delegation, decentralizing of decision making. But decentralization in turn raises problems of integration that call for additional coordinating devices—planning procedures, reports, formal reviews. But these mechanisms multiply, causing a crisis of red tape, which in turn is solved by greater emphasis on trust and informal collaboration. And so development is accompanied by a series of more or less predictable crises.

Greiner's model is instructive in that each solution at one stage becomes the problem at the next. A leadership style or a structural arrangement that is adaptive at one level of size and complexity is unsuitable for another. Similarly, one would expect to observe changes over time in the relevance and utility of different types of personnel and resources. The problems encountered and hence the types of resources required vary with the stage of development. Obtaining sufficient capital resources to expand operations may be critical at the earlier stages of growth—and may represent a much greater challenge, since the risks to investors are higher—but less important in later stages, when capital will be easier to raise and may be available through internalized savings mechanisms. Resource acquisition is a necessary, but variable, process that continues throughout the life of the organization.

Up to the 1980s, most research on organizational life cycles emphasized development and omitted decline. But, reflecting changes in some important sectors of the U.S. economy, more recent work has examined decline: both factors causing it and management strategies for dealing with it. (For reviews, see Greenhalgh, 1983; Whetten, 1987.) Among the strategies that have been identified and examined are turnaround, downsizing, divestment, and executive succession (Cameron, Sutton, and Whetten, 1988). Some of these approaches are discussed in Chapters 8 and 10.

The ecologists in particular stress the difficulties confronting all organizations as they attempt to acquire and maintain a flow of resources adequate to perpetuate themselves. By contrast, institutional theorists such as Meyer and Rowan emphasize the ease with which some types of resources can be assembled to constitute an organization. To repeat their summary of the situation: in developed societies, "the building blocks for organizations come to be littered around the societal landscape; it takes only a little entrepreneurial energy to assemble them into a structure" (Meyer and Rowan, 1977: 345). That is, the more institutionalized the environment—the more it contains rules, accepted procedures, licensed actors, and taken-for-granted frameworks for carrying out specified actions—the less difficult it is to create and sustain organizations. However, although organizations in these circumstances may be able to more readily assemble various elements and actors, whether these resources can be fully mobilized by their managers is open to question. We pursue these matters in Chapter 10.

SUMMARY

Organizations, as we know them, have not always existed. They evolved during the past few centuries as part of a dual-level process. The same social changes that brought about the development of individualism—the freeing of resources (including the individual) from all-absorbing social structures—are responsible for the growth of organizations. Both developments celebrate the legitimation of specialized, particularized goals and the freedom to own and mobilize resources in their pursuit.

From a rational system perspective, organizations arise to take advantage of the production economies offered by an elaborate division of labor and to meet the cognitive and control challenges posed by complex and uncertain environments. From a natural system perspective, institutionalists propose that organizations emerge as an embodiment of rationalized belief systems that proliferate in the wider social structure; Marxists argue that organizations arise as structures created by capitalists to expropriate surplus value from productive labor. All of these explanations can be correct, but for different times and places and types of organizations.

The costs and benefits of creating organizations are more easily evaluated if organizations are compared with alternative social forms for carrying on complex work. Organizations are viewed as having advantages over market mechanisms when the tasks to be carried out are sufficiently complex and uncertain as to exceed the information-processing capacities of individuals, and when so few potential buyers or sellers exist that they may attempt to take advantage of one another. Under these conditions, organizations offer mechanisms for reducing transaction costs and for constraining opportunistic behavior. Organizations are viewed as superior to informal peer groups as mechanisms for overseeing and coordinating complex work. However, conventional hierarchies in organizations may function poorly on ambiguous or highly complex tasks that require the exercise of individual discretion and the exchange of large amounts of information.

All organizations must secure a continuing supply of resources—including participants—from their environment. The initial mix of resources that are mobilized at the creation of a particular organization are critical in that they constitute a structural pattern that tends to persist—imprinting the organization with characteristics that are preserved over time. The types of incentives for participants to contribute and the mix of participants have important consequences for the structural features and flexibility of the organization. All organizations compete for resources, but the consequences and costs of obtaining them vary with the type of organization and environment as well as with the stage of development an organization has reached.

Boundary Setting and Boundary Spanning

The organizational world bubbles and seethes. Observed for a lengthy interval, the configuration of organizations within it changes like the patterns of a kaleidoscope. Organizations expand, contract, break up, fuse. Some surfaces become thick and opaque, reducing exchanges between their interior contents and the external environment, while others etherealize and permit heavier traffic in one or both directions. Shapes are altered. Some processes are depressed, some intensified. Levels of activity rise and fall. Organizations disintegrate and vanish as others form in droves, and the birth and death rates vary over time and space. Nothing stays constant.*

Herbert Kaufman (1975)

The central insight emerging from the open system model is that all organizations are incomplete: all depend on exchanges with other systems. All are open to environmental influences as a condition of their survival. By contrast, both the rational and natural system perspectives insist that organizations, as a condition of their existence, must maintain boundaries that separate them from their environments. In the absence of distinguishable boundaries, there can be no organizations as we understand that term. In this chapter we explore the interdependence and the independence of organizations, and we examine the types of mechanisms used to set (and reset) and to span their boundaries.

THE SOCIAL BOUNDARIES OF ORGANIZATIONS

The problems confronting organizations in setting and policing their boundaries are complex and subtle. Given the essence of organizations as open sys-

*Excerpt from "The Natural History of Human Organizations" by Herbert Kaufman is reprinted from *Administration and Society*, Vol. 7, No. 2 (August 1975), p. 143, by permission of the publisher, Sage Publications, Inc.

tems, their boundaries must necessarily be sieves, not shells, admitting the desirable flows and excluding the inappropriate or deleterious elements. Determining what is desirable or harmful can be a difficult decision, in part because the criteria can vary from time to time and from location to location in the organization. To explicate these issues, we first concentrate on the social boundaries of organizations, examining the various indicators used to mark those boundaries and the criteria employed by organizations in determining whom to admit or reject.

Determining Organizational Boundaries

Early in Chapter 1, after laboring over the concepts of normative and behavioral structure, we quietly slipped in the concept of *collectivity*. This concept serves to bring together the two components of structure but also adds a new element: the notion of boundary. A collectivity is a specific instance of social organization—an identifiable "chunk" of the social order. As noted, the criteria for the existence of a collectivity are (1) a *delimited* social structure—that is, a *bounded* network of social relations—and (2) a normative order *applicable to the participants* linked by the network. All collectivities—including informal groups, communities, organizations, and entire societies—possess, by definition, boundaries that distinguish them from other systems.

Accepting the view that organizations, as a type of collectivity, possess boundaries is one thing, but deciding what and where they are is another. Establishing the boundaries of an organization is a difficult business, raising both theoretical and empirical problems.

To embrace the notion of organizations as open systems is to acknowledge that organizations are penetrated by their environments in ways that blur and confound any simple criterion for distinguishing the one from the other. How are we to regard customers? Clients? Stockholders? A second difficulty is the growing number of organizations that are subsumed under broader structures—for example, schools within districts, local banks that are branches of larger financial enterprises, and firms or establishments that are parts of multidivisional corporations or cooperative networks. Such connections may strongly influence many aspects of the structure and performance of the local units, so that treating them as independent units may create serious errors. Third, because more of our studies include measures taken at more than one point in time, we need to realize that organizational boundaries are very likely to fluctuate over time (see Freeman, 1978).

Laumann, Marsden, and Prensky (1983) note that two approaches and, within each, three substantive foci are used to define boundaries. The two approaches are the realist and the nominalist. In the *realist* approach, the investigator adopts the "vantage point of the actors themselves in defining the boundaries" of the system, assuming that this view will importantly influence their behavior. Under the *nominalist* strategy, the "analyst self-consciously imposes a conceptual framework constructed to serve his own analytic purposes" (p. 21). Regardless of the approach selected, the investigator must also determine what feature of the situation to emphasize as the criterion for determining boundaries. Laumann and associates distinguish among three alternatives—the characteristics of the actors (or nodes), their relations, and their activities.

Many investigators define the boundaries of an organization by focusing on its *actors*—for example, attempting to determine who is and who is not regarded as a member. Members also are likely to share other attributes, such as interests, training, or ethnicity. A second approach—favored by network analysts—is to establish the boundaries of the system by noting which actors are involved in *social relations* of a specified type. Network analysts prefer measures of relations to measures of actors' attributes, arguing that the former provides a better measure of social structure. A widely used behavioral indicator of relatedness is frequency of interaction. Although no social unit is completely separated from its environment on the basis of this criterion, Homans (1950: 85) suggests that it is possible to locate system boundaries where the web of interaction shows "certain thin places."[1] A third possibility is to focus on the nature of the *activities* performed. We would expect to observe a change in the activities conducted by individuals as they cross a system boundary.[2] Pfeffer and Salancik favor this criterion, arguing that organizational boundaries are coterminous with activity control:

> When it is recognized that it is behaviors, rather than individuals, that are included in structures of coordinated behavior, then it is possible to define the extent to which any given person is or is not a member of the organization. . . . The organization is the total set of interstructured activities in which it is engaged at any one time and over which it has discretion to initiate, maintain, or end behaviors. . . . The organization ends where its discretion ends and another's begins. (1978: 32)

A focus on relationships or activities emphasizes behavioral criteria for defining the limits of organizations. Since both interactions and activities require time and space, two useful indicators of significant boundaries are an organization's spatial barriers and their guardians (for example, fences, walls, doors, guards, receptionists) and the temporal systems (for example, working hours and activity schedules) it creates to contain them. By contrast, a focus on the characteristics of actors emphasizes normative criteria for defining the significant characteristics of membership.

Membership, interaction, and activity boundaries often do not coincide. The operational systems—as revealed by studies of patterns of interaction and of interdependent activities—through which organizations actually accomplish their tasks may cross-cut formal or membership boundaries. Research and development laboratories for corporations are increasingly located on university campuses under complex joint-venture and contract

---

[1] It is not only social scientists who wrestle with the question of how to bound a system under study. Other social analysts, such as novelists, confront a similar problem. The strategy proposed by Henry James is not dissimilar to that adopted by scientific investigators:

> Really, universally, relations stop nowhere, and the exquisite problem of the artist is eternally but to draw, by a geometry of his own, the circle within which they shall happily appear to do so. (1907: vii)

[2] Barnard took the position that activities, not participants, are the basic elements of organizations. Thus, he defined an organization as "a system of coöperative activities of two or more persons." (1938: 75)

agreements; on the output side, innovative marketing departments are engaged in close association with their bellwether customers in developing and testing new products. And in the public sector, many implementation arrangements entail the complex cooperation of federal, state, and local agencies or some form of public-private collaboration—for example, the contracting out of services to for-profit or nonprofit firms. It is wise to conclude that, in many cases, formal organizational boundaries do not circumscribe vital activities and relations.

Nevertheless, most groups, and particularly organizations, carefully differentiate members from nonmembers and develop explicit criteria for recruiting and selecting the former. Why is this true? What is the importance of membership boundaries for the functioning of organizations?

Recruitment Criteria

Rational system theorists are quite certain that they understand the functions of organizational boundaries: boundaries contribute to organizational rationality. Several of the characteristics Weber (1968 trans.) identified as defining rational-legal systems may be viewed as bounding or insulating the organization from its social context. For example, his stipulation that officials be appointed by free contract according to their technical qualifications is intended to ensure that selection criteria are organizationally relevant and that the selection process will be relatively free from the influence of other social affiliations, whether religious, economic, political, or familial.

Udy's (1962) study of thirty-four production organizations in thirty-four different nonindustrialized societies lends empirical support to Weber's concerns. Udy sought to determine how the internal features of an organization's structure are related to the type of recruitment criteria used by the organization. His measures of structure are rather crude because the data are drawn from a systematic file of secondary data sources—the Human Relations Area File—based primarily on anthropological field studies. However, because the sample of organizations is drawn from nonindustrialized societies, it contains much greater variation in environmental and organizational characteristics than would be present in a comparable sample of organizations in industrialized societies. Udy differentiated five types of recruitment, ranging from participation in a production organization because of "voluntary self-commitment and self-defined interest" (high social insulation) to participation that was "required by compulsory political ascription" (high social involvement). To assess the structural characteristics of the thirty-four organizations, Udy developed a scale that measured the extent to which they reflected rational principles of organization. The presence or absence of seven indicators—including the organizational pursuit of limited objectives, rewards based on performance criteria, specialization, and rewards controlled by superiors—assessed the degree of structural rationality within each organization. Analysis of the data revealed that the higher the degree of social insulation the organization achieved, the more likely it was to exhibit rational structural features.

Udy's findings do not seem surprising. Consider the case of a family that decides to run a retail store. The father might feel obliged to pay the older son a higher wage, in recognition of his superior status in the family structure, even if he does not contribute more than others toward achieving the goals of the organization. The more an organization is insulated from its social environment—in this case the family's kinship structure—the more it can select, deploy, and reward its participants according to organizationally relevant criteria.

Organizationally controlled recruitment criteria are but one important mechanism fostering insulation of the organization from its social environment; Weber (1968 trans.) pointed to the need for others. His insistence that officials, once recruited, should regard their office as their sole, or at least their primary, occupation indicates his recognition that other occupational affiliations of members may affect their performance within organizations. And it is not only other occupational demands that can create claims on participants that may conflict with those of the focal organization. As the kinship example emphasizes, any social identity may become the basis of conflicting expectations and behavior patterns. Externally reinforced status characteristics such as age, sex, ethnicity, and social class are an important source of these expectations and obligations (see Hughes, 1958: 102–15; Dalton, 1959; Kanter, 1977a). And as the number and variety of other special-purpose organizations grow, membership in them supplies new identities and sources of power that can impinge on the participant's role performance in the organization. Salient identities can also develop as the result of interactions and exchange processes among participants within the organization, and these give rise to informal status distinctions (see Homans, 1961; Blau, 1964).

The nonorganizational identities of individual participants play a relatively small role in rational system views of organization: they are viewed primarily as a problem to be managed by appropriate recruitment criteria and control mechanisms. By contrast, the many faces of participants are of great interest to natural system analysts. To begin, from a natural system perspective, it is impossible for any organization to eliminate completely these sources of "disturbance": social identities—externally validated roles, qualities, interests—are among the most portable of baggage. Some extreme types of organizations do attempt to eliminate the external status connections of a subset of their participants. This is the case for such *total institutions* as prisons, early mental hospitals, monasteries, and army barracks. As Goffman explains:

> The barrier that total institutions place between the inmate and the wider world marks the first curtailment of self. In civil life, the sequential scheduling of the individual's roles, both in the life cycle and in the repeated daily round, ensures that no one role he plays will block his performance and ties in another. In total institutions, in contrast, membership automatically disrupts role scheduling, since the inmate's separation from the wider world lasts around the clock and may continue for years. Role dispossession therefore occurs. (1961: 14)

In addition to imposing these time and physical barriers, many such institutions forbid all contact with outsiders, strip the inmate of personal possessions, segregate sex or age groups, issue institutional garb, and restrict interaction among inmates (see also, McEwen, 1980). It is possible to view these measures as a set of mechanisms for ensuring that organizations will be buffered from the disturbing effects of the external roles occupied by participants. However, in our view they are sufficiently rare and extreme that they serve better to remind us of how difficult it is for any organization to eliminate the influence on its participants of their nonorganizational roles and relationships. Total institutions are best viewed as a limiting case—as defining one extreme on a continuum.

Most organizations do not erect excessive barriers or engage in elaborate stripping tactics; hence, we should expect most organizations to be composed of participants who possess multiple identities and behave accordingly. Certainly, natural system analysts embrace this view. We have already noted (in Chapter 3) the interest of human relations investigators in the effects of sex, class, and ethnicity on the allocation of workers to roles and on worker behavior. And Selznick's analysis of individual "commitments" and the constraints they place on the rational deployment of personnel (also reviewed in Chapter 3) is highly germane to these issues.

Most natural system theorists do not portray participants' other roles as disruptive; rather they view these characteristics as a vital resource for the organization. Even within a rational-system, performance-oriented context, natural system analysts point out that most organizations do not themselves train their members to talk, to think, or to use specialized tools: these fundamental skills are typically acquired in different settings and imported into the organization. Also, from the natural system perspective, goal-attainment considerations are secondary to survival, and many participants are recruited precisely because they possess extraorganizational characteristics viewed as valuable to this end. For most organizations—and especially for those operating in more institutionalized environments—it is important to recruit the "right" participants, for symbolic as well as for technical considerations. Schools need to hire certificated instructors; nursing homes, licensed administrators; universities, instructing staffs with Ph.D.'s; and financial organizations, certified public accountants. Such environmental connections ensure legitimacy and increased confidence in the organization.

Organizations also conform to the expectations of their social environments by maintaining some consistency between their own status systems and the stratification criteria used in the larger society (Anderson et al., 1966). For example, it remains the case up to the present time that women are rarely appointed to high managerial positions in U.S. corporations,[3] partly because their special social identities were viewed by their male colleagues as introducing additional sources of uncertainty into transactions requiring high trust (Kanter, 1977a), but also because organizations wish to inspire confidence in outsiders with whom they conduct business, and so try not to violate widely shared community norms. Further, for certain types of boundary-spanning roles, such as being a member of a board of directors, an indi-

---

[3]A review of the proxy statements of 799 public companies of the 1,000 largest U.S. industrial and service organizations in 1990 revealed that only one-half of 1 percent of the highest paid officers and directors were women. Examinations of the listings of upper management officials contained in the annual reports of 255 major corporations indicated that about 5 percent were women (Fierman, 1990).

vidual's selection may depend entirely on his or her external roles and connections. Thus, a banker may be asked to serve on the board of directors of a hospital because of ties with the financial community.

Natural system theorists emphasizing the conflict perspective observe that participants enter organizations with different and often conflicting interests, and that organizational resources are often deflected to serve personal ends (Perrow, 1986). Worker interests can differ from those of managers or directors; human resource professionals may prefer longer-term and more diffuse employment systems that build employee loyalty, whereas financial specialists emphasize the advantages of narrow and short-term contracts and externalization of work. At more macro levels, Marxist theorists note that appointments to the board of directors may serve the interests of the elite class rather than those of the individual organization. (See the discussion of organizational fields at the societal level later in this chapter.)

Feminist theorists, in particular, stress the hidden agenda underlying attempts to distinguish formal roles from other, informal or "private" roles. The distinction both delegitimates and diminishes other, nonorganizational sources of power (abilities, resources, connections) and at the same time shores up and formalizes existing organizationally based inequalities in power (see Acker, 1990; Martin, 1990).

An interesting instance of combining multiple roles—business and personal—is represented by direct sales organizations, which currently employ about 5 percent of the U.S. labor force, and a disproportionate number of women. In her study of such organizations as Tupperware, Amway, and Mary Kay, Biggart observes that:

> Whereas bureaucratic firms seek to exclude nonwork social relations in order to control workers, the direct selling industry pursues profit in the opposite way: by making social networks serve business ends. (1989: 8)

Direct sales organizations encourage the inclusion of family members, relatives, and friends in the business organization; they combine business and personal relationships as well as business and social occasions; and they reverse the process, "making the economic ties of sponsorship the basis for familylike social relations." The combination of economic and affective ties creates "a double-stranded bond far stronger than either one alone" (p. 85).

These types of organizational arrangements support the contention of the natural system theorists that the external identities and connections of participants—far from being disruptive and restrictive—are, under many conditions, a primary resource for the organization, providing skills, legitimacy, and valued connections with the larger social environment.

Social Insulation and Social Engulfment

The strategic question facing all organizations is how to recruit participants and harness their roles and resources in the service of organizational goals (whether goal attainment or survival), while avoiding or minimizing the danger of becoming captive to participants' external interests or personal agendas. Once pipelines are established, resources may flow in either direction!

Katz and Eisenstadt (1960) discuss this issue from a less organization-centered point of view. They note that problems can occur from either of two types of imbalance—when an organization imposes too many or too few restrictions on the other roles held by its participants. When nonorganizational roles impinge on organizational roles inappropriately, then we have the problem of *debureaucratization.* The simplest examples are those of nepotism or corruption. The reverse problem occurs when organizational roles improperly assume priority over nonorganizational roles, leading to *overbureaucratization.* Examples of this process are provided by the early best-seller, *The Organization Man* (Whyte, 1956) and the more recent *Company Man* (Sampson, 1995), which describe the unreasonable requirements placed by some corporations on the personal lives of upwardly mobile managers and their families. It is by no means a simple or noncontroversial matter to determine when external roles are or are not properly impinging on organizational roles, and vice versa. There is, for example, much current discussion, fueled by feminist concerns, of modifying work arrangements to better accommodate family requirements (see Hochschild, 1989; Roman and Blum, 1993). More organizations are experimenting with flextime hours, work sharing, and off-site work locations, and more are providing family-oriented benefits, including maternity/paternity leave and day-care services. Still, critics complain that such programs are not widely available—U.S. government policies and most company practices lag behind their counterparts in Western Europe—and fall far short of meeting the need, particularly of women employees, who still bear disproportionate responsibility for both child care and parental care. (Other problems associated with overbureaucratization are discussed in Chapter 12.)

The extreme case of debureaucratization involves the dissolution of the organization. An organization no longer exists when it does not maintain a delimited network of social relations to which a distinctive normative order is applicable. Diamond (1958) provides an interesting case study of a disappearing organization: the fabled Virginia Company, associated with the founding of the Jamestown colony. This company was established in 1607 to exploit the riches of a new continent and the labors of its native peoples. Virginia proved to be different from previous English colonial sites in that native labor refused to be mobilized and mineral wealth was not to be found. It became necessary to establish an agricultural community based on voluntary labor imported from England. Over time, the company was forced to supply more and more inducements to its colonists: land became easier to acquire, women were recruited to become the wives of settlers, and company discipline was limited as representatives of the settlers acquired some voice in government. Diamond summarizes these changes:

> At one time in Virginia, the single relationship that existed between persons rested upon the position they occupied in the Company's table of organization. As a result of the efforts made by the Company to get persons to accept that relationship, however, each person in Virginia had become the occupant of several statuses, for now there were rich and poor in Virginia, landowners and renters, masters and servants, old residents and newcomers, married and single, men and women; and the simultaneous possession of these statuses

involved the holder in a network of relationships, some congruent and some incompatible, with his organizational relationship. (1958: 471)

Gradually, settlers came to regard their roles outside the company as more important and were no longer willing to accept their organizational position as the primary basis of legitimate order. Thus, a society emerged where before there had been only an organization.

Note that we have now located both ends of the continuum of organizational control over the relevant properties of participants. At one end of this continuum of social insulation–involvement, the organization is highly insulated from its social environment, the limiting case being that of the *total institution* as defined by Goffman. At the other end, the organization is highly involved in its social environment, the extreme case being the *engulfed organization*, exemplified by the Virginia Company as described by Diamond.[4] Of course, the majority of organizations are somewhere between these two extremes, able to exert some control over the multiple roles participants bring into the organization or informally develop within its confines, but rarely in a position to eradicate or exclude them. In most cases organizations do not wish to eliminate these external roles but prefer to mobilize them in their service.

From a broader historical perspective, there is no doubt that organizations have helped to bring about basic changes in societal stratification systems (see Eisenstadt, 1981). To the extent that kinship and other ascribed criteria are less employed in determining employment and career advancement, organizations have helped to produce "the great transformation" described by Polanyi (1944) by which market processes are less governed by other types of institutional criteria. Still, as Granovetter (1985) reminds us, we should not overstate the extent to which economic activities—including hiring, pay, and promotion decisions—are insulated from more diffuse social constraints. Economic processes are embedded in broader social networks and institutions.

Labor Markets and Organizational Boundaries

The current debate on the relative advantages of relying on internal labor markets in order to cement the loyalties of employees to the company versus utilizing more part-time or short-term workers provides an instructive example of the alternative ways in which modern organizations manage their social boundaries. The classical economic assumption that workers move freely from job to job and firm to firm, governed by pressures to maximize the fit between their skills and the requirements of their job, and hence between their productivity and their earnings, has been severely challenged by labor and institutional economists such as Kerr (1954) and Doeringer and

---

[4]Note that Katz and Eisenstadt (1960) have in mind a different continuum. One end point, debureaucratization, is the same as Udy's high social involvement, but the other end point, overbureaucratization, extends beyond the point where the organization insulates itself from the environment (as a total institution) to include situations in which the organization inappropriately imposes its normative system on formerly autonomous external systems.

Piore (1971). The latter analysts emphasize the extent to which information, opportunities, mobility, and rewards are differentially structured and shaped by varying occupational, industry, and organizational arrangements. Among the more important distinctions they introduce is that between internal and external labor markets. Doeringer and Piore (1971: 1) define *internal labor markets* as those within "an administrative unit, such as a manufacturing plant, within which the pricing and allocation of labor is governed by a set of administrative rules and procedures."

The key features of internal labor markets are (1) a cluster of jobs that (2) are hierarchically structured into one or more job ladders representing a progression in knowledge or skills, and that (3) include a few "entry ports" at the lower levels connecting them with wider, external labor markets (Althauser and Kalleberg, 1981). Note that in this conception it is not necessarily the case that all jobs in a given firm are organized as internal labor markets (Althauser, 1989). Estimates based on data collected on a representative sample of employees in the United States suggest that approximately half of the establishments in which these employees worked, sampled in 1991, met minimal criteria for internal labor markets for their key or "core" occupations (Kalleberg et al., 1996: 94). The use of internal labor markets by a firm represents one strategy for exercising increased control over its social boundaries.

What are the factors that lead to the creation of internal labor markets? As might be expected, rational and natural system theorists have posed alternative explanations. Working within the transaction cost framework—a rational open system model—Williamson (1981) argues that the most important influence on what type of labor market is created is the specificity of the human assets. The "human assets" of an organization are, of course, the skills and knowledge of its personnel. "Specificity" refers not simply to the extent of specialization of knowledge and skills, but to the degree to which these skills are transferable across employers. The deeper and more specialized one's skills are in the view of a specific employer, the more dependent is that employer on that employee, and vice versa, so that it is in the interests of both to create a "protective governance structure, lest productive values be sacrificed if the employment relation is unwittingly severed" (1981: 563). An internal labor market serves the employee's interests by providing the prospects of upward mobility through a regularized career of advancement, with increased earnings accompanying progression in skills. And the employer's interests are served because valuable workers in whom investments in training have been made are less likely to desert to a competitor.

In a related discussion, Williamson and Ouchi distinguish between "hard" and "soft" contracting:

> Under hard contracting, the parties remain relatively autonomous, each is expected to press his or her interests vigorously, and contracting is relatively complete. Soft contracting, by contrast, presumes much closer identity of interests between the parties, and formal contracts are much less complete. (1981: 361)

Soft contracting is characteristic of internal labor markets. It assumes a more elaborate governance structure (job ladders, grievance procedures, pay scales) and a higher level of investment and trust on the part of both employ-ers and employees. In this sense, internal labor markets may be viewed as mechanisms for bringing employees more fully and firmly within the bound-aries of an organization than is the case with external labor markets, in which the hard bargaining between employers and employees more closely resem-bles that occurring between two independent contractors.

The existence of internal labor markets is explained in a rather differ-ent manner by natural open system theorists. Marxist theorists such as Edwards (1979) argue that internal labor markets are more likely to arise in "core" segments of the economy—in large and powerful firms that have obtained an oligopoly, or near monopoly, in their industries (see Averitt, 1968). As these firms grow in size and complexity, they shift from simple hier-archical to technical to bureaucratic control systems. Edwards explains:

> *Bureaucratic* control, like technical control, differs from the simple forms of con-trol in that it grows out of the formal structure of the firm, rather than simply emanating from the personal relationships between workers and bosses. But while *technical* control is embedded in the physical and technological aspects of production and is built into the design of machines and the industrial architec-ture of the plant, bureaucratic control is embedded in the social and organiza-tional structure of the firm and is built into job categories, work rules, promotion procedures, discipline, wage scales, definitions of responsibilities, and the like. Bureaucratic control establishes the impersonal force of "company rules" or "company policy" as the basis for control. [Emphasis added.] (1979: 131)

Because they rely on social definitions rather than technical distinctions, bureaucratic control structures can be elaborated with ease: the number of offices, levels, titles, and salary levels can be multiplied without limit. Moreover, incentives can be added to reward not simply effort and produc-tivity but also such qualities as dependability, loyalty, and commitment to the organization.

Marxists view internal labor markets as reflecting the greater power of some classes of workers to wrest economic advantages from employers, but they also view these structures as:

> graded hierarchies that foster a docile "status" orientation and dissuade work-ers from utilizing the power implicit in their skills. Internal labor markets also institutionalize cleavages among workers along racial, sexual, and ethnic lines, thereby reducing the likelihood of working-class cohesion. (Baron, 1984: 40)

Pfeffer and Cohen (1984) employed data from a sample of about 300 large organizations in the San Francisco Bay area to test alternative explana-tions of internal labor markets. Degree of specificity of skills, as measured by extensiveness of employer training, somewhat predicted internal markets, providing support for the transaction cost arguments. But so did extent of unionization and being located in the core industries, providing support for a Marxist interpretation. In addition, Pfeffer and Cohen report that the development of internal labor markets was associated with the existence of a personnel department, a finding that supports an institutional interpretation of the spread of this structural form. Once such structures have been created in the more advanced organizations, they are apt to be picked up and promoted by professional personnel officers as being consistent with the principles of modern human resources management (see Baron, Dobbin, and Jennings, 1986). These results are largely corroborated by Kalleberg and colleagues (1996). In their study of a nationally representative sample of organizations, Kalleberg and associates found internal labor markets more likely to occur in organizations that were larger, more bureaucratic ("taller"), faced with asset specificity problems, were unionized, and whose personnel decisions were made by a centralized personnel office.

All of this theoretical and empirical attention to internal labor markets, their causes and consequences, seems a bit outdated given recent developments in United States corporations. Beginning during the mid-1980s and continuing up to the present time, many large corporations have been engaged in extensive "downsizing" efforts that, increasingly, affect not only blue-collar and lower-level employees but also white-collar workers and middle-and upper-level managers. Between 1979 and 1993, employment totals of the Fortune 500—the 500 largest manufacturing organizations in the United States—declined annually—from 16.2 million employees in 1979 to 11.5 million in 1993 (Useem, 1996). As a consequence, there is much speculation in the popular and academic press about whether the "implicit contract" between management and workers—which promised promotion and job security to faithful and productive workers—has been repealed (see Bluestone and Bluestone, 1992; Kochan, Katz, and McKersie, 1994). Informed observers suggest that conventional career paths through corporations no longer work: the rules for success in organizations have changed (see Kotter, 1995).

Increasingly, firms have discovered the benefits of various forms of *externalization* of the workforce. Pfeffer and Baron (1988) identify three ways in which the attachment between firms and workers may be decreased: locational, temporal, and administrative. Reduced *locational* attachment is exemplified by the increasing number of workers who perform their activities off-site, for example, "home work" or "flexiplace" arrangements. Such arrangements are encouraged by developments in computers that not only support home work through rapid information transfer but also enable work to be readily monitored. Reduction in *temporal* attachment refers to the increasing tendency for organizations to employ part-time or short-term workers, who often lack job benefits or job security. As many as one-fifth of the United States labor force as of 1978 worked part-time, defined as permanent employees working less than 35 hours per week (see Rotchford and Roberts, 1982). Finally, an increasing number of workers are *administratively* detached from the employment setting in the sense that they are hired on specific short-term contracts or are employed on another firm's payroll—for example, work for a temporary staffing agency. Temporary employment organizations have grown rapidly during the past two decades as have contracting-out arrangements. More than 6 million workers were employed by companies that supplied services to other companies, including temporary help agencies, in 1994 compared with just over 3 million in 1984 (Powell, 1996; see also, Warme, Lundy, and Ludy, 1992).

Organizations pursue externalization strategies for numerous reasons, including evading restrictions on hiring (public sector organizations often circumvent hiring restrictions by contracting out), focusing attention and resources on the firm's distinctive competence, paying reduced salaries and eliminating benefits, and to increase flexibility, both with respect to number of employees and mix of skills. Pfeffer and Baron comment:

> Ironically, then, because externalization enhances flexibility and focus, it may actually be an essential concomitant of human resource policies that emphasize long-term employment, commitment of the permanent workforce, and a shared vision or distinctive competence. In order to adapt to changes in the environment, firms need to have some way of changing staffing levels and work assignments and to do so without reneging on the implicit contracts held with the permanent workforce. Thus, the very elements of bureaucratic control and clan control that promise careers and continuity in return for loyalty and commitment may require a buffer workforce to absorb fluctuations in environmental demand. (1988: 274)

Economic "dualism" may not only be an important characteristic of the economy; it may be an increasingly important characteristic of many individual firms. These trends are accompanied by problems for workers and firms, which we discuss in Chapter 12.

The downsizing and outsourcing by corporations of work and workers is also occurring in response to the growing power of stockholders, who provide the necessary capital and who increasingly take a financial conception of the firm. Short-term financial gains can be achieved by reducing workers or selling off parts of the company, although such steps may not be in the long-range interest of the firm or of the society in which it operates.

Returning to the primary theme of social boundaries, current trends suggest that the boundaries of many work organizations are being redrawn such that labor—in particular, workers not connected to the core functions of the organizations—is becoming more peripheral and even external to the organization while investors—especially key stockholders—are being incorporated more fully into the firm (see Chapter 11). A new brand of "investor capitalism" is enabling corporate owners to exercise tighter control over managerial action (see Useem, 1996).

MANAGING TASK ENVIRONMENTS

In Chapter 6, following Dill (1958), we defined the task environment as those features of the environment relevant to the organization viewed as a production system—in particular, the sources of inputs, markets for outputs, competitors, and regulators. Since no organization generates all the resources necessary for its goal attainment or survival, organizations are forced to enter into exchanges, becoming interdependent with other environmental groups, typically other organizations. Unequal exchange relations can generate power and dependency differences among organizations; hence, organizations are expected to enter into exchange relations cautiously and to pursue strategies that will enhance their own bargaining position. This general perspective, labeled the resource dependence approach (see Chapter 5), has given rise to considerable theoretical and empirical work since the early 1970s (see Pfeffer and Salancik, 1978; Burt, 1983). Closely related work, on competitive strategies appropriate for firms confronting varying market configurations, has been carried out by Porter (1980). The level of analysis most often associated with this approach is that of the organization set: the environment is viewed as it relates to and impinges on some particular organization, which serves as the primary focus of the analysis.[5] Using a different set of assumptions, transaction cost theorists and population ecologists have also examined the relation of task environments to organizational forms.

As discussed in Chapter 6, determining the nature and scope of its domain is a critical concern for any organization. In arriving at their domain definition, organizations must negotiate and bargain with members of their organization set so that their claims to be in a given business are recognized as legitimate by others to whom they must relate. The higher the consensus on an organization's domain, the easier it will be for its members to conduct routine transactions.

Domain definition concerns not simply the general arena of activity, but what particular roles or functions the organization will perform. The manufacturer decides not simply to produce toys, but particular types or lines of toys targeted to particular types of customers—distributors and consumers. Porter (1980) regards decisions concerning product differentiation—the creation of relatively distinctive products and services—and focus—the identification of a selected buyer group or segment of a product line—to be among the most significant made by organizations in determining their comparative strategies. Among other effects, these decisions determine the identity of the organization's most significant competitors and partners—its strategic location within the broader industry or sector.

In addition, organizations must determine what subset of all the stages involved in producing a particular product or service they are going to embrace. The toy company does not ordinarily produce its own steel or plastic, but purchases these inputs, in varying stages of completion, from other firms. All organizations are confronted by basic decisions concerning which items or services they will make and which they will purchase from others. As Williamson (1975; 1981) points out, these "make or buy" decisions are tantamount to defining the technical boundaries of the organization. To "make" goods or services is to bring these activities within your own boundaries; to "buy" them is to relinquish them to the environment. As we would expect, Williamson predicts that firms will set their boundaries in such a manner as to minimize their transaction costs. Even if we do not accept this account as the only or even the most important basis for setting boundaries, it is clear that these are critical boundary-defining decisions. And it is important to see that organizations can and do regularly review and revise these decisions,

---

[5]However, Burt's (1983) work is conducted at a broader network or field level of analysis. He gives more attention than do most resource dependence theorists to constraints imposed on an organization's action by the wider structure of relations (see Davis and Powell, 1992).

eliminating former departments (for example, by contracting out these services) and adding new units (for example, through vertical integration). They can also decide to change domains (for example, by merging with a company in a different business).

We continue our discussion of managing task environments by reviewing the main concerns and contributions of the resource dependence theorists. In general, two lines of argument may be distinguished. The first focuses on the central work processes of the organization and asks how they may be protected from disturbances arising from the task environment. The strategies considered are those designed to *buffer* the organization's technical core—to amplify its protective boundaries. This argument emphasizes the need to close the system artificially to enhance the possibilities of rational action.[6] The second line of argument recognizes that among the most important actions organizations can take is the modification of their boundaries, more or less drastically and more or less formally. These actions include boundary-spanning and boundary-shifting strategies that *bridge* between organizations and their exchange partners, competitors, or regulators.

Buffering Strategies

Organizations may be viewed as technological systems—as mechanisms for transforming inputs into outputs. It is almost always possible to identify one or more central sets of tasks around which an organization is constructed. Teaching in schools, treatment and patient care in hospitals, investigatory work in research organizations, assembly work in automobile plants, legislating in Congress—these are examples of central tasks in varying types of organizations. Following James Thompson (1967), we will refer to the arrangements developed to perform these central tasks—including the skills of personnel employed to carry them out—as the *core technology* of the organization.

A key proposition formulated by Thompson is that "under norms of rationality, organizations seek to seal off their core technologies from environmental influences" (1967: 19). This proposition follows from Thompson's attempt to reconcile the rational, natural, and open system perspectives, as described in Chapter 5. He argues that the rational system perspective is most applicable at the technical level of the organization. Here, if anywhere, there is expected to be a concern with the careful selection of means to pursue ends and an attempt to reduce to a minimum the extraneous forces that can upset these connections. The purest example of these tendencies, which are expected to be present to some degree in all organizations, is the organization that is able to develop a *long-linked technology*, a series of sequential, interdependent production activities, exemplified by the assembly line in a manufacturing company (1967: 15–16).

Long-linked technologies can be created only when certain conditions are met. They require (1) a clear understanding of the cause-effect relations linking inputs with outputs, so that by carrying out the proper activities it is

---

[6]Some kinds of task demands and environmental conditions make it impossible to exclude uncertainty from the technical core. Structural accommodations for dealing with these situations are examined in Chapter 9.

possible to produce the desired effect regularly; (2) a stable supply of appropriate inputs; and (3) a continuing demand for the standardized outputs. The last two conditions require the organization to deal with its environment. The long-linked technology, while effective and efficient for achieving specific objectives, is quite inflexible and, hence, vulnerable to change or uncertainty.

All organizations, but especially those with long-linked technologies, are highly motivated to secure enough stability, determinateness, and certainty to be able to function efficiently and effectively in environments that contain unknowns and uncertainties. Organizations seeking to buffer their technical flows from environmental perturbations may pursue a number of strategies. These strategies come in many forms and guises, but they all may be regarded as intraorganizational techniques aimed at reducing uncertainty for the technical core. As with all strategies, there are potential costs as well as gains for the organization, and in our brief review we will touch on both.

Coding. Organizations can classify inputs before inserting them into the technical core. Preprocessing of inputs aids their proper routing and, if necessary, their exclusion. If inappropriate or inadequately processed inputs inadvertently gain entry, they can cause delays, create machinery problems, or require special attention, often from supervisory personnel. For example, on an automobile assembly line, the parts are carefully inspected and rejects are culled before they are placed on the conveyor belt. Coding is not restricted to long-linked technologies or even to industrial concerns; for example, human-service agencies classify clients as a means of determining their eligibility for service and facilitating their routing to the appropriate service units.

The costs of coding should not be overlooked. The coding process itself consumes resources and is always imperfect. No set of codes can capture all of the relevant properties of the raw materials; codes always simplify, sometimes in useful, but sometimes in distorting or biasing ways. Also, we should recall Weick's admonition that while organizations need to reduce equivocality (by coding) in order to ensure some stability, they also need to retain some equivocality in order to learn how their environment is changing and to retain flexibility (Weick 1979; 1995; see also, Chapter 4).

Stockpiling. Organizations can collect and hold raw materials or products and thereby control the rate at which inputs are inserted into the technical core or outputs released to the environment. Organizations are likely to stockpile critical resources, those whose supply is uncertain or whose price fluctuates greatly over time. The hope is that regardless of vicissitudes on the supply side, the organization will be assured of a continuous flow of resources. Similarly, on the output side, products may be held in warehouses in order to be released on the market at the most propitious time. But the capital tied up in reserves is not productive, and the costs of stockpiling include storage costs and possible loss through spoilage, damage, deterioration, or obsolescence.[7] The problem confronting all organizations is to

---

[7]Stockpiling is one source of organizational *slack*: unused resources. New procedures, such as "just-in-time" inventory control systems represent attempts to reduce this source of inefficiency. These procedures are discussed in Chapter 9.

ensure that inventories are sufficient to meet all needs—both on the supply and demand sides—while defending against the possibility of obsolescence as production needs or customer demands change.

Leveling.   Leveling, or smoothing, is an attempt by the organization to reduce fluctuations in its input or output environments. Whereas stockpiling is a relatively passive technique, leveling entails a more active attempt to reach out into the environment to motivate suppliers of inputs or to stimulate demand for outputs. Organizations use advertising to stimulate demand for their products; retail stores schedule sales during slack periods, utilities stimulate or discourage use of their power supplies by variable time-of-day rates, and colleges hold conferences in the summer to use idle facilities. Even hospitals smooth their work flow by scheduling elective surgery during slack periods. The costs associated with such efforts are self-evident: seeking out suppliers or customers consumes energy and resources, and many of the techniques used, such as advertising, tend to combine high costs and uncertain returns.

Forecasting.   If environmental fluctuations cannot be handled by stockpiling or by leveling, organizations may have to settle for forecasting: anticipating changes in supply or demand conditions and attempting to adapt to them. Environmental changes are often patterned, exhibiting a weekly or a seasonal cycle. Organizations taking account of such regularities can often accommodate them. For example, taxi companies anticipate changes in demand for their services over a twenty-four-hour period and arrange drivers' schedules accordingly; beaches or amusement parks make educated guesses about crowd size based on school and holiday schedules. Costs associated with forecasting, in addition to those entailed in guessing wrong, include the difficulties of expanding and contracting capacity, in particular the problems and inefficiencies of using part-time or short-term help. As discussed earlier, externalized labor sources, such as temporary agencies and contracts for outsourcing of specific tasks, are among the devices used by organizations to achieve flexibility.

Adjusting scale.   Changing the scale of the technical core, in response to information provided by forecasting, or for other reasons, is one of the most general buffering strategies available to organizations. Technological factors may encourage growth: there are favorable economies of scale for virtually every kind of technical process, and Thompson argues that organizations will tend to expand "until the least-reducible component is approximately fully occupied" (1967: 46). Other, probably more compelling factors encourage growth as well. Larger size, particularly relative to one's competitors, is typically associated with increased power. Thus, larger firms are better able to set prices, control how much they produce, and influence the decisions of related organizations. Pfeffer and Salancik summarize the advantages of size:

> Organizations that are large have more power and leverage over their environments. They are more able to resist immediate pressures for change and, more-

over, have more time in which to recognize external threats and adapt to meet them. Growth enhances the organization's survival value, then, by providing a cushion, or slack, against organizational failure. (1978: 139)

Organizations grow, but they also shrink. They go into decline, for lack of resources, and they may also shrink for strategic reasons. As noted, many organizations have engaged in downsizing, often to focus more intensively on their distinctive competence. Some types of organizations must know how to both grow and shrink rapidly. Military organizations are examples of organizations that maintain structures in place to support both rapid mobilizing and demobilizing efforts.

The buffering strategies just described represent standard operating procedures for conventional organizations. They achieve the benefits of increased stability and predictability so as to support the use of standardized routines and mass production machines. However, as the environment becomes more competitive and demand more customized, these costs associated with stability rise and the benefits of flexibility increase. We reserve for Chapter 9 a consideration of techniques employed by organizations to be more responsive to dynamic environments.

We have argued that buffering strategies are employed to help seal off or cushion the technical core from disturbances in the environment. Organizations also use bridging strategies, some of which are intended to benefit the technical core. More often, however, bridging strategies are oriented toward enhancing the security of the organization in relation to its environment. Safety, survival, and an improved bargaining position are the prizes that motivate bridge building, rather than improving the performance of its technical core.

Bridging Strategies

While buffering strategies are primarily associated with the technical core, bridging strategies are oriented toward the security of the entire organization in relation to its environment. They address, in particular, the power position of an organization vis-à-vis its exchange partners.

Virtually all of the formulations of power and exchange relations among organizations build on the conception of power developed by Emerson (1962). Emerson emphasizes that one actor's power over another is rooted in the latter's dependence on resources controlled by the former. As expressed by Emerson, "the power of A over B is equal to, and based upon, the dependence of B upon A" (1962: 33). Further, the dependence of one actor on another varies as a function of two factors: B's dependence on A (1) is directly proportional to the importance B places on the goals mediated by A, and (2) is inversely proportional to the availability of these goals to B outside the A-B relationship. Obviously, the actors involved may be individuals, groups, or organizations (see also Chapter 11).

Emerson's formulation is useful for several reasons when applied to a given organization and the set of organizations to which it relates (see Thompson, 1967). Power is not viewed as some generalized capacity but as a function of specific needs and resources that can vary from one exchange partner to another. Thus, it is possible for an organization to have relatively little power in relation to its suppliers, but considerable power in relation to its buyers. Further, we would expect each supplier's power to vary with the importance of the resources it supplies and the extent to which alternative suppliers are available. This approach avoids a zero-sum view of power, in which it is assumed that when one actor gains power another must lose it. Rather, it becomes possible for two actors to each gain in power over the other—through an increase in the extent of their interdependence.

Bridging strategies may be viewed as a response to increasing organizational interdependence. Interdependence can occur when two or more different kinds of organizations exchange resources. Such *symbiotic* interdependence can give rise, as noted, to power differences if the resources exchanged are not of equal importance. Interdependence also occurs when two or more similar organizations compete for the resources of another party. Such *competitive* or commensalistic interdependence is often resolved by differentiation, former competitors becoming exchange partners (Blau and Scott, 1962: 217–21). For example, an automobile manufacturer may be unable to compete successfully by selling automobiles but survive by supplying parts to other automobile companies.

The most complete analysis of bridging strategies to date is that provided by Pfeffer and Salancik; our summary draws heavily on their work. Their general thesis is simply stated: "The typical solution to problems of interdependence and uncertainty involves increasing coordination, which means increasing the mutual control over each other's activities" (1978: 43). Although all bridging strategies share this feature, they are quite varied in the strength and the nature of the connections forged. Some of the more common types of bridging strategies are described below.

Bargaining. We use the term *bargaining* to refer not to one but to a large family of strategies by which an organization attempts to ward off dependence. To be compulsively precise, bargaining is not really a bridging but a prebridging strategy: it consists of things to do before calling in the bridge builders or while waiting for them to arrive. Much of the bargaining pertains to defining and defending the organization's domain. Other types are aimed at helping the organization increase its independence and improve its competitive position. Students of organizations are increasingly aware that bargaining and negotiating are complex activities, requiring knowledge of one's own interests and priorities, those of others, information about the current and likely future states of affairs, knowledge of rule systems and norms governing agreements, and related matters (see Bazerman and Neale, 1992).

Contracting. According to Thompson, contracting is "the negotiation of an agreement for the exchange of performances in the future" (1967: 35). Contracts may be more or less formally drawn up and more or less legally binding. The critical point is that they represent attempts by organizations to reduce uncertainty by coordinating their future behavior, in limited and specific ways, with other units. As we have learned from Williamson (1975), there is a limit to how much uncertainty can be hedged or handled by contracts (see Chapter 7), but Williamson himself notes (pp. 90–95) that contracts can be modified to handle considerable uncertainty; contingent claims contracts, incomplete long-term contracts, and sequential spot contracts are examples. The negotiation of contracts with labor unions and principal suppliers and buyers is one of the chief ways in which organizations assure themselves of some degree of certainty in a changing environment.

While contracts take a legal or quasi-legal form, in practice they typically involve considerable latitude and informal renegotiation. Because it is so costly, both in monetary terms and in the damage it inflicts on the ongoing relation, litigation is rare (see Macaulay, 1963). However, dispute resolution processes are certainly strengthened because they take place "in the shadow of the law."

Co-optation. As defined in Chapter 3, co-optation is the incorporation of representatives of external groups into the decision-making or advisory structure of an organization. The significance of this practice in linking organizations with their environments was first described by Selznick (1949), who also noted its possible costs. Selznick argued that by co-opting representatives of external groups, organizations are, in effect, trading sovereignty for support.

Most studies of co-optation have focused on boards of directors, investigating the extent of interlocking ties among various types of organizations.[8] It is argued that allowing representatives of other organizations to participate in decision making in the focal organization is an important indication of interdependence and an effort by the linked organizations to coordinate their activities. Such representatives may range from strong, controlling directors imposed by one organization on another to common messengers transmitting information of mutual interest (Pennings, 1981). Not all board members are environmental representatives: some are there to provide specialized expertise, to oversee and augment the administrative skills of management.

To the extent that directorate ties function as a co-optative strategy for dealing with the interdependence of organizations, we would expect board appointments to vary with the amount and type of resource needs and flows confronting the focal organization. Although it is often difficult to measure needs and flows, and although co-optation is only one possible means of managing interdependence, there is considerable evidence to support this interpretation. For example, studies by Pfeffer of eighty randomly selected

[8]Two different, but related, perspectives have been employed in the study of interlocking directorates. The first is an interorganizational approach that assumes organizations are entities pursuing interests, during which they establish connections with other organizations. The resource dependence approach embraces this perspective. The second, a Marxist perspective, is an intraclass approach that assumes that individual actors, such as members of the business elite, have interests and that organizations are the agents they use to establish relations with other individuals sharing their class interests (see Palmer, 1983; Mizruchi, 1982; Pfeffer, 1987). These two perspectives take basically similar views of the functions of interlocks—they secure resources, information, and support, for example—but differ as to what set of interests is being promoted—organizational versus class.

nonfinancial corporations (1972a) and fifty-seven hospitals in Illinois (1973) provide empirical support for the expectation that board appointments are used by organizations to establish linkages with important segments of the environment on which they are dependent. Thus, the corporations that exhibited a high debt-equity ratio were observed to have a higher proportion of representatives from financial institutions on their boards. And hospitals having larger budgets, and those receiving a higher proportion of their capital budgets from private donations and lacking federal or religious affiliations, were more likely to stress fund-raising ability as a criterion for selecting board members.

More convincing evidence is provided by Burt and his colleagues (Burt, Christman, and Kilburn, 1980; Burt, 1983), who examined the extent of interlocking directorates, among a sample of the largest manufacturing firms from each of twenty industries in the United States for 1967. In their approach, the economy is viewed as a network of industrial sectors, differing in degree of concentration and extent of interconnections as measured by empirical studies of interindustry sales (input-output ratios). The analysts propose that firms in more highly concentrated sectors that buy and sell to many other sectors that are less highly concentrated are likely to be more profitable and to have less need to establish interlocks. Interlocks are expected to be more common among firms in less highly concentrated industries and among firms having to deal with buyers and sellers in more highly concentrated sectors. These predictions were confirmed for profitability and for three types of directorate ties: firms owned by the same corporation (and thus having the same directors); firms owned by two corporations sharing one or more directors; and firms owned by two corporations sharing a director with the same financial institution. Burt and associates conclude that:

> Each of the three types of directorate ties tends to occur where there is market constraint and tends not to occur in the absence of constraint. Further, the three types of ties are coordinated as multiplex directorate ties. Where establishments in one sector constrain those in another, there is a strong tendency for all three types of directorate ties to exist between the two sectors. . . . Whatever the cooptive intent of the directorate ties described, they are patterned as if they were intended to coopt market constraints on corporate pricing discretion. (1980: 821)

Finally, Burt and associates note that the use of interlocks to manage dependence is much more common between firms in different industries than between firms in the same industry, probably because of antitrust regulations that prohibit such visible techniques of cooperation (collusion?) among competitors.

Co-optation is also widely employed as a coordinating strategy among public agencies and nonprofit associations. From the mid 1960s, the era of the Great Society programs, to the late 1970s, a great many federally sponsored organizations were created whose hallmark was decentralized decision making combined with mandated participation of representatives from the areas affected. Such programs included community action agencies, model cities programs, community mental health programs, area agencies for the aged, and health systems agencies (see Piven and Cloward, 1971; Sundquist, 1969). Analysts disagree about the effects of such ties: some see them as compromising agency objectives; others as providing a useful voice for suppressed interests. More generally, network theorists suggest that, in contested arenas, which interests prevail is determined by the relative strength of supportive relations in which they are embedded (see Padgett and Ansell, 1992).

With the coming of more conservative policies in the 1980s, including the reduction in the federal role and in funding for community services, co-optation has shifted from being a primarily vertical strategy to being a horizontal strategy. Community agencies employ numerous co-optation mechanisms—joint board memberships, liaison roles, interorganizational brokers—as a way to increase resources, reduce uncertainty, and increase legitimacy (see Galaskiewicz, 1985). Indeed, federal and state programs currently place great emphasis on coordination among community agencies, often as a condition of being eligible for funding. Whereas federal regulations proscribe co-optation among competing organizations in the for-profit sector, they mandate it as a means of coordination among public and non-profit agencies.

Hierarchical contracts. Stinchcombe (1985) has identified an important class of coordinating mechanisms that combine some of the "arms-length" features of contracts with other control features usually associated with authority relations exercised within organizational boundaries. He observes that these augmented contracts are employed as the principal control mechanisms even under conditions of extraordinary complexity and uncertainty—for example, in relations between defense agencies and supplier firms or between nation-states and oil construction and production companies—where we would expect, under formulations such as Williamson's, to find the exclusive use of internal organizational controls. The contracts developed to manage such interdependence involve a variety of conditional clauses to handle possible contingencies and to resolve disputes. For example, defense contractors may allow the purchaser to inspect compliance to requirements and progress toward objectives as necessary; to change requirements or specifications as the work proceeds; and to renegotiate the allocation of costs and benefits depending on what outcomes occur. Such hierarchical rights undermine the autonomy of the independent contractors and constitute a step in the direction of creating a joint venture between the contracting parties—except that the "venture" is a specific project rather than a continuing program of cooperative activity. Such admittedly complex contracting arrangements are widely employed in high-cost–high-gain (high-risk) situations, such as large-scale construction and defense and space technology.

Strategic alliances. An increasingly popular way to obtain the benefits of larger scale and differentiation without the costs of investing in and maintaining facilities and personnel is to participate in strategic alliances. *Alliances* involve agreements between two or more organizations to pursue joint objectives through a coordination of activities or sharing of knowledge or resources. Airline firms may coordinate schedules, exchange maintenance service, or jointly purchase fuel; manufacturing companies may share production technology or R&D costs; medical care organizations may share laboratories or pharmacies, or agree to regularly refer patients to particular providers for specialized care. Alliances can allow cooperating firms to parlay strengths in one arena into advantages in another in which they are currently weak. For example, a company may have efficient production facilities but lack effective distribution systems or access to desirable markets. Alliances operate on the premise that dependable coordination and control does not require joint ownership, but can be built on contractual arrangements supported by trust (see Alter and Hage, 1993; Harrigan, 1985; Kanter, 1994; Kaluzny, Zuckerman, and Ricketts, 1995). As we discuss in Chapter 10, strategic alliances, or "network forms," provide an important and increasingly popular alternative to integrated firms and multidivisional companies.

Joint ventures. A joint venture occurs when two or more firms create a new organization to pursue some common purpose. Joint ventures differ from mergers, discussed below, in that they entail only a limited pooling of resources by the participating organizations. For example, several wholesale companies may combine resources to purchase a trucking operation, or a wholesale company may combine assets with a farmers' cooperative to build a canning company. As these examples suggest, joint ventures may occur among either competitors or exchange partners. Testing the hypothesis that joint ventures tend to reflect resource interdependencies, Pfeffer and Nowak (1976) examined data from 166 joint ventures occurring over a decade. In support of the hypothesis, they found that the more exchanges taking place between different industry groups, as measured by interindustry sales figures, the more likely firms from these industries were to enter into joint ventures. Pfeffer and Nowak also tested the prediction that firms within industry groups facing higher competition would be more likely to develop joint ventures as a means of reducing competitive pressures. Again, the data supported the prediction: joint ventures were found to be more frequent within industries exhibiting an intermediate level of concentration, a situation of maximum competitive pressure.[9]

Of course, competition does not just stem from domestic competitors. In the interests of maintaining competitive markets within this country, many types of joint ventures are prohibited by U.S. antitrust laws. However, because of increasing pressure from international competitors, such policies are being reviewed and, in some cases, modified. The National Cooperative Research Act passed in 1984, for example, allows competitive firms within this country to develop joint ventures in order to pool basic research activities. As of 1990, more than 150 U.S. cooperative research and development consortia have developed. These joint ventures can be large and complex undertakings. For example, one of the earliest and largest to develop is the Microelectronics and Computer Technology Corporation (MCC), a venture

[9]Industry groups with high concentration ratios are those dominated by a relatively small group of firms. These firms are more likely to have developed an "understanding" with one another, and together they control the conditions of survival for the smaller firms within the industry. On the other hand, industry groups with low concentration ratios are, by definition, composed of a great many small firms, no one of which is able to generate great competitive pressures on its neighbors.

owned by twenty-two corporations in semiconductor, computer, and aerospace industries designed to carry out long-range research in computer and semiconductor technology (see Gibson and Rogers, 1988).

Mergers.   No doubt the most drastic strategy used by organizations in relating to critical units of their environment is to absorb these units: two or more independent organizations form a single collective actor. Three major types of mergers have been identified:

1. *Vertical integration,* in which organizations engaged in related functions but at different stages in the production process merge, backward or forward, with one another. Vertical integration, of course, takes place between exchange partners—organizations that are symbiotically related. For example, furniture manufacturers may merge (backward) with lumber companies or (forward) with furniture distributors or showrooms.
2. *Horizontal merger,* in which organizations performing similar functions merge to increase the scale of their operation. For example, two car dealerships that formerly handled only one line of automobiles may merge into one dealership handling two or more brands.
3. *Diversification,* in which one organization acquires one or more other organizations that are neither exchange partners nor similar organizations competing with each other, but organizations operating in different domains. For example, in the 1960s International Telegraph and Telephone, an electronics-manufacturing company, acquired a rent-a-car company, a major hotel chain, a home-building company, a baking company, a producer of glass and sand, a consumer-lending firm, and a data-processing organization. The extreme form of diversification is the *conglomerate.*

The United States has experienced several waves of mergers, each of a differing type. Drucker (1970) argues that most mergers at the turn of the century involved horizontal or vertical integration as a dominant industrialist or financier attempted to gain control within a single industry. Mergers occurring in the 1920s represented a "defensive" reaction to these earlier developments as smaller companies jockeyed for position in the second tier. Most recent mergers involve the creation of conglomerates, either as a result of organizations attempting to diversify or as a result of their being taken over by aggressive asset managers who promise stockholders a better return on capital (see Chandler, 1990).

Research by Pfeffer (1972b) supports the expectation that mergers involving vertical integration are more likely to occur among companies in industries engaged in frequent transactions. His study of 854 large mergers of companies in manufacturing and mining shows that mergers tended to occur more often among types of firms highly interdependent in their resource flows. Further, his findings on the effects of competitive interdependence replicated those reported for joint ventures: horizontal mergers were more likely to occur among firms located in industries exhibiting intermediate levels of concentration—situations of maximum intraindustry competition. Finally, Pfeffer and Salancik argue that mergers involving diversification are most likely to occur "when exchanges are very concentrated and when capital or statutory constraints" limit the use of other options for managing interorganizational interdependence (1978: 127).

As we have seen, the resource dependence approach emphasizes the extent of interorganizational resource flows and the degree of market concentration as the basis for generating predictions about mergers in general and vertical integration in particular. And as noted earlier, Williamson (1975; 1981) suggests that decisions concerning vertical integration can also be explained as attempts to reduce transaction costs. It is expected that as the assets required by an organization become more specific, firms will elect to produce them internally to avoid becoming overly dependent on a small number of external suppliers. This prediction was tested by Monteverde and Teece (1982) in a study of decisions made by General Motors and by Ford for a list of 133 automotive components. Measuring asset specificity by the amount of development effort required to produce a given component, they reported that, as expected, specificity was positively associated with the decision to integrate-in the manufacture of the component. Walker and Weber (1984) studied sixty decisions made in a component division of a large United States automobile manufacturer, decisions both to integrate (make rather than buy) and to deintegrate (buy rather than make) components. Consistent with transaction cost predictions, the division was more likely to manufacture components itself if there were few competing suppliers and if the volume of parts needed was uncertain. A recent review of empirical research testing transaction cost arguments concludes that asset specificity appears to be "an important determinant of vertical integration, particularly when examined together with uncertainty and product complexity" (Shelanski and Klein, 1995).

Resource dependence and transaction cost explanations of mergers are not necessarily in conflict, although the former place greater stress on the organization's interest in reducing uncertainty and dependence while the latter stress its interest in increasing economic efficiency.

Associations. Associations are arrangements that allow similar or diverse organizations to work in concert to pursue mutually desired objectives. They operate under many names, including trade associations, cartels, leagues, coordinating councils, and coalitions.

Both similar and dissimilar organizations enter into associations at the community or local level. We find many associations of similar organizations—for example, hospital councils and associations of retail merchants—as well as associations of diverse organizations—the community chest and chambers of commerce. Individual organizations join associations in order, variously, to garner resources, secure information, exercise influence, or obtain legitimacy and acceptance. The structure and strength of associations vary greatly: some are informal and weak, others are formally structured and exercise great power over their members (see Warren, 1967).

The trade association is an important type of association operating at the field or sector, national, and even international level. It is "a coalition of firms or businessspersons who come together in a formal organization to cope with forces and demands to which they are similarly exposed" (Staber and Aldrich, 1983: 163; see also, Staber, 1985). There is some evidence that trade associations are more likely to form in less highly concentrated sectors where too many firms are present to permit more tacit coordination (Pfeffer and Salancik, 1978: 179).

The power of trade associations varies markedly from society to society. Trade associations in the United States are more numerous, more specialized, and much less influential than those in most Western European countries, Japan, and Korea. Most trade associations in the United States are not sufficiently strong or organized to serve as vehicles for centralizing and representing the interests of industries, as do trade associations in the more corporatist states[10] (see Berger, 1981; Okimoto, 1984; Streeck and Schmitter, 1985). Institutional theorists increasingly attend to these structures as important examples of governance systems at the organization field level (see Campbell, Hollingsworth, and Lindberg, 1991; Scott, 1994).

Government connections. The nation-state is the prime sovereign in the modern world, the major source of legitimate order, the agent defining, managing, and overseeing the legal framework of society. Whereas early views regarded organizations in the private sector as sometimes being subject to governmental intervention, contemporary theorists insist that the nation is always a relevant actor, although the ways in which the state acts varies from place to place and time to time (Block, 1994). Although often treated as a monopolistic agency, the state—particularly liberal states such as the United States—is more realistically treated as a highly differentiated, multifaceted, often loosely coupled congeries of organizations. For example, many semi-independent agencies regulate and fund various aspects of health care in the United States. Federal systems also divide powers between national, state, and local governmental units.

All nation-states exercise extensive powers over economic and other types of exchange processes, playing a central role in enforcing the general rules governing technical environments (see North, 1990). Although these functions are broadly institutional in nature, because they directly impact the exchange of resources, we consider them here rather than in the following section dealing with institutional environments.

Lindblom has pointed out that "an easy way to acknowledge the special character of government as an organization is simply to say that governments exercise authority over other organizations" (1977: 21). Although Lindblom goes on to caution that governmental authority is sometimes contested, it is nevertheless essential to take account of governments' special powers and of the unique role a government plays as an organization among organizations.

Agencies of the modern state in general exercise considerable authority over the many arenas that make up a society, but observers have noted that the amount and nature of authority exerted varies considerably from one

---

[10]Corporatism is a political system involving the development of a set of "noncompetitive, hierarchically ordered and functionally differentiated" private interests who are allowed legitimate and privileged access to and participate in public decision making (Schmitter 1974: 93). It is more characteristic of some Latin American and northern European state systems.

sector or field to another (see Campbell, Hollingsworth, and Lindberg, 1991; Schmitter, 1990). Moreover, the kinds of controls also vary. Campbell and Lindberg (1990) usefully distinguish between the influence that states exercise as *institutional actors* and that exerted because of the *institutional texture* they present. As *actors*, states affect sectors through their allocation decisions—for example, supplying government-guaranteed loans or purchasing goods or services—but also by their power to define and enforce property rights—for example, antitrust, regulatory, and labor policies. Through such actions, states help to define "the balance of power among a wide variety of actors in civil society" (Campbell and Lindberg, 1990: 636).

Some laws and regulations apply to all types of organizations—for example, those specifying general property rights, rules of fair trade, and employee benefits such as workmen's compensation and social security. Their impact is determined by the specific wording of the statutes, regulations, and court interpretations by which they are implemented. Individual organizations and associations of organizations are therefore motivated to influence these policies. Thus, when laws are being formulated or revised, organizations will see to it that their concerns and interests are expressed in testimony before legislative committees, in lobbying efforts directed at individual legislators, and in commentaries on the "feasibility" and fairness of proposed administrative regulations. Many laws as written are ambiguous until their meaning is "clarified" by collective interpretation on the part of organizational representatives and rulings by the courts (see Edelman, 1992).

Governments also place special constraints on the transactions of certain categories of organizations. Many types of organizations confront governmental regulatory bodies that monitor closely the quality of their products or services or their transactions with exchange partners or competitors. Utilities, railroads, banks, and pharmaceutical companies, for example, have long operated under the close scrutiny of public regulatory bodies. Numerous observers have pointed out that although such surveillance may, as intended, help to protect the public interest, it also has the unintended effect of protecting the interests of the organizations being regulated—by restraining competitive pressures, restricting the entry of new firms, and managing prices (see Stigler, 1971; Wilson, 1980; Noll, 1985). Co-optative processes operate as organizations influence regulatory agents in an attempt to reduce the uncertainties in their environments.

In addition to regulating economic transactions, public organizations also enter into them. Many public agencies are a major provider of resources. Some resource flows are indirect, coming in the form of tax breaks or exemptions; others are more direct, involving outright transfers of funds in the form of subsidies or grants; and still others involve the government's acting not as an interested third party but as a direct participant in the transaction—as a buyer of products or a client of services. Some departments of the federal government, such as the Pentagon, are the primary purchasers of the products of a vast complex of organizations. And some populations of organizations—for example, applied research organizations such as RAND and SRI—exist largely on contracts to conduct studies and provide services for a large range of governmental agencies.

The tactics organizations employ to influence governmental organizations are not the same ones they use with private organizations. In particular, as Pfeffer and Salancik (1978: 192) have noted, private organizations requesting special treatment from governmental agencies must justify their private claims on the grounds that they serve the public interest. Thus, the Chrysler Corporation's successful pursuit of $1.5 billion in loan guarantees from the federal government was justified in the name of preserving competition in the automobile industry and safeguarding the jobs of American workers.

Viewed as a complex of governance units exhibiting varying institutional *texture*, state agencies provide varied contexts for taking action and resolving disputes. With respect to some sectors, the state is relatively unified (for example, atomic energy); with respect to others, it is fragmented and conflictful (for example, education). A number of studies have demonstrated that organizations operating in environments containing more fragmented and conflicting sources of authority are more likely to develop more complex and elaborated administrative structures (Meyer, Scott, and Strang, 1987; Scott and Meyer, 1991a). The state also offers arenas of political access to private interests, and provides forums for decision making and dispute resolution, all of which vary by sector (see Hult and Walcott, 1990).

Selecting among bridging strategies. Several general types of bridging strategies have been described. The construction of a theoretical argument that allows us to be able to view such diverse organizational activities as alternative strategies for managing interdependence is one of the major contributions of the resource dependence approach. An important issue requiring further study is to determine the conditions under which one rather than another strategy is likely to be used. Davis, Kahn, and Zald (1990) begin to address this question by developing the framework depicted in Figure 8–1. Two principal dimensions underlie their approach: (1) whether the interdependence being managed is symbiotic or commensalistic and (2) the degree or extent of coordinative structure constructed. Depending on the extent and importance of the symbiotic interdependence involved, the mechanisms employed range from short-term contracts at the low end to vertical mergers at the high. Responses to commensalistic interdependence range from co-optative strategies to manage modest levels of competition to horizontal mergers to resolve high levels.

From a strategic point of view, all of these bridging devices can be viewed as varying types of strategic connections. From negotiating specific contracts to full-scale mergers, organizations strive to improve their position by developing advantageous linkages with other units. For most of this century, it has been assumed (by both practitioners and theorists) that the strongest and most effective ties were those based on ownership: joint ventures, acquisitions, mergers. In recent years, however, many organizations have entered into contracts and alliances that do not entail changes in ownership; and organization theorists have begun to recognize the importance of these forms. Strong alliances or networks between independent organizations permit participating units to combine many of the advantages that come from being independent (and perhaps also the flexibilities that come from being small) with some of the security and strength that comes from being in league with others (see Powell, 1990; Harrison, 1994; see also Chapter 10).

Symbiotic	*Commensalistic*
┌Vertical mergers	┌Horizontal mergers
├"Symbiotic" joint ventures	├Cooperative joint ventures
├Hierarchical contracts	├Trade associations
├Contracting	├Co-optation/collusion
▼ Markets	▼ Markets

FIGURE 8–1 Symbiotic and Commensalistic Bridging Strategies. *Source:* Adapted from Davis, Kahn, and Zald (1990), Figures 2.1, 2.2, pp. 34–35.

Determing which bridges to build and which to dismantle. It is not feasible for organizations to build connections with all relevant parties who are in a position to affect their behavior or outcomes. During the heyday of diversification, many organizations appeared to be attempting to follow this strategy, reaching out to incorporate a wide range of allies, but the 1990s have been marked by much more restricted growth—indeed, by downsizing and outsourcing strategies. How do organizations determine which units to keep and which to let go? How do organizations decide with which independent organizations to develop linkages?

Stinchcombe argues that in times of uncertainty and rapid change, information about the future is of critical importance. For each organization some types of information are more valuable than others, and this information is located in "distinct social locations." In search of the "earliest available information that will show what direction the actor ought to be going," organizations will grow "toward those locations where information for resolving uncertainty is chiefly located" (Stinchcombe, 1990: 2). As organizations increasingly move from serving large, mass markets to meeting the needs of more diversified customers, they need to be able, on the one hand, to keep track of changes in consumer demand and, on the other, to rapidly change their mix of production technologies (See Piore and Sable, 1984). To track consumer demand, in addition to making increasing use of a wide range of information technologies to track their own and competitors' sales in various markets, they develop partnerships with leading customers. Customer representatives are quizzed about problems with products or services; they are invited to test and critique prototypes; they are even allowed to participate directly in design sessions. They are increasingly incorporated within the boundaries of the firm. On the production side, workers key to the mission of the firm are accorded greater participation in decision making and provided incentives to encourage them to share their ideas and reveal their "tacit" knowledge. Flexibility is increasingly achieved by negotiating "relational contracts" with a number of favored suppliers. Connections with these contractors involve not just the increased sharing of information but also mutual investments in machinery and training, and sometimes the exchange of personnel (see Kanter, 1994; Harrison, 1994). On both the input and the output sides, contemporary organizations continually draw and redraw their technical boundaries to incorporate or ensure the regular supply of critical knowledge, skills, and resources.[11]

[11]Organizational flexibility has its costs, both in terms of increased demands on core participants and in its effects on workers who are externalized. We discuss these problems in Chapter

MANAGING INSTITUTIONAL ENVIRONMENTS

As discussed in earlier chapters, ideas concerning institutional environments are more recent and less well developed than those concerning technical environments, and we know less about these institutional requirements and how organizations relate to them.

Theorists suggest that, at least in modern societies, the two major types of collective actors who generate institutional rules—cognitive categories, normative beliefs, regulatory policies—are governmental units and professional groups. DiMaggio and Powell assert that:

> Bureaucratization and other forms of homogenization [are] effected largely by the state and the professions, which have become the great rationalizers of the second half of the twentieth century. (1983: 147)

We have already discussed the important role played by nation-states, so let us briefly comment on the professions. More so than other types of collective actors, the professions exercise control by defining social reality—by devising ontological frameworks, proposing distinctions, creating typifications, and fabricating principles or guidelines for action. They define the nature of many problems—from physical illness to economic depression—monopolizing diagnostic techniques as well as treatment regimes. They underwrite the legitimacy of providers as well as practices.

Meyer (1994) argues that scientists and other professionals increasingly operate at a world-system level, holding conferences, issuing statements, promulgating recipes for reforming and rationalizing one after another sphere of activity—from standards for health and education to procedures for protecting the environment. Such activities greatly encourage the proliferation of organizations, viewed as the "natural" or appropriate instruments for effecting such change.

There appears to be at least one clear difference between organizational responses to technical and institutional aspects of their environments. Most connections with technical environments involve flows or exchanges—of information, resources, personnel. Although some connections with institutional environments also involve flows—particularly of information—a more important linkage process is absorption or incorporation. Whereas organizations *exchange* elements with their technical environments, they are *constituted* by elements drawn from their institutional environments. Technical elements are secured, combined, and transformed by organizational processes so that they commonly are no longer visible in their original state. By contrast, institutional elements—cognitive forms and cultural rules—are secured and utilized or copied without being transformed. Great efforts are made to ensure their visibility to outsiders, and it is essential that their distinctive features remain intact.

As with technical environments, organizations employ both buffering and bridging strategies in relating to their institutional environments.

Buffering Strategies

Symbolic coding. All organizations make extensive use of coding mechanisms; it is a key component of the process by which work is rationalized. Even in highly technical environments, coding involves symbolic—especially cognitive—processes. Various facets of the objects and subjects being processed must be selected, identified, classified, and labeled. Categorical rules are the essence of institutional frameworks; they provide the distinctions that are coded into the fabric of the organization and into the standard operating procedures employed in sorting and routing inputs. Sometimes the coding rules are generated by organizations in local interaction as they collectively confront and solve problems; in other cases, the rules have been developed in other locations, and are imported into the situation, often by professional problem solvers such as consultants (see Suchman, 1995). In all cases, symbolic coding is an important aspect of the more general organizing process described by Weick as "sense-making" (Weick, 1995).

Decoupling. Meyer and Rowan (1977) suggest that organizations responding to institutional requirements are likely to "decouple" their normative or prescriptive structure from their operational structure. This enables them to incorporate and display structural elements that conform to institutionalized conventions and, at the same time, preserve some autonomy of action. For example, Westphal and Zajac (1994) report that many corporations, responding to the norms of the investment community, adopted CEO compensation incentive plans tieing the earnings of executives to company profits, but that only a small number actually implemented the plans. While disparities between policies and practice are often observable, it is important that we not assume that they always exist, but examine the individual circumstances. We discuss decoupling in more detail in Chapter 10.

Other defensive strategies. While early institutionalists sometimes appeared to suggest that organizations had no alternative but to conform to institutional requirements, later theorists have argued that organizations respond to institutional demands in more strategic ways. Oliver (1991) identified five general strategies that organizations might pursue: acquiescence, compromise, avoidance, defiance, and manipulation. The meaning of these strategies is quite self-evident, and Oliver and others provide numerous examples of organizations that do not automatically comply but engage in some kind of defensive action. Two caveats. First, we would expect these reactions to be much more common in the face of regulative rather than normative institutional demands, and more likely in the face of normative rather than cognitive rules. In short, some institutional forms are more basic and less easily contested than others. Second, we would expect strategic reactions to be more likely in the presence of conflicting or ambiguous institutional regimes. Actors perceive themselves to have choices when institutional systems are not unified. Thus, Goodrick and Salancik (1996) report that hospital physicians exercised more discretion—and hence varied more in their treatments—when professional rules about the treatment of patients were uncertain.

Bridging Strategies

Both Meyer and Rowan (1977) and DiMaggio and Powell (1983) propose that *isomorphism* is the master bridging process in institutional environments: by incorporating institutional rules within their own structures, organizations become more homogeneous, more similar in structure, over time. Such processes, however, are expected to occur only within a particular institutional sphere or organizational field, so that to the extent that the fields are differentiated, we would expect organizational forms to diverge (see Scott, 1983). DiMaggio and Powell (1983) identify three general mechanisms conducive to isomorphism: (1) coercive, resulting when one organization adopts structures or procedures because they are compelled to do so; (2) mimetic or imitative, resulting when one organization simply elects to copy or mimic another, often because of uncertainty; and (3) normative, occurring when an organization adopts procedures or forms because they are purported to be superior. These three mechanisms are associated with the three conceptions of insitutions described in Chapter 6, coercive with regulative institutions, normative with normative, and mimetic with cognitive institutions (see Table 6–1; see also, Scott, 1995). These mechanisms, in varying combinations, give rise to a number of institutional bridging strategies.

Categorical conformity. This is the broadest and most general strategy, and can easily be extended to include as special cases the other three types. Categorical conformity is the process whereby institutional rules in the form of typifications, or taken-for-granted distinctions, provide guidelines to organizations on the basis of which they pattern their structures. These distinctions are the aspects of institutionalization emphasized by Berger and Luckmann (1967) and by Meyer and Rowan (1977) (see Chapters 5 and 6). Thus, knowledge is seamless, but conventional distinctions have developed between various scientific and humanistic disciplines with the result that most colleges and universities exhibit the same or very similar collections of schools and departments. Illness is varied and its sources often unknown, but most medical care organizations develop around a recognized and limited set of diagnoses and specialties (see Thornton, 1992). In general, we would expect categorical conformity to be produced primarily by mimetic and normative mechanisms.

Because cognitive categories provide the bases around which work in organizations and structures becomes differentiated, Meyer and Rowan (1977: 349) refer to them as "vocabularies of structure." Organizations incorporate these cognitive belief systems because doing so enables them to make themselves understandable to others and, in this manner, enhances their legitimacy and increases their access to resources and survival capacities.

Structural conformity. Sometimes environmental actors impose very specific structural requirements on organizations as a condition for acceptance and support. Organizations are required to adopt specific structural elements—tables of organization, departments, roles—in order to merit approval. DiMaggio and Powell (1983: 152) point out that organizations confronting high levels of uncertainty often borrow structural forms, sometimes by consciously modeling a successful form, sometimes by bringing in personnel from other organizations who are known to be capable of importing innovative forms, and sometimes by seeking assistance from consulting firms, "which, like Johnny Appleseeds, spread a few organizational forms throughout the land."

The nation-state is an important source of structural isomorphism, creating fields of organizations with virtually identical forms or requiring existing organizations to adopt particular structural units as a condition of eligibility for funding. During the 1960s and 1970s, in particular, the U.S. government imposed considerable structural unity on many types of regional, state, and local agencies. In arenas ranging from mental health and community cancer control to museums and arts councils, many federal programs specified in considerable detail the structures and components to be established (see Foley and Sharfstein, 1983; DiMaggio, 1983; Kaluzny, Warnecke et al., 1996). Also, governmental statutes frequently require that particular offices or units be added to existing structures—for example, affirmative-action officers or safety units.

But it is not only governmental organizations that impose structural uniformity on numerous other types of organizations. Many quasi-public bodies, such as foundations and professional associations, have similar effects. Thus, the Joint Commission on Hospital Accreditation—a "private" joint venture involving the American College of Physicians and Surgeons and the American Hospital Association—requires as a condition of accreditation that hospitals have specific structural features, such as a medical staff organization with specific subcommittees to review staff admissions, quality assurance, medical records, and so forth. Although no hospital is compelled to conform to these requirements, there are strong normative pressures to do so, which are reinforced by financial policies that often restrict reimbursement to care received in accredited institutions.

Thus, both by choice and by coercion, organizations frequently exhibit structural isomorphism as a mechanism for adapting to their institutional environment.

Procedural conformity. Organizations are often placed under pressure from institutions in their environments to carry out specified activities or to carry them out in specified ways. As with structural conformity, such pressures are sometimes the result of uncertainty—the procedures being adopted or copied by organizational choice—and sometimes the result of explicit normative or coercive pressures that require their adoption under threat of informal or formal sanctions.

Many of the rational myths described by Meyer and Rowan (1977) define procedures, spelling out in greater or lesser specificity the steps to be followed in carrying out certain types of activities. In a sense, rational myths are institutionally defined technologies specifying means-ends chains an organization is to follow in order to realize desired objectives. A vast range of procedural rules—from committing mental patients, to incorporating organizations, to baptizing new church members, to implementing PERT (planning, evaluation, and review techniques)—are devised in institutional environments and incorporated into organizations as part of their standard operating procedures.

As with other types of institutional elements, governmental units and professionals are in the forefront of constructing procedures. In some situations, particularly when professional groups are strong, the nation-state will collaborate with professionals in attempting to rationalize an arena of activity. For example, in the quality-assurance programs mandated by the federal government in the 1970s and 1980s, such as the Professional Stanford Review Organizations and the Peer Review Organizations, dominant decision-making roles were reserved for physicians (see Scott, 1982a). In other areas, such as social welfare, legislation has reduced the discretion of social workers, lowered the qualifications they must meet for employment, and in general substantially deprofessionalized the public welfare program in the United States (Simon, 1983). Rationalization can take many forms and can locate discretion at more or less centralized nodes in the organizational structures created. The state is more likely to prefer more centralized structures, and the professions, more decentralized systems of procedures (Scott, 1987).

Lawyers, particularly in the United States, operate under the mantle of both state power and professional authority. They occupy most of the positions in our legislative bodies and our courts, as well as a large proportion of the positions in public administrative agencies. They are the acknowledged experts in devising procedural approaches to dispute resolution and problem solving. Even when the demands being enforced are primarily technical, the requirements are often couched in procedural language—the language of lawyers—rather than in language that attempts to specify outcomes, such as costs and benefits (see Ackerman, 1985). Regulatory units as varied as the Health Systems Agencies, the Food and Drug Administration, and the Environmental Protection Agency operate primarily by specifying elaborate procedures—certificates of need, clinical trials, environmental impact reports—to be followed in justifying the introduction of new products or constructions (Taylor, 1984). Critics have noted that these procedures readily become disconnected from outcomes, creating legalistic mazes and bureaucratic rituals rather than providing a framework to support rational decision making (see Bardach and Kagan, 1982). But institutionalists emphasize that adherence to procedural specifications is one way in which stable organizational forms can be created and legitimated to work in conflict-ridden arenas. That the decisions are technical is irrelevant in these arenas since the decisions involve value conflicts: How or in whose interests is the technology to be used? Since any outcome will be controversial, the resolution of the matter must rest on the legitimacy of the decision process. Deciding rightly is more important than making the right decision.

Personnel conformity. One of the primary building blocks of complex, differentiated, formal organizations is the large number of educated, often certified workers who assume specialized roles within them. As Meyer points out, cultures vary considerably in where in the social structure rationality is institutionalized, but in contemporary Western societies, there is heavy emphasis on the individual as the prime locus. The Western cultural conception is one of:

> The competent, achieving individual, whose productive action brings rewards to the self and corresponding gains to the collectivity (in such conceptions as the gross national product). This individual is institutionally located and managed primarily in the system of education. (Meyer, 1985: 593)

Institutional environments often specify what types of actors—in terms of their (primarily educational) qualifications—are to be allocated to particular functions or roles. Conformity to institutional rules often entails the hiring of specific types of personnel. The most obvious examples involve certification and licensure. To be licensed as a "skilled nursing facility" an institution must include on its staff a specified proportion of registered nurses; governmentally mandated audits must be performed by certified public accountants; and accreditation bodies require that university faculties contain sufficient numbers of Ph.D.'s. In a great many arenas, organizational designers and managers have no or little control over the definition of jobs or the types of personnel recruited to fill them: these decisions have been made by external certification, licensure, and accreditation agencies. For example, once a hospital decides to offer a particular service, it is highly constrained by licensing rules in its decisions on what types of personnel are to be hired and how work is to be allocated among them (Freidson, 1986). Even when licensure is not required as a condition of operation or of funding, it is often used by occupations and organizations as a means of assuring the public that employees are qualified to perform their duties. From aerobics instructors and bartenders to tree surgeons and television repairmen, certification is looked to as an important source of legitimation.

More generally, a number of analysts have argued that education provides an important base for most personnel systems within organizations. Modern employment and promotion structures are heavily interlaced with educational requirements, which are justified in terms of technical skills and specialized knowledge required by the job. Yet, a number of analysts have assembled evidence that challenges the presumed association between education and job qualifications or between education and productivity (see Berg, 1971; Collins, 1979). It has been proposed that the connection between education and occupational attainment is better viewed as having an institutional rather (or more) than a technical basis. Hiring certified or educated employees signals to the environment that the employer is a modern, responsible firm employing rational criteria of personnel selection and promotion. Without insisting that education and certification have no relation to performance, it is possible to embrace the institutional insight that, independent of performance, the hiring of individuals with appropriate educational credentials enhances the legitimacy of the employing organization and secures for it additional support and resources.

ADAPTATION AND SELECTION

To this point, our discussion of the social and technical boundaries of organizations and the buffering and bridging strategies they employ to defend, define, and redefine these boundaries has focused on the organization set level of analysis. And we have drawn primarily on resource dependence and institutional theories in developing the arguments and interpretations. Now we shift to view the terrain from higher levels: from the population and organizational field levels; and we use ecological and Marxist theory to supplement resource dependence and institutional frameworks. We consider first the problem of defining populations of organizations, which involves, in effect, determining the boundaries of organizational forms.

Bounding Organizational Forms

In Chapters 6 and 7 we described earlier attempts by ecologists to specify the concept of organization form, most commonly by emphasizing distinctive structural features associated with the operation of a core technology. In their more recent work, Hannan and Freeman (1989) shift their focus from organizational technologies to boundary-setting activities, emphasizing the "segregating" and "blending" processes by which populations of organizations establish their boundaries. Drawing on the ideas of Barth (1969), who has examined the ways in which ethnic groups draw and redraw their boundaries over time, Hannan and Freeman suggest that analysts examine the changing nature of technological processes and requirements that shape organizational structures as well as changes in transaction costs, which cause organizations to revise their "efficient boundaries." Of even greater importance are successful collective action—for example, the creation of industry associations or regulatory agreements developed with governmental agencies—and institutional processes that come to define particular forms as legitimate or appropriate for carrying out specified types of work. Thus, in this revised view, the clarity of boundaries defining an organizational form is a variable, different not only from one type of organization to another, but for a given type of organization through time. Hospitals in the United States, for example, until recently assumed only a limited number of forms—most typically, that of the "voluntary," nonprofit, free-standing hospital—but now exhibit a bewildering variety of types (see Alexander and D'Aunno, 1990). Blending processes have dominated segregating ones, producing exotic combinations of for-profit and nonprofit forms and ambulatory and in-service care, and various types of multihospital systems have appeared. Determining which organizations should be classified as "hospitals" is no longer a simple or straightforward matter.

Change in Organizations

Most theorists that work at the level of the organization set—contingency, resource dependence, transaction cost theorists—assume that organizational structures can be modified, that they are subject to manipulation by participants who are attempting to improve their adaptation. The buffering and bridging strategies we have reviewed presume the presence of decision makers who survey the situation, confront alternatives as well as constraints, and select a course of action. They presume, in short, that organizational structures can be changed by modifications of existing structures.

This assumption is challenged by ecologists studying organizations at the population level of analysis. They argue that much of the variation in structural forms is due to environmental *selection* rather than adaptation (see Aldrich and Pfeffer, 1976). It is not necessary to insist that organizations exhibit no structural changes in attempting to adapt to their environments, but only that many organizations fail to modify their structures as quickly as their environments change (Hannan and Freeman, 1984).

In an earlier discussion, Hannan and Freeman (1977: 931–32) cite a large number of constraints upon change in organizations. Their list includes such internal limitations as the organization's investment in capital equipment and trained personnel, constraints on the transfer and processing of information, the costs of upsetting the internal political equilibrium, and the conservative forces of history and tradition. Equally important are the external constraints, including legal and fiscal barriers to entry and exit from markets, environmental limitations on the flow of information, and the difficulty of securing the external political and social support needed to legitimate any change. Evidence regarding the stability of organizational structures over time is provided by Stinchcombe's (1965) analysis, described in Chapter 7, of the link between time of founding and current structural characteristics of organizations. Stinchcombe's thesis of organizational imprinting is consistent with the view that organizations do not easily or quickly change their structural features. Thus, structural inertia is an important cause of environmental selection: structural forms are unable to keep pace with environmental change.

Resisting change is not, however, necessarily a liability for an organization. As discussed in Chapter 1, Hannan and colleagues point out that inertia is associated with both reliability of performance (a virtue in terms of technical criteria) and with accountability (a virtue from the standpoint of institutional judgments) (Hannan and Freeman 1984; Hannan and Carroll, 1995). Organizations that exhibit high reliability and/or high accountability are more likely to survive, given a reasonable degree of environmental stability. Nevertheless, under conditions of higher environmental uncertainty, inertia becomes a liability rather than an asset, preventing the organization from changing enough, or quickly enough, to survive.

Organizations change but at differing rates. Moreover, different aspects of the organization change at differing rates. Thus, Hannan and Freeman (1989: 77) postulate a "hierarchy of inertial forces." For example, the primary mission embodied in the core technology is more inertial than the structure and staffing of the ancilliary units, whose work may be discontinued or contracted out. This is only another way of asserting that organizations exhibit not one but many boundaries, and that the size and height of the protective barriers raised against instability or interference varies across different activities and arenas.[12]

Probably the single best indicator of an organization's capacity to adapt successfully to its environment is its continued existence—its survival. Population ecologists, hence, have devoted much research effort to examining the factors determining mortality rates among organizations. Results of a large number of studies of organizational populations—including restaurants, semiconductor firms, newspapers, unions, telephone companies, breweries, and social service organizations—have been summarized by Carroll (1984), by Singh and Lumsden (1990), and by Baum (1996). Among the general factors leading to higher mortality rates are (1) liability of newness: the tendency for newer and younger organizations to fail; (2) liability of

---

[12]It is because different forces shape the core and peripheral structures of organizations that we consider them separately, treating the core technology in Chapter 9 and the more peripheral structures in Chapter 10.

smallness: the tendency for smaller organizations to fail at higher rates than larger organizations; and (3) density dependence: the greater likelihood for organizations to fail if confronted at their founding with many organizations of the same type. Characteristics of political and institutional environments have also been demonstrated to influence the survival of organizations. Research by Carroll (1987) and others indicates that one of the most important predictors of both founding and failures of newspapers was the amount of political turmoil experienced in that year. Singh, Tucker, and House (1986) and Baum and Oliver (1991) show that social service organizations that received authorization from external legitimation agencies—for example, listing in a community directory or obtaining a registration number from the provincial government—were less likely to fail than organizations that did not obtain such legitimation.

Two sets of distinctions related to explaining organizational mortality deserve closer attention. First, organizations "fail" in a number of ways that are important to distinguish. They may dissolve completely, be acquired through purchase, or cease to exist as a legal entity through acquisition or merger. These clearly represent quite different kinds of end-states, and, as we would expect, research demonstrates that they have diverse determinants and correlates (Carroll, 1984). Second, organizations of the same type vary in terms of the extent of their specialization. Research suggests that generalist organizations make different demands and have different survival potential than do specialists (see Freeman and Hannan, 1983; Hannan and Freeman, 1989).[13]

The adaptation arguments of the resource dependence school and the selection arguments of the population ecologists are not necessarily incompatible and in fact can be viewed as complementary. Specifically, the population ecology approach seems to us to be particularly useful in focusing on the core features of organizations, and accounting for changes in organizational forms over longer periods. By contrast, the resource dependence approach emphasizes the more peripheral features of organizations, and stresses changes occurring over shorter periods. Let us briefly amplify these sources of divergence.

The population ecology approach usefully emphasizes that there are important constraints on the variability and adaptability of organizational structures. This argument applies particularly to those characteristics that are closely associated with the core technology: it is here that we find the major investments in capital equipment and skilled personnel, investments not readily changed. On the other hand, the resource dependence advocates are correct in pointing out the many possibilities open to organizations in modifying their peripheral structures—their buffers and bridges. To label these structures as peripheral is not to regard them as superficial or of little adaptive consequence. As we have tried to argue throughout this chapter, the strategies employed by organizations to buffer and bridge can have profound

---

[13]Ecologists distinguish between environmental variability (the extent of change observed in resources, etc.) and grain (the frequency or "patchiness" of change). Broadly speaking, generalist organizations are better adapted to highly variable and coarse grained environments; specialists to less variable and fine grained environments.

effects on their chances for survival and their level of functioning (see Chapter 10).

The population ecology approach is best suited to explain changes in the distribution of organizational forms over the long run—over a period of decades or centuries. For example, it is better used for explaining changes over time in the number of community colleges in relation to other organizational forms in higher education than for explaining structural changes made by one college in reaction to some environmental challenge. The resource dependence approach is best employed to account for adaptive responses of specific organizations over a relatively short period.

Although the founding ecological theorists emphasized the connection between ecological and population-level analyses and stressed the distinction between selection and adaptation arguments, the second generation of ecological researchers has relaxed these strictures. Thus, Carroll (1984) argues that ecological arguments can be appropriately applied to individual organizations and to organization fields as well as to populations. At the level of the individual organizations, an ecological perspective "involves the study of demographic events and life-cycle processes across individual organizations" (p. 72). And Singh and Lumsden (1990) insist that while population ecologists have correctly emphasized the impact of organizational founding and failure rates—selection processes—as they contribute to change, that ecologists should also examine the rates at which organizations change their structures—adaptation processes.

These developments are constructive. Early ecologists no doubt overemphasized the extent of structural inertia in order to call attention to change processes at the population level.[14] That insight having been achieved, it is appropriate to conduct studies that examine factors affecting change at both the organization and the population levels.

Adaptation of Organizational Fields

Adaptation is not the exclusive province of the individual organization or the organizational population, but also occurs at the level of the organizational field. Biological ecologists observe that adaptation processes may involve the behavior of isolated organisms, the behavior of populations, or more elaborate, interspecies communal responses. Similarly, human ecologists have long insisted that human communities are usefully analyzed as collective adaptative responses of differing but interdependent populations to the constraints and opportunities posed by specific environments (see Hawley, 1950). Ecological perspectives emphasize the more "natural" and unwitting aspects of such adaptive behavior, but strategic management theory and more political approaches stress that such collective mechanisms are also created by purposeful actors joining forces to improve the circumstances for all their constituents. Although resource dependence ideas are typically applied at the organization-set level in examinations of the adaptive capabilities of

---

[14]Organizational ecologists were also perhaps overinfluenced by the models developed by biological ecologists. Although there are important analogies between biological and social forms, we agree with open system theorists in insisting that an important hallmark of the latter is their unusual capacity for structural modification and elaboration.

individual organizations, many of the specific strategies employed—for example, contracts, co-optation, joint ventures, and associations—involve the creation of interorganizational systems that are themselves vehicles of collective action and adaptation operating at a different level of analysis (see Astley and Van de Ven, 1983; Astley, 1985).

These conceptions of communal or collective adaptation have been applied most frequently to examinations of the adaptive functions of interorganizational systems within a given community, but they are also applicable to the analysis of broader organizational fields: industry and societal. Applications at each of these levels are briefly reviewed.

Organizational fields at the community level. A large literature has developed on community structures analyzed as interorganizational systems (see Galaskiewicz, 1985, for a review). An important axis around which community interests may turn is local versus extralocal dependence. Some organizational interests—local businesses, financial institutions, local media, realtors, and lawyers—are highly dependent on and greatly advantaged by community growth and have strong incentives to combine forces to forge their community into a "growth machine" (Molotch, 1976; Whitt, 1989). These are the groups that are most likely to be active in and centrally connected with local interorganizational networks (Galaskiewicz, 1979). By contrast, local plants or branch offices of national corporations headquartered elsewhere are less likely to be involved in such communal systems.

Even though nonlocal organizations are not strongly connected to community systems, they can exercise great influence when and if their interests are affected (Friedland, 1980). The power of such organizations is based not only on their economic dominance, but also on their capacity to "exit": to move out of a specific community. While "dominant and mobile actors participate less than nondominant, immobile ones" (Friedland and Palmer, 1984: 410), their influence may be exerted in less direct ways. They can apply informal pressure on political leaders or their business associates, and they are likely to influence what is put on the agenda for decision making more than they determine what decisions are made on those matters that do reach the agenda[15] (see Chapter 11).

Organizational fields at the industry level. One of the most interesting studies conducted to date at this level of analysis is that of Miles (1982), who studied the response of the "Big Six" corporations in the United States tobacco industry to the threat posed by the demonstration of a causal link between smoking and impaired health. Although there was some early warning, the publication of the surgeon general's report linking smoking and cancer and subsequent actions taken by various federal agencies constituted a major environmental crisis for these organizations. Although each corporation adopted a variety of strategies ranging from product innovation to diversifi-

[15]Preventing issues or questions from being raised and shaping the agenda of decision making have been identified as important, albeit difficult-to-investigate, modes of power. These types of power have been variously labeled structural or systemic, and this area of inquiry has been termed the study of *nondecisions* (see Bachrach and Baratz, 1962; Alford and Friedland, 1975).

cation, they also engaged in collective action. For example, during the first signs of trouble, they created the Tobacco Industry Research Committee to conduct their own studies of the effects of tobacco use. Following the surgeon general's report, they collectively engaged in a wide variety of lobbying efforts, providing cancer-research grants to the American Medical Association and various universities and monitoring closely and attempting to influence legislative and administrative actions affecting their interests.[16]

Numerous studies have been conducted of the extent to which organizational fields within particular industries or societal sectors have developed networks or structures to support collective action. For example, Hirsch (1975) has contrasted the relatively successful efforts of companies within the pharmaceutical industry to organize to protect their interests with the much less successful activities of firms within the record industry. Although the two industries are somewhat similar in their level of technical development, reliance on batch processing, and dependence on external gatekeepers (physicians and disc jockeys) to mediate between themselves and their customers, pharmaceutical firms have been much more successful in obtaining legislation protecting brand-name drugs, in securing patent protections, and in co-opting physician groups in support of their interests. By contrast, record companies have been unable to obtain much collective control over pricing or distribution, have not secured exclusive copyright protections, and have not been able to co-opt disc jockeys to represent their interests. (The payola scandals of the 1950s and mid-1980s—attempts by record companies to bribe the staffs of radio stations—represent a notably crass and unsuccessful attempt to secure disc jockeys' loyalties.) It is not clear why pharmaceutical firms have been more successful in their collective efforts than record companies, but it is obvious that the degree of success associated with collective action by organizations within the same field can greatly affect the environment confronting each firm.

Two concepts that have proved to be useful in analyzing institutional structures are particularly helpful in examining adaptation processes at the organizational field level. They are governance systems and institutional logics. *Governance systems* are arrangements that support the regularized control of the actions of one set of social actors by another. These arrangements may be coercive power structures, legitimate authority systems, or mutually enforced, informal systems of control. They may or may not involve governmental bodies, but at the industry level, they usually do. If so, as already described earlier in this chapter, the exercise of power by state agencies may vary considerably across societies, from sector to sector, and over time.

But governance structures are not simply about the exercise of state power. Organizations in most industries or sectors are permitted to develop associations of various types that not only attempt to influence state actions but also directly engage in control activites. Trade associations, trade unions, professional associations—these and other collective forms exercise substan-

---

[16]Hannan and Freeman (1989) point out that alongside these adaptive actions, selective processes were also invoked. Miles focused on the Big Six: the larger, more successful companies. During the period of his study, "of the 78 companies in the U.S. tobacco business in 1956, 49 had left the industry by 1986" (pp. 32–33); 12 of these shifted into other business lines, but 37 firms disappeared.

tial control, both formal and informal, over one or another arena of social life. Moreover, inequalities in economic power as expressed, for example, in different degrees of industry concentration, provide an important basis for differential control within and across industries.

The adaptation of fields is often carried out by existing governance systems; and changes in adaptation at the field level are often signified by changes in governance systems—both in their composition or membership and in their mechanisms. For example, DiMaggio (1983) has described how the field of performing arts (orchestras, theaters) in the United States was transformed when the National Endowment for the Arts was created and, for the first time, community-based companies competed for a common pool of resources at the state and national levels. By contrast, Alexander (1996) examines a later period in which art museums were forced to rely increasingly on corporate sponsorship and considers the effects of such sponsorship not only on their organizational structure but on the types of art displayed. And Leblebici and colleagues (1991) describe changes in governance arrangements in the U.S. radio broadcasting industry during the period 1920–1965, as dominant organizations were forced to respond to innovations introduced by marginal participants in the market.

The second concept, *institutional logics*, refers to the cognitive frames and underlying assumptions that constitute the "organizing principles" for pursuing goals in a given arena (see Friedland and Alford, 1991: 248).[17] They provide much of the stability and continuity that underlies practice in differing industries, and these assumptions act to differentiate, for example, schools from factories from hospitals. Such logics also change over time.

Major changes are currently under way in the logics and governance structures that underpin the delivery of medical care services in the United States (see Starr, 1982). My colleagues and I suggest that three different logics can be discerned during the last half century in this field: the logic of "professional dominance" (1920–1965), which asserted the authority of the medical profession and the overriding importance of quality as determined by professional standards; the logic of "public responsibility" (1965–1982), which witnessed the vastly increased federal presence to ensure equity of access for the elderly and the poor; and "managerial and corporate logics" (1982–present), which emphasize deregulation, the virtues of competition, and the use of market criteria to allocate medical resources (Scott, Mendel, and Pollack, forthcoming). Note that each of these logics is associated with different criteria of success and different ways of thinking about the nature of the work to be done; and each privileges different classes of actors and organizations; and each entails different governance structures and mechanisms.

Organizational fields at the societal level. Fligstein's study of changes during this century in the nature of the largest corporations in the United States argues that these large, diversified firms no longer relate to industry boundaries, but operate at the national or international level, sharing common strategies and structures. He proposes that, over time, the strategies or institutional

---

[17]A closely related concept is Bourdieu's (1977) notion of *habitus,* which emphasizes the extent to which cultural rules are internalized and provide the basis for stable dispositions that allow individuals to meaningfully structure their behavior within situations.

logics of these firms have shifted from a product or manufacturing conception to a sales or marketing conception to a financial conception. Executives are no longer "committed to any given industry and no longer identify their firms in market terms," but rather in financial measures of success (Fligstein, 1990: 32). Relatedly, the governance structures of these firms have shifted from unified companies to multidivisional systems (see Chapter 10).

Other analysts have studied the changing nature of organization fields in public service arenas at the national level. Employing network analysis techniques, Laumann and Knoke (1987) examined the ways in which shifting populations of public and private organizations become active in the setting of national policy in the sectors of health and energy during the 1970s. The boundaries of such interorganizational policymaking systems are vague, with participation being determined by interest in the issue (domain), capacity to mobilize relevant resources—such as staff, funds, and expertise—and centrality of location in the system. Policy systems differ in the nature and extent of their order. The health policy system in the United States is dominated more by governmental decision-making units than the energy sector; moreover, "consensus about who matters appears to be much more systematically—indeed, almost institutionally—organized in the health domain" (Laumann and Knoke, 1987: 188). Energy is a newer focus for national policy in the United States, and stable patterns of interaction and influence among organizational interests, both private and public, have not yet emerged.

A continuing stream of studies has examined the extent to which private organizations are linked into networks of collective assistance that span industries or sectors. As we have already noted, many of these connections are intraorganizational, involving the acquisition of many formerly independent firms and/or merger with these firms into vertically integrated or functionally diversified corporations. (We will consider these connections further in Chapter 10.) But other connections entail varying types of bridges among formally independent units that join forces to secure mutual benefits. There is disagreement over what interests are being served by such arrangements. Marxist theorists tend to emphasize class-based interests, focusing on connections among the elite families controlling major corporations, who utilize a variety of social networks—connections developed in elite colleges and social clubs but extended to corporate boards—to safeguard their class advantages (see Domhoff, 1983; Useem, 1984). One influential line of research concludes that corporate interests in the United States reflect the existence of a structure of "financial hegemony" whereby banks and insurance companies monopolize the flow of investment capital, allowing their directors and top executives to exercise broad control over the development of the corporate economy as a whole (see Mintz and Schwartz, 1985). The evidence for the existence of ties among firms—for example, ownership, interlocking directorates (individuals who are officers or directors of one company serving on the board of another); capital flows, trading relations—is stronger than that demonstrating the effects of these ties on decisions or actions. The types of control exercised appear to be indirect—operating via a system of structural constraints—rather than through the direct exercise of power (see Mizruchi, 1996).

Increasingly, the research on this topic involves comparisons across societies. John Scott (1991) suggests that similar patterns of indirect control are characteristic of Canada (see Carroll, 1986) and of the United Kingdom (see J. Scott, 1986); by contrast, the banks in Germany and Austria exercise more direct controls whereas those in France and Italy exhibit controls through a number of investment holding companies (see also, Chandler, 1990).

Whereas the Marxist perspective views organizations as instruments used by members of the capitalist class to pursue their interests, resource dependence theorists stress that organizations are "real," possessing their own interests "apart from serving as settings and apart from the various people who [are] in them at any point in time" (Pfeffer, 1987). More specifically, organizations are coalitions of interests, the directors and owners being only one among many sets of participants. We examine later (see Chapter 11) arguments concerning the divergence of the interests of owners (stockholders) and managers.

In addition to comparative research on corporate elite structures, we are also beginning to see studies of cross-societal differences in managerial control strategies or logics. Guillen (1994) compares the changing managerial models utilized by managers in the United States, Germany, Spain, and Great Britain during this century, arguing that while a set of general models can be discerned across these rather diverse societies, that there is considerable variance in when one or another model was ascendant, in response to differing "organizational problems facing the employer and managerial class during different time periods" as well as to varying "institutional factors favoring or impeding the adoption of particular organizational paradigms as solutions to those problems."

In his comparative studies of business practices in Europe and Asia, Whitley (1992a,b,c) examines differences across societies in institutional logics or, what he terms "business recipes."

> These business recipes, or systems, are particular ways of organizing, controlling and directing business enterprises that become established as the dominant form of business organization in different societies. They reflect successful patterns of business behavior and understanding of how to achieve economic success that are reproduced and reinforced by crucial institutions. (Whitley, 1992c: 125)

Such recipies vary somewhat across European countries (see also, Chandler 1990), but widely between European and Asian societies, as numerous analysts have demonstrated. Asian organizations tend to have less distinct boundaries and to be embedded in stable networks of interorganizational partnerships based on personal, particularistic, and diffuse ties among firms to a greater extent than Western counterparts (see also, Dore, 1973; Abegglen and Stalk, 1985; Hamilton and Biggart, 1988; Fruin, 1992; Orrù, Biggart, and Hamilton, 1997).

SUMMARY

At one and the same time, organizations must be open to their environments and attentive to their boundaries. This poses an intricate problem with respect to the recruitment of participants. Organizations require some control over the criteria by which individuals are admitted and rewarded, and in some extreme cases organizations hold sufficient power to eliminate participant characteristics or identities that are based on their involvement in other social systems. In the more usual case, however, an organization has neither the power nor the desire to eliminate such identities, which can be put to use by the organization. How to mobilize these characteristics in the service of organizational goals while preventing participants from using organizational resources in the service of other goals is a continuing challenge for managers of all organizations.

To varying degrees, organizations try to internalize labor market processes exerting a major effect on individuals' mobility chances—determining what positions are to be filled, what positions are open to entry from outside, what linkages exist among positions, and how individuals are selected to positions. Deciding what work and which workers to internalize and which to externalize is a continuing issue confronting designers and managers of organizations.

Two broad classes of strategies have been identified by which organizations relate to their task environments. Organizations employ buffering techniques—coding, stockpiling, leveling, forecasting, and adustments in scale—to seal off their technical core from environmental disturbances. They use bridging techniques—bargaining, contracting, co-optation, alliances, joint ventures, mergers, associations, and governmental connections—to increase the number and variety of their linkages with competitors and exchange partners and thereby enhance their security in technical environments. Other types of buffering strategies—symbolic coding, decoupling—and bridging strategies—categorical, structural, procedural, and personnel conformity—are employed in securing legitimacy and support in institutional environments. Analysis of such strategies is most readily conducted at the level of the organization set and presumes that the managers of an organization can fashion its activities so as to enhance its security or effectiveness. This assumption is challenged by analysts working at the population level, who emphasize the inertia of organizations and insist that most change occurs because of natural selection—the differential survival of different organizational types—rather than rational selection—conscious design by organizational managers.

Adaptation occurs not only at the level of the individual organization but also at the organization field level: community, industry, and society. Both adaptation and selection approaches—which are addressed to different aspects of organizations and to different time periods—are useful for examining organization-environment interdependencies.

Sources of Structural Complexity: The Technical Core

Every organized human activity—from the making of pots to the placing of a man on the moon—gives rise to two fundamental and opposing requirements: the division of labor into various tasks to be performed, and the coordination of these tasks to accomplish the activity. The structure of an organization can be defined simply as the sum total of the ways in which it divides its labor into distinct tasks and then achieves coordination among them.

Henry Mintzberg (1979)

Whether by natural or rational selection—by evolution or learning—organizations tend to move toward higher levels of complexity. This thesis will be amplified at two levels. First, in this chapter we examine the sources of structural complexity that develop within the technical core of an organization. The prime source of core complexity is the nature of the work being carried out—the demands made by the technology on the structure. Second, in Chapter 10 we consider the sources of structural complexity that occur outside the technical core, in the peripheral sectors of the organization, including the managerial and institutional levels. These structures respond in particular to demands posed by the size or scale of the organization and by the task and institutional environments. At the conclusion of Chapter 10 we examine the relation between the core and peripheral structures.

The structural features of organizations that are of primary interest are those defining the division of labor—structural differentiation, including occupational and role specialization, departmentalization, and multidivisional forms—and those relating to coordination and control of work—formalization, hierarchy, centralization, and various structures for facilitating lateral information flows.

Contingency theory provides the primary orienting framework for the topics addressed in this chapter, although we also draw on socio-technical perspectives and introduce the ideas of organizational culture theorists. As described in Chapter 4, contingency theory insists that there is no single best way in which to design the structure of an organization. Rather, what is the best or most appropriate structure depends—is contingent—on what type of work is being performed and on what environmental demands or conditions confront the organization. Lawrence and Lorsch and Jay Galbraith utilize a rational-open perspective and stress formalized responses to task complexity. Other theorists, such as the Tavistock group, Burns and Stalker, Cole, and Ouchi, assume a natural-open system perspective and emphasize the value of more diffuse and informal control systems. Both groups will inform our attempts to account for the complexity of the technical core.

To the extent possible, organizations attempt to seal off their technical core from environmental disturbances. This central proposition developed by James Thompson (1967) helps to account for the defensive behavior of many types of organizations. The specific strategies devised by organizations to buffer their technical core were reviewed in the previous chapter. But what if the buffers are inadequate and uncertainty penetrates the technical core? In many ways, the conception of sealing off the organization from uncertainty seems dated—outmoded and ill-advised—to today's organizations, which, in order to survive, need to attend more closely to what the customers want and what their competitors are doing. As organizations take on more complex and unpredictable tasks, it is no longer reasonable to assume that all traces of uncertainty will be buffered out of the core. How can the structure of the technical core be modified so as to accommodate more demanding tasks and more uncertain prospects? To address this question, we need to develop a clearer conception of how to define and measure the work performed in the technical core.

DEFINING AND MEASURING TECHNOLOGY

As we pointed out in Chapter 1, *technology* is the term that has come to refer to the work performed by an organization. This concept can be narrowed so as to include only the hardware—"the equipment, machines and instruments" individuals use in productive activities (Orlikowski 1992: 399). However, most organization theorists have embraced the broader view that technology includes not only the hardware used in performing work but also the skills and knowledge of workers, and even the characteristics of the objects on which work is performed. We must acknowledge at the outset that there is considerable overlap between *technology, technical system, task environment,* and *environment* as these terms are employed by organizational analysts. *Environment* is the more inclusive term and incorporates political, technological, and institutional aspects of the organizational context. *Task environment* emphasizes those features of the environment relevant to its supply of inputs and its disposition of outputs but also includes the power-dependence relations within which the organization must make its exchanges. *Technology* refers to "the physical combined with the intellectual or knowledge processes by which materials in some form are transformed into outputs" (Hulin and Roznowski, 1985: 47). Finally, *technical system* refers to "a specific combination of machines and methods employed to produce a desired outcome" (Sproull and Goodman, 1990: 255). The distinction between technology and technical system calls attention to the difference between the general state of knowledge in some domain and the particular manner in which that knowledge is deployed and embedded in a given work situation. Technology constrains but does not dictate the precise configuration of machines and methods that make up a specific technical system (see Weick, 1990).

It is important to emphasize the extent to which an organization's technology—although an "internal" element—links the organization to its environment: the environment not only is the source of inputs and the recipient of outputs but also is the major source of the work techniques and tools employed by the organization. Most organizations do not themselves invent their technologies but import them from the environment.

Earlier students of industrial and organizational sociology noted the impact of technical and production features of the work process on worker behavior and work-group structure (for example, Sayles, 1958; Trist and Bamforth, 1951; Walker and Guest, 1952; Whyte, 1948). But it was the empirical research of Woodward (1958; 1965) and a theoretical article by Thompson and Bates (1957) that first called attention to technology as a general determinant of organizational structure. Woodward's conception of technology as applied to industrial organizations was broadened and generalized by Thompson (Thompson and Bates, 1957; Thompson, 1967), by Litwak (1961), and by Perrow (1967; 1970) so as to be applicable to all types of organizations.

Literally dozens of specific indicators have been developed by students of technology to capture its salient dimensions. Some emphasize the nature of the inputs obtained, for example, their uniformity (Litwak, 1961) or their variability (Perrow, 1970); others the operations performed in terms of their complexity (Woodward, 1965) or "work-flow" integration (Pugh et al., 1969); and still others focus on the knowledge requirements, for example, knowledge of cause-effect relations (Thompson, 1967) or programmability (Sproull and Goodman, 1990).[1]

Although a great many specific measures of technology have been generated, it is possible to identify three general underlying dimensions that encompass most of the more specific measures and, more to the point, isolate the most critical variables needed to predict structural features of organizations. These three dimensions are complexity or diversity, uncertainty or unpredictability, and interdependence.[2] We will discuss each briefly.

Complexity or diversity. This dimension refers to the number of different items or elements that must be dealt with simultaneously by the organiza-

---

[1]A summary classification of these and other measures will be found in Scott (1992: 229). The two dimensions underlying the classification are facets of technology—materials, operations, or knowledge—and stage of processing—inputs, throughputs, or outputs.

[2]Given the degree of overlap between the concepts of technology and environment, it should not surprise us to find very similar analytic dimensions employed to characterize the features of each.

tion. Specific measures such as multiplicity and customization of outputs and variety of inputs tap this dimension.

Uncertainty or unpredictability. This dimension refers to the variability of the items or elements upon which work is performed or to the extent to which it is possible to predict their behavior in advance. Some of the general factors affecting the degree of uncertainty of the organization's task environment described in Chapter 6 are also relevant here. Specific measures of uncertainty include uniformity or variability of inputs, the number of exceptions encountered in the work process, and the number of major product changes experienced.

Interdependence. This dimension refers to the extent to which the items or elements upon which work is performed or the work processes themselves are interrelated so that changes in the state of one element affect the state of the others. Thompson (1967: 54–55) has proposed a useful typology for assessing degree of interdependence. Three levels are identified: (1) *pooled* interdependence, in which the work performed is interrelated only in that each element or process contributes to the overall goal (for example, selecting fabrics and color schemes for the inside decor of a jet airplane is related to the plane's aerodynamic design only in that both contribute to the overall objective or final product); (2) *sequential* interdependence, which exists when some activities must be performed before others (for example, component parts of a jet engine must be produced before they all can be assembled into a single functioning unit); and (3) *reciprocal* interdependence, which is present to the degree that elements or activities relate to each other as both inputs and outputs (for example, design decisions regarding the weight and thrust of a jet engine and the aerodynamic design of the fuselage and wings must take each other into account). Thompson points out that these three levels of interdependence form a Guttman-type scale, in that elements or processes that are reciprocally interdependent also exhibit sequential and pooled interdependence, and processes that are sequentially interdependent also exhibit pooled interdependence.

As indicated, these dimensions are of interest because they can be employed to predict the structural features of organizations.

TECHNOLOGY AND STRUCTURE: RATIONAL SYSTEM VIEWS

Since matters can rapidly become complicated, we will state at the outset the major linkages that are expected to exist between an organization's technology and its structure. In noting these main effects, we recognize that the interaction effects—the effects produced by two or more of the variables in combination—are more powerful and frequently of greater interest. The predictions are as follows:

1. The greater the technical complexity, the greater the structural complexity. The structural response to technical diversity is organizational differentiation.

2. The greater the technical uncertainty, the less formalization and centralization.
3. The greater the technical interdependence, the more resources must be devoted to coordination. More specifically, Thompson (1967: 55–56) argues that pooled interdependence can be managed by standardization, the development of rules or routines; sequential interdependence requires the development of plans or schedules, which specify timing and order in the work processes; and reciprocal interdependence requires the use of mutual adjustment or coordination by feedback, in which the interrelated parties must communicate their own requirements and respond to the needs of each other. Each coordination strategy is increasingly costly in terms of resources.

Basic Coordination Mechanisms

Galbraith (1973; 1977) has usefully argued that one way in which the varying demands of technologies on structures can be summarized is to ask how much information must be processed during the execution of a task sequence. He argues that information requirements increase as a function of increasing diversity, uncertainty, and interdependence of work flows, and that these factors interact such that the effects of complexity are much greater if, for example, it is accompanied by uncertainty. Using this simple formula to gauge information-processing demands, Galbraith then outlines a series of structural modifications organizations can make in their technical core as a means of adapting to increased demands for the processing of information. The following formal structures, discussed in order of increasing complexity, may be employed to manage the work flow.

Rules and programs. Organizations performing the simplest and most routine tasks rely primarily on rules and performance programs to secure acceptable outcomes. And, of course, organizations carrying on even the most complex types of work perform many activities that can be regulated by rules and programs. These structural devices represent agreements about how decisions are to be made or work is to be processed that predate the work performance itself. Often rules and programs are embedded in the forms and documents that workers must complete—forms that specify what information is to be collected or what activities are to be completed. Such forms, along with procedural manuals, can be designed to accommodate considerable complexity and some uncertainty, particularly as regards the sequence of events. For example, it is possible to develop rules for carrying out specific task activities and to add "switching rules" that signal which of several clusters of activities is to be performed or the order of their performance (see March and Simon, 1958: 142–50).

Schedules. Schedules are necessary when different kinds of activities are to be carried on in the same location or when sequential interdependence is present. To information concerning the what and how of task performance, schedules add the dimension of when. Schedules also specify the period they are in force, and so are subject to modification. Galbraith suggests that

increasing uncertainty can be handled by shortening the plan-replan cycle—
that is, the period during which a given set of rules and schedules is in force.

Departmentalization. One of the most difficult and critical of all decisions facing an organization is how work is to be divided: what tasks are to be
assigned to what roles and what roles to what departments. As described in
Chapter 2, early administrative theorists suggested that homogeneous activities be placed in the same organizational units, but critics noted that there
are often several, competing bases for determining homogeneity (see March
and Simon, 1958: 22–32). Thompson (1967: 57) has proposed that organizations will seek to group tasks according to their degree of interdependence, with reciprocally related tasks placed in the same or closely adjacent
units, sequentially related tasks placed in less closely adjacent units, and tasks
exhibiting pooled interdependence placed in the least closely adjacent units.
Organizations are expected to behave in this manner because the type of
coordination mechanism needed to cope with reciprocal tasks—mutual
adjustment—is the most costly in terms of organizational resources; schedules, which are used to cope with sequential tasks, are the next most costly;
and rules are the least costly. In short, Thompson argues that organizations
attempt to group tasks so as to minimize coordination costs. It is instructive
to note that Thompson's principle of minimizing coordination costs as an
explanation for the location of departmental boundaries can be viewed as a
special case of Williamson's (1975) principle of minimizing transaction costs
as an explanation for the location of organizational boundaries[3] (see
Chapter 7).

Hierarchy. Hierarchy can be used to respond to increased information
flows in two ways. First, as Fayol and other administrative theorists emphasized
early in this century (see Chapter 2), officials can be used to deal with unexpected or irregular occurrences on an "exception" basis. Of course, this practice can provide a satisfactory solution only if the exceptions do not arise too
frequently. Second, as suggested by open system theorists (see Chapter 4), hierarchies can be used to group tasks (Simon, 1962). According to Thompson:

> It is unfortunate that [hierarchy] has come to stand almost exclusively for
> degrees of highness or lowness, for this tends to hide the basic significance of
> hierarchy for complex organizations. Each level is not simply higher than the
> one below, but is a more inclusive clustering, or combination of interdepen-
> dent groups, to handle those aspects of coordination which are beyond the
> scope of any of its components. (1967: 59)

---

[3]Williamson's concept of transaction costs is broader than Thompson's concept of coordination costs because it includes the costs of negotiations between prospective exchange partners as well as the negotiations needed to cordinate exchanges once an agreement has been
established. Within most organizations the former negotiations do not occur: one department
is not allowed to determine whether or not to enter into exchanges with another unit in the
same organization. However, in some very large organizations an attempt is made to simulate
a market situation, and departments are allowed to decide whether to enter into exchange
agreements with other internal units or to seek more favorable exchange rates externally (see
Chapter 10).

As the amount of interdependence among organizational tasks increases, it becomes more difficult to handle it by departmentalization—to contain, for example, all of the instances of reciprocal interdependence within an organizational unit. As interdependence overflows departmental units, a heavier burden of information processing is placed on hierarchical officers who are expected to provide links across units.

Delegation. Rather than attempting to program and regulate closely the work of all participants and requiring that all decisions be made above the level of the performers, organizations confronting increased complexity and uncertainty can delegate some autonomy to workers. Galbraith (1973) refers to this arrangement as targeting or goal setting, indicating that coordination is secured not by minute descriptions of work procedures but by specification of the desired outcomes. Organizations often incorporate professionals or other specialists to accomplish particular tasks whose work they do not control in detail but by specifying the nature of the outputs required. Delegation is present to some extent and for some positions in most organizations. However, it reaches its most highly developed form in professional organizations, a form to be discussed more fully later in this chapter.

Microcoordination. An important coordination device, often overlooked, but used by many organizations is to rely on the capacity of the "task object"—the customer or client—to monitor and guide the services received. Professional organizations such as universities and hospitals often recognize their task objects to be subjects who can, to some extent, look out for their own interests. Students, for example, may be told that it is their responsibility to meet all graduation requirements. They are expected to call attention to any problems or defects in their treatment. And many manufacturing organizations, particularly those providing customized products to knowledgeable customers, have come to realize the value of recognizing these "external" groups as valuable interested participants. The extent to which clients and customers are capable of and permitted to exercise such microcoordination varies greatly across organizations.

Rules and programs, schedules, departmentalization, hierarchy, and some delegation: these are the ubiquitous features of complex formal organizations. By means of these conventional structural mechanisms, organizations are able to respond to task demands posing moderate information-processing requirements. But what if the levels of diversity, uncertainty, and interdependence are higher still so that conventional solutions prove inadequate? Galbraith argues that an organization confronting excessive levels of task complexity and uncertainty can choose one of two general responses: it may elect to (1) "reduce the amount of information that is processed," or (2) "increase its capacity to handle more information" (1973: 15). Although these two responses push in different directions, they are not necessarily incompatible. Moreover, each response may be made through one of several strategies, and an organization may pursue more than one strategy at the same time.

Additional Coordination Strategies: Reducing Information

Product versus process organization.   We have noted that information-processing costs can be reduced by placing highly interdependent tasks in the same or adjacent work units. This principle underlies the creation of product-based departments. For example, a publishing organization may begin with a departmental structure based on function or process criteria: editorial, production, and marketing divisions. Suppose that two product lines develop: college texts and trade (commercial bookstore) publications. At some point, the costs of attempting to handle the information that must accompany these quite different types of products across the three divisions may become sufficiently high that the company decides to reorganize on a product basis. Now we have two divisions: text and trade, each with its own departments of design, production, and marketing. The diversity of information processing required to operate within the process-based structure has been substantially reduced by the adoption of a product structure.

The costs accompanying a shift to product departments are primarily those associated with the loss of economies of scale. The scale of each unit has been reduced, and this may prevent the use of specialized personnel or machinery that can be supported only by a large volume of work. Product-based organization also reduces the likelihood that the benefits of variety—stimulation, transfer of learning, overlap of domains—will be available to enrich the organization or its participants.

Slack resources.   An organization can reduce its information-processing demands simply by reducing the required level of performance (see Galbraith, 1973). Higher performance standards increase the need for coordination: lowered standards create slack—unused resources—which provides some ease in the system. For example, if delivery deadlines are not set so as to challenge the production units, then the need for information processing is reduced. If there are few constraints on inventory levels, then rapid response to changes in supply and demand messages is less essential. And, to use a nonmanufacturing example, if every third-grade teacher uses the first several weeks to reteach the basic lessons and skills of the second grade, then the sequential interdependence between second- and third-grade teachers is reduced, and there is less need for coordination of their efforts.

In addition to storing extra components and introducing redundancy into task performances, an organization can store surplus task or work-flow information. In his study of the complex structures that supply repair services for the electronic equipment required to support the U.S. Naval Air Systems Command, Kmetz (1984: 272) details the use of information buffers—"pools or collections of information formed to support decision making or monitoring of workflow variables." At critical junctures in the repair process, varying types of information—samples of data, knowledge of legitimate and unsanctioned routines, backup guides and records—develop as alternatives to or supports for the official communications and data packages. For example, "a relatively formalized buffer, such as a work-around notebook, supports repair of a WRA [weapon replaceable assembly] independently of the accuracy of the test program" (1984: 273). Such slack resources allow looser coupling of interdependent work systems.

Some slack in the handling of resources, including information, is not only inevitable but essential to smooth operations. All operations require a margin of error—an allowance for mistakes, waste, spoilage, and similar unavoidable accompaniments of work. The question is not whether there is to be slack but how much slack is to be permitted. Excessive slack resources increase costs for the organization that are likely to be passed on to the consumer. Since creating slack resources is a relatively easy and painless solution available to organizations, whether or not it is employed is likely to be determined by the amount of competition confronting the organization in its task environment.[4]

While Galbraith emphasizes that slack resources reduce information-processing requirements by lowering standards, it is equally important to emphasize that they reduce the need for information processing by reducing interdependence. Conventional organizational routines of mass and batch production assume pooled or, at most, sequential interdependence: design engineers are departmentally buffered from production workers who, in turn, are separated from marketing personnel. Designs are "tossed over the wall" to production workers who have little say in the design but are expected to produce products for salespeople who often have little say in what is being produced. These functionally specialized and insulated departments—"chimney" structures—are considered by most contemporary students of organizations as hopelessly old-fashioned and noncompetitive.

Additional Coordination Strategies: Increased Capacity

Other strategies are intended, not to reduce the need for information processing, but to increase the information-processing capacity of the organization. We describe here only the more formalized strategies—those that rely on the explicit design of new roles and relations to process heightened information flows. Informal approaches are described in the following section.

Augmented hierarchies. Many analysts have observed that although hierarchies can assist the coordination of work by imposing patterns and constraints on the flow of information, if the messages sent become too numerous or the content too rich, a hierarchical system can quickly become overloaded (see Chapter 7; see also Rogers and Agarwala-Rogers, 1976; Kreps, 1986). The capacity of the hierarchical system can be increased in two ways: (1) by increasing the information flows between nodes and (2) by increasing the information-processing capacity of the nodes. Often organizations do both.

In earlier times, and at the present time for many functions, information flows are increased by adding specialized administrative and clerical person-

---

[4]March and colleagues have pointed out that organizational slack is also a critical resource supporting organizational experimentation and learning (Cyert and March, 1963; Levitt and March, 1988). March (1988: 4) notes that search activities motivated by slack—rather than by immediate problem-solving pressures—are "less likely to solve immediate problems, more likely to be directed to subunit or individual objectives, and more likely to discover distinctively new alternatives."

nel—inspectors, accountants, clerks—charged with gathering and summarizing the information needed for decision making. More recently, some of these functions have been taken over by increasingly sophisticated electronic monitoring, transmission, and data-reduction systems. The design of systems that will permit the rapid transmission of relevant, "on-line" information through feedback loops to appropriate decision centers is one of the major aims and achievements of the modern systems design movement (see Sprague and Watson, 1986; Zmud, 1983). Huber (1990) argues that the employment of advanced information technologies tends to increase the number of information sources but reduce the number of intermediate human actors involved in its transmission.

The capacity of decision nodes is also increased by adding personnel or electronic resources. The addition of "staff" personnel to assist the "line" officers is one of the earliest and most widely used modifications of the hierarchy. This innovation increases information-processing capacity without formally decentralizing decisions or sacrificing the unity-of-command principle. Staff "experts" give technical assistance and specialized advice to the generalist managers who are empowered to make the final decision. However, we know from a large number of studies that although the staff-line distinction may preserve the appearance of a unified command system, much actual power passes from the hands of line officers to staff associates (see Dalton, 1959; Goldner, 1970). In addition to these staff-line arrangements, the modern executive is likely to be supported not only by technical specialists but also by a variety of "assistants," "assistants-to," "deputies," and "associates" who perform stable or shifting duties but always act on behalf of and subject to the approval of their superiors (see Hamilton and Biggart, 1984: 15–54). All, however, contribute to the capacity of the system to process information.

The new information technologies—in particular, computers—affect not only the gathering and transmission of information but also its use in decision making. Although more research is required, Huber (1990) suggests that such technologies tend to support the more rapid and accurate identification of problems and opportunities, increase the availability of relevant and timely information and, in this way, improve both the speed and quality of decision making.

Lateral connections. Consider the following situation. An aircraft company has reorganized, grouping workers within divisions by product, and one of the divisions is responsible for the development and testing of new types of jet engines. The departments have been created on a functional basis: there is a department housing the scientists and engineers responsible for design, a production department composed of the mechanical engineers and technicians responsible for building prototype engines, and a department of engineers responsible for evaluating and testing the models. Clearly this situation involves high levels of task complexity, uncertainty, and interdependence and will require the exchange of large amounts of information as the work is carried on. In a normal hierarchical structure, the communications required to coordinate performance among departments would be expected to flow up the chain of command from workers through supervisors to departmental managers. The managers would be expected to exchange information among themselves and with the division manager, arrive at a common definition of how the work was to proceed, and then communicate detailed instructions back down the hierarchies within each department. Given the extent of interdependence and the amount of information to be processed, such a process would entail long delays and great inefficiencies.

In situations of such heavy information flow, the development of more direct, lateral connections across work groups and departments is an obvious response. That is, lateral connections allow information to flow more directly among participants in interdependent departments or work groups, rather than up and over through hierarchical channels. Although the opening of such channels may seem both simple and obvious, it represents an organizational revolution! Informal communications and arrangements among interdependent workers exist in virtually all organizations and undoubtedly often save them from floundering because of inadequacies of the vertical channels. But we are dealing here not with informal but formal structures: we are discussing the official legitimation of connections among workers across departmental boundaries. To permit such developments is to undermine the hierarchical structure: department heads are no longer fully in control of, and so cannot be held fully accountable for, the behavior of their subordinates. This is why organizations— even organizations facing fairly high degrees of uncertainty and interdependence—long resisted the development of formal lateral connections. But increasingly they are compelled to do so, and, when they do, can choose among several types of arrangements, including the following:

Liaison Roles. Liaison roles are specialized positions or units created to facilitate interchange between two or more interdependent departments. The responsibilities of such integrating roles may include troubleshooting, conflict resolution, and anticipation of problems. These positions are similar to staff roles except that they relate to two or more managers rather than to one. Lawrence and Lorsch (1967) examine the functions of such positions in organizations and discuss the characteristics of individuals who fill them successfully. Note that the creation of liaison roles makes for a more complex management structure but does not undermine the hierarchical principle.

Task Forces. A task force is by definition a temporary group that is given a delimited problem to solve. The expectation is that the group will be dissolved once its work is completed. The task force may involve its members full- or part-time. Participants are drawn from several departments, and frequently from several levels, and are selected not only because of their interest or ability with respect to the work of the task force but also because of their stature in their own departments. In the case of the jet engine division, a task force involving representatives from all three departments might be created to codify the technical terms and symbols used by members of that division. The strength of the task force is that it allows multiple representatives to interact intensively over a short period to achieve a specific objective. Status distinctions that hinder free interaction are typically suspended during the group's existence. That such distinctions are present but ignored contributes to the special atmosphere of a task force[5] (see Miles, 1964). Because the task force is defined

---

[5]A particularly interesting and dramatic example is provided by President Kennedy's creation of a task force—the Excom, composed of trusted advisers and associates—to make recommendations to him on the course of action to be pursued during the Cuban missile crisis of 1962. The best account of this group's structure and deliberations is provided by the president's brother, Robert Kennedy (1969). (See also, Allison, 1971.)

as temporary, its existence is compatible with the maintenance of the hierarchy. Indeed, task forces may function as safety valves, reducing tensions and solving problems generated by the continuation of the hierarchy.

Project Teams. Whereas task forces are temporary systems created to solve nonrecurring problems, project teams are groupings of personnel across departmental lines that carry on some portion of the regular work of the organization. In the jet engine example, a team comprising several members from each department may be built around the design and testing of a highly experimental prototype engine. Members would be released from their regular duties over an extended period in order to better contribute to this effort. The typical project team would have a leader or manager responsible for planning and coordinating the work of the team as long as it performed as a unit. Departmental officers would, in effect, delegate authority to the project manager to act on their behalf during the project but would see to it that their own personnel were being used and treated appropriately.

Many of the new innovations in production processes—CAD (computer-aided design), CAM (computer-aided manufacturing), JIT (just-in-time inventory controls)—do not simply entail the use of new computer technology but also involve significant structural changes as buffers between departments are reduced and interdependence increased (see Susman and Chase, 1986; Adler, 1990). Designers are expected to interact with manufacturing workers as they take into account the "producibility" of the product; and marketing personnel—who best know their customer's needs—are expected to exercise increased influence in both the design and production process (see Chase and Tansik, 1983). Permitting such interaction among workers across departments escalates interdependence from pooled to sequential to reciprocal levels.

Some project teams span the boundaries of formal organizations, as members are selected and combined in order to accomplish a specified goal. Eccles and Crane (1988) have analyzed the use of project teams in the investment banking industry. Here, although the basic structure is functional in form—including investment banking, sales, trading, and research activities—the working out of a "deal" for a specific client requires the rapid, short-term mobilization of varying combinations of specialists—sometimes from more than one investment bank—working in close combination with related specialists in the customer firm. The resulting structures are "flexible, flat, complex, and rife with conflict" (p. 133). High differentiation results from the high degree of specialization; but integration of efforts is equally important and achieved through various mechanisms, including the delegation of considerable discretion and power to the lead banker (project manager) and the creation of special liaison roles termed "relationship managers," who are responsible for integrating the efforts of all specialists within a given firm who share a common customer.

In some organizations, work is organized so that project teams become the primary basis for the organization of work, replacing functional departments and even prescribed job descriptions. Rather than relying on an elaborate fixed division of labor, organizations institute flexible teams composed of individuals with diverse training but not fixed responsibilities who are assigned targets or goals that are subject to modification based on experience and learning (see Powell, 1996). A formal structure remains intact, but its units are teams rather than departments.

Matrix Structures. The hallmark of the matrix is its multiple command structure: vertical and lateral channels of information and authority operate simultaneously. The ancient and sacred principle of unity of command is set aside, and competing bases of authority are allowed to jointly govern the work flow. The vertical lines are typically those of functional departments that operate as "home bases" for all participants; the lateral lines represent project groups or geographical arenas where managers combine and coordinate the services of the functional specialists around particular projects or areas (see Davis and Lawrence, 1977; Hill and White, 1979). This type of structure is illustrated in Figure 9–1, which depicts the formal structure of the rocket division of a space agency.

The constituent units of matrix structures may be relatively permanent or shifting (Sayles, 1976). The permanent matrix structure is illustrated by the rocket division (Figure 9–1), the products and requirements of which are relatively stable. Examples of organizations employing a shifting matrix structure are those that must maintain a fairly stable set of specialists but allocate them across a changing mix of project teams. Examples are research organizations such as RAND and SRI that perform research under contract to clients whose interests vary greatly—from assessing an experimental health care system to designing an airport complex for a developing nation. An economist might be involved in both types of projects, but would play quite a different role in each. All participants are responsible both to their functional superior and to their project leader.

The conflicts between an orientation to function or product that exist in at least a latent form in most organizations are elevated by the matrix organization into two competing structural principles. Although such institutionalization of conflict does not resolve it, it does ensure that both the functional and the product interests are viewed as legitimate and have managerial representatives who will continually define and defend them. Moreover, assigning specific roles the responsibility for defending particular values gives them higher visibility and makes trade-offs or compromises more evident: conflicts between decision makers are more visible than conflicts internalized within a single decision maker.

Some of the overt interrole conflicts built into the matrix structure are managed by sequential attention to one or another set of priorities. In what has been called the "matrix swing," functional priorities may receive more attention at the beginning and ending of a project cycle as personnel are hired or released and as budgets are negotiated, but once a project is under way, attention and authority shift to the project leader. Still, much ambiguity must be tolerated and competing claims accommodated for the matrix to function. For many participants, matrix structures are high-demand, high-stress work environments (see Davis and Lawrence, 1977; Larson and Gobeli, 1987).

Empirical Evidence

Empirical studies examining the relations between technology and structure have produced a body of evidence that is generally supportive of the predictions of contingency theory, but also suggests that the relations are relatively weak. (For reviews, see Gerwin, 1981; Scott, 1990b; Donaldson, 1996; Roberts and Grabowski, 1996.) Many technical problems beset these studies, includ-

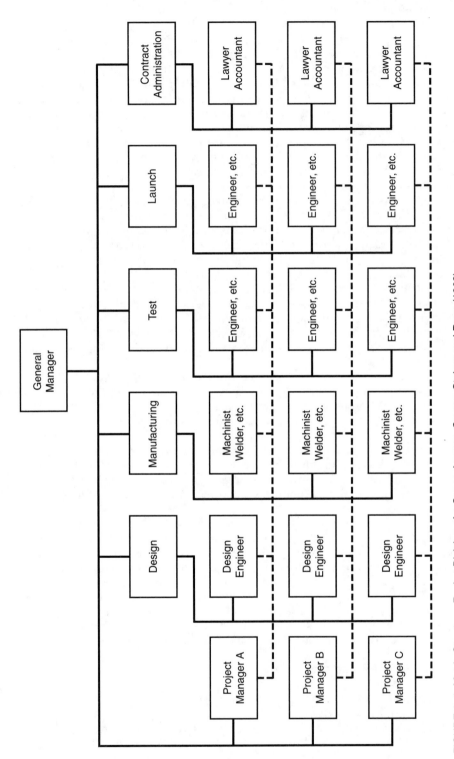

FIGURE 9–1 Matrix Structure: Rocket Division of a Space Agency. *Source:* Steiner and Ryan (1968).

ing problems in employing different types of measures, in ignoring or confusing levels of analysis, in failing to specify the expected form of the contingency relation, and in focusing on only a few selected relations rather than combinations or patterns of relations.

With respect to measures, we have already called attention to the wide variety of technology measures employed; and similar creativity has characterized the development of structural measures (see Van de Ven and Ferry, 1980). Clearly, all these measures are not interchangeable: they assess different facets of technologies or structures. Also, different data sources are often employed including the judgments of officials acting as informants, the reports of rank-and-file participants, observations, and documents. Pennings (1973) has noted the low convergent validity of varying sources of information (see also, Stablein, 1996).

Some studies relating technology and structure are conducted at the level of the organization as a whole; others use the work group or department as the unit of study; still others examine the nature of individual tasks and associated work arrangements. Efforts to relate technical and structural measures at the organizational level are extremely hazardous because organizations tend to employ a variety of technologies and to be structurally complex. An example of an attempt to develop an organization-wide measure is provided by the work of the Aston group—associated with Aston University in Great Britain—who aggregated data gathered by interviews with chief executives and a number of department heads into a single-measure, work-flow integration, to characterize the technology of the organization as a whole (Hickson, Pugh, and Pheysey, 1969).

Analysts studying technology and structure at the departmental level confront less severe, but similar, problems caused by technical and structural heterogeneity. Many work groups and most departments include different types of work, particularly in the case of product-based organizational structures. Further, studies (for example, Mohr, 1971) that measure the characteristics of tasks performed by individual workers and aggregate them to form measures of some modal task characteristics may not only cause the analyst to overlook variance across individual workers but fail to capture those characteristics of technology that are distinctive to the group level, such as work variety or complexity at the departmental level (see Comstock and Scott, 1977).

Even at the level of the individual worker we must be prepared to encounter multiple types of work and varied work structures (see Dornbusch and Scott, 1975). The range of tasks performed is likely to vary in complexity and uncertainty; and control structures often take such differences into account. For example, universities employ different arrangements to manage teaching than to oversee research.

In summary, given the great diversity and complexity of the types of work and the structures encompassed by most organizations, we should not be surprised to learn that many specific studies report varying and contradictory findings. When the subject of study is variable and complex, findings will be highly susceptible to differences in the variables and indicators employed, the sample drawn, the level of organization studied, and similar research decisions.

Another factor that inhibits the strength of observed associations between technology and structure is that most contingency theorists are vague about the expected form of the relations (see Schoonhoven, 1981). Some of the most interesting and consistent findings are those reporting nonlinear associations. Woodward (1965), for example, observed that as the extent of technical complexity increased from low (batch processing) through medium (mass production) to high levels (process production), the span of control exhibited a curvilinear (inverted U-shaped) pattern, with narrow spans of control occurring at the two extremes. Although such curvilinear patterns have been widely reported for a number of measures of control (see Lincoln, Hanada, and McBride, 1986), most analysts continue to apply statistical tests that incorporate assumptions of linearity. Better specified theoretical and statistical models are needed if progress is to be made in understanding these relations.

Yet another limitation of efforts to test contingency predictions is that most studies examine only one relation at at time—for example, the relation between uncertainty and formalization—although the theory implies that technologies and structures consist of multiple-variable, patterned relations or *configurations* (see Meyer, Tsui, and Hinings, 1993). An interesting attempt to evaluate such a framework is reported by Drazin and Van de Ven (1985), who studied 629 employment security offices. They examined the relation between technology (task difficulty and variability), and eleven measures of structure (for example, specialization, standardization) and process (for example, mode of communication, methods of conflict resolution). The pattern of results supported contingency predictions: for example, high-performing units under varying task conditions were observed to vary significantly in their structure/process characteristics from low-performing units and to exhibit the predicted profile of structural and process characteristics.

The examination of the technology-structure relation has been extended during the past decade by a number of cross-cultural studies, many of which were motivated by an interest in determining whether contingency arguments are "culture-free."[6] Two sets of studies are of particular interest. The first, conducted by the Laboratory for the Economic and Sociological Study of Work in Aix-en-Provence, France, under the leadership of Maurice, examined the organization of work in nine factories—three each in Great Britain, France, and Germany—matched for technology using Woodward's categories of "mass production," "small batch," and "process" modes. Embracing a natural system perspective (elaborated in the next section), these researchers emphasized more qualitative comparisons which recognize "that organizational features have to be seen as socially constructed in different ways, rather than measured along a standardized dimension" (Maurice, Sorge, and Warner, 1980: 72). They report relatively large and consistent differences by country in the organization of work. German firms, regardless of technological complexity, exhibited higher levels of worker expertise, flexibility, and autonomy; British firms were intermediate, while French firms concentrated expertise and decision making in top managers and staff specialists.

---

[6]It is possible for contingency theory to accommodate cultural variables simply by treating such differences as another kind of contingency affecting organizational design. However, to do so carries us far from the rational -system model, which assumes that technology, far from being shaped, is itself the shaper, operating to produce similar structures in varying cultures and social settings (see Lincoln, 1990).

Maurice and colleagues interpret such differences as reflecting broad variations in the three societies' educational institutions and industrial relations practices (see Maurice, 1979; Rose, 1985).

The second set of studies, conducted by Lincoln and colleagues (Lincoln, Hanada, and McBride, 1986; Lincoln and Kalleberg, 1990), contrasts a sample of fifty-five American and fifty-one Japanese manufacturing plants. This research reports differences between firms in the two countries, with Japan exhibiting less specialization and taller hierarchies than the United States regardless of technology, and also some differences in the effects of technology, with Japan exhibiting weaker relations between workflow rigidity and centralization measures.[7] The important conclusion is drawn that "the impact of technology on structuring is stronger among U.S. organizations" than Japanese organizations of the same type, suggesting that in the Japanese context "the design of the organization becomes detached to some degree from the technology process and more attuned to the needs of the human workforce" (Lincoln, Hanada, and McBride, 1986: 358, 362).

The mixed and, at best, weak empirical support for the contingency theory predictions coupled with the growing evidence that technology-structure relations are influenced by broader social context has stimulated important critiques and alternative theoretical formulations that modify and challenge rational system formulations. In particular, early work based on the contingency framework embraced what Orlikowski (1992) has labeled the "technological imperative" model: a view that technology "exerts unidirectional, causal influences over humans and organizations." Natural system theorists challenge this conception.

TECHNOLOGY AND STRUCTURE: NATURAL SYSTEM VIEWS

Analysts embracing natural system assumptions are increasingly reevaluating and reformulating rational system arguments concerning technology and structure. These critiques can, somewhat crudely, be organized around three themes: (1) social factors affecting technology; (2) rethinking the relation between technology and structure; and (3) emphasizing the utility of informal, in contrast to formal, structure.

The Social Shaping of Technology

A growing number of social historians and sociologists have begun to recognize that the development of technologies does not represent a working out of some sort of inexorable logic of technical determinism or economic efficiency but, instead, some combination of what is technically possible and socially acceptable. In this view, technologies are, in good measure, socially constructed. As Noble argues:

---

[7]Two different kinds of cultural effects are distinguished: (1) variable *level* effects, for example, the assertion that Japanese organizations exhibit lower levels of specialization than their U.S. counterparts; and (2) variable *causal* effects, for example, the assertion that task complexity is associated with different degrees of centralization in Japan than in the United States (see Przeworski and Teune, 1970; Lammers and Hickson, 1979b).

> Because of its very concreteness, people tend to confront technology as an irre-
> ducible brute fact, a given, a first cause, rather than as hardened history, frozen
> fragments of human and social endeavor. . . . The process of technological
> development is essentially social, and thus there is always a large measure of
> indeterminancy, of freedom, within it. Beyond the very real constraints of ener-
> gy and matter exists a realm in which human thoughts and actions remain deci-
> sive. (1984: xi)

A wide spectrum of views has developed regarding the social determinants of technology, ranging from the relatively uncontroversial arguments
that science and technology are influenced by their social and political context to the much more radical view that technologies are socially constructed—that both designers and users determine what technologies are, what
they do, how they work, even what it means to say that they work (See Bijker,
Hughes, and Pinch, 1987).

A number of the "new" social historians have attempted to examine how
social and political factors have influenced which technologies are developed
and adopted (see, for example, Hounshell, 1984; Shaiken, 1985). Noble
(1984), for example, argues that numerical control approaches won out over
record-playback approaches to the design of automatically controlled
machine tools because they located control in the hands of programmers and
managers rather than among machine operators on the shop floor and so better served a number of powerful interests including the U.S. Air Force, aerospace contractors, and the engineering community.

And, in a more general, speculative historical review, Piore and Sabel
(1984) suggest that the choice made by industrializing societies to replace generalized tools with specialized machinery was not dictated by economic necessity but by political interests. "Power in the market, not efficiency (in the sense of
a uniquely appropriate application of technology), decided the contest" (p. 40).

It is typical of these new histories of technology to emphasize the
unevenness and unexpectedness of change, the diversity of causes and connections. Sabel observes that "The fit between what needs to be done and how
it can be done is seldom as tight as the determinists imagine" (1982: 5). An
important concern of these histories is to uncover "roads not taken" (Noble
1984)—to document alternative technical solutions and/or organizational
arrangements that were possible or were developed, but did not become dominant. Most of these accounts also emphasize the role played by organizational politics, by vested interests, and by institutional arrangements in shaping
and selecting the technologies that succeeded.

In these views, then, technology is itself a socially shaped if not constructed reality. The causal arrrows are shifted to examine how social structures shape technology rather than how technology shapes social, including
organizational, structure.

The Strategic Connection of Technology and Structure

In addition to challenging rational system conceptions of the nature of technology, natural system theorists assert that while the choice of technologies
may constrain the design of structures, it does not determine them. Theorists

such as Child (1972) insist that the state of technology and other environmental conditions pose only broad and general constraints on structural design. Contingency theorists place too much weight on external constraints and do not give sufficient attention to actors and their capacity for choice. This line of argument, labeled *strategic contingency,* emphasizes that a given set of circumstances can support many alternative adaptive responses, many alternative strategies. Accordingly, what is an effective structure for a given organization is shaped not only by its technology and task environment but also by the strategy adopted. (We also consider strategy in Chapters 10 and 11.)

Strategic contingency theorists also remind us that the division of labor and the differential contacts of participants with others inside and outside the organizations create divergent perspectives and interests as well as new sources of power that can be used to pursue these interests (Hickson et al., 1971). The recognition of multiple interests within organizations has led to the coalitional model of organizations: many organizations are in no sense unified actors but are instead shifting combinations of varying interest groups moving in and out of the organization and up and down in relative power. If a particular group has a corner on some valued resource, such as legal expertise or scientific creativity, and there is no readily available alternative, it is likely to acquire power within the organization. And one of the uses to which power is put is to shape the structure of the organization.[8] More powerful actors are likely to attempt to locate more discretion in the positions they occupy and to attempt to reduce that located in other positions. Such struggles are not confined to blue-collar workers and supervisors or managers; they are equally likely among school teachers and principals, between physicians and managers.

Of course, when we shift from technology to technical system, the opportunity for social and political forces to operate is greatly enlarged. The complexity and uncertainty of work are strongly influenced by the specific technical systems that are created, and by the way and the extent to which work is divided. Similarly, interdependence is not only a function of the technical processes per se, but the ways in which they are distributed among workers. Through differentiation, complex tasks can be divided, made simpler, and made more interdependent. Alternatively, by emphasizing a craft approach or through professionalization, complex tasks can be constructed, delegated to individual performers, and made less interdependent. Differentiation, deskilling, and interdependence (simplifying evaluation, increasing the need for coordination) are more likely to occur when managers exercise power; craft expertise, professionalization, and skill enhancement (rendering external control more difficult, justifying increasing autonomy) occur when performers exercise power (Dornbusch and Scott, 1975). Such arguments are not limited to, but are clearly consistent with, those developed by Marxist theorists, who point to the continuing struggle for discretion and control occurring in the workplace (see Chapter 7).

The emphasis that strategic contingency theorists place on the flexibility of connections—loose coupling—between technology and structure and on the role of power in shaping these connections is echoed by analysts exam-

---

[8]A related use to which power is put is shaping the goals of the organization (see Chapter 11).

ining effects associated with the introduction of new information technologies. Zuboff (1988) argues that these technologies—variously combining microelectronics, computer systems, telecommunications—exhibit two critical characteristics: first, they enhance automation, carrying forward the logic of nineteenth-century machine systems that "enables the same processes to be performed with more continuity and control." Second, however, the new technologies differ fundamentally from earlier machines because of their capacity to "informate" work processes by simultaneously generating:

> information about the underlying productive and administrative processes through which an organization accomplishes its work. It provides a deeper level of transparency to activities that had been either partially or completely opaque. (Zuboff, 1988: 9)

More specifically:

> The intelligence of the microprocessor that resides at the base of virtually every application not only applies instructions to equipment but can convert the current state of product or process into information. (Zuboff, 1985: 105)

Recalling Galbraith's insight that technologies affect structures by determining how much information must be processed during the task sequence, it is possible to see that some aspects of new technologies absorb information: such technologies as automation and robotics eliminate the need for the information-processing capacities of social structures. By contrast, other aspects of the new technologies create new information: they are able to not only "apply programmed instructions to equipment but also convert the current state of equipment, product, or process into data" (Zuboff, 1988: 9). However, whether this new information is employed primarily to exercise greater control over the work process or provides the basis for increased innovation and autonomy among performers is not determined by the technology, but by choices made by those exercising influence in these work sites.

Rather than making the unsatisfactory if not impossible choice regarding the causal priority of either technology over structure or the reverse, a better alternative formulation has been proposed by Barley and by Orlikowski. They adapt Gidden's conception of the "duality" of social structure (see Chapter 1), applying it to the relation of technology and structure. Orlikowski summarizes the conception as containing two premises. First, technology exhibits duality: it is both product and object:

> Technology is the product of human action, while it also assumes structural properties. That is, technology is physically constructed by actors working in a given social context, and technology is socially constructed by actors through the different meanings they attach to it. . . . However, it is also the case that once developed and deployed, technology tends to become reified and institutionalized, losing its connection with the human agents that constructed it or gave it meaning, and it appears to be part of the objective, structural properties of the organization. (Orlikowski, 1992: 406)

But, second, even though undergoing reification, technologies vary in their "interpretive flexibility" (see Pinch and Bijker, (1987):

> [There are] differences among technologies in the degree to which users can effect redesign. While we can expect a greater engagement of human agents during the initial development of a technology, this does not discount the ongoing potential for uses to change it (physically and socially) throughout their interaction with it. (Orlikowski, 1992: 408)

Both premises are persuasively illustrated in a study by Barley (1986) of changes occurring in the social order of two radiology departments of hospitals at the time when computer tomography (CAT) scanners were first introduced. Far from viewing it as determinant in its effects, Barley regards the introduction of the new technology as "an occasion" for restructuring of the technical system. "The scanners occasioned change because they became social objects whose meanings were defined by the context of their use" (p. 106). He documents how the interaction patterns exhibited by radiologists and technicians changed over time by isolating "scripts" that defined identifiable sequences in the changing order. Because of differences in the surrounding contexts, the varying expertise of personnel, and the specific course of interactions, identical technologies gave rise to different structural outcomes. Although "each department changed in similar directions, one department became far more decentralized" (p. 105).

Thus, in Barley's study the general predictions of contingency theory receive support: the greater complexity and uncertainty of the new technology is associated with increasing decentralization. But so too do those of the strategic contingency theorists who emphasize variable reactions and connections and stress the diversity of interests and the role of power.

Two final comments on the limitations of conventional contingency theory. First, it overemphasizes the role of intraorganizational forces. We have attempted throughout this discussion to stress the importance of wider social and institutional forces in shaping technology and technical-structural relations. Here we supply one additional example. The major incentive for many organizations to develop a project-management structure came not from within as a rational response to information processing demands but from outside the organization. The Department of Defense required its contractors to use this structural arrangement in the 1950s as a condition for obtaining financial support! (Wieland and Ullrich, 1976: 39). Government contract officers were tired of getting the runaround from functional department heads, each of whom had only partial control over any given project. The development of a project-management format gave these officers someone they could more easily relate to and hold responsible for the successful and timely completion of the project. Second, contingency theory overlooks the importance of informal structures as a response to uncertainty and complexity.

Reliance on Informal Rather Than Formal Structure

Contingency theory approaches to structural design, like all rational system models, stress the benefits of formalization. The rational system response to increasing task demands is to shorten and strengthen the leash: provide superiors with more and faster information so they can more rapidly change the instructions to performers; increase the ratio of superiors to performers so that more information can be processed more quickly and revised guidelines supplied to performers. Some of these modifications move in the direction of decentralization: power and authority are more widely dispersed as hierarchies are augmented and, particularly, as lateral connections are added. But formalization is, if anything, increased in these systems.[9] New types of roles are created and new linkages specified that increase the complexity, flexibility, and capacity for change in the structure. But the flexibility involved is designed, not spontaneous, and the changes reflect capacity to shift rapidly from one set of formal rules and roles to another.

We know, of course, that this central assumption is challenged by natural system theorists, who stress the advantages of informal structures, particularly as strategies for dealing with task uncertainty. These alternative approaches, which have received much recent attention, rely primarily on enlarged roles, internalized and peer controls, and informal structures to confront high levels of uncertainty and complexity. Rather than augmenting hierarchies, they minimize vertical distinctions and flatten hierarchies, and rather than creating new, specialized lateral roles and relations, they encourage more direct, face-to-face communications among any or all participants as required. Decision making and the exercise of control become more decentralized, and organizational roles less formalized. We review several bodies of theory and research that emphasize the value of informal structures in work organization.

Socio-technical systems and work design.   We have briefly described the socio-technical system approach developed at the Tavistock Institute in London following World War II (see Chapter 5.) One of the guiding premises of this approach is that work involves a combination of social and technical requisites and that the object of design is to "jointly optimize" both components—not sacrifice one for the other. By contrast, rational system approaches are more likely to focus on the demands of the technical system, ignoring the psychological and social needs of workers. Technical systems are designed; then human workers are "fitted in" to their requirements. And to fit human behavior into a prespecified technical system requires that it be highly programmed, that the activities and interactions be specified and predictable—in a word, formalized.

If human as well as technical requirements are to be served, then it is necessary to determine what kinds of work situations motivate and satisfy workers. The Tavistock group emphasizes both individual task features and social organizational, particularly work-group, features. At the task level, repetitive, undemanding, isolated jobs undermine commitment and performance motivation. And at the work-group level, competition and close supervision foment stress, petty deceptions, scapegoating, and low morale. These effects were observed when more highly mechanized approaches were introduced in British coal mines—technical approaches that disrupted worker

---

[9]The relation between formalization and decentralization is discussed in Chapter 10.

autonomy and work-group cohesion (Trist and Bamforth, 1951). The solution was to restructure the situation so as to give more attention to its social components. In the restructured situation:

> Groups of men are responsible for the whole task, allocate themselves to shifts and to jobs within the shift, and are paid on a group bonus. Thus the problems of overspecialized work roles, segregation of tasks across shifts with consequent scapegoating and lack of group cohesion were overcome. (Pugh and Hickson, 1996: 86)

The rational system assumption that worker performance is enhanced when work demands are routinized and standardized—when complexity is factored into simple tasks and when uncertainty is removed—is strongly challenged by this approach. Organizations may thrive on certainty, but individuals do not! This counterassumption originating in the socio-technical school has given rise to a large body of theory and research pursued primarily at the social psychological level of the individual worker. The most influential of these are job characteristics theory and its elaboration in work design and individual needs approaches.

Briefly, research on job characteristics pursues the assumption that specific attributes of the job, such as variety, autonomy, and required interaction, are associated with worker motivation and work performance. Turner and Lawrence (1965) developed and tested these predictions by measuring the characteristics of forty-seven industrial jobs, but found the expected relations held only for workers in rural areas, who were presumed to have different needs or expectations for work than urban workers. Later research has pursued this "contingent" assumption that the relation between job characteristics and worker responses is mediated by worker expectations or needs (see Hackman and Oldham, 1980). The same types of job characteristics—variety, task identity, autonomy—are identified as important, as having "high motivating potential," but whether the potential is recognized depends on the psychological needs of the particular worker. Although a number of empirical tests of this more complex model of task characteristics and performance have been conducted (see, for example, Brief and Aldag, 1975; Stone, Mowday, and Porter, 1977; Steers and Spencer, 1977), the support is at best weak, and the research has been criticized on both methodological and theoretical grounds (see Roberts and Glick, 1981; Pfeffer, 1982; Staw, 1984). Many of the criticisms made are similar to those leveled at the contingency theory approach to technology-structure.

The socio-technical approach has placed greater emphasis on the social organization of work groups—together with the necessary support features at higher organizational levels—than on the narrower matter of the design of individual jobs. Work groups, properly structured, can provide workers with an ongoing source of incentives, error correction, assistance, and social support that no amount of attention to individual job design can hope to match. The restructured semiautonomous work groups developed for the British coal mines suggests the type of approach deemed suitable to mechanized organizations with moderate levels of uncertainty and interdependence. A similar solution was developed by Volvo of Sweden when it decided to replace the traditional conveyor line for assembling its automobiles with movable automobile carriers that would permit more task variety and worker discretion embedded within a system empowering work groups as the central work elements (see Gyllenhammar, 1977). And Cole (1979) has described how, on the other side of the globe, Toyota Auto Body of Japan reorganized its work process to enrich worker skills, enlarge worker discretion, and activate workgroup incentives and controls in the now-famous "quality circles." These work groups are ordinarily organized around a particular type of job and are granted primary responsibility for such matters as safety and quality control. They become involved with "almost every other kind of problem, including improvement of productivity, the speed and way of stopping the conveyor belt, job procedures, job training, and human relations problems" (Cole, 1979: 161).[10]

When the organizational environment becomes more turbulent and the work demands more uncertain, a socio-technical design suggests that redundancy of function is superior to redundancy of parts (Emery and Trist, 1965). Pugh and Hickson (1996: 89) summarize the critical difference between these two emphases:

> The traditional technocratic bureaucracy is based on redundancy of parts. The parts are broken down so that the ultimate elements are as simple as possible; thus an unskilled worker in a narrow job who is cheap to replace and who takes little time to train would be regarded as an ideal job design. But this approach also requires reliable control systems—often cumbersome and costly.
>
> An alternative design, based on the redundancy of functions, is appropriate to turbulent environments. In this approach individuals and units have wide repertoires of activities to cope with change, and they are self-regulating. For the individual they create roles rather than mere jobs; for the organization, they bring into being a variety-increasing system rather than the traditional control by variety reduction. . . . Autonomous working groups, collaboration rather than competition (between organizations as well as within them) and reduction of hierarchical emphasis, are some of the requirements for operating effectively in modern turbulence.

Organizational routines and tacit knowledge. From the insights of March and Simon (1958), if not before, students of organizations have appreciated the importance of "performance programs"—sets of activities that are performed in a regular and predictable way to carry out the work of the organization. Rational system theorists emphasize that these programs can and should be rationalized: engineers and technical staff must analyze the work requirements and design the necessary operations so as to minimize time and resource use. This orientation is best exemplified by Taylor's scientific management approach (see Chapter 2), but is still a widely utilized approach.

---

[10]In a later study, Cole contrasts efforts to establish worker participation structures in Japan, Sweden, and the United States. They are more widely diffused in Japan than in Sweden and in Sweden than in the United States. His analysis shows that these practices are much more highly institutionalized in Japan and Sweden, receiving support from industry groups and the state (see Cole, 1989).

Natural system theorists also recognize the importance of these patterned activities or routines but see them as more often the accomplishment of the worker rather than the expertise of the designer. Natural system views have been reinforced by the arguments of evolutionary and learning theorists who stress the importance of encouraging variation (variety), experiential learning, and gradual accumulation of experience and tacit knowledge (Miner, 1990). Much of the knowledge on which the organization relies is contained in the skills and tacit knowledge of its workforce—such routines are the "genes" of the organization (Nelson and Winter, 1982). Rather than such knowledge being:

> represented in the firm in a form that makes alternative ways of doing things accessible to an effective survey, leading to a choice founded on economic criteria . . . organizational capabilities are fragmented, distributed, and embedded in organizational routines. No individual knows how the organization accomplishes what it actually does, much less what alternatives are available. (Winter, 1990: 99)

The recent movement aimed at improving organizational performance, known as "total quality management" (TQM), recognizes the importance of these routines and the wisdom they contain, but seeks to capture tacit knowledge and make it accessible to all through discovering "best practices" that can then be codified and widely disseminated. Innovations such as quality circles and team problem solving are attempts to provide occasions for making explicit what some performers "know" but may not be aware that they know. While TQM offers more autonomy to teams for collective problem solving, it tends to resort to more conventional, top-down approaches, as Hackman and Wageman point out:

> Once such practices are identified and documented, they are diffused throughout the organization and standarized, with the result that work-unit members may wind up with very little discretion about how they perform their tasks. The potential for overspecification of work procedures is so great that one is reminded of industrial engineering during the heyday of scientific management. . . . The motivational costs of this approach are well documented. (1995: 326–327)

So, the old battles between rational and natural system views of organizations continue under new labels. (TQM approaches are further reviewed in Chapter 13.)

Organic systems and clans. During the early 1960s, Burns and Stalker studied a rather diverse group of about twenty industrial firms in Great Britain. Their sample included rather traditional textile companies, engineering firms, and a number of firms attempting to move into the rapidly growing market of electronics. Early in their field research, the investigators were struck by the presence of two quite distinct management styles—which they labeled the mechanistic and the organic. They noted that the two approaches tended to be associated with differing industries, or, more accurately, with differing types of industrial environments. The mechanistic firms were to be found in relatively stable environments, the organic in more rapidly changing environments. Burns and Stalker describe these two organizational systems as follows:

> In mechanistic systems the problems and tasks facing the concern as a whole are broken down into specialisms. Each individual pursues his task as something distinct from the real tasks of the concern as a whole, as if it were the subject of a subcontract. "Somebody at the top" is responsible for seeing to its relevance. The technical methods, duties, and powers attached to each functional role are precisely designed. Interaction within management tends to be vertical. . . .
>
> Organic systems are adapted to unstable conditions, when problems and requirements for action arise which cannot be broken down and distributed among specialist roles within a clearly defined hierarchy. Individuals have to perform their special tasks in the light of their knowledge of the tasks of the firm as a whole. Jobs lose much of their formal definition in terms of methods, duties and powers, which have to be redefined continually by interaction with others participating in a task. Interaction runs laterally as much as vertically. Communication between people of different ranks tends to resemble lateral consultation rather than vertical command. (1961: 5–6)

Organic systems, in response to conditions of high complexity and uncertainty, represent instances "where organization becomes an invertebrate process rather than a structure" (Grandori, 1987: 93).

More recent analyses have added to our understanding of this type of system. Ouchi (1980; 1981) defines it as a *clan system.* Building on the distinctions proposed by Williamson, he argues that just as hierarchies replace markets when transactions become moderately uncertain and complex, in a parallel fashion hierarchies fail and are replaced by clan systems when the transactions reach levels of extreme complexity and uncertainty.[11] Ouchi suggests that the costs of monitoring very complex exchanges by conventional or augmented authority systems is prohibitive and will increasingly give rise to "organizational failures" and the search for alternative structures. One viable alternative is the clan—a group that may or may not be linked by kinship ties but is based on common internalized goals and strong feelings of solidarity.[12]

Although clan systems are distinguished from formalized bureaucracies by a number of elements—including nonspecialized roles and career paths, implicit and internalized control mechanisms, holistic rather than segmented concerns, and slow and diffuse evaluation—Ouchi argues that their most important feature is the long-term, often lifetime, employment that they offer their participants. This characteristic was identified quite early as a distinctive

---

[11]Note that whereas the structural mechanism—informal, diffuse ties among participants—is one associated with the natural system perspective, the argument—reduction in transaction costs—is one stemming from the rational system perspective.

[12]Granovetter (1985) argues that Williamson greatly exaggerates the effectiveness of hierarchies in combating opportunism and underestimates the importance of informal, interpersonal controls in building trust and discouraging malfeasance. Thus, from this perspective, Ouchi's concept of clan is only a more highly developed instance of control processes operating in all organizations.

feature of Japanese organizations (see Abegglen, 1958; Dore, 1973); Ouchi proposes it as a defining characteristic of all clan organizations—which include not only Japanese organizations but many others including some of the most "modern" and progressive U.S. firms, such as Hewlett-Packard, IBM, and Eastman Kodak (see Ouchi, 1981).

The expectation of long-term employment creates the conditions for a different type of control system. The employee sees his or her career prospects as being directly linked to the company's success. Conflicting interests are reduced and goal congruence enhanced (Grandori, 1987). And the long-term commitment provides both incentive and opportunity for the organization to "invest" in its employees, not only increasing their specific work skills and knowledge by providing extensive training and varied job experience but also developing their general understanding of organizational needs and programs and increasing their commitment to its goals and values. In short, we have the conditions for the development of elaborated internal labor markets (see Chapter 8).

These discussions that emphasize internalized controls and more diffuse, long-term attachments have been supplemented by analyses that stress the importance of creating and sharing a common corporate culture. Cultural symbols and meanings are held to be an important alternative to structural forms (see Deal and Kennedy, 1982; Trice and Beyer, 1993). We discuss and evaluate these arguments in Chapter 11.

From Structure to Process?

Whereas well into the last decade of this century the language of organization has been dominated by a focus on structure—divisions, departments, positions, or jobs—a shift is now clearly under way in the direction of emphasizing process. This fundamental shift—involving not simply vocabulary, but mind-set—occurred first, and is better reflected, in the more popular management tracts than in the scholarly literature (with the exception of theorists like Weick—see Chapter 4). Management consultants and other close observers of current practice in innovative companies stress that as global competition increases and technological advances occur at an increasing rate, organizations must develop new models and metaphors:

> Organization action in the new model needs to be viewed in terms of clusters of activity sets whose membership, composition, ownership, and goals are constantly changing, and in which projects rather than positions are central. (Kanter, Stein, and Jick, 1992: 13)

> The rigidity and regimentation of the industrial company are being replaced by the flexibility and fluidity of the information company. (Naisbitt and Aburdene, 1985: 137)

> Competition is now a "war of movement" in which success depends on anticipation of market trends and quick response to changing customer needs. Successful competitors move quickly in and out of products, markets, and sometimes even entire businesses—a process more akin to an interactive video game than to chess. In such an environment, the essence of strategy is *not* the

structure of a company's products and markets, but the dynamics of its behavior. (Stalk, Evans, and Shulman, 1992: 62)

There is little doubt that in recent years organizations have developed new kinds of flexibilities, including more reliance on contingent workers, the development of more loosely coupled and flexible connections among work units and divisions—some of which operate outside the formal boundaries of the organization—and more reliance on project teams, whose goals, composition, and division of labor shift over time.

On the other hand, it may be too early to proclaim the death of structure. Research by Eisenhardt and colleagues over a period of several years observing organizations operating in highly competitive, fast-paced environments suggests that the most successful organizations are not those who replace their structures—problem-solving, decision-making, production—with shifting organic improvisation, but those who are able to combine conditions supporting openness and experimentation with structures providing direction and coherence (Eisenhardt and Tabrizi, 1995). Brown and Eisenhardt describe these arrangements as "semi-structures":

> By semi-structures we mean organizations in which some features are prescribed (e.g., roles, project priorities, time intervals between projects), but other aspects are not. For example, we observed that the firms with successful product portfolios remained betweeen mechanic and organic structures. Some roles, meetings, and priorities were prescribed, but the actual design process was unfettered. These firms also probed the future between rigidly planning and chaotically reacting, and executed transition processes that were between haphazard and rigid. (Brown and Eisenhardt, forthcoming)

Considering these issues theoretically, we are drawn to Gidden's formulation, which, we believe, successfully overcomes the false dichotomy between structure-process or structure-action. Giddens (1979) suggests the concept "structuration" to remind us that structure is both performance and product: that to exist it must be reproduced in action; and it is changed in and through actions that differ more or less from earlier action. As a social product, social structure always serves as a context for ongoing action—both as facilitator and as contraint—but all action contains the possibility of innovation and renewal—often only incremental, but sometimes revolutionary.

PROFESSIONAL ORGANIZATIONS

Certainly the most elaborate and intricate organizational arrangements yet devised for coping with high orders of complexity and uncertainty in production systems are to be found in the professional organization. We began the discussion of technology and structure by stating three general principles relating characteristics of technology and structure: greater technical complexity is associated with greater structural complexity, greater technical uncertainty is related to lower formalization and centralization, and greater interdependence is associated with more elaborate coordination structures. We now call attention to an important exception to the first principle. Technical complexity does not invariably give rise to greater complexity of structure; it may give rise instead to greater "complexity" of the performer. That is, one way to manage greater task complexity is not to divide the work and parcel it out among differentiated work groups or departments, but to confront the complexity with more highly qualified and flexible performers—with professionals (Scott, 1966; Stinchcombe, 1990). This response is particularly effective when (1) the work is also uncertain, a condition that militates against preplanning and subdivision, and (2) the work does not involve high levels of interdependence among workers. As an example of the latter, the teaching by faculty members in universities, the work of lawyers in law firms, and the work of physicians in clinics as customarily performed tend to involve relatively little interdependence. Whether complexity and uncertainty of work give rise to complex organizations or to complex performers is determined partly by the characteristics of the work itself but is also influenced by the political and social power of the performer group, as we have emphasized (see also, Larson, 1977; Abbott, 1988).

As complexity, uncertainty, and interdependence increase, professionals are more likely to work within organizational structures, becoming subject to a more explicit division of labor and more formalized coordination mechanisms. Thus, complex performers enter into and are supported and constrained by complex organizational structures.

Professionals perform the core tasks of the organization under two general types of arrangements. The first, which I have labeled the *autonomous* professional organization, exists to the extent that "organizational officials delegate to the group of professional employees considerable responsibility for defining and implementing the goals, for setting performance standards, and for seeing to it that standards are maintained" (Scott, 1965b: 66). The professional performers organize themselves—as a "staff" in hospitals, as an "academic council" in universities—to assume these responsibilities. Usually, a fairly well demarcated boundary is established between those tasks for which the professional group assumes responsibility and those over which managers have jurisdiction. Examples of types of professional organizations likely to conform to the autonomous pattern include general hospitals, therapeutic psychiatric hospitals, medical clinics, elite colleges and universities, and scientific institutes oriented to basic research (see Clark, 1963; Smigel, 1964; Freidson, 1975; Galanter and Palay, 1991; Wallace, 1995).

Current developments in medical care in the United States suggest that the maintainence of such structural arrangements, as for any type of structure, is not simply a matter of rational design. Physicians have lost social power and legitimacy during recent decades for many reasons—fragmentation of specialities, increased competition as the numbers of physicians have grown, inability to curtail treatment costs, the rise of the consumer movement—and as a consequence, are increasingly subordinated to corporate structures and managers. Although mangers still do not directly control diagnostic and treatment decisions, the controls they do exercise in setting patient loads and cost ceilings is resulting in severe constraints on professional discretion (see Hafferty and McKinlay, 1993; Salmon, 1994).

I have labeled the second type the *heteronomous* professional organization because in this arrangement "professional employees are clearly subordinated to an administrative framework," and the amount of autonomy granted them is relatively small (Scott, 1965b: 67). Employees in these settings

are subject to administrative controls, and their discretion is clearly circumscribed. Unlike their autonomous counterparts, they are subject to routine
supervision. This type of professional organization is exemplified by many
public agencies—libraries, secondary schools, social welfare agencies—as well
as some private organizations, such as small religious colleges, engineering
companies, applied research firms, and public accounting firms (see Bidwell,
1965; Etzioni, 1969; Kornhauser, 1962; Montagna, 1968). Also, as Hall (1968)
has pointed out, the distinction between autonomous and heteronomous
structures can be applied to organizational departments as well as to entire
organizations. Thus, the research and development department of a manufacturing company is likely to be organized as a heteronomous structure.

The structure of heteronomous professional organizations is in many
respects similar to the arrangements already described in which organizations
handle somewhat complex and uncertain tasks by delegation. The work of the
professionals takes place within a structure of general rules and hierarchical
supervision, but individual performers are given considerable discretion over
task decisions, particularly those concerning means or techniques. Thus, individual teachers make choices regarding instructional techniques, and individual engineers make decisions concerning design or construction strategies.

The organization of autonomous professionals takes many forms, depending in particular on the degree of interdependence among the individual performers and performer groups. One of the primary strengths of the full-fledged
professional is that he or she is deemed capable of independent decision making and performance, and this includes coordinating work with others as
required by the situation. However, more explicit structural forms for coordinating work are required as professionals themselves become more highly specialized and are expected to coordinate not only their own work but the work
of a growing number of paraprofessional workers, and as interdependence
among work groups and departments increases. In many cases project teams
are used. In hospitals such teams may be built around a particular type of surgical procedure—open-heart surgery is a dramatic example—or around the
care of a particular group of patients—for example, children with cancer (see
Fox, 1959; Beckhard, 1972). And faculty members in universities conduct an
increasing amount of their research in project teams, each of which has a coor-
dinator or leader, often designated the principal investigator. These arrangements support collaborative effort across disciplinary or departmental lines.
Matrix designs are common in research organizations such as RAND (Smith,
1966) and are used in some hospital departments (Neuhauser, 1972). In many
of these organizations professional participants and administrators exercise
roughly equivalent power—an arrangement termed the "conjoint" professional
organization (see Scott, 1982b). Such arrangements attempt to combine the
advantages of both professional and bureaucratic forms.

Organizations that in one way or another utilize lateral relationships as
legitimate avenues of information and influence flows constitute the new generation of organizational forms. As we have attempted to illustrate, a number of
different lateral structural arrangements are in use—including project teams,
matrix structures, organic or clan systems, and professional organizations. All
move us away from unitary hierarchical arrangements, "beyond bureaucracy,"
or "from bureaucracy to adhocracy." Futurists and social commentators such as

Bell (1973), Toffler (1970; 1980), Naisbitt (1982), Davis (1987), and Galbraith and Lawler (1993) agree that these new organizational forms offer new opportunities and challenges to participants but at the same time impose greater pressures and requirements on them.

SUMMARY

Most efforts to explain the structural complexity within the technical core of an organization focus on the characteristics of the work being performed—on the technology. While a great many specific measures of technology have been proposed, it appears that the most important dimensions to represent in attempting to relate technology to structure are complexity, uncertainty, and interdependence. In general, we expect technical complexity to be associated with structural complexity or performer complexity (professionalization); technical uncertainty with lower formalization and decentralization of decision making; and interdependence with higher levels of coordination. Complexity, uncertainty, and interdependence are alike in at least one respect: each increases the amount of information that must be processed during the course of a task performance. Thus, as complexity, uncertainty, and interdependence increase, structural modifications need to be made that will either (1) reduce the need for information processing—for example, by lowering the level of interdependence or by lowering performance standards—or (2) increase the capacity of the information-processing system, by increasing the channel and node capacity of the hierarchy or by legitimating lateral connections among participants.

Empirical studies of the relation between technology and structure show mixed and often conflicting results. Among the factors contributing to this confusion are methodological problems, such as lack of consensus on measures or on measurement strategies, and theoretical problems, including misspecifications of the level of analysis at which the measures apply and lack of clarity about the causal connections between technology and structure. Recent analysts have emphasized the extent to which social structures—both societal and organizational—shape technology as well as the strategic connection beween technology and structure.

Although significant attention has been devoted to the relation between technology and formal structures such as rules, schedules, hierarchies, and coordinating roles, much recent work emphasizes the importance of informal structures, particularly when high levels of uncertainty are confronted. Organic systems or clan structures are viewed as simultaneously fostering reliability and flexibility and as increasing worker motivation and commitment.

Complexity of performers in the form of professionals can substitute for complexity of organizational structure, but rather than being alternative modes of rationalizing work, professionals are increasingly incorporated into organizations. Professional organizations combine elements from both formal and informal approaches, stressing internalization of controls and worker autonomy and at the same time employing more formalized control systems, such as project teams and matrix structures.

CHAPTER

10

Sources of Structural Complexity: The Peripheral Components

> The device by which an organism maintains itself stationary at a fairly high level of orderliness . . . really consists in continually sucking orderliness from its environment.
>
> *Erwin Schrödinger (1945)*

The division between the technical core and the peripheral components of an organization is admittedly somewhat arbitrary. It is intended to emphasize that organizations are composed of different units that respond to different forces. The previous chapter emphasized those portions of the organization—labeled the technical core—that are most directly shaped by the technologies utilized to perform its key tasks. We argued that the characteristics of the work performed are related to the characteristics of the structures created to contain the work. (Whether work characteristics produce structural characteristics or the reverse was discussed but not fully resolved.) Attention was limited to the characteristics of those structures that contain, control, or are otherwise close to the organization's central work flow.

In this chapter the focus is widened to include broader structural features of organizations. In general—we will note important exceptions—these are less directly tied to the technical core. They are peripheral in this sense and only in this sense: peripheral is not synonymous with marginal. The peripheral structures, for present purposes, encompass many aspects of the managerial and the institutional levels as defined by Parsons (see Chapter 3). We examine, first, the structural changes at these levels that accompany the organization's attempt to buffer its technical core and construct bridges to other social units. These changes accompany the organization's efforts to adapt to and modify its task environment. We next examine structural features associated with the size of the organization. As we will learn, the meaning of size is far from clear, but its importance as a determinant of structural characteristics is well established. Third, we describe three of the major changes that have occurred in business organizations during this century: first, the rise of the multidivisional firm, second, recent efforts to divest and downsize, and third, the development of network forms. In the final section, relations between the core and peripheral structures are discussed.

A brief methodological note: Examinations of the structural features of organizations, their determinants, and their interrelationships require the collection of data from a large, diverse sample of organizations. In these studies, the organizations are themselves the units of analysis. Ideally, what is required is a large sample of organizations randomly drawn from a population of independent organizations. To date, only one such study has been conducted (Kalleberg et al., 1996).[1] A series of early comparative studies was conducted by Blau and his associates and by the Aston group in Great Britain. More recently, studies have focused on comparing organizations operating in different societies or cultures (for example, Hofstede, 1984; Lincoln and Kalleberg, 1990). The use of survey studies, collecting original data from respondents in numerous organizations, is, however, much less common today than during the 1960s and 1970s. Increasingly, researchers rely on secondary data sources, such as those available from public agencies, trade associations, and investment companies.

SIZE AND STRUCTURE

Defining and Measuring Size

What is size? Some analysts treat it as a dimension of organizational structure like formalization or centralization—one of several structural properties of an organization (see, for example, Hall and Tittle, 1966). Others treat size more as a contextual variable that measures the demand for an organization's services or products and thereby provides opportunities for and imposes constraints on its structure (see, for example, Blau and Schoenherr, 1971; Pugh et al., 1969). Like technology, size appears to be a variable that is on the interface between the organization and its environment: both variables are, on the one hand, internal features interacting with other structural properties and, on the other hand, features strongly shaped by external conditions. And, because it is externally driven like technology, size is more likely to be treated as an independent variable that shapes and determines other structural variables. If technology assesses what type of work is performed by the organization, size measures how

---

[1]Kalleberg and associates developed an ingenious design to generate their sample. Because there is no existing census of organizations, they began by drawing a random sample of adults in the United States who were asked who their principal employer was, and then, as a second step, data were gathered from organizational informants regarding selected features of each of these employment settings, in particular, human resources practices. This procedure resulted in a random sample of employment organizations (establishments), weighted by size of organization (see Kalleberg et al., 1996, ch. 2).

much of that work the organization carries on—the scale on which the work is conducted.[2]

As Kimberly (1976) notes, several different indicators of organizational size have been employed by researchers, each measuring a somewhat different aspect of size. Some, like square footage of floor space in a factory or number of beds in a hospital, measure the physical capacity of an organization to perform work. Others, such as the sales volume or number of clients served during a given period, focus less on potential capacity and more on current scale of performance. And indicators such as net assets provide a measure of discretionary resources available to the organization.

Most studies of the relation between organizational size and structure have used the number of participants (usually employees) as an indicator of size. The advantages of this measure are that it tends to reflect both the capacity of the organization for performing work as well as the current scale of actual performance. Also, most of the dependent variables of interest—formalization, centralization, bureaucratization—are measures of methods for controlling and coordinating people, so that numbers of individuals are of more relevance than other possible indicators of size. However, using the number of participants as an indicator of size poses some problems. As previously discussed, it is often difficult to determine how to set the boundary between participants and nonparticipants or "partial" participants (short-term, part-time, and contract workers). Also, comparisons of numbers of participants across different types of organizations can be misleading, since some types of organizations are much more labor-intensive than others.

We turn now to consider the major predicted and empirical relations between size and structure.

Size, Bureaucracy, and Differentiation

Early interest in the effects of size focused on its relation to the degree of bureaucratization, defined as the relative size of the administrative component of an organization. A number of critics of large organizations, such as Parkinson (1957), insisted that they invariably develop a disproportionate number of administrative employees. Several decades of empirical research found contradictory findings, in part because the administrative category is made up of a number of different kinds of employees—managerial, professional and technical, and clerical—each of which tends to relate differently to changes in size (Rushing 1966).

A second basic reason for the absence of consistent associations between organizational size and administrative size is that size produces two different effects that have opposing consequences for the size of the administrative component. On the one hand, organizational size is positively associated with structural differentiation. Studies of a wide variety of

---

[2]Size can also be given an institutional interpretation. Size, particularly relative size, is closely associated with visibility and respectability. Larger organizations are more likely to be the targets of institutional actors (for example, state regulatory bodies) and are also more likely to provide the models imitated by other organizations.

organizations show reasonably consistent and positive associations between size of organization and various measures of structural differentiation, including number of occupational categories, number of hierarchical levels, and spatial dispersion of the organization—for example, the number of branch offices (see Blau and Schoenherr, 1971; Meyer, 1979; and Pugh et al., 1969). Larger organizations tend to be structurally more complex. (For a recent overview of the empirical research, see Donaldson, 1996.) On the other hand, size is positively associated with the presence of more activities of the same general type. Size involves an increase in the scale of operations, which means not necessarily more kinds of operations (that is, differentiation) but more operations of the same kind.

As noted, these two effects of size have opposing consequences for the size of the administrative component. In a remarkable series of propositions, Blau (1970) attempts to summarize and resolve these conflicts, as follows. Large size is associated with structural differentiation, and differentiation, in turn, creates pressures to increase the size of the administrative component. This occurs because differentiation increases the heterogeneity of work among the various subunits and individuals, creating problems of coordination and integration. The administrative component expands to assume these responsibilities. On the other hand, organizational size is associated with increases in the average size of units, within which the work performed is relatively homogeneous. The larger the number of persons engaged in similar work, the smaller the number of administrative personnel needed to supervise them. In sum, larger organizational size, by increasing structural differentiation—that is, by increasing the number of different types of organizational subunits—increases the size of the administrative component, which coordinates the work of these units; at the same time, larger organizational size, by increasing the volume of homogenous work within organizational subunits, reduces the size of the administrative component, which supervises work within these units.

In their analysis of the fifty-three state employment security agencies, Blau and Schoenherr conclude that:

> Large size, by promoting differentiation, has the indirect effect of enlarging the managerial component, but the savings in managerial manpower resulting from a large scale of operations outweigh these indirect effects, so that the overall effect of large size is a reduction in the managerial component. (1971: 91)

Such a conclusion may well hold for the type of organization studied, but is not necessarily applicable to other types of organizations. Whether the administrative component is, on balance, affected positively or negatively by size would seem to depend primarily on what type of differentiation is involved. For example, differentiation that merely creates new units of the same type (segmentation) would be expected to have a less positive effect on the administrative component than functional differentiation, which creates new types of units. And how much functional differentiation occurs would be determined primarily by the type of work the organization is performing—that is, by its technology—and by the type of environment—both technical and institutional—in which it is operating.

Size, Formalization, and Centralization

We have defined *formalization* as the extent to which roles and relationships are specified independently of the personal characteristics of the occupants of positions. Most empirical studies of formalization emphasize the extent to which rules such as formal job definitions and procedural specifications govern activities within the organizations. A Weberian model of structure would lead us to expect that the larger the size of the organization, the more formalized its structure would be, and indeed, most empirical studies support this prediction. Hall, Haas, and Johnson (1967) report only moderate but fairly consistent positive correlations between size and six indicators of formalization, including "concreteness" of positional descriptions and formalization of the authority structure. Blau and Schoenherr's (1971) study of state employment security agencies reports a positive association between organizational size and the extent of written personnel regulations in the state's civil service system.[3] And the Aston group (Pugh et al., 1969), in their study of forty-six work organizations, reports a strong positive correlation between size and scales measuring formalization and standardization of procedures for selection and advancement.

The conventional view of the bureaucratic model of organizational structure would also lead to the prediction that large organizations will have more highly *centralized* systems of decision making (see Hage, 1965). However, the studies by Blau and Schoenherr and the Aston group do not support this expectation. Rather, both research groups found that organization size was negatively correlated with several indicators of centralization. (For example, Blau and Schoenherr used measures of the decentralization of influence to division heads and the delegation of responsibility to local office managers, and Pugh and his colleagues developed scales for determining the level in the hierarchy where executive action could be taken subject only to pro forma review.) Consistent with the positive association between size and formalization, centralization was negatively associated with most of the measures of formalization. This pattern of results was also reported by Child (1972), who applied the scales developed by the Aston group to a national sample of eighty-two business organizations in Britain. And Mansfield (1973) reanalyzes these data to show that although the relationships are not very strong, the negative association between measures of centralization and standardization or formalization persist when the effects of size are controlled. These results were also replicated in the recent study based on a nationally representative sample of organizations. Kalleberg and associates (1996) report positive relations between size, differentiation, and formalization, but negative relations between size and bureaucratization and size and centralization.

Blau and Schoenherr explain this unexpected pattern of results by suggesting that centralization and formalization may be viewed as alternative

---

[3]Noting that this relation might better be tested at the state rather than the agency level, Blau and Schoenherr (1971: 58–59) also report a strong positive correlation between the total number of all state employees, as an indicator of the size of the state government, and the extent of formalized personnel regulations in the state's civil service system.

control mechanisms: more formalized arrangements permit more decentralized decision making. They argue that:

> Formalized standards that restrict the scope of discretion make decentralized decisions less precarious for effective management and coordination, which diminishes the reluctance of executives to delegate responsibilities way down the line to local managers far removed in space as well as in social distance from top management at the headquarters. (1971: 121)

Mansfield, perhaps with the aid of hindsight, scolds his colleagues for expecting a positive relation between formalization and centralization in the first place, arguing that Weber has been misread:

> It can be argued, paradoxically, that the only method by which the directorate in large organizations can retain overall control of the organization's functioning is by decentralizing much of the decision making within the framework of bureaucratic rules. It is reasonable to interpret Weber as implying a moderate negative relationship between the bureaucratic variables and the centralization of decision making. This proposition, however, runs counter to everyday notions of bureaucracy. (1973: 478)

Mansfield's interpretation of Weber's view is supported by our conclusion (in Chapter 2) that Weber's model of rational-legal authority provides a structure of roles that supports the exercise of relatively greater independence and discretion, within specified constraints, than are found in earlier administrative arrangements. The extent of bureaucratization and centralization is also affected by the organization's technology and the wider social and cultural environment in which it operates[4] (see Hofstede, 1984).

Worker Competence, Formalization, and Centralization

In Chapter 9, we discussed the relation between the qualifications of workers and the structural features of the technical core. We noted that employing personnel with greater expertise, such as craft workers or professionals, also affected the characteristics of more remote administrative structures. Hall's study (1968) of varying occupational groups in twenty-seven organizations provides more complete information on the relation between worker competence and organizational structure. Hall assessed six structural features of these organizations: hierarchy of authority or centralization (defined as the extent to which the locus of decision making is prestructured); the division of labor (extent of functional specialization); presence of rules; extent of procedural specification; impersonality (degree of formalization); and technical competence (extent to which universalistic standards such as qualifications and education are used in selection and promotion). Reasonably strong, positive correlations were found among all

---

[4]A limitation of all of the studies just reviewed is that they were based on cross-sectional data. Studies (e.g., Freeman and Hannan, 1975; Meyer, 1979) employing longitudinal data show that the effects of organizational growth on structure are quite different from the effects of reduction in size or downsizing.

of these dimensions with the exception of technical competence. This variable was negatively correlated with all of the other structural attributes! The more highly qualified workers were found in those organizations that exhibited fewer "bureaucratic" attributes, as Weber defined the term: that is, those organizations with lower levels of task specialization, formalization, and standardization.

These results suggest that whether work is simplified and divided among less highly skilled participants or assigned to workers with higher skills who are granted more autonomy of action has implications not only for the immediate structure of the technical core but also for the general structural characteristics of organizations.

An apparent exception to our expectation that less extensive task subdivision and higher worker qualifications will be associated with greater decentralization of decision making is reported by Lincoln, Hanada, and McBride (1986). In their study of United States and Japanese manufacturing plants exhibiting similar ranges of technological complexity (as described in Chapter 9), these researchers found, as expected, Japanese plants to exhibit lower levels of job specialization: Japanese workers were more likely to be generalists, performing a range of job functions. But contrary to expectations, centralization of formal decision making in Japanese firms was found to be higher than in U.S. firms. Further study, however, revealed that de facto or informal decision making was more decentralized in Japanese than in U.S. plants. Lincoln and colleagues conclude that "the Japanese organizations delegate less formal authority than U.S. plants, but in practice they permit greater involvement in decisions by employees lower in the hierarchy" (p. 353). The de facto structuring of decision making in Japan is consistent with the general expectation that more highly skilled workers are more likely to be found in more decentralized organizational structure.

It appears that one of the great watersheds in the design of organizations is the decision concerning whether tasks are divided and hierarchically coordinated or left in larger clusters and delegated to more highly skilled workers or to self-organizing teams. Both represent instances of rational organization, but each is associated with a different structural form.

ENVIRONMENT AND STRUCTURE

Buffering, Bridging, and Structural Complexity

Chapter 8 described some of the specific mechanisms used by organizations to buffer their technical cores from disturbing environmental influences and to build bridges to essential exchange partners and allies. Such organizational responses to the technical environment are not a simple matter of utilizing selected techniques or mechanisms. Associated with their use are fundamental changes in the structure of the organization.

Mapping environmental complexity. What changes may be expected when organizations employ one or more of the several buffering techniques we have described: coding, stockpiling, leveling, or forecasting? Such activities will require the development or recruitment of personnel with new and different skills from those employed in the technical core itself. These participants require additional space and special equipment. In short, as the need for such buffering techniques increases, we expect to observe the development and growth of new specialized staff roles and departments at either end of the technical core—in other words, buffering units that interface with the input and output environments of the organization.

Consider also the use of the simpler bridging techniques, such as bargaining, contracting, and co-optation. As the task environment becomes more differentiated and active with the development of segmented labor markets, rapid technical and scientific developments, multiple types of buyers and sellers, subcontractors to oversee, and competitors to watch and attempt to outmaneuver, the organization responds by adding new types of occupational groups and specialists to deal with each of these environmental sectors. Organizations hire personnel officers and labor relations experts to deal with more complex labor markets; scientists, engineers, research administrators, and patent lawyers to participate in and keep pace with scientific developments; purchasing agents and marketing specialists to relate to the input and output environments; contract specialists and auditors to negotiate with and police contractors, market analysts, and sometimes even industrial spies, to look after competitors. Most of these additions to the organizational structure involve the creation of new staff or support departments attached to the managerial level of the organization.

Structural elaboration may also occur at the institutional level as the size of boards of directors is increased to allow for the addition of new types of board members, who will connect the organization with sectors or units of importance in their environment. Or it may occur as advisory structures are created to broaden the linkage of the organization to its task environment. Thus, the increasing complexity of the task enviroment is adapted to by increased structural complexity—differentiation—on the part of the organization.

This adaptation occurs not only in response to technical environments but also as a reaction to institutional environments. Organizations enhance their chances for survival and resource acquisition by adhering closely to the institutionally defined patterns, by incorporating them in their own structures, by becoming structurally isomorphic with them (Meyer and Rowan, 1977; DiMaggio and Powell, 1983).

Where—in what part of the organizational structure—the external complexity is mapped can vary. Public schools in more complex funding and regulatory enviroments become more administratively complex, but much of this reaction occurs at the level of the district office rather than in the structure of the individual school (see Meyer, Scott, and Strang, 1987; Scott and Meyer, 1988). Similarly, individual hospitals respond differently to the constraints of their regulatory environments than do hospitals belonging to multihospital systems (Fennell and Alexander, 1987).

As might be expected, organizations are very sensitive to the nuances of the normative climate in their institutional environments: they take account of the amount of support for and conflict over particular reforms and proposed changes. Rowan (1982) has examined changes in the staffing of a sample of California school districts between 1930 and 1970. He reports that the hiring of district specialists in the areas of health, psychology, and curricular matters was highly responsive to the level of support and attention to these domains that was reflected in broader educational movements and national and state political acts. The higher the consensus—or in Rowan's words, the more "balanced" the institutional environment—the more widely diffused were officials identified with these movements; the more unbalanced the domain, the more irregular were the patterns traced by the districts in hiring and retaining appropriate specialists.

Organizational structures are also shaped by broader, societal-level changes. Baron, Dobbin, and Jennings (1986) have examined how the federal government's intervention in labor relations during World War II fostered bureaucratization of employment by (1) providing "models of employment practices that often extended to entire industries" and (2) providing "strong incentives to establish or extend personnel departments that could analyze and justify labor needs and institute bureaucratic mechanisms to reduce turnover" (p. 373). The latter development, in particular, stimulated the spread of rationalized employment systems as professional personnel administrators continued to expand and assume control over additional functions long after the original occasion for mobilization had passed.

Whether differentiation of organizational structure occurs as a rational system response designed to support the buffering and bridging activities of organizations attempting to regulate critical resource flows, or as a natural system response designed to coalign the structure with its institutional environment or to serve the interests of one or another constituency, the more general processes at work here are best depicted by the open system perspective. This approach insists that an organization, as an open system, adapts to more complex environments by itself becoming more complex: it is a type of system "whose persistence and elaboration to higher levels depend upon a successful mapping of some of the environmental variety and constraints into its own organization on at least a semipermanent basis" (Buckley, 1967: 63).

It is important to stress that the organization's "mapping," or incorporating, of portions of the "environmental variety" into its own structure introduces new and different, and sometimes alien and hostile, elements into its own system. For example, the hiring of a labor relations specialist by a personnel department presumably introduces a person with expertise in, and experience with, labor unions. Such persons are hired because of their ability to understand, communicate, and negotiate with unions and their representatives. They may be more similar in background and training and attitudes to their counterparts in the unions than to their colleagues in the personnel department (see Goldner, 1970). Similarly, as stock investors have become more organized and influential, corporations have responded by creating investor relations offices, staffed by personnel with close relations to investment analysts and brokers (see Useem, 1996). The same is true for hundreds of other types of occupational groups whose services are required by the organization but whose value depends on their marginality to the system and on their connections with similar groups in other organizations. These associations among persons in similar occupational groups—accountants, computer specialists, labor lawyers, public relations experts, advertising managers—across different organizations are among the most important bridges linking contemporary organizations. The flow of individuals back and forth across these bridges sometimes creates problems for the larger society (see Chapter 12) but always creates challenges—both threats and opportunities— for the host organization, which must attempt to control and integrate their activities.

Conflict, integration, and loose coupling. The study by Lawrence and Lorsch (1967) of plastics manufacturing companies, which has been referred to several times in this volume, illustrates many of the major points we wish to emphasize.[5] As will be recalled (see Chapter 4), their research showed that (1) the task environments confronting the plastics manufacturing companies were highly varied, differing for research, production, and marketing functions; (2) this environmental variety was mapped into the structure of the organization, resulting in the creation of separate departments to confront these diverse environments; (3) however, the more differentiated the departments within each organization, the more likely were disagreements and conflicts to develop and the more difficult the problems of coordinating and integrating their work; and (4) therefore, the more differentiated the departments and the more successful the organization in integrating their efforts, the more effective the organization.[6]

The primary integrating mechanism used in the plastics companies studied was that of liaison roles: special roles were created to help integrate the work of the three basic departments and resolve conflicts among them. Lawrence and Lorsch (1967: 54–83) report that the more successful integrators possessed attributes and orientations intermediate to those of the units they bridged, exercised influence based on technical competence, were oriented to the performance of the system as a whole, and enjoyed high influence throughout the organization. Walton and his colleagues (Walton, Dutton, and Fitch, 1966; Walton and Dutton, 1969) have also studied interdepartmental conflict in organizations and strategies for resolving it. They note that such conflicts often develop out of mutual task dependence, task-related asymmetries, conflicting performance criteria, dependence on common resources, communication obstacles, and ambiguity of goals as well as organizational differentiation. Such conflicts can be met with varying responses, from structural redesign to third-party consultation and attempts at reeducation of participants (see Blake, Shephard, and Mouton, 1964; Likert and Likert, 1976; Rahim, 1986).

---

[5]The results of interest in the present context are based on a study by Lawrence and Lorsch of only six plastics companies. Since the organizations themselves were the units of analysis, this is a very small sample on which to base any firm conclusions. We prefer to treat their research as a stimulating exploratory study valuable chiefly for the ideas generated, not for the hypotheses confirmed.

[6]To arrive at a composite rating of effectiveness, Lawrence and Lorsch (1967: 40) combined objective measures of change in profits, sales volume, and number of new products with subjective ratings by managers of how well their companies were performing. We examine these and other measures of effectiveness in Chapter 13.

Note however, that it is a rational system perspective that underlies most of these concerns with the integration of structurally differentiated departments. It is assumed that the organization is primarily a production system and that when conflicts occur among subunits, they must be resolved. Conflict interferes with goal attainment, and its resolution is associated with greater effectiveness of performance. A quite different view of conflict and conflict resolution processes is associated with the natural system perspective, which presumes that interdepartmental conflict is not primarily a product of error, ambiguity, and ignorance but results from fundamental divergences in group interests, and that the struggles are concerned not simply with means but with the goals to be served by the organization. These matters will be discussed in Chapter 11.

The assumption that integration is required because differentiation is present is also consistent with the rational system assumption that the various parts of the organization should be tightly coupled, each harnessed in the service of unified objectives. By contrast, the open system model of organizations envisages a system of more or less loosely coupled elements, each capable of autonomous action (see Chapter 4). Weick (1976) and Orton and Weick (1990) note a number of ways in which loose coupling of these structural elements may be highly adaptive for the organization, particularly when it confronts a diverse, segmented environment. To the extent that department units are free to vary independently, they may provide a more sensitive mechanism for detecting environmental variation. Loose coupling also encourages opportunistic adaptation to local circumstances, and it allows simultaneous adaptation to conflicting demands. Should problems develop with one department, it can be more easily sealed off or severed from the rest of the system. Moreover, adjustment by individual departments to environmental perturbation allows the rest of the system to function with greater stability. Finally, allowing local units to adapt to local conditions without requiring changes in the larger system reduces coordination costs for the system as a whole.

Obviously some organizations effect tighter coupling among their department than others, and within a given organization we will see variation in the degree of coupling. In general, we would expect to observe tighter coupling between units within a technical core linked by serial or reciprocal interdependence than between core units and those operating on the boundaries. Nevertheless, two words of caution merit emphasis. First, the extent of the interdependence, coordination, or coupling between any two organizational subunits is a matter for empirical determination, not assumption. Second, whether looser or tigher coordination or coupling is adaptive for the organization depends on the specific circumstances confronted.

MACRO STRUCTURAL ADAPTATIONS

From Unitary to Multidivisional Structures

Before concluding our discussion of the structural consequences of buffering and bridging strategies, we need to consider the effects of large changes in the scale of the organization such as those associated with merger or divestitures. Based on results reported in the previous section, we would expect increased size to be associated with increased structural differentiation. But we can be more specific than this. Chandler and Williamson argue that when firms grow beyond a certain point, not just further differentiation but a structural reorganization is likely to take place.

The canonical account of the history of American business enterprise is provided by Chandler (1977), who identifies four phases of growth for industrial enterprise. The first period, just after the Civil War, was a time of rapid expansion and resource accumulation. This was the age of the larger-than-life entrepreneurs who expanded their organizations, most often through vertical integration. In the second phase, a new generation of professional managers, differentiated from the owners or the founding entrepreneurs, developed "methods for managing rationally the larger agglomerations of men, money, and materials" (1962: 388). Attention was concentrated on the reduction of unit costs and the coordination of diverse functional activities. The first two phases are best represented in the United States by the development of the railroads. Chandler points out that:

> The safe, reliable movement of goods and passengers, as well as the continuing maintenance and repair of locomotives, rolling stock, and track, roadbed, stations, roundhouses, and other equipment, required the creation of a sizable administrative organization. It meant the employment of a set of managers to supervise these functional activities over an extensive geographical area; and the appointment of an administrative command of middle and top executives to monitor, evaluate, and coordinate the work of the managers, responsible for the day-to-day operations. It meant, too, the formulation of brand new types of internal administrative procedures and accounting and statistical controls. Hence, the operational requirements of the railroads demanded the creation of the first administrative hierarchies in American business. (1977: 87)

Railroads were, hence, associated with the development of the *unitary* form, the now conventional structure composed of a management unit and several functionally organized departments. This structure was the great achievement of the nineteenth century when, as scale and complexity increased, individual entrepreneurial forms gave way to those which relied on technical expertise, specialization, and salaried managers. Of course, the expansion of the railroads had a significant impact on the development of all types of businesses, the availability of reliable and inexpensive transportation enabling them to vastly expand their input and output markets.

Phase three, lasting from the turn of the century to the First World War, witnessed the filling out of existing product lines as firms continued to expand. And, in order to ensure the continuing and efficient use of their resources, firms began to diversify, moving into related fields that would capitalize on their technical skills and marketing contacts.

In the fourth phase, following World War I, a few major companies that had diversified and were attempting to manage several related product lines found it necessary to reorganize in order to ensure the efficient employment of their resources. Thus, a new business form first appeared in this country during the early 1920s having been independently developed at about the same time by a number of major companies, including du Pont, General Motors, Standard Oil of New Jersey, and Sears, Roebuck (Chandler, 1962).

The new form that emerged was the *multidivisional* or *M-form* structure, which consisted of a general corporate office and several product-based or regional divisions, each of which contains functionally differentiated departments. These departmental units are subdivided into work units (establishments) that are distributed on a geographical or product basis (see Figure 10–1).

Firms can undertake horizontal mergers in order to increase the size of their markets, or vertical mergers in order to incorporate more phases of the production or distribution process and still fit comfortably into a unitary structure. However, as the firm begins to diversify its products and attempts to enter markets related or unrelated to those presently served—as it expands its *scope* rather than only its scale—it will benefit from moving into a multidivisional form (Chandler, 1990). This is the sense in which Chandler insists that a firm's structure should be suited to its strategy. He argues that:

> Unless structure follows strategy, inefficiency results. This certainly appears to be the lesson to be learned from the experience of our four companies [du Pont, General Motors, Standard Oil, and Sears, Roebuck]. Volume expansion, geographical dispersion, vertical integration, product diversification, and continued growth by any of these basic strategies laid an increasingly heavy load of entrepreneurial decision making on the senior executives. If they failed to reform the lines of authority and communication and to develop information necessary for administration, the executives throughout the organization were drawn deeper and deeper into operational activities and often were working at cross purposes to and in conflict with one another. (1962: 314–15)

Chandler argues that, given a diversified strategy, the new multidivisional form is superior to the unitary form because it frees some officials from the tyranny of daily operational decisions and allows them to concentrate on positioning the organization in its environment and determining the proper mix of product lines and markets and thereby the allocation of resources among divisions.[7] The M-form is also particularly well suited to supporting a multinational strategy, in which numerous divisions offering the same general product lines are situated to take advantage of multiple national markets (see Vaupel and Curhan, 1969; Tsurumi, 1977).

Chandler's general predictions receive empirical support from research by Rumelt (1986), who examined changes in the strategy and structure of a random sample of 100 of the 500 largest U.S. corporations in 1949, 1959, and 1969. Rumelt devised a set of categories to characterize company strategy, ranging from single business through dominate business to related businesses to unrelated businesses. During the period of study the number of

---

[7]Based on a detailed analysis of the workings during the period 1924 to 1958 of General Motors, one of Chandler's exemplar companies, Freeland (1996) argues that there is little evidence that the M-form produced a clear distinction between strategic and tactical planning. Rather, the lines between corporate and divisional decision making were both blurred and contested, and the resulting participative decentralization was better suited to generating consent among middle managers than to simplifying information processing.

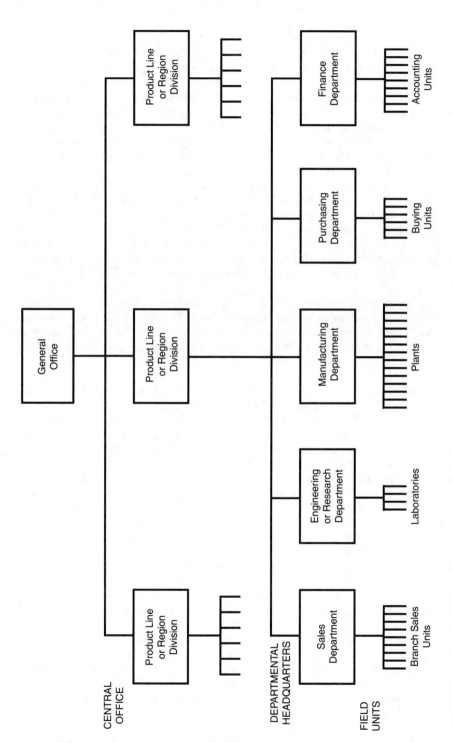

FIGURE 10–1 The Multidivisional Structure. *Source:* Chandler (1962), p. 10.

CENTRAL
OFFICE

DEPARTMENTAL
HEADQUARTERS

FIELD
UNITS

General
Office

Product Line
or Region
Division

Product Line
or Region
Division

Product Line
or Region
Division

Sales
Department

Engineering
or Research
Department

Manufacturing
Department

Purchasing
Department

Finance
Department

Branch Sales
Units

Laboratories

Plants

Buying
Units

Accounting
Units

diversified corporations more than doubled, the percent of firms carrying on related or unrelated business strategies growing from 30 to 65 percent. With respect to structural change, during the same period, the percent of firms employing a product-division (M-form) structure increased from 20 to 76 percent. Diversification strategies were strong predictors of structural form, particularly during the 1949–1959 period. Contrary to ecological assumptions, "the vast preponderance of the change in the distribution of organizational forms among the 500 was caused by firms changing their form of organization rather than exiting firms being replaced by firms with different structures" (Rumelt, 1986: 65).

In a later, more extensive study, Fligstein assembled a data file containing information on 216 large U.S. firms spanning the period 1919 to 1979. His sample contains the 100 largest nonfinancial corporations in existence during each of three periods: 1919–1939, 1939–1959, and 1959–1979. His analysis reveals that whereas less than 2 percent of these corporations had adopted the multidivisional structure before 1929, over 84 percent had done so by 1979. Again, Chandler's central predictions were confirmed:

> Industries where product-related strategies dominated, like machine, chemical and transportation industries, adopted the MDF [M-form] in large numbers relatively early; while industries that were more likely to be vertically integrated, like mining, metalmaking, lumber and paper, and petroleum, adopted the MDF later and to a lesser extent. (Fligstein, 1985: 386)

While the spread of M-form structures generally parallels the development of diversified strategies, institutional forces also appear to be at work. Thus, Rumelt (1986) reports that, after 1959, business firms regardless of strategy moved to adopt the M-form structure because "divisionalization has been accepted as the norm" (p. 77). Similarly, Fligstein (1985) observed a mimetic effect beginning in 1939 "whereby firms in industries with other firms who have already changed to the MDF are more likely to do so" independent of firm strategy. Rumelt concludes: "The data gave strong support to Chandler's proposition that 'structure follows strategy,' but forced the addition of the proposition that 'structure also follows fashion'" (1986: 149).

Williamson (1975: 132–54) points out that Chandler's historical account of the problems accompanying diversification and the structural solution to these problems is consistent with predictions generated by the transaction cost framework. He argues that the principal problem created by diversification is that it creates increasing complexity and uncertainty—this time *within* the organization rather than in the environment—up to a level that exceeds the information-processing and decision-making capacity of the managers. The structural development that occurs is one that simplifies the informational and decision situations by clearly differentiating between the long-range policy decisions to be handled by the general office and the short-run operational decisions to be determined at the divisional level.

In Chandler's terms, the general office is responsible for strategic decisions, the divisions, for operational decisions. *Strategic* decisions determine what business one is in. Chandler stresses major choices, but strategic decisions are better viewed as a continuum: from modest changes in product/service mix—for example, a hardware store must decide whether to include garden supplies or lumber; a hospital, whether to provide long-term care or emergency services—to major changes involving a move into a different industry—for example, an automobile company decides whether to manufacture boats; a hotel corporation, whether to diversify into managing movie theaters. In all cases, strategic decisions involve a choice of domain(s). They determine the nature of the organization's technical core—or how many different kinds of technical cores will be included within the framework of the organization. In traditional organizations, strategic and operational decisions are made by the same individuals; in M-form structures, they become differentiated.

The individual divisions (or "strategic business units" or "profit centers") within the M-form structure present the interesting case of operating on the interface "between market and hierarchy." On the one hand, they are subject to the authority system of the parent organization; on the other hand, they are expected to effectively compete against other providers in a given market. Williamson (1985) emphasizes the advantages of utilizing both market and hierarchical controls as central office executives, who make decisions about whether or not to continue, enlarge, or divest a given division, can make use of competitive market information—how well the unit is doing in competition with other providers—as well as information obtained through audits and other hierarchical control systems. By contrast, Eccles and White (1988) point out that the transaction costs associated with exchanges between divisions are often higher than those between independent units. This is because managers of divisions must ascertain for any given transaction whether firmwide criteria or division-specific criteria are to be employed. In some situations, managers will be rewarded for minimizing costs by purchasing outside the company; in other situations, they will be expected to be a "team-player" and purchase inputs supplied by other divisions within their own company, even though these are more costly than those available outside the company. The presence of a hierarchy can distort the operation of market processes.

The more that the central office of an M-form company is divorced from the specifics of the work performed by the individual divisions, the more it must rely on financial indicators of performance. The internalization of capital markets is yet another way in which the modern corporation attempts to reduce, for its constituent units, the uncertainty of the environment. Thus, in important respects, the emergence of the conglomerate firm represents a further extension of M-form logic. *Conglomerate* firms are those containing divisions engaged in unrelated businesses: the diversification spans industry groups, not simply product lines. But, as Williamson notes, its development builds logically on the M-form structure:

> Once the merits of the M-form structure for managing separate, albeit related, lines of business (e.g., a series of automobile or a series of chemical divisions) were recognized and digested, its extension to manage less closely related activities was natural. (1985: 288)

In such firms, divisions are treated primarily as profit centers: the prime criteria for their continuation and support is their current or future profitability, and the general office functions as an (internal) capital market, by which cash flows are directed to high-yield uses.

In comparing the American experience with that of comparably developed societies, Chandler (1990) reconsidered his earlier views that the factors driving the evolution of firm structure throughout the late nineteenth and twentieth centuries were largely those of strategic responses to economic competion. He recognized for the first time the important role played by the nation state and its regulatory policies.[8] He concludes that the passage of the Sherman Antitrust Act had "a profound impact on the evolution of modern industrial enterprises in the U.S." (p. 72). By defining as illegal many attempts to acquire firms within the same industry, it forced companies seeking to expand to diversify.

> This legislation, amplified by the Supreme Court's decision in the 1890s and enforced by the executive branch in the early years of the next century, remained uniquely American; no other nation adopted a comparable law before World War II. That legislation and the values it reflected probably marked the most important noneconomic cultural difference between the United States and Germany, Britain, and indeed the rest of the world insofar as it affected the long-term evolution of the modern industrial enterprise. (Chandler, 1990: 72–73)

The movement of U.S. corporations from same-industry to related and then into unrelated business ventures was further encouraged by the passage in 1950 of the Celler-Kefauver Act. This act together with subsequent court decisions further curtailed corporate efforts to increase market share within the same industry and, in effect, forced corporate expansion to occur in product-unrelated areas—that is, through conglomerate strategies. As Fligstein (1985; 1990) points out, the shift to conglomerate forms was the adaptive response of expansionist-oriented firms to governmental restrictions imposed on earlier, successful product-related strategies.

Divesting and downsizing.   A hundred-year-long chronicle of increasing scale and scope by business enterprise now shows clear signs of coming to an end. Although the number of mergers and acquisitions continues unabated, beginning during the 1980s, and continuing up to the present, we have witnessed an unexpected turnaround as a number of large corporations have been purchased only to be broken up and their component units sold off, other companies have voluntarily elected to sell off divisions or engaged in other types of downsizing maneuvers.

Evidence began to appear in the 1980s that conglomerate forms were not performing as well as their more unitary counterparts. Rumelt's (1986) empirical assessment of Chandler's strategy-stucture thesis was among the

---

[8]Dobbin (1994b) has compared the role played by the nation-state from the earliest stages of the development of railroads in France, England, and the United States and shows how the state pursued very different policies in each case, exerting enormous influence, and yet its role was largely overlooked by participants and observers who ascribed developments in each case to the working out of "natural" economic laws.

first to report that the highly diversified, unrelated business corporations performed less well than those firms that, in Peters and Waterman's phrase (1982), "stuck to their own knitting." Changes in regulatory policies and innovative practices in financing (the development of "junk bonds") supported the emergence during this period of a "takeover market" such that investors bought out corporations thought to be undervalued in order to "bust them up" and sell off the separate components (Coffee, Lowenstein, and Rose-Ackerman, 1988). During a ten-year period from 1980 to 1990, roughly one-quarter of the Fortune 500 firms—the 500 largest industrial firms by sales—disappeared through being taken over and broken up. Moreover, during this period:

> the level of total diversification . . . among firms in this population dropped from 1.0 in 1980, to .90 in 1985, and to .67 in 1990—a one-third drop over a decade. Even more dramatic is the decline in the level of unrelated diversification, which declined from .63 in 1980 to .59 in 1985, and to .35 in 1990—a 44 percent drop. . . . Thus, there was a marked migration toward more focused organizational forms over the course of the decade. (Davis, Diekmann, and Tinsley, 1994: 562)

Davis and colleagues argue that the image of the corporation that gained currency in the 1960s as being merely a "financial portfolio," rather than a productive organic entity, helped to legitimate the takeover and bust-up tactics of corporate raiders during this period of rapid change. How we think about our organizations affects how we treat them: cognitive models have behavioral consequences.

In addition to deintegration and divestiture, many companies have also engaged in *downsizing*—reducing the numbers of their full-time employees, either by contracting out jobs formerly handled within their boundaries, reorganizing work in ways that enabled fewer employees to perform the tasks formerly requiring larger numbers, or hiring temporary or part-time employees. During the period 1982–1990, a time when total employment increased only very slightly, temporary employment increased more than 300 percent (see Callaghan and Hartmann, 1991). Many of the largest and best-known organizations in the United States, including General Motors, IBM, and IT&T, were substantially smaller in 1995 than they were in 1985. As noted in Chapter 1, the average size of business organizations in the United States is smaller today than three decades ago.

From independent to interdependent, network forms. The widely held assumption that bigger is better, that all the advantages are on the side of bringing more and more activities and resources under the control of a single hierarchy, has begun to give way to the recognition that important strengths are associated with alliances or loose confederations of organizational forms. We reviewed in Chapter 8 the diverse types of bridging mechanisms available to organizations wishing to develop cooperative or coordinative arrangements. Some of these mechanisms—for example, mergers—involve changes in the ownership and in the formal boundaries of organizations, but many—for example, contracting and co-optation, and entering into alliances and associations—do not. The latter, looser types of connections have gained in popularity in recent years, and have begun to receive more research attention.

The development of an explicit set of alliances among organizations is only the most visible sign of the many and varied types of connections that link organizations in modern society. Granovetter has suggested that the Coase-Williamson question regarding why it is that firms develop to mediate transactions among individual buyers and sellers might well be replicated one level higher, taking firms rather than individuals as the object of inquiry and:

> asking why it is that in every known capitalist economy, firms do not conduct business as isolated units, but rather form cooperative relations with other firms, with legal and social boundaries of variable clarity around such relations. In no case do we observe an economy made up of atomized firms doing business at arms length with other firms across a market boundary. (Granovetter, 1994: 453)

Transaction costs at both levels are reduced by the presence of more diffuse relations among economic agents and the construction of various types of governance structures.

Analysts have observed that varying combinations of small, independent, but interdependent firms have been able to successfully compete in many types of markets with larger corporations. Developments in information technologies as well as the increasingly specialized nature of consumer markets have helped to create conditions favoring more flexible production regimes. Long-linked technologies are ill suited to provide customized goods or to respond to rapidly changing consumer tastes. Examples of successful small-scale firms range from family-based textile manufacturers in Japan (Dore, 1983) to firms producing engineering components and motorcycles in Italy (Brusco, 1982) to software firms in Silicon Valley (Saxenian, 1994). Piore and Sabel (1984) point out that such complexes of flexible firms and workshops are embedded in and supported by some sort of broader institutional base, often developing out of kinship ties or some kind of municipal or regional political structure. Such arrangements encourage cooperative behavior and allow longer term relational contracting to coexist along with competitive practices. Such alliances or network forms provide yet another viable form of organizing "between markets and hierarchies," (see Powell and Smith-Doerr, 1994).

Rather than assuming that networks represent only a hybrid or halfway form combining elements from more conventional models, however, Powell argues that they constitute a distinct form that is "neither market nor hierarchy." Powell (1990) summarizes the key features that distinguish *network* forms from either market arrangement or hierarchical (conventional authority) structures (see Table 10–1). As the listing of features suggests, networks entail more enduring and diffuse connections than markets but more reciprocal and egalitarian arrangements than hierarchies.

In an insightful field study contrasting "arms-length" market-based with more "embedded" network relations among firms in a sample of New York-based apparel firms, Uzzi (1996: 678–9) notes that the latter alliances among firms were based on trust and supported the transfer among firms of more fine-grained information—including "strategic and tacit know-how that boosts a firm's transactional efficacy and responsiveness to the environ-

TABLE 10–1   Three Models of Economic Organization

	Models		
Key Factors	*Market*	*Hierarchy*	*Network*
Normative basis	Contract— Property rights	Employment relationship	Complementary strengths
Means of communication	Prices	Routines	Relational
Mode of conflict resolution	Haggling— Resort to courts	Administrative fiat—supervision	Norms of reciprocity
Degree of flexibility	High	Low	Medium
Amount of commitment among parties	Low	Medium to high	Medium to high
Tone or climate	Precision and/or suspicion	Formal, bureaucratic	Open-ended, mutual benefits
Actor preference or choices	Independent	Dependent	Interdependent

Source: Adapted from Powell (1990), Table 1, p. 300.

ment"—and the creation of joint problem-solving arrangements "that enable actors to coordinate functions and work out problems "on the fly.'" Organizations involved in such embedded relations were more likely to survive than organizations relying primarily on market-based relations.

Network forms come in a wide variety of guises. A useful typology has been proposed by Harrison (1994) who differentiates between four types:

1. *Networks in craft-type industries*
   In these forms, work is organized around specific projects and involves the temporary cooperation of varying combinations of skilled workers. Examples include construction projects and artistic productions such as publishing or film projects (see Stinchcombe, 1959; Hirsch, 1972; Becker, 1982).
2. *Small-firm-led industrial districts*
   These network forms include the northern Italian industrial districts, including textile companies such as Benetton (Belussi, 1989) and the semiconductor firms in Silicon Valley (Saxenian, 1994).
3. *Geographically clustered big-firm-led production systems*
   These forms include the well-known Asian examples of *keiretsu* ("societies of business," see Abegglen and Stalk, 1985) as well as connections that have developed between central assembly firms and multitudes of small suppliers, for example, Volvo of Sweden (see Håkansson, 1989) or U.S. automobile companies (see Helper, 1991).
4. *Strategic alliances*
   Alliances of this type are increasingly found among firms of all sorts, but especially large firms attempting to secure competitive advantage in a global environment (see Kanter, 1989; Dunning, 1993).

Whereas some analysts such as Piore and Sabel (1984) and Perrow (1992) have proclaimed that small-firm alliances are the wave of the future and likely to outcompete and outmanuever larger and presumably less flexible forms, others such as Kanter (1989) and Harrison (1994) argue that large-scale firms have both the power and the resources to prevail in the long run. Harrison describes these ascendant systems as composed of one lead firm orchestrating the contributions of a "core-ring" set of related, subordinate firms, whether suppliers or merchandizers.

Roughly parallel developments have occurred in the public sector. During the past two decades, the range and variety of organizational forms and relations in the public sector have greatly increased. Many traditional government agencies—the archetype bureaucracy—have undergone restructuring and downsizing. Public agencies have been joined by hybrid forms, such as government corporations and government-sponsored enterprises, which attempt to build in various types of market controls. Moreover, more and more governmental agencies contract out particular tasks to private companies, both for-profit and nonprofit forms, in the belief that competition among such providers will improve the efficiency of governmental services (see Brooks, Liebman, and Schelling, 1984; Osborne and Gaebler, 1992).

In short, the earlier dichotomy between markets and hierarchies, as well as the related distinction between private and public, is not very helpful in describing existing organizational forms. And alliances of smaller and larger organizations, including mixtures of public agencies and private firms, are under some circumstances a viable alternative to large-scale corporations and public bureaucracies.

CONNECTING THE CORE AND PERIPHERAL STRUCTURES

Tight and Loose Coupling

Much of what passes for organizational structure consists of varying types of mechanisms for controlling the behavior of participants. Hierarchy, formalization, centralization, modes of coordination—all are devices to help ensure that the organizational managers can shape and influence the behavior of other participants charged with carrying on the production activities of the organization. Indeed, a primary justification for the existence of managers is the impact of their ideas and decisions and designs and plans on the behavior of other participants. Many accounts of organizational structure—or, alternatively, many types of organizational structure—emphasize the tight coupling of managers and performers' behavior. Managers decide, performers implement; managers command, performers obey; managers coordinate, performers carry out specialized tasks. Organizations or segments of organizations of this type certainly exist, particularly in situations in which work activities have been divided and routinized. Rational system analysts emphasize this view of organizational structure.

By contrast, early natural system analysts, with their interest in behavioral rather than normative structures, looked more carefully at the operation of these supposedly tightly coupled systems and failed to observe the presence of the taut command systems described by the textbooks in administrative science. Rather, their studies revealed that workers were reluctant to accept close supervision and likely to develop protective work-group mechanisms or understandings with their supervisors that allowed them some leeway and breathing space in defining and meeting requirements. The control systems were less tightly coupled in operation than in theory.

All formal structural devices, however, connote tight coupling of activities. Decentralization, delegation, professionalization, even the creation of the staff-line distinction—these are mechanisms for ensuring *some* coordination and control but also for legitimating and supporting the exercise of discretion. They build in flexibility and encourage initiative in the technical core of the organization and so reduce its dependence on and its responsiveness to hierarchical directives. Moreover, as Parsons (1960) pointed out when he distinguished among the technical, managerial, and institutional levels of organization, a qualitative break in the line-authority relation exists at the points where the three levels connect (see Chapter 3). Parsons argues that only within a level can a superior directly supervise the work of subordinates and assume responsibility for it, since differences in the nature of the work performed at each level are too great to permit strict control of the lower by the higher levels. Thus, board members functioning at the institutional level would not be expected to exercise direct, routine line authority over managers but to grant them considerable freedom in exercising their managerial responsibilities; managers, in turn, would not ordinarily exercise direct line authority over the technical functions of workers. In short, the functions performed at each level are seen to be somewhat distinct and not readily linked to one another. Thus, even the relatively conventional views of rational and natural system theorists recognize the presence of considerable loose coupling as an important structural and operational feature of most organizational systems.

Meyer and Rowan (1977) take a more extreme view of the possibilities of loose coupling in organizations. They suggest that organizations responding to institutional pressures will be inclined to selectively decouple their formal structures from the activities carried on in their technical core. The rationalized myths that provide meaning and legitimacy to the formal structures often do not provide clear and consistent guidelines for technical activities. The result is that the organization conforms closely to the ritually defined meanings and categories supplied by the environment but does not attempt seriously to implement them at the operational level. For example, Meyer and Rowan argue that educational organizations adhere closely to the ritual categories of education: "There seem to be centralized and enforced agreements about exactly what teachers, students, and topics of instruction constitute a particular school" (1978: 84). But at the operational level, there is little organizational coordination or control over instructional activities. These activities are delegated to teachers, and there is little or no attempt to evaluate and control their performance—either hierarchically or collegially. The solution of decoupling is particularly likely to occur when environmental rules impose conflicting requirements on organizations. Thus, schools may be simultaneously required to give special treatment to educationally handicapped children but at the same time to "mainstream" them, not seg-regate them from their fellow students. Organizations can adapt to conflict-ing demands by creating appropriate programs and offices at the administrative level that can create the required reports, but then decou-pling these offices from the operational level. (See also, Brunsson, 1989).

Decoupling is only one possible response by organizations to institution-al pressures. In some cases, organizations abide by both the letter and spirit of the law, in others they conform in more ceremonial ways; in still others, they may engage in defiant or overt nonconformist acts, as noted in Chapter 8. We need to observe organizational responses, not presume what they will be.

Still, the decoupling arguments of institutional theorists are important because they suggest that the formal structures of organizations have mean-ing and importance regardless of whether they affect the behavior of per-formers in the technical core. Formal structures can symbolize meaning and order. And, as Meyer and Rowan have emphasized, organizations that devise structures that conform closely to institutional requirements "maximize their legitimacy and increase their resources and survival capabilities" (1977: 352).

Managing Up and Down

It is certainly obvious that over the course of this century, organizational forms have become more and more top-heavy. As Bendix (1956) and others have pointed out, the proportion of administrators to production workers has grown continuously throughout this period (see Chapter 1). A number of factors con-tributing to this result have been described in previous portions of this volume: the augmentation of the hierarchy to increase the information-processing capacity of the organization as the tasks performed become more complex and uncertain; the elaboration of managerial and staff positions in response to the need to buffer core departments and build connections with other units in the task environment; the incorporation of representatives from external units at the managerial or institutional level in order to relate more adequately to these interests, either as exchange partners or symbolically.[9] All of these develop-ments imply the growth of peripheral roles and structures in relation to the technical core. However, only some of them orient the managerial level in and down toward the activities of the technical core. Many direct their attention up and out to the larger social and political environment. Managers of today's orga-nizations must devote as much time and energy to "managing" their environ-ments as to managing their production system.

Marxist theorists point out the close, interdependent connections between control arrangements within organizations and political systems in the wider society. Economic enterprises always rest on a political base. Whereas the prevailing rhetoric in capitalist societies stresses that enterprise is free and independent from state interference, Burawoy (1985) argues that political regimes within firms and in the wider polity are always linked. Capitalist systems differ from state socialism not in the absence of connec-tions but in the directness and visibility of those connections that do exist.

---

[9]In addition to these changes in the "numerator," important changes in the "denomina-tor" have also transpired. The number of production workers has continuously declined in many industries because of technological developments substituting capital equipment for labor.

When institutional forces are intense, managers have their work cut out for them. Although, as we have already noted, Meyer and Rowan (1977: 345) suggest that "it takes only a little entrepreneurial energy to assemble" the relevant components—roles, rules, rituals—which are "littered around the societal landscape," to assemble these components is one thing and to fully mobilize them is another (see Chapter 7). Tilly (1978: 69) has proposed that the level of mobilization is a function of the product of two factors: the value of the resources acquired and the probability of "delivering" them when needed. He further suggests that the variables affecting delivery include "the extent of competing claims on the resources involved, the nature of the action to which the resources are to be committed, and how organized the mobilizing group is" (p. 71). It is apparent that many of the resources managers acquire in order to adapt to institutional requirements incorporate elements—whether professional roles or legal rules—that are subject to many competing claims, and are not likely to be readily assimilated or mobilized in the service of organizational objectives.

These conditions help to account for Meyer's assertion that as the larger societal structures become more "rationalized," individual organizations attempting to operate within them become less "rational."

> Modern rationality has a vastly expanded jurisdiction, and many fewer aspects of society are organized in other ways. All these rationalized perspectives enter into the life of typical formal organizations, which contain and must legitimate the rationalistic perspecitves of citizen-members, representatives of various occupational perspectives, carriers of bodies of authoritative knowledge, and organized representatives of a variety of external perspectives that penetrate the organizations and have some sovereign standing. It is exactly this rationalization of so many aspects of society that limits the rationality of formal organizational structure: modern formalized organizations are built up around the acknowledgment of the external legitimation, definition, and control of their internal processes. (1983: 269)

In this fashion, modern organizations "look less like rational organizations than holding companies incorporating various institutionally defined packages" (p. 262). The packages can be acquired and exhibited, but are not readily mobilized in the service of specific goals.[10] The increasingly rationalized institutional structures to be found in modern societies constitute a normative exoskeleton that both supports and constrains its constituent organizations.

Managing Sideways

While some units within organizations will remain loosely coupled under some conditions, and some groups will be difficult to mobilize in the service of specific organizational goals, numerous organizations are attempting to

---

[10]Is the glass half full or half empty? Perrow (1991) argues that organizations increasingly assume control of more activities and functions which used to be performed by the wider society. Meyer and I stress the reverse process: "Although organizations may have absorbed society, as Perrow claims, society has no less absorbed organizations." (Scott and Meyer, 1994: 4)

radically redesign their organizational arrangements to shift from a primarily vertical to a more horizontal model and from a model based on functional differentiation to one based more on the identification of key processes. Such organizations have been driven to rethink how they conduct work and do business by the pressures of increasing global competition.

Such organizations are typically built around flexible and self-managing teams who combine personnel from across functional areas. These organizations emphasize lateral connections among their workers, making use of liaison roles, task forces, and, particularly, project teams (see Chapter 9), but extend these connections to incorporate participants in peripheral departments, such as research and development, marketing and sales, and service personnel (see Galbraith and Lawler, 1993). In some cases, these teams cross formal organizational boundaries to incorporate representatives of supplier firms on the input side and of major customers on the output side.

Some organizations go well beyond simple restructuring, with its emphasis on reducing the number or size of departments or reconfiguring organizational units, to attempt to *reengineer* the work (Hammer and Champy, 1993). "Whereas restructuring is concerned with moving, shrinking, or eliminating units ('boxes') reengineering has to do with changing the way work is carried out" (Keidel, 1994: 15). Reengineering attempts to identify a core set of business processes, each with an identifiable beginning and ending point—such as developing a new product, or designing, producing, and distributing a given product or service, and attempts to incorporate within the team (or task force) all those whose work relates to that process. All tasks are identified and analyzed in an attempt to eliminate unnecessary work and, more important, reduce misunderstandings, delays, and errors occurring as tasks are passed between workers and departments. Most of the new process techniques for improving performance involve the creation of increased interdependence among workers, as pooled and sequential arrangments are converted into reciprocal relations, reducing slack and increasing information-processing requirements. The new electronic modes of information transmission and processing are essential to these systems.

Conventional organizations are designed to support vertical decision making, and we should not underestimate how difficult it is to radically restructure organizations to emphasize the management of changing processes rather than stable routines, and shifting responsibilities rather than fixed duties and jurisdictions. To shift from more vertical to more horizontal arrangements requires changes in performance measures, incentives, job descriptions, reporting relations, information systems, and career incentives, to name only the most relevant factors. Workers require multiple skills and must relate to one another flexibly as the situation requires; there needs to be an atmosphere of security and trust if task-oriented problems are to be the focus of decision making. Managers need to be generalists rather than trained as narrow specialists; and there must be incentives for learning and for exposing errors. However, what is needed and what is available are not always the same. It does not appear that such conditions are present in most employment settings at the present time. (We discuss these issues further in Chapter 13.)

SUMMARY

This chapter has examined some of the factors affecting the larger structure of the organization: the extent of its bureaucratization, centralization, formalization, and differentiation. Although the characteristics of the organization's core technology influence its peripheral features, the latter also respond to other forces, in particular, the organization's size and its task and institutional environments. A number of empirical studies show that larger organizations are more highly differentiated and more formalized than smaller organizations. However, these studies also reveal that larger organizations tend to be less bureaucratized and centralized in their decision-making structures. It is suggested that reductions in bureaucratization occur because of administrative economies resulting from the managing of more of the same type of work, although these savings are counteracted and may be offset by increased administrative costs associated with greater differentiation—the costs of managing different kinds of work. Decentralization is both necessary, because of information overload at the top caused by increased size and differentiation, and possible, because formalization promotes consistency of decision making.

Technology also affects the characteristics of peripheral structures; in particular, the division and routinization of work are associated with higher levels of differentiation, formalization, and bureaucratization, but the delegation of work to more highly skilled personnel is associated with the opposite structural effects. Whether the effects of size or of technology dominate in determining structural features of organizations cannot be determined from existing studies: longitudinal studies designed to test explicit causal models based on better samples of organizations are required.

The peripheral structures of organizations are also affected by the buffering and bridging strategies employed by organizations in relating to their task environment. Associated with all of these specific techniques are structural modifications—additions of new roles and departments and representatives of external interests. Open systems map critical features of their environments into their own structures as a major adaptive strategy. Structural reorganization is also associated with organizational growth. A prime example of such reorganization is the shift during the first half of this century in many major corporations from a unitary to a multidivisional structure. Recent developments suggest, however, that organizational growth has important limits. Conglomerate organizations are now out of fashion, and current trends favor smaller and leaner forms supplemented by alliances or networking arrangements.

The extent to which managerial units control and coordinate work in the technical core varies by type of organization but has probably been overstated. Considerable looseness of coupling has not only been observed in most organizations in the behavior of supervisors and workers but is legitimated by many types of formal arrangements. Recent analysts have called attention to some of the adaptive features of loosely coupled systems—whether the coupling involves boundary units relating to specific environmental segments, connections among boundary units, or connections between boundary and core units. The symbolic importance of structure has also been noted. Changes in structure at the institutional or managerial level are symbolically important whether or not they are associated with changes in procedures or behaviors within the technical core.

Managers must expend as much time and energy in relating to environmental demands as in directing the internal affairs of the organization. And, increasingly, managers must learn how to create systems that will allow participants to interact more effectively and efficiencly across functional boundaries. Managers need to manage laterally across work units as well as up and down, between levels of the hierarchy and between the organization and its environment.

CHAPTER 11

Goals, Power, and Control

Group decision-making extends deeply into the business enterprise. Effective participation is not closely related to rank in the formal hierarchy of the organization. This takes an effort of mind to grasp. Everyone is influenced by the stereotyped organization chart of the business enterprise. . . . Power is assumed to pass down from the pinnacle. Those at the top give orders; those below relay them on or respond.

   This happens, but only in very simple organizations—the peacetime drill of the National Guard or a troop of Boy Scouts moving out on Saturday maneuvers. Elsewhere the decision will require information. Some power will then pass on to the person or persons who have this information. If this knowledge is highly particular to themselves then their power becomes very great.

John Kenneth Galbraith (1967)

The subjects of goals, power, and control have recurred frequently enough throughout the preceding chapters that their importance must now be established. Although we have touched on these topics in many places—and have skirted them in others—we have not yet confronted them directly. We begin by discussing the concept of organizational goals, indicating some of the reasons it has proved so obstreperous. We will find that it is helpful to change the questions: What are goals? and Do organizations have goals? to the question: Who sets the goals in organizations? It is here that the questions of goals and power come together. It is also instructive to ask whether there are organizations that lack goals, and, if so, what effect this has on their structure and functioning.

   We also examine control systems in organizations. What are the sources of power, and how does power become authority? Some organizations employ internal rather than external control systems, relying heavily on shared cultural beliefs. These types of controls are also examined.

GOAL SETTING IN ORGANIZATIONS

Problems in Conceptualizing Organizational Goals

The varying uses of goals.   The concept of organizational goals is among the most slippery and treacherous of all those employed by organizational analysts. Many factors contribute to the confusion in this area. A brief description of some of these factors may not resolve all of the questions but at least will clarify some of them. One source of difficulty is that statements of organizational goals are used in a number of ways by those who discuss organizations. Thus, rational system analysts emphasize that goals provide criteria for generating and selecting among alternative courses of action (Simon, 1964; 1976). These analysts stress the *cognitive* functions of goals: goals provide directions for and constraints on decision making and action. Natural system analysts, such as Barnard (1938) and Clark and Wilson (1961), emphasize that goals serve as a source of identification and motivation for participants. And Selznick (1949) notes that goals may be employed as ideological weapons with which to overcome opposition and garner resources from the environment. These analysts all emphasize the *cathectic* (motivational) properties of goals: goals serve as bases of attachment for both organizational participants and external publics. Note that a goal statement that is satisfactory for analysts concerned with the cathectic properties of goals may be unsatisfactory for analysts interested in their cognitive contributions. Vague and general goals may suffice for motivational purposes—indeed, they may be especially suited to this function—but be unsatisfactory for cognitive guidance. For example, colleges may be able to attract students or funds with the claim that they are "preparing tomorrow's leaders," but such goal statements will provide little help in designing the curriculum or hiring the faculty.

Institutional analysts stress the *symbolic* functions of goals. Whereas the cognitive and cathectic properties of goals emphasize their effects on organizational participants, the symbolic aspect of goals points to their significance for organizational audiences: publics, clients, taxpayers, regulators. The goals an organization espouses, the goals it appears to be serving, the goals it embodies and is perceived to represent—these symbolic goals have important effects on the organization's ability to acquire legitimacy, allies, resources, and personnel.

Still other analysts challenge the conventional view of behavior in which goals precede actions. Weick has insisted on the relevance of dissonance theory as formulated by Festinger (1957) and others to decision making in organizations. Weick argues that:

> Rationality seems better understood as a postdecision rather than a predecision occurrence. Rationality makes sense of what has been, not what will be. It is a process of justification in which past deeds are made to appear sensible to the actor himself and to those other persons to whom he feels accountable. (Weick, 1969: 38)

In short, behavior sometimes precedes goals, and goals are then invented to serve as a *justification* for the actions taken (Staw, 1980).

Goal statements also serve as a basis for *evaluating* the behavior of participants or of entire organizations (see Scott, 1977). They provide criteria for identifying and appraising selected aspects of organizational functioning. We will examine goals used as evaluation criteria applied to organizational performance in Chapter 13. The criteria used to evaluate performance may or may not be the same as those employed to direct it.

More generally, the various types of goal statements—goals used to guide behavior, to motivate it, to symbolize it, to justify it, or to evaluate it—may not coincide closely not only because they serve different functions but also because they emanate from different sources. Symbolic goals are likely to be promulgated at the institutional level of the organization, which seeks to legitimate organizational purposes by stressing their larger social functions. The top managers of a company are likely to stress cathectic goals as a way of developing commitment among their participants. From Barnard (1938) to Selznick (1957) to Peters and Waterman (1982) the "functions of the executive" are to articulate and inculcate commitment to corporate values. Middle-level managers, in concert with their technical staff, are expected to translate general aspirations into specific products and services, and so may be expected to emphasize the cognitive aspects of goals. Evaluators at all levels employ goals as a source of criteria for evaluating participants as they carry on the work of the organization, and participants at all levels employ goal statements to help them justify their past actions when asked to give an accounting.

Goals and strategies. Many organizational analysts prefer the concept of strategy to that of goal. Chandler (1962: 13) defines *strategy* as "the determination of the basic long-range goals and objectives of an enterprise, and the adoption of courses of action and the allocation of resources necessary for carrying out these goals." This widely accepted definition identifies several distinctive features of strategy. First, the primary focus is on external concerns: the linkage of the organization to its environment. Second, two types of goals are differentiated: (1) selection of domain ("What businesses shall we be in?") and (2) selection of competitive stance ("How shall we compete in each business?") (see Chaffee, 1985). Porter (1980) has identified a number of "generic" competitive strategies among which firms may choose:

- *overall cost leadership*—producing in high volume and holding costs low relative to competitors
- *differentiation*—creating a product that is perceived industrywide as being unique, such as a design or brand image
- *focus*—emphasizing a particular buyer group, segment of the product line, or geographic market

Third, as emphasized by natural system analysts, treatments of strategy—like all discussions of goals—often confuse intentions with actions, official with operational goals. To avoid this difficulty, Mintzberg (1987) suggests that distinctions be made between "intended" strategy (plans), "emergent" strategy (unplanned patterns of behavior), and "realized" strategy (actual behavior whether planned or unplanned).

Finally, many discussions of strategy presume that such decisions are made exclusively by executives high up in the organization. Indeed, as described in Chapter 10, Chandler stresses the value of segregating operational and strategic decisions and reserving the latter for top officials. By contrast, analysts such as Burgelman and Sayles point out that innovations (new products, new processes) in companies typically develop deep down in the research and operational units of organizations, receive support from middle managers, and, after the fact, become recognized and legitimated by top executives. They insist that:

> Their [middle managers'] initiatives, when successful, change the direction(s) and the strategic plans of the corporation. . . . Thus, relatively autonomous, unplanned initiatives from the operational and middle levels of the organization help to shape corporate strategy. (Burgelman and Sayles, 1986: 144)

Eccles and Crane (1988) make similar arguments with respect to investment banking, referring to a "grass-roots" process of strategy formulation as individual investment bankers—"those closest to the markets"—make decisions that, within broad management constraints, determine business strategy (p. 49).

In sum, strategies can be viewed as a subset of organizational goals, but a very important subset.

Individual and organizational goals.   Simon (1964; 1976) has most forcefully urged the distinction between individual goals that govern a participant's decision to join or remain in an organization, and organizational goals that are expected to govern the decisions of individuals as participants (see Chapters 2 and 7). Simon proposes that for the sake of clarity such individual goals be labeled *motives*. This rational system conception of a relatively clear distinction between individual motives and organizational goals is challenged by the natural system perspective, which insists that individuals are not completely contained within their roles but may be expected to impose their own preferences on the choices that confront them as participants. Simon (1964) does not deny the operation of such processes but insists that the distinction retains value. He notes, for example, that many requirements organizations impose on their participants are orthogonal to their motives—for example, it is often a matter of indifference to individuals who have accepted employment as production workers or salespersons what particular products they manufacture or sell. More generally, one would need to deny the existence of formal roles and their impact on individual behavior to assert that organizational goals are indistinguishable from individual motives. The separation of these concepts is also aided by Clark and Wilson's (1961) discussion of incentive systems (see Chapter 7). Their typology reminds us that in only a limited set of organizations—which they label *purposive*—do individual motives and organizational goals coincide. In most organizations the goals toward which participants direct their behavior are different from the goals that motivate them to participate in the organization.

One implication of these considerations is that we will not want to survey individual participants and then aggregate their individual objectives to arrive at a description of the organization's goals. In escaping from this reductionist fallacy, however, we must be careful not to go to the opposite extreme and posit the existence of some type of metaphysical corporate mind in which collective goals are formulated. To do so is inappropriately to reify the organization, granting it anthropomorphic properties it does not possess. We can avoid both reductionism and reification by reformulating the question. Instead of asking, Do organizations have goals? we will ask, Who sets organizational goals? and How are organizational goals set?

The Dominant Coalition

The most satisfactory answer to date to the question of who sets organizational goals is provided by Cyert and March (1963). They note that the classic economist's response to this question is to point to the goals of the entrepreneur and to equate the organization's goals with this person's objectives: the firm is seen as the shadow of one powerful actor. A second proposed solution is to presume that goals are consensually defined: all participants share equally in goal setting. Both of these models of goal setting are rejected as exceptional patterns found only rarely in nature. Cyert and March (1963: 27–32) propose the alternative conception of organizational goals being set by a negotiation process that occurs among members of the *dominant coalition.*

Organizations are viewed as composed of coalitions—groups of individuals pursuing certain interests. Each group attempts to impose its preferences (goals) on the larger system, but in the typical case, no single group will be able to determine completely what goals are to be pursued. Group members seek out as allies other groups whose interests are similar, and they negotiate with those groups whose interests are divergent but whose participation is necessary. One group will make a "side payment" to another to secure its cooperation, that is, will accede to that group's demands. For example, a management group, to secure its goal of continued growth, will agree to provide a given level of return on investment to its stockholders and will agree to pay a specified level of wages to its employees. Note, however, that what is a goal for one group is viewed as a side payment by another group, and vice versa. Each group whose interests must be taken into account helps to define the goals of the organization.

All such groups are, by definition, members of the dominant coalition. Each negotiated agreement provides guidance to the organization and places constraints on what may be regarded as an acceptable course of action. And the goals themselves are complex preference statements that summarize the multiple conditions any acceptable choice must satisfy. Simon amplifies this point.

> In the decision-making situations of real life, a course of action, to be acceptable, must satisfy a whole set of requirements, or constraints. Sometimes one of these requirements is singled out and referred to as the goal of the action. But the choice of one of the constraints, from many, is to a large extent arbitrary. For many purposes it is more meaningful to refer to the whole set of requirements as the (complex) goal of the action. (1964: 7)

The conception of the dominant coalition, though certainly not the last word on the subject of who sets organizational goals, avoids many problems that have plagued earlier explanations. We embrace this conception because:

- The problem of reification is avoided: individuals and groups have interests, and the process by which these preferences come to be imposed on the organization is specified.
- It is recognized that although individuals and groups are allowed to specify the goals of the organization, there is no presumption that they do so on an equal footing, nor is it assumed that they hold common objectives.
- It is recognized that although individuals and groups impose goals on the organization, in most cases no single individual or group is powerful enough to determine completely the organization's goals; hence, the organization's goals are distinct from those of any of its participants.
- Allowance is made for differences in interests among participants. Some, but not all, of these differences may be resolved by negotiation, so at any time, conflicting goals may be present.
- It is recognized that the size and composition of the dominant coalition may vary from one organization to another and within the same organization from time to time.

Coleman points out that another advantage to this general approach to goal setting in organizations is that it easily permits the analyst to shift the level of analysis from, for example, the individual groups and their interests to the organization as a unit comprising their interests. He asserts that:

> If we conceive of this system [the organization] as an actor at the next level (which I shall call a "corporate actor"), then its interests are given by the values of events at the lower level. In such an integrated system, the organization acts as if it were a single actor, and the directions in which it acts are given by the values of events generated at the lower level. . . .
>
> Thus the shift between levels in this theory is accomplished by conceiving of organizations as continuing systems of action, subject to internal analysis, and also as corporate actors, with interests derivable from that internal analysis. (Coleman, 1975: 86)

Coleman's explication helps to clarify the model, but in so doing calls attention to a major weakness.

With all of its advantages over previous conceptions, the coalition model of goal setting remains basically an aggregative model. Individual actors and even groups are allowed to have genuine interests, but organizations are not: they are viewed simply as collections of interests or, in Pfeffer and Salancik's words, "as settings in which groups and individuals with varying interests and preferences come together and engage in exchanges" (1978: 26). Such a conception may suffice for a coalitional or open system theorist but cannot be expected to be acceptable to a rational or natural system analyst. Wallace voices the latter's concerns in his critique of Coleman's view that "'interests' are fixed in individuals" and that "causal dominance" is located at the bottom rather than the top of the hierarchy.

> Coleman appears to deny or ignore the reverse possibility that the values of events at the higher level may "give" the interest of the individual actor; he also

appears to overlook the possibility that genuinely new interests may emerge from a new arrangement (especially a hierarchical arrangement) of individual actors. (Wallace, 1975: 127)

Although interests are certainly brought to the organization and imposed on it by some powerful participant groups, it seems equally likely that interests are also generated within the organization. Managers who stand to profit from economies realized by increased scale or technical innovation may be expected to coalesce around these "new" interests, and others whose power is closely associated with the condition and survival prospects of the larger enterprise may be expected to champion the interests of the organization as a whole.

The natural system theorists are correct in assuming that in most cases a set of participants will perceive that their interests are served by the survival and strengthening of the organization. Thus, we need to allow for the possibility that new interests and new coalitions will emerge over time in response to the opportunities and dangers created by the existence of the organization itself. The dominant coalition model can thereby be modified and interpreted so as to avoid the reductionist fallacy.

As noted, all organizations are not expected to look alike in the size and composition of their dominant coalitions. We need to examine what factors account for these differences.

Factors Affecting the Size and Composition of the Dominant Coalition

There are many potential sources of power in modern organizations. Those who own property, whether in the form of capital, land, machinery, or disposable goods, have "a socially defensible right to make a decision on how to use" these resources (Stinchcombe, 1983: 131). *Ownership* is an important basis of power in most economic systems. However:

> Usually the person or group that has a socially and legally defensible right to make a decision on the use of the resource does not do so directly. . . . Instead, the fund of resources is entrusted to an administrative apparatus, of which the property-owning group (the board of directors) is the formal head. . . . The property rights are . . . used to make the activities of an administrative apparatus controlling the resources legitimate. (Stinchcombe, 1983: 135–36)

Owners delegate control over resources to *managers*, who are expected to act on their behalf—to serve as their agents. But, as numerous analysts from Berle and Means (1932) to Galbraith (1967) to agency theorists such as Pratt and Zeckhauser (1985) have noted, the interests of owners—whether capitalists or widely dispersed middle-class stockholders—and managers may diverge; managers develop their own power base as owners become dependent on their expertise and detailed knowledge of the administration of the enterprise.[1]

---

[1] See Chapter 12 for a discussion of the same process in public bureaucracies: the power of administrative officials grows to challenge that of the political rulers.

Managerial power has recently been severely tested by the efforts of corporate raiders to buy undervalued corporations, unseat existing managers, and sell off profitable divisions. This effort to create a "market for corporate control" (Herman, 1981) can be viewed at least in part as an "attempt to reestablish the link between ownership and control that the managerial revolution allegedly severed" (Davis, 1990). But after a decade of struggle in the United States, during which time about 10 percent of the Fortune 500 companies were either acquired or went private as a result of hostile takeover bids, it appears as though managers have been largely successful in consolidating their position of control within corporations. They have been able to secure the adoption of a variety of mechanisms—for example, poison pills, shark repellents, and related measures—that reduce the desirability of and, hence, the likelihood of hostile takeover.

Organizations also depend on the energies and skills of workers or *labor* who carry out the work of transforming resources. Although as individuals they may exercise relatively little power, collectively workers are often able to acquire considerable power by engaging in or threatening strikes, slowdowns, or sabotage and expressing their demands through collective bargaining or other forms of negotiation. However, it is important to recognize that the power of organized labor in the United States has declined substantially, as exemplified by a drop in the number of union members from a high point of 36 percent of the labor force in 1945 to under 17 percent in 1990 (Cornfield, 1991). As of today, the United States "has, in proportionate numerical terms, the weakest labor movement in the industrial world" (Lipset, 1986: 421). Even though union power is at an all-time low, it is still the case that many workers, acting both individually and collectively, exercise considerable power within their organizations. In part, simply the threat of unionization helps them in their negotiations with employers, who provide benefits and procedural safeguards to employees in order to forestall unionization (see Sutton et al., 1994).

Finally, power accrues to those who occupy critical *boundary roles* in the organization. Individuals and work groups that connect with important resource suppliers, mediate the demands of critical regulatory agencies, or embody the concerns of institutional actors obtain power within the organizations they serve.

Hickson and colleagues (1971) have proposed a useful set of dimensions for explaining power in organizations based on the division of work. Like the resource dependence theorists, they build on Emerson's (1962) formulation of power-dependence relations, but rather than applying these ideas to interorganizational relations, they focus on explaining the distribution of power within organizations, employing a strategic contingency approach (see Chapter 10).

Hickson and associates offer three general propositions relating to the acquisition of intraorganizational power. First, building on the insights of Crozier, they propose that subunits that cope more effectively with uncertainty are more likely to acquire power. The source of uncertainty may vary from technical to environmental disturbances. Crozier (1964), in an intensive case study of the French tobacco manufacturing industry, observed that mechanics held considerable power—much more than their formal position in the organization would suggest—because they were capable of dealing with machine breakdowns, the major source of uncertainty in the highly mechanized plants. The importance of environmental uncertainty for internal power is further illustrated by Goldner's study of the industrial relations (IR) unit in a manufacturing organization. Goldner writes that:

> The major source of IR's power over specific plant-level issues was . . . the use of the union as an outside threat. Recognition that their nominal antagonists were the source of their internal power was even made explicit by one IR manager: "As I told one of the (other IR) guys who was damning the unions—Don't bite the hand that feeds you." (1970: 104–5)

What sources of uncertainty are confronted and their relative importance shifts over time. Whereas labor was a major source of uncertainty for many organizations earlier in this century, financial markets have become both more volatile and more important in recent years. Thus, those boundary roles within the firm that can deal with shareholders and their intermediaries—financial analysts—have become increasingly powerful. Most corporations now have an office for dealing with "investor relations," and these units are exploring new ways in which to "manage" this source of uncertainty (see Useem, 1996).

Note that the main contribution of this first proposition by Hickson and colleagues is its insistence that it is not the presence of uncertainty alone but the *successful coping with uncertainty* that produces power for the subunit. Only if the subunit can effectively manage the uncertainty confronted, and in doing so protect the other units from its disturbing effects, can the subunit parlay uncertainty into power.

The second proposition is "the lower the substitutability of the activities of a subunit, the greater its power within the organization" (Hickson et al., 1971: 221). This prediction is a direct application of Emerson's principle that power is inversely affected by alternative sources. In operational terms, this variable can be measured by the extent to which an organization can obtain alternative services to those provided by the unit or by the extent to which the personnel within the unit are replaceable.

The third proposition relates to the centrality of the subunit, which is defined as having two components: pervasiveness—"the degree to which the workflows of a subunit connect with the workflows of other units"—and immediacy—"the speed and severity with which the workflows of a subunit affect the final outputs of the organization" (1971: 221–22). Hickson and colleagues predict that the higher the centrality—pervasiveness and immediacy—of the subunit, the greater its power.[2]

These researchers have tested these propositions in a study of four principal subunits—the engineering, marketing, production, and accounting departments—in each of seven small manufacturing organizations, or twenty-

---

[2]Those interested in designing more egalitarian organizations must not only be attentive to the design of the formal authority system but must also guard against these sources of differential power. Among the techniques employed are task and worker rotation, demystification of expertise, and dedifferentiation of work roles—attempts to ensure that coping skills are shared, work is substitutable, and centrality is shared and thus neutralized (see Rothschild-Whitt, 1979; Rothschild and Whitt, 1986).

eight subunits in all (Hinings et al., 1974). A sample of organizations was selected so as to vary the uncertainty faced by the subunits, in particular, marketing. Independent variables were measured by scales based on both questionnaire and interview responses. The dependent variable, power, was measured in several ways: perceived influence attributed to the subunits over a variety of task areas; perceived formal authority over the same task areas; and reported participation in decision making. The several power indicators showed, in general, high and positive intercorrelations. Generally speaking, the data provided support for the three propositions. In terms of relative importance, coping with uncertainty was observed to have the greatest impact on power, followed, in order, by immediacy, nonsubstitutability, and pervasiveness.

But alongside these technical arguments, we need to add the institutionalist perspective. As Meyer points out:

> Organizations and their internal units derive legitimacy, power, and authority from their status in social environments. . . . The social validity of a given unit— a professional group, a technical procedure, or a departmentalized function— is often defined more importantly in the environment than by internal technical efficacy. (1978: 357)

Such units have power—based on their external connections and supports— that is *independent* of their contributions to internal operations.

Power over organizations is not restricted to those within its formal boundaries. Regulative agencies, tax authorities, planning commissions, and host communities—these and many other "stakeholders" exert varying levels of influence over organizational decision making. There is considerable controversy over the legitimacy of these multiple interest groups. Many economists insist that firms in capitalist systems exist for one primary purpose: to return profits to investors. By contrast, sociologists are more likely to view as legitimate the claims of participants and others affected by the organization and to condemn the "culture of shortsightedness," which views organizations as only tools of whatever combination of financial interests is currently in place (see Selznick, 1992).

Which interests are in control changes as environmental conditions vary. Thus, Perrow's (1961) case study of a community hospital documents the gradual transition of power from the owners and trustees to the physicians, as a result of the increasing ability of the latter group to effectively cope with medical uncertainties presented by patients, and the more recent shift of power from the physicians to the professional managers, as a result of the importance of internal coordination and external boundary management and the administrators' capacity to deal with these problems. Similarly, Fligstein (1987) has shown that as the environments confronting major corporations have changed over this century, the composition of the dominant coalition has also varied. Using as an indicator of power shifts the type of department from which the chief executive officer (CEO) is selected, Fligstein examined the departmental background of the top executive in his sample of 216 major corporations and observed how this background changed between 1919 and 1979. He reports that whereas entrepreneurs—

the founders and builders of corporations—dominated during the period 1880–1920, CEOs tended to be selected from manufacturing departments between 1920 and 1940, from sales departments between 1940 and 1960, and from finance departments from 1960 into the 1980s. He argues that these shifts mirror the changing challenges confronting corporations: production problems dominated in the 1920s and 1930s, distributional problems in the 1940s and 1950s, and financial problems from the 1960s to the present.

The number of potential powerholders and the various sources of power help to explain why the size of the dominant coalition has increased in most organizations in recent years. Rather than highly centralized hierarchies in which one or a few persons exercise most of the power and make most of the decisions, most contemporary organizations exhibit power and decision-making structures that include a substantial number of individuals. Galbraith (1967) argues that one of the most fundamental changes in the organization of the modern corporation has been the shift from an entrepreneurial mode, in which a single powerful person dominates the enterprise, to a flatter structure in which power is more widely diffused.

More so than Galbraith, Thompson (1967: 127–36) makes clear the reason for the increasing size of the organization's power structure. Consistent with the views of Crozier and Hickson, Thompson argues that the number of positions of power within the organization and hence the size of the dominant coalition, is affected both by the nature of the organization's technology and by its task and institutional environments. The more uncertain the technology and the greater the number of sources of uncertainty in the organization's environment, the more bases for power there are within the organization and the larger will be the dominant coalition. When organizations embrace more uncertain technologies, as in the case of professional organizations, and when the sources of uncertainty increase in the environment of the organization, we may expect those who cope with these problems to demand and receive a place in the decision-making councils of the organization.

What difference, if any, does it make when power shifts from one group to another or is shared with a larger proportion of the participants? The difference should be reflected, of course, in the goals pursued by the organization. Admission to the dominant coalition is an empty victory if the new partners cannot affect the definition of the goals to be served. On the basis of his case study of the community hospital, Perrow (1961) asserts that as doctors replaced trustees, and then were themselves displaced by managers, hospital goals shifted from community welfare to professional to business objectives. Similarly, within business corporations, as the entrepreneur-owner began to share power with managers and professionals, Galbraith argues that the goal of owners/stockholders to increase dividends and profits gave way to a different goal preferred by the new dominant managerial coalition, namely, "the greatest possible rate of corporate growth as measured in sales." This goal was valued by the managers because expansion of output meant expansion of the managerial component itself, "including more jobs with more responsibility and hence more promotion and more compensation" (1967: 171). More recently, as noted in Chapter 8, stockholders have found new ways to protect and extend their interests within corporate governance systems and, accordingly, organizations are pursuing downsizing and other strategies that serve not managerial, but stockholder interests (see Useem, 1993).

Fligstein (1987; 1990) also observes changes in goals associated with changes in the composition of the dominant coalition. He asserts that associated with changes in the origins of the types of persons assuming command within the corporations are basic changes in the goals of these organizations—the types of strategies being pursued. Founding entrepreneurs pursued strategies of horizontal merger in attempting to control the market. As the scale of production increased, coordination and resource problems came to the fore and manufacturing officials became dominant, pursuing strategies of vertical integration. Functional (unitary) forms were constructed to support these strategies.

> Once production is routinized, power shifts to sales and marketing personnel as the key issue for the organization becomes growth. . . . A sales and marketing strategy focuses on attempting to broaden the firm's markets by expanding across regions and countries. (Fligstein, 1985: 380)

This strategy is supported by the creation of multidivisional forms to support production and product-related distribution systems. Finally, governmental actions in the 1950s designed to prevent further concentration forced the development of alternate strategies: corporations were forced to abandon their attempt to increase their market share and began to pursue growth through multiple, unrelated product lines. Financial experts were in the best position to devise these strategies, and the conglomerate form was best suited to their support.

Environmental changes, shifting power-dependency relations, changing goals and strategies, and new structural forms—while the temporal sequence and the causal ordering of these elements are not clear, and will often be difficult to establish, it does appear that there are strong interdependencies among them.

In more differentiated and loosely coupled systems such as universities, power differences among subunits may be reflected not so much in direct attempts to redefine the goals of the larger system but in efforts to lay claim to a disproportionate share of the organization's resources. This process is well illustrated in a study by Pfeffer and Salancik (1974) of the allocation of general university resources among twenty-nine academic departments examined over a thirteen-year period. These researchers convincingly show that the greater the power of individual departments, as measured by indicators such as perceived influence and representation on powerful university committees, the greater the proportion of general university funds they received. Also, departments with higher amounts of research funding or other types of external support were able to leverage other types of university resources (see Pfeffer, 1992). Although such budgetary decisions may appear remote from the general goals of the university, they are in reality highly relevant: the allocation of scarce resources among diverse university programs is one of the clearest indicators available of the "real" goals of the institution.

Power and Interests

Organization theorists are in general agreement that power differences exist in organizations and that the use of power is necessary to establish objectives and to secure contributions to them. However, rational and natural system theorists disagree about the extent to which power is employed to serve official and collective goals in contrast to covert and personal ends. In particular, conflict theorists argue that much of the power generated by organizations is not placed in the service of achieving espoused goals but is used to perpetuate an exploitative system, to preserve class privilege, and to secure narrow, private gain. Such arguments have been advanced and pursued at least since the time of Marx, and are reflected currently in the work of analysts such as Burawoy (1985), Clegg and Dunkerley (1980), Perrow (1986), and Sabel (1982). These conflict theorists have recently been joined by a number of feminist theorists, including Acker (1990), Calas and Smircich (1996), and Martin (1994), who examine the ways in which women are prevented from rising to the top rungs of power and systematically excluded from equal benefits and protections. The increasing disparity between the compensation of executives and pay levels of rank-and-file employees (see Crystal, 1991), the protections and advantages executives have secured for themselves in the event of a hostile takeover (see Davis, 1990), and the extent to which minorities and women remain in segregated jobs and lower-paying and less secure positions are among the most visible evidence cited by these researchers to support their arguments (see also, Chapter 13).

Surveying the effects of the presence of an ever-increasing number of organizations on their surrounding social structures, it is difficult to disagree with Perrow's conclusion:

> Organizations generate power; it is the inescapable accompaniment of the production of goods and services; it comes in many forms from many sources; it is contested; and it is certainly used. (Perrow, 1986: 265)

Anarchies, Adhocracies, and Learning

Both the bureaucratic-administrative model of the rational system perspective and the coalitional-bargaining model of the natural and open system perspectives provide for the development of a set of goals by which organizational decisions can be made. Both allow for the construction of relatively clear criteria or preference orderings in terms of which priorities can be set and selections made among alternative courses of action. But there are classes of organizations—and, more important, classes of decision situations within many organizations—in which no clear preference orderings have been determined. Such organizations are on the fringe if not beyond the pale of those collectivities included within the conventional definitions and theories of organizations (see Chapter 1). Yet they present both interesting and instructive lessons.

Thompson and Tuden (1959) focus on these situations by constructing a typology that combines two dimensions: (1) how much agreement there is among participants of the organization about the goals or preferred outcomes of the system, and (2) how much agreement there is about the means or the causal processes by which these outcomes can be realized. The cross-classification of this simple ends-and-means distinction produces four types of decision contexts, each of which is argued to be associated with a different decision strategy:

Beliefs about Causation	*Preferences about Outcomes*	
	Agreement	Disagreement
Agreement	*Computation*	*Compromise*
Disagreement	*Judgment*	*Inspiration*

We are most interested here in the right-hand column—situations in which participants lack consensus on goals—but let us briefly comment on the simpler and more familiar situations in which such agreement is present. Thompson and Tuden use the term *computation* to denote those decisions most suited to the typical bureaucratic decision-making structure, which, as we have often noted, is most appropriate in situations in which goals are clearly defined and the technology relatively certain. The term *judgment* is employed to refer to the strategies required when agreement on goals exists but the means of achieving them is uncertain. This situation is best confronted with a collegium and is illustrated by the structure of professional organizations previously described.

As for the column of interest, Thompson and Tuden argue that there are sometimes situations in which participants agree about how to accomplish some objective or about what the expected consequences of available alternatives are, but disagree over which alternative is preferable. Such situations call for *compromise*. A mild version of this situation is provided by the coalitional view of decision making—which, as we have described, is resolved by negotiation, bargaining, and sequential attention to goals. More extreme instances of disagreement and conflict can sometimes be resolved through the creation of representative bodies that allow for the expression of differences and the engineering of compromises. Most such forums—for example, the United Nations and the United States Congress—presume the existence of substantive differences in preferences but rely on procedural agreements—such as Robert's Rules of Order—for resolving them.

The fourth and final decision situation is characterized by the absence of agreement about either ends or means. Thompson and Tuden suggest these anomic situations are more often found in and among organizations than conventional theories suggest. They propose that such circumstances, if they are not to result in complete system disintegration, call for *inspiration*, perhaps of the type suggested by Weber's (1968 trans.) description of the charismatic leader. This is not inconsistent with Weber's own views, described in Chapter 2, in which charismatic leaders are viewed as more likely to emerge in crisis situations—times when conventional goals are being challenged and established procedures are not working. And, like Weber, Thompson and Tuden expect such leadership to give rise over time to a computational (bureaucratic) structure based on a new definition of goals and accepted procedures, as charisma is routinized.

March and his colleagues (March and Olsen, 1976, 1989; Cohen, March, and Olsen, 1972, 1976; Cohen and March, 1976; March, 1988) have also examined decision making under conditions of "inconsistent and ill-defined preferences," "unclear technologies," and "fluid participation"—the shifting involvement of members in decision situations (Cohen, March, and Olsen, 1972: 1). They label these conditions *organized anarchies*. But unlike Thompson and Tuden, March and associates do not view these circumstances as crises or as transitory states. Rather, they insist that they have been "identified often in studies of organizations," "are characteristic of any organization in part," and "are particularly conspicuous in public, educational, and illegitimate organizations" (Cohen, March, and Olsen, 1976: 25).

The portrait of organized anarchies is set within a more general framework that stresses the ambiguity in decision making. March and Olsen comment on their approach:

> We remain in the tradition of viewing organizational participants as problem-solvers and decision-makers. However, we assume that individuals find themselves in a more complex, less stable, and less understood world than that described by standard theories of organizational choice; they are placed in a world over which they often have only modest control. (1976: 21)

The organizational world depicted here is similar to that described by Weick (1969; 1995; see also Chapter 4): individual decision makers have cognitive and attention limits; external conditions constrain alternatives and affect outcomes but often go unnoticed; and choices by individuals in decision-making positions may not eventuate in organizational action. Under such conditions, all choices are somewhat ambiguous.

> Although organizations can often be viewed conveniently as vehicles for solving well-defined problems or structures within which conflict is resolved through bargaining, they also provide sets of procedures through which participants arrive at an interpretation of what they are doing and what they have done while in the process of doing it. From this point of view, an organization is a collection of choices looking for problems, issues and feelings looking for decision situations in which they might be aired, solutions looking for issues to which they might be the answer, and decision makers looking for work. (Cohen, March, and Olsen, 1972: 2)

Under conditions of organized anarchy, the ambiguity of choice present in all decision-making situations reaches its apex. Here problems, solutions, participants, and choice opportunities are viewed as flows that move relatively independently into and out of the decision arena—metaphorically labeled a "garbage can." Which solutions get attached to which problems is largely determined by chance—by what participants with what goals happened to be on the scene, by when the solutions or the problems entered, and so on. Although the system described seems bizarre and even pathological when compared with the conventional model of rational decision making, it does produce decisions under conditions of high uncertainty: that is, some solutions do get attached by some participants to some problems.

Cohen, March, and Olsen (1972) have developed and examined some of the implications of their garbage-can model under varying assumptions by using computer-simulation techniques. However, this model of decision making was originally suggested to them on the basis of observations of decision-making processes in colleges and universities:

> Opportunities for choice in higher education can easily become complex "garbage cans" into which a striking variety of problems, solutions, and participants may be dumped. Debate over the hiring of a football coach can become connected to concerns about the essence of a liberal education, the relations of the school to ethnic minorities, or the philosophy of talent. (Cohen and March, 1976: 175)

Perhaps it is due specifically to the characteristics of universities, or perhaps they intend their comments to apply more generally to all organized anarchies, but unlike Thompson and Tuden, Cohen and March (1974: 1976) do not look for a charismatic leader to ride in on horseback bringing inspiration for new goals. They perceive the role of leaders—for example, university presidents—in such situations in much more problematic and pessimistic terms. They do suggest that leaders can improve their performance if they take into account the unusual nature of decision-making situations in these organizations. By carefully timing issue creation, by being sensitive to shifting interests and involvement of participants, by recognizing the status and power implications of choice situations, by abandoning initiatives that have become hopelessly entangled with other, originally unrelated problems, by realizing that the planning function is largely symbolic and chiefly provides excuses for interaction, leaders in organized anarchies can maintain their sanity and, sometimes, make a difference in the decision made.

One major factor often accounting for the absence of clearly specified goals is the unstable nature of some organizational environments. If environments are turbulent, then it is difficult to establish clear and specific objectives around which to design a structure and orient participant activities. Under unsettled conditions, tents may be preferable to palaces:

> In constant surroundings, one could confidently assemble an intricate, rigid structure combining elegant and refined components—an organizational palace. . . .
>
> However, systematic procedures offer weak protection against unpredictability, just as increased rigidity does not effectively prepare a building for earthquakes. Some flaws of systematic procedures are inherent in the concept of strategic planning: drafting plans, dismantling an old structure, and erecting a new structure take so long that designers need to forecast how the environment will shift. Since forecasts are only conjunctures derived from the past experiences, greater reliance on forecasts induces greater design errors. Systematic procedures also sap an organization's flexibility by strengthening its rationality.
>
> . . . Residents of changing environments need a tent. An organizational tent places greater emphasis on flexibility, creativity, immediacy, and initiative than on authority, clarity, decisiveness, or responsiveness; and an organizational tent neither asks for harmony between the activities of different organizational components, nor asks that today's behavior resemble yesterday's or tomorrow's.

Why behave more consistently than one's world does? (Hedberg, Nystrom, and Starbuck, 1976: 44–45)

Unstable environments undermine clear and consistent goals, just as they unsettle rigid formalized structures (see Chapter 9).

Still, some elements of consistency can be found in the goal structures of organizations operating under unstable conditions. If, following Mintzberg and McHugh (1985), strategies are defined as "a pattern in a stream of decisions or actions," then it may be possible to retrospectively identify underlying motifs. Not all intended strategies are realized, and those that are realized may be emergent rather than deliberate. In their case study of the National Film Board (NFB) of Canada from its inception in 1939, Mintzberg and McHugh were able to discern a number of patterns in its products and approach that, although unplanned, nevertheless provided a fabric with discernible designs. The filmmakers provided the warp, but the environment furnished the woof.

> . . . the NFB had an ironic relationship with its environment. In one sense, it was highly responsive—to social trends, new fashions, new media, social turmoil. Ultimately, the NFB found its purpose—when it did—in the world around it, not in itself: it truly was a mirror for its society. . . . Yet in another sense, this was truly an organization that "did its own thing." Except during the war years, the NFB as a whole catered largely to its own needs, for the most part selecting those parts of the environment to which it cared to respond. . . .
>
> The essence of adhocracy, in contrast to machine bureaucracies that seek to control their environments in order to support their standardized systems of mass production, would seem to be rapid and continuous responsiveness to the environment, with minimal organizational momentum. (Mintzberg and McHugh, 1985: 191)

Organizations such as the NFB that rely less on long-term strategic planning and more on ad hoc, emergent strategies may also be said to replace coventional rational decision-making techniques with *experiential learning* (see Hedberg, 1981; March 1988). Whereas rational system models assume that goals are stable, learning modes assume that they are subject to change, that many choices are not guided by preestablished intentions but result in the discovery of new purposes. And whereas rational system models propose that technologies are known, learning models stress that they must be continuously invented, shaped, and modified in the light of feedback from the environment. Learning approaches embrace the open system conception of organizations:

> Learning in open, cognitive systems takes the form of positive feedback which changes the systems or their knowledge, whereas learning in closed, natural systems is the function of negative feedback which aims at maintaining the genotype unchanged. (Hedberg, 1981: 5)

Learning that "changes the system," that results not simply in new decisions but in new rules and methods for deciding, is what Argyris (1982) terms double-loop learning. It requires the "unlearning" of the old ways as well as the acquisition of new ones.

March (1991) contrasts two types of adaptive processes in organizations: exploitation and exploration. *Exploitation* involves taking advantage of what one already knows: cashing in on the investments made in existing machinery and skills. By contrast, *exploration* involves a search for new knowledge and skills, learning new ways of thinking and working. Organizations must determine the proper balance between these modes, deciding how much effort to invest in turning out goods and services and how much to invest in developing future products. Exploration is, by definition, always risky. There is no guarantee of returns on investments made. But, under conditions of even modest change, some investment in exploration—for example, research and development—is essential to ensure long-term survival.

We should not underestimate, however, how difficult it is for organizational systems to learn anything useful—and how easy it is to derive the wrong lessons—given a rapidly changing environment, selective attention and inattention processes, cognitive limits, the changing behavior of competitors, and the ambiguity of feedback.

Conceptions of Goals and Theoretical Models

Grandori (1987) argues that there is a close relation between an analyst's conception of organizational goals and the choice of a theoretical model for explaining organization structure. She takes contingency theory as the baseline model, a model that assumes that organizations are pursuing single or consistent objectives and that they are capable of rationally adapting their structure to fit changing circumstances. To the extent that analysts are aware that there are multiple, conflicting objectives that are associated with varying types of participants, the theoretical model adopted tends to be that of resource dependence. Resource dependence theorists also assume that organizations do not simply adapt to their environments but are capable of influencing or choosing among them. Population ecologists question the assumption of both contingency and resource dependence theorists that organizations adapt or react to their environments by emphasizing the inertia of organizational structure. Finally, theorists who relax the assumption that organizations have fixed objectives—whether unified or conflicting, whether to attain particular goals or simply to survive—embrace models of anarchy and learning. Actors in such organizations are viewed as lacking a priori preferences, but instead discover what their goals are in the course of acting.

Note that the theoretical models vary not only in how goals are conceived, but also in the extent to which rationality of action is posited. Organizations vary and so do the perspectives we employ to understand them.

CONTROL SYSTEMS

It is one thing to set goals; it is another to see that energies are directed toward their accomplishment. To this end, control must be exercised. Of course, all collectivities control their members. As we have previously argued in defining them, if collectivities do not show evidence of a distinctive normative structure and some regular patterns of participant behavior, we cannot even establish their existence. But, as Etzioni has argued, the problems of control in organizations are especially acute:

> The artificial quality of organizations, their high concern with performance, their tendency to be far more complex than natural units, all make informal control inadequate and reliance on identification with the job impossible. Most organizations most of the time cannot rely on most of their participants to internalize their obligations to carry out their assignments voluntarily, without additional incentives. Hence, organizations require formally structured distribution of rewards and sanctions to support compliance with their norms, regulations, and orders. (1964: 59)

Perhaps this explains why so many of the topics discussed in connection with organizations relate more or less directly to the subject of control. Consider the following list: administration, authority, automation, boundaries, bureaucratization, centralization, contracts, coordination, culture, decision premises, discipline, evaluation, formalization, hierarchy, incentives, integration, internalization, performance programs, power, procedures, routinization, rules, sanctions, socialization, supervision—these are some of the specific manifestations and instruments of control.

We begin this section by discussing the interpersonal control system—the structure of power and authority in organizations. Then we consider how these arrangements are supplemented and, in some measure, replaced by various impersonal control mechanisms. Finally, we discuss culture as a mode of control present in all organizations but dominant in some types.

Power

A great many pages have been filled with discussions of power, and many definitions of this important concept have been proposed (see Cartwright, 1965). One of the simplest and most satisfactory approaches to this topic is that of Emerson:

> It would appear that the power to control or influence the other resides in control over the things he values, which may range all the way from oil resources to ego-support, depending upon the relation in question. In short, power resides implicitly in the other's dependence.[3] (1962: 32)

Emerson views power as *relational, situational,* and at least potentially *reciprocal.* Thus, his approach emphasizes that power is to be viewed not as a characteristic of an individual but rather as a property of a social relation. To say that a given person has power is meaningless unless we specify over whom he or she has power. We must take into account the characteristics of both the

---

[3]An important advantage to this approach is that it is applicable to relations among varying types of units: individuals, groups, organizations. Here we apply the conception to relations among individuals; in Chapter 8, we used it to examine power relations among organizations.

superordinate and the subordinate individual in describing a power relation. The power of superordinates is based on their ability and willingness to sanction others—to provide or withhold rewards and penalties—but we must recognize that what constitutes a reward or a penalty is ultimately determined by the goals or values of subordinates in the relation. To use two extreme examples, a gunman has no power over the individual who does not value his or her life, nor does a person with money have power over another who does not value money or the things it will buy. Emerson's formulation also provides a means of determining the degree of power in a relation: recall his suggestion that A's power over B is (1) directly proportional to the importance B places on the goals mediated by A, and (2) inversely proportional to the availability of these goals to B outside the A-B relation (1962: 32).

It is consistent with this approach that power can have many bases. An individual's power is based on all the resources—money, skills, knowledge, strength, sex appeal—that he or she can employ to help or hinder another in the attainment of desired goals. What types of resources will function as sanctions will vary from one individual to another and from situation to situation. Thus, if workers in an office value the quality of their technical decisions, then expertise becomes an important resource that can be used as a sanction by them (see Blau, 1955); if boys at a camp prefer to avoid black eyes and to be on winning teams, then such characteristics as strength and athletic prowess will become important bases of power for them (see Lippitt et al., 1953).

Emerson's formulation also allows for the possibility of mutual dependency. Power relations can be reciprocal: one individual may hold resources of importance to another in one area but be dependent on the same person because of resources held by the latter in a different area. And just as the degree of individual dependence may vary by situation, so may the degree of mutual dependence, or interdependence.

We will define interpersonal *power* as the potential for influence that is based on one person's ability and willingness to sanction another person by manipulating rewards and punishments important to the other person. That is, power has its origin in the dependency of one person on resources controlled by another, but power itself is best defined as a potential for influence. We turn now to discuss briefly the emergence of power structures in informal and formal systems.

Power in informal groups.   During the late 1950s a large number of studies examined the operation of power in informal groups and, in particular, the emergence of power differences in previously undifferentiated task groups. The emergence of power was examined in field studies (Lippitt et al., 1953; Sherif and Sherif, 1953) as well as in the laboratory (Bales, 1952; Bales and Slater, 1955). These studies describe the way in which certain personal qualities that differ among members become the basis for differences in sanctioning ability. As analyzed by Homans (1961) and Blau (1964), the process of differentiation occurs through a series of exchanges among group participants. Over time, some members emerge who are both more willing and more able to make important contributions to goal attainment, whether to the goals of individual members or to those of the group as a whole: they can manipulate sanctions of importance to others. As Blau notes, "a person who commands services others need, and who is independent of any at their command, attains power over others by making the satisfaction of their need contingent on their compliance" (1964: 22). Both Blau and Homans see the origin of power structures as a product of unequal exchange relations that occur when some individuals become increasingly dependent on others for services required in reaching their objectives. A person lacking resources to repay the other for these services, who is unwilling to forgo them and unable to find them in other relations, has but one alternative: "he must subordinate himself to the other and comply with his wishes, thereby rewarding the other with power over himself as an inducement for furnishing the needed help" (Blau, 1964: 21–22). In this manner, exchange processes that involve asymmetries give rise to a differentiated power structure.

Pfeffer (1992) reviews a number of individual attributes that research has shown to be the source of power. These include energy and physical stamina; an ability to focus one's interests and energies; sensitivity to others, their interests and needs; flexibility as conditions change; an ability to tolerate conflict, and to submerge one's ego in the interest of building coalitions and alliances (see also, Cialdini, 1988). These abilities allow individuals to develop the resources needed in mobilizing others in one's cause.

In addition to these exchange views of power, Tyler (1993) has proposed a social identification model suggesting that individuals conform primarily because of their interest in their social standing in the group. This work stresses the importance of relational as against more instrumental types of rewards as sources of control.

In a network-based conception, Burt (1992) argues that power is a function not only of an actor's material resources (financial capital) and personal attributes or skills (human capital) but also of his or her *social capital*. Social capital consists of one's social relations with other actors and is of two types: first, the extent to which one has access to others who themselves control valued resources; second, the structure of the network itself. Burt argues that individuals who are in networks that allow them nonredundant contacts to many different types of other actors enjoy a competitive advantage compared with those who have an equal number of contacts but to others similar to themselves. Diversity of contacts is an important source of social capital and, hence, of power (see also, Granovetter, 1973).

Power in formal organizations.   Power in informal groups is based on the characteristics and relations of individuals—differences that can function as resources allowing some to reward and punish others. It is the differential distribution and use of such characteristics or resources that give rise in informal groups to a power structure. By contrast, power in formal organizations is determined at least in part by design. Most organizations are designed in such a manner that a hierarchy of positions is created: one position is defined as controlling another. A supervisory position, for example, is defined as being more powerful than that of a worker, and in accordance with this definition, sanctioning powers are attached to the position. Thus, supervisors may be allowed to evaluate the work of their subordinates, determining by these evaluations who receives what rate of pay and who is to be recommended for promotion. Such powers are attached to the position: they are available to any individual who occupies it, regardless of his or her personal qualities.

Rational system theorists emphasize the importance of formal power structures in the functioning of organizations. They argue that it is possible to design power structures in such a manner that sanctioning power may be made commensurate with responsibilities and distributed so as to facilitate the organization's requirements for coordination and control of participants' contributions. They also note that although the theoretical range of subordinates' values and, hence, of power bases is quite broad, the actual range is quite narrow: certain values are widely shared, so that it is possible to identify resources, such as money and status, that will function as sanctions for most participants most of the time. They further note the quite palpable advantages associated with the formalization process itself, which results in the "domestication" of power. Thus, tensions associated with the generation of power differences are avoided; the organization is freed from the necessity of finding "superior" individuals to fill superior positions; and power is more readily transferred from one person to another as position occupants come and go (see Chapter 2). Formalization is one of the important ways in which the "personal" element is removed from interpersonal control systems.

Natural system theorists insist, on the other hand, that no organization ever succeeds in completely controlling all sources of power or in rationally allocating power among its positions. There are two reasons for this. First, we come again to the chief thesis of the natural system perspective: positions are filled by persons, and persons possess diverse and variable characteristics, some of which may become the basis for informal power differences in formal organizations. Differences among individuals in intelligence, motivation, training, social relations, and other respects can serve as resources that sometimes supplement and sometimes contradict and erode the formal distribution of power. Second, in the organization's allocation of resources to positions, some participants inevitably obtain access to resources that can be used in ways not intended by the organizational designers. For example, access to information is an important resource that can become the basis for sanctioning and controlling others. A position such as secretary can make its occupants privy to sensitive information that they can use to enhance their own power and influence. And, as we have learned from Hickson and associates (1971), a strategic location in the structure—confronting a high degree of uncertainty or the centrality of the work performed—can be an important, unanticipated source of sanctioning ability and hence of influence.

Research by Tannenbaum and associates (Tannenbaum, 1968; Tannenbaum et al., 1974) supplies evidence for the general expectation that amount of control or influence is positively associated with position in the formal hierarchy. If individuals are asked to describe how much influence is associated with each type of position in the organization, then it is possible to construct a "control graph" that depicts how centralized or decentralized is the distribution of power in the organization. The centralization of power varies from organization to organization, largely as a function of differences in ideology or goals that directly affect the formal definitions of how power is to be distributed: for example, power was more evenly distributed in the League of Women Voters, a voluntary agency emphasizing member participation, and in European companies emphasizing worker participation than in more traditional U.S. business and industrial concerns. (However, as Tannenbaum emphasizes, power was somewhat centralized in all of these organizations, ideology and preferences notwithstanding.) Of more interest is Tannenbaum's demonstration that aside from its distribution, the total amount of control exercised varies from one organization to another. That is, in some organizations none of the positions is perceived as exercising very much influence over others, whereas in other organizations all or most of the positions are seen to exercise considerable power. This finding underlines our earlier point that organizations may be expected to vary in the amount of mutual dependence or interdependence they display.

Authority

Weber has pointed out that in his experience no organization:

> voluntarily limits itself to the appeal to material or affectual motives as a basis for guaranteeing its continuance. In addition, every such system attempts to establish and to cultivate the belief in its "legitimacy." (Weber, 1947 trans.: 325)

In other words, no organization is likely to be content with establishing a power structure; in addition, it will attempt to create an authority structure. Most social scientists define authority as legitimate power. *Legitimacy* is the property of a situation or behavior that is defined by a set of social norms as correct or appropriate. Thus, to speak of legitimate power is to indicate (1) a set of persons or positions linked by power relations and (2) a set of norms or rules governing the distribution and exercise of power and the response to it.

In the case of informal groups, we refer to the exercise of power as legitimate to the extent that there emerges a set of norms and beliefs among the members subordinate to the power wielder that the distribution and exercise of power is acceptable to them and is regarded as appropriate. The emergence of such norms significantly alters the control structure, as Blau and I have argued:

> Given the development of social norms that certain orders of superiors ought to be obeyed, the members of the group will enforce compliance with these orders as part of their enforcement of conformity to group norms. The group's demand that orders of the superior be obeyed makes obedience partly independent of his coercive power or persuasive influence over individual subordinates and thus transforms these other kinds of social control into authority. (Blau and Scott, 1962: 29)

In sum, a set of dyadic power relations between the superior and each subordinate is transformed by the emergence of legitimacy norms into a multiperson control structure in which each subordinate now participates in the control of each of his or her colleagues. Peer-group controls are harnessed in the support of the power structure. Another way of describing these important developments is to say that a stable role structure has emerged that guides the expectations of participants, making it possible for a leader to lead and for followers to follow without the generation of disruptive emotional responses. As Thibaut and Kelley suggest, in an authority structure, in contrast with a power structure:

> Nonadherence is met with the use of power to attempt to produce conformity, but the influence appeal is to a supra-individual value ("Do it for the group" or "Do it because it's good") rather than to personal interests ("Do it for me" or "Do it and I'll do something for you"). (1959: 129)

The emergence of legitimacy norms deflects the actors' attention from their personal preferences to the requirements of the system and of their roles within it. In this sense, as Kelman and Hamilton emphasize:

> the person acts as if he were in a nonchoice situation. . . . when a person is presented with a demand in a situation that has all the earmarks of legitimacy, he does not usually ask himself what he would like to do. The central question he confronts is what he must do or should do—his obligations rather than his preferences. (1989: 90)

Rules and role requirements replace preferences and choice.

For all of these reasons—involvement of subordinate participants in the control system, development of differentiated expectations among participants, depersonalization of power processes with consequent reduction of interpersonal tensions, elevation of role requirements over personal preferences—authority structures tend to be much more stable and effective control systems than power structures. Like formalization, authority helps to clothe personal power in impersonal garb.

There is, however, another equally important consequence of the legitimation process. The emergence of social norms not only allows a greater measure of control of subordinates by the power wielder but also regulates and circumscribes the exercise of power. Emerson (1962) points out that the emergence of legitimacy norms among subordinates allows them to act as a coalition vis-à-vis the power wielder, defining the arena within which he or she can appropriately exercise power. Subordinates are individually weaker but collectively stronger than the superior, allowing them to place some limits on his or her power. Legitimacy norms specify the orders to which subordinates are expected to comply—and hence support the exercise of power—but also identify demands that the power wielder cannot appropriately make of subordinates—and hence limit the exercise of power. In sum, legitimacy norms cut both ways: they permit greater and more reliable control of subordinates within certain limits defined as appropriate areas of control—Barnard (1938) referred to these areas as the "zone of indifference"—and they restrict the exercise of power to these areas. We conclude that *authority is legitimate power* and that *legitimate power is normatively regulated power.*

Two types of authority: endorsed and authorized power.   Dornbusch and I (Dornbusch and Scott, 1975) have raised a question that has not been explicitly asked by previous students of authority. Having determined that social norms that regulate power relations provide the basis for legitimate control structures, we sought to determine who—what group of participants—defines and enforces these norms. In most informal groups, there is only one possible source: the set of participants who are subject to the exercise of power and hence are subordinates of the power wielder. We have noted how, by acting as a coalition, this subordinate group can limit and regulate the exercise of power over them by a superordinate. We label this type of situation *endorsed power,* or authority by endorsement. A number of theorists—in particular, Barnard (1938)—view the enforcement of norms by subordinates, or endorsement, as the basic mechanism underlying authority in formal organizations. While we do not deny this process operates in organizations, in our opinion it is secondary to another process.

An important characteristic of formal organizations is the presence of persons superordinate to as well as persons subordinate to a given power wielder. Most hierarchies are multilevel, so that norms may be developed and enforced by persons superior to the power wielder. Indeed, this is one of the primary features of a hierarchy of offices. As Weber states:

> The principles of office hierarchy and of levels of graded authority mean a firm-ly ordered system of super- and subordination in which there is a supervision of the lower offices by the higher ones. (Weber, 1946 trans.: 197)

A familiar safeguard built into most hierarchies is the principle of appeal, by which subordinates who feel that their immediate superior is making unfair or unreasonable demands on them, may turn to their superior's boss with the expectation that he or she will enforce authority norms that curb the superi-or's power. We label a situation in which power is regulated by those superior to the power wielder *authorized power,* or authority by authorization.[4]

For authorization to operate as a source of normative control, there must be a level of the hierarchy above that of the person or position whose exercise of power is at issue. What happens at the very top of the hierarchy, where there is no superordinate level to regulate the exercise of power? In the usual case, as Parsons (1960) has pointed out, the managerial hierarchy ends with its top position being responsible to a different type of office: the insti-tutional level, exemplified by the board of directors or board of trustees. These offices are defined as being legitimated by—normatively regulated by—some different, nonhierarchical principle. Often they are legitimated by some type of electoral process (for example, election of officers by stockholders), or officers are appointed to represent the interests of the ultimate beneficia-ries—for example, the owners or the citizenry.

It is important to emphasize that a principle function of the institution-al level—one noted several times throughout this volume—is to secure the legitimation of the organization's hierarchy. This is accomplished by linking the norms and values supporting the hierarchy to broader institutionalized normative systems, demonstrating their congruence and consistency. Weber's famous typology of authority systems, described in Chapter 2, is based on dif-

---

[4]Another possible source of the creation and enforcement of norms in organizations is the colleagues or equals of the power wielder—those occupying the same formal position in the organization. This source may be expected to be of particular importance in professional orga-nizations, and is labeled *collegial* power.

ferences in the types of norms that legitimate power systems. Recall that he distinguished between traditional, charismatic, and bureaucratic systems, each of which justifies and regulates an existing structure of power on a different basis. Weber (1968 trans.), Bendix (1956), and Guillén (1994) have examined how these broadly accepted normative beliefs change over time, causing and reflecting changes in power arrangements within specific administrative systems. For example, the legitimacy of the nation-state is no longer likely to be justified by the doctrine of the divine right of kings, but is instead supported by beliefs in its consistency with constitutional documents or the "people's will." Similarly, the authority systems of more limited organizations are justified by beliefs in property rights, or procedural correctness, or the legitimacy of specialized expertise.

It is equally important to recognize that in most situations there exist multiple, competing sets of norms and beliefs supporting alternative authority regimes. Such divided authority is especially associated with the Judeo-Christian tradition, which early insisted on the differentiation of the ecclesiastical polity from the secular polity. As Berman notes, "Perhaps the most distinctive characteristic of the Western legal tradition is the coexistence and competition within the same community of diverse jurisdictions and diverse legal systems" (1983: 10). Such legal pluralism is especially prevalent in the Western democracies, which take great pains to create divided and off-setting authorities. One of the most important strategic choices confronting all organizations, although it is seldom recognized as a conscious choice, is the selection of the set of authority norms with which to become aligned. The existence of competing regimes also enables individual participants to engage in "principled disobedience" (Kelman and Hamilton, 1989), as discussed in Chapter 12.

Returning to our basic distinction, it is possible for some control attempts to be authorized—that is, supported by superiors of the power wielder—but not endorsed—that is, not supported by subordinates of the power wielder—or vice versa. It is also possible for control attempts to be both authorized and endorsed. An instance of the first type would be the authority exercised by a police officer in an urban neighborhood whose residents are suspicious or hostile toward police activities; the second type is illustrated by the authority exercised by an informal leader in a work group. The third type—authority that is both authorized and endorsed—is represented by an individual serving as a supervisor who is also a natural leader. Authority that is both authorized and endorsed may be said to enjoy greater legitimacy and may be expected to be more effective and more stable than that which receives support from only one source (Dornbusch and Scott, 1975: 56–64; see also, Zelditch and Walker, 1984).

Structural Control

Authority and power are usually regarded as personal or interpersonal control systems, but as we have noted, in moving from informal to formalized power and from power to authority, we introduce more impersonal supports. Formal power is attached to positions rather than persons, and authority is power justified—authorized or endorsed—by normative beliefs.

As Edwards (1979) has pointed out, simple and more personal power systems tend to give way over time to more complex and impersonal forms—to technical and bureaucratic structures (see Chapter 8). Controls are built into technical production systems in the form of machine pacing or, in the case of continuous-flow systems, in the layout and speed of the assembly line. These "built-in" controls reduce the need for personal direction and in this manner change the role of supervisors from overseer to troubleshooter (see Walker and Guest, 1952; Blau and Scott, 1962: 176–83). The new information technologies can both inform and support work as well as monitor and regulate it. These controls are so effective that they enable some types of work to be performed off-site, isolated from the typical, multiple controls in place in all organized work settings (see Zuboff, 1988).

Even more elaborate and less visible controls are embedded in the organization structure itself—in the layout of offices, functions, rules, and policies. Edwards emphasizes that the force of these bureaucratic arrangements resides in their seemingly impersonal character.

> Above all else, bureaucratic control institutionalized the exercise of capitalist power, making power appear to emanate from the formal organization itself. Hierarchical relations were transformed from relations between (unequally powerful) people to relations between jobholders or relations between jobs themselves, abstracted from the specific people or the concrete work tasks involved. "Rule of law"—the firm's law—replaced rule by supervisor command. And indeed, the replacement was not illusory. To the extent that firms were successful in imposing bureaucratic control, the method, extent, and intensity of sanctions imposed on recalcitrant workers were specified by organizational rules. (1979: 145–46)

Technical and bureaucratic control structures thus represent important instances of *structural* controls. Differences in power are built into the design of the technologies or into the definition of relations among positions, and these power differences are normatively justified. There are two major advantages to power wielders in gaining structural control. The first is that one's power advantages are partially concealed: all participants—both those with greater power and those with lesser power—appear to be commonly subordinated to a normative framework exercising control over all. The second advantage is that those with structural power do not need to mobilize resources in order to have their interests taken into account. It is automatically assumed that they are "entitled" to be represented in any matter affecting their interests. By contrast, interests that are not structured have to become mobilized if they are to be heard (see Alford, 1975). It is in this sense that power functions less as a "wild card" and more like a "trump suit" in the game of politics within organizations (see Heilbroner, 1980: 146).

Culture

Some types of organizations, as described in Chapter 9, rely less on formalized control systems than on the development of a set of beliefs and norms that participants employ to orient and govern their contributions. These types of controls denote the existence of a *corporate culture*. Pointing to culture as one basis of control should come as no surprise, since anthropologists have long believed most of the orderliness and patterning found in social life is accounted for by cultural systems, but such views have only recently been employed by students of organizations.[5]

Smircich (1983: 339) points out that the concept of culture is used in two quite different ways by organizational analysts: "as a critical variable and as a root metaphor." In the first usage, culture is something that an organization *has;* in the second, it is something an organization *is*. We restrict attention here to the first meaning and consider the second in the following section. Viewed as a variable (or set of variables):

> The term "culture" describes an attribute or quality internal to a group. We refer to an organizational culture or subculture. In this sense culture is a possession— a fairly stable set of taken-for-granted assumptions, shared beliefs, meanings, and values that form a kind of backdrop for action. (Smircich, 1985: 58)

Culture so defined may be employed either as an external independent variable that may affect the organization—for example, organizations in France are molded by a distinctive set of cultural beliefs unique to that society (Crozier, 1964)—or as an internal variable that characterizes the values or style of a particular organization.

Most of the analysts focusing on culture as a variable embrace a functionalist perspective and focus on the contributions that cultural elements make to "organizational unification and control" (Smircich and Calas, 1987: 238; see also, O'Reilly and Chatman, 1996). Schein, for example, suggests that the concept of culture should be reserved for the "deeper level of basic assumptions and beliefs that are shared by members of an organization" and embraces the functionalist assumption that: "These assumptions and beliefs are learned responses to a group's problems of survival in its external environment and its problems of internal integration" (Schein, 1992: 6).

Trice and Beyer (1993) distinguish between the substance and the forms of cultures. They suggest that cultural substance consists of the "shared, emotionally charged belief systems we call ideologies," whereas cultural forms are the "observable entities, including actions, through which members of a culture express, affirm, and communicate the substance of their culture to one another" (p. 2).

Every organization necessarily has a culture, but cultures vary in their attributes. Much attention has been devoted in the popular organizations literature to the competitive advantages for organizations of creating "strong" cultures—belief systems that define a general mission sustaining commitment to something larger than self; that provide guidelines by which participants can choose appropriate activities; that create sources of meaning and identification such that participants not only know what they are to do for the good of the organization but want to do it. Such beliefs are inculcated and reinforced by rituals and ceremonies that provide collective occasions for express-

---

[5]Recall, however, the similar arguments of Barnard (1938) and Selznick (1957), who emphasized the importance of symbolic controls.

ing solidarity and commitment; by the raising up of heroes that personify common goals; and by the creation of slogans and symbols that signify shared values (Deal and Kennedy, 1982; Peters and Waterman, 1982). Precisely how such strong cultures are created and maintained is the subject of much current study (see Jelinek, Smircich, and Hirsch, 1983; Frost et al., 1985; Schneider, 1990; Cameron and Quinn, 1996).

A major concern raised by the cultural controls in organizations is their potential development into an authoritarian system that is subject to abuse precisely because its controls are internalized and individual participants are unconstrained in the demands that they place on themselves and their colleagues. Peters and Waterman describe this darker side of cultural controls in the corporate setting:

> So strong is the need for meaning . . . that most people will yield a fair degree of latitude or freedom to institutions that give it to them. The excellent companies are marked by very strong cultures, so strong that you either buy into their norms or get out. (1982: 77)

This high level of commitment to special-purpose organizations is of concern in a society based on pluralism and committed to democratic institutions. We regard this kind of commitment as a potential source of pathology and comment further on its implications in the next chapter. On the other hand, Kunda (1992) suggests that individuals are not "cultural dopes," and that while, on the one hand, they can experience and respond to direct and overt cultural pressures they, on the other hand, can be aware that they are being manipulated, and "cognitively distance" themselves from the prevailing ideologies.

Other students of organizational culture emphasize its diversity and variety. Martin (1992), for example, contrasts dominant approaches that stress the unity of cultural beliefs within an organization with others that stress the extent of differentiation—the identification of subcultures—or still others that acknowledge the absence of a shared, integrated set of values: a fragmented culture. Martin treats these differences as paradigms—analytic models applicable to any organization—but also recognizes that the cultures of specific organizations may be better characterized by one rather than another perspective.

MODERN AND POSTMODERN ORGANIZATIONS

Our decision to discuss organizational goals in the same chapter that considers power and control processes was not an arbitrary one. As noted earlier, the concept of a dominant coalition as the agent by which organizational goals are selected and imposed highlights the linkage of power and goal setting. Recent discussions of modern versus postmodern views of organizations emphasize the significance of this association and point to alternative models.

Postmodernism is a recent intellectual movement and still a work in progress. During the past decade, a steady stream of loosely related ideas and critiques, primarily generated by European social and cultural theorists, has

begun to challenge many of the central assumptions underlying contemporary social science, including views of organizations. This work shares much in
common with other natural open system perspectives. Like resource dependence theory, it emphasizes the central role of power in shaping social institutions; like Marxist theory, it does not accept at face value the rationalist
claims of organizational designers and officials; and, like institutional theory,
it stresses the overriding importance of cultural beliefs and symbolic processes. But its critique is more far-reaching than any of these. The principal archi-
tects of this approach include Foucault (1977) and Lyotard (1984); Nietzsche
was the early guiding spirit.[6]

Postmodernists stress the importance of the symbolic, cultural elements
of the social world. Our social world is socially constructed; and what we "see"
or believe depends on the social situation and our location in it. Emphasis
shifts from seeking explanations to providing interpretations, a development
that signifies a number of important changes. First, as Agger observes, "postmodernism rejects the view that science can be spoken in a singular, universal
voice" (1991: 121). Rather, "every knowledge is contextualized by its historical
and cultural nature." Different truths are associated with differing social or
temporal locations. "Social science becomes an accounting of social experience from these multiple perspectives of discourse/practice, rather than a
larger cumulative enterprise committed to the inference of general principles
of social structure and organization" (p. 117). A related difference: all knowledge is self-referential or reflexive; that is, we as interpreting subjects understand events in the world not only in their relation to one another, but to
ourselves.

> Culture—the shared meanings, practices, and symbols that constitute the
> human world—does not present itself neutrally or with one voice. It is always
> multivocal and overdetermined, and both the observer and the observed are
> always enmeshed in it; that is our situation. There is no privileged position, no
> absolute perspective, no final recounting. (Rabinow and Sullivan, 1987: 7–8)

And there is a power-knowledge connection in that "the impossibilities in separating power from knowledge are assumed and knowledge loses a sense of
innocence and neutrality" (Alvesson and Deetz, 1996: 205).

The more open one's conception of organization, the more vague and
permeated its boundaries, the more varied its constituent elements, the more
diverse the actors and their interests, the more discordant their conceptions
and cognitive frames, the less possible it is to embrace a single, simple view of
organization as rational system. Rationalities become multiple, interests and
purposes are differentiated and contextualized. All organizations, being composed of multiple, different individuals, each with his or her own unique history and constellation of interests and affiliations, are open systems, but they
vary greatly in the extent to which these differences are recognized, legitimat-

---

[6] Related perspectives include critical theory, for example, the work of Marcuse (1964)
and Habermas (1971); poststructuralism, for example, Derrida (1976); and some modes of feminist theory, for example, Moi (1985). For a thoughtful overview of the relation between postmodernism and social science, see Rosenau (1992).

ed, and taken into account in the organizing process. A "modernist" mentality seeks to impose order on the chaos, to resolve or suppress the contradictions, to integrate the competing interests and agendas so that a single, harmonious vision guides decisions and a consistent set of premises governs the conduct of participants. Clearly, in doing so, power will need to be invoked, conflicts resolved by negotiation or by recourse to authority, some participants excluded from decisions, or even from continued involvement in the organization. These are the instruments by which a uniform rationality is forged.

A postmodernist view emphasizes the diversity of elements that make up organizations. If uniformity exists, it is because diversity has been suppressed; if consistency dominates, it has been arbitrarily imposed. At the present time, postmodernism exists more as a critical approach than as an alternative model of organizing. As an approach to examining organizations, it resonates with the work of those theorists who insist that organizations *are* cultures: that their essence is to be found in their symbolic order. This order is constructed in and through social interactions of particular individuals in a particular setting (Smircich and Calas, 1987). One mode of analysis is, therefore, to "deconstruct" (Derrida, 1976) this order, to show that "meaning and understanding are not naturally intrinsic to the world and that they have to be constructed" (Cooper and Burrell, 1988). Postmodernists also would not privilege the formal structure, but insist that this version of what is necessary or "rational" must be set alongside the various informal systems that represent attempts to resist any such single vision of order. The task of the analyst is to understand "what is 'going on' in a situation," recognizing that there is no one correct version, including that developed by the analyst. Truth is recognized to have many aspects and to speak with many voices.

As noted, it is less clear what a "postmodern" organization might look like. Presumably, its culture would support diversity, pluralism, and ambiguity (see Martin, 1992). Such a model would also push in the direction of de-differentiation, as Lash (1988) argues. This process would occur both internally, as specialized roles are eschewed and formalized hierarchies disestablished, but also externally, as organizational boundaries are disregarded, and actors allowed to mobilize support and pursue interests across lines that are regarded as artificial and arbitrary. Under such circumstances, organizational boundaries operate less and less to contain and support individual behavior. Perhaps the organic forms described in Chapter 9 or the "network" forms discussed in Chapter 10 provide illustrations of postmodernist organizations (see also Clegg, 1990; Alvesson and Deetz, 1996).

Alternatively, it may be that the major contribution of postmodernist work will not be to serve as a guide for designing new forms of organizations but to undermine or challenge the hegemony of existing modernist discourse that permeates most contemporary treatments of organization.

SUMMARY

Goals are put to many uses by organizational participants. They serve cognitive functions, guiding the selection of alternative courses of action; they have cathectic properties, serving as a source of identification and commitment for participants and as symbolic properties appealing to external constituencies; they provide present justifications for actions taken in the past; they provide criteria for the evaluation of performances, participants, and programs of action; and under some conditions they provide ideological guidance for the contributions of participants. Moreover, individual participants bring their own private goals or motives with them into the organization, and these rarely coincide with those of the organization.

Strategies refer to a subset of goals focusing on the orientation of the organization to its environment. They emphasize the choice of domain and the selection of a competitive stance within that domain. While strategies are often described as determined by top executives, under many circumstances, they are influenced by the decisions of middle- and lower-level participants.

The concept of a dominant coalition that determines goals in organizations solves some of the mysteries of goal setting. It helps to avoid reification of the organization as a single purposeful actor but at the same time allows the organization's goals or preference structures to differ from those of all its human agents. The concept allows for the possibility that groups and individual participants have different interests and agendas and indicates how, through negotiation and the making of side payments, bargains are struck and a basis for common action developed. The concept of dominant coalitions also reminds us that individual participants do not have equal power in decision making and that the preferences and interests of some will receive more attention than those of others. Although individuals and groups bring preferences and interests with them into the organization, organizations are more than a setting where existing interests come together: they are places where new interests are created.

The size and shape of the dominant coalition changes over time in response to the changing external conditions to which the organization must adapt. As new sources of uncertainty and challenge develop in its environment, the organization creates offices to deal with them. Officers who can successfully cope with such problems may be expected to acquire power within the organization, since others are dependent on them for critical services. As environments become more complex and turbulent, the dominant coalition grows and its shape changes to incorporate more and different specialists capable of managing one or another boundary problem. And as the composition of the membership of the dominant coalition changes, the goals of the organization also change, reflecting these shifts in power.

Some organizations lack clear goals or efficacious technologies. Such conditions are not very hospitable to the formation and maintenance of organizations, but when they exist several alternative strategies are possible. Organizations may suffer and hope for the millennium, awaiting the appearance of a charismatic leader who will clarify ends and supply means. They may attune themselves to high ambiguity, recognizing that almost-random connections among streams of problems, participants, and solutions will produce some decisions. Or they may engage in experiential learning, interpreting environmental cues in order to improvise changing strategies.

All collectivities control their members, but some distinctive control arrangements are to be found in organizations. Power is the potential for influence based on sanctioning ability, and authority is normatively regulated power. In informal groups authority tends to exist as endorsed power—power constrained by norms enforced by subordinates—but in formal organizations authority exists primarily as authorized power—power circumscribed and supported by norms enforced by officers superior to the power wielder. In some types of organizations, control may reside more in organizational cultures—that is, in shared, internalized beliefs and norms that provide meaning and guidance to individual members engaged in collective action.

Modernist views of organizations see them as structures for coordinating activities in the pursuit of specialized goals. Postmodernist critics assert that such structures can only be created by power used to suppress diverse interests and delegitimate alternative interpretations and rationalities.

ORGANIZATIONS AND SOCIETY

We have emphasized throughout this volume that organizations are only subsystems of larger social systems and are connected in numerous and vital ways to them. What differentiates the focus of the next two chapters from previous ones is not a concern with these connecting links but a shift in reference. Thus far, the organization itself has served as the primary point of reference. We have explored goals, structures, technologies, and participants from the standpoint of what they can reveal about the system of which they are parts. Now we adopt a different benchmark: that of the host society. We ask in these two concluding chapters what organizations can do to and for the societies that support them. We examine unintended as well as intended effects.

Chapter 12 explores some of the problems and dangers associated with the operation and growth of organizations. In particular, we focus on power and its potential misuse. Organizations generate power as a consequence of their functioning. Previous chapters have examined how power can be employed in the service of organizational goals—whether those goals be certain outputs or the survival of the organization. Chapter 12 investigates the side effects of the power that is generated—its unanticipated consequences for both internal participants and external publics. As might be imagined, these are issues raised primarily by the natural system perspective on the functioning of organizations.

From the rational system perspective, organizations are instruments for the attainment of goals. We have asked numerous questions about the implications of this view for the organization. However, a crucial question for the larger society within which organizations operate is how effective and efficient they are in meeting their goals. Are they sufficiently adept in their functions—in achieving their respective goals and in producing high quality goods and services—that they merit social support in spite of problems they raise? Although the question of effectiveness is most readily addressed from the rational system perspective, we shall quickly discover that different questions regarding organizational effectiveness are raised by natural and open system points of view. These queries and issues are addressed in Chapter 13.

CHAPTER 12

Organizational Pathologies

> Bureaucracy has been and is a power instrument of the first order. . . . The individual bureaucrat cannot squirm out of the apparatus in which he is harnessed. . . . In the great majority of cases, he is only a single cog in an ever-moving mechanism which prescribes to him an essentially fixed route of march. . . .
>
> The ruled, for their part, cannot dispense with or replace the bureaucratic apparatus of authority once it exists. For this bureaucracy rests upon expert training, a functional specialization of work, and an attitude set for habitual and virtuoso-like mastery of single, yet methodically integrated functions. . . . This holds for public administration as well as for private economic management. More and more the material fate of the masses depends upon the steady and correct functioning of the increasingly bureaucratic organizations of private capitalism. The idea of eliminating these organizations becomes more and more utopian.
>
> *Max Weber (1947 trans.)*

Weber was aware of the use and the possible misuse of power in modern organizations. Inappropriate applications can occur both internally, when participants are exploited or stunted or in other ways damaged by their involvement, and externally, when publics who rely on organizations for goods and services find that organizations are unresponsive to their needs or interests. Internal problems may appear to be an issue only for the individuals involved, but a moment's reflection will convince us that damage done to organizational participants is a social, and not simply a personal, problem. As has been noted, individuals are only partially involved in any given organization: injury inflicted on participants in one setting may be expected to affect their performance in others. Three types of problems for individual participants are frequently cited: alienation, inequity, and overconformity or ritualism. They are examined in the first section of this chapter.

Turning to problems involving publics, we first examine the issue of responsiveness. What can be done to ensure that organizations are attentive to the needs and interests of external constituencies? This is a particularly acute problem for public organizations, which are expected to be oriented primarily to public interests, but is by no means restricted to them. We also examine the broader issue of corporate versus individual interests, which raises more general questions about the distribution and use of power in contemporary society.

Throughout this chapter, we endeavor to show that it is not necessary to develop new concepts or arguments to explain organizational pathologies. There is a close correspondence between many of the best and the worst features of organizations. In some cases, similar processes, with slight variations, produce both an organization's strengths and its weaknesses. In other cases, the organization's strengths *are* its weaknesses, when viewed from a different perspective.

PROBLEMS FOR PARTICIPANTS

Alienation

Much time and attention has been devoted over the years to the impact of organizations on the personal characteristics of their participants. There are many claims and considerable evidence regarding these effects—and most of them are conflicting! At least since the time of Adam Smith and down to the present, observers have pointed to the debilitating consequences of organizational involvement, and in particular, employment, for individual participants. These destructive processes are often summarized under the concept of alienation—a concept with enough facets and varied interpretations to serve as an adequate umbrella under which to gather a quite varied set of criticisms.

Even Marx, who more than any other theorist called attention to the importance of alienation of workers, identified several possible forms of alienation (see Marx, 1963 trans.; Faunce, 1968). Workers may be alienated from the product of their labor. Labor gives value to the objects it creates, but as a worker loses control over his product, it comes to exist "independently, outside himself, and alien to him and . . . stands opposed to him as an autonomous power" (Marx, 1963 trans.: 122–23). Workers can also be alienated from the process of production. This occurs to the extent that:

> the work is external to the worker, that it is not part of his nature, and that, consequently, he does not fulfil himself in his work but denies himself, has a feeling of misery rather than well-being, does not develop freely his mental and physical energies but is physically exhausted and mentally debased. . . . His work is not voluntary but imposed, forced labor. (Marx, 1963 trans.: 124–25)

As a consequence of the first two processes, workers become alienated from others in the work setting. Marx explains:

> The alien being to whom labour and the product of labour belong, to whose service labour is devoted, and to whose enjoyment the product of labour goes,

can only be man himself. If the product of labour does not belong to the worker, but confronts him as an alien power, this can only be because it belongs to a man other than the worker. (1963 trans.: 130)

Enter the capitalist. And enter the argument that it is not work that alienates, but exploitation of workers by the misuse of power.

Before turning to some evidence regarding the pervasiveness and distribution of alienation, a second influential formulation deserves mention. Like Marx, Seeman (1959; 1975) views alienation as a multifaceted concept; he identifies six varieties: (1) powerlessness—the sense of little control over events; (2) meaninglessness—the sense of incomprehensibility of personal and social affairs; (3) normlessness—use of socially unapproved means for the achievement of goals; (4) cultural estrangement—rejection of commonly held values and standards; (5) self-estrangement—engagement in activities that are not intrinsically rewarding; and (6) social isolation—the sense of exclusion or rejection. Seeman has argued that powerlessness and self-estrangement are the two types of alienation that have most meaning in the workplace, and these seem most consistent with Marx's distinctions. A great many measures, including several multiple-item scales, have been developed to assess one or the other of these dimensions (see Seeman, 1975); most of them treat these conditions as internal, social psychological states. Israel (1971) has taken strong exception to this practice, insisting that alienation is more accurately and usefully viewed as an objective condition of the social structure, not a subjective attitude or disposition. Individuals may not be able to recognize that they are alienated: sentiments may not accurately reflect circumstances.

In spite of Israel's concerns, most empirical studies on alienation are based on data obtained from individual respondents who report their feelings or attitudes—for example, work satisfaction and dissatisfaction, levels of interest or commitment—or their behavior—for example, turnover, absenteeism, physical and mental health symptoms. Most surveys conducted in this country over the past half century report (1) generally high levels of worker satisfaction and morale but (2) large variation in satisfaction and symptoms across differing occupational strata and work situations. These surveys also show that higher satisfaction tends to be associated with such factors as intrinsic interest of the work, level of control, level of pay and economic security, and opportunities for social interaction (see Blauner, 1964; Sheppard and Herrick, 1972; Special Task Force, 1973).

Whereas much of this earlier work was based on a relatively passive model of worker behavior, more contemporary studies embrace the view that workers respond more "proactively" to their environments (see J. Scott, 1985). A quantitative analysis of a large number of ethnographic studies of worker responses to a variety of workplace conditions by Hodson (1996) suggests that while workers respond more positively to organizations supporting worker participation in decision making than to more bureaucratic or assembly-line systems; craft organizations continued to evoke the highest levels of worker satisfaction and pride.

An impressive body of research relating characteristics of work to personality measures—more enduring and basic attributes than attitudes—is that conducted by Kohn and associates (see Kohn and Schooler 1983; for a summary and assessment, see Spenner, 1988). Variables employed to measure jobs included complexity of work and closeness of supervision, job pressures, risks and rewards, and location in the hierarchy. Personality dimensions include intellectual flexibility, self-directedness, and sense of well-being or distress. The nature of the data (longitudinal) and analysis techniques (structural equations) allowed the investigators to distinguish effects in both directions: more of the effects of job on personality were contemporaneous, whereas more of the effects of personality on (reports of) job conditions were lagged, that is, only apparent after several years. The most important effects were associated with work complexity. In general:

> Men in self-directed jobs become less authoritarian, less self-deprecatory, less fatalistic, and less conformist in their ideas while becoming more self-confident and more responsible to standards of morality. (Spenner, 1988: 75)

These and related studies provide convincing evidence that the nature of work and working conditions can have significant effects on personality.

As the number and variety of service occupations expand in contemporary society, an interesting new variant of self-estrangement has arisen that requires workers to simulate emotions they do not feel. Workers such as flight attendants, retail clerks, and food servers perform "emotional labor" in that they are required to "induce or suppress feeling in order to sustain the outward countenance that produces the proper state of mind in others" whom they serve (Hochschild, 1983: 7; see also, Rafaeli and Sutton, 1987). The manipulation of emotion exacts its costs on the performer, who is subject to "burnout" and to feelings of insincerity and inauthenticity; and their audiences may come to discount such "phony" commercialized feelings. Hochschild estimates that about one-third of all U.S. workers currently have jobs that require them to engage in such emotional labor; however, more than half of all women workers hold such jobs (p. 11).

A number of analysts have claimed that the impact of organizations on their participants extends far beyond the walls of the organization itself. Argyris (1957; 1973) summarizes several studies that indicate that workers who experience "constraint and isolation" on the job carry these attitudes into their free time: such workers are less involved in organized leisure, community, or political activities. Kanter (1977b) reviewed a number of studies that suggest that both men's and women's occupational experiences have important implications for their family roles. She asserts that these studies contradict the "myth of separate worlds" perpetuated by companies that do not wish to assume responsibility for the effects of their policies and practices on the "personal" lives of their employees (and also by social scientists who tend to specialize in studying organizations or families but not their interdependence) (see also, Gerstel and Gross, 1987). Similarly, Ouchi argues that organizations have a vested interest in failing to recognize their psychological casualties:

> The costs of psychological failure are not borne entirely by the firm, but rather are externalized to the society generally. That is, employees who reach the

point of emotional disability, who become unsatisfactory workers, are the first to be laid off during depressions or, in extreme cases, are fired. The firm which has "used up" people emotionally does not have to face the cost of restoring them. In much the same manner that firms were able until recently to pollute the air and the water without paying the costs of using up these resources, they continue to be able to pollute our mental health with impunity. (1979: 36–37)

Kanter asserted in the late 1970s that "a major social welfare issue of the decades to come" is likely to be focused on the question "Can organizations more fully and responsibly take into account their inevitable interface with the personal lives of their participants?" (1977b: 89), but two decades later, most obsevers would conclude that little has changed.

Social critics correctly accuse many organizations of generating alienation among their participants that spills over into the wider social structure. While such problems require attention and correction, a long line of social analysts from Saint-Simon (1952 trans.) through Barnard (1938) to Ouchi (1981) and Peters and Waterman (1982) have gone to the opposite extreme, looking to organizations to provide the primary source of social integration, personal identity, and meaning in modern society. Wolin calls attention to the underlying anxiety and elitist stance that nurtures this point of view:

The fondness for large scale organization displayed by contemporary writers largely stems from anxieties provoked by the emergence of the mass. They see organizations as mediating institutions, shaping disoriented individuals to socially useful behavior and endowing them with a desperately needed sense of values. These large entities supply the stabilizing centers, which not only integrate and structure the amorphous masses, but control them as well. (1960: 427)

On the one hand, we embrace the concern that organizations should not be a source of alienation and estrangement to their participants, but, on the other hand, we cannot accept the opinion that employment organizations should serve as the principal centers of meaning and of moral and social integration in contemporary society. As indicated in Chapter 7, we see the development of special-purpose organizations as being closely associated with the emergence of the ideology of individualism, including the doctrine of natural rights and the value of individual freedom. The development of the rational-legal out of the traditional forms, to use Weber's terms, signals the emergence of norms and structures that place restrictions on the hierarchy of the organization and reduce the leverage of any particular organization in relation to the individual. We endorse these developments and view with alarm proposals to expand the power and influence of an organization over its members. This argument will be amplified at the end of this chapter.

Inequity

Formal organizations are expected to be fair in their treatment of personnel: universalistic criteria of hiring, promotion, and pay are purported to operate; achievement is supposed to replace ascription as the basis for distributing rewards. There is no question that in the United States there is long-term evidence that more universalistic, equalitarian standards of employment are being utilized, with improvements in occupational status attainment for both women and nonwhites (see Featherman and Hauser, 1978; Farley, 1984). These trends continue during the recent period as shown by an examination of data from the General Social Survey for the period 1972 to 1987. Analyses conducted by DiPrete and Grusky (1990) show that ascriptive processes continue to recede; however, there is also evidence of a gradual slowdown in the rate of change. The timing of this slowdown coincides with the onset of more conservative federal policies during the 1980s, when many of the earlier equal opportunity initiatives were either weakened or eliminated.

In spite of advances throughout the twentieth century, a substantial disparity remains between the advancement and earnings of men in comparison to women and whites in comparison to nonwhites. Race and gender characteristics of employees continue to be important factors affecting their opportunities and outcomes. In the United States in the early 1980s, for example, African American males earned 72 percent as much as white males per hour but, because of less stable employment, 56 percent as much as white males per year (see Jaynes and Williams, 1989: 297). More important, these differences persist between whites and blacks with similar amounts of education. Similarly, in the United States during the 1980s, women earned only about 70 percent of the wage rate of men, and these differences have changed little between 1920 and 1980 (see Smith and Ward, 1984; Marini, 1989). Although women—including women with children—have rapidly moved into the labor force since World War II, they have largely found employment in the lower-wage occupations and industries, primarily the services and retail trades.

Recent sociological analyses of labor markets emphasize that, in order to understand the distribution of social and economic rewards to workers, we must not only examine the "supply side" characteristics of the individual workers but also the "demand side" characteristics of jobs, their numbers, variety, and connections. And, as emphasized in our discussion of labor markets in Chapter 8, most jobs are defined by and embedded in organizations (see Baron and Bielby, 1980).

The conventional assumption is that jobs exist independently of their occupants, but research by Baron, Bielby, and others suggests that the more powerful and advantaged groups (for example, white males) are able to develop more elaborate and differentiated job positions and titles than less privileged groups. Jobs remain highly segregated by gender. In 1990, in the United States, the sex segregation index for occupations was .57, meaning that roughly six out of ten employed women (or men) would have to change occupations to achieve an equal gender distribution (see Reskin, 1993). At the organizational level, gender segregation of jobs is even more pronounced. Research conducted in a diverse sample of organizations within California by Bielby and Baron shows that even within seemingly integrated occupations:

> Work done by both men and women is often done in distinct organizational settings, and when enterprises employ both sexes in the same occupation, they typically assign them different job titles. Once established, sex labels of job titles

acquire tremendous inertia, even when similar work is done by the opposite sex elsewhere in the same establishment or in other settings. (1986: 787)

Research comparing the occupations dominated by men or women shows that "women's jobs are not usually *less* skilled than men's, but women's and men's jobs generally require *different kinds* of skills" (England, 1992). These are the types of findings that fuel efforts to ensure comparable pay for comparable work.

Feminist theorists carry the critique of modern organizations well beyond the accusation that qualified women do not receive equal treatment or compensation.[1] Martin and Knopoff (forthcoming), for example, argue that although Weber's classic discussion of the defining features of bureaucracy appears to be gender-neutral and universal in its depiction of administration based on expertise, its emphasis on full-time commitment of personnel and on training as the main qualification for officeholding disadvantages those who, like women, confront conflicting commitments—for example, to the care of family members—and lack equal access to education and training programs. Conventional discussions that ignore the interdependence of work and family responsibilities, that treat the former as public and masculine and the latter as private and feminine, distort reality in a manner that disadvantages women (see Bose, Feldberg, and Sokoloff, 1987; Martin, 1990).

A different kind of inequity has arisen among organizations in their treatment of employees during the last two decades. The downsizing activities of many organizations during the past decade have removed large numbers of regular, secure positions from these mainstream organizations and have increasingly substituted the use of part-time, temporary, low-wage employees. In addition to giving organizations greater flexibility, the use of contract and temporary workers also enables companies to secure major savings because they are not obligated to provide employees benefits such as health insurance and contributions to pension funds. Harrison (1994) cites U.S. government statistics showing that the number of year-round, full-time employees with annual earnings below the poverty line increased from 12 percent of all employees in 1979 to 18 percent in 1990. Harrison regards these trends toward increasing polarization in earnings as "the dark side of flexible production": corporate flexibility is purchased at the cost of decreased job security and reduced benefits for millions of workers (see also, Harrison and Bluestone, 1988; Warme, Lundy, and Lundy, 1992).

Overconformity

In his justly famous essay "Bureaucratic Structure and Personality," Robert Merton calls attention to a set of processes by which "the very elements which conduce toward efficiency in general produce inefficiency in specific

---

[1]My colleague Joanne Martin has taken me to task for relegating feminist theory to this chapter devoted to organizational pathologies. In her mind, this treatment constitutes a marginalization of feminist scholarship (see Martin, 1994: 419). Such is not my intent. Rather, my reading of feminist scholarship on organizations is that it is a body of work that is attempting to point out the limitations of existing organizational forms and to document, in particular, the human costs associated with the operation of these structures as they are presently constituted. In short, this literature, up to the present time, has focused primarily on organizational pathologies.

instances" (1957: 200). He argues that structural devices established to ensure reliability and adequacy of performance—rules, discipline, a graded career—can "also lead to an over-concern with strict adherence to regulations which induces timidity, conservatism, and technicism" (1957: 201). Merton also argues that:

> Adherence to the rules, originally conceived as a means, becomes transformed into an end-in-itself; there occurs the familiar process of displacement of goals whereby an instrumental value becomes a terminal value. (1957: 199)

Other possible sources of goal displacement are described by natural system analysts, such as Selznick (1949) and Dalton (1959), who emphasize the commitments individuals develop to their tools, working arrangements, procedures, and work groups (see Chapter 3). Rational system analysts March and Simon (1958: 150–58) examine the manner in which means-ends chains designed to support rationality of decision making (see Chapters 2 and 4) also foster goal displacement, which they refer to as "sub-goal formation." They point out that cognitive processes operating at the individual, group, and organizational levels all contribute to such developments, supplementing the cathectic process emphasized by Merton, Selznick, and Dalton. Since goals are divided and factored among individuals and groups, goal displacement is encouraged by selective perception and attention processes among individuals, the selective content of in-group communication, and the selective exposure to information occasioned by the division of labor within the larger organization. Goals assigned to individuals and groups as means are viewed as ends in themselves. Scientists in research and development units emphasize creativity without regard to feasibility; manufacturing units emphasize producibility without attention to marketability; and so on.

If we take a somewhat larger view, however, we will see that goal displacement is not confined to organizations but is quite widespread in modern societies. Indeed, we would argue that it is synonymous with differentiation of the social structure and elaboration of the cultural system. As societies and cultures develop, activities formerly regarded as means become ends in themselves: eating becomes dining; buildings and garments needed for protection from the elements take on symbolic importance and give rise to architecture and fashion; sexual relations intended "by nature" as a means to the survival of the species become a terminal value, elaborated in romantic love and sex as play. The myriad occupations that emerge in modern societies may be viewed as instances of means transformed into ends: scientists pursue truth for its own sake; physicians prolong life as an ultimate value; and teachers devote their lives to socialization of the young. And we have noted, time and again, that the goals of organizations can be viewed as specialized functions or means from the perspective of the larger society.

Once we realize that goal displacement is the hallmark of any advanced civilization, it seems unfair and somewhat disingenuous to single out bureaucrats and accuse them of unique vices. They are involved in a process in which we all participate.

It appears to us that the basis for concern is not the displacement of ends by means but the continued pursuit of means that have somehow become disconnected from, or are at odds with, the ends they were designed to serve. In times of rapid change, we can easily imagine such dislocations becoming more common: primary goals change, but it is difficult to rapidly design and implement necessary adjustments down the chains of means-ends connections. As we have noted, organizations structured around functional roles and categories are likely to be dysfunctional when speed of adjustment is required. Efforts to modify organizational structures to enable them to process information more rapidly—augmenting the hierarchy and developing lateral connections (see Chapter 9)—may be interpreted as attempts to shorten and improve the consistency of these chains. Also, attempting to ensure that all participants are using their specialized knowledge and skills in the service of the same objectives—for example, meeting customer demands—is increasingly important for survival in a competitive environment (see Chapter 13).

To return to the narrower topic of rigidity or overconformity, results from two large surveys suggest that rather than increasing rigidity, participation in organizations encourages individual flexibility and openness to new ideas. The first study, conducted by Inkeles (1969), reports the results of a cross-national survey of 1,000 men from each of six developing societies. The study identified a series of interrelated attitudes labeled "modernity," which included such specific attitudes as openness to new experiences, assertion of increasing independence from the authority of traditional figures, abandonment of passivity and fatalism, interest in planning and punctuality, and interest in political issues and in keeping abreast of the news. The two most important influences on individuals' development of "modern" attitudes were school attendance and work in a factory. On the role of schools, Inkeles comments:

> These effects of the school, I believe, reside not mainly in its formal, explicit, self-conscious pedagogic activity, but rather are inherent in the school as an organization. . . . It teaches ways of orienting oneself toward others, and of conducting oneself, which could have important bearings on the performance of one's adult roles in the structure of modern society. (1969: 213)

And as for the factory experience:

> Just as we view the school as communicating lessons beyond reading and arithmetic, so we thought of the factory as training men in more than the minimal lessons of technology and skills necessary to industrial production. We conceived of the factory as an organization serving as a general school in attitudes, values, and ways of behaving which are more adaptive for life in a modern society. (1969: 213)

Inkeles found organizational participation to be a liberating, consciousness-expanding experience for individuals in developing societies.

Kohn (1971) used survey data from a sample of over 3,000 men employed in a variety of civilian occupations to examine the effect of bureaucratic employment on individuals' attitudes. Characteristics of employment settings were measured simply in terms of the number of levels of supervision and the size of the organization; individual attitudes were assessed in terms of three dimensions: (1) emphasis placed on conformity or respectability, (2) intolerance or rigid conformity and resistance to change, and (3) intellectual rigidity. The resulting associations were not particularly strong but were consistent. Kohn found that:

> Men who work in bureaucratic firms or organizations tend to value, not conformity, but self-direction. They are more open-minded, have more personally responsible standards of morality, and are more receptive to change than are men who work in nonbureaucratic organizations. They show greater flexibility in dealing both with perceptual and with ideological problems. (Kohn, 1971: 465)

Like Inkeles, Kohn emphasizes the liberalizing effects of organizational involvement on individual participants.

Whereas the general experience of participating in an organization may have salutary effects on individual characteristics, we know that organizations vary greatly in their cultures and control regimes. Not only do organizations differ one from another, but, as already described, to maximize their flexibility, a given organization may pursue polarized labor policies, confronting their participants with a spectrum of alternatives, the extremes of which may pose serious problems for individuals. At the bottom end, some participants must settle for low-wage, insecure, arms-length connections lacking due-process protections and benefits; while at the top end, participants may be offered a more protected and privileged place within an internal labor market, but one that demands obeisance to the prevailing cultural ideologies. Kunda (1992) provides a revealing portrait of these two extremes of employee involvement in his study of employment in a high-tech corporation located along Route 61 in Massachusetts. The upwardly mobile, mainstream employees are expected to put in long hours in the corporation and must constantly wrestle with the insatiable demands of a work culture whose values they have internalized: "one has to combat both the company's demands and one's own impulses, not easily distinguishable, to allocate more time to work and to the organizational self that is formed in its context" (p. 167).

> By choice they have entered into a contract that is more than economic, one that must contend with overt external claims on self-definition. Behavioral conformity and evidence of a vaguely defined "loyalty" are not enough. A demonstration of "incorporation" of the culture, of adoption of an organizationally defined and sanctioned self, is required. Consequently, the appearance of personal autonomy—a condition naturally (and ideologically) associated with the high status they seek—is threatened. Although it is not immediately apparent, the price of power is submission: not necessarily to demands concerning one's behavior, as is typical of low-status work, but to prescriptions regarding one's thoughts and feelings, supposedly the most cherished belonging of autonomous beings. (p. 214)

At the other end of the spectrum are the temporary workers who are so marginal, they are virtually nonpersons.

The worker's inner experience attracts no managerial attention: since the body is replaceable, leverage of the soul is deemed unnecessary. (p. 210)

. . . these people are in a position to be truly marginal—belonging neither to home nor host cultures, governed by few regulations, often invisible, yet an increasingly necessary feature of corporate life. In this sense, the "extra-culturals" are equivalent to the homeless, forced to depend on the kindness of strangers. (p. 225)

The upper limits to which conformity pressures can rise has been usefully (and frighteningly) explored by Milgram (1973; 1974) in a series of experiments. Milgram's design called for a three-person situation in which a scientist-teacher is assisted by a second person in attempting to teach a student a series of word pairs. The experiment is described as examining the effects of punishment on learning, and it is the task of the assistant to administer punishments—electrical shocks—to the student when he or she gives an incorrect answer. Intensity of the shocks administered increased systematically throughout the experiment, from a low of 15 volts to a maximum of 450 volts: the upper end of the scale on the generator is labeled "Extreme Intensity/Shock: Danger, Severe Shock," and the final position, "XXX." In reality, the assistant is the true subject of the experiment; both the teacher and the student are actors, and no real shocks are administered. The true purpose of the study is to determine how much (apparent) pain one individual will inflict on another when ordered to do so.

The results are unsettling, to say the least. Across a wide variety of types of subjects—from Yale undergraduates to adult professionals and blue-collar workers to individuals from many different countries—approximately 60 percent of the subjects conformed to the demands of the scientist and administered shocks at the highest levels possible to the student. The possibility that all these subjects were sadists was ruled out: left to their own devices, with no instruction from the scientist as to "appropriate" shock levels, the great majority of subjects administered very low, apparently painless shocks.

On examination, the experimental setting is a powerful one: it is what social psychologists would term a "strong situation." It has many features we associate with a Weberian bureaucracy: the scientist-teacher enjoys both the authority of office as well as apparent expertise. The setting—a university laboratory—exudes propriety and legitimacy. The goals are specific and the roles are clearly defined. The subject has "contracted with" the experimenter—each was paid a nominal sum for their participation—and hence has committed himself or herself to conform to the demands of the experimenter. Thus, although an apparently simple experiment, Milgram created in the laboratory a number of the features that are characteristic of totalitarian structures: a strong, unitary hierarchy, the absence of legitimate alternatives, an implicit agreement to perform whatever actions were required by the authority figure without questioning the purposes of those actions.

Milgram argues that such conditions induce individuals to focus attention on the requirements of their position rather than on the consequences of their behavior:

The person feels responsible to the authority directing him but feels no responsibility for the content of the actions that the authority prescribes. Morality does not disappear—it acquires a radically different focus: the subordinate person feels shame or pride depending on how adequately he has performed the actions called for by authority. (1973: 77)

Such situations strangle independence and induce "normal" individuals to behave in ways that, to external observers, are incomprehensible. The most extreme instance in modern history of the terrible consequences that may attend individuals' mindlessly following orders is surely represented by Hitler's death camps.

Kelman and Hamilton (1989) provide a useful analytic framework within which to interpret, and attempt to learn from, the disturbing results of Milgram's experiments. Compliance to authority differs from more conventional influence situations, as we have argued in Chapter 11, in that the focus shifts from the personal preferences of the subject to the obligations of the situation and the requirements of the role. Kelman and Hamilton suggest that, for authority to be accepted, the subject must accept as legitimate the system, the agent, and the specific demands of the agent. Although each of these elements is present in all authority situations, organizations vary in the relative emphasis placed on them; and individuals differ in the extent to which they are more oriented to "rules"—the specific demands made on them—"roles"—their definition of their job and relation to their superior— or "values"—their ideological commitment to the larger system.[2]

Variations in the conditions of the Milgram experiments can be used to illustrate these differing orientations. Results from the baseline conditions suggest that a good many individuals regarded the orders they were given as inappropriate even though they had no reason to question the legitimacy of the official or the larger organization. Thus, while 62 percent of the experimental subjects conformed, 38 percent refused to complete the experiment. The situation changed dramatically when subjects had information leading them to challenge the legitimacy of the experimenter or the system itself. Under one condition, two experimenters of apparently equal authority ran the experiment. At the point where the learner began to protest the shocks received, one experimenter called for a halt while the other insisted that the subject continue to administer shocks. In this condition, the level of conformity quickly fell to zero. In another experimental variation, the subject was joined by fellow "assistants," some of whom "chose" (by preinstruction) to disobey. Under these conditions, only 10 percent of the subjects continued to obey to the end.

It appears obvious that structural factors such as divided authority or the presence of others who challenge authority dramatically alters the power of a legitimate hierarchy. The main impact appears to be in "breaking the cognitive frame" imposed on the subordinate. The situation is redefined from being one in which the focus is on one's duty as determined by existing

---

[2]Each of these orientations is associated with a different process supporting conformity. The processes that support rule orientation give rise to compliance behaviors; those that support role orientation, to identification with the superior; and processes that link individuals to systemic values, to internalization behaviors (see Kelman and Hamilton, 1989: 103–22).

role relations to one's responsibility for actions viewed in a wider context (or in terms of varying value criteria).

The logic and incentives of most organizational hierarchies reinforce and reward an upward orientation. But it is possible to counter these pressures with others (for example, from external reference groups) and to build in mechanisms that will encourage independent reflection and more responsible action. These include flatter hierarchies, participative decision making, multiple channels permitting upward communications, and special incentives to encourage "whistle-blowing" when inappropriate behaviour is observed. Clearly, making more rather than less information available to all participants will encourage subordinates to develop independent views. Other structural supports include the creation of specialized roles (for example, ombudspersons; "devil's advocates" who are expected to challenge the consensus) and specially defined occasions (for example, "brainstorming" sessions; Q-circle meetings) during which opinions may be aired and problems addressed under more egalitarian norms.

The larger message is that situational factors account for much of the variance in conformity-independence (see Nisbett and Ross, 1980). If we are concerned about the extent to which individuals are overly compliant, we need to change the structures within which they are embedded and the cultural definitions that constrain their self-conceptions.

PROBLEMS FOR PUBLICS

Unresponsiveness

All organizations must provide benefits to external publics—customers, clients, citizens—as a condition for their continued existence. The contributions required from these publics vary according to the nature of the organization but may involve direct payments for products or services received, indirect support in the form of taxes, and normative support in the form of goodwill and legitimacy. A concern with organizational responsiveness to the demands of external publics is most often raised in connection with public organizations, since the public is expected to be the primary beneficiary of their activities. However, problems can also develop in the relations between publics and organizations in the private sector. We will examine both situations.

Responsiveness of public sector organizations. Weber, in company with many other past and present political analysts, believed that the most serious challenge facing contemporary societies was to maintain control over the expanding state bureaucracies. Numerous observers before Weber, including Mill, Bagehot, Le Play, and Mosca, noted the growth in numbers and power of government officials, but Weber's analyses provide the most complete and systematic conceptualization of this major change in governmental systems (see Albrow, 1970). Unlike some of the previous critics, Weber insisted that the primary problem with the growth of bureaucracy was not that of inefficiency or mismanagement. Indeed, Weber cogently argued that in comparison with earlier administrative forms, the bureaucratic structures were highly efficient and reliable (see Chapter 2). But for Weber, these characteristics—the administrative virtues—also constituted bureaucracies' most serious threat.[3] Accompanying increased bureaucratization was the strong likelihood of growth in the power of public officials. Weber argued:

> Under normal conditions, the power position of a fully developed bureaucracy is always overpowering. The "political master" finds himself in the position of the "dilettante" who stands opposite the "expert," facing the trained official who stands within the management of administration. This holds whether the "master" whom the bureaucracy serves is a "people" . . . or a parliament. . . . It holds whether the master is an aristocratic, collegiate body, legally or actually based on self-recruitment, or whether he is a popularly elected president, a hereditary and "absolute" or a "constitutional" monarch. (1946 trans.: 232–33)

Weber's explanation for this development was quite straightforward: "More and more the specialized knowledge of the expert became the foundation for the power position of the officeholder" (1946 trans.: 235). Recall in this connection Weber's description of the transition from patrimonial to bureaucratic administrative forms (see Chapter 2). As a ruler's territory expanded, it would increasingly become necessary to decentralize operations and delegate authority to members of the administrative staff. The division of labor among the staff members becomes more fixed; specialized competence of officers increases, and, at the same time, the ruler's ability to oversee each operation is reduced. Relative to the ruler, each staff member becomes more knowledgeable in each specific area of operation. The staff also becomes more aware of itself as a distinct social group with common interests. We have, in brief, a classic instance of a shift in power-dependence relations: each subordinate is individually less powerful than the ruler, but collectively the subordinates have become more powerful, and by acting in concert they can impose conditions on the ruler's exercise of power (see Chapter 11). These constraints on the ruler's power, which developed slowly and haltingly over long periods, include such bureaucratic "safeguards" as civil service commissions and elaborate codes of conduct. Rosenberg has described the effects of these developments in his analysis of the evolution of the Prussian state:

> The raising of standardized prerequisites for admission had a profound effect upon the bureaucracy as a social elite and as a political group. Whatever the motives and ostensible objectives of the ministerial sponsors of the reformed merit system, the new service tests turned out to be, in the hands of the bureaucratic nobility, a wonderful device for consolidating its control over personnel recruitment and for gaining greater freedom from royal molestations in this crucial area. (1958: 180)

---

[3]Weber was not alone in admitting the likely efficiency of the bureaucracy but expressing reservations about the use of this instrument. Thus, in one of his celebrated essays on bureaucracy, the poet Ezra Pound responds to the claim that bureaucrats are active and attentive to their duty by noting that "the idea of activity as a merit is, when applied to bureaucrats, as deadly as the idea of activity among tuberculous bacillae" (1973: 219).

The increasing dependence of the dilettante on the expert goes a long way toward accounting for the shift of power "down" from titular rulers to the nominal subordinates—the administrative officials.[4]

In the case of democratic systems, where power is expected to reside in the hands of the governed, other factors operate to shift power "up" from the people to administrative elites. The most influential analysis of these processes is that provided by Michels (1949 trans.). Rather than focusing exclusively on state bureaucracies, Michels insists that processes that withdraw power from the people and place it in the hands of bureaucrats can be studied equally well in organizations such as political parties that are expected to serve the interests of their rank and file.[5] Michels's (1949 trans.) major work is based on a case study of the Social Democratic party in pre–World War I Germany (see Chapter 3). His famous aphorism "Who says organization, says oligarchy" summarizes his central argument that oligarchic tendencies to shift power from the majority and place it in the hands of an elite minority are built into the very structure of organization. They are an unintended consequence of organization. He points to the division of functions, which creates specialized knowledge; to the hierarchy of offices, which fosters and legitimates the uneven distribution of information and decision-making privileges; and to the structure of incentives, which encourages officials to remain in office but discourages rank-and-file members from involvement in the day-to-day business of the party. Michels's theoretical formulation emphasizes the internal factors giving rise to oligarchical processes; his descriptive account of the development of the Social Democratic party, however, places equal importance on the organization's relation with its environment. Throughout the period from 1890 to 1910, this party, the first of the strong working-class parties, was fighting for its existence. Leaders emphasized the need to present a unified front; internal disagreement and dissent were viewed as a luxury to be forgone until the party came to power; and leaders were reluctant to engage in any activities that weakened the strength of the organization in relation to its external environment.

Michels thus poses the following dilemma: a party or a union must build a strong organization and ensure its survival to achieve its objectives, yet preoccupation with such organizational problems leads to the surrender of these very objectives. "Thus, from a means, organization becomes an end" (1949 trans.: 390). Experience since Michels's time tends to confirm his thesis. Most unions, most professional associations and other types of voluntary associations, and most political parties exhibit oligarchical leadership structures; the democratic machinery established to prevent such arrangements functions primarily as a feeble device allowing rank and file participants to

---

[4]Note that the same arguments were used in Chapter 11 to account for the increasing shift of power in individual organizations—both governmental and nongovernmental—from the owners and general managers to the technical experts and specialist managers. This process results, as noted, in increases in the size of the dominant coalition within organizations.

[5]Lipset (1960: 357) refers to such organizations as private governments. Blau and I (Blau and Scott, 1962: 45) refer to them as mutual benefit associations. They include such organizations as political parties, unions, and professional associations. Since they are formed to serve the interests of their members, most such organizations develop ideologies and procedures that support the participation of the majority in setting organizational goals.

rubber-stamp executive decisions and "elect" slates of nominees running in uncontested elections (see Editors of the Yale Law Journal, 1954; Wilson, 1973). Even the well-known study by Lipset, Trow, and Coleman (1956) of a "deviant case," a democratically run union, suggests that although such processes are not inevitable, the conditions—both internal and external—causing the drift of power from the rank and file to the upper levels of the organization are sufficiently widespread to vindicate Michels's pessimistic generalization.

The focus of the present discussion, however, is on responsiveness: the degree to which administrative and political bodies reflect the interests of those whom they are presumed to serve. Michels insists that the leaders of the German Social Democratic party forsook the values and interests of its membership, betraying socialist values and working-class interests for bourgeois values and selfish interests. Although it is true that the party's goals shifted over time, it is not obvious that this process was resisted by the members or was contrary to their interests. Thus, Coser (1951) has argued that the shift to the right in the party's program may not have resulted primarily from the bureaucratic conservatism of the leaders but from the rapid improvement in the social and economic situation of the working class during this period. Not only the party administrators but also the party members were becoming more conservative.

Shifting attention from processes at work at the top of the bureaucracy that may insulate bureaucrats from responding appropriately to political controls, let us turn to consider the "street level" where public officials relate to citizens, clients, and, increasingly, customers. First, it is important to recognize that there exist many different types of public agencies, and they exhibit, correspondingly, a wide variety of relations to their publics. Wilson (1989) proposes a simple but useful typology of public agencies based on the nature and organization of interests that they confront. A *client* agency faces one dominant client group that favors the agency's goals; for example, the Civil Aeronautics Board as it relates to constituents in the civil aviation industry. An *entrepreneurial* agency deals with a single interest on which it imposes costs; for example, the National Highway Traffic Safety Administration. An *interest-group* agency must deal with two well-organized and contending interests, for example, the National Labor Relations Board. A fourth type, the *majoritarian* agency, faces a collection of scattered and varied interests. Obviously, how "responsive" these agencies are judged to be will vary not only over time but also depending on which interests are privileged. Analysis of large numbers of public agencies suggests that many are subject to "capture" by one or another special interest (see Wilson, 1980).

An overly cozy relation between political bureaus and private interests has already been discussed in a different context. In Chapter 8, considerable attention was devoted to describing bridging strategies as an important means of increasing the security of organizations in their task environments. As noted, the increasing scale and scope of governmental activity encourages organizations of all types to view public agencies as salient features of their environments and as targets of co-optation. Government officials, for their part, are vulnerable to influences from such groups for many reasons: they must relate to these organized interests on a regular basis, and they may become dependent on them for information, cooperation, political support, and even future employment (see Heclo, 1977; Wilson, 1989). Thus, many contemporary governmental agencies appear to have insufficient social insulation from specific sources of power in their environment; they are often unresponsive to the public interest because they are overly responsive to the interests of special publics.

Some of the recent reforms aimed at "reinventing" government specifically target increased responsiveness to client groups. Because in most agencies officials are not dependent on client services as a source of revenue, special measures are required to focus attention on client reactions. Among the techniques that agencies have employed are the following: customer surveys, community surveys, supervisory contact with selected customers, the creation of customer councils and focus groups, use of inspectors and ombudsmen, complaint tracking systems, and quality guarantees (for example, a training program guarantees the qualifications of their graduates to employers) (see Osborne and Gaebler, 1992; Gore, 1993). Such approaches can be of use to service bureaucracies, particularly when they are not employed simply to provide feedback to frontline workers but utilized to rethink the mission of the agency, redesign work, work structures, and incentive and control systems. But public organizations differ in a number of important ways from private firms, and techniques like TQM invented in the private sector must be carefully applied in the public arena. Part of that care requires that we think clearly about how to identify the "customer" in this setting.

Responsiveness of private sector organizations.   Recent analysts are increasingly concerned with the responsiveness of private organizations to the interests of their clients and the larger public. In an important and influential essay, *Exit, Voice, and Loyalty,* Hirschman (1970) distinguishes between two general options open to disgruntled publics wishing to express dissatisfaction with the types and quality of services received. The first, *exit,* involves the withdrawal of patronage. Dissatisfied customers simply withdraw from a relation with one firm and seek another that is expected to serve their interests more adequately. Exit is the typical economic response; it is typified in the relations between private firms and their customers and presumes the existence of alternatives. The second option, *voice,* is broadly defined as "any attempt at all to change, rather than to escape from, an objectionable state of affairs" (Hirschman, 1970: 30). Voice is the typical political option—expressed through elections, petitions, complaints, protests, and riots—because it is more likely to be exercised in situations in which a monopoly exists. Voice is a more costly option than exit, demanding at a minimum the investment of time and energy; in extreme cases, its exercise can entail personal risk and sacrifice.

Hirschman argues that private firms can greatly benefit from publics who take the trouble to exercise the option of voice rather than exit. He notes that the quality of services provided by firms can deteriorate when alternative suppliers are available to some, since the more discerning customers withdraw their business, leaving those who are less quality-conscious—or who have no alternatives—to endure substandard service. Such problems are especially characteristic of "lazy monopolies," such as subsidized railroads or public educational systems. Hirschman argues that publics would benefit from the use of mixed options. Incentives need to be provided to encourage quality-conscious customers to exercise voice before resorting to exit—this is one of the major functions of *loyalty*.

A major theme of recent, popular business literature is the central, and often overlooked, importance of the customer. Levitt (1986: xxii) asserts that: "The purpose of a business is to get and keep a customer." Peters and Waterman (1982) emphasize that "excellent" companies are those who stay "close to the customer." While such advice begs the question as to which of many possible types of customers a particular business should get, keep, and stay close to, it does contain an important truth that some contemporary organizations and executives seem to have forgotten. Organizations that take advantage of customer needs, ideas, and reactions enjoy important advantages in a competitive marketplace. If closely attended to, discerning customers can provide invaluable feedback on existing products and services as well as ideas for future developments. For market-based organizations, the customer is the ultimate arbiter of utility and quality. Quality enhancement approaches to improving organizational effectiveness emphasize the importance of customer-driven criteria. We consider these approaches in Chapter 13.

But many private organizations are not well attuned to market signals. Meyer and Zucker (1989) observe that older organizations are more likely to survive than newer organizations, in spite of the fact that "organizational performance does not improve with age." This observation once again underlines the fact that economic interests are not the only factors affecting human behavior, as we have tried to emphasize, but agency theorists are correct to underline the importance of the appropriate structuring of incentives. Managers often lack direct incentives that closely align their own interests with performance objectives. There is, for example, little correlation between executive compensation and company performance (see Crystal, 1991). They may also lack the information or controls necessary to effectively pursue these objectives. For their part, owners are traditionally assumed to be attentive to the performance and long-range development of their company, but the current dispersion and rapid turnover of stock ownership that is characteristic of publicly traded U.S. and British corporations militates against effective oversight by the ownership group as a whole. The corporate board, which is expected to act as agent to protect owners' interests, is often not effective, typically meeting only a few days a year and being dependent on the CEO and other top managers for much of their information. Board acquiescence to the recent demands of managers to embrace poison pill defenses against hostile takeovers gives priority to the interests of managers over those of stockholders (see Coffee, Lowenstein, and Rose-Ackerman, 1988; Davis, 1990). It is no simple matter to design structures in such a manner that all participants will be motivated to serve customer/client interests.

Relentlessness

A final concern associated with the functioning of organizations in relation to publics is the relentlessness of their behavior. This problem, though neglected by most critics and analysts, is in our view the most serious one raised by the existence of organizations. It consists not in a malfunction of the organization but in the pathological aspects of "normal" organizational activities.

Coleman's (1974) analysis is most compelling. As noted earlier (see Chapter 7), Coleman distinguishes between natural persons, like you and me, and corporate actors—organizations. Organizations are composed not of persons but of positions, and persons are not completely contained within organizations. Persons contribute to and invest in organizations' specific resources over which they lose full control. (The corporate actor is empowered to make decisions concerning the use of the resources available to it, and except in the rare and debilitating case in which an individual retains veto power over the use of his or her resources, individuals must be willing to give up a measure of control over their resources as the price for collective action.) With the creation of a corporate actor, a new set of interests comes into existence.

From the perspective of the natural person, organizations are agencies for achieving desired objectives. However, from the point of view of the corporate actor, individuals are agents hired to pursue the goals of the collective actor. Individual actors are means for attaining corporate ends. Coleman clearly spells out the implications of this view:

> It is the corporate actors, the organizations that draw their power from persons and employ that power to corporate ends, that are the primary actors in the social structure of modern society.
>
> What does this mean in practice? It means a peculiar bias in the direction that social and economic activities take. It means that among the variety of interests that men have, those interests that have been successfully collected to create corporate actors are the interests that dominate society. (1974: 49)

Nonorganized interests of persons are neglected in a society dominated by corporate actors. Further, corporate interests differ from those of natural persons in being more narrow, more intense, more refined, and more single-minded.

> Decisions about the employment of resources are more and more removed from the multiplicity of dampening and modifying interests of which a real person is composed—more and more the resultant of a balance of narrow intense interests of which corporate actors are composed. (1974: 29)

Individual administrators are constrained by organizational goals and the definitions of their roles. They are expected to act as agents of the organization and as stewards of its resources. University trustees cannot in good conscience use the resources of their institution to relieve poverty or to build low-cost housing for members of the surrounding community. Pentagon officials are expected to build our armaments and strengthen our defenses regardless of the deleterious effects of such activities on the national economy or on the long-range prospects for survival of the human race. Organizations do not speak with one voice, as we have seen, and they are frequently loosely coupled coalitions of interests, but compared with natural persons, they are relatively specialized in their purposes and organized so as to pursue them unreservedly.

Ashby, the noted general system theorist, has pointed out that all "synthetic" organisms, including organizations, exhibit this tendency toward specialization of a sort likely to be dysfunctional for those who create them:

> There is no difficulty, in principle, in developing synthetic organisms as complex, and as intelligent as we please. But we must notice two fundamental qualifications: first, their intelligence will be an adaptation to, and a specialization toward, their first particular environment, with no implication of validity for any other environment such as ours; and secondly, their intelligence will be directed toward keeping their own essential variables within limits. They will be fundamentally selfish. (1968: 116)

Given the expectation that organizations will take a relatively narrow band of interests and pursue them unremittingly, our reluctance to enshrine organizations as the social and moral centers of the new society may seem more intelligible. This reluctance is shared. For example, Hart and W. G. Scott express alarm at the growing acceptance of a new set of values they label "the organizational imperative," which presumes that "whatever is good for man can only be achieved through modern organization" and "therefore, all behavior must enhance the health of such modern organizations" (1975: 261; see also Scott and Hart, 1979).

In a more extreme form, corporate pressures may not only cause participants to pursue a limited set of goals without regard to their effect on other values; they may also induce participants to engage in actions that are illegal or immoral. Corporate crime is a matter of growing concern. And much of the deviant behavior identified is encouraged by such "normal" organizational conditions as limitations on information, circumscribed responsibilities, and strong performance pressures (see Clinard and Yeager, 1980; Ermann and Lundman, 1982; Greenberg and Scott, 1996).

In our introduction to Part Four, we commented that all of the pathologies of organizations to be identified relate in some manner to the problem of power. This statement applies to the current topic. Coleman (1974) points out that in a social structure containing both natural persons and corporate actors, it is possible for one natural person to lose power without a corresponding gain on the part of another natural person. Persons can lose power to corporate actors. Coleman argues that this loss or transfer is currently going on at a rapid rate, a situation giving rise to a widespread feeling of powerlessness among individuals. And Coleman points out that as a result of this transfer:

> The outcome of events is only partly determined by the interests of the natural persons, giving a society that functions less than fully in the interests of the persons who make it up. (1974: 39)

This seems to us to represent the ultimate form of alienation. In Marx's simpler world, power stripped from one person (the worker) belonged to another (the capitalist). In today's more complex world, power lost by one person may not be gained by any similar person but absorbed by a corporate actor and employed in pursuit of its specialized purposes.

SUMMARY

Pathologies in the operation of contemporary organizations afflict both individual participants and external publics. We emphasize those that are based on the abuse of power.

Problems affecting individual participants include alienation, inequity, and overconformity. Alienation can be defined either subjectively as a sense of powerlessness and self-estrangement or objectively as a condition under which workers lose control over the products of their labor or the value created by it. Most empirical studies are based on the subjective conception and reveal that the level of alienation among workers in this country is not high but that it varies greatly by the type of occupation, and that similar objective positions are experienced and reacted to differently by individuals. We take exception to the proposal that work organizations should function as the primary center of social and moral integration for individuals.

Organizational advocates, especially rational system theorists, assert that they operate in a relatively universalistic fashion, providing equal (or improved) opportunity to qualified participants irrespective of race, gender, or other ascribed attributes. The evidence suggests otherwise. Minority groups, such as African Americans, and women do not experience equal treatment or equal returns to their investments in education and skills. Feminist theorists, in particular, assert that most organizations are severely biased in favor of white, male virtues and values.

Organizational participants are frequently castigated for ritualism in the sense that they convert means into ends. Such transformations are, however, widespread throughout highly differentiated societies and do not become problematic unless there is a disjunction between means and ends. Studies reveal that organizational participation can be a source of flexibility and liberation as well as of timidity and overconformity. Job insecurity and uncertainty appear to be powerful factors governing conformity.

The responsiveness of organizations to the needs of external publics is of concern for all types of organizations, but especially those in which the public is designated as the prime beneficiary. The central problem with the growth of public organizations is that of maintaining their responsiveness to public interests. Responsiveness may be curtailed by the specialization and increasing expertise of administrative officials, the developing class interests of the administrative cadre, the uneven distribution of information and incentives for participation, and pressures for unity in the face of external threats. It is suggested that some of the difficulties that beset public organizations are also created by their overresponsiveness to public interests—the interests of special publics.

Private sector organizations are expected to be responsive to economic signals—for example, the withdrawal of business by customers searching for better quality or lower prices. However, the dispersed structure of ownership and the controls and incentives for managers do not always encourage responsiveness to customer concerns. Recent reforms have attempted to redress some of these problems by refocusing attention on the interests of clients and customers.

Even when organizations perform effectively and efficiently, they may nevertheless cause difficulties for the larger society because of their tendency to embody and mobilize support for relatively narrow goals. Individual interests that happen to coincide with organizational domains are well served; those that do not are liable to be seriously neglected. Our interests as individuals may be alienated not only by the actions of powerful others who strip us of our rights and resources but also by the normal functioning of impersonal organizations to whom we bequeath our resources and over which we lose control.

Organizational Effectiveness

There is no such thing as "good organization" in any absolute sense. Always it is relative; and an organization that is good in one context or under one criterion may be bad under another.

W. Ross Ashby (1968)

In recent years organizational analysts have become increasingly interested in the topic of organizational effectiveness. During the 1950s and early 1960s, the topic was generally neglected, in part because of the belief that considerations of effectiveness represented only an applied or practical, not a theoretical, concern. Gradually, however, analysts began to perceive that there could be as much theoretical justification in examining the consequences of varying structural arrangements as in probing their determinants. And an important boost to the topic occurred when contingency theorists began to argue that some types of structures were better suited than others to certain tasks or environments. The question was raised, Better suited in what sense? and the answer given was often couched in terms of effectiveness. In this sense, effectiveness is argued by some theorists to be a determinant as well as a consequence of organizational structure.

In addition to theoretical justifications, the topic of effectiveness has become highly salient in recent years because of the increased intensity of global competition. Attention to enhanced productivity—one important aspect of effectiveness—has, for many market-oriented firms, become critical to survival.

The topic of organizational effectiveness is eschewed by some analysts on the ground that it necessarily deals with values and preferences that cannot be determined objectively. Such criticisms, however, apply not to the general topic but only to certain formulations of it. We will not seek to determine, for example, whether a given organization is or is not effective in some general sense. Rather, we shall attempt to learn what types of criteria of effectiveness are suggested by what constituencies and what types of indicators of effectiveness are proposed with what implications for organizational assessment. In sum, as was the case in our discussions of such value-loaded topics as decision making, goal setting, and power, we will attempt to remain descriptive and analytic in our approach rather than normative and prescriptive. (We confess that some of our comments in the previous chapter on pathologies were value-laden and prescriptive.)

Three major questions are addressed in the following discussion: What are the major criteria that have been proposed to define effectiveness? What are the approaches to assessing effectiveness? and What types of explanations are given to account for differences in effectiveness? As we will see, each of these topics is affected by the type of organization examined and, in particular, by whether the organization is or is not responsive to market mechanisms.

DETERMINING CRITERIA OF EFFECTIVENESS

To the novice, defining and determining the effectiveness of an organization must seem a relatively straightforward affair: to inquire into effectiveness is to ask how well an organization is doing, relative to some set of standards. This is not wrong, but by this time, we experts in organizational analysis know that the pursuit of this simple question will lead us into some complex and controversial issues. There are many possible bases for generating criteria of effectiveness, and as we would expect, many different constituencies have an interest in the effectiveness of any organization and seek to propose criteria that reflect this interest.

Multiple Criteria

Steers (1977), Campbell (1977), and Cameron and Whetten (1983) as well as others have assembled lengthy lists of criteria that have been used by one or more analysts in measuring effectiveness. Campbell, for example, lists thirty different criteria, ranging from productivity and profits to growth, turnover, stability, and cohesion. In attempting to understand why so many and such varied criteria of effectiveness have been proposed, we do not need to search very far beyond the thesis of this volume; quite diverse conceptions of organizations are held by various analysts, and associated with each of these conceptions will be a somewhat distinctive set of criteria for evaluating the effectiveness of organizations. Although several schemata for differentiating among these conceptions have been proposed, we argue that our old friends—the rational, natural, and open system perspectives—account for much of the variance in measures of effectiveness (Scott, 1977).

Under a rational system model, since organizations are viewed as instruments for the attainment of goals (see Chapter 2), the criteria emphasized focus on the number and quality of outputs and the economies realized in transforming inputs into outputs. General criteria include measures of total output and of quality, productivity, and efficiency. More so than for the other two models, measures of effectiveness from a rational system perspective take the specific goals of the organization as the basis for generating effectiveness criteria. Thus, automobile companies focus on how many cars are manufactured during a given period in absolute numbers or in relation to cost measures; employment bureaus access how many clients are placed in positions, perhaps in relation to the number of persons processed.[1]

As we know, the natural system model views organizations as collectivities that are capable of achieving specified goals but are engaged in other activities required to maintain themselves as a social unit. Thus, natural system analysts insist on adding a set of support goals to the output goals emphasized by the rational system model. Further, these support goals are expected to dominate output goals if the two do not coincide: organizations are governed by the overriding goal of survival (see Chapter 3). The criteria generated by this conception include measures of participant satisfaction and morale (indicators of whether the organization's inducements are sufficient to evoke contributions from participants adequate to ensure survival), the interpersonal skills of managers, and survival itself.

The open system perspective views organizations as being highly interdependent with their environments and engaged in system-elaborating as well as system-maintaining activities. Information acquisition and processing are viewed as especially critical, since an organization's long term well-being is dependent on its ability to detect and respond to subtle changes in its environment (see Chapter 4). Yuchtman and Seashore specify one criterion that they argue is most appropriate for assessing the effectiveness of organizations from the open system perspective: "bargaining position, as reflected in the ability of the organization, in either absolute or relative terms, to exploit its environment in the acquisition of scarce and valued resources" (1967: 898). Criteria such as profitability, which may be viewed as the excess of returns over expenditures, are also emphasized by open system analysts. And a great many theorists stress the importance of adaptability and flexibility as criteria of effectiveness. Weick (1977) emphasizes these dimensions when he insists that effective organizations are characterized by a diversity of linguistic forms, techniques for breaking out of normal cognitive and normative constraints, means of simultaneously crediting and discrediting information received, and structural units that are loosely articulated so as to maximize sensitivity to the environment and diversity of response.[2]

Analysts' diverse conceptions of organizations are not the only source of variation in effectiveness criteria. Other important bases of diversity include time perspective and level of analysis. Time considerations enter into the generation and application of effectiveness criteria in two senses. First, the criteria employed may vary depending on whether a relatively shorter or longer

---

[1]Because of its focus on goals, the rational system is virtually synonymous with the "goals model" described by Etzioni (1960). Several critics have pointed out that because of the emphasis placed by the rational system or goals model on the specific types of goals pursued, these models do not provide an adequate basis for comparing the effectiveness of differing types of organizations (see Yuchtman and Seashore, 1967).

[2]In his inimitable fashion, Weick summarizes his criteria as follows: "Specifically, I would suggest that the effective organization is (1) garrulous, (2) clumsy, (3) superstitious, (4) hypocritical, (5) monstrous, (6) octopoid, (7) wandering, and (8) grouchy" (1977: 193–94).

time frame is adopted. As noted, organizations may focus attention on short-range financial indicators to the neglect of other more enduring measures of performance. How critical a time frame is may depend on how rapidly the environment is changing. Hannan and Freeman (1977: 116), working from an ecological perspective, point out that highly specialized organizations well adapted to their environment may outperform generalist organizations at a given point in time, but may fare much less well over a longer period to the extent that the environment has changed. Second, organizations are necessarily at different stages of their life cycles, and criteria appropriate for assessing effectiveness at one stage may be less so for another. As Seashore has noted, "the meaning of growth for the health, survival, and overall effectiveness of the organization was very different at different stages of the organizational life cycle" (1962).

We have stressed the importance of level of analysis throughout this volume, and it is a critical factor in accounting for variations in effectiveness criteria. Our conclusions concerning the relative effectiveness of organizations will vary greatly depending on whether we emphasize their impact on individual participants, on the organization itself, or on broader, external systems. Cummings argues for the first, social psychological–level criterion for assessing organizational effectiveness. He proposes that:

> An effective organization is one in which the greatest percentage of participants perceive themselves as free to use the organization and its subsystems as instruments for their own ends. (Cummings, 1977: 60)

Most analysts take the organization itself as the appropriate level of analysis for assessing effectiveness. Yuchtman and Seashore (1967: 896) explicitly adopt this posture, suggesting that a relevant view of effectiveness answers the question How well is the organization doing for itself? Still other investigators adopt a more ecological framework and propose that organizations should be evaluated in terms of their contributions to other, more general systems. For example, a police department may be evaluated in terms of the contributions it makes to community peace and safety.

Variations in theoretical perspectives on organizations, in time horizons and developmental stage, and in level of analysis—these help to account for the diversity of criteria proposed in analyzing effectiveness. Yet another source of diversity is to be found in the varying sets of participants and constituents associated with organizations (see also, Zammuto, 1982).

Participants, Constituents, and Criteria

Whether organizations are viewed as rational, natural, or open systems, our conceptions of their goals, participants, and constituencies have become progressively more complex. We have been instructed by Simon to view even "simple" output goals as complex and multifaceted (see Chapters 2 and 11), and we have learned from Etzioni and Perrow to add support or maintenance goals to output goals (see Chapter 3). This more complex conception of goals is reinforced by viewing organizations as collections of subgroups of participants who possess various social characteristics, are in different social locations, and exhibit divergent views and interests regarding what the organization is and what it should be doing (see Chapters 4 and 11). This conception of the organization as a political system can be expanded to include outside constituencies who seek to impose their goals on the organization.

It is important to emphasize that when we speak of goals in relation to ascertaining the effectiveness of organizations, we are focusing on the use of goals to supply evaluation criteria. As argued in Chapter 11, goals are used to evaluate organizational activities as well as to motivate and direct them. In a rational world, we would expect the criteria that are developed to direct organizational activities to be the same as those employed to evaluate them, but, as we have emphasized, events in organizations are not always as rational and tightly coupled as some theorists would have us believe. Instead, we must be prepared to observe different criteria employed by those who assign tasks and those who evaluate performance (see Dornbusch and Scott, 1975). Discrepancies are more likely to occur when the control system becomes differentiated and these functions are assigned to different actors, but they can occur when the same persons or groups perform both directing and evaluating activities. An oft-cited problem in organizations develops when vague and broad criteria are used to direct task activities but very explicit criteria are employed to evaluate them, with the consequence that evaluation criteria deflect attention and effort from the original stated objectives to a different or narrower set of goals embodied in the evaluation system. Evaluation criteria often focus on the more easily measured task attributes and ignore others less readily assessed. Thus, social workers may be directed by their supervisors to provide therapeutic casework services but be evaluated primarily on the basis of the number and timeliness of their visits to clients and the correctness of their calculation of budgets (see Scott, 1969). Such discrepancies are likely to result in a displacement of goals as participants come to realize what criteria are used to determine evaluations and to disperse rewards (see Kerr, 1975).

Varying goals—viewed both as directive and as evaluative criteria—will be held by different participant groups and constituencies in organizations. The managers of organizations may not speak with one voice but with many, since they may be composed of a shifting coalition of interests. Similarly, top managers' goals for directing and evaluating activities may not coincide with or be completely reflected in the criteria used by middle-level personnel such as supervisors or technical specialists. Performers vary in the extent to which their own conceptions of their work coincide with those of their superiors, and also in their capacity to enforce their preferences. Finally, many "external" constituencies, often referred to as *stakeholders*—investors, clients, suppliers and buyers, regulators, community leaders, and news media—have genuine interests in the functioning of an organization and may be expected to attempt to advocate and, if possible, impose their own effectiveness criteria on the organization. In general, the number of persons and groups who propose criteria for evaluating the performance of an organization will be much larger than the number who can legitimately direct its activities. "A cat may look at a king," and a reporter for the hometown newspaper may scrutinize the performance of the town's leading industry.

According to this conception of organizations, we would expect little commonality in the criteria employed by the various parties who assess organizational effectiveness. This expectation is shared by Friedlander and Pickle, who impute appropriate interests to such groups as owners, employees, creditors, suppliers, customers, governmental regulators, and the host community. Their data on a sample of small business organizations show that performance assessed by these varying criteria results in a pattern of low and often negative correlation coefficients: to do well on a criterion preferred by one constituency is to do poorly on a criterion favored by another. Friedlander and Pickle conclude that "organizations find it difficult to fulfill simultaneously the variety of demands made upon them" (1968: 302–3).

Another consideration complicating the examination of effectiveness is the recent challenges to the assumption that organizations necessarily exhibit a unified or consistent set of performances. The political models just reviewed allow for divergence and conflict of interests among participants but presume their resolution through negotiation and power processes. In the end, the organization is presumed to pursue a single program. Alternative models suggest the utility of viewing some organizations as "organized anarchies" or as loosely coupled systems containing subunits that exhibit a high degree of autonomy and are capable of pursuing inconsistent objectives (see Chapter 11). This conception admits the possibility that, with respect to any specific criterion of effectiveness, an organization can be both effective and ineffective depending on what components are being evaluated!

Given the wide variety of participants, groups, and constituencies that can attempt to set criteria for organizational effectiveness, what generalizations, if any, can be suggested to guide investigations in this area? We offer three predictions. First, the criteria proposed by each group will be self-interested ones. Customers will desire higher quality at lower costs, suppliers will wish to sell more dearly and wholesalers to buy more cheaply, workers will prefer higher wages and greater fringe benefits, and managers will seek higher profits and lower costs. We should not look for heroes or villains but for parties with varying interests. And all parties will evaluate the performance of the organization in terms of criteria that benefit themselves. Second, although no criteria are disinterested—each benefits some groups more than others—all will be stated so as to appear universalistic and objective. This generalization receives support from Pfeffer and Salancik's (1974) study of the allocation of resources among university departments. They report that the stronger departments succeed in budget allocation contests not by imposing particularistic criteria on decisions but by ensuring that the universalistic criteria selected favor their own position. For example, strong departments that have larger graduate-student enrollments will favor this criterion in allocating resources while departments with larger numbers of undergraduate majors will seek to impose this criterion as a distribution rule. Third, given multiple sets of actors pursuing their own interests and a situation of scarce resources, we would expect little commonality or convergence and some conflicts in the criteria employed by the various parties to assess organizational effectiveness, a prediction supported by the study conducted by Friedlander and Pickle (1968).

The existence of diverse constituencies with multiple interests provides an explanation for the paradox that older organizations are less likely to fail even though performance does not improve with age, according to Meyer and Zucker (1989). They argue that "permanently failing organizations"—organizations that fail to be productive or profitable in the pursuit of their official goals—often continue to survive because their existence serves varied interests. A diverse array of stakeholders is attached to an organization—no doubt, the older the organization, the larger and more diverse the accumulated interests. Meyer and Zucker assert that "Most people are more concerned with maintaining existing organizations than with maximizing organizational performance" (p. 23). Note, however, that this assertion accepts a rational system view of performance: it privileges the interests of those who define the official objectives as against others who contribute to and benefit from the continued existence of the organization.

One final constituency remains to be considered. Researchers who attempt to assess the effectiveness of organizations are not immune to these political processes. Which, and whose, criteria we choose to emphasize in our studies of organizations will depend on our own interests in undertaking the study. We must be willing to state clearly what criteria we propose to employ, recognizing that whatever they are and whoever espouses them, they are always normative conceptions, serving some interests more than others, and likely to be both limited and controversial.

The Total Quality Management Movement

During the last two decades, a substantial change has occurred in the ways that many individuals in organizations think and talk about organizational effectiveness. This change is largely related to the emergence of the "total quality management" movement or TQM. Because of ideas fostered by this movement, the concept of effectiveness has begun to be displaced by an emphasis on "quality." Moreover, the meaning attached to quality has also undergone change. In earlier formulations, quality was treated as referring to selected, specific attributes of a given product or service, such as realibility or durability. Juran (1989) refers to this usage as a "little q" approach, in contrast to the "big Q" view of quality as referring to a wide range of attributes, from waste reduction to partnering with suppliers and customers, to human resources management. Three values are uppermost in the new quality paradigm (big Q): (1) customer focus, (2) continuous improvement, and (3) teamwork (Dean and Bowen, 1994).

Customer focus emphasizes the importance of bringing customer needs—in particular, the end user of the product or service—into every part of the organization. Techniques are developed to cultivate extensive relations with customers, utilizing surveys, focus groups, and similar tools for identifying their unmet needs and concerns. These techniques are sometimes extended to identify "internal" customers—those whose work depends on others prior to them in the production stream. Continuous improvement replaces the older quality emphasis on "conformance to standards" with a drive to relentlessly improve all products and services as well as the processes that create them. Teamwork stresses the need to break down the conventional barriers and buffers that have been erected in traditional organizations—between levels of the hierarchy, between staff and line, between functional departments—and to design teams that can be held accountable for the "total quality" of specific products and services.

Three themes are pervasive in the new TQM paradigm. First, there is recognition of the value of collaboration between all partners involved in the task—designers and engineers, suppliers, production personnel, human resource managers, sales personnel, and the customers themselves. Second, there is awareness of the importance of organizational learning on the part of all participants, who are expected to be constantly searching for new and better ways to work and new and better products and services to produce. Third, it is emphasized that quality is not a specialized, technical function to be assigned to control officers; quality is not what you check for at the end of the production line. Rather, quality is built in to every step and is part of every participant's job description (see Cole, 1994).

The quality movement enjoyed its early acceptance and success in Japan, a number of whose companies embraced and implemented principles espoused by Deming (1986) and Juran (1974). U.S. managers were slow to respond to the competitive challenge posed by the success of Japanese companies, and were reluctant to learn from their Japanese counterparts. In many ways, the movement needed to be reinvented and repackaged, by consultants such as Crosby (1979), to be acceptable to American companies (see Cole, forthcoming). The development in 1987 of the Malcolm Baldrige program, which specified particular structures and practices, regularly updated, and which stimulated competition among companies for recognition by setting up the Baldrige award, has helped to diffuse quality ideology and practice.

Much research remains to be conducted to determine what types of practices have been adopted and implemented by what kinds of companies with what kinds of results (Dean and Bowen, 1994). Research in this domain lags practice. Many critics and cynics believe that the quality movement is only the latest among a succession of management fads. One cause for skepticism is the great demands the ideology places on an organization to change its conventional way of doing business. Sustained support from top management is critical since the full implementation of the model requires changes in virtually every aspect of the organization. It is particularly difficult to stimulate trust among participants and to cultivate a learning environment in the face of current pressures to downsize and to focus on short-term financial targets. Achieving continuous learning is also at odds with the requirement that members adhere closely to standardized best practice (Hackman and Wageman, 1995). As is so often the case, there is great tension between those who see the company primarily as a rational production system that needs to be reengineered and those who see it as a natural social system in which participant commitment and motivation are essential if learning and change are to support improved quality.

High Reliability Organizations

The complexity of modern society and the increasing power and sophistication of technology has heightened the salience and value of organizations capable of performing at a high level of reliability. Complex military systems such as aircraft carriers and submarines, traffic control systems, power distribution grids, nuclear plants—these are examples of organizations whose failure can produce major disasters. Key defining characteristics of these systems include high complexity (containing many parts that are themselves complex), tight coupling (the parts exhibiting relatively time-dependent, invariant, and inflexible connections with little slack), and processes that are interactive in nonlinear ways (following unexpected sequences that are not visible or not immediately comprehensible) (Perrow, 1984). Such systems become problematic when they have "catastrophic potential": when their failure can result in substantial loss of life and property.

Investigators have endeavored to learn from the failures—for example, the Three Mile Island nuclear accident (Perrow, 1984); the Bhopal plant explosion (Shrivastava, 1986); the Challenger disaster (Vaughan, 1996); the "near-misses" (Sagan, 1993)—as well as the successes—the routine operation of aircraft carriers (Roberts, 1990) and of the U.S. air traffic system (LaPorte, 1988)—of such systems. As might be expected, selection and training of personnel, redundancy of functions (equipment, procedures), reliance on collegiality and negotiation within a tight formal command structure, and a culture emphasizing cooperation and commitment to high standards are among the organizational elements promoting high reliability.

Nevertheless, commentators such as Perrow insist that there are some types of systems, such as nuclear plants, that are sufficiently complex and lethal that they are guaranteed to fail sooner or later. Accidents in such systems must be regarded as inevitable, as "normal." In Perrow's view, these systems are "hopeless and should be abandoned because the inevitable risks outweigh any reasonable benefits." (1984: 304)

Organizations demanding high reliability place extraordinary demands on all organizational components. They represent systems that devote much energy and attention to monitoring their own performance—but they do not fare well under the present conditions of increasing production pressures and reduced resources facing many organizations (see Vaughan 1996).

Market and Nonmarket Organizations

Most observers emphasize the importance of the distinction between market and nonmarket organizations, especially when issues of effectiveness or performance are under consideration. The conventional view is that when properly functioning, the market provides a mechanism for linking the interests of organizational participants and external constituencies in such a manner that the former do not prosper unless they serve the interests of the latter. The effectiveness of market-controlled organizations is directly determined by their customers: if their interests are satisfied, then they will continue to supply the inputs required by the organization; if not, then they can withhold their contributions, causing the organization to suffer and perhaps ultimately to fail. Under ideal market conditions an organization's output goals and system-maintenance goals are tightly linked.

A contrasting view is developed by Fligstein (1990; 1996), who emphasizes that, like all social structures, markets themselves are socially constructed. Markets vary from one another in their characteristics, and they change over time. Viewed in this way:

> Markets in the abstract do not suggest anything about how to organize production. That organization is an outcome of social processes whereby firms inter-

act with one another and the state to produce what can be called a market. (Fligstein, 1990: 19–20)

If markets are social constructions that vary over time and space, it follows that what is meant by "effectiveness" or "efficiency" also varies. When markets are expanding and firms growing, efficiency refers to economies of scale; under different circumstances—of uncertainty and specialization of markets—efficiency will relate to the spreading or risks among many businesses. What type of strategy produces effective performance varies with the nature of the market. And, most important, market structures are not exogenous to and independent of the actions and interactions of the firms operating within them; markets are created by these interactions, as mediated by agents of the state.

As already noted, research by Burt (1983) has shown that the structure of industrial markets varies greatly in degree of concentration and, hence, the level and nature of the competition confronted (see Chapter 8). This in turn affects profitability: firms operating in industries characterized by many ties among producers but few ties among their suppliers or customers reap higher profits. Moreover, Burt (1988) has recently shown that a cross-section of U.S. markets exhibited high stability of structural relations during the 1960s and 1970s.

We hasten to add, however, that the market situation confronting many U.S. corporations has undergone dramatic changes during the recent decade as a result of increasing global competition. The Big Three U.S. automobile corporations, to take just one dramatic example, were long regarded as highly effective corporations until their markets were invaded and transformed by German and Japanese imports. The transition now under way to a global marketplace for many industries changes once again the structure of the market and with it the criteria of effectiveness and strategies for success (see Porter, 1986).

Many organizations, most notably, many public organizations, operate in nonmarket environments. Downs (1967: 25) employs as his major criterion for defining a government bureau the condition that "the major portion of its output is not directly or indirectly evaluated in any markets external to the organization by means of voluntary quid pro quo transactions." This means that "there is no direct relationship between the services a bureau provides and the income it receives for providing them" (p. 30). This does not imply, however, that such organizations are uncontrolled. Attention to the institutional aspects of environments will show that such organizations are subject to extensive controls, but of a different type: controls that emphasize process over outcome indicators of performance. We discuss these differences later in this chapter. During the late 1960s and 1970s, extensive efforts were made to develop techniques for assessing the effectiveness of governmental agencies. Evaluation research, both as a set of methodologies and as a collection of professional service firms, has been developed to perform this function. Although these efforts began with quite naive assumptions regarding techniques for assessing program and agency effectiveness, they have rapidly become more sophisticated, both technically and politically (see Suchman, 1967; Weiss, 1972; Cronbach et al., 1980).

Evaluation research has proved to be no panacea, however, and general discontent with the effectiveness of public organizations has continued to mount.

> Just as the widespread perception of the failures of private enterprise and the market system in the 1930s generated the political impetus for the creation of the welfare state, which reached its climax in the Great Society programs of the 1960s, so have the recent critiques of federal efforts gradually generated a new reaction back toward belief in the magic of the marketplace and the virtues of private sector dynamism and local initiative. (Brooks, 1984: 5)

The drive toward "privatization" of the public sector has taken several routes. Increasingly, publicly owned and operated services are expected at least in part to "pay their own way"—to take in enough revenue to cover most if not all the services provided. Indeed, the variety of organizational forms allowing some degree of governmental ownership or sponsorship combined with some degree of reliance on the marketplace is quite remarkable. These forms range from fully owned governmental corporations (such as the U.S. Postal Service) to a wide variety of government-sponsored enterprises (for example, COM-SAT [Communications Satellite Corporation] and the Corporation for Public Broadcasting) (see Seidman, 1975). Alternatively, many organizations supplying public services are supported by public funds but are privately owned. This is the case, for example, with defense contractors. A large and increasing proportion of public services—health care, education, police and fire protection—are contracted to private agencies (see Brooks, Liebman, and Schelling, 1984; Smith and Lipsky, 1993). It is argued that contracting out goods and services fosters competition and hence greater efficiency and effectiveness, but small numbers of suppliers and the widespread use of sole-source bidding greatly reduce the utility of such safeguards, as has been demonstrated by recurrent overpricing and mismanagement scandals involving weapons procurement by the Pentagon. Reliance on the market also presumes that consumers can evaluate the quality of products and services being purchased. But such an assumption is not tenable for many types of services; indeed, this is one of the major reasons why nonmarket organizations came into existence!

Nonmarket organizations are particularly likely to lack clear output measures. When the goals are to provide for an adequate defense, to negotiate advantageous treaties with other countries, or to fight poverty, it is difficult to determine how effective performances are. Of course, other types of organizations also pursue goals that are vague and difficult to assess. Two problems are involved: how to select indicators—the evidence to employ in evaluating performances—and how to set standards—the criteria to be used in judging whether a given performance is good or poor. Issues of standard setting and indicator selection are discussed later in this chapter.

ASSESSING EFFECTIVENESS

In order for an evaluation of a performance to occur, criteria must be selected, including the identification of properties or dimensions and the setting of standards; work must be sampled, with decisions made concerning the types of indicators to be employed and the nature of the sample to be drawn; and sampled values must be compared with the selected standards (see Dornbusch and Scott, 1975). In our view, the same components are applicable whether the intent is to evaluate an individual performer or an entire organization. To this point, we have discussed only the problems encountered in determining the properties or dimensions of the organizational performance to be evaluated. In the current section, we discuss the setting of standards and the selection of indicators for assessing organization effectiveness and briefly comment on decisions regarding selection of the sample.

Setting Standards

The setting of standards is a central component in establishing criteria for evaluating the effectiveness of an organization. By definition, standards are normative and not descriptive statements. The problem of how standards for assessing organizations are set is an interesting one but has received relatively little attention from social scientists. Cyert and March have attempted to adapt the psychological concept of aspiration level to explain how organizations establish goals for use as evaluative standards. They argue that:

> Organizational goals in a particular time period are a function of (1) organizational goals of the previous time period, (2) organizational experience with respect to that goal in the previous time period, and (3) experience of comparable organizations with respect to the goals dimension in the previous time period. (1963: 123)

More generally, aspirations adapt to performances. "Aspirations change over time, and they change endogenously. . . . In general, as performances improve, so do aspirations; as performances decline, so do aspirations" (March, 1994: 31). When performance exceeds standards, organizational slack increases and success-induced search may be triggered. Such exploratory learning is more free and open, less purposeful, more likely to fail, but increases variety in the system and may support long-run adaptation. By contrast, failure-induced search is more constrained and involves less risk taking. In short, organizational learning is affected by how performance relates to standards. As noted above, the new quality paradigm emphasizes the value of continually ratcheting up the standards governing performance.

Selecting Indicators

Among the most critical decisions to be made in attempting to assess organizational effectiveness is the choice of the measures or indicators to be employed. Three general types of indicators have been identified: those based on outcomes, on processes, and on structures (see Donabedian, 1966; Suchman, 1967; Scott, 1977).

Outcomes. Outcome indicators focus on specific characteristics of materials or objects on which the organization has performed some operation.

Examples of outcome indicators are changes in the knowledge or attitudes of students in educational organizations, or changes in the health status of patients in medical institutions. Outcomes are often regarded as the quintessential indicators of effectiveness, but they also may present serious problems of interpretation. Outcomes are never pure indicators of quality of performance, since they reflect not only the care and accuracy with which work activities are carried out but also the current state of the technology and the characteristics of the organization's input and output environments. These matters are of little import when cause-effect knowledge is relatively complete and when organizations are able to exercise adequate controls over their input and output sectors—that is, when the organization is well buffered from its environment. In such situations, represented by the manufacture of standardized equipment in competitive markets, outcomes serve as safe indexes of quality and quantity of organizational performance. However, many types of organizations lack such controls over their work processes and task environments. For example, a patient's medical condition following surgery will reflect not only the quality of care rendered by the surgical staff and the hospital personnel but also the state of medical science with respect to the particular condition treated, as well as the patient's general physical condition and extent of surgical disease at the time of the operation. Such problems are too much for some analysts, who dismiss the attempt to use outcome measures to assess effectiveness under these circumstances. Thus, Mann and Yett reason:

> There are those who argue that the output of a health facility should be specified in terms of its effect on the patient. . . . We reject this definition of hospital output for the same reason that we do not regard the output of a beauty salon as beauty. (1968: 196–97)

In our view, the use of outcome measures presents difficult, but not unsolvable, problems in assessing effectiveness of organizations such as hospitals and schools. The problem of inadequate knowledge of cause-effect relations can be handled by the use of relative rather than absolute performance standards, so that the performance of an organization is compared against others carrying on similar work. This approach presumes that the organizations assessed can—or should—participate in the same cultural system and have access to the same general knowledge pool. A particular organization possessing more relevant knowledge—for example, having better-trained personnel—would be expected to perform better than one possessing less knowledge, but the use of relative standards ensures that an organization is not penalized for lacking knowledge that no one has.

The problem posed by the contribution of variations among input characteristics to variations in outcomes experienced is less easily resolved. Although we can safely assume that organizations have access to the same knowledge, we cannot assume that they have access to the same client pool or supply sources. Indeed, one of the principal ways in which organizations vary is in the amount and quality of inputs they are able to garner. The pattern of inputs characterizing various types of organizations is not as simple as might appear on superficial examination. For example, as might be expected, prestigious universities recruit highly intelligent students, as indicated by scores on standard entrance examinations or past performance in academic settings, whereas less highly regarded institutions accept higher proportions of less qualified students. By contrast, highly regarded teaching hospitals focus primarily on the care of the very sick or on those whose problems pose the greatest challenge to medical science. In these organizations, there is an inverse relation between presumed quality of institution and patient condition. We would expect organizations to seek or take credit for acquiring inputs that enhance their outcomes—a widely used indicator of quality for universities is the characteristics of the student body they are able to attract—but to resist being held accountable for inputs that negatively affect outcomes. Thus, teaching hospitals insist that if patient outcome measures are employed as indicators of performance quality, they be standardized to take account of differences in patient mix. Statistical techniques are available that allow analysts to adjust outcome measures to take into account differences in characteristics of inputs (see Flood and Scott, 1987; Heithoff and Lohr, 1990).

Outcome measures may also be affected by the characteristics of output environments. For example, indicators of outcomes relating to sales for products, or to placement or rehabilitation for prisoners or mental patients, will reflect not simply organizational performance but also market conditions or the receptivity of community groups external to the organization. As with inputs, we would expect organizations to prefer to take credit for conditions enhancing outcomes but insist that conditions having a negative effect be taken into account if outcomes are evaluated.

More generally, the decision as to how to treat input characteristics and output environments is not primarily a methodological but a theoretical issue. Do we wish to adjust for differences in student intelligence among universities in assessing student performance, or do we wish to regard student recruitment as an important aspect of a university's performance? Do we wish to adjust for market conditions in assessing a firm's retail sales, or do we wish to consider ability to build a solid market niche an important component of the firm's performance? Answers to these and similar questions depend on whether we seek to concentrate simply on the organization's throughput processes—its technical-core activities—or to include in our assessment the performance of the organization's bridging units—its input and output components.

Still other issues are involved in the use of outcome measures to assess organizational effectiveness. Briefly, it is difficult to determine the appropriate timing of such measures. Some organizations insist that their full effects may not be apparent for long periods following their performance. For example, some educators claim that relevant academic outcomes can only be assessed long after the students have left school and have attempted to apply their knowledge in the "real world." And when is the appropriate time to assess a hospital's effect on a patient's health—immediately following a major therapeutic intervention such as surgery, at discharge, or following a posthospitalization recovery period? Another problem in employing outcome indicators is the lack of relevant information. Many types of organizations have little or no data on outcomes achieved: they quickly lose contact with their "products"—whether these be human graduates or manufactured commodities. The collection of relevant outcome data can become very costly indeed if it entails tracking down such products after they are distributed throughout the environment.

Partly because of these quite formidable difficulties in assessing and interpreting outcome measures, other types of indicators of organizational effectiveness are often preferred. These measures—of processes and structures—can be more briefly described.

Processes. Process measures focus on the quantity or quality of activities carried on by the organization. As Suchman (1967: 61) notes, this type of indicator "represents an assessment of input or energy regardless of output. It is intended to answer the questions, 'What did you do?' and 'How well did you do it?'" Process measures assess effort rather than effect. Some process measures assess work quantity—for example, staying with our hospital illustration, we may ask how many laboratory tests were conducted during a given period or how many patients were seen per hour in the emergency room. Others assess work quality—for example, hospitals might be rated by the frequency with which medication errors occur or by the proportion of healthy tissue removed from patients during surgery. Still other measures assess the extent of quality-control efforts—for instance, the autopsy rate in hospitals or the proportion of X rays reviewed by radiologists.

In some respects, process measures are more valid measures of the characteristics of organizational performance. Rather than requiring inferences from outcomes to performance characteristics, process measures directly assess performance values. On the other hand, it is important to emphasize that all process measures evaluate efforts rather than achievements, and when the focus is on quality of performance rather than quantity, they assess conformity to a given program but not the adequacy or correctness of the programs themselves. Process measures are based on the assumption that it is known what activities are required to ensure effectiveness. Students of medical care have challenged the assumption that there is a strong correlation between conformity to current standards of medical practice and improvements in patient outcomes (see Brook, 1973), as well as the assumption that higher levels of medical care result in improved health status (see Fuchs, 1974). More generally, social critics such as Illich (1972; 1976) claim that the substitution of process for outcome is one of the great shell games perpetrated by modern institutions against individuals. Illich argues that contemporary individuals are trained:

> to confuse process and substance. Once these become blurred, a new logic is assumed: the more treatment there is, the better are the results; or, escalation leads to success. The pupil is thereby "schooled" to confuse teaching with learning, grade advancement with education, a diploma with competence, and fluency with the ability to say something new. His imagination is "schooled" to accept service in place of value. Medical treatment is mistaken for health care, social work for the improvement of community life, police protection for safety, military poise for national security, the rat race for productive work. Health, learning, dignity, independence, and creative endeavor are designed as little more than the performance of the institutions that claim to serve these ends, and their improvement is made to depend on allocating more resources to the management of hospitals, schools, and other agencies in question. (1972: 1)

Recognizing that Illich's broad accusations have some merit, we would, however, express two sorts of reservations. The first relates to an argument we made in Chapter 12. Focusing on processes rather than outcomes represents a type of goal displacement. However, as noted earlier, goal displacement is a very widespread phenomenon and need not be regarded as pathological. Only when means and ends become disconnected is there cause for distress. Our second demurring relates to the case of organizations confronting strong institutionalized pressures, in which, to a large extent, process *is* substance. In these organizations, conformity to ritually defined procedures produces a successful outcome, by definition. Ceremony is substance in many contemporary organizations, including religious bodies, legal firms, and many professionally staffed organizations (see Chapter 6).

Organizations are more likely to compile data on work processes than on outcomes. Performance quality and quantity are often regularly monitored. Gathering information on work processes, however, can still be problematic. Inspections based on observation of ongoing performances are both expensive and reactive—that is, likely to influence the behavior observed. In most work situations there are numerous barriers to work visibility, and workers often resist attempts to directly observe their work in progress. Many kinds of work occur under circumstances that render routine inspection impossible, and other kinds, such as those emphasizing mental activities, are by their nature difficult to observe. Because of such difficulties, organizations may rely on self-reports of activities performed. However, such data are likely to be both biased and incomplete representations of work processes (see Dornbusch and Scott, 1975: 145–62). Because of these and related difficulties in obtaining process measures, many organizations rely on structural indicators of effectiveness.

Structures.   Structural indicators assess the capacity of the organization for effective performance. Included within this category are all measures based on organizational features or participant characteristics presumed to have an impact on organizational effectiveness. Manufacturing organizations can be assessed by the value and age of their machine tools; hospitals are assessed by the adequacy of their facilities and equipment and by the qualifications of the medical staff as reflected in past training and certification; and schools are assessed by the qualities of their faculties measured in terms of types of degrees acquired, and by such features as the number of volumes in their libraries. These types of measures form the basis of accreditation reviews and organizational licensing systems.

If process measures are once removed from outcomes, then structure indicators are twice remote, for these measures index not the work performed by structures but their *capacity* to perform work—not the activities carried out by organizational participants but their qualifications to perform the work. Structural indicators focus on organizational inputs as surrogate measures for outputs. Economists warn us that quality of outputs should not be confused with quality (or cost) of inputs, although many current measures of productivity make precisely this association (see Panel to Review Productivity Statistics, 1979).

As was the case with measures of organizational process, a number of observers have suggested that an emphasis on structural measures may have detrimental consequences for quality of outcomes. For example, numerous observers have argued that personnel licensure requirements have become a major obstacle to innovation in work procedures and to the optimal deployment of workers (see Tancredi and Woods, 1972). Thus, we have the interesting situation in which some measures of organizational effectiveness based on the assessment of process or of structure are argued to adversely affect other measures of effectiveness based on outcomes.

Selecting Samples

Once indicators have been selected, decisions must still be made regarding the gathering of information relevant to these measures. We leave aside here discussion of specific techniques of data gathering as well as decisions pertaining to sample size, ensuring of representativeness, and other technical considerations, in order to emphasize the critical importance of the definition of the universe from which the sample is to be drawn. A basic decision confronting the analyst who assesses the effectiveness of any organization is whether to focus on the actual work performed by the organization or instead to ask whether the organization is attending to the appropriate work. The first option takes as given the current program of the organization—its structures, processes, or outcomes—and seeks to ascertain its quality or effectiveness. The second option assumes a broader perspective, asking whether the organization is engaged in the right program. Never mind whether the organization is doing things right; is it doing the right things? Reinhardt (1973) labels the first criterion microquality and the second, macroquality. If this distinction were applied to a service organization, an assessment of microquality would focus on the quality of structures, processes, or outcomes actually experienced by clients who were the recipients of the organization's services. By contrast, an assessment of macroquality would seek to determine whether the appropriate services were being provided or, more critically, whether the proper clients were receiving services. The effectiveness of a medical care organization might be assessed in terms of the health status of the clients who had received services (microquality) or by the health status of the population residing within the organization's service area (macroquality).

Participants, Constituents, and Measures

Just as with evaluation criteria, we would expect differing participant and constituency groups to prefer some types of measures over others. Generally, we expect organizational managers to emphasize structural measures of effectiveness, in part because these reflect factors that are more under their control than other types of indicators. Thus, organizational administrators are likely to have considerable influence over the types of facilities provided or the standards used in hiring personnel. By contrast, we would expect performers or rank-and-file participants to emphasize process measures of effectiveness. Skilled and semiskilled workers, who have little or no discretion in the selection of their activities, will prefer to be evaluated on the basis of their conformity to their performance programs rather than on the basis of the efficacy of these programs. And professional personnel, who are granted discretion in their choice of activities, will also usually prefer to be evaluated on the basis of process measures—their conformity to "standards of good practice"—since inadequacies in the knowledge base mean that they lack full control over outcomes.

Clients who use the products or receive the services are likely to focus primarily on outcome measures of effectiveness. They will evaluate the organization's product in terms of the extent to which it has met their own needs and expectations. Did the motor run? Was something of interest or use learned? Was pain relieved or functioning improved? In addition, clients who receive personal services are likely to place considerable value on process measures having to do with promptness, courtesy, and sensitivity of treatment. In circumstances where outcomes are difficult to evaluate, process measures will receive more weight from clients than outcome indicators. The most extreme cases involve institutionalized environments in which outcomes are inseparable from processes, so that both performers and recipients devote attention to evaluating conformity to established norms of practice.

The two most vigorous movements to improve the quality of organizational performance—the ISO 9000 quality certification process, which is dominant in Europe, and TQM, which has influenced organizational practice in Asia and, increasingly, in the United States—differ in their focus of attention. The International Organization for Standardization (ISO) focuses attention on the assessment of a comprehensive quality system, emphasizing conformity to a set of primarily procedural and structural guidelines. Emphasis is placed on the extent to which the organization has a documented "quality" system in place, represented by an overall "quality manual" (see Lamprecht, 1993; Mendel, 1996). By contrast, the quality movement in Asia and America places highest priority on outcome measures as defined by client needs, but also gives attention to procedural and structural elements, viewed in terms of their contributions to quality outcomes.

All of the interest groups considered to this point—organizational managers, performers, and consumers—are likely to focus on microquality indicators of effectiveness. They will prefer to focus on the structures, processes, and outcomes associated with the work that the organization is actually performing. But another interest group consisting of the public at large, including some public regulatory bodies, will be more likely to emphasize measures of macroquality. Is the organization concentrating its attention and resources on the proper products or problems? Do eligible clients have access to its services? Is the community as a whole benefiting from its operation?

Our final constituency is composed of researchers dedicated to the objective, scientific analysis of organizational effectiveness. We would hope to find this group busily engaged in analyzing all types of indicators of effectiveness, exploring their interrelation, and employing criteria variously drawn from all of the interested parties. Although we have not conducted the type of systematic survey of the literature required to support such a conclusion, it appears that we analysts have emphasized the structural and process measures of effectiveness—those measures preferred by organization managers and performers—to the neglect of outcome measures—those preferred by clients and the larger public. Both ideological and economic factors help to produce this bias in orientation. It is our belief that organizational analysts are more likely to identify with organizational managers and professional performers than with client and public interests. Indeed, most of the research on organizations is conducted by persons who train future managers while consulting for present ones. Also, most of the data available to us for analysis are collected by the organizations for their own purposes or are based on information supplied by organizational managers. Organizations, as noted above, are much less likely to collect data on outcomes than data based on their structural features and processes. If we want data on outcomes—and especially on outcomes that represent measures of macroquality—we will have to collect them for ourselves, or persuade governmental agencies to collect them for us. We should not minimize the cost or the value of such data in correcting the bias that currently exists in indicators of organizational effectiveness.

EXPLAINING EFFECTIVENESS

Given the multiple possible meanings and measures of effectiveness that have been proposed, our comments on explanations of effectiveness can be brief since they are mostly by way of warning. When effectiveness can be viewed as comprising such varied criteria as flexibility, low turnover, and growth, we must seek explanatory variables as varied as what they are asked to account for. Given that many of the proposed measures of effectiveness are uncorrelated or even negatively correlated, we should not expect to find general explanations that will distinguish effective from ineffective organizations. We must agree to settle for modest and limited measures of specific aspects of organizational structures, processes, and outcomes.

Also given the complexity and openness of organizations as detailed in this volume, we would not expect any single set of factors to account for organizational effectiveness. This is the major defect, in our opinion, of some best-sellers in the organizational literature. For example, such studies as Ouchi's *Theory Z* and Peters and Waterman's *In Search of Excellence*, while they provide valuable insights into new managerial techniques, convey the message that organizational performance is primarily a matter of management effectiveness—of management's capacity to create the right culture and motivational structure. Overlooked or underemphasized are such factors as industrial location, positioning in various markets—resource, labor, capital, sales—critical alliances and connections, information systems, and institutional supports. Effective organizations require more than enthusiastic managers and motivated workers.

Since the appearance of the open system perspective, a popular approach to explaining variations in effectiveness has involved the use of contingency models: organizations whose internal features best match the demands of their technologies or task environments are expected to be most effective (see Chapter 4). The adequacy of such models depends, among other things, on the quality of our ideas about the appropriate relation (match) between task or environmental demands and organizational arrangements. We have attempted to summarize some of these evolving principles in Chapters 8 through 10, and while we do not apologize for the current state of knowledge, there is clearly much room for improvement. The principles developed are generally vague and need to be carefully adapted for application to specific settings. That this is not a straightforward task is illustrated by Perrow's critique of Neuhauser's attempt to apply these ideas to the organization of doctors' work in hospitals. Neuhauser (1971) embraces the widely accepted design principle that when work is complex and uncertain, attempts to control performance with the use of highly specified procedures—high formalization—will lower work quality. Perrow would certainly subscribe to this general principle, but he takes issue with Neuhauser's specific application of it to the hospital setting.

> Tasks are complex on the medical side of the hospitals, so when dealing with doctors, specification of procedures should be low. But the specifications of what kind of procedures? Any, it seems. For example, he includes the number of tests required at admissions . . . and the number of limitations placed upon the surgery that people can perform (a general practitioner cannot do heart surgery). Using knee-jerk theorizing, he says that if there are a lot of specifications of these kinds, quality should be low. Presumably he could have included scrubbing before surgery as a specification of procedures that would lower quality when tasks are complex. (1972: 420)

Perrow's tone is overly caustic, but his point is well-taken, and the problem illustrated is all too common in organizational analysis. We are too often in thralldom before a general principle, applying it mindlessly to situations whose complexity swamps whatever truth might have been revealed by a more thoughtful approach. Let us not be misunderstood. We need the guidance of general principles. But we also require sufficiently detailed knowledge of the organizations and their technologies and environments to be able to select valid indicators of the variables to be assessed. Surgeons do need to be able to exercise discretion in some critical areas of their work, but this requirement need not be inconsistent with the precise specification of other aspects of their performance. If we wish to explain effects, there is no substitute for a knowledge of the specific causal processes linking them with relevant inputs, technologies, and work arrangements.

Contingency models often overlook the open system concept of equifinality: that many different causal paths can lead to the same effect (but see Doty, Glick, and Huber, 1993). In particular, it is often presumed that an organization's ability to maximize its productivity or its profits is due to the superior design of its production structures and the resulting technical efficiency. However, we should know by this time that organizations are technical systems but not simply technical systems. As Katz and Kahn remind us:

> The textbook path to organizational survival is internal efficiency: build the better mousetrap or build the old trap less expensively. There is, however, a whole class of alternative or supplementary solutions—the political devices that maximize organizational return at some cost to other organizations or individuals. (1978: 249)

Pfeffer and Salancik stress the importance of these political solutions throughout their analysis of organizational functioning, concluding that "the effectiveness of an organization is a sociopolitical question" (1978: 11). Consumers and (some) regulators seek ways to link an organization's effectiveness in goal attainment to its effectiveness in resource acquisition and survival. Sometimes they succeed but often they fail: an organization's resource acquisition and survival are not always tightly linked with the quality of its services to the publics it claims to benefit.

SUMMARY

Criteria for evaluating organizational effectiveness cannot be produced by some objective, apolitical process. They are always normative and often controversial, and they are as varied as the theoretical models used to describe organizations and the constituencies that have some interest in their functioning. Similarly, the indicators to be used in assessing organizational effectiveness must be chosen from among several possible types, and data gathered from several possible sampling frames. Measures based on outcomes, processes, and structural features of organizations are likely to produce inconsistent conclusions and are differently favored by various constituencies.

The recent quality movement seeks to focus attention on the outcomes of interest to customers, and attempts to foster efforts to devise systems that will motivate continuous, incremental improvements across all segments of the organization.

We should not seek explanations for organizational effectiveness in general, since such general criteria are not available, and we must be cautious in celebrating the truism that organizations that are better adapted to their environments are more effective. Adaptation can be achieved in numerous ways, many of which contribute to the survival of the organization but fail to serve the interests of external constituencies.

References

Abbott, Andrew (1988). *The System of Professions: An Essay on the Division of Expert Labor.* Chicago: University of Chicago Press.

Abegglen, James C. (1958). *The Japanese Factory: Aspects of Its Social Organization.* Glencoe, IL: Free Press.

Abegglen, James C., and George Stalk, Jr. (1985) *Kaisha: The Japanese Corporation.* New York: Basic Books.

Acker, Joan (1990). "Hierarchies, Jobs, Bodies: A Theory of Gendered Organizations," *Gender & Society*, 4:139–58.

Ackerman, Bruce A. (1985). "Cost Benefit and the Constitution," in *Regulatory Policy and the Social Sciences*, 351–57, ed. Roger G. Noll. Berkeley: University of California Press.

Adams, J. Stacey (1965). "Inequity in Social Exchange," in *Advances in Experimental Social Psychology*, vol. 2, pp. 267–300, ed. Leonard Berkowitz. New York: Academic Press.

Adler, Paul S. (1990). "Managing High-Tech Processes: The Challenge of CAD/CAM," in *Managing Complexity* in *High-Technology Industries, Systems and People*, ed. M. A. Von Glinow and S. A. Mohrman. Oxford: Oxford University Press.

Agger, Ben (1991). "Critical Theory, Poststructuralism, Postmodernism: Their Sociological Relevance," *Annual Review of Sociology*, 17, 105–31.

Aiken, Michael, and Jerald Hage (1968). "Organizational Interdependence and Intra-organizational Structure," *American Sociological Review*, 33, 912–29.

Albrow, Martin (1970). *Bureaucracy.* New York: Praeger.

Alchian, A. A., and H. Demsetz (1972). "Production, Information Costs, and Economic Organization," *American Economic Review*, 62, 777–95.

Aldrich, Howard E. (1979). *Organizations and Environments.* Englewood Cliffs, NJ: Prentice Hall.

———— (1992). "Incommensurable Paradigms? Vital Signs from Three Perspectives," in *Rethinking Organization: New Directions in Organization Theory and Analysis*, 17–45, ed. Michael Reed and Michael Hughes. Newbury Park, CA: Sage.

Aldrich, Howard E., and C. Marlene Fiol (1994). "Fools Rush In? The Institutional Context of Industry Construction," *Academy of Management Review*, 19, 645–70.

Aldrich, Howard E., and Sergio Mindlin (1978). "Uncertainty and Dependence: Two Perspectives on Environment," in *Organization and Environment*, pp. 149–70, ed. Lucien Karpit. Beverly Hills, CA: Sage.

Aldrich, Howard E., and Jeffrey Pfeffer (1976). "Environments of Organizations," *Annual Review of Sociology*, 2, 79–105.

Aldrich, Howard E., and Roger Waldinger (1990). "Ethnicity and Entrepreneurship," *Annual Review of Sociology*, 16, 111–35.

Aldrich, Howard E., and David A. Whetten (1981). "Organization-Sets, Action-Sets, and Networks: Making the Most of Simplicity," in *Handbook of Organizational Design*, vol. 1, pp. 385–408, ed. Paul C. Nystrom and William H. Starbuck. New York: Oxford University Press.

Alexander, Jeffrey A., and Thomas A. D'Aunno (1990). "Transformation of Institutional Environments: Perspectives on the Corporatization of U.S. Health Care," in *Innovations in Health Care Delivery: Insights for Organization Theory*, 53–85, ed. Stephen S. Mick. San Francisco: Jossey-Bass.

Alexander, Jeffrey C. (1982). *Theoretical Logic in Sociology*, vol. 4, *The Modern Reconstruction of Classical Thought: Talcott Parsons*. Berkeley: University of California Press.

Alexander, Victoria D. (1996). *Museums and Money: The Impact of Funding on Exhibitions, Scholarship and Management*. Bloomington, IN: Indiana University Press.

Alford, Robert R. (1975). *Health Care Politics*. Chicago: University of Chicago Press.

Alford, Robert R. and Roger Friedland (1975). "Political Participation and Public Policy," *Annual Review of Sociology*, 1, 429–79.

Allison, Graham T. (1971). *Essence of Decision: Explaining the Cuban Missile Crisis*. Boston: Little, Brown.

Alter, Catherine, and Jerry Hage (1993). *Organizations Working Together*. Newbury Park, CA: Sage.

Althauser, Robert P. (1989). "Internal Labor Markets," *Annual Review of Sociology*, 15, 143–61.

Althauser, Robert P., and Arne L. Kalleberg (1981). "Firms, Occupations, and the Structure of Labor Markets: A Conceptual Analysis and Research Agenda," in *Sociological Perspectives on Labor Markets*, 119–49, ed. Ivar Berg. New York: Academic Press

Alvesson, Mats, and Stanley Deetz (1996). "Critical Theory and Postmodernism Approaches to Organizational Studies," in *Handbook of Organization Studies*, 191–217, ed. Stewart R. Clegg, Cynthia Hardy, and Walter R. Nord. Thousand Oaks, CA: Sage.

Ancona, Deborah, Thomas Kochan, Maureen Scully, John Van Maanen, and D. Eleanor Westney (1996). *Managing for the Future: Organizational Behavior and Processes*. Cincinnati, OH: Southwestern College Publishing.

Anderson, Bo, Joseph Berger, Bernard P. Cohen, and Morris Zelditch, Jr. (1966). "Status Classes in Organizations," *Administrative Science Quarterly*, 11, 264–83.

Arendt, Hannah (1963). *Eichmann in Jerusalem*. New York: Viking.

Argyris, Chris (1957). *Personality and Organization*. New York: Harper.

_____ (1973). "Personality and Organization Theory Revisited," *Administrative Science Quarterly*, 18, 141–67.

_____ (1982). *Reasoning, Learning and Action: Individual and Organizational*. San Francisco: Jossey-Bass.

Arrow, Kenneth J. (1974). *The Limits of Organization*. New York: Norton.

Ashby, W. Ross (1952). *A Design for a Brain*. New York: Wiley.

_____ (1956). "The Effect of Experience on a Determinant System," *Behavioral Science*, 1, 35–42.

_____ (1968). "Principles of the Self-Organizing System," in *Modern Systems Research for the Behavioral Scientist*, pp. 108–18, ed. Walter Buckley. Chicago: Aldine.

Astley, W. Graham (1985). "The Two Ecologies: Population and Community Perspectives on Organizational Evolution," *Administrative Science Quarterly*, 30, 224–41.

Astley, W. Graham, and Andrew H. Van de Ven (1983). "Central Perspectives and Debates in Organization Theory," *Administrative Science Quarterly*, 28, 245–73.

Averitt, Richard T. (1968). *The Dual Economy: The Dynamics of American Industry Structure*. New York: Norton.

Bachrach, Peter, and Morton S. Baratz (1962). "The Two Faces of Power," *American Political Science Review*, 56, 947–52.

Bales, Robert F. (1952). "Some Uniformities of Behavior in Small Social Systems," in *Readings in Social Psychology* (2nd ed.), pp. 146–59, ed. Guy E. Swanson, Theodor M. Newcomb, and Eugene L. Hartley. New York: Holt, Rinehart and Winston.

_____ (1953). "The Equilibrium Problem in Small Groups," in *Working Papers in the Theory of Action*, pp. 111–61, by Talcott Parsons, Robert F. Bales, and Edward A. Shils. Glencoe, IL: Free Press.

Bales, Robert F., and Philip E. Slater (1955). "Role Differentiation in Small Decision-Making Groups," in *Family, Socialization and Interaction Process*, pp. 259–306, ed. Talcott Parsons and Robert F. Bales. New York: Free Press.

Bardach, Eugene, and Robert A. Kagan (1982). *Going by the Book: The Problem of Regulatory Unreasonableness*. Philadelphia: Temple University Press.

Barker, E. (1944). *The Development of Public Services in Western Europe, 1660–1930*. New York: Oxford University Press.

Barley, Stephen R. (1986). "Technology as an Occasion for Structuring: Evidence from Observations of CT Scanners and the Social Order of Radiology Departments," *Administrative Science Quarterly*, 31, 78–108.

Barnard, Chester I. (1938). *The Functions of the Executive*. Cambridge, MA: Harvard University Press.

Barnett, William P., and Glenn R. Carroll (1987). "Competition and Mutualism among Early Telephone Companies," *Administrative Science Quarterly*, 32, 400–21.

Baron, James N. (1984). "Organizational Perspectives on Stratification," *Annual Review of Sociology*, 10, 37–69.

Baron, James N., and William T. Bielby (1980). "Bringing the Firms Back In: Stratification, Segmentation, and the Organization of Work," *American Sociological Review*, 45, 737–65.

Baron, James N., Frank R. Dobbin, and P. Deveraux Jennings (1986). "War and Peace: The Evolution of Modern Personnel Administration in U.S. Industry," *American Journal of Sociology*, 92, 350–83.

Barth, Fredrik, ed. (1969). *Ethnic Groups and Boundaries*. Boston: Little, Brown.

Bateson, Gregory (1972). *Steps to an Ecology of Mind*. New York: Ballantine.

Baum, Joel A. C. (1996). "Organizational Ecology," in *Handbook of Organization Studies*, pp. 77–114, ed. Stewart R. Clegg, Cynthia Hardy, and Walter Nord. Thousand Oaks, CA: Sage.

Baum, Joel A. C., and Christine Oliver (1991). "Institutional Linkages and Organizational Mortality," *Administrative Science Quarterly*, 36, 187–218.

Baum, Joel A. C., and Jitendra V. Singh, ed. (1994). *Evolutionary Dynamics of Organizations*. New York: Oxford University Press.

Bavelas, Alex (1951). "Communication Patterns in Task-Oriented Groups," in *The Policy Sciences*, pp. 193–202, ed. Daniel Lerner and Harold D. Lasswell. Stanford, CA: Stanford University Press.

Bazerman, Max H., and Margaret A. Neale (1992). *Negotiating Rationally*. New York: Free Press.

Becker, Howard S., (1982). *Art Worlds*. Berkeley: University of California Press.

Beckhard, Richard (1972). "Organizational Issues in the Team Delivery of Comprehensive Health Care," *Milbank Memorial Fund Quarterly* 50 (part 1), 287–316.

Bedeian, Arthur G. (1984). *Organizations: Theory and Analysis* (2nd ed.). Chicago: Dryden Press.

Beer, Stafford (1964). *Cybernetics and Management*, New York: Wiley.

Bell, Daniel (1960). "Work and Its Discontents: The Cult of Efficiency in America," in *The End of Ideology*, pp. 222–62, by Daniel Bell. Glencoe, IL.: Free Press.

_____ (1973). *The Coming of Post-Industrial Society*. New York: Basic Books.

Belussi, Fiorenza (1989). "Benneton Italy: Beyond Fordism and Flexible Specialization to the Evolution of the Network Firm Model," in *Information Technology and Women's Employment: The Case of the European Clothing Industry*, ed. S. Mitter. Berlin: Springer Verlag.

Bendix, Reinhard (1956). *Work and Authority in Industry*. New York: Wiley.

_____ (1960). *Max Weber: An Intellectual Portrait*. Garden City, NY: Doubleday.

Bendix, Reinhard, and Lloyd H. Fisher (1949). "The Perspectives of Elton Mayo," *Review of Economics and Statistics*. 31, 312–19.

Beniger, James R. (1986). *The Control Revolution: Technological and Economic Origins of the Information Society*. Cambridge, MA: Harvard University Press.

Bennis, Warren G. (1959). "Leadership Theory and Administrative Behavior," *Administrative Science Quarterly*, 4, 259–301.

_____ (1966). *Changing Organizations*. New York: McGraw-Hill.

Bennis, Warren G., and Philip E. Slater (1968). *The Temporary Society*. New York: Harper & Row.

Berg, Ivar (1971). *Education and Jobs: The Great Training Robbery*. New York: Praeger.

Berger Peter L., Brigitte Berger, and Hansfried Kellner (1973). *The Homeless Mind: Modernization and Consciousness*. New York: Random House.

Berger, Peter L., and Thomas Luckmann (1967). *The Social Construction of Reality*. New York: Doubleday.

Berger, Suzanne, ed. (1981). *Organizing Interests in Western Europe: Pluralism, Corporatism and the Transformation of Politics*. New York: Cambridge University Press.

Berle, A. A., and Gardiner C. Means (1932). *The Modern Corporation and Private Property*. New York: Macmillan.

Berman, Harold J. (1983). *Law and Revolution: The Formation of the Western Legal Tradition*. Cambridge, MA: Harvard University Press.

Bertalanffy, Ludwig von (1956). "General System Theory," in *General Systems: Yearbook of the Society for the Advancement of General Systems Theory*, ed. Ludwig von Bertalanffy and Anatol Rapoport, 1, 1–10.

_____ (1962). "General System Theory: A Critical Review," in *General Systems: Yearbook of the Society for General Systems Research*, ed. Ludwig von Bertalanffy and Anatol Rapoport, 7, 1–20.

Bidwell, Charles E. (1965). "The School as a Formal Organization," in *Handbook of Organizations*, pp. 972–1022, ed. James G. March. Chicago: Rand McNally.

Bielby, William T., and James N. Baron (1986). "Men and Woman at Work: Sex Segregation and Statistical Discrimination," *American Journal of Sociology*, 91, 759–99.

Biggart, Nicole Woolsey (1989). *Charismatic Capitalism: Direct Selling Organizations in America*. Chicago: University of Chicago Press.

Bijker, W. E., Trevor Pinch, and Thomas Hughes, eds. (1987). *The Social Construction of Technological Systems: New Directions in the Sociology and History of Technology*. Cambridge, MA: MIT Press.

Bittner, Egon (1967). "The Police on Skid Row: A Study of Peace Keeping," *American Sociological Review*, 32, 699–715.

Blake, R. R., and J. S. Mouton (1964). *The Managerial Grid*. Houston: Gulf.

Blake, R. R., H. A. Shephard, and J. S. Mouton (1964). *Intergroup Conflict in Organizations*. Ann Arbor, MI: Foundation for Research on Human Behavior.

Blau, Peter M. (1955). *The Dynamics of Bureaucracy*. Chicago: University of Chicago Press (rev. 1963).

_____ (1956). *Bureaucracy in Modern Society*. New York: Random House.

_____ (1957). "Formal Organization: Dimensions of Analysis," *American Journal of Sociology*, 63, 58–69.

_____ (1964). *Exchange and Power in Social Life*. New York: Wiley.

_____ (1970). "A Formal Theory of Differentiation in Organizations," *American Sociological Review*, 35, 201–18.

Blau, Peter M., Wolfe V. Heydebrand, and Robert E. Stauffer (1966). "The Structure of Small Bureaucracies," *American Sociological Review*, 31: 179–91.

Blau, Peter M., and Richard A. Schoenherr (1971). *The Structure of Organizations*. New York: Basic Books.

Blau, Peter M., and W. Richard Scott (1962). *Formal Organizations: A Comparative Approach*. San Francisco: Chandler.

Blauner, Robert (1964). *Alienation and Freedom*. Chicago: University of Chicago Press.

Block, Fred (1994). "The Roles of the State in the Economy," in *The Handbook of Economic Sociology*, 691–710, eds., Neil J. Smelser and Richard Swedberg. Princeton, NJ: Princeton University Press and the Russell Sage Foundation.

Bluestone, Barry, and Irving Bluestone (1992). *Negotiating the Future: A Labor Perspective on American Business*. New York: Basic Books.

Blumberg, Paul (1968). *Industrial Democracy: The Sociology of Participation*. New York: Schocken Books.

Boas, Max, and Steve Chain (1977). *Big Mac: The Unauthorized Story of McDonald's.* New York: New American Library.

Boguslaw, Robert (1965). *The New Utopians: A Study of System Design and Social Change.* Englewood Cliffs, NJ: Prentice Hall.

Bose, Christine, Roslyn Feldberg, and Natalie Sokoloff, eds. (1987). *Hidden Aspects of Women's Work.* New York: Praeger.

Boulding, Kenneth E. (1956). "General Systems Theory: The Skeleton of Science," *Management Science,* 2, 197–208.

Bourdieu, Pierre (1977 trans.). *Outline of a Theory of Practice.* Trans. by Richard Nice. New York: Cambridge University Press (first published in 1972).

Boyd, Brian K., Gregory G. Dess, and Abdul M. A. Rasheed (1993). "Divergence between Archival and Perceptual Measures of the Environment: Causes and Consequences," *Academy of Management Review,* 18, 204–26.

Braverman, Harry (1974). *Labor and Monopoly Capital: The Degradation of Work in the Twentieth Century.* New York: Monthly Review Press.

Brayfield, Arthur H., and Walter H. Crockett (1955). "Employee Attitudes and Employee Performance," *Psychological Bulletin,* 52, 396–424.

Brief, Arthur P., and Ramon J. Aldag (1975). "Employee Reactions to Job Characteristics: A Constructive Replication," *Journal of Applied Psychology,* 60, 182–86.

Brook, Robert H. (1973). *Quality of Care Assessment: A Comparison of Five Methods of Peer Review.* Washington, DC: Bureau of Health Services Research and Evaluation.

Brooks, Harvey (1984). "Seeking Equity and Efficiency: Public and Private Roles," in *Public-Private Partnership: New Opportunities for Meeting Social Needs,* pp. 3–29, ed. Harvey Brooks, Lance Liebman, and Corinne S. Schelling. Cambridge, MA: Ballinger.

Brooks, Harvey, Lance Liebman, and Corinne S. Schelling, eds. (1984). *Public-Private Partnership: New Opportunities for Meeting Social Needs.* Cambridge, MA.: Ballinger.

Broom, Leonard, and Philip Selznick (1955). *Sociology.* 2nd ed. Evanston, IL: Row, Peterson.

Brown, Richard Harvey (1978). "Bureaucracy as Praxis: Toward a Political Phenomenology of Formal Organizations," *Administrative Science Quarterly,* 23, 365–82.

Brown, Shona L., and Kathleen M. Eisenhardt (forthcoming). "Product Innovation as Core Capacity: The Art of Continuous Change," *Administrative Science Quarterly.*

Brunsson, Nils (1985). *The Irrational Organization.* New York: Wiley.

_____ (1989). *The Organization of Hypocrisy: Talk, Decisions and Actions in Organizations.* New York: Wiley.

Brusco, Sebastiano (1982). "The Emilian Model: Productive Decentralisation and Social Integration," *Cambridge Journal of Economics,* 6, 167–84.

Buckley, Walter (1967). *Sociology and Modern Systems Theory.* Englewood Cliffs, NJ: Prentice Hall.

Burawoy, Michael (1979). *Manufacturing Consent: Changes in the Labor Process under Monopoly Capitalism.* Chicago: University of Chicago Press.

_____ (1982). "Introduction: The Resurgence of Marxism in American Sociology," in *Marxist Inquiries: Studies of Labor, Class, and States.* Supplement to *American Journal of Sociology,* 88, S1–S30, ed. Michael Burawoy and Theda Skocpol. Chicago: University of Chicago Press.

_____ (1985). *The Politics of Production.* London: Verso.

Burgelman, Robert A., and Leonard R. Sayles (1986). *Inside Corporate Innovation: Strategy, Structure, and Managerial Skills.* New York: Free Press.

Burgess, John William (1902). *Political Science and Comparative Constitutional Law.* Boston: Ginn.

Burns, Tom R., and Helena Flam (1986). *The Shaping of Social Organization: Social Rule System Theory and Its Applications.* London: Sage.

Burns, Tom, and George M. Stalker (1961). *The Management of Innovation.* London: Tavistock.

Burrell, Gibson, and Gareth Morgan (1979). *Sociological Paradigms and Organizational Analysis.* London: Heinemann.

Burt, Ronald S. (1980). "Models of Network Structure," *Annual Review of Sociology,* 6, 79–141.

_____ (1983). *Corporate Profits and Cooptation.* New York: Academic Press.

_____ (1988). "The Stability of American Markets," *American Journal of Sociology,* 94, 356–95.

_____ (1992). *Structural Holes*. Cambridge, MA: Harvard University Press.

Burt, Ronald S., Kenneth P. Christman, and Harold C. Kilburn, Jr. (1980). "Testing a Structural Theory of Corporate Cooptation: Interorganizational Directorate Ties as a Strategy for Avoiding Market Constraints on Profits," *American Sociological Review*, 45, 821–41.

Calás, Marta B., and Linda Smirich (1996). "From 'The Women's' Point of View: Feminist Approaches to Organization Studies," in *Handbook of Organization Studies*, 218–57, ed. Stewart R. Clegg, Cynthia Hardy and Walter R. Nord. Thousand Oaks, CA: Sage.

Callaghan, Polly, and Heidi Hartmann (1991). *Contingent Work: A Chart Book on Part-Time and Temporary Employment*. Washington, DC: Economic Policy Institute.

Calvert, Monte A. (1967). *The Mechanical Engineer in America, 1830–1910: Professional Cultures in Conflict*. Baltimore: Johns Hopkins University Press.

Cameron, Kim S., and R. E. Quinn (1996). *Diagnosing and Changing Organizational Culture*. San Francisco: Jossey-Bass.

Cameron, Kim S., Robert I. Sutton, and David A. Whetten, eds. (1988). *Readings in Organizational Decline: Frameworks, Research, and Prescriptions*. Cambridge, MA: Ballinger.

Cameron, Kim S., and David A. Whetten, eds. (1983). *Organizational Effectiveness: A Comparison of Multiple Models*. New York: Academic Press.

Campbell, Donald (1969). "Variation and Selective Retention in Socio-Cultural Evolution," *General Systems: Yearbook of the Society for General Systems Research*, 16, 69–85.

Campbell, John L., J. Rogers Hollingsworth, and Leon N. Lindberg, eds. (1991). *Goverance of the American Economy*. Cambridge: Cambridge University Press.

Campbell, John L., and Leon N. Lindberg (1990). "Property Rights and the Organization of Economic Activities by the State," *American Sociological Review*, 55, 634–47.

Campbell, John P. (1977). "On the Nature of Organizational Effectiveness," in *New Perspectives on Organizational Effectiveness*, pp. 13–55, ed. Paul S. Goodman and Johannes M. Pennings. San Francisco: Jossey-Bass.

Carey, Alex (1967). "The Hawthorne Studies: A Radical Criticism," *American Sociological Review*, 32, 403–16.

Carroll, Glenn R. (1984). "Organizational Ecology," *Annual Review of Sociology*, 10, 71–93.

_____ (1987). *Publish and Perish: The Organizational Ecology of Newspaper Industries*. Greenwich, CT: JAI Press.

_____ (1994). "Organizations . . . The Smaller They Get," *California Management Review* 37 (1), 28–41.

Carroll, Glenn R., and Jacques Delacroix (1982). "Organizational Mortality in the Newspaper Industries of Argentina and Ireland: An Ecological Approach," *Administrative Science Quarterly*, 27, 169–98.

Carroll, W. K. (1986). *Corporate Power and Canadian Capitalism*. Vancouver: University of British Columbia Press.

Cartwright, Dorwin (1965). "Influence, Leadership, Control," in *Handbook of Organizations*, pp. 1–47, ed. James G. March. Chicago: Rand McNally.

Carzo, Rocco, Jr, and John N. Yanouzas (1967). *Formal Organization: A Systems Approach*. Homewood, IL: Richard D. Irwin: Dorsey.

Chaffee, Ellen Earle (1985). "Three Models of Strategy," *Academy of Management Review*, 10, 89–98.

Chandler, Alfred D., Jr. (1962). *Strategy and Structure: Chapters in the History of the American Industrial Enterprise*, Cambridge, MA: MIT Press.

_____ (1977). *The Visible Hand: The Managerial Revolution in American Business*. Cambridge, MA: Belknap Press of Harvard University Press.

Chandler, Alfred D., Jr, with the assistance of Takashi Hikino (1990). *Scale and Scope: The Dynamics of Industrial Capitalism*. Cambridge, MA: Belknap Press of Harvard University Press.

Chase, Richard B., and David A. Tansik (1983). "The Customer Contact Model for Organization Design," *Management Science*, 29, 1037–50.

Child, John (1972). "Organizational Structure, Environment and Performance: The Role of Strategic Choice." *Sociology*, 6, 1–22.

_____ (1981). "Culture, Contingency and Capitalism in the Cross-National Study of Organizations," in *Research in Organizational Behavior*, vol. 3, pp. 303–56, ed. L. L. Cummings and Barry M. Staw. Greenwich, CN: JAI Press.

Christie, L. S., R. S. Luce, and J. Macy, Jr. (1952). "Communication and Learning in Task-Oriented Groups." Technical Report No. 231. Cambridge, MA: Research Laboratory of Electronics, MIT.

Cialdini, Robert B. (1988). *Influence: Science and Practice* (2nd ed.). Glenview, IL: Scott, Foresman.

Cicourel, Aaron (1968). *The Social Organization of Juvenile Justice.* New York: Wiley.

Clark, Burton R. (1956). *Adult Education in Transition.* Berkeley: University of California Press.

_____ (1963). "Faculty Organization and Authority," in *The Study of Academic Administration*, pp. 37–51, ed. Terry F. Lunsford. Boulder, CO: Western Interstate Commission for Higher Education.

_____ (1970). *The Distinctive College: Antioch, Reed and Swarthmore.* Chicago: Aldine.

_____ (1972). "The Organizational Saga in Higher Education," *Administrative Science Quarterly*, 17, 178–183.

_____ (1983). *The Higher Education System.* Berkeley: University of California Press.

Clark, Peter M., and James Q. Wilson (1961). "Incentive Systems: A Theory of Organizations," *Administrative Science Quarterly*, 6, 129–66.

Clegg, Stewart R. (1990). *Modern Organizations: Organization Studies in the Postmodern World.* London: Sage.

Clegg, Stewart R., and D. Dunkerley (1977). *Critical Issues in Organizations.* London: Routledge & Kegan Paul.

_____ (1980). *Organization, Class and Control.* London: Routledge and Kegan Paul.

Clemmer, Donald (1940). *The Prison Community.* Boston: Christopher.

Clinard, Marshall B. and Peter C. Yeager (1980). *Corporate Crime.* New York: Free Press.

Coase, R. H. (1937). "The Nature of the Firm," *Economica*, 4, 386–405.

Coch, L., and J. R. P. French, Jr. (1948). "Overcoming Resistance to Change," *Human Relations*, 1, 512–32.

Coffee, John C., Jr., Louis Lowenstein, and Susan Rose-Ackerman, eds. (1988). *Knights, Raiders, and Targets: The Impact of the Hostile Takeover.* New York: Oxford University Press.

Cohen, Bernard P. (1972). "On the Construction of Sociological Explanations," *Synthese*, 24, 401–9.

Cohen, Michael D., and James G. March (1974). *Leadership and Ambiguity: The American College President.* New York: McGraw-Hill.

_____ (1976). "Decisions, Presidents, and Status," in *Ambiguity and Choice in Organizations*, pp. 174–205, ed. James G. March and Johan P. Olsen. Bergen, Norway: Universitetsforlaget.

Cohen, Michael D., James G. March, and Johan P. Olsen (1972). "A Garbage Can Model of Organizational Choice," *Administrative Science Quarterly*, 17, 1–25.

_____ (1976). "People, Problems, Solutions and the Ambiguity of Relevance," in *Ambiguity and Choice in Organizations*, pp. 24–37, ed. James G. March and Johan P. Olsen. Bergen, Norway: Universitetsforlaget.

Cole, Robert E. (1979). *Work, Mobility, and Participation.* Berkeley: University of California Press.

_____ (1989). *Strategies for Learning: Small Group Activities in American, Japanese, and Swedish Industry.* Berkeley, CA: University of California Press.

_____ (1994). "Different Quality Paradigms and their Implications for Organizational Learning," in *The Japanese Firm: Sources of Competitive Strength*, pp. 66–83, ed. Masahiko Aoki and Ronald S. Dore, Oxford: Clarendon Press.

_____ (forthcoming). *Fads, Imitation, and Learning: The Case of the American Quality Movement.*

Coleman, James S. (1974). *Power and the Structure of Society.* New York: Norton.

_____ (1975). "Social Structure and a Theory of Action," in *Approaches to the Study of Social Structure*, pp. 76–93, ed. Peter M. Blau. New York: Free Press.

_____ (1990). *Foundations of Social Theory.* Cambridge, MA: Belknap Press of Harvard University Press.

Colignon, Richard A. (1996). *Power Plays: Critical Events in the Institutionalization of the TVA.* Albany: State University of New York Press.

Collins, Orvis (1946). "Ethnic Behavior in Industry: Sponsorship and Rejection in a New England Factory," *American Journal of Sociology*, 21, 293–98.

Collins, Randall (1975). *Conflict Sociology: Toward an Explanatory Science.* New York: Academic Press.

_____ (1979). *The Credential Society.* New York: Academic Press.

Commons, John R. (1924). *Legal Foundations of Capitalism.* New York: Macmillan.

Comstock, Donald E., and W. Richard Scott (1977). "Technology and the Structure of Subunits: Distinguishing Individual and Workgroup Effects," *Administrative Science Quarterly,* 22, 177–202.

Cooley, Charles Horton (1956 ed.). *Social Organization.* NY: Charles Scribner's Sons (first published in 1902).

Cooper, Robert, and Gibson Burrell (1988). "Modernism, Postmodernism and Organizational Analysis: An Introduction," *Organization Studies,* 9, 91–112.

Cornfield, Daniel B. (1991). "The U.S. Labor Movement: Its Development and Impact on Social Inequality and Politics," *Annual Review of Sociology,* 17, 27–49.

Coser, Lewis (1956). *The Functions of Social Conflict.* Glencoe, IL: Free Press.

Coser, Rose Laub (1951). "An Analysis of the Early German Socialist Movement." Unpublished M.A. Thesis, Department of Sociology, Columbia University.

Cote, Owen, and Harvey M. Sapolsky (1990). "Militaries: Familiar but Unusual Organizations." Paper presented at a Conference on Organizational Issues in U.S. Nuclear Policy, Berkeley, CA.

Creighton, Andrew L. (1990). "The Emergence of Incorporation as a Legal Form for Organizations." Unpublished Ph.D. Dissertation, Department of Sociology, Stanford University.

Cronbach, Lee J., and Associates (1980). *Toward Reform of Program Evaluation.* San Francisco: Jossey-Bass.

Crosby, Philip B. (1979). *Quality is Free: The Art of Making Quality Certain.* New York: New American Library.

Crozier, Michel (1964). *The Bureaucratic Phenomenon.* Chicago: University of Chicago Press.

Crystal, Graef S. (1991). *In Search of Excess: The Overcompensation of American Executives.* New York: Norton.

Cummings, Larry L. (1977). "Emergence of the Instrumental Organization," in *New Perspectives on Organizational Effectiveness,* pp. 56–62, ed. Paul S. Goodman and Johannes M. Pennings. San Francisco: Jossey-Bass.

Cyert, Richard M., and James G. March (1963). *A Behavioral Theory of the Firm.* Englewood Cliffs, NJ: Prentice Hall.

Dahrendorf, Ralf (1959 trans.). *Class and Class Conflict in Industrial Society.* Stanford, CA: Stanford University Press (first published in 1957).

Dalton, Melville (1950). "Conflicts between Staff and Line Managerial Officers," *American Sociological Review,* 15, 342–51.

_____ (1959). *Men Who Manage.* New York: Wiley.

Davis, Gerald F. (1990). "Agents Without Principles? The Spread of the Poison Pill Through the Intercorporate Network." *Administrative Science Quarterly,* 36, 583–613.

Davis, Gerald F., Kristina A. Diekmann, and Catherine H. Tinsley (1994). "The Decline and Fall of the Conglomerate Firm in the 1980s: The Deinstitutionalization of an Organizational Form," *American Sociological Review,* 59, 547–70.

Davis, Gerald F., Robert L. Kahn, and Mayer N. Zald (1990). "Contracts, Treaties, and Joint Ventures," in *Organizations and Nation-States: New Perspectives on Conflict and Cooperation,* 19–54, ed. Robert L. Kahn and Mayer N. Zald. San Francisco: Jossey-Bass.

Davis, Gerald F., and Walter W. Powell (1992). "Organization-Environment Relations," in *Handbook of Industrial and Organizational Psychology,* vol. 3 (2nd ed.), pp. 315–75, ed. Marvin Dunnette. Palo Alto, CA: Consulting Psychologists Press.

Davis, Kingsley (1949). *Human Society.* New York: Macmillan.

Davis, Louis E., and James C. Taylor (1976). "Technology, Organization, and Job Structure," in *Handbook of Work, Organization, and Society,* pp. 379–419, ed. Robert Dubin. Chicago: Rand-McNally.

Davis, Stanley M. (1987). *Future Perfect.* Reading, MA: Addison-Wesley.

Davis, Stanley M., and Paul R. Lawrence (1977). *Matrix.* Reading, MA.: Addison-Wesley.

Deal, Terrence E., and Allan A. Kennedy (1982). *Corporate Cultures.* Reading MA.: Addison-Wesley.

Dean, James W., Jr., and David E. Bowen (1994). "Management Theory and Total Quality: Improving Research and Practice Through Theory Development,"*Academy of Management Review* 19, 392–418.

Deming, W. Edwards (1986). *Out of the Crisis.* Cambridge, MA: MIT Center for Advanced Engineering Study.

Derrida, J. (1976). *Speech and Phenomenon.* Evanston, IL: Northwestern University Press.

Diamond, Sigmund (1958). "From Organization to Society," *American Journal of Sociology,* 63, 457–75.

Dibble, Vernon K. (1965). "The Organization of Traditional Authority: English County Government, 1558 to 1640," in *Handbook of Organizations,* pp. 879–909, ed. James G. March. Chicago: Rand McNally.

Dill, William R. (1958). "Environment as an Influence on Managerial Autonomy," *Administrative Science Quarterly,* 2, 409–43.

DiMaggio, Paul J. (1983). "State Expansion and Organizational Fields," in *Organizational Theory and Public Policy,* pp. 147–61, ed. Richard H. Hall and Robert E. Quinn. Beverly Hills, CA: Sage.

_____ (1986). "Structural Analysis of Organizational Fields: A Blockmodel Approach." in *Research in Organizational Behavior,* 8, 355–70, ed. Barry M. Staw and L. L. Cummings. Greenwich, CT: JAI Press.

_____ (1988). "Interest and Agency in Institutional Theory," in *Institutional Patterns and Organizations: Culture and Environment,* pp. 3–21, ed. Lynne G. Zucker. Cambridge, MA: Ballinger.

_____ (1991). "Constructing an Organizational Field as a Professional Project: U.S. Art Museums, 1920–1940," in *The New Institutionalism in Organizational Analysis,* pp. 267–92, ed. Walter W. Powell and Paul J. DiMaggio. Chicago: University of Chicago Press.

DiMaggio, Paul J., and Walter W. Powell (1983). "The Iron Cage Revisited: Institutional Isomorphism and Collective Rationality in Organizational Fields," *American Sociological Review,* 48, 147–60.

_____ (1991). "Introduction," in *The New Institutionalism in Organizational Analysis,"* pp. 1–38, ed. Walter W. Powell and Paul J. DiMaggio. Chicago: University of Chicago Press.

DiPrete, Thomas A. (1989). *The Bureaucratic Labor Market: The Case of the Federal Civil Service.* New York: Plenum.

DiPrete, Thomas A., and David B. Grusky (1990). "Structure and Trend in the Process of Stratification for American Men and Women," *American Journal of Sociology* 96, 107–43.

Dobbin, Frank R. (1994a). "Cultural Models of Organization: The Social Construction of Rational Organizing Principles," in *The Sociology of Culture: Emerging Theoretical Perspectives,* pp. 117–53, ed. Diana Crane. Cambridge, MA: Blackwell.

_____ (1994b). *Forging Industrial Policy: The United States, Britain, and France in the Railway Age.* New York: Cambridge University Press.

Dobbin, Frank R., Lauren Edelman, John W. Meyer, W. Richard Scott, and Ann Swidler (1988). "The Expansion of Due Process in Organizations," in *Institutional Patterns and Organizations: Culture and Environment,* pp. 71–98, ed. Lynne G. Zucker. Cambridge, MA: Ballinger.

Doeringer, Peter B., and Michael J. Piore (1971). *Internal Labor Markets and Manpower Analysis.* Lexington, MA: Heath.

Domhoff, G. William (1983). *Who Rules America Now? A View for the 80s.* Englewood Cliffs, NJ: Prentice Hall.

Donabedian, Avedis (1966). "Evaluating the Quality of Medical Care," *Milbank Memorial Fund Quarterly,* 44 (part 2), 166–206.

Donaldson, Lex 1985. *In Defence of Organization Theory: A Reply to the Critics.* Cambridge: Cambridge University Press.

_____ 1995. *American Anti-Management Theories of Organization: A Critique of Paradigm Proliferation.* Cambridge: Cambridge University Press.

_____ 1996. "Structural Contingency Theory," in *Handbook of Organization Studies*, pp. 57–76, ed. Stewart R. Clegg, Cynthia Hardy, and Walter R. Nord. Thousand Oaks, CA: Sage.

Dore, Ronald (1973). *British Factory–Japanese Factory.* Berkeley: University of California Press.

_____ (1983). "Goodwill and the Spirit of Market Capitalism," *British Journal of Sociology*, 34, 459–82.

Dornbusch, Sanford M., and W. Richard Scott, with the assistance of Bruce C. Busching and James D. Laing (1975). *Evaluation and the Exercise of Authority.* San Francisco: Jossey-Bass.

Doty, D. Harold, William H. Glick, and George P. Huber (1993). "Fit, Equifinality, and Organizational Effectiveness: A Test of Two Configurational Theories," *Academy of Management Journal*, 36: 1196–1250.

Downs, Anthony (1967). *Inside Bureaucracy.* Boston: Little, Brown.

Drazin, Robert, and Andrew H. Van de Ven (1985). "Alternative Forms of Fit in Contingency Theory," *Administrative Science Quarterly*, 30, 514–39.

Drucker, Peter (1970). "The New Markets and the New Capitalism," *Public Interest*, 21 (Fall), 44–79.

_____ (1976). "What Results Should You Expect? A User's Guide to MBO," *Public Administration Review*, 36, 1–45.

Duncan, Robert B. (1972). "Characteristics of Organizational Environments and Perceived Environmental Uncertainty," *Administrative Science Quarterly*, 17, 313–27.

Dunning, John H. (1993). *Multinational Enterprises and the Global Economy.* Reading, MA: Addison-Wesley.

Durkheim, Emile (1949 trans.). *Division of Labor in Society.* Glencoe, IL: Free Press (first published in 1893).

_____ (1961 trans.). *The Elementary Forms of Religious Life.* New York: Collier (first published in 1912).

Eccles, Robert G., and Dwight B. Crane (1988). *Doing Deals: Investment Banks at Work.* Boston, MA: Harvard Business School Press.

Eccles, Robert G., and Harrison C. White (1986). "Firm and Market Interfaces of Profit Center Control," in *Approaches to Social Theory*, pp. 203–20, ed. Siegwart Lindenberg, James S. Coleman, and Stefan Nowak. New York: Russell Sage Foundation.

_____ (1988). "Price and Authority in Inter-Profit Center Transactions," *American Journal of Sociology*, 94, Supplement, S17–S51.

Edelman, Lauren B. (1992). "Legal Ambiguity and Symbolic Structures: Organizational Mediation of Civil Rights Law," *American Journal of Sociology*, 97, 1531–76.

Editors of the Yale Law Journal (1954). "The American Medical Association: Power, Purpose, and Politics in Organized Medicine," *Yale Law Journal*, 63, 938–1022.

Edwards, Richard (1979). *Contested Terrain: The Transformation of the Workplace in the Twentieth Century.* New York: Basic Books.

Eisenhardt, Kathleen M. (1988). "Agency and Institutional Theory Explanations: The Case of Retail Sales Compensation," *Academy of Management Journal*, 31, 488–511.

Eisenhardt, Kathleen M., and Behnam N. Tabrizi (1995). "Accelerating Adaptive Processes: Product Innovation in the Global Computer Industry, *Administrative Science Quarterly*, 40, 84–110.

Eisenstadt, S. N. (1958). "Bureaucracy and Bureaucratization: A Trend Report and Bibliography," *Current Sociology*, 7(2), 99–164.

_____ (1981). "Interactions between Organizations and Societal Stratification," in *Handbook of Organizational Design*, vol. 1, pp. 309–22, ed. Paul C. Nystrom and William H. Starbuck. Oxford: Oxford University Press.

Ellul, Jacques (1964 trans.). *The Technological Society.* New York: Knopf (first published in 1954.)

Elsbach, Kimberly D., and Robert I. Sutton (1992). "Acquiring Organizational Legitimacy Through Illegitimate Actions: A Marriage of Institutional and Impression Management Theories," *Academy of Management Journal*, 35, 699–738.

Elster, Jon (1983). *Explaining Technical Change: A Case Study in the Philosophy of Science.* Cambridge: Cambridge University Press.

Emerson, Richard M. (1962). "Power-Dependence Relations," *American Sociological Review*, 27, 31–40.

Emery, Fred E. (1959). *Characteristics of Socio-Technical Systems*. Tavistock Document 527. London: Tavistock.

Emery, Fred E., and E. Thorsrud (1969, trans.). *Form and Content in Industrial Democracy*. London: Tavistock (first published in 1964).

_____ (1976). *Democracy at Work*. Leiden: Martinus Nijhoff.

Emery, Fred E., and E. L. Trist (1965). "The Causal Texture of Organizational Environments," *Human Relations*, 18, 21–32.

England, Paula (1992). *Comparable Worth: Theories and Evidence*. New York: Aldine de Gruyter.

Ermann, M. David, and Richard J. Lundman (1982). *Corporate Deviance*. New York: Holt, Rinehart and Winston.

Etzioni, Amitai (1960). "Two Approaches to Organizational Analysis: A Critique and a Suggestion," *Administrative Science Quarterly*, 5, 257–78.

_____ (1961). *A Comparative Analysis of Complex Organizations*. New York: Free Press of Glencoe (rev. 1975).

_____ (1964). *Modern Organizations*. Englewood Cliffs, NJ: Prentice Hall.

_____, ed. (1969). *The Semi-Professions and Their Organization*. New York: Free Press.

Evan, William M. (1966). "The Organization Set: Toward a Theory of Interorganizational Relations," in *Approaches to Organizational Design*, pp. 173–88, ed. James D. Thompson. Pittsburgh: University of Pittsburgh Press.

Evans, Peter B., Dietrich Rueschemeyer, and Theda Skocpol, eds. (1985). *Bringing the State Back In*. Cambridge: Cambridge University Press.

Farley, Reynolds (1984). *Blacks and Whites: Narrowing the Gap?* Cambridge, MA: Harvard University Press.

Fama, Eugene F. (1980). "Agency Problems and the Theory of the Firm," *Journal of Political Economy*, 88, 288–307.

Faunce, William A. (1968). *Problems of an Industrial Society*. New York: McGraw-Hill.

Fayol, Henri (1949 trans.). *General and Industrial Management*. London: Pitman (first published in 1919).

Featherman, David L., and Robert M. Hauser (1978). *Opportunity and Change*. New York: Academic Press.

Fennell, Mary L., and Jeffrey A. Alexander (1987). "Organizational Boundary Spanning in Institutionalized Environments," *Academy of Management Journal*, 30, 456–76.

Ferguson, Kathy E. (1984). *The Feminist Case against Bureaucracy*. Philadelphia: Temple University Press.

Ferree, Myra Marx, and Patricia Yancey Martin, eds. (1995). *Feminist Organizations: Harvest of the New Women's Movement*. Philadelphia: Temple University Press.

Festinger, Leon (1957). *A Theory of Cognitive Dissonance*. Evanston, IL: Row, Peterson.

Fiedler, Fred E. (1964). "A Contingency Model of Leadership Effectiveness," in *Advances in Experimental Social* Psychology, ed. Leonard Berkowitz. New York: Academic Press.

_____ (1971). "Validation and Extension of the Contingency Model of Leadership Effectiveness: A Review of Empirical Findings," *Psychological Bulletin*, 76, 128–48.

Fierman, Jaclyn (1990). "Why Women Still Don't Hit the Top," *Fortune*, 122 (July 30), 40–62.

Fligstein, Neil (1985). "The Spread of the Multidivisional Form among Large Firms, 1919–1979," *American Sociological Review*, 50, 377–91.

_____ (1987). "The Intraorganizational Power Struggle: The Rise of Finance Presidents in Large Corporations," *American Sociological Review*, 52, 44–58.

_____ (1990). *The Transformation of Corporate Control*. Cambridge, MA: Harvard University Press.

Fligstein, Neil, and Iona Mara-Drita (1996). "How to Make a Market: Reflections on the Attempt to Create a Single Market in the European Union," *American Journal of Sociology*, 102,1–33.

Flood, Ann Barry, and W. Richard Scott (1987). *Hospital Structure and Performance*. Baltimore: Johns Hopkins University Press.

Foley, Henry A., and Steven S. Sharfstein (1983). *Madness and Government: Who Cares for the Mentally Ill?* Washington, DC: American Psychiatric Press.

Follett, Mary Parker (1942). *Dynamic Administration.* New York: Harper.

Form, William (1987). "On the Degradation of Skills," *Annual Review of Sociology*, 13, 29–47.

Foucault, Michel (1977). *Discipline and Punish.* New York: Pantheon.

Fox, Renée (1959). *Experiment Perilous.* Glencoe, IL: Free Press.

Francis, Arthur, Jeremy Turk, and Paul Willman, eds. (1983). *Power, Efficiency and Institutions: A Critical Appraisal of the `Markets and Hierarchies' Paradigm.* London: Heinemann.

Franke, Richard Herbert, and James D. Kaul (1978). "The Hawthorne Experiments: First Statistical Interpretation," *American Sociological Reivew,* 43, 623–43.

Freeland, Robert F. (1996). "The Myth of the M-Form? Governance, Consent, and Organizational Change," *American Journal of Sociology* 102, 483–526.

Freeman, John H. (1978). "The Unit of Analysis in Organizational Research," in *Environments and Organizations,* pp. 335–51, ed. Marshall W. Meyer. San Francisco: Jossey-Bass.

_____ (1986). "Data Quality and the Development of Organizational Social Science: An Editorial Essay," *Administrative Science Quarterly,* 31,298–303.

Freeman, John H., and Jack W. Brittain (1977). "Union Merger Process and Industrial Environment," *Industrial Relations,* 16, 173–85.

Freeman, John H., and Michael T. Hannan (1975). "Growth and Decline Processes in Organizations," *American Sociological Review,* 40, 215–28.

_____ (1983). "Niche Width and the Dynamics of Organizational Populations," *American Journal of Sociology,* 88, 1116–45.

Freidson, Eliot (1970). *Profession of Medicine.* New York: Dodd, Mead.

_____ (1975). *Doctoring Together: A Study of Professional Social Control.* New York: Elsevier.

_____ (1986). *Professional Powers: A Study of the Institutionalization of Formal Knowledge.* Chicago: University of Chicago Press.

_____ (1994). *Professionalism Reborn: Theory, Prophecy, and Policy.* Chicago: University of Chicago Press.

Freidson, Eliot, and Buford Rhea (1963). "Processes of Control in a Company of Equals," *Social Problems,* 11 (Fall), 119–31.

Friedland, Roger (1980). "Corporate Power and Urban Growth: The Case of Urban Renewal," *Politics and Society,* 10, 203–24.

Friedland, Roger, and Robert R. Alford, "Bringing Society Back In: Symbols, Practices, and Institutional Contradictions," in *The New Institutionalism in Organizational Analysis,* 232–63, ed. Walter W. Powell and Paul J. DiMaggio. Chicago: University of Chicago Press.

Friedland, Roger, and Donald Palmer (1984). "Park Place and Main Street: Business and the Urban Power Structure," *Annual Review of Sociology,* 10, 395–416.

Friedlander, Frank, and Hal Pickle (1968). "Components of Effectiveness in Small Organizations," *Administrative Science Quarterly,* 13, 289–304.

Frost, Peter J., Larry F. Moore, Meryl Reis Louis, Craig C. Lundberg, and Joanne Martin, eds. (1985). *Organizational Culture,* Beverly Hills, CA: Sage.

Fruin, W. M. (1992). *The Japanese Enterprise System: Competitive Strategies and Cooperative Structures.* Oxford: Clarendon.

Fuchs, Victor R. (1974). *Who Shall Live? Health, Economics, and Social Choice.* New York: Basic Books.

Galanter, Mark, and T. Palay (1991). *Tournament of Lawyers.* Chicago: University of Chicago Press.

Galaskiewicz, Joseph (1979). "The Structure of Community Organizational Networks," *Social Forces,* 57, 1346–64.

_____ (1985). "Interorganizational Relations," *Annual Review of Sociology,* 11, 281–304.

Galbraith, Jay R. (1973). *Designing Complex Organizations.* Reading, MA: Addison-Wesley.

_____ (1977). *Organization Design.* Reading, MA: Addison-Wesley.

Galbraith, Jay R., and Edward E. Lawler III, eds. (1993). *Organizing for the Future: The New Logic for Managing Complex Organizations.* San Francisco: Jossey-Bass.

Galbraith, John Kenneth (1967). *The New Industrial State.* Boston: Houghton Mifflin.

Gall, John (1978). *Systematics.* New York: Simon & Schuster, Pocket Books.

Gamson William (1975). *The Strategy of Protest.* Homewood, IL: Dorsey.

Garfinkel, Harold (1967). *Studies in Ethnomethodology.* Englewood Cliffs, NJ: Prentice Hall.

Geertz, Clifford (1973). *The Interpretation of Cultures.* New York: Basic Books.

Georgopoulos, Basil S. (1972). "The Hospital as an Organization and Problem-Solving System," in *Organization Research on Health Institutions,* pp. 9–48, ed. Basil S. Georgopoulos. Ann Arbor: Institute for Social Research, University of Michigan.

Gereffi, Gary, and Miguel Korzeniewicz (1994). *Commodity Chains and Global Capitalism.* Westport, CT: Praeger.

Gerstel, N., and Gross, H. E., eds. (1987). *Families and Work.* Philadelphia: Temple University Press.

Gerwin, Donald (1981). "Relationships between Structure and Technology," in *Handbook of Organizational Design,* vol. 2, 3–38, ed. Paul C. Nystrom and William H. Starbuck. New York: Oxford University Press.

Ghoshal, Sumantra, and Christopher B. Bartlett (1990). "The Multinational Corporation as an Interorganizational Network," *Academy of Management Review,* 15, 603–25.

Ghoshal, Sumantra, and D. Eleanor Westney, ed. (1993). *Organization Theory and the Multinational Corporation.* New York: St. Martin's Press.

Gibson, David V., and Everett M. Rogers (1988). "The MCC Comes to Texas," in *Measuring the Information Society: The Texas Studies,* ed. F. Williams. New York: Sage.

Giddens, Anthony (1979). *Central Problems in Social Theory.* Berkeley: University of California Press.

_____ (1983). *Profiles and Critiques in Social Theory.* Berkeley: University of California Press.

Gilbreth, F. B., and L. M. Gilbreth (1917). *Applied Motion Study.* New York.

Gilligan, Carol (1982). *In a Different Voice: Psychological Theory and Women's Development.* Cambridge, MA: Harvard University Press.

Glasberg, Davita Silfen, and Michael Schwartz (1983). "Ownership and Control of Corporations," *Annual Review of Sociology,* 9, 311–32.

Glassman, Robert (1973). "Persistence and Loose Coupling in Living Systems," *Behavioral Science,* 18, 83–98.

Glennon, Lynda M. (1979). *Women and Dualism.* New York: Longman.

Goffman, Erving (1961). *Asylums.* Garden City, NY: Doubleday, Anchor Books.

Goldner, Fred H. (1970). "The Division of Labor: Process and Power," in *Power in Organizations,* pp. 97–143, ed. Mayer N. Zald. Nashville, TN.: Vanderbilt University Press.

Goodman, Paul (1968). *People or Personnel* and *Like a Conquered Province.* New York: Random House.

Goodrick, Elizabeth, and Gerald R. Salancik (1996). "Organizational Discretion in Responding to Institutional Practices: Hospitals and Caesarean Births," *Administrative Science Quarterly,* 41, 1–28.

Gordon, David M., Richard Edwards, and Michael Reich (1982). *Segmented Work, Divided Workers.* Cambridge: Cambridge University Press.

Gore, Al (1993). *The Gore Report on Reinventing Government: Report of the National Performance Review.* New York: Random House.

Gosnell, Harold F. (1937). *Machine Politics: Chicago Model.* Chicago: University of Chicago Press.

Gould, Steven J., and N. Eldredge (1977). "Punctuated Equilibria: The Tempo and Mode of Evolution Reconsidered," *Paleobiology,* 3, 115–51.

Gouldner, Alvin W. (1954). *Patterns of Industrial Bureaucracy.* Glencoe, IL: Free Press.

_____ (1959). "Organizational Analysis," in *Sociology Today,* pp. 400–28, ed. Robert K. Merton, Leonard Broom, and Leonard S. Cottrell, Jr. New York: Basic Books.

Grandori, Anna (1987). *Perspectives on Organization Theory.* Cambridge, MA: Ballinger.

Granovetter, Mark (1973). "The Strength of Weak Ties," *American Journal of Sociology,* 78: 1360–80.

_____ (1985). "Economic Action and Social Structure: The Problem of Embeddedness," *American Journal of Sociology*, 91, 481–510.

_____ (1994). "Business Groups," in *The Handbook of Economic Sociology*, 453–75, ed. Neil J. Smelser and Richard Swedberg. Princeton, NJ: Princeton University Press and Russell Sage Foundation.

Granovetter, Mark, and Charles Tilly (1988). "Inequality and Labor Processes," in *Handbook of Sociology*, pp. 175–221, ed.Neil J. Smelser. Newbury Park: Sage.

Greenberg, Jerald, and Kimberly S. Scott (1996). "Why Do Workers Bite the Hand that Feeds Them? Employee Theft as a Social Exchange Process," in *Research in Organizational Behavior*, 18, ed. Barry M. Staw and L. L. Cummings. Greenwich, CT: JAI Press.

Greenhalgh, Leonard (1983). "Organizational Decline," in *Research in the Sociology of Organizations*, vol. 2, 231–76, ed. Samuel B. Bacharach. Greenwich, CT: JAI Press.

Greiner, Larry E. (1972). "Evolution and Revolution as Organizations Grow," *Harvard Business Review*, 50 (July–August), 37–46.

Gross, Edward (1953). "Some Functional Consequences of Primary Controls in Formal Work Organizations," *American Sociological Review*, 18, 368–73.

_____ (1968). "Universities as Organizations: A Research Approach," *American Sociological Review*, 33, 518–44.

Gross, Edward, and Amitai Etzioni (1985). *Organizations in Society*. Englewood Cliffs, NJ: Prentice Hall.

Gross, Neal, Ward S. Mason, and Alexander W. McEachern (1958). *Explorations in Role Analysis*. New York: Wiley.

Guetzkow, Harold, and Herbert A. Simon (1955). "The Impact of Certain Communication Nets upon Organization and Performance in Task-Oriented Groups," *Management Science*, 1, 233–50.

Guillén, Mauro F. (1994.) *Models of Management: Work, Authority, and Organization in Comparative Perspective*. Chicago: University of Chicago Press.

Gulick, Luther, and L. Urwick, eds. (1937). *Papers on the Science of Administration*. New York: Institute of Public Administration, Columbia University.

Gusfield, Joseph R. (1968). "The Study of Social Movements," in *International Encyclopedia of the Social Sciences*, vol. 14, pp. 445–52. New York: Macmillan.

Gyllenhammar, P. G. (1977). *People at Work*. Reading, MA: Addison-Wesley.

Habermas, Jurgen (1971). *Knowledge and Human Interests*. Boston: Beacon Press.

Haberstroh, Chadwick J. (1965). "Organization Design and Systems Analysis," in *Handbook of Organizations*, pp. 1171–211, ed. James G. March. Chicago: Rand McNally.

Hackman, J. Richard, and Greg R. Oldham (1980). *Work Redesign*. Reading, MA: Addison-Wesley.

Hackman, J. Richard, and Ruth Wageman (1995). "Total Quality Management: Empirical, Conceptual and Practical Issues," *Administrative Science Quarterly*, 40, 309–42.

Hafferty, Frederic W., and John B. McKinlay, eds. (1993). *The Changing Medical Profession: An International Perspective*. New York: Oxford University Press.

Hage, Jerald (1965). "An Axiomatic Theory of Organizations," *Administrative Science Quarterly*, 10, 289–320.

Håkansson, Hakan (1989). *Corporate Technological Behavior: Cooperation and Networks*. London: Routledge.

Hall, A.D., and R. E. Fagen (1956). "Definition of System," *General Systems: The Yearbook of the Society for the Advancement of General Systems Theory*, 1, 18–28.

Hall, Richard H. (1963). "The Concept of Bureaucracy: An Empirical Assessment," *American Journal of Sociology*, 69, 32–40.

_____ (1967). "Some Organizational Considerations in the Professional-Organizational Relationship," *Administrative Science Quarterly*, 12, 461–78.

_____ (1968). "Professionalization and Bureaucratization." *American Sociological Review*, 33, 92–104.

Hall, Richard H., J. Eugene Haas, and Norman J. Johnson (1967). "Organizational Size, Complexity, and Formalization," *American Sociological Review*, 32: 903–12.

Hall, Richard H., and Charles R. Tittle (1966). "Bureaucracy and Its Correlates," *American Journal of Sociology*, 72, 267–72.

Hamilton, Gary G., and Nicole Woolsey Biggart (1984). *Governor Reagan, Governor Brown: A Sociology of Executive Power.* New York: Columbia University Press.

_____ (1988). "Market, Culture, and Authority: A Comparative Analysis of Management and Organization in the Far East," *American Journal of Sociology,* 94 (supplement), S52–S94.

Hammer, Michael, and James Champy (1993). *Reengineering the Corporation: A Manifesto for Business Revolution.* New York: Harper Business.

Hannan, Michael T., and Glenn R. Carroll (1995). "An Introduction to Organizational Ecology," in *Organizations in Industry: Strategy, Structure and Selection,* pp. 17–31, ed. Glenn R. Carroll and Michael T. Hannan. New York: Oxford University Press.

Hannan, Michael T., Glenn R. Carroll, Elizabeth A. Dundon, and John Charles Torres (1995). "Organizational Evolution in a Multinational Context: Entries of Automobile Manufactureres in Belgium, Britain, France, Germany, and Italy," *American Sociological Review,* 60, 509–28.

Hannan, Michael T., and John Freeman (1977). "The Population Ecology of Organizations," *American Journal of Sociology,* 82, 929–64.

_____ (1984). "Structural Inertia and Organizational Change," *American Sociological Review,* 49, 149–64.

_____ (1987). "The Ecology of Organizational Founding: American Labor Unions, 1836–1985," *American Journal of Sociology,* 92, 910–43.

_____ (1989). *Organizational Ecology.* Cambridge: Harvard University Press.

Harrigan, K. R. (1985). *Strategies for Joint Ventures.* Lexington, MA: Lexington Books.

Harris, Douglas H., ed. (1994). *Organizational Linkages: Understanding the Productivity Paradox.* Washington, DC: National Academy Press.

Harrison, Bennett (1994). *Lean and Mean: The Changing Landscape of Corporate Power in the Age of Flexibility.* New York: Basic Books.

Harrison, Bennett, and Barry Bluestone (1988). *The Great U-Turn: Corporate Restructuring and the Polarizing of America.* New York: Basic Books.

Hart, David K., and William G. Scott (1975). "The Organizational Imperative," *Administration and Society,* 7, 259–85.

Hawley, Amos (1950). *Human Ecology.* New York: Ronald Press.

Heclo, Hugh (1977). *A Government of Strangers: Executive Politics in Washington.* Washington, DC: Brookings Institution.

Hedberg, Bo (1981). "How Organizations Learn and Unlearn," in *Handbook of Organizational Design,* vol. 1, pp. 3–27, ed. Paul C. Nystrom and William H. Starbuck. Oxford: Oxford University Press.

Hedberg, Bo L. T., Paul C. Nystrom, and William H. Starbuck (1976). "Camping on Seesaws: Prescriptions for a Self-Designing Organization," *Administrative Science Quarterly,* 21, 41–65.

Heilbroner, Robert L. (1980). *An Inquiry into the Human Prospect.* (rev. ed.). New York: Norton.

Heinz, John P., and Edward O. Laumann (1982). *Chicago Lawyers: The Social Structure of the Bar.* New York: Russell Sage Foundation and American Bar Association.

Heithoff, Kim A., and Kathleen N. Lohr, ed. (1990). *Effectiveness and Outcomes in Health Care.* Washington, DC: National Academy Press.

Helper, Susan (1991). "How Much Has Really Changed between U.S. Automakers and their Suppliers?" *Sloan Management Review,* 32 (Summer), 15–28.

Herman, Edward S. (1981). *Corporate Control, Corporate Power.* New York: Cambridge University Press.

Herzberg, Frederick (1966). *Work and the Nature of Man.* Cleveland, OH: World.

Hickson, David J., C. R. Hinings, C. A. Lee, R. E. Schneck, and J. M. Pennings (1971). "A Strategic Contingencies' Theory of Intraorganizational Power," *Administrative Science Quarterly,* 16, 216–29.

Hickson, David J., D. S. Pugh, and Diana C. Pheysey (1969). "Operations Technology and Organization Structure: An Empirical Reappraisal," *Administrative Science Quarterly,* 14, 378–97.

Hill, Raynard E., and Bernard J. White (1979). *Matrix Organization and Project Management.* Ann Arbor: University of Michigan Press.

Hillery, George A., Jr. (1968). *Communal Organization: A Study of Local Societies.* Chicago: University of Chicago Press.

Hind, Robert R., Sanford M. Dornbusch, and W. Richard Scott (1974). "A Theory of Evaluation Applied to a University Faculty," *Sociology of Education,* 47, 114–28.

Hinings, C. R., D. J. Hickson, J. M. Pennings, and R. E. Schneck (1974). "Structural Conditions of Intraorganizational Power," *Administrative Science Quarterly,* 19, 22–44.

Hirsch, Paul M. (1972). "Processing Fads and Fashions: An Organization-Set Analysis of Cultural Industry Systems," *American Journal of Sociology,* 77, 639–59.

———— (1975). "Organizational Effectiveness and the Institutional Environment," *Administrative Science Quarterly,* 20, 327–44.

———— (1985). "The Study of Industries," in *Research in the Sociology of Organizations,* vol. 4, 271–309, ed. Samuel B. Bacharach and Stephen M. Mitchell. Greenwich, CN: JAI Press.

Hirschman, Albert O. (1970). *Exit, Voice, and Loyalty.* Cambridge, MA: Harvard University Press.

Hobsbawn, Eric, and Terence Ranger, ed. (1983). *The Invention of Tradition.* Cambridge: Cambridge University Press.

Hochschild, Arlie Russell (1983). *The Managed Heart: Commercialization of Human Feeling.* Berkeley: University of California Press.

———— (1989). *The Second Shift: Working Parents and the Revolution at Home.* New York: Viking.

Hodgson, Geoffrey (1988). *Economics and Institutions: A Manifesto for a Modern Institutional Economics.* Philadelphia: University of Pennsylvania Press.

Hodson, Randy (1996). "Dignity in the Workplace Under Participative Management: Alienation and Freedom Revisited." *American Sociological Review,* 61, 719–38.

Hofstadter, Richard (1945). *Social Darwinism in American Thought, 1860–1915.* Philadelphia: University of Pennsylvania Press.

Hofstede, Geert (1984). *Culture's Consequences: International Differences in Work-Related Values* (abridged ed.). Beverly Hills, CA: Sage.

Hofstede, Geert, and M. S. Kassem, eds. (1976). *European Contributions to Organization Theory.* Assen, The Netherlands: Van Gorcum.

Holdaway, Edward A., and Thomas A. Blowers (1971). "Administrative Ratios and Organizational Size: A Longitudinal Examination," *American Sociological Review,* 36, 278–86.

Hollander, Edwin P., and James W. Julian (1969). "Contemporary Trends in the Analysis of Leadership Processes," *Psychological Bulletin,* 71, 387–97.

Homans, George C. (1950). *The Human Group.* New York: Harcourt.

———— (1961). *Social Behavior: Its Elementary Forms.* New York: Harcourt, Brace & World.

Hopkins, Terence K., and Immanuel Wallerstein (1986). "Commodity Chains in the World-Economy Prior to 1800," *Review,* 10 (1), 157–70.

Hopwood, Anthony, and Peter Miller, eds. (1994). *Accounting as Social and Institutional Practice.* New York: Cambridge University Press.

Hounshell, David A. (1984). *From the American System to Mass Production, 1900–1932: The Development of Manufacturing Technology in the United States.* Baltimore: Johns Hopkins University Press.

Huber, George P. (1990). "A Theory of the Effects of Advanced Information Technologies on Organizational Design, Intelligence, and Decision Making," *Academy of Management Review,* 15, 47–71.

Hughes, Everett C. (1958). *Men and Their Work.* Glencoe, IL: Free Press.

Hulin, Charles L., and Milton R. Blood (1968). "Job Enlargement, Individual Differences, and Worker Responses," *Psychological Bulletin,* 69, 41–55.

Hulin, Charles L., and M. Roznowski (1985). "Organizational Technologies: Effects on Organizations' Characteristics and Individuals' Responses," in *Research in Organizational Behavior,* vol. 7: 39–85, ed. L. L. Cummings and Barry M. Staw. Greenwich, CT: JAI Press.

Hult, Karen M., and Charles Walcott (1990). *Governing Public Organizations: Politics, Structures, and Institutional Design.* Pacific Grove, CA: Brooks/Cole.

Ianni, Francis A. J. (1972). *A Family Business: Kinship and Social Control in Organized Crime.* New York: Russell Sage Foundation.

Illich, Ivan (1972). *Deschooling Society*. New York: Harper & Row.

_____ (1976). *Medical Nemesis*. New York: Random House.

Inkeles, Alex (1969). "Making Men Modern: On the Causes and Consequences of Individual Change in Six Developing Countries," *American Journal of Sociology*, 75, 208–25.

Israel, Joachim (1971). *Alienation: From Marx to Modern Sociology*. Boston: Allyn & Bacon.

James, Henry (1907). Preface to *Roderick Hudson*. New York: Scribner.

Jaques, Elliott (1951). *The Changing Culture of a Factory*. London: Tavistock.

Jaynes, Gerald David, and Robin M. Williams, Jr., eds. (1989). *A Common Destiny: Blacks and American Society*. Washington, DC: National Academy Press.

Jelinek, Mariann, Linda Smircich, and Paul Hirsch, eds. (1983). "Organizational Culture," *Administrative Science Quarterly*, 28 (September), entire issue.

Jenkins, J. Craig (1979). "What Is to Be Done: Movement or Organization?" *Contemporary Sociology*, 8, 222–28.

Jensen, Michael C., and William H. Meckling (1976). "Theory of the Firm: Managerial Behavior, Agency Costs, and Ownership Structure," *Journal of Financial Economics*, 3, 305–60.

Johnson, H. Thomas, and Robert S. Kaplan (1987). *Relevance Lost: The Rise and Fall of Management Accounting*. Boston, MA: Harvard Business School Press.

Jones, Stephen R. G. (1990). "Worker Interdependence and Output: The Hawthorne Studies Reevaluated," *American Sociological Review* 55, 176–90.

_____ (1992). "Was There a Hawthorne Effect?" *American Journal of Sociology*, 98, 451–68.

Juran, Joseph M. (1974). *The Quality Control Handbook* (3rd ed.). New York: McGraw-Hill.

_____ (1989). *Juran on Leadership for Quality*. New York: Free Press.

Kahn, Robert L. (1990). "Organizational Theory and International Relations: Mutually Informing Paradigms," in *Organizations and Nation-States: New Perspectives on Conflict and Cooperation*, pp. 1–15, ed. Robert L. Kahn and Mayer N. Zald. San Francisco: Jossey-Bass.

Kahn, Robert L., D. M. Wolfe, R. P. Quinn, J. D. Snoek, and Robert A. Rosenthal (1964). *Organizational Stress*. New York: Wiley.

Kahneman, Daniel, P. Slovic, and Amos Tversky (1982). *Judgment under Uncertainty: Heuristics and Biases*. Cambridge: Cambridge University Press.

Kalberg, Stephen (1980). "Max Weber's Types of Rationality: Cornerstones for the Analysis of Rationalization Processes in History," *American Journal of Sociology*, 85, 1145–79.

Kalleberg, Arne L., David Knoke, Peter V. Marsden, and Joe L. Spaeth (1996). *Organizations in America: Analyzing Their Structures and Human Resource Practices*. Thousand Oaks, CA: Sage.

Kaluzny, Arnold D., and Richard B. Warnecke, eds. (1996). *Managing a Health Care Alliance: Improving Community Cancer Care*. San Francisco: Jossey-Bass.

Kaluzny, Arnold D., Howard S. Zuckerman, and Thomas C. Ricketts III (1995). *Partners for the Dance: Forming Strategic Alliances in Health Care*. Ann Arbor, MI: Health Administration Press.

Kanter, Rosabeth Moss (1972). *Commitment and Community: Communes and Utopias in Sociological Perspective*. Cambridge, MA: Harvard University Press.

_____ (1977a). *Men and Women of the Corporation*. New York: Basic Books.

_____ (1977b). *Work and Family in the United States: A Critical Review and Agenda for Research and Policy*. New York: Russell Sage Foundation.

_____ (1989). *When Giants Learn to Dance: Mastering the Challenges of Strategy, Management and Careers in the 1990s*. New York: Simon & Schuster.

_____ (1994). "Collaborative Advantage: The Art of Alliances," *Harvard Business Review*, 72 (July–August), 96–108.

Kanter, Rosabeth Moss, Barry A. Stein, and Todd D. Jick (1992). *The Challenge of Organizational Change*. New York: Free Press.

Katz, Daniel, and Robert L. Kahn (1952). "Some Recent Findings in Human Relations Research in Industry," in *Readings in Social Psychology* (2nd ed.). pp. 650–65, ed. Guy E. Swanson, Theodore M. Newcomb, and Eugene L. Hartley. New York: Holt.

Katz, Daniel, Nathan Maccoby, and Nancy Morse (1950). *Productivity, Supervision and Morale in an Office Situation*. Ann Arbor: Institute for Social Research, University of Michigan.

_____ (1966). *The Social Psychology of Organizations.* New York: Wiley (rev. 1978).

Katz, Elihu, and S. N. Eisenstadt (1960). "Some Sociological Observations on the Response of Israeli Organizations to New Immigrants," *Administrative Science Quarterly,* 5, 113–33.

Kaufman, Herbert (1975). "The Natural History of Human Organizations," *Administration and Society,* 7, 131–49.

_____ (1976). *Are Government Organizations Immortal?* Washington, DC: Brookings Institution.

Keidel, Robert W. (1994). "Rethinking Organizational Design," *Academy of Management Executive,* 8(4), 12–30.

Kelman, Herbert C., and V. Lee Hamilton (1989). *Crimes of Obedience: Toward a Social Psychology of Authority and Responsibility.* New Haven: Yale University Press.

Kennedy, Robert F. (1969). *Thirteen Days: A Memoir of the Cuban Missile Crisis.* New York: Norton.

Kerr, Clark (1954). "The Balkanization of Labor Markets," in *Labor Mobility and Economic Opportunity,* pp. 92–110, ed. E. Wight Bakke. Cambridge, MA: MIT Press.

Kerr, Clark, John T. Dunlop, Frederick Harbison, and Charles A. Myers (1964). *Industrialism and Industrial Man* (2nd ed.). New York: Oxford University Press.

Kerr, Steven (1975). "On the Folly of Rewarding A, while Hoping for B," *Academy of Management Journal,* 18, 769–783.

Khandwalla, Pradip N. (1977). *The Design of Organizations.* New York: Harcourt Brace Jovanovich.

Kimberly, John R. (1976). "Organizational Size and the Structuralist Perspective: A Review, Critique and Proposal," *Administrative Science Quarterly,* 21, 571–97.

Kimberly, John R., Robert H. Miles, and Associates (1980). *The Organizational Life Cycle.* San Francisco: Jossey-Bass.

Klandermans, Bert, and Sidney Tarrow (1988). "Mobilization into Social Movements: Synthesizing European and American Approaches," in *From Structure to Action: Comparing Movement Participation across Cultures, International Social Movement Research,* vol. 1, 1–38, ed. Bert Klandermans, Hanspeter Kriesi, and Sidney Tarrow. Greenwich, CN: JAI Press.

Kmetz, John L. (1984). "An Information Processing Study of a Complex Workflow in Aircraft Electronics Repair," *Administrative Science Quarterly,* 29, 255–80.

Kochan, Thomas A., Harry C. Katz, and Robert B. McKersie (1994). *The Transformation of American Industrial Relations* (2nd ed.). New York: Basic Books.

Kohn Melvin L. (1971). "Bureaucratic Man: A Portrait and an Interpretation," *American Sociological Review,* 36, 461–74.

Kohn, Melvin L., and Carmi Schooler (1973). "Occupational Experience and Psychological Functioning: An Assessment of Reciprocal Effects," *American Sociological Review,* 38, 97–118.

_____ (1983). *Work and Personality: An Inquiry into the Impact of Social Stratification.* Norwood, NJ: Ablex.

Kornhauser, William (1962). *Scientists in Industry: Conflict and Accommodation.* Berkeley: University of California Press.

Korten, David C. (1995). *When Corporations Rule the World.* San Francisco: Berrett-Koehler.

Kotter, John P. (1995). *The New Rules: How to Succeed in Today's Post-Corporate World.* New York: Free Press.

Kreps, Gary L. (1986). *Organizational Communication: Theory and Practice.* New York: Longman.

Krupp, Sherman (1961). *Pattern in Organization Analysis.* Philadelphia: Chilton.

Kuhn, Thomas S. (1962). *The Structure of Scientific Revolutions.* Chicago: University of Chicago Press.

Kunda, Gideon (1992). *Engineering Culture: Control and Commitment in a High-Tech Corporation.* Philadelphia: Temple University Press.

Lammers, Cornelis J., and David J. Hickson, eds. (1979). *Organizations Alike and Unlike: International and Interinstitutional Studies in the Sociology of Organizations.* London: Routledge & Kegan Paul.

Lamprech, James L. (1993). *Implementing the ISO 9000 Series.* New York: Marcel Dekker.

Landsberger, Henry A. (1958). *Hawthorne Revisited.* Ithaca, NY: Cornell University Press.

_____ (1961). "Parsons' Theory of Organizations," in *Social Theories of Talcott Parsons*, pp. 214–49, ed. Max Black. Englewood Cliffs, NJ: Prentice Hall.

Langlois, Richard N., ed. (1986). *Economics as a Process: Essays in the New Institutional Economics.* New York: Cambridge University Press.

LaPorte, Todd R. (1982). "On the Design and Management of Nearly Error-Free Organizational Control Systems," in *Accident at Three Mile Island: The Human Dimensions*, ed. David L. Sills, C. P. Wolf, and Vivian B. Shelanski. Boulder, CO: Westview Press.

_____ (1988). "The United States Air Traffic System: Increasing Reliability in the Midst of Rapid Growth," in *The Development of Large Scale Technical Systems,* pp. 215–44, ed. Thomas Hughes and Renata Mayntz. Boulder, CO: Westview Press.

Larson, Magali Sarfatti (1977). *The Rise of Professionalism.* Berkeley: University of California Press.

Larson, Erik W., and David H. Gobeli (1987). "Matrix Management: Contradictions and Insight," *California Management Review*, 29, 126–38.

Lash, S. (1988). "Postmodernism as a Regime of Signification," *Theory, Culture and Society*, 5, 311–36.

Laumann, Edward O., Joseph Galaskiewicz, and Peter V. Marsden (1978). "Community Structure as Interorganizational Linkages," *Annual Review of Sociology*, 4, 455–84.

Laumann, Edward O., and David Knoke (1987). *The Organizational State: Social Choice in National Policy Domains.* Madison: University of Wisconsin Press.

Laumann, Edward O., Peter V. Marsden, and David Prensky (1983). "The Boundary Specification Program in Network Analysis," in *Applied Network Analysis*, 18, 34, ed. Ronald S. Burt and Michael J. Minor. Beverly Hills, CA: Sage.

Lawrence, Paul R. (1993). "The Contingency Approach to Organization Design," in *Handbook of Organizational Behavior*, pp. 9–18, ed. Robert T. Golembiewski. New York: Dekker.

Lawrence, Paul R., and Jay W. Lorsch (1967). *Organization and Environment: Managing Differentiation and Integration.* Boston: Graduate School of Business Administration, Harvard University.

Leavitt, Harold J. (1951). "Some Effects of Certain Communication Patterns on Group Performance," *Journal of Abnormal and Social Psychology*, 46, 38–50.

_____ (1965). "Applied Organizational Change in Industry: Structural, Technological and Humanistic Approaches," in *Handbook of Organizations*, pp. 1144–70, ed. James G. March. Chicago: Rand McNally.

Leavitt, Harold J., William R. Dill, and Henry B. Eyring (1973). *The Organizational World.* New York: Harcourt Brace Jovanovich.

Leblebici, Husayin, Gerald R. Salancik, Anne Copay, and Tom King (1991). "Institutional Change and the Transformation of Interorganizational Fields: An Organizational History of the U.S. Radio Broadcasting Industry," *Administrative Science Quarterly*, 36, 333–63.

Lembrecht, James L. (1993). *Implementing the ISO 9000 Series.* New York: Marcel Dekker.

Levine, Sol, and Paul E. White (1961). "Exchange as a Conceptual Framework for the Study of Interorganizational Relationships," *Administrative Science Quarterly*, 5, 583–601.

Levitt, Barbara, and James G. March (1988). "Organizational Learning," *Annual Review of Sociology*, 14, 319–40.

Levitt, Theodore (1986). *The Marketing Imagination.* New York: Free Press.

Levy, David (1994). "Chaos Theory and Strategy: Theory, Applications, and Managerial Implications," *Strategic Management Journal*, 15, 167–78.

Lewin, Kurt (1948). *Resolving Social Conflicts.* New York: Harper.

Light, Ivan H. (1972). *Ethnic Enterprise in America.* Berkeley: University of California Press.

Light, Ivan H., and Edna Bonacich (1988). *Immigrant Entrepreneurs.* Berkeley: University of California Press.

Likert, Rensis (1961). *New Patterns of Management.* New York: McGraw-Hill.

Likert, Rensis, and Jane C. Likert (1976). *New Ways of Managing Conflict.* New York: McGraw-Hill.

Lilienthal, David E. (1944). *TVA: Democracy on the March.* New York: Harper & Brothers.

Lincoln, James R. (1979). "Organizational Differentiation, in Urban Communities: A Study in Organizational Ecology," *Social Forces*, 57, 915–29.

_____ (1982). "Intra- (and Inter-) Organizational Networks," in *Research in the Sociology of Organizations*, vol. 1, pp. 1–38, ed. Samuel B. Bacharach. Greenwich, CN: JAI Press.

_____ (1990). "Japanese Organization and Organization Theory, in *Research in Organizational Behavior*, 12, 256–93, ed. Barry M. Staw and L. L. Cummings. Greenwich, CT: JAI Press.

Lincoln, James R., Mitsuyo Hanada, and Kerry McBride (1986). "Organizational Structures in Japanese and U.S. Manufacturing," *Administrative Science Quarterly*, 31, 338–64.

Lincoln, James R., and Arne L. Kalleberg (1990). *Culture, Control and Commitment: A Study of Work Organization and Work Attitudes in the United States and Japan.* New York: Cambridge University Press.

Lincoln, James R., and Kerry McBride (1987). "Japanese Industrial Organization in Comparative Perspective," *Annual Review of Sociology*, 13, 289–312.

Lindblom, Charles E. (1977). *Politics and Markets.* New York: Basic Books.

Lippitt, Ronald, Norman Polansky, Fritz Redl, and Sidney Rosen (1953). "The Dynamics of Power," in *Group Dynamics*, pp. 462–82, ed. Dorwin Cartwright and Alvin Zander. Evanston, IL: Row, Peterson.

Lipset, Seymour Martin (1960). *Political Man.* New York: Doubleday.

_____ (1986). "North American Labor Movements: A Comparative Perspective," in *Unions in Transition: Entering the Second Century*, pp. 421–77, ed. Seymour Martin Lipset. San Francisco: Institute for Contemporary Studies.

Lipset, Seymour Martin, Martin A. Trow, and James S. Coleman (1956). *Union Democracy.* Glencoe, IL: Free Press.

Litwak, Eugene (1961). "Models of Bureaucracy Which Permit Conflict," *American Journal of Sociology*, 67, 177–84.

Litwak, Eugene, and Lydia F. Hylton (1962). "Interorganizational Analysis: A Hypothesis on Coordinating Agencies," *Administrative Science Quarterly*, 6, 395–420.

Litwak, Eugene, and Henry J. Meyer (1966). "A Balance Theory of Coordination between Bureaucratic Organizations and Community Primary Groups," *Administrative Science Quarterly*, 11, 31–58.

Lowin, Aaron, and James R. Craig (1968). "The Influence of Level of Performance on Managerial Style: An Experimental Object-Lesson in the Ambiguity of Correlational Data," *Organizational Behavior and Human Performance*, 3, 440–58.

Lyden, F. J. (1975). "Using Parsons' Functional Analysis in the Study of Public Organizations," *Administrative Science Quarterly*, 20 (March), 59–70.

Lyotard, J-F. (1984). *The Postmodern Condition: A Report on Knowledge.* Minneapolis: University of Minnesota Press.

McEwen, C. A. (1980). "Continuities in the Study of Total and Nontotal Institutions," *Annual Review of Sociology*, 6, 143–85.

McGregor, Douglas (1960). *The Human Side of Enterprise*, New York: McGraw-Hill.

MacIver, Robert M. (1947). *The Web of Government.* New York: Macmillan.

McKelvey, Bill (1982). *Organizational Systematics.* Berkeley: University of California Press.

McLuhan, Marshall (1964). *Understanding Media: The Extensions of Man.* New York: Signet.

McNeil, Kenneth (1978). "Understanding Organizational Power: Building on the Weberian Legacy," *Administrative Science Quarterly*, 23, 65–90.

McNeil, Kenneth, and James D. Thompson (1971). "The Regeneration of Social Organizations," *American Sociological Review*, 36, 624–37.

McPherson, J. Miller (1983). "An Ecology of Affiliation," *American Sociological Review*, 48, 519–35.

Macaulay, Stewart (1963). "Non-Contractual Relations in Business: A Preliminary Study," *American Sociological Review*, 28, 55–69.

Mailer, Norman (1968). "The Steps of the Pentagon," *Harper's*, 236 (March), 47–142.

Maines, David R. (1977). "Social Organization and Social Structure in Symbolic Interactionist Thought," *Annual Review of Sociology*, 3, 235–59.

Mann, Judith K., and Donald E. Yett (1968). "The Analysis of Hospital Costs: A Review Article," *Journal of Business*, 41, 191–202.

Mannheim, Karl (1950 trans.). *Man and Society in an Age of Reconstruction*, trans. Edward Shils. New York: Harcourt Brace Jovanovich (first published in 1935).

Mansfield, Roger (1973). "Bureaucracy and Centralization: An Examination of Organizational Structure," *Administrative Science Quarterly*, 18, 77–88.

March, James G., ed. (1965). *Handbook of Organizations*. Chicago: Rand McNally.

_____ (1981). "Decisions in Organizations and Theories of Choice," in *Perspectives on Organization Design and Behavior*, pp. 205–44, ed. Andrew H. Van de Ven and William F. Joyce. New York: Wiley-Interscience.

_____ (1988). *Decisions and Organizations*. Oxford: Blackwell.

_____ (1991). "Exploration and Exploitation in Organizational Learning," *Organization Science*, 2, 71–87.

_____ (1994). *A Primer on Decision Making: How Decisions Happen*. New York: Free Press.

March, James G., and Johan P. Olsen (1976). *Ambiguity and Choice in Organizations*. Bergen, Norway: Universitetsforlaget.

_____ (1989). *Rediscovering Institutions: The Organizational Basis of Politics*. New York: Free Press.

March, James G., and Herbert A. Simon (1958). *Organizations*. New York: Wiley.

Marcuse, Herbert (1964). *One-Dimensional Man*. Boston: Beacon Press.

Marglin, Stephen (1974). "What Do Bosses Do?: The Origins and Functions of Hierarchy in Capitalist Production," *Review of Radical Political Economics*, 6 (Summer), 60–112.

Marini, Margaret Mooney (1989). "Sex Differences in Earnings in the United States," *Annual Review of Sociology*, 15, 343–80.

Marsden, Peter M. (1990). "Network Data and Measurement," *Annual Review of Sociology*, 16, 435–63.

Martin, Joanne (1981). "Relative Deprivation: A Theory of Distributive Injustice for an Era of Shrinking Resources," in *Research in Organizational Behavior*, vol. 3, pp. 53–107, ed. L. L. Cummings and Barry M. Staw. Greenwich, CN: JAI Press.

_____ (1990). "Deconstructing Organizational Taboos: The Suppression of Gender Conflict in Organizations," *Organization Science*, 1, 339–59.

_____ (1992). *Cultures in Organizations: Three Perspectives*. New York: Oxford University Press.

_____ (1994). "The Organization of Exclusion: Institutionalization of Sex Inequality, Gendered Faculty Jobs and Gendered Knowledge in Organizational Theory and Research," *Organization*, 1, 401–31.

Martin, Joanne, and Kathy Knopoff (forthcoming). "The Gendered Implications of Apparently Gender-Neutral Theory: Re-reading Weber," in *Ruffin Lectures Series*, vol. 3: *Business Ethics and Women's Studies*, ed. Ed Freeman and Andrea Larson. Oxford: Oxford University Press.

Marx, Karl (1954 trans.). *Capital*. Moscow: Foreign Languages Publishing House (first published in 1867).

_____ (1963 trans.). *Karl Marx: Early Writings*, trans. and ed. T. B. Bottomore. London: Watts (first published as *Economic and Philosophical Manuscripts*, 1844).

_____ (1972 trans.). "Economic and Philosophic Manuscripts of 1844: Selections," in *The Marx-Engels Reader*, ed. Robert C. Tucker. New York: Norton.

Marx, Karl, and Frederick Engels (1955 trans.). *Manifesto of the Communist Party*. Moscow: Foreign Languages Publishing House (first published in 1848).

Maslow, Abraham (1954). *Motivation and Personality*. New York: Harper.

Massie, Joseph L. (1965). "Management Theory," in *Handbook of Organizations*, pp. 387–422, ed. James G. March. Chicago: Rand McNally.

Maurice, Marc (1979). "For a Study of 'The Societal Effect': Universality and Specificity in Organization Research," in *Organizations Alike and Unlike: Inter-Institutional Studies in the Sociology of Organizations*, pp. 42–60, ed. Cornelis J. Lammers and David J. Hickson. London: Routledge & Kegan Paul.

Maurice, Marc, Arndt Sorge, and Malcolm Warner (1980). "Societal Differences in Organizing Manufacturing Units: A Comparison of France, West Germany, and Great Britain," *Organizational Studies*, 1, 59–86.

Maynard, Douglas W., and Steven E. Clayman (1991). "The Diversity of Ethnomethodology," *Annual Review of Sociology*, 17, 385–418.

Mayo, Elton (1945). *The Social Problems of an Industrial Civilization.* Boston: Graduate School of Business Administration, Harvard University.

Mead, George Herbert (1934). *Mind, Self and Society.* Chicago: University of Chicago Press

Mendel, Peter (1996). "ISO 9000 Quality Certifications: Institutionalization of a Global Model of Quality Systems." Unpublished paper, Department of Sociology, Stanford University.

Merton, Robert K. (1957). *Social Theory and Social Structure* (2nd ed.). Glencoe, IL: Free Press.

Merton, Robert K., Ailsa P. Gray, Barbara Hockey, and Hanan C. Selvin, eds. (1952). *Reader in Bureaucracy.* Glencoe, IL: Free Press.

Meyer, Alan D., Anne S. Tsui, and C. R. Hinings (1993). "Configurational Approaches to Organizational Analysis," *Academy of Management Journal,* 36: 1175–95.

Meyer, John W. (1977). "The Effects of Education as an Institution," *American Journal of Sociology,* 83, 55–77.

_____ (1983). "Institutionalization and the Rationality of Formal Organizational Structure," in *Organizational Environments: Ritual and Rationality,* pp. 261–82, by John W. Meyer and W. Richard Scott. Beverly Hills, CA: Sage.

_____ (1978). "Strategies for Further Research: Varieties of Environmental Variation," in *Environments and Organizations,* 352–68, ed. Marshall W. Meyer. San Francisco: Jossey-Bass.

_____ (1985). "Institutional and Organizational Rationalization in the Mental Health System," *American Behavioral Scientist,* 28, 587–600.

_____ (1994). "Rationalized Environments," in *Institutional Environments and Organizations: Structural Complexity and Individualism,* pp. 28–54, ed. W. Richard Scott and John W. Meyer. Thousand Oaks, CA: Sage.

Meyer, John W., John Boli, and George M. Thomas (1987). "Ontology and Rationalization in the Western Cultural Account," in *Institutional Structure: Constituting State, Society, and the Individual,* pp. 12–37, ed. George M. Thomas, John W. Meyer, Francisco O. Ramirez, and John Boli. Newbury Park, CA: Sage.

Meyer, John W., and Brian Rowan (1977). "Institutionalized Organizations: Formal Structure as Myth and Ceremony," *American Journal of Sociology,* 83, 340–63.

_____ (1978). "The Structure of Educational Organizations," in *Environments and Organizations,* pp. 78–109, ed. Marshall W. Meyer. San Francisco: Jossey-Bass.

Meyer, John W., and W. Richard Scott, with the assistance of Brian Rowan and Terrence E. Deal (1983). *Organizational Environments: Ritual and Rationality.* Beverly Hills, CA: Sage.

Meyer, John W., W. Richard Scott, and David Strang (1987). "Centralization, Fragmentation, and School District Complexity," *Administrative Science Quarterly,* 32, 186–201.

Meyer, Marshall W. (1979). *Change in Public Bureaucracies.* Cambridge: Cambridge University Press.

_____ (1990). "The Weberian Tradition in Organizational Research," in *Structures of Power and Constraint: Papers in Honor of Peter M. Blau,* pp. 191–215, ed. Craig Calhoun, Marshall W. Meyer, and W. Richard Scott. Cambridge: Cambridge University Press.

Meyer, Marshall W., and Lynne G. Zucker (1989). *Permanently Failing Organizations.* Newbury Park, CA: Sage.

Mezias, Stephen J. (1990). "An Institutional Model of Organizational Practice: Financial Reporting at the Fortune 200," *Administrative Science Quarterly,* 35, 431–57.

Michels, Robert (1949 trans.). Political Parties, trans. Eden and Cedar Paul. Glencoe, IL: Free Press (first published in 1915).

Miles, Matthew B. (1964). "On Temporary Systems," in *Innovations in Education,* pp. 437–90, ed. Matthew B. Miles. New York: Teachers College, Columbia University.

Miles, Robert H. (1982). *Coffin Nails and Corporate Strategies.* Englewood Cliffs, NJ: Prentice Hall.

Milgram, Stanley (1973). "The Perils of Obedience," *Harper's* (December), 62–66; 75–77.

_____ (1974). *Obedience to Authority.* New York: Harper & Row.

Milgrom, Paul, and John Roberts (1992). *Economics, Organization and Management.* Englewood Cliffs, NJ: Prentice Hall.

Miller, E. J., and A. K. Rice (1967). *Systems of Organization.* London: Tavistock.

Miller, George A. (1953). "What Is Information Measurement?" *American Psychologist,* 8, 3–12.

Miller, James Grier (1978). *Living Systems.* New York: McGraw-Hill.

Mills, C. Wright (1956). *The Power Elite.* New York: Oxford University Press.

Miner, Anne S. (1987). "Idiosyncratic Jobs in Formalized Organizations," *Administrative Science Quarterly,* 32, 327–51.

_____ (1990). "Seeking Adaptive Advantage: Evolutionary Theory and Managerial Action," in *Evolutionary Dynamics in Organizations,* pp. 76–89, ed. Joel A. C. Baum and Jitendra V. Singh. New York: Oxford University Press.

Miner, Anne S., and Pamela R. Haunschild (1995). "Population Level Learning," in *Research in Organizational Behavior,* 17, 115–66, ed. L. L. Cummings and Barry M. Staw. Greenwich, CT: JAI Press.

Mintz, Beth, and Michael Schwartz (1985). *The Power Structure of American Business.* Chicago: University of Chicago Press.

Mintzberg, Henry (1971). "Managerial Work: Analysis from Observation," *Management Science,* 18 (October), B97–B110.

_____ (1973). *The Nature of Managerial Work.* New York: Harper & Row.

_____ (1979). *The Structure of Organizations.* Englewood Cliffs, NJ.: Prentice Hall.

_____ (1983). *Power in and around Organizations.* Englewood Cliffs, NJ: Prentice Hall.

_____ (1987). "The Strategy Concept I: Five Ps for Strategy,"in *Organizational Approaches to Strategy,* pp. 7–20, ed. Glenn R. Carroll and David Vogel. Cambridge, MA: Ballinger.

Mintzberg, Henry, and Alexandra McHugh (1985). "Strategy Formation in an Adhocracy," *Administrative Science Quarterly,* 30, 160–97.

Mises, Ludwig von (1944). *Bureaucracy.* New Haven: Yale University Press.

Mizruchi, Mark S. (1982). *The American Corporate Network,* 1904–1974. Beverly Hills, CA: Sage.

_____ (1996). "What Do Interlocks Do? An Analysis, Critique, and Assessment of Research on Interlocking Directorates," *Annual Review of Sociology* 22. Palo Alto, CA: Annual Reviews.

Mizruchi, Mark, and Michael Schwartz, eds. (1986). *The Structural Analysis of Business.* Cambridge: Cambridge University Press.

Mohr, Lawrence B. (1971). "Organizational Technology and Organizational Structures," *Administrative Science Quarterly,* 16, 444–59.

Moi, T. (1985). *Sexual/Texual Politics: Feminist Literary Theory.* New York: Methuen.

Molotch, Harvey (1976). "The City as a Growth Machine: Toward a Political Economy of Place," *American Journal of Sociology,* 82, 309–32.

Montagna, Paul D. (1968). "Professionalization and Bureaucratization in Large Professional Organizations," *American Journal of Sociology,* 72, 138–45.

Monteverde, Kirk, and David J. Teece (1982). "Supplier Switching Costs and Vertical Integration in the Automobile Industry," *Bell Journal of Economics,* 12, 206–13.

Mooney, James D. (1937). "The Principles of Organization," in *Papers on the Science of Administration,* pp. 89–98, ed. Luther Gulick and L. Urwick. New York: Institute of Public Administration, Columbia University.

Mooney, James D., and Allan C. Reiley (1939). *The Principles of Organization.* New York: Harper.

Naisbitt, John (1982). *Megatrends.* New York: Warner Books.

Naisbitt, John, and Patricia Aburdene, (1985). *Re-inventing the Corporation.* New York: Warner Books.

National Training Laboratories (1953). *Explorations in Human Relations Training.* Washington, DC: National Training Laboratories.

Nelson, Richard R., and Sidney G. Winter (1982). *An Evolutionary Theory of Economic Change.* Cambridge, MA: Belknap Press of Harvard University Press.

Neuhauser, Duncan (1971). *The Relationship between Administrative Activities and Hospital Performance.* Research Series 28. Chicago: Center for Health Administration Studies, University of Chicago.

_____ (1972). "The Hospital as a Matrix Organization," *Hospital Administration,* 17 (Fall), 8–25.

Newton, Kenneth (1975). "Voluntary Associations in a British City," *Journal of Voluntary Action Research,* 4, 43–62.

Nisbett, Richard, and Lee Ross (1980). *Human Inference: Strategies and Shortcomings of Social Judgment.* Englewood Cliffs, NJ: Prentice Hall.

Noble, David F. (1977). *America By Design: Science, Technology and the Rise of Corporate Capitalism.* New York: Oxford University Press.

————— (1984). *Forces of Production: A Social History of Industrial Automation.* New York: Oxford University Press.

Nohria, Nitin, and Robert G. Eccles (1992). *Networks and Organizations: Structure, Form and Action.* Boston: Harvard Business School Press.

Noll, Roger G., ed. (1985). *Regulatory Policy and the Social Sciences.* Berkeley: University of California Press.

North, Douglass C. (1990). I*nstitutions, Institutional Change and Economic Performance.* Cambridge: Cambridge University Press.

Oberschall, Anthony (1973). *Social Conflict and Social Movements.* Englewood Cliffs, NJ: Prentice Hall.

Oberschall, Anthony, and Eric M. Leifer (1986). "Efficiency and Social Institutions: Uses and Misuses of Economic Reasoning in Sociology," *Annual Review of Sociology*, 12, 233–53.

Ocasio, William (1997). "Toward an Attention-Based View of the Firm," *Strategic Management Journal*, 18 (Summer).

O'Connor, James (1973). *The Fiscal Crisis of the State.* New York: St. Martin's Press.

Odione, George S. (1965). *Management by Objective.* New York: Pitman.

Okimoto, Daniel I. (1984). *Competitive Edge: The Semiconductor Industry in the United States and Japan.* Stanford, CA: Stanford University Press.

Oliver, Christine (1991). "Strategic Responses to Institutional Processes," *Academy of Management Review*, 16, 145–79.

Olson, Mancur, Jr. (1965). *The Logic of Collective Action.* Cambridge, MA: Harvard University Press.

O'Reilly, Charles A., and Jennifer A. Chatman (1996). "Culture as Social Control: Corporations, Cults, and Commitment," in *Research in Organizational Behavior*, 18, 157–200, ed. Barry M. Staw and L. L. Cummings. Greenwich, CT: JAI Press.

Orlikowski, Wanda J. (1992). "The Duality of Technology: Rethinking the Concept of Technology in Organizations," *Organization Science*, 3, 398–427.

Orru, Marco, Nicole Woolsey Biggart, and Gary G. Hamilton. (1977). *The Economic Organization of East Asian Capitalism.* Thousand Oaks, CA: Sage.

Orton, J. Douglas, and Karl E. Weick (1990). "Loosely Coupled Systems: A Reconceptualization," *Academy of Management* Review, 15, 203–23.

Osborne, David, and Ted Gaebler (1992). *Reinventing Government.* Reading, MA: Addison-Wesley.

O'Toole, J., ed. (1972). *Work in America: A Report to the Secretary of State for Health, Education and Welfare.* Cambridge, MA: MIT Press.

Ouchi, William G. (1979). "Markets, Bureaucracies and Clans." Unpublished paper, Graduate School of Management, University of California, Los Angeles.

————— (1980). "Markets, Bureaucracies and Clans," *Administrative Science Quarterly*, 25, 129–41.

————— (1981). *Theory Z.* Reading, MA: Addison-Wesley.

Ouchi, William G., and Alfred M. Jaeger (1978). "Type Z Organization: Stability in the Midst of Mobility," *Academy of Management Review*, 3, 305–14.

Padgett, John F., and Christopher K. Ansell (1992). "Robust Action and the Rise of the Medici, 1400–1434," *American Journal of Sociology*, 101: 993–1028.

Palmer, Donald (1983). "Broken Ties: Interlocking Directorates and Intercorporate Coordination," *Administrative Science Quarterly*, 28, 40–55.

Panel to Review Productivity Statistics (1979). *Measures and Intrepretation of Productivity.* Washington, DC: National Academy of Sciences.

Parkinson, C. Northcote (1957). P*arkinson's Law and Other Studies in Administration.* Boston: Houghton Mifflin.

Parsons, Talcott (1947). Introduction to *The Theory of Social and Economic Organization*, pp. 3–86, by Max Weber. Glencoe, IL: Free Press.

————— (1951). *The Social System.* Glencoe, IL: Free Press.

————— (1953). "A Revised Analytical Approach to the Theory of Social Stratification," in *Class, Status and Power: A Reader in Social Stratification*, pp. 92–129, ed. Reinhard Bendix and Seymour M. Lipset. Glencoe, IL: Free Press.

_____ (1960). *Structure and Process in Modern Societies*. Glencoe, IL: Free Press.

_____ (1966). *Societies: Evolutionary and Comparative Perspectives*. Englewood Cliffs, NJ: Prentice Hall.

Parsons, Talcott, Robert F. Bales, and Edward A. Shils (1953). *Working Papers in the Theory of Action*. Glencoe, IL: Free Press.

Patchen, Martin (1961). *The Choice of Wage Comparisons*. Englewood Cliffs, NJ: Prentice Hall.

Pelz, Donald C. (1952). "Influence: A Key to Effective Leadership in the First-Line Supervisor," *Personnel*, 29, 209–17.

Pennings J. (1973). "Measures of Organizational Structure: A Methodological Note," *American Journal of Sociology*, 79, 686–704.

_____ (1981). "Strategically Interdependent Organizations," in *Handbook of Organizational Design*, vol. 1, pp. 433–55, ed. Paul C. Nystrom and William H. Starbuck. Oxford: Oxford University Press.

Perrow, Charles (1961). "The Analysis of Goals in Complex Organizations," *American Sociological Review*, 26, 854–66.

_____ (1965). "Hospitals: Technology, Structure and Goals," in *Handbook of Organizations*, pp. 910–71, ed. James G. March. Chicago: Rand McNally.

_____ (1967). "A Framework for the Comparative Analysis of Organizations," *American Sociological Review*, 32, 194–208.

_____ (1970). *Organizational Analysis: A Sociological View*. Belmont, CA: Wadsworth.

_____ (1972). "Review of Neuhauser, D.: *The Relationship between Administrative Activities and Hospital Performance*," *Administrative Science Quarterly*, 17, 419–21.

_____ (1973). "The Short and Glorious History of Organizational Theory," *Organizational Dynamics*, 2 (Summer), 2–15.

_____ (1982). "Three Mile Island: A Normal Accident," in *The International Yearbook of Organizational Studies 1981*, pp. 1–25, ed. David Dunkerley and Graeme Salaman. London: Routledge & Kegan Paul.

_____ (1984). *Normal Accidents: Living with High-Risk Technologies*. New York: Basic Books.

_____ (1986). *Complex Organizations: A Critical Essay* (3d ed.). Glenview, IL: Scott, Foresman.

_____ (1991). "A Society of Organizations," *Theory and Society*, 20: 725–62.

_____ (1992). "Small-Firm Networks," in *Networks and Organizations*, pp. 445–470, ed. Nitin Nohria and Robert G. Eccles. Boston: Harvard Business School Press.

Peters, Thomas J., and Robert H. Waterman, Jr. (1982). *In Search of Excellence*. New York: Harper & Row.

Pfeffer, Jeffrey (1972a). "Size and Composition of Corporate Boards of Directors: The Organization and Its Environment," *Administrative Science Quarterly*, 17, 218–28.

_____ (1972b). "Merger as a Response to Organizational Interdependence," *Administrative Science Quarterly*, 17, 382–92.

_____ (1973). "Size, Composition, and Function of Hospital Boards of Directors: A Study of Organization-Environment Linkage," *Administrative Science Quarterly*, 18, 349–64.

_____ (1978). "The Micropolitics of Organizations," in *Environments and Organizations*, pp. 29–50, ed. Marshall W. Meyer. San Francisco: Jossey-Bass.

_____ (1981). *Power in Organizations*. Marshfield, MA: Pitman.

_____ (1982). *Organizations and Organization Theory*. Boston: Pitman.

_____ (1983). "Organizational Demography," in *Research in Organizational Behavior*, vol. 5, 299–357, ed. L. L. Cummings and Barry M. Staw. Greenwich, CN: JAI Press.

_____ (1987). "A Resource Dependence Perspective on Intercorporate Relations," in *Intercorporate Relations: The Structural Analysis of Business*, pp. 25–55, ed. Mark S. Mizruchi and Michael Schwartz. New York: Cambridge University Press.

_____ (1992). *Managing with Power: Politics and Influence in Organizations*. Boston: Harvard Business School Press.

_____ (1993). "Barriers to the Advance of Organizational Science: Paradigm Development as a Dependent Variable," *Academy of Management Review*, 18, 599–620.

Pfeffer, Jeffrey, and James N. Baron (1988). "Taking the Workers Back Out: Recent Trends in the Structuring of Employment," in *Research in Organizational Behavior*, 10, 257–303, ed. Barry M. Staw and L. L. Cummings. Greenwich, CT: JAI Press.

Pfeffer, Jeffrey, and Yinon Cohen (1984). "Determinants of Internal Labor Markets in Organizations," *Administrative Science Quarterly*, 29, 550–72.

Pfeffer, Jeffrey, and Phillip Nowak (1976). "Joint Ventures and Interorganizational Dependence," *Administrative Science Quarterly*, 21, 398–418.

Pfeffer, Jeffrey, and Gerald R. Salancik (1974). "Organizational Decision Making as a Political Process: The Case of a University Budget," *Administrative Science Quarterly*, 19, 135–51.

_____ (1978). *The External Control of Organizations*. New York: Harper & Row.

Pinch, Trevor J., and W. E. Bijker (1987). "The Social Construction of Facts and Artifacts," in *The Social Construction of Technological Systems*, pp. 17–50, ed. W. E. Bijker, Thomas P. Hughes, and Trevor Pinch, ed. Cambridge, MA: MIT Press.

Piore, Michael J., and Charles F. Sabel (1984). *The Second Industrial Divide: Possibilities for Prosperity*. New York: Basic Books.

Piven, Frances Fox, and Richard A. Cloward (1971). *Regulating the Poor*. New York: Pantheon.

Polanyi, Karl (1944). *The Great Transformation*. New York: Holt.

Pondy, Louis R., and Ian I. Mitroff (1979). "Beyond Open System Models of Organization," in *Research in Organizational Behavior*, 1, 3–39, ed. Barry M. Staw. Greenwich, CN: JAI Press.

Porter, Lyman W., and Edward E. Lawler III (1968). *Managerial Attitudes and Performance*. Homewood, IL: Irwin.

Porter, Lyman W., Edward E. Lawler III, and J. R. Hackman (1975). *Behavior in Organizations*. New York: McGraw-Hill.

Porter, Michael E. (1980) *Competitive Strategy*. New York: Free Press.

_____, ed. (1986). *Competition in Global Industries*. Boston: Harvard Business School Press.

Pound, Ezra (1973). *Selected Prose, 1909–1965*, ed. William Cookson. New York: New Directions.

Powell, Walter W. (1988). "Institutional Effects on Organizational Structure and Performance," in I*nstitutional Patterns and Organizations: Culture and Environment*, pp. 115–36, ed. Lynne G. Zucker. Cambridge, MA: Ballinger.

_____ (1990). "Neither Market Nor Hierarchy: Network Forms of Organizations," in *Research in Organizational Behavior*, 12, 295–336. ed. Barry M. Staw and Larry L. Cummings. Greenwich, CT: JAI Press.

_____ (1991). "Expanding the Scope of Institutional Analysis," in *The New Institutionalism in Organizational Analysis*, 183–203, ed. Walter W. Powell and Paul J. DiMaggio. Chicago: University of Chicago Press.

_____ (1996). "The Capitalist Firm in the 21st Century: Emerging Patterns." Paper presented at the Annual Meetings of the American Sociological Association, New York, August.

Powell, Walter W., and Paul DiMaggio, eds. (1991). *The New Institutionalism in Organizational Analysis*. Chicago: University of Chicago Press.

Powell, Walter W., and Laurel Smith-Doerr. "Networks and Economic Life," in *The Handbook of Economic Sociology*, 368–402, ed. Neil J. Smelser and Richard Swedberg. Princeton, NJ: Princeton University and Russell Sage Foundation.

Pratt, John W., and Richard J. Zeckhauser, (1985). "Principals and Agents: An Overview," in *Principals and Agents: The Structure of Business*, pp. 1–25, ed. John W. Pratt and Richard J. Zeckhauser. Boston: Harvard Business School Press.

Przeworski, Adam, and Henry Teune (1970). *The Logic of Comparative Social Inquiry*. New York: Wiley.

Pugh, D. S., and D. J. Hickson (1976). *Organizational Structure in Its Context: The Aston Programme I*. Lexington, MA: Heath.

_____ ed. (1996). *Writers on Organizations* (5th ed.). Thousand Oaks, CA: Sage.

Pugh, D. S., D. J. Hickson, and C. R. Hinings (1969). "An Empirical Taxonomy of Structures of Work Organizations," *Administrative Science Quarterly*, 14, 115–26.

Pugh, D. S., D. J. Hickson, C. R. Hinings, and C. Turner (1968). "Dimensions of Organization Structure," *Administrative Science Quarterly*, 13, 65–91.

_____ (1969). "The Context of Organization Structures," *Administrative Science Quarterly*, 14, 91–114.

Rabinow, Paul, and William M. Sullivan (1987). "The Interpretive Turn: A Second Look," in I*nterpretive Social Science: A Second Look*, pp. 1–30, ed. Paul Rabinow and William M. Sullivan. Berkeley: University of California Press.

Rafaeli, Anat, and Robert I. Sutton (1987). "Expression of Emotion as Part of the Work Role," *Academy of Management Review*, 12, 23–37.

Rahim, M. Afzalur (1986). *Managing Conflict in Organizations*. New York: Praeger.

Reed, Theodore L. (1978). "Organizational Change in the American Foreign Service, 1925–1965: The Utility of Cohort Analysis," *American Sociological Review*, 43, 404–21.

Regier, Darrel A., Irving D. Goldberg, and Carl A. Taube (1978). "The de facto US Mental Health Services System: A Public Health Perspective," *Archives of General Psychiatry*, 35, 685–93.

Reinhardt, Uwe E. (1973). "Proposed Changes in the Organization of Health-Care Delivery: An Overview and a Critique," *Milbank Memorial Fund Quarterly*, 51, 169–222.

Reskin, Barbara (1993). "Sex Segregation in the Workplace," *Annual Review of Sociology* 19, 241–70.

Ritzer, George (1993). *The McDonaldization of Society: An Investigation into the Changing Character of Contemporary Social Life*. Thousand Oaks, CA: Pine Forge Press.

Roberts, Karlene H. (1990). "Some Characteristics of One Type of High Reliability Organization," *Organization Science*, 1, 160–76.

Roberts, Karlene H., and William Glick (1981). "The Job Characteristics Approach to Task Design: A Critical Review," *Journal of Applied Psychology*, 66, 193–217.

Roberts, Karlene H., and Martha Grabowski (1996). "Organizations, Technology and Structuring," in *Handbook of Organization Studies*, 409–23, ed. Stewart R. Clegg, Cynthia Hardy, and Walter R. Nord. Thousand Oaks, CA: Sage.

Roethlisberger, F. J., and William J. Dickson (1939). *Management and the Worker*. Cambridge, MA: Harvard University Press.

Rogers, Everett M., and Rekha Agarwala-Rogers (1976). *Communication in Organizations*. New York: Free Press.

Roman, Paul M., and Terry C. Blum (1993). "Work-family Role Conflict and Employer Responsibility: An Organizational Analyis of Workplace Responses to a Social Problem," in *Handbook of Organizational Behavior*, pp. 299–326, ed. Robert T. Golembiewski. New York: Dekker.

Romanelli, Elaine (1991). "The Evolution of New Organizational Forms," *Annual Review of Sociology*, 17, 79–103.

Rose, Michael (1985). "Universalism, Culturalism, and the Aix Group: Promise and Problems of a Societal Approach to Economic Institutions," *European Sociological Review*, 1, 65–83.

Rosenau, Pauline Marie (1992). *Post-Modernism and the Social Sciences: Insights, Inroads, and Intrusions*. Princeton, NJ: Princeton University Press.

Rosenberg, Hans (1958). *Bureaucracy, Aristocracy and Autocracy: The Prussian Experience 1660–1815*. Cambridge, MA: Harvard University Press.

Rosenberg, Nathan, and L. E. Birdzell, Jr. (1986). *How the West Grew Rich: The Economic Transformation of the Industrial World*. New York: Basic Books.

Rosenzweig, Philip M., and Jitendra V. Singh (1991). "Organization Environments and the Multinational Enterprise," *Academy of Management Review*, 16, 340–61.

Rothschild-Whitt, Joyce (1979). "The Collectivist Organization: An Alternative to Rational Bureaucratic Models," *American Sociological Review*, 44, 509–27.

Rothschild, Joyce, and J. Allen Whitt (1986). *The Cooperative Workplace: Potentials and Dilemmas of Organizational Democracy and Participation*. Cambridge: Cambridge University Press.

Rowan, Brian (1982). "Organizational Structure and the Institutional Environment: The Case of Public Schools," *Administrative Science Quarterly*, 27, 259–79.

Roy, Donald (1952). "Quota Restriction and Goldbricking in a Machine Shop," *American Journal of Sociology*, 57, 427–42.

Rumelt, Richard (1986). *Strategy, Structure, and Economic Performance*. Boston: Harvard Business School Press (first published in 1974).

Rushing, William A. (1966). "Organizational Size and Administration," *Pacific Sociological Review*, 9 (Fall), 100–108.

_____ (1968). "Hardness of Material as an External Constraint on the Division of Labor in Manufacturing Industries," *Administrative Science Quarterly*, 13, 229–45.

Sabel, Charles F. (1982). *Work and Politics: The Division of Labor in Industry*. Cambridge: Cambridge University Press.

Sagan, Scott D. (1993). *The Limits of Safety: Organizations, Accidents, and Nuclear Weapons.* Princeton, NJ: Princeton University Press.

Sage, Andrew P. (1981). "Designs for Optimal Information Filters," in *Handbook of Organizational Design*, vol. 1, pp. 105–21, ed. Paul C. Nystrom and William H. Starbuck. London: Oxford University Press.

Saint-Simon, Henri Comte de (1952 trans.). *Selected Writings*, trans. F. M. H. Markham. New York: Macmillan (first published in 1859).

Salancik, Gerald R., and Jeffrey Pfeffer (1977). "An Examination of Need-Satisfaction Models of Job Attitudes," *Administrative Science Quarterly*, 22, 427–56.

Salmon, J. Warren, ed. (1994). *The Corporate Transformation of Health Care: Perspectives and Implications.* Amityville, NY: Baywood.

Sampson, Anthony (1995). *Company Man.* New York: HarperCollins.

Satow, Roberta Lynn (1975). "Value-Rational Authority and Professional Organizations: Weber's Missing Type," *Administrative Science Quarterly*, 20, 526–31.

Saxenian, Annalee (1994). *Regional Advantage: Culture and Competition in Silicon Valley and Route 128.* Cambridge, MA: Harvard University Press.

Sayles, Leonard R. (1958). *Behavior of Industrial Work Groups.* New York: Wiley.

_____ (1976). "Matrix Organization: The Structure with a Future," *Organizational Dynamics*, (Autumn), 2–17.

Schein, Edgar H. (1992). *Organizational Culture and Leadership* (2nd ed.). San Francisco: Jossey-Bass.

Schmitter, Philippe C. (1974). "Still the Century of Corporatism?" in *The New Corporatism: Social-Political Structures in the Iberian World*, pp. 85–131, ed. Frederick B. Pike and Thomas Stritch. Notre Dame, IN: University of Notre Dame Press.

_____ (1990). "Sectors in Modern Capitalism: Models of Governance and Variations in Performance," in *Labour Relations and Economic Performance*, pp. 3–39, ed. Renato Brunetta and Carlo Dell-Aringa. Houndsmills, England: Macmillan Press.

Schneider, Benjamin, ed. (1990). *Organizational Climate and Culture.* San Francisco: Jossey-Bass.

Schoonhoven, Claudia Bird (1981). "Problems with Contingency Theory: Testing Assumptions Hidden within the Language of Contingency Theory," *Administrative Science Quarterly*, 26, 349–77.

Schrödinger, Erwin (1945). *What Is Life?* Cambridge: Cambridge University Press.

Schumpeter, Joseph A. (1934 trans.). *The Theory of Economic Development.* Cambridge, MA: Harvard University Press, (first published in 1926).

_____ (1947). *Capitalism, Socialism and Democracy* (2nd ed.). New York: Harper & Row.

Schutz, Alfred (1962 trans.). *Collected Papers*, vols. 1 and 2. The Hague: Nijhoff.

Schwab, Donald P., and Larry L. Cummings (1970). "Theories of Performance and Satisfaction: A Review," *Industrial Relations*, 9, 408–30.

Schwab, J. J. (1960). "What Do Scientists Do?" *Behavioral Science*, 5 (January), 1–27.

Scott, James C. (1985). *Weapons of the Weak.* New Haven, CT: Yale University Press.

Scott, John P. (1979). *Corporations, Classes and Capitalism.* New York: St. Martin's Press.

_____ (1986). *Capitalist Property and Financial Power.* New York: New York University Press.

_____ (1991). "Networks of Corporate Power," *Annual Review of Sociology*, 17, 181–203.

Scott, W. Richard (1964). "Theory of Organizations," in *Handbook of Modern Sociology*, pp. 485–529, ed. Robert E. L. Faris. Chicago: Rand McNally.

_____ (1965a). "Field Methods in the Study of Organizations," in *Handbook of Organizations*, pp. 261–304, ed. James G. March. Chicago: Rand McNally.

_____ (1965b). "Reactions to Supervision in a Heteronomous Professional Organization," *Administrative Science Quarterly*, 10, 65–81.

_____ (1966). "Professionals in Bureaucracies—Areas of Conflict," in *Professionalization*, pp. 265–275, ed. Howard M. Vollmer and Donald L. Mills. Englewood Cliffs, NJ: Prentice Hall.

_____ (1969). "Professional Employees in a Bureaucratic Structure: Social Work." in *The Semi-Professions and Their Organization*, pp. 82–144, ed. Amitai Etzioni. New York: Free Press.

_____ (1970). *Social Processes and Social Structures: An Introduction to Sociology.* New York: Holt, Rinehart and Winston.

_____ (1975). "Organizational Structure," *Annual Review of Sociology*, 1, 1–20.

_____ (1977). "Effectiveness of Organizational Effectiveness Studies," in *New Perspectives on Organizational Effectiveness*, pp. 63–95, ed. Paul S. Goodman and Johannes M. Pennings. San Francisco: Jossey-Bass.

_____ (1981). *Organizations: Rational, Natural and Open Systems* (1st ed.). Englewood Cliffs, NJ: Prentice Hall.

_____ (1982a) "Health Care Organizations in the 1980s: The Convergence of Public and Professional Control Systems," in *Contemporary Health Services: Social Science Perspectives*, 177–95, ed. Allen W. Johnson, Oscar Grusky, and Bertram H. Raven. Boston: Auburn House.

_____ (1982b). "Managing Professional Work: Three Models of Control for Health Organizations," *Health Services Research*, 17, 213–40.

_____ (1983). "The Organization of Environments: Network, Cultural, and Historical Elements," in *Organizational Environments: Ritual and Rationality*, pp. 155–75, by John W. Meyer and W. Richard Scott. Beverly Hills, CA: Sage.

_____ (1985a). "Conflicting Levels of Rationality: Regulators, Managers, and Professionals in the Medical Care Sector," *Journal of Health Administration Education*, 3 (Spring), 113–31.

_____ (1985b). "Systems within Systems: The Mental Health Sector," *American Behavioral Scientist*, 28, 601–18.

_____ (1986). "The Sociology of Organizations," in *Sociology: From Crisis to Science?* Vol. 2: *The Social Reproduction of Organization and Culture*, pp. 38–58, ed. Ulf Himmelstrand. Beverly Hills, CA: Sage.

_____ (1987). "The Adolescence of Institutional Theory," *Administrative Science Quarterly*, 32, 493–511.

_____ (1990a). "Symbols and Organizations: From Barnard to the Institutionalists," in *Organization Theory: From Chester Barnard to the Present and Beyond*, pp. 38–55, ed. Oliver E. Williamson. New York: Oxford University Press.

_____ (1990b). "Technology and Structure: An Organizational-Level Perspective," in *Technology and Organizations*, pp. 109–43, ed. Paul S. Goodman and Lee S. Sproull. San Francisco: Jossey-Bass.

_____ (1992). *Organizations: Rational, Natural and Open Systems* (3rd ed.). Englewood Cliffs, NJ: Prentice Hall.

_____ (1993). "The Organization of Medical Care Services: Toward an Integrated Theoretical Model," *Medical Care Review*, 50, 271–303.

_____ (1994). "Conceptualizing Organizational Fields: Linking Organizations and Societal Systems," in *Systemrationalitat und Partial Interesse [System Rationality and Partial Interests]*, pp. 203–221, ed. Hans-Ulrich Derlien, Uta Gerhardt, and Fritz W. Scharpf. Baden-Baden, Germany: Nomos Verlagsgesellschaft.

_____ (1995). *Institutions and Organizations*. Thousand Oaks, CA: Sage.

Scott, W. Richard, and Elaine V. Backman (1990). "Institutional Theory and the Medical Care Sector," in *Innovations in Health Care Delivery: Insights for Organization Theory*, pp. 20–52, ed. Stephen S. Mick. San Francisco: Jossey-Bass.

Scott, W. Richard, and Søren Christensen, eds. (1995). *The Institutional Construction of Organizations: International and Longitudinal Studies*. Thousand Oaks, CA: Sage.

Scott, W. Richard, Peter Mendel, and Seth Pollack (forthcoming). "Environments and Fields: Studying the Evolution of a Field of Medical Care Organizations," in *Remaking the Iron Cage: Institutional Dynamics and Processes*, ed. Walter W. Powell. Chicago: University of Chicago Press.

Scott, W. Richard, and John W. Meyer (1988). "Environmental Linkages and Organizational Complexity: Public and Private Schools," in *Comparing Public and Private Schools*, vol. 1, 128–60, ed. Thomas James and Henry M. Levin. New York: Falmer Press.

_____ (1991a). "The Organization of Societal Sectors: Propositions and Early Evidence," in *The New Institutionalism in Organizational Analysis*, 108–40, ed. Walter W. Powell and Paul DiMaggio. Chicago: University of Chicago Press.

_____ (1991b). "The Rise of Training Programs in Firms and Agencies: An Institutional Perspective," in *Research in Organizational Behavior*, vol. 13, 297–326, ed. L. L. Cummings and Barry Staw. Greenwich CT: JAI Press.

_____, eds. (1994). *Institutional Environments and Organizations: Structural Complexity and Individualism.* Thousand Oaks, CA: Sage.

Scott, William G. (1992). *Chester I. Barnard and the Guardians of the Managerial State.* Lawrence: University of Kansas Press.

Scott, William G., and David K. Hart (1979). *Organizational America.* Boston: Houghton Mifflin.

Searle, John R. (1995). *The Construction of Social Reality.* New York: Free Press.

Seashore, Stanley E. (1954). *Group Cohesiveness in the Industrial Work Group.* Ann Arbor: Institute for Social Research, University of Michigan.

_____ (1962). *The Assessment of Organizational Performance.* Ann Arbor: Survey Research Center, University of Michigan.

Seavoy, Ronald E. (1982). *The Origins of the American Business Corporation, 1784–1855: Broadening the Concept of Public Service During Industrialization.* Westport, CT: Greenwood Press.

Seeman, Melvin (1959). "On the Meaning of Alienation," *American Sociological Review,* 24, 783–91.

_____ (1975). "Alienation Studies," *Annual Review of Sociology,* 1, 91–123.

Seidman, Harold (1975). "Government-Sponsored Enterprise in the United States," in *The New Political Economy: The Public Use of the Private Sector,* pp. 83–108, ed. Bruce L. R. Smith. New York: Wiley.

Selznick, Philip (1948). "Foundations of the Theory of Organization," *American Sociological Review,* 13, 25–35.

_____ (1949). *TVA and the Grass Roots.* Berkeley: University of California Press.

_____ (1952). *The Organizational Weapon.* New York: McGraw-Hill.

_____ (1957). *Leadership in Administration.* New York: Harper & Row.

_____ (1969). *Law, Society, and Industrial Justice.* New York: Russell Sage Foundation.

_____ (1992). *The Moral Commonwealth: Social Theory and the Promise of Community.* Berkeley: University of California Press.

_____ (1996). "Institutionalism 'Old' and 'New'," *Administrative Science Quarterly,* 41, 270–277.

Shaiken, Harley (1985). *Work Transformed: Automation and Labor in the Computer Age.* New York: Holt, Rinehart and Winston.

Shannon, Claude E., and Warren Weaver (1963). *The Mathematical Theory of Communication.* Urbana: University of Illinois Press.

Shaw, M. E. (1954). "Some Effects of Problem Complexity upon Problem Solution Efficiency in Various Communication Nets," *Journal of Experimental Psychology,* 48, 211–17.

_____ (1964). "Communication Networks," in *Advances in Experimental Social Psychology,* vol. 1, pp. 111–47, ed. Leonard Berkowitz. New York: Academic Press.

Shelanski, Howard A., and Peter G. Klein (1995). "Empirical Research in Transaction Cost Economics: A Review and Assessment," *Journal of Law, Economics, & Organization,* 7, 335–61.

Shenhav, Yehouda (1995). "From Chaos to Systems: The Engineering Foundations of Organization Theory, 1879–1932," *Administrative Science Quarterly,* 40, 557–85.

Sheppard, Harold L., and Neal Herrick (1972). *Where Have All the Robots Gone?* New York: Free Press.

Sherif, Muzafer, and Caroline W. Sherif (1953). *Groups in Harmony and Tension.* New York: Harper & Row.

Shrivastava, P. (1986). *Bhopal.* New York: Basic Books.

Shulman, Arthur D. (1996). "Putting Group Information Technology in its Place: Communication and Good Work Group Performance," *Handbook of Organization Studies,* pp. 357–74, ed. Stewart R. Clegg, Cynthia Hardy, and Walter R. Nord. Thousand Oaks, CA: Sage.

Silverman, David (1971). *The Theory of Organizations.* New York: Basic Books.

Simmel, Georg (1955 trans.). *Conflict* and *The Web of Group-Affiliations.* Glencoe, IL: Free Press. (The first essay was first published in 1908, the second in 1922.)

Simon, Herbert A. (1962). "The Architecture of Complexity," *Proceedings of the American Philosophical Society,* 106, 467–82.

_____ (1964). "On the Concept of Organizational Goal," *Administrative Science Quarterly,* 9, 1–22.

_____ (1966). *The New Science of Management Decision*. New York: Harper.

_____ (1976). *Administrative Behavior* (3rd ed.). New York: Macmillan. (Originally published in 1945).

_____ (1979). "Rational Decision Making in Business Organizations," *American Economic Review*, 69, 493–513.

Simon, Herbert A., Donald W. Smithberg, and Victor A. Thompson (1950). *Public Administration*. New York: Knopf.

Simon, William H. (1983). "Legality, Bureaucracy, and Class in the Welfare System," *Yale Law Journal*, 92, 1198–1269.

Singh, Jitendra V., ed. (1990). *Organizational Evolution: New Directions*. Newbury Park, CA: Sage.

Singh, Jitendra V., and Charles J. Lumsden (1990). "Theory and Research in Organizational Ecology," *Annual Review of Sociology*, 16, 161–95.

Singh, Jitendra V., David J. Tucker, and Robert J. House (1986). "Organizational Legitimacy and the Liability of Newness," *Administrative Science Quarterly*, 31, 171–93.

Slater, Philip E. (1955). "Role Differentiation in Small Groups," *American Sociological Review*, 20, 300–310.

Smigel, Erwin O. (1964). *The Wall Street Lawyer: Professional Organization Man?* New York: Free Press.

Smircich, Linda (1983). "Concepts of Culture and Organizational Analysis," *Administrative Science Quarterly*, 28, 339–58.

_____ (1985). "Is the Concept of Culture a Paradigm for Understanding Organizations and Ourselves?" in *Organizational Culture*, pp. 55–72, ed. Peter J. Frost, Larry F. Moore, Meryl Reis Louis, Craig C. Lundberg, and Joanne Martin. Beverly Hills, CA: Sage.

Smircich, Linda, and Marta B. Calás (1987). "Organization Culture: A Critical Assessment," in *Handbook of Organizational Communication*, pp. 228–63, ed. Fredric M. Jablin, Linda L. Putnam, Karlene H. Roberts, and Lyman W. Porter. Newbury Park, CA: Sage.

Smith, Adam (1957). *Selections from the Wealth of Nations*, ed. George J. Stigler. New York: Appleton Century Crofts (originally published in 1776).

Smith, Bruce L. R. (1966). *The RAND Corporation*. Cambridge, MA: Harvard University Press.

Smith, J. P., and M. P. Ward (1984). *Women's Wages and Work in the Twentieth Century*. Santa Monica, CA: RAND.

Smith, Steven Rathgeb, and Michael Lipsky (1993). *Nonprofits for Hire: The Welfare State in the Age of Contracting*. Cambridge, MA: Harvard University Press.

Smith, Thomas Spence, and R. Danforth Ross (1978). "Cultural Controls on the Demography of Hierarchy: A Time-Series Analysis of Warfare and the Growth of the United States Army, 1960–68." Unpublished paper, University of Rochester.

Snyder, David, and Charles Tilly (1972). "Hardship and Collective Violence in France, 1830 to 1960," *American Sociological Review*, 37, 520–32.

Special Task Force to the Secretary of Health, Education and Welfare (1973). *Work in America*. Cambridge, MA: MIT Press.

Spenner, Kenneth I. (1988). "Social Stratification, Work, and Personality," *Annual Review of Sociology*, 14, 69–97.

Sprague, R. H., and H. J. Watson (1986). *Decision Support Systems: Putting Theory into Practice*. Englewood Cliffs, NJ: Prentice Hall.

Sproull, Lee S. (1981). "Response to Regulation: An Organizational Process Framework," *Administration and Society*, 12, 447–70.

Sproull, Lee S., and Paul S. Goodman (1990). "Technology and Organizations: Integration and Opportunities," in *Technology and Organizations*, pp. 254–65, ed. Paul S. Goodman and Lee S. Sproull. San Francisco: Jossey-Bass.

Sproull, Lee S., and Sara Kiesler, eds. (1991). *Connections: New Ways of Working in the Networked Organization*. Cambridge, MA: MIT Press.

Staber, Udo (1985). "A Population Perspective on Collective Action as an Organizational Form: The Case of Trade Associations," in *Research in the Sociology of Organizations*, vol. 4, pp. 181–220, ed. Samuel B. Bacharach and Stephen M. Mitchell. Greenwich, CN: JAI Press.

Staber, Udo, and Howard Aldrich (1983). "Trade Association Stability and Public Policy," in *Organizational Theory and Public Policy*, pp. 163–78, ed. Richard H. Hall and Robert E. Quinn. Beverly Hills, CA: Sage.

Stablein, Ralph (1996). "Data in Organization Studies," in *Handbook of Organization Studies*, 509–25, ed. Stewart R. Clegg, Cynthia Hardy, and Walter R. Nord. Thousand Oaks, CA: Sage.

Stalk, George, Philip Evans, and Lawrence E. Shulman (1992). "Competing on Capabilities: The New Rules of Corporate Strategy," *Harvard Business Review* (March/April): 57–69.

Stark, David (1980). "Class Struggle and the Transformation of the Labour Process: A Relational Approach," *Theory and Society*, 9, 89–130.

Starr, Paul 1982. *The Social Transformation of American Medicine*. New York: Basic Books.

Staw, Barry M. (1980). "Rationality and Justification in Organizational Life," in *Research in Organizational Behavior*, vol. 2, pp. 45–80, ed. Barry M. Staw and Larry L. Cummings. Greenwich, CT: JAI Press.

_____ (1984). "Organizational Behavior: A Review and Reformulation of the Field's Outcome Variables," *Annual Review of Psychology*, 35, 627–66.

Steers, Richard M. (1977). *Organizational Effectiveness: A Behavioral View*. Pacific Palisades, CA: Goodyear.

Steers, Richard M., and Daniel G. Spencer (1977). "The Role of Achievement Motivation in Job Design," *Journal of Applied Psychology*, 62, 472–79.

Steinbruner, John D. (1974) *The Cybernetic Theory of Decision*. Princeton, NJ: Princeton University Press.

Steiner, George A., and William G. Ryan (1968). *Industrial Project Management*. New York: Crowell-Collier and Macmillan.

Stern, Robert N. (1979). "The Development of an Interorganizational Control Network: The Case of Intercollegiate Athletics," *Administrative Science Quarterly*, 24, 242–66.

Stigler, George J. (1971). "The Theory of Economic Regulation," *Bell Journal of Economics and Management Science*, 2 (Spring), 3–21.

Stinchcombe, Arthur L. (1959). "Bureaucratic and Craft Administration of Production: A Comparative Study," *Administrative Science Quarterly*, 4, 168–87.

_____ (1965). "Social Structure and Organizations," in *Handbook of Organizations*, pp. 142–93, ed. James G. March. Chicago: Rand McNally.

_____ (1968). *Constructing Social Theories*. Chicago: University of Chicago Press.

_____ (1983). *Economic Sociology*. New York: Academic Press.

_____ (1985). "Contracts as Hierarchical Documents," in *Organization Theory and Project Management*, by Arthur Stinchcombe and Carol Heimer. Bergen, Norway: Universitetsforlaget.

_____ (1990). *Information and Organizations*. Berkeley: University of California Press.

Stogdill, R. M., and A. E. Coons, ed. (1957). *Leader Behavior: Its Description and Measurement*. Research Monograph 88. Columbus, OH: Bureau of Business Research, Ohio State University.

Stolzenberg, Ross M. (1978). "Bringing the Boss Back In: Employer Size, Employee Schooling, and Socioeconomic Achievement," *American Sociological Review*, 43, 813–28.

Stone, Eugene F., Richard T. Mowday, and Lyman W. Porter (1977). "Higher Order Need Strengths as Moderators of the Job Scope–Job Satisfaction Relationship," *Journal of Applied Psychology*, 62, 466–71.

Streeck, Wolfgang, and Philippe C. Schmitter, eds. (1985). *Private Interest Government: Beyond Market and State*. Beverly Hills, CA: Sage.

Street, David, Robert Vinter, and Charles Perrow (1966). *Organization for Treatment*. New York: Free Press.

Suchman, Edward A. (1967). *Evaluative Research*. New York: Russell Sage Foundation.

Suchman, Mark C. (1995). "Localism and Globalism in Institutional Analysis: The Emergence of Contractual Norms in Venture Finance," in *The Institutional Construction of Organizations: International and Longitudinal Studies*, pp. 39–63, ed. W. Richard Scott and Søren Christensen. Thousand Oaks, CA: Sage.

_____ (forthcoming). "Constructed Ecologies: Reproduction and Structuration in Emerging Organizational Communities," in *Remaking the Iron Cage: Institutional Dynamics and Processes*, ed. Walter W. Powell. Chicago: University of Chicago Press.

Sundquist, James L. (1969). *Making Federalism Work*. Washington, DC: Brookings Institution.

Susman, Gerald I., and Richard B. Chase (1986). "A Sociotechnical Analysis of the Integrated Factory," *Journal of Applied Behavioral Science*, 22, 257–70.

Sutton, John, Frank Dobbin, John W. Meyer, and W. Richard Scott (1994). "Legalization of the Workplace," *American Journal of Sociology*, 99: 944–71.

Swanson, Guy E. (1976). "The Tasks of Sociology," *Science*, 192, 665–67.

Swinth, Robert L. (1974). *Organizational Systems for Management: Designing, Planning and Implementation*. Columbus, OH: Grid.

Tancredi, Laurence R., and J. Woods (1972). "The Social Control of Medical Practice: Licensure versus Output Monitoring," *Milbank Memorial Fund Quarterly*, 50 (part 1), 99–126.

Tannenbaum, Arnold S. (1968). *Control in Organizations*. New York: McGraw-Hill.

Tannenbaum, Arnold S., Bogdan Kavcic, Menachem Rosner, Mino Vianello, and Georg Wieser (1974). *Hierarchy in Organizations*. San Francisco: Jossey-Bass.

Taylor, Donald W. (1965). "Decision Making and Problem Solving," in *Handbook of Organizations*, pp. 48–86, ed. James G. March. Chicago: Rand McNally.

Taylor, Frederick W. (1911). *The Principles of Scientific Management*. New York: Harper.

_____ (1947). *Scientific Management*. New York: Harper & Brothers.

Taylor, Serge (1984). *Making Bureaucracies Think: The Environmental Impact Statement Strategy of Administrative Reform*. Stanford, CA: Stanford University Press.

Taylor, Verta (1995). "Watching for Vibes: Bringing Emotions in the Study of Feminist Organizations," in *Feminist Organizations: Harvest of the New Women's Movement*, pp. 223–33, ed. Myra Marx Feree and Patricia Yancey Martin. Philadelphia: Temple University Press.

Terreberry, Shirley (1968). "The Evolution of Organizational Environments," *Administrative Science Quarterly*, 12, 590–613.

Thibaut, John W., and Harold H. Kelley (1959). *The Social Psychology of Groups*. New York: Wiley.

Thietart, R. A., and B. Forgues (1995). "Chaos Theory and Organization," *Organization Science*, 6, 19–31.

Thomas, George M., and John W. Meyer (1984). "The Expansion of the State," *Annual Review of Sociology*, 10, 461–82.

Thompson, E. P. (1967). "Time, Work Discipline and Industrial Capitalism," *Past and Present*, 38, 56–97.

Thompson, James D. (1967). *Organizations in Action*. New York: McGraw-Hill.

Thompson, James D., and Frederick L. Bates (1957). "Technology, Organization, and Administration," *Administrative Science Quarterly*, 2, 325–42.

Thompson, James D., and Arthur Tuden (1959). "Strategies, Structures, and Processes of Organizational Decision," in *Comparative Studies in Administration*, pp. 195–216, ed. James D. Thompson et al. Pittsburgh: University of Pittsburgh Press.

Thompson, Kenneth (1980). "The Organizational Society," in *Control and Ideology in Organizations*, pp. 3–23, ed. Graeme Salaman and Kenneth Thompson. Cambridge, MA: MIT Press.

Thompson, Victor A. (1961). *Modern Organization*. New York: Knopf.

Thornton, Patricia H. (1992). "Psychiatric Diagnosis as Sign and Symbol: Nomenclature as an Organizing and Legitimating Strategy," in *Research on Social Problems*, vol. 4, ed. Gale Miller and James Holstein. Greenwich, CT: JAI Press.

Tilly, Charles (1978). *From Mobilization to Revolution*. Reading, MA: Addison-Wesley.

Toffler, Alvin (1970). *Future Shock*. New York: Random House.

_____ (1980). *The Third Wave*. New York: Morrow.

Tolbert, Pamela S., and Lynne G. Zucker (1983). "Institutional Sources of Change in the Formal Structure of Organizations: The Diffusion of Civil Service Reform, 1880–1935," *Administrative Science Quarterly*, 28, 22–39.

Trahair, R. C. S. (1992). *The Humanist Temper: The Life and Work of Elton Mayo*. New Brunswick, NJ: Transactions Books.

Trice, Harrison M., and Janice M. Beyer (1993). *The Cultures of Work Organizations*. Englewood Cliffs, NJ: Prentice Hall.

Trist, Eric L. (1981). "The Evolution of Sociotechnical Systems as a Conceptual Framework and as an Action Research Program," in *Perspectives on Organization Design and Behavior,* pp. 19–75, ed. Andrew H. Van de Ven and William F. Joyce. New York: Wiley-Interscience.

Trist, Eric L., and K. W. Bamforth (1951). "Social and Psychological Consequences of the Longwall Method of Coal-Getting," *Human Relations* 4, 3–28.

Tsurumi, Y. (1977). *Multinational Management.* Cambridge, MA: Ballinger.

Turk, Herman (1977). *Organizations in Modern Life.* San Francisco: Jossey-Bass.

Turner, Arthur N., and Paul R. Lawrence (1965). *Industrial Jobs and the Worker.* Boston: Harvard Graduate School of Business Administration.

Tushman, Michael L., and Philip Anderson (1986). "Technological Discontinuities and Organizational Environments," *Administrative Science Quarterly,* 31, 439–65.

Tyler, Tom R. (1993). "The Social Psychology of Authority," in *Social Psychology in Organizations: Advances in Theory and Research,* pp. 141–160, ed. J. Keith Murnighan. Englewood Cliffs, NJ:Prentice Hall.

Udy, Stanley H., Jr. (1959a). "'Bureaucracy' and 'Rationality' in Weber's Organization Theory," *American Sociological Review,* 24, 791–95.

_____ (1959b). *Organization of Work.* New Haven: Human Relations Area Files Press.

_____ (1962). "Administrative Rationality, Social Setting, and Organizational Development," *American Journal of Sociology,* 68, 299–308.

_____ (1970). *Work in Traditional and Modern Society.* Englewood Cliffs, NJ: Prentice Hall.

Useem, Michael (1984). *The Inner Circle.* New York: Oxford University Press.

_____ (1993). *Executive Defense: Shareholder Power and Corporate Reorganization.* Cambridge, MA: Harvard University Press.

_____ (1996). *Investor Capitalism: How Money Managers Are Changing the Face of Corporate America.* New York: Basic Books.

U.S. Bureau of the Census (1984). *Statistical Abstracts of the United States 1985.* Washington, DC: Government Printing Office.

U.S. Department of Labor, Bureau of Labor Statistics (1979). *Employment and Wages, 1976.* Springfield, VA: National Technical Information Service.

U.S. Office of the Federal Register, General Services Administration (1992). *The United States Government Manual.* Washington, DC: Government Printing Office.

Uzzi, Brian (1996). "The Sources and Consequences of Embeddedness for the Economic Performance of Organizations: The Network Effect," *American Sociological Review,* 61: 674–98.

Van de Ven, Andrew H., and Diane L. Ferry (1980). *Measuring and Assessing Organizations.* New York: Wiley-Interscience.

Van de Ven, Andrew H., and Raghu Garud (1989). "A Framework for Understanding the Emergence of New Industries," in *Research on Technological Innovation, Management and Policy,* 4, 195–225, ed. Richard S. Rosenbloom. Greenwich, CT: JAI Press.

Van Maanen, John (1973). "Observations on the Making of Policemen," *Human Organization,* 32, 407–17.

Vaughan, Diane (1996). *The Challenger Launch Decision: Risky Technology, Culture and Deviance at NASA.* Chicago: University of Chicago Press.

Vaupel, James W., and Joan P. Curhan (1969). *The Making of Multinational Enterprise.* Cambridge, MA: Harvard University Press.

Veblen, Thorstein (1904). *The Theory of Business Enterprise.* New York: Scribner's.

Verba, Sidney (1961). *Small Groups and Political Behavior.* Princeton, NJ: Princeton University Press.

Verba, Sidney, and Norman H. Nie (1972). *Participation in America: Political Democracy and Social Equality.* New York: Harper & Row.

Vroom, Victor H. (1969). "Industrial Social Psychology," in *The Handbook of Social Psychology* (2nd ed.), vol. 5, pp. 196–268, ed. Gardner Lindzey and Elliot Aronson. Reading, MA: Addison-Wesley.

Walder, Andrew G. (1986). *Communist Neo-Traditionalism: Work and Authority in Chinese Industry.* Berkeley: University of California Press.

Walker, Charles R., and Robert H. Guest (1952). *The Man on the Assembly Line*. Cambridge, MA: Harvard University Press.

Walker, Gordon, and David Weber (1984). "A Transaction Cost Approach to Make-or-Buy Decisions," *Administrative Science Quarterly*, 29, 373–91.

Wallace, Jean (1995). "Organizational and Professional Commitment in Professional and Nonprofessional Organizations," *Administrative Science Quarterly*, 40, 228–55.

Wallace, Walter L. (1975). "Structure and Action in the Theories of Coleman and Parsons," in *Approaches to the Study of Social Structure*, pp. 121–34, ed. Peter M. Blau. New York: Free Press.

Walton, Richard E., and John M. Dutton (1969). "The Management of Interdepartmental Conflict: A Model and Review," *Administrative Science Quarterly*, 14, 73–84.

Walton, Richard E., John M. Dutton, and H. Gordon Fitch (1966). "A Study of Conflict in the Process, Structure, and Attitudes of Lateral Relationships," in *Some Theories of Organization* (rev. ed.), pp. 444–65, ed. Chadwick J. Haberstroh and Albert H. Rubenstein. Homewood, IL: Irwin; Dorsey.

Wamsley, Gary L., and Mayer N. Zald (1973). *The Political Economy of Public Organizations*. Lexington, MA: Heath.

Ward, John William (1964). "The Ideal of Individualism and the Reality of Organization," in *The Business Establishment*, pp. 37–76, ed. Earl F. Cheit. New York: Wiley.

Waring, Stephen P. (1991). *Taylorism Transformed: Scientific Management Theory Since 1945*. Chapel Hill: University of North Carolina Press.

Warme, Barbara D., Katherina L. P. Lundy, and Larry A. Lundy, eds. (1992). *Working Part-Time: Risks and Opportunities*. New York: Praeger.

Warner, W. Lloyd, and J. O. Low (1947). *The Social System of the Modern Factory*. New Haven: Yale University Press.

Warren, Roland L. (1963). *The Community in America*. Chicago: Rand McNally (rev. ed. 1972).

_____ (1967). "The Interorganizational Field as a Focus for Investigation," *Administrative Science Quarterly*, 12, 396–419.

Weber, Max (1946 trans.). *From Max Weber: Essays in Sociology*, ed. Hans H. Gerth and C. Wright Mills. New York: Oxford University Press (first published in 1906–24).

_____ (1947 trans.). *The Theory of Social and Economic Organization*, ed. A. H. Henderson and Talcott Parsons, Glencoe, IL: Free Press (first published in 1924).

_____ (1958 trans.). *The Protestant Ethic and the Spirit of Capitalism*, trans. Talcott Parsons. New York: Scribner's (first published in 1904–5).

_____ (1968 trans.). *Economy and Society: An Interpretive Sociology*, 3 vols., ed. Guenther Roth and Claus Wittich. New York: Bedminister Press (first published in 1924).

Weick, Karl E. (1969). *The Social Psychology of Organizing*. Reading, MA: Addison-Wesley (2nd ed. 1979).

_____ (1974). "Middle Range Theories of Social Systems," *Behavioral Science*, 19, 357–67.

_____ (1976). "Educational Organizations as Loosely Coupled Systems," *Administrative Science Quarterly*, 21, 1–19.

_____ (1977). "Re-Punctuating the Problem," in *New Perspectives on Organizational Effectiveness*, pp. 193–225, ed. Paul S. Goodman and Johannes M. Pennings. San Francisco: Jossey-Bass.

_____ (1987). "Organizational Culture as a Source of High Reliability," *California Management Review*, 29 (Winter), 116–36.

_____ (1990). "Technology as Equivoque: Sensemaking in New Technologies," in *Technology and Organizations*, pp. 1–44, ed. Paul S. Goodman and Lee S. Sproull. San Francisco: Jossey-Bass.

_____ (1995). *Sensemaking in Organizations*. Thousand Oaks, CA: Sage.

Weiss, Carol H. (1972). *Evaluation Research*. Englewood Cliffs, NJ: Prentice Hall.

Westney, D. Eleanor (1987). *Imitation and Innovation: The Transfer of Western Organizational Patterns to Meiji Japan*. Cambridge, MA: Harvard University Press.

Westphal, James D., and Edward J. Zajac (1994). "Substance and Symbolism in CEO's Long-Term Incentive Plans," *Administrative Science Quarterly*, 39: 367–90.

Whetten, David A. (1987). "Organizational Growth and Decline Processes," *Annual Review of Sociology*, 13, 335–58.

White, Harrison C., Scott A. Boorman, and Ronald L. Breiger (1976). "Social Structure from Multiple Networks: 1. Blockmodels of Roles and Positions," *American Journal of Sociology*, 81, 730–80.

White, Ralph, and Ronald Lippitt (1953). "Leader Behavior and Member Reaction in Three 'Social Climates,'" in *Group Dynamics*, pp. 586–611, ed. Dorwin Cartwright and Alvin Zander. Evanston, IL: Row, Peterson.

Whitehead, Alfred North (1925). *Science and the Modern World*. New York: Macmillan.

_____ (1929). *The Aims of Education*. New York: Macmillan.

Whitley, Richard (1992a). *Business Systems in East Asia: Firms, Markets and Societies*. London: Sage.

_____ ed. (1992b). *European Business Systems: Firms and Markets in Their National Contexts*. London: Sage.

_____ (1992c) "The Social Construction of Organizations and Markets: The Comparative Analysis of Business Recipes," in *Rethinking Organizations: New Directions in Organization Theory and Analysis*, pp. 120–43, ed. Michael Reed and Michael Hughes. Newbury Park, CA: Sage.

Whitt, J. Allen (1989). "Organizational Ties and Urban Growth," in *Networks of Power: Organizational Actors at the National, Corporate, and Community Levels*, pp. 97–109, ed. Robert Perrucci and Harry R. Potter. New York: Aldine de Gruyter.

Whyte, William Foote, ed. (1946). *Industry and Society*. New York: McGraw-Hill.

_____ (1948). *Human Relations in the Restaurant Industry*. New York: McGraw-Hill.

_____ (1951). "Small Groups and Large Organizations," in *Social Psychology at the Crossroads*, pp. 297–312, ed. John H. Rohrer and Muzafer Sherif. New York: Harper.

_____ (1959). *Man and Organization*. Homewood, IL: Irwin.

Whyte, William Foote, et al. (1955). *Money and Motivation: An Analysis of Incentives in Industry*. New York: Harper.

Whyte, William H., Jr. (1956). *The Organization Man*. New York: Simon & Schuster.

Wieland, George F., and Robert A. Ullrich (1976). *Organizations: Behavior, Design, and Change*. Homewood, IL: Irwin.

Wiener, Norbert (1956). *I Am a Mathematician*. New York: Doubleday.

Wildavsky, Aaron B. (1979). *Speaking Truth to Power: The Art and Craft of Policy Analysis*. Boston: Little, Brown.

Williamson, Oliver E. (1975). *Markets and Hierarchies: Analysis and Antitrust Implications*. New York: Free Press.

_____ (1981). "The Economics of Organization: The Transaction Cost Approach," *American Journal of Sociology*, 87, 548–77.

_____ (1985). *The Economic Institutions of Capitalism*. New York, Free Press.

_____, ed. (1990). *Organization Theory: From Chester Barnard to the Present and Beyond*. New York: Oxford University Press.

_____ (1991). "Comparative Economic Organization: The Analysis of Discrete Structural Alternatives," *Administrative Science Quarterly*, 36, 269–96.

_____ (1994). "Transaction Cost Economics and Organization Theory," in *The Handbook of Economic Sociology*, pp. 77–107, ed. Neil J. Smelser and Richard Swedberg. Princeton: Princeton University Press and Russell Sage Foundation.

Williamson, Oliver E., and William G. Ouchi (1981). "The Markets and Hierarchies and Visible Hand Perspectives," in *Perspectives on Organization Design and Behavior*, pp. 347–70, ed. Andrew H. Van de Ven and William E. Joyce. New York: Wiley.

Wilson, James Q. (1962). *The Amateur Democrat*. Chicago: University of Chicago Press.

_____ (1973). *Political Organizations*. New York: Basic Books.

_____ (1978). *The Investigators: Managing FBI and Narcotics Agents*. New York: Basic Books.

_____, ed. (1980). *The Politics of Regulation*. New York: Basic Books.

_____ (1989). *Bureaucracy: What Government Agencies Do and Why They Do It*. New York: Basic Books.

Winter, Sidney G. (1990). "Organizing for Continuous Improvement: Evolutionary Theory Meets the Quality Revolution," in *Evolutionary Dynamics of Organizations*, pp. 90–108, ed. Joel A. C. Baum and Jitendra V. Singh. New York: Oxford University Press.

Wolin, Sheldon S. (1960). *Politics and Vision: Continuity and Innovation in Western Political Thought.* Boston: Little, Brown.

Woodward, Joan (1958). *Management and Technology.* London: H.M.S.O.

_____ (1965). *Industrial Organization: Theory and Practice.* New York: Oxford University Press.

Yuchtman, Ephraim, and Stanley E. Seashore (1967). "A System Resource Approach to Organizational Effectiveness," *American Sociological Review,* 32, 891–903.

Zald, Mayer N. (1970). "Political Economy: A Framework for Comparative Analysis," in *Power in Organizations,* pp. 221–61, ed. Mayer N. Zald. Nashville, TN: Vanderbilt University Press.

Zald, Mayer N., and Patricia Denton (1963). "From Evangelism to General Service: The Transformation of the YMCA," *Administrative Science Quarterly,* 8, 214–34.

Zald, Mayer N., and John D. McCarthy, eds. (1987). *Social Movements in an Organizational Society.* New Brunswick, NJ: Transaction Books.

Zammuto, Raymond F. (1982). *Assessing Organizational Effectiveness.* Albany: State University of New York Press.

Zelditch, Morris, Jr. (1969). "Can You Really Study an Army in the Laboratory?" in *A Sociological Reader on Complex Organizations* (2nd ed.), pp. 528–39, ed. Amitai Etzioni. New York: Holt, Rinehart and Winston.

Zelditch, Morris, Jr., and Henry A. Walker (1984). "Legitimacy and the Stability of Authority," in *Advances in Group Processes: Theory and Research,* vol. 1, pp. 1–25, ed. Edward J. Lawler. Greenwich, CT: JAI Press.

Zey-Ferrell, Mary, and Michael Aiken, eds. (1981). *Complex Organizations: Critical Perspectives.* Glenview, IL: Scott, Foresman.

Zimmerman, Don H. (1970). "The Practicalities of Rule Use,"in *Understanding Everyday Life,* ed. J. D. Douglas. Chicago: Aldine.

Zimmerman, Don H., and D. Wieder (1970). "Ethnomethodology and the Problem of Order," in *Understanding Everyday Life,* pp. 287–95, ed. J. D. Douglas. Chicago: Aldine.

Zmud, R. W. (1983). *Information Systems in Organizations.* Glenview, IL: Scott, Foresman.

Zuboff, Shoshana (1985). "Technologies that Informate: Implications for Human Resource Management in the Computerized Industrial Workplace," in *Human Resources Management Trends and Challenges,* pp. 103–39, ed. Richard E. Walton and Paul R. Lawrence. Boston: Harvard Business School Press.

_____ (1988). *In the Age of the Smart Machine.* New York: Basic Books.

Zucker, Lynne G. (1977). "The Role of Institutionalization in Cultural Persistence," *American Sociological Review,* 42, 726–43.

_____ (1983). "Organizations as Institutions," in *Research in the Sociology of Organizations,* vol. 2, pp. 1–47, ed. Samuel B. Bacharach. Greenwich, CN: JAI Press.

_____ ed. (1988). *Institutional Patterns and Organizations: Culture and Environment.* Cambridge, MA: Ballinger.

Name Index

Subject Index